BUILDING LOVE
THAT LASTS

T0405873

BUILDING LOVE THAT LASTS

Secrets for Creating an Extraordinary Life and Profound Intimacy with Your Partner

CLINTON CALLAHAN

HOHM PRESS
Chino Valley, Arizona

© 2020, Clinton Callahan.

All rights reserved. It is copyright law that no part of this book may be reproduced in any manner without written permission from the publisher, except in the case of quotes used in critical articles and reviews. And, copyright owner hereby grants permission for readers to copy and use portions of this book as study material in discussion groups, seminars, trainings, websites, newsletters, ezines or power-point presentations provided that the material is given for free, that proper reference is given for maps and exercises to Possibility Management, and that copies include the following copyright block:

© World Copyright 2020 by Clinton Callahan. Excerpted from the book *Building Love That Lasts*. You are granted permission to copy and distribute this excerpt as long as it is given for free and this author, copyright and website block is included on each copy. All other rights are reserved. To get a free email subscription to SPARKs click on the PUBLICATIONS/NEWSLETTER button of http://clintoncallahan.org. Thanks for experimenting with Possibility Management!

To the One who pushes the ones who push the pens.

Acknowledgements

I am grateful to:

Pauline Aiko Lamprecht who first introduced me to the experience of "Countenance," without warning, one Monday afternoon in a noisy, smoke-filled Viennese café in the fall of 1994. As my reality horizon expanded into infinity and I could hardly breathe, she calmly said that she never opens this door for anyone. She just waits until someone visits.

Mayli, Aiko's teacher, who obviously trains her students with a rare deference.

Clinton Callahan Jr., my father, a King who read this whole manuscript out loud to my mother Virginia, who couldn't read anymore, just so she could hear what it says.

My ex-wives; my not-ex-daughters; and every person who has ever encouraged me to learn more about love.

Sue Nestrud, who spent hundreds of unpaid hours transforming piles of badly recorded talk tapes into words on paper that built the foundation for this project.

Tilman and Dagmar Neubronner of Genius Verlag, whose unmitigated enthusiasm for our work and for revolutions in general helped entice this book out of the womb.

Regina Sara Ryan and the Hohm Press team, who excel in the compassionate art of working kindly with cantankerous authors to make a better book.

Werner and Hannelore Lutz, whose creative financial ideas and simple exuberance for life greatly supported the final writing of this book.

Mike McDonnell, for all those hours talking to me about responsibility under the streetlights on the far side of midnight.

Anyone who has ever tried (or even wanted to try) to write a book that would somehow help people, because many of those books have helped me.

Everyone who participated in Possibility Management Laboratories experimenting together to discover what works and what does not work.

Marion Lutz, for being the listening into which I could write *Building Love That Lasts*.

Lee Lozowick, a man who has many secrets but none worth telling, because he knows that a person keeps only what they authentically discover themselves. You are a space through which Archetypal Love does its work in the world (just my opinion). This manuscript was completed only because you said, "I want to see the book." Where the words are best the words are yours. Thank you for never ceasing to kick the ass connected to this one.

NOTE: This book intends to empower you as an experimenter. We have found that experimenting builds 'matrix' for holding more consciousness. Each section in this book that invites you to try new behavior has been given a Matrix Code, for example, BLTLCH00.01, which deciphers as Experiment 01 in Chapter 00 (the Introduction) of *Building Love That Lasts*. Reading this entire book earns you 3 Matrix Points. The Matrix Code for reading this whole book is BLTL000.00.

The theory is that through trying new behavior you earn real Matrix Points by weaving new distinctions into your Being. The more matrix you build, the more consciousness your Being catches. The idea is that if together we can earn one million new Matrix Points we will upgrade the morphogenetic field of the human race and change the status quo for the better.

You can register your Matrix Points by setting up a free account at http://StartOver.xyz., an entryway into our massively-multiplayer online-and-offline personal-transformation thoughtware-upgrade game.

The game has the same purpose as this book: to upgrade thoughtware for what it means to be human. Through your StartOver.xyz account you will be able to see the global number of Matrix Points we have built in each category, and also the total number of Matrix Points we've all earned together. Will you help us do this experiment?

We made an online catalog of all the website 'bubbles' in the StartOver.xyz 'bubble-net' at http://StartOverHere.xyz.

We are populating over 250 StartOver.xyz websites with distinctions and experiments as fast as our little Team at GeneralMemetics.org can do it. If you ever made a website before, you know that those things are alive! They don't stand still for long. They evolve and morph into new territories of their own accord... and sometimes they die. Don't be surprised if you find a few of our websites to be incomplete or with a dead link. Please let us know what you need and we will regard your necessity as kick-butt. Thanks for being an experimenter!

Contents

It's No Secret

A man tells me he wants to leave his wife because they have not had sex in a year and their relationship is dead. Well, what did they expect? The couple had no chance from the beginning. It is not their fault. They were given no classes about how to stay ecstatically in love, no guidance for enduring intimacy's intense delights. How could they have learned to create anything different from what was modeled by their parents? The couple tries to have relationship but the man does not know how to protect his woman's feminine dignity. How *could* she risk revealing her true sensuality to him? He holds no safe sanctuary for her to unfold into! The man has no reference point for directing his attention or keeping his center, no connection to his feelings at all. He does not recognize that the thinness of his personality is his true source of power. The man *could* use uncertainty as a way for making right-angled turns at light-speed, bringing his woman along for the adventure. Instead he regards his inner spaciousness as a handicap and masks it with a show of toughness or professionalism. He turns to whatever the culture offers to prove his manliness – an expensive car, a corner office, the latest mobile phone. But the man himself remains adolescent, having undergone no rite of passage to shock pulses of life into his archetypal masculine structures. So the revolutionary in him who could make changes to benefit the world watches videos instead. The courageous inventor who could generate wonderful new viewpoints to lift the hearts of humanity goes gambling. The noble leader in him stays home and masturbates. This adolescent, dressed in a man's body, remains "hook-able," defensive, and self-centered. And his communication sucks – talking to him is like reading emails, so much is missing. He gives smart reasons instead of deriving power from admitting what he does not know. He stands arrogantly aloof instead of consoling fears through simply listening, or vaporizing barriers through speaking clearly about what else is possible. Like the rest of us who attended school he has been forced to sever his internal connection to deep imagination, so no flood of dynamic nonlinear actions brings his life to life. He *is* dead. *He* is dead. He thinks of his woman as something to consume like a candy bar, like a movie, like a plate of food that you can send back to the cook if you don't like it, instead of something to create, like a possible goddess, like a temple of tenderness, like a trembling love poem. Forced to constrict himself to a mental world, it's no secret that the only ecstasy he feels is intellectual. Thus blinded, he forfeits his natural gifts for unlocking the sensual feminine "being" before him, aching to explore worlds of sexuality beyond his wildest dreams.

Introduction

If you could learn to create intimacies that lead directly to true love would you be willing to start over again in relationship? If the love your heart and soul yearn to bathe in was proven to be a direct result of certain behaviors rather than a fantasy would you be willing to forget your hopelessness, forgive your partner and try again? If clear practical instructions could be given for building love that lasts would you begin the practices? That is the challenge of this book: What are you willing to actually try?

The main idea of this book is quite simple. From moment to moment, no matter who you are relating to, you choose one of three kinds of love to set the tone for your relating: ordinary, extraordinary, or Archetypal.

Our culture does not teach us to distinguish among ordinary, extraordinary or Archetypal Relationship, so you have little clarity for consciously determining the quality of relationship that you create.

If the possibilities offered to you in this book were already provided by our culture you would not need to read this book. You would already be living in radiant joy and brilliant Love.

A culture can only teach the level of relationship skills that is already woven into its fabric. To learn more you must venture beyond traditional limits. Our culture does not teach you how to go beyond its own limits. It could, but it does not. In many ways our present culture takes our dignity away, subjugates women, deceives men and prepares us for a lifetime of relational mediocrity. Without consciously taking actions that seem unusual by normal standards you will rarely if ever leave the familiar but heartbreaking conditions of "ordinary human relationship."

This book recognizes your interest in discovering further possibilities. This book is strong support for "people" people, whose success and joy come from creatively relating with others, including

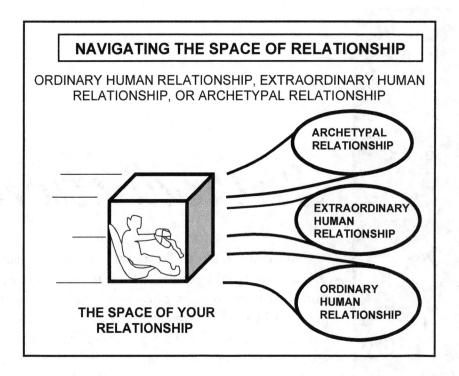

NAVIGATING THE SPACE OF RELATIONSHIP

ORDINARY HUMAN RELATIONSHIP, EXTRAORDINARY HUMAN RELATIONSHIP, OR ARCHETYPAL RELATIONSHIP

ARCHETYPAL RELATIONSHIP

EXTRAORDINARY HUMAN RELATIONSHIP

ORDINARY HUMAN RELATIONSHIP

THE SPACE OF YOUR RELATIONSHIP

parents, managers, nurses, educators, entertainers, stewardesses, therapists, trainers, waiters, public speakers, caregivers, leaders, consultants, customer relations personnel, climbing expedition members, astronauts, sports teams, personal development coaches, spiritual students, mediators, directors, healers, film makers, conductors, sales persons, counselors, or anyone longing to enter these vocations. This book supports you in taking a different series of actions, actions that shift your relating into new worlds of relationship. Years of experimenting confirm that the human body, mind, heart and soul thrive in a breath-by-breath and glance-by-glance whole-body experience of radiant joy and brilliant Love. An endless abundance of love can be directly experienced by any human being who prepares himself or herself. It is specifically this preparation that interests me.

As one of my heroes, Buckminster Fuller, said, "You never change things by fighting the existing reality. To change something, build a new model that makes the existing model obsolete." This book is about building new models for relationship.

The Challenge

This book is a call for men to grow up and for women to wake up. Life in a patriarchy – the form of our current culture – does not require men to grow up. Since the patriarchy protects adolescent men from the consequences of their actions, adolescence never matures. As a result, much of what the patriarchy promotes is irresponsible, designed for short-term indulgence and consumption rather than for long-term holistic sustainability. The patriarchy does not introduce men to the wide and creative future that is crying out for mature masculine intelligence. Men are not shown that there are more challenging aims than how to maximize quarterly profits. A man discovers who he is and what his life can actually be about through growing up and struggling toward authenticity. These discoveries allow a man to find his power and his destiny in the world, and to experience the rewards of using masculine kindness and attention for creating the possibility of relationship.

This book is a call for women to wake up and for men to grow up. Women are smarter, faster, and in many instances stronger than men. Women live longer and have better orgasms. Women have known this about themselves all along but have also been using it to complain and manipulate. It is now time for women to own their strengths and put them to use responsibly. It is a waste of effort to try to beat the patriarchy at its own game. Women can, of course. But what do women get if they play the men's games better than the men? They get more of what they already do not want: fear, hatred and aggression from men. The invitation in this book is for women to play a different game. Play Woman. Woman can enact and serve the Archetypal Feminine even within a patriarchy. As women distinguish between feminine and masculine power and take more and more possession of feminine responsibilities, they will find that they have jobs of the highest importance to do with plenty of power and challenges. Not the least of which is bringing men into experiencing a greater depth and breadth of intimate relationship.

Every word in this book is written for both men *and* women readers. Even if a section seems written specifically for women it is actually intended for both men *and* women, and vice versa. In other words, read the whole book. Most of the clarity and perspectives in *Building Love That Lasts* originate from a context that is broader than our familiar culture. That context is woven into every word. The new context is what provides you with new possibilities, so try to get as much of that into you as you can.

About Me

I almost gave up attending the university in my third year because I was dissatisfied with what I was being taught. I loved my field of physics but I was immensely disillusioned about what I thought a university should be. It was 1973 when I took a three-month sabbatical from school to read books from a list of titles I had gathered from respected friends. The questions I wrestled with felt immense and complex. What is a human being? What is a life? What is a man? My three months quickly came to an end with no definitive results. I stuffed my writings into a manila envelope and returned to classes. My unanswered questions sank into subconsciousness to fester for a year and a half.

In the fall of 1974 I discovered that the magic of the mind had been busily weaving a new set of neural networks for me. Complete concepts began bubbling into my awareness. I decided to create an experimental laboratory, not out of stainless steel and glass but rather out of intention and agreement. The laboratory would be energetic, a meeting format in which it was very okay to be yourself, to ask unusual questions, to try out new ideas and new ways of being. It would be an opportunity to be together that was at the same time safe, stimulating and active. One night I dared to share this idea with three friends. I proposed that we get a group of students together for discovering what was really going on that was not being taught in classes. They were in. The laboratory would start with an introductory meeting. We set the date for Friday, January 10, 1975. We reserved a room at the University Union and cobbled together some flyers to post around campus. The game was on.

I figured a few people might show up for an evening's discussion. The meeting was set for 7:00 PM and by 6:30 people were arriving. I sat, pretending to be one of the audience. I had never spoken to a group of people before and had no idea what to do. As more and more people entered I sat there nervously sweating, waiting for some kind of inspiration to move me to my feet, but nothing came. Finally, at ten after seven, my friend Roger Taber elbowed me in the ribs. "Hey! You have to go up there. You are the guy who thought of this." I remember creeping to the front of the room and facing more than seventy-five eager listeners.

I don't remember what I said that night, but the next week, on Thursday evening, fifteen people showed up at my apartment for a meeting. They continued showing up every week for the whole school year. The experiment worked. Wherever I lived after that, I would put up flyers and assemble a new team of experimenters, from local townspeople, to meet every week and explore the edges of what was possible.

The material in this book comes from working directly in these small groups; from our committment to provide for each other whatever was needed so that we could take the steps we wanted to take for authentic personal development. We found that the commitment needed to come first, before we knew how to produce the results needed. Such commitments took either foolishness or courage, and as I look back I can see we had both. We learned that authentic commitment created a necessity to which the universe could respond. Things would turn out unexpectedly well for people at our meetings – they had fun and they would keep coming back to do the experiments.

We used a simple method that I now refer to as "rapid learning," a method of trying something immediately, extemporaneously, instead of figuring a strategy out in advance. In such an approach it doesn't matter *what* you try, because whatever you try produces some kind of results – either favorable or a flop. The universe is a giant feedback generator, quite dependable for saying what works and what doesn't. Rapid learning was simple: if it was working, we kept going. If it wasn't, then we shifted our approach and tried again.

I was and still am a rampaging note taker. From these early stages on, I wrote down the feedback we got from the universe. My bookshelves are filled with three-ring binders overstuffed with hand-drawn diagrams and experimental process descriptions. I paid very careful attention to what worked and what did not. Things not working did not stop us from proceeding. They challenged our imaginations to invent entirely new procedures. The distilled results slowly collected themselves into what I now call "Possibility Management," a new way of working with people both individually and in groups, both personally and professionally; a way that creates clear communications, responsible enlivening relationship, imaginative innovations, and effective results.

My commitment to the universe was that whatever secrets it revealed to me I would document impeccably and share as widely as possible. That is why I worked so hard to bring this book together: to complete my end of the bargain – because the universe has certainly kept its end!

What Was Learned

Working in small groups in trainings and in Possibility Labs we figured out how to "voyage" into spaces of incredible clarity. That is, we learned to use group intelligence in nonlinear ways to bypass ordinary limits of perceiving and relating and could enter new territory repeatedly. We learned how to plug directly into the source of unlimited possibility, which turns out to be an Archetypal Principle, a "force of nature" as George Bernard Shaw called it, a facet of Archetypal Love out of which the entire universe is made.

We learned how to navigate our group to the center of the "Great Labyrinth of Spaces," predictably, repeatably, as a felt sensation, and then to stay there for three or five days in a row and work for what people wanted and needed. We discovered entryways into the same spaces that other explorers and researchers had entered to retrieve the clarity and poetry that they brought to the world. People like John and Antonietta Lilly, Charles Tart, John Holt, Joseph Chilton Pearce, Eric Berne, Martin Heidegger, Thomas Gordon, Linda Adams, Stephen Karpman, Valerie Lankford, Rupert Sheldrake, David Bohm, William Glasser, Ilya Prigogine, Carlos Castaneda. Even the way that healers and saints reportedly work with people became familiar to us.

I spent a number of years attempting to establish workable alternative cultures, only to find that the experiment failed each time due to human emotional conflicts. My focus turned to learning more about relationship. I became hungry for guidance and sought input from a series of traditions, including Maharishi Mahesh Yogi's Transcendental Meditation, Jose Silva's UltraMind System as taught by John Magera, Paramahansa Yogananda's Self Realization Fellowship, and Gurdjieff Foundation meetings with Ron Bosanquet in Australia. And, since 1989 I have been a student of Lee Lozowick and the Western Baul tradition.

In 1990, I changed careers – from designing computer hardware for biomedical research, to designing human "thoughtware" for developing "relationship intelligence." In 1995, I moved to Europe. In 1998, I started our training academy in Germany. Today the work continues in corporate trainings, Possibility Labs and Trainer Labs.

How to Use This Book

First, I ask you to be patient with the jargon that shows up in this book. In order to investigate conditions not normally addressed, I use quite a few words in unusual ways, borrowing terminology from Possibility Management. When introducing a term for the first time I have tried to put it in "quotes" and give you a brief working definition. For further explanation these quoted words are listed in the "Glossary of Possibility Management Terms" in the back of the book. Reading the Glossary is in itself an education in Possibility Management, *and* that is not the point of this book. Try not to get stuck in the new terms. If you find that while reading you do not understand something, my suggestion is to just keep reading on. The book says things in many different ways so that people with different ways of thinking and different personal experiences can still understand. You are not expected to understand everything. Later on you can return to what was not clear if you want to.

There is a lot in here. Don't anticipate getting everything all at once. I didn't. This book is a culmination of more than fifty years of learning, and not much of that learning was easy. Give yourself some slack. I hope that, as you read along, the new terminology makes understanding these ideas easier for you, and that the words become more and more familiar or even comfortable through usage.

About "Archetype"

One word used quite frequently is the term "Archetype." The Archetypal terminology used in *Building Love That Lasts* comes from Possibility Management and is *not* derived from or associated with the popular work of Carl Gustav Jung. Jung evolved his understanding of deep-psychology archetypes in reference to the psychoanalytical context that he inherited from his teacher Sigmund Freud. Instead of relying on Jung's experiences, we have done our own empirical research for over thirty years. These experiments brought us directly into contact with the same sources that Jung must have tapped into to formulate his particular terminology. Instead of a *psychological* context we researched from a *possibility* context. Because we went fishing with a different net, we caught a different sort of fish, although we fished in the same sea.

In Possibility Management, Archetypes are potential configurations hardwired into the energetic structure of human beings. Archetypes are either responsible or irresponsible. Irresponsible Archetypes are awakened during childhood and used to create a workable defense strategy. Responsible Archetypes lie dormant until they are turned on through an adolescent rite of passage (which is notably missing from our culture). Much is written in later chapters to further explore Archetypes, so this is enough for now. I have capitalized Archetypal words in this book because they are … well … Archetypal.

Everything Is Changing

Implied here is the understanding that nothing in this book is perfect. Nothing is final. All of it is in the process of development. Over the years of using and sharing these ideas and procedures I have watched them change before my eyes. They change even while I am speaking about them in public or using them in trainings. These ideas do not come from the known and the certain, rather they seem to be alive and continuously evolving.

I am not writing this book because I am a scholar who is recognized as an authority on the subject material. If I were writing from scholastic authority then I would say, "I will explain to you what is possible," or "I will reveal to you what is possible." Instead I say, "Let us investigate together what is possible." Fortunately for you *I do not know what I am talking about*. If I originated this writing in what I know for certain, then we would have a very short and boring conversation.

Instead of writing from certainty I am willing to be at risk. Being at risk means that I am willing to be in the uncomfortable position of *not knowing* and still responsibly proceeding. (I tell you this so that you can do the same kinds of experiments yourself.) Even in this moment I am on the spot, and because of my commitment to you, the reader, I am using everything I can to create useful results, even

though I do not already know how to do that. Together, like this, we enter and investigate what could be possible in unknown territory.

Prove It for Yourself

In no instance should you use the fact that you have a book in your hands as an excuse for giving away your "personal bullshit detector." No matter what this book says, it also insists that you prove it for yourself. There are no *shoulds* or *should nots* in this book, no good/bad, right/wrong, better/worse, positive/negative. There is no system of beliefs, no precepts, no moral codes, no rules. There is no ideal relationship to try to emulate, no model behavior to try to remember. Neutrality derives from the simple understanding that every action creates its own consequences. This book proposes new actions to cause new consequences, tested through your own experimentation. You get a chance to rethink your decisions about speaking, listening, feeling or being in relationship. Deep new clarity comes to you about how you create what you are creating, and how you could, if you wanted to, create something completely different. You have in your hands all that you need to further your own research.

Therefore, do not be surprised if you find yourself writing notes in the margins of this book, and adding details and dimensions of clarity to the diagrams based on what you yourself discover. Possibility Management is "open code," meaning, in this case, that its origins cannot be hidden because its origins are Archetypal. If you can understand Possibility Management, then, you are standing at the source of Possibility Management, and have the ability to further develop it. Just like open code computer software, Possibility Management will continue to be developed by you, the responsible user. If you eventually get copies of your findings back to me we can share what you have discovered in future editions. Or write your own books and articles if you want. You are encouraged to use these tools and techniques however you can to serve people. Make this material your own. At the same time please keep in mind that the value of referencing Possibility Management as your source is that Possibility Management will then hang together as a body of knowledge that will continue to serve people for many generations to come. We can continue developing it together. If you, however, mix these maps with new-age metaphysical esoteric psychology, rename them and pass them on to other people, then Possibility Management will be scattered and diluted. I hope you make choice A.

Keep Experimenting
Your Life as a Laboratory (BLTLCH00.01.)
This book is not a work of logic and the mind. This book is an investigation into "experiential reality," that is, reality before it is influenced by words. This book is *not* about saying how it is. This book is an invitation for you to make experiments to *discover for yourself* how it is. Talk is cheap – worthless in many instances. Especially talk about the possibility of directly experiencing Archetypal Love. Doing experiments – now *that* has value. Hopefully, while reading this book, doing experiments will become your way.

Over and over again this book will beg you, entice you, even trick you into actually trying new behaviors. Because what you *do* and what you *stop doing* is what creates the results you have in your life, not what you *think*. Understanding what this book says is not enough to make a difference for you. Certainly, understanding is involved. But understanding is not sufficient. Satisfaction in human relationship comes less from how you think about it and more from how you experience it. How you experience relationship will come through the novelty of your actions.

As you explore the new terrains yourself, personally, under your own volition and at your own risk, your authority becomes authentic. When your authority is authentic then the stories that you tell about your life can awaken a long-forgotten longing in other people to experience radiant joy and brilliant Love. Hearing such stories is how we remember that true love is possible. Going *first* is what makes you a leader. Changing *yourself* simultaneously changes your culture.

Keep in mind that this book cannot be your final guide. The real-time feedback and coaching needed to adjust your attitudes and behaviors only comes from other living, breathing, feeling human beings, not from a book, and not from your own mind. So, plan to talk with people about what you are learning and trying. Getting a group together to discuss and practice these ideas can prove to be exceptionally productive, especially as an aid to digesting the new ideas and creating practical ways to apply them.

When experimenting, be generous and kind with yourself. Give yourself plenty of space and time. Spending a part of your day exploring Archetypal Love is time well spent. Consider in comparison how much time you spend watching television commercials, sitting in traffic jams, or waiting in line at the post office.

Please remember that experiencing wild phenomena is *not* the goal of this work. The goal is for you to get into the laboratory and start doing experiments yourself rather than watching safely from the observation room. Should some delightful experience actually occur for you, regard your ecstasy as an accident, *and* take careful notes. Developing the discipline to experiment invites more than the usual number of fortuitous accidents.

"But What If My Partner ... ?"
You might be quite enthusiastic about the possibility of self-development that this book represents. You might feel inspired by

the thought of entering new domains of relationship and of exploring deeper intimacies with your partner. You might also imagine that to make use of this book your partner should be at the same place as you in their development with an equivalent enthusiasm for doing experiments. The third part of this misery-making formula is noticing that your partner is neither at the same place as you nor do they carry the same level of interest. At this point the whole proposal of developing relationship intelligence devolves into a painfully insoluble paradox with you being the victim of the joke.

I don't know where this fantasy of harmonious growth got its beginnings, but it is arguably *never* the case that two people are at the same place in their development or have the same level of enthusiasm about relationship experiments, *ever*. We are human beings, living organisms. We have the possibility of being reborn into a new experience of life with every breath. Stasis and orderliness are nowhere in the picture.

The procedure for using this book equally applies in *any* quality of relationship: you read the book and you practice the experiments. You have fun. You try your best and crash and burn, pick yourself up and try again. Play around. Stretch beyond your limits. These experiments open fabulous new universes of perception and experience – *your* perception and *your* experience. Your partner will do whatever they will do. Sure you can invite them to play along with you. Either they will play or they won't. But the moment you expect *anything* from your partner the possibility of authentic relationship is killed, because what you then have is your expectation instead of the relationship.

Even if your partner is thoroughly antagonistic to creating an extraordinary life and profound intimacy, this never had nor ever will have any impact on what you decide to learn about and explore. No matter if you take huge risks in being vulnerable and communicative and every effort you make seems to explode in your face, *no effort is wasted*. Your matrix builds regardless of your apparent lack of success. One thing I have been learning about is having faith. One thing I see worthy of great respect and faith is evolution. Your actual circumstances turn out to be irrelevant. What matters is your relationship to those circumstances. You can have faith in evolution happening in whatever your circumstances.

There are no failed relationships, because in every relationship evolution is happening. Even if you live in total denial of what is really going on in your relationship, something is cooking in you, and sooner or later it will come to the surface for your benefit. So relax about your partner, and keep making efforts; see what you can learn. Do whatever you can to accept things as they are – accept things deep within yourself and completely outside of yourself. In the moment you accept, those things are free to suddenly change form.

When Nothing Happens

Even after reading this book and doing the experiments off and on for five or ten years, nothing might happen. This is not a problem. There is nothing wrong with you. Trying experiments and having nothing happen does not mean that Archetypal Love does not exist. The fact that the possibility of experiencing something great is just a possibility does not detract from its greatness.

Building Love That Lasts is a tough book, a difficult book. You will look directly in the face of your own incompetencies, your unconsciousness, your irresponsibilities, and your "underworld." This is painful, and the pain will not go away. You will learn that what has been motivating your actions is not what you thought. You will see that you have hurt the people you love; that in fact you wanted to hurt them because you thought you had no other options. Now you will have other options to try, and they are simple, solid, and clearly explained options to create more Love and intimacy than you may have thought existed.

Suddenly, relationship may take on a value and importance that will draw from you the highest regard. Suddenly, being with your partner might become delightful in ways never before imagined.

Probably the best overall guideline for how to use this book is: Have fun!

PART I

Expansive Learning

CHAPTER 1

Learning About Joy and Love

In school we are taught to learn by fitting new information into our already existent understanding like fitting pieces into a jigsaw puzzle. This is what I call "defensive learning." Defensive learning assumes that we already know the most important things there are to know. Anything new is an extra puzzle piece that must be fitted into the portion of the puzzle we have already assembled. If we encounter something that does not fit into our current "knowledge continent" we tend to ignore the new thing as irrelevant. Our relevancy filters are so fast that many times we do not even recognize when we have decided to ignore something because it does not fit in anywhere. If we ignore something before realizing we have ignored it then that thing becomes invisible to us.

Defensive learning, although widely used, is extremely linear: it allows us to only learn more about what we already know. When we gain maturity and have a wish to enter "the unknown" we may discover that our defensive approach that at first seemed to protect us has now become our prison.

Expansive Learning

The secrets in this book will be discovered through stepping out of the defensive learning prison and experimenting with a nonlinear learning method that I call "expansive learning." Expansive learning is what we did as children *before* we went to school. Think of how much a child learns in his or her first years: hand-eye coordination, standing, walking, speaking, social etiquette, to name a few skills. Compare that with how much you learned in this past year.

Expansive learning assumes that we know almost nothing. It encourages us to accept new puzzle pieces on their own merits. It allows unrecognizable information to stand alone in us, still permitting us to use it without demanding that it fit anywhere into our present field of understanding.

Expansive learning occurs in parallel by allowing us to build understanding on many isolated construction sites simultaneously. It is nonlinear because some pieces may not fit together for years, perhaps ever, while other pieces may come together in moments, sliding into place whole chunks at a time.

Expansive learning is not about trying to create one all-encompassing unified field theory, such as Einstein sought during the later part of his life. The expansive approach involves staying open and flexible – keeping new options available even if they make no sense (at first) compared with what we already know. Expansive learning is therefore indispensable as the foundation for *Building Love That Lasts*, which explores domains of human relationships and love – fields interlaced with much that we do not know.

With expansive learning it is okay to *not know*. You simply move into the unknown and start looking around, already assuming that you will not understand everything. While not knowing, you allow yourself to *see what you see* and *feel what you feel*, without trying to fit it in anywhere. This means that you might not know what it is that you *are* experiencing, at first, or how it works, or how it all fits together. In time, the new things that you notice will become more and more familiar. Eventually they can establish whole new continents of understanding for you that vastly enrich the quality of your life and your relationships.

The challenge of expansive learning is that if you are accustomed to defensive learning, expansive learning may seem disorderly. In the midst of these explorations you may have the sensation that you are no longer standing on a solid foundation of logic, with defendable reasons, and that you are less in control of the learning process. This is exactly how expansive learning feels.

Observations and arguments encountered in these pages will tend to be less heady and more experiential. *Building Love That Lasts* will instruct you in using language as a bridge to communicate new experiences based on your own internal reference points – *your* personal sensations in the immediate present.

While expansive learning includes diversity and chaos, don't assume that it will only cause anxiety or disruption. As you venture further into the territories that this book explores, you may be quite surprised to find that you can actually relax and be effective without being in total control or having your usual level of certainty. You may even find a sense of empowerment and experiential freedom when you no longer need to carry around a heavy platform of linear arguments on which to defend your actions or inactions. You may discover a refreshing excitement in uncertainty, as the experience of *not knowing* indicates that you have entered a gateway to new possibilities.

Discoveries do not come without some reorientation, however. The wilder the reorientation, the more interesting the discovery! If you guard yourself against disillusionment and disassembly, you eliminate the chance of discovery. Conversely, the more accepting you are of wild reorientation, the more interesting your discoveries will be.

You can rely on your mind's astonishing ability to establish new definitions for normal. Think how quickly you adopted into your daily life new technologies like microwave ovens, fax, DVD, CD, mobile telephony, personal computers and Internet. The mind can quickly adjust what it calls normal to include new ways of thinking, feeling, acting and being. During continual expansive learning new normals do not last long. Soon the next disorientation comes along and you again experience the uncertainty of being in strange territory. Such is the life of an explorer.

A true explorer can count on being periodically uncomfortable for the rest of his days. Learning about building Love that lasts is comparable to being in a space pilot training school where becoming functional in groundlessness is part of the program .

If you question whether or not you qualify as such an explorer, lay your worries to rest. If you have read this far, you can be assured that you *are already* an explorer. If not, you would have put this book aside long ago. Welcome aboard!

This chapter will present ten essential actions and attitudes of expansive learning to guide you through everything that follows in this book. Considering these perspectives can help you catalyze a significant deepening of your relationship intelligence.

Expansive Learning Includes:
1. Building/expanding matrix
2. Making vital distinctions
3. Getting on the One Team
4. Thinking beyond separation
5. Taking your time
6. Letting your patterns disintegrate
7. Being okay with looking bad
8. Avoiding naiveté
9. Apprenticing to a guide, and
10. Being lovable.

By making sincere efforts to blend these actions and attitudes into the basic mix of your daily life you become an expansive learner. The surprise awaiting your discovery is that the precious innocence and raw passion of expansive learning makes you an authentic aphrodisiac exuding the scent of radiant joy and brilliant Love.

1. Building/Expanding Matrix

There are secrets you cannot understand even if they stare you in the face for decades. This kind of secret keeps itself. It stands invisibly before you until something in you changes. This book does not intend to reveal this kind of secret to you – it cannot. But by you doing the expansive learning experiments in *Building Love That Lasts* you gradually build in yourself something that makes it possible to see what you could not see before: consciousness – commonly defined as greater awareness or expanded view. Consciousness does not grow until it has something to grow on. What you build is called "matrix."

Matrix is the energetic framework upon which consciousness can grow. Learning that matrix exists and how matrix can be built adds tremendous clarity to the whole issue of personal development. For example: Noticing that one person can easily learn and retain a new soft skill, like expressing feelings honestly, while another person struggles and falters merely indicates differences in their matrixes. Proceeding with personal development begins with building matrix.

Think of a climbing rose bush. Before it can climb it needs some kind of trellis to support its growth. Likewise, before human consciousness can grow there needs to be a structure for consciousness to expand onto. The trellis for consciousness is matrix (in no way related to the film of the same name). Many of the exercises and experiments described in this book are specifically designed to build matrix.

Keep in mind that understanding *how* to do an experiment does not build matrix. Only *doing* the experiment builds matrix. Doing an experiment is called "practice," and practice is the means to building Love that lasts.

The primary way in which we "practice," and thereby build matrix in relationship, is by living and "being-with" others as determined by our commitments, rather than as determined by our circumstances. For example, you might decide to be more patient with your children, and to spend more time simply sharing your presence with them, without an agenda. However, when the day is done and you notice that you had no more patience, you might want to attribute the failure to circumstances, like: a conflict in your schedule; things starting too late; everyone being too tired; an unexpected visitor. This is not practice; this is defense! As an expansive learner building a new matrix for relationship, your practice would entail creating new ways to meet your commitments rather than caving in to the circumstances. Practicing would be to produce the promised results regardless of reasons, excuses or conditions.

Practice builds matrix for holding additional consciousness. Consciousness is everywhere. The more matrix you build, the more consciousness can show up through you. At the same time, however, it is useful to know that no matter how sincerely or how diligently you practice, matrix can only grow at a certain maximum rate of speed. While you can slow the growth of matrix to a minimum, the upper speed limit for building matrix cannot be broken. It can also be useful to know that there is no "top end" to building matrix.

MAP OF BUILDING MATRIX

WITHOUT MATRIX:

WITH MATRIX:

Consciousness is everywhere. The more elegant the being, the more consciousness it reflects. Consciousness shows up as responsibility. A person's being starts out about the size of a grapefruit. Matrix is the framework upon which being can grow. Without a matrix, being does not take elegant form. Matrix can be built through exposing yourself to beneficial stresses (such as visiting a foreign culture or trying to understand this book), certain radiations (such as being in the company of saints or sacred artifacts), certain substances (such as a true alchemical elixir, like Tonic Gold™), the efforts to stay awake (such as by paying attention to your attention and staying aware of what you are aware of), and your efforts to practice (such as flossing your teeth every night before you go to bed no matter how late it is or how tired you are). No one can build matrix for you.

Expanded matrix automatically gives you the ability to venture into new territories of awareness. (The corollary to this is that if you are surprised and suddenly find yourself experiencing unfamiliar territory, it could be simply that your matrix has been growing further than you thought!) At first, the idea of taking a journey into new territory sounds romantic and adventurous. And, well, it is romantic and adventurous, better than any tropical island white-beach-and-warm-seas fantasy. But, as you may already know, the experience of *actually entering* new territory can awaken hidden emotional surprises. Unexpected reactions can come from long-repressed insecurities, outdated irrelevant decisions about yourself, emotional wounds from communications never expressed or never heard, and so on. Since this book is designed to build matrix, any or all of these reactions may occur for you. I suggest that you take a breath and prepare yourself mentally and emotionally for meeting the unexpected before each reading session. Don't be dismayed if you find that some parts of your life turn upside down, or you feel unusually agitated, while reading this book.

Feeling uncomfortable while reading this book does not mean that anything is wrong, or that you should turn around and try to find your way back to the illusionary safety of what you formerly regarded as solid ground. Feeling uncomfortable or disoriented, as we've noted before, simply indicates that you are in the process of expansive learning; you are building matrix.

2. Making Vital Distinctions

A distinction divides one set of things into two or more sets of things through discerning important but previously unnoticed differences. For example, a bowl of apricots is only a bowl of apricots until you distinguish between under-ripe, exactly-ripe and over-ripe apricots. The apricot distinction can make a difference in your breakfast. The distinctions in this book can make a difference in your relationship.

Making distinctions is a foundation for expansive learning. Distinction-making creates clarity that you did not have before, which reveals options that you did not see to choose from. New options permit you to take relationship actions that you never took before; actions that can awaken previously undreamed-of aliveness, pleasures, and possibilities in your relationships.

The relationship distinctions made in this book are not made in our culture at large. We could not learn them from our parents, for example, because they did not have them. We did not learn them from teachers in school for the same reason. Without making and living these distinctions, and knowing what sort of relationship we are creating in each moment, we will automatically tend to create what this book refers to as "ordinary human relationship." There is nothing wrong with creating Ordinary human relationship; it simply produces predictable, mechanical experiences in relating with other human beings. Without making new distinctions we may never even suspect that anything other than ordinary human relationship is possible.

But, then again, maybe we had hopes. Maybe, after looking around at hundreds of "ordinary" couples, we developed a deep heart's desire to create something more profound with our life and our connection with another person. We may have had a silently pulsating wish, without knowing how, to make the moments of our relating into a sanctuary for ecstatic love.

Fortunately, in the domain of expansive learning, not knowing how does not matter. Rather, it is our intentions and our efforts that matter. This book can inflame our intentions with clear distinctions, and educate those efforts with practices. If we live out the rest of our lives and waste our potential, we will lose a precious opportunity and suffer a painful loss. With these distinctions in place, however, we have the potential to bring our relationships out of a shadowy chaos and into a bright vibrancy.

As you read over the relationship distinctions listed below don't struggle to try to fully understand them all right now. They are presented here to give you an overview of where we will be going in following chapters.

Relationship Distinctions
1. Relationship is ongoing moment-to-moment creation in one of three domains: ordinary human relationship, extraordinary human relationship, or Archetypal Relationship.
2. We are either conscious that we create the quality of our relationship or we are not conscious of it and we try to avoid that responsibility.
3. If we try to avoid responsibility for creating the quality of our relationship then we unconsciously create ordinary human relationship.
4. If we *are* conscious that we create the quality of our relationship and take responsibility for our thoughts, feelings and actions as an adult man or woman, then we can create extraordinary human relationship.
5. If we consciously create the quality of our relationship *and* take responsibility for the Archetypal context of that relationship then we can create Archetypal Relationship.
6. We cannot create either extraordinary human relationship or Archetypal Relationship unconsciously. Both take conscious efforts.
7. We cannot create Archetypal Relationship without first being able to consciously and sustainably create extraordinary human relationship.

8. We cannot consciously create extraordinary human relationship until we become (painfully) aware of how, when, and why we unconsciously create ordinary human relationship. (Welcome to your underworld!)
9. Gaining all that is required to create and enter the domain of Archetypal Relationship can take a long time and a lot of (guided) effort.
10. There is no better life than taking the time and making the efforts to learn to create Archetypal Relationship. (This last, of course, is not a distinction; it is just my own personal opinion.)

3. Getting on the One Team

All the readers of this book together form one exploration team. There are no passengers. On this adventure everyone has jobs to do. We are all crew. It is not an *us vs. them* situation, the *haves* and the *have nots*, the privileged and the marginalized. The work we are doing is taking place at the edge of the known, the edge of culture. You are here, so you too are responsible for the success of this journey. If you sense that you have something to say, we depend on you to say it. This might not be fair, but as science fiction writer David Gerrold says, "Nobody is the enemy; we're all just martyrs to evolution."

This conversation we are having right now is the leading edge of the evolution of consciousness in human relationship. Your experiments cut new forms of consciousness that open pathways for others to more easily follow. There are thousands of people around the world on the edge of discovery waiting for someone to go first. As mentioned in the Introduction, when you go first everyone benefits. We are one team. So, document your discoveries and let them be known. Use your intelligence to test everything. Use your voice to share what you find.

If you think that what you are discovering is already common knowledge, go stand in a bus station for a couple of hours. Hang around in a Wal-Mart and watch people interact with their kids. Out of a million people, what percentage do you think are doing experiments like those described in this book? Look around. The answer is: almost none. Every effort you make to learn about radiant joy expands the limits of human consciousness and human understanding. Every moment longer that you can tolerate the intensity of the experience of brilliant Love creates a building-block substance that is used to transform the world. I beg you to keep doing whatever you can.

4. Thinking Beyond Separation

This book is not a course in philosophy, religion, or exobiology. We are here to expand our learning, and thus expand our competence in creating relationship. Expansive learning includes asking a number of dangerous questions, like where does the urge for relationship come from? And what is it that does the relating? These are questions we may not commonly consider. Exploring answers to these questions can provide us with insights for taking actions that create results we do not commonly achieve. Let's begin with a question about consciousness.

How many consciousnesses are there?

Relationship originates between unique and separate human beings. If people were not unique and separate there could be no distinguishing relationship. We would just be together, all as one. The fact that we can conceive of so-called relationships, and the fact that we act as if relationships exist as something to speak about and to develop, causes us to assume that individual people are separate from each other. This could be a false assumption. It could be the case that all people who have ever existed, who exist now, and who

ever will exist are but uniquely reflecting facets of one, whole, brilliantly jeweled, radiant consciousness.

For a moment, let's consider this possibility that our assumption of separation is false. Let's ask the question: If instead of separate, individuated consciousnesses, we are all manifestations of one consciousness, *where* is that consciousness?

Let's start by imagining the possible "one consciousness" as the light from the sun. You do not see light from the sun until it hits something, which is why the night sky looks black. At night, we are in the shadow of the Earth, so the sun does not hit the atmosphere. In space, the only things out there for sunlight to hit are the moon, comets, and satellites. Even though just as much sunlight "goes by" at night as goes by in the daytime, we don't see the sunlight "go by" when there is nothing for it to hit. In this same way we do not experience omnipresent consciousness until it prisms through a physical object. Consciousness could be everywhere, but between objects there is nothing to indicate the presence of that consciousness.

When light strikes an object, the quality of the light that we see (for example, the color, transparency, shape, texture, brightness) is determined by the physical quality of the object that reflects the light. Similarly, the quality of consciousness that we experience (for example, intelligence, attention span, flexibility, radiance, creativity, presence) with any animal, vegetable or mineral is determined by the physical structure of the object reflecting the one consciousness. The more sophisticated and complex the structure, the more sophisticated and complex the consciousness that it manifests. For instance, a stone is less conscious than a flower is less conscious than a worm is less conscious than a bird is less conscious than a cat is less conscious than a human is less conscious than those structures that manifest a consciousness greater than the human being, and therefore too complex for us to perceive their existence.

The fact that we human beings tend to regard each other as separate beings is not wrong. It is just that the separatist view is only a partial picture, a distortion created by circumstance and perspective.

We human beings can act as individual particles when we hold and defend our personal opinions, preferences, territories and attitudes. We also sometimes act as connected wave formations such as during mass hysteria, shopping sprees (7 million copies of Harry Potter sold in one day!), and the experience of communion. A more holistic picture of a human being, then, would allow that we are neither solely particles nor solely waves. We are, instead, potentially capable of expressing both particle and wave behavior.

We contain this potential to act as either a wave or a particle within us at all times. In physics, an object with such qualities is called a "wavicle." Human behavior is more like the behavior of wavicles than the behavior of either waves or particles. As you recognize your wavicleness, you expand your learning and add dimensions to your abilities to interact.

5. Taking Your Time

This book will explore ordinary, extraordinary and Archetypal domains. Through taking the time to study the maps and practice the soft skills presented here you will be discovering previously unrevealed dimensions of relationship. You obviously want these skills … and now! Right away! Perhaps you are already asking, "Does true love itself exist? If so, prove it. How do I get there?"

The answer to this and every other "how to" question is, "You get there one step at a time." Learning in excruciating detail exactly what we are up to *now* is the first step to the possibility of being up to something else.

Seeing how we trap ourselves in the ordinary propels us to leave the ordinary and enter the extraordinary and the Archetypal.

While you are reading this book and experimenting with these ideas the possibility is open that you may encounter the extraordinary. If the extraordinary happens to you try not to overreact. This whole universe is extraordinary. If you notice and appreciate extraordinariness happening in the microcosm around you, make the time to write it down. Writing down your experience changes it from subjective to objective, which is the same as saying if you don't write it down it didn't happen. Keeping notes on your journey can prove to be invaluable for building matrix.

There are some hints that make your writing more effective in transforming extraordinary experience into objective reality. When you write, try to not figure it all out or psychologize it. Don't write what it means to you personally. Just write down "what happened." Allow yourself to savor the deep sensual nuances of the experience and keep exploring. Don't get off the elevator at the first floor; instead stay with it and keep going as high as the elevator can take you. Practice tolerating the extraordinary for as long as you can endure it. Practice this every chance you get, over and over again. Ask the next question. Do the next experiment. Write what happens by splitting off only ten percent of your attention. Write as a side effect without laboring over the writing, while using the rest of your attention to have the experience.

Do not succumb to the temptation of being reasonable by going into your head to analyze, judge and criticize what you are experiencing. *Slow down.* Stay on the edge. Thinking about experience brings you into your head. Going into your head when you are having an experience removes you from the experience, so you don't get to have it. Just because you have been trained to go into your head by your culture and times does not mean that you have to do it.

Experience is rare. It only happens now. If an experience turns out to be a wondrous experience you can think about it later. *Have the wondrous experience now.* Love only happens now. Not going into your head when love is happening takes practice. Take the time to practice.

And, while we are on the subject of time and experience, remember that the good news and the bad news is the same news: all things pass, including wondrous experience. A heavenly experience is just as temporary as a hellish experience. The Tibetan Vajrayana Buddhist Master Chögyam Trungpa said, "When you are in heaven, be in heaven. When you are in hell, be in hell." The rest of the time you can think about it.

Without experiencing true love personally you may not suspect that relationship can offer such surprising possibilities. This book invites you to start over again with relationship and *this time* to come in through a different doorway. The new path blows away the mists of fairy tales and confusion, outrage and doubt, and enables you to create a relationship full of mystery and ecstasy that will take a lifetime to explore.

Building Love that lasts is completely possible, *and* you need to be cautioned: it takes focused intentional efforts, and time. Unfolding the Archetypal Woman and Man takes time. It may even take luck. But certainly lots of time.

6. Letting Your Patterns Disintegrate

We have been trained that learning involves pattern recognition. To an even greater degree, however, learning (especially expansive learning) also involves pattern disintegration.

Patterns disintegrate through learning new core ideas, called "memes." A meme is a fundamental instruction for the design of your mind in the same way that a gene is a fundamental instruction for the design of your body. This book is filled with "memetic viruses" that can spring back to life in a moment through contact with the living medium of your mind.

The memes in this book are very clear and have a tendency to replace any memes you presently have that are less clear than the new ones. Developing new competence in creating relationship means the old patterns must be released from their grip. Our old view must disassemble. Give yourself permission to wholly experience the annihilation of your present relationship memes.

Our usual modes for being in relationship are simply patterns of behavior that we learned long ago and continue to implement because they are familiar. What you are doing by reading this book and experimenting with new behavior is saying, "The buck stops here. With me. Now. I want to make changes." By taking responsibility for starting new patterns you simultaneously destroy old patterns.

During the reordering of your understanding you may experience some moments of confusion. This is normal. Confusion is one sign of grief; you may be grieving the passing of the old familiar ways. For example, you may see that you've been mistrusting and even denying your own intuition in favor of what others tell you, or in favor of some system of doctrinal belief. When this awareness hits, head on, let it come with honest wails and tears, if that's what it does, rather than trying to keep an already dead thing alive so as to avoid the pain of recognizing that it is dead. As Marilyn Ferguson said so long ago in *The Aquarian Conspiracy*, "a falling apart precedes a falling together." I encourage you to let the reordering happen uninterrupted, and as thoroughly as you can. You short-circuit the process when you attempt to cover it up or deny it. Take care to nurture yourself through it all. Go for a walk. Take a long hot bath. Listen to sweet music. Enjoy the sunset and a good meal. Go to bed early.

If you succeed in leaving your known territory and entering the unknown where everything seems new, one thing you can be sure of is that the mind will not leave you alone for long. It is uncanny how the mind will rustle through the ashes of our burnt down house of cards and without effort construct another way of looking at things in almost no time. Pattern disintegration is a prelude to a new world view. The mind puts itself back together without you having to do much of anything.

If you experience pattern disintegration and renewal often enough you will start to see that this is how evolution happens. Expansive learning means that you can learn to recognize and participate in the evolutionary flow. As the bright warmth of summer fades into fall, so too does the deathly chill of winter inevitably blossom into spring. Such transitions are natural and, in the big picture, unstoppable. The force of evolution does its mysterious work during the transitions between solid phases. Get used to being in transition.

Through making efforts to shift your basic life strategy from mere survival to full-out living you align yourself with forces that are greater than yourself. You start to play a role in what author Rogan Taylor calls the "death and resurrection show." In the heat of unexpected opportunities your old ideas blaze and crisp, making way for new ideas to sprout. Through fire after fire you slowly come to discover what philosopher Karlfried Graf Durckheim refers to as "that which is indestructible." Life can be more intensely profound and exciting than we have ever been led to believe, including our life of relationship.

7. Being Okay with Looking Bad

You are going to look bad in this expansive learning process. There is no way around

it. In the paradigm of defensive learning we have been convinced that looking bad is the worst possible circumstance: If we look bad to our peer group they might cast us away. Deep down we fear that being banished from our core group is a death sentence. And a long time ago it used to be. In some cases now it still is. But, look at it this way – seeking peer acceptance is typical herd behavior. Survival through herd behavior is an instinct we acquired long before we crept down from the trees and stood upright on two feet. Although the urge to follow our ancient herd instincts may feel strong, we do not have to follow them. In particular, herd instincts do not serve us when we are doing un-herd-like things, such as learning. Expansive learning is not herd behavior. Expansive learning is individual behavior. When learning expansively you may tend to stand out in a crowd.

Learning something new, which you are doing as you work with this book, automatically makes you look bad to your peers because you look strangely different from how you looked before. You also look bad to yourself because now that you know what you know now, you can see that you did not know it before. There is no way to avoid looking bad if you are on the learning team.

You get to choose between the "looking good team" and the "learning team." As a member of the looking good team you might be looking good, but as Ken Windes – my first trainer and a student of Dr. Eric Berne's Transactional Analysis – used to say, "Looking good, going nowhere." The way you join the learning team is to keep studying, keep practicing, going to talks, seminars, workshops and trainings, doing your own personal experimenting, and implementing new behaviors. In this particular case the way you join the learning team is to keep reading.

If while reading you begin to experience a painfully clear perspective of yourself and what your relationship-life has been about, let that experience go on and on for a long time, as long as it can go. Not as guilt. Not as self-flagellation. Merely as clear self-recognition about what you have actually been up to. It takes time for your self-image to adjust to the new view. It takes time to hit bottom satisfactorily so that wisdom, humbleness and compassion can ripen out of the pain of disillusionment.

You may find that you have some resistance to seeing clearly what you have been up to. By seeing the new clarity and at the same time having resistance to seeing the new clarity you are actually holding two things in the same place at the same time. Two things cannot normally occupy the same space at the same time. Holding two things in the same place at the same time is called "cathexis." Cathecting (allowing cathexis) produces a valuable kind of stress energy, similar to isometric exercises. Conscious cathexis builds your matrix. Cathecting certain energies and exposing yourself to certain experiences and influences produces evolutionary change, which is not necessarily a pretty sight.

Try to avoid explanatory, justificatory, diversionary or anesthetizing tactics to avoid the discomfort of realizing what you have been up to in your relationship-life. The discomfort is the birth pain of new consciousness within you.

8. Avoiding Naïveté

There are real pitfalls to eating hamburgers, driving to work, or taking a bath. There are also real pitfalls along this journey toward building Love that lasts. Don't be naïve. Stay alert to the "dangers" of expansive learning, especially in learning what you did not know that you did not know about. For example, you might be shocked when you first recognize the level and intensity of delusion generally circulated in our culture. Or, you might find that you are changing faster than

your present circle of friends and notice that they have little interest in talking about what you now most want to talk about. You might suddenly start remembering surprising little incidents that occurred in your childhood – events that reflect badly on the fantasy image you've had of your parents or relatives. You might unexpectedly discover a deep inner inspiration for working in a career that is very different from the career path you are presently following. The dangers along the journey toward building Love that lasts are that some parts of your life might change.

It is naïve to assume that many changes can all happen at once for you, because the matrix for holding greater understanding can only be built at a certain rate. You avoid naïveté in this process when you practice patience, allowing yourself to persist even when changes are not happening as fast as you think they should. Changes unwrap layer by layer. Old wounds are healed one feeling at a time. Expired invalid decisions are re-cognized and re-made one decision at a time. As we discussed in number 5 above, these things take time.

During the unfolding process, as we build Love that lasts, I have observed that imbalances can occur. Pay attention. Watch out that your naïveté doesn't get you trapped in them. For example, the habit for some women to hate men runs deep in the female heart. There are so many reasons to hate men. Thousands of years of man-hating can vibrate in your nerves, nerves that you inherited directly from the body of a woman who also had reasons to hate men. When you start getting your clarity back, your voice back, and your center back, it is wise to be vigilant that your newfound power is not used by your unconscious commitment to despise and destroy men. You would be surprised how many spiritually developed women languish in a self-made righteous hell of unconscious man-hating. And we wonder why more men are not attracted to personal development!

For men, we are so deeply terrified of our innate nothingness that stepping into self-reflective opportunities is not exactly our cup of tea. Either we act out being a sensitive, nice boy still hiding behind our mama's apron or we have shut our feelings down altogether, preferring the adrenaline highs provided by money, power and impersonal sex. Give us a better cell phone or a BMW with GPS and we are satisfied as deeply as we are willing to be satisfied, especially when there are still wars so easy to cook up.

9. Apprenticing to a Guide

Consider not trying to make this journey alone. The guidance of someone who has gone before you and can provide you with timely feedback and coaching is highly recommended. A guide may even be necessary for success.

How do you find such a guide? Stay open and pay attention. Keep talking with people about what you are doing. It is said that, "When the student is ready the teacher appears." It is also said that, "When the teacher is ready the students appear." Both of these axioms can be extremely misleading, rich with opportunities for betrayal and self-delusion for the unwary. (Even for the wary! So be very wary!)

Human beings tend to succeed better when they work *together* on an evolutionary journey, because support for evolution is contextual; that is, encouragement and support for evolution come from your culture, the people you bring around you. Trying to wing it on your own cannot usually generate enough momentum to escape the gravitational pull toward "normal," especially within a culture that does not promote personal development and transformation. Feedback and coaching from a skilled guide clarifies and ignites your innate rocket fuel and simultaneously establishes a new cultural context for you to work from.

But finding a qualified guide in these days of computer learning may not be so easy. In any case, keep trying. You may discover that outrageous coincidences favor people who make courageous efforts to build Love that lasts.

Do not be afraid to apprentice yourself to a lover of love. At the same time, do not be naïve about giving authority to just any so-called guide. There are many self-proclaimed teachers who use their power and the name of love to slide themselves into your purse, your psychology or your panties for their own personal benefit. Pay attention and trust your intuition more than their words. Take your time and observe anyone else working with that guide. If other apprentices seem to be empowered, clear, gentle, open, and able to communicate with you, you may have just found yourself an authentic guide.

10. Being Lovable

The biggest stumbling block in relationship is often the unwavering notion that we are unlovable. We can be easily convinced that we are unlovable during incidental childhood events, especially in a modern industrialized culture where childraising has been relegated to the category of chores below that of washing clothes and putting dishes away. After once concluding that we are not loved we may continue to prove ourselves right by selectively editing our perceptions so we only see confirming evidence. Even a tiny scrap of circumstantial evidence suffices to support our commitment to self-hatred. From then on, we live our life in self-fulfilling prophecy, shadowy loneliness, stale resentment and poorly disguised despair.

If this scenario applies to you, perhaps you are reasoning that, since you are obviously not lovable now, you were never lovable. The problem is, *you have already been loved.* If you look, you *could* find the memory of a moment in your life in which you were loved

– otherwise you would not know what being loved is all about and being loved would not matter to you! You have already been loved by a friend, a teacher, a neighbor, a grandparent, an aunt or uncle, a colleague, a brother or sister, and, God forbid, in moments – and although you may find this hardest of all to accept – even by your own parents. You know that this is true.

If you have ever been loved in your life, even for a moment, *then you are already lovable*. It is too late to think, even for a moment, no less for the rest of your life, that you are unlovable.

But, you may have a persistent feeling that you want to be loved *more*. This is great. I want to be loved more too. (I also want to win the lottery.) In the meantime, while we wait around for our fantasies to maybe come true, we can learn more about loving and being the source of love so that wherever we go love happens. Then we can ourselves discover the true abundance of Love, for real, right here and right now, wherever we are.

So. Good. Now that we are done with *that little thing* and you can trust yourself to be lovable right now *forever*, we can get on with the rest of the book.

These ten basics of expansive learning will start us roving in a propitious direction. As consciousness explorer and educator Joseph Chilton Pearce says, "Perhaps the scope of this work sounds a bit broad for a single volume, and I can hear complaints that this book attempts too much. But I argue that all too often we attempt too little. Better an impossible task of splendid proportion than a sure but piddling one of no consequence. We learn from failures as well as successes." And as my teacher Lee Lozowick says, "If it is not impossible, why bother doing it?"

PART II

The Ordinary

CHAPTER 2

Ordinary Relationship/ Ordinary Love

Human relationship skills at the beginning of the twenty-first century may be regarded by future generations as still being in the Dark Ages.

If you have the desire to create relationship differently, this book can help you tremendously. But you cannot jump to a new level when standing on thin air. You have to stand on something solid to leap from. The platform we will build to stand on here is that of clarity about your present relationship skills. How can you figure out ways to create extraordinary relationship without first knowing, in exacting detail, how you create relationship the way it shows up for you now. This chapter will explore the qualities and technologies for creating ordinary human relationship.

MAP OF THREE KINDS OF RELATIONSHIP

ARCHETYPAL RELATIONSHIP

EXTRAORDINARY HUMAN RELATIONSHIP

ORDINARY HUMAN RELATIONSHIP

We begin with a "thought-map," an energetic diagram representing ways that we might be thinking about possible kinds of relationship.

With a map like this you do not have many options. If you want to create relationship and all you know about is ordinary human relationship, then you have very little chance of creating anything other than ordinary human relationship.

Ordinary Relationship / Ordinary Love

Each of us is doing the best that we can. There is nothing wrong or bad or stupid about being involved in ordinary human relationship. If the best that we can do is eventually proven to be lacking in some way, that is not necessarily our fault. It is perhaps the fault of our education.

The quality of our relationships is related to the quality of our soft skills education, our so-called relationship intelligence. Relationship intelligence is built out of emotional intelligence, social intelligence, communication skills, listening skills, problem solving skills, our imagination, our relationship to fear and other feelings, the level of our emotional healing, our ability to engage actionless presence with another person, and other skills of this nature. Think about this: Where did we learn how to create relationship?

Many of us have never participated in a human relationship class or training. We acquired most of our relationship intelligence by the time we were four or five years old, before going to school, by directly imitating our parents. Where did our parents acquire their relationship intelligence? From imitating their parents. Where did our parents' parents acquire their relationship intelligence? From their parents, and so on. We are probably using a level of relationship intelligence that has been passed on from generation to generation for thousands of years. Newer, more effective, relationship intelligence soft skills do exist, but we probably lack them because neither our parents nor our teachers could demonstrate them.

This is actually great news! It means you have a real chance to improve your relationship intelligence. The new soft skills are learned when you take personal responsibility for going step-by-step beyond the limits of standard education, just as you are doing right now by studying this book. Let's examine what we presently use for relationship intelligence.

This chapter explores the first and most common kind of love, called "ordinary human love." Ordinary human relationship is built around ordinary human love.

Because ordinary human love is so widespread and so widely accepted, it may at first be difficult to understand what is being said here. Later in the book, after comparing ordinary human love with extraordinary human love or Archetypal Love, what is said here about ordinary human love may make better sense.

In any field, our first efforts at unfolding the available knowledge are often sloppy and ineffective. Nonetheless, where we begin can

```
┌─────────────────────────────────────────────────┐
│         ┌──────────────────────────────┐         │
│         │  MAP OF THREE KINDS OF LOVE  │         │
│         └──────────────────────────────┘         │
│                                                   │
│  1.  Ordinary Human Love, self-referenced,        │
│      neurotic, "I need you" love, dependent       │
│      on certain expected circumstances and        │
│      experiences.                                 │
│                                                   │
│  2.                                               │
│                                                   │
│                                                   │
│  3.                                               │
│                                                   │
└─────────────────────────────────────────────────┘
```

be deeply respected simply because it is the place where we begin. Without the first step there is no next step. In the field of love, where we begin is with ordinary human love.

Ordinary human love originates within a consumer perspective – that of *wanting to be* loved. We focus on obtaining love and long to have our unmet childhood needs finally fulfilled. When someone appears to fulfill our needs and we say to them, "I love you," what we actually mean is, "I need you to keep fulfilling my needs. I want to own you, to have you, to possess you and to control you so that you keep taking care of me." We conclude that this is love.

Our intention in ordinary human relationship is to arrange it so that the other person takes care of us. If they stop automatically fulfilling our needs, we wonder if they still love us. After all, if they are not fulfilling our needs, why are we in relationship with them?

To continue getting our needs met we may complain ("You always leave the breakfast dishes in the sink for me to wash."); manipulate ("The kids feel really neglected when you won't play with them."); barter ("If you come with me to visit my mother I will come with you to your business party."); threaten ("Come to dinner right now or I will feed it to the dog!"); cajole ("C'mon, a big strong man like you should be able to tell our neighbor to stop letting his dog shit in our yard."); play victim ("Did you ever wonder if *I* have enough clean underwear in *my* drawer to wear this week?"), and so on. Such interactions are so normal we may already be wondering, "What else is there?"

Ordinary human love is based on seeing the *evidence* of love, such as flowers, chocolates, birthday cards, and having our expectations met. Ordinary human love is also based on having the *experience* of love, some kind of warm fuzzy feeling in our tummy. If we do not see the evidence that we expect to see, or if we do not feel that warm fuzzy feeling we think of as *being in love,* then we conclude that the other person does not love us anymore. This makes ordinary human love extremely conditional and unstable. It goes up, down and around like a roller coaster ride. We can never trust that such love is truly there or that love will truly stay. This instability forms the erratic basis of ordinary human relationship.

If we regard the other person as the source of love for us, then it is up to the other person to make us happy. If we are not happy, then it must be our partner's fault. If our unhappiness is our partner's fault, then we have proof that we are not with the right person. Day in and day out we live with neurotic insecurity.

Infatuation

Our training about relationship is to look for Mr. or Mrs. Right. If we convince ourselves that we have found such a person, we fall into a sensation known as infatuation. Infatuation is the illusion that the person we are with matches our fantasy image of someone who will perfectly fulfill our needs even if we do not deserve it.

Infatuation temporarily enlarges our world because it sidesteps the natural territoriality of our defense strategy. For a short time we feel like we are in (or, if we are lucky, back in) our father's protective arms or nursing at our mother's nurturing breasts. We might let our partner physically touch us in ways that are definitely taboo for us when our defenses snap back into their usual place. Or we might let our partner look more closely into our private matters – our personal diary, our kinkiness, our past experiences of being wounded – and then, without knowing exactly why, we may close back up again.

The experience of infatuation lasts only as long as we keep a heavy fog bank over our natural defendedness using the fantasy that we have found an endless source of love for ourselves. As soon as we collect enough evidence about the other person's behavior and character to prove they don't love us, the fog burns away. We come out of denial, and our self-generated fantasy image of our partner dies badly. So does our infatuation. We may conclude that "love has ended" and the shock of this disillusionment may unhinge our world. We may feel betrayed (again). Being betrayed gives us justification for unleashing our usual vengeance. Thus occupied we don't see that chasing an illusion distracts us from making use of treasures that lie within easy reach.

Years may go by; decades of frustration, confusion, desperation and loneliness. We may be tempted to give up on relationship altogether, and instead stay busily distracted, but alone, for the rest of our days. Or we may compromise our authenticity and "play dead" just to have a warm body in bed with us at night.

Our culture provides us with plenty of exciting distractions and numbness-inducing substances so that we can avoid consciously encountering the core discrepancies between what we are actually doing with our lives and what we really want to be doing. By staying numb or distracted we continue creating Ordinary human relationship without a clue that something else is possible. Since infatuation could well be the best kind of intimacy we know, we may design our moves so as to snatch as many moments of infatuation as possible. But, over time, we cannot continue to stay naïve. Moments of ecstasy become jaded. Infatuation seems to fade away ever more quickly. We feel like we are driving along this relationship highway with a flat tire. Nobody has ever told us that there is a spare tire and a jack packed into the bottom of our trunk.

This book can provide you with the tools and possibilities for using previously unknown resources.

SECTION 2-B
Ordinary Human Communication

To clarify how ordinary human communication works I will use Dr. Eric Berne's *Map of Parent Adult Child Ego States,* one of the central thought-maps from his system of Transactional Analysis. Berne's map is simple and effective. Later in this book you will see this map evolve to provide even greater clarity.

Right now we will use the map in its original form. To understand the map we must first understand what is meant by the term "ego state." (In a later chapter we will replace the term "ego state" with the term "Box.")

An ego state is a set of ideas, beliefs, attitudes and behaviors with which we are identified. Using the term "state" implies that our identification is only temporary, that we change from one ego state to another ego state. And that is exactly the point. When we are identified with a certain set of ideas, beliefs, attitudes or behaviors, we are certain that these are the only ideas possible. We regard this set of attitudes as who we are, and we assume that it encompasses all that is. We think that no option exists other than the worldview we are currently seeing and using.

Human psychology's imperative to have and to know its own identity is astonishing. By packaging itself into one identity, the mind blinds itself to the existence of any other possible identity, even if a moment before it was packaged into a completely different identity. Then, when the circumstances change, the mind shifts identities again. The mind has dozens of prepackaged identities in store and chooses whichever identity best assures survival for us in a particular circumstance.

We are identified with the "identification mechanism" in our mind, meaning that we do not notice when our mind shifts from one identity to the next. For us it is a seamless segue, as unnoticed as blinking. We notice the identity shifting in other people, but not in ourselves. For example, remember a time when you were with a friend and their telephone rang. Your friend stops talking with you and speaks to the caller, who might be their mother, child, boss, or the police. Right before your eyes your friend's identity instantly shifts to a strange character, with a voice, speech patterns, vocabulary, posture and attitude that you have never seen in them before. As soon as the call ends they shift smoothly back into the character who talks to you, never realizing that they shifted at all. The drastic identity shift in your friend might cause a shock in you, but more likely you will play along as if you saw nothing unusual. Ignoring the identity shift in each other is an agreement we make amongst ourselves to keep the show rolling. Nonetheless, we shift identity many times each day, most of the time without being conscious about it.

Knowing that the human mind has a bias toward identification and an uncanny deftness with shifting identity is such a radical piece of knowledge that even though this idea is presented to you in a precise and useable form in these paragraphs, you will probably forget it in the next few moments. Then, when the next person leaves the room and forgets to shut the door behind them, the identity in your mind who must have the door closed to feel secure will get offended and regard its own reality limits of greater importance than maintaining a respectful relationship with the other person. This is how we begin to get a feel for the insidious difficulties involved in ordinary human communications.

Dr. Eric Berne's map indicates that there are three generalized ego states with which a person would normally be identified. These are the "Parent ego state," the "Adult ego state," or the "Child ego state." We are typically identified with one ego state or another during most of our waking and sleeping hours. In this chapter we will investigate the Parent and Child ego states. In a later chapter we will investigate the Adult ego state.

The Parent ego state includes both the "nurturing Parent," with a voice that praises and approves, and the "critical Parent," with a voice that blames and disapproves. These two voices speak into our mind or out of our mouth in many of our daily conversations. Nurturing Parent voices might say things like, "You are wonderful! You are the best! You are so beautiful! You are so smart! You are so good! You are perfect!" Critical Parent voices might say, "You are not good enough. You are a failure. You are stupid. You will never make it. You are a loser. You are a slob. You are ugly. You are a reject." And so on into creative infinity.

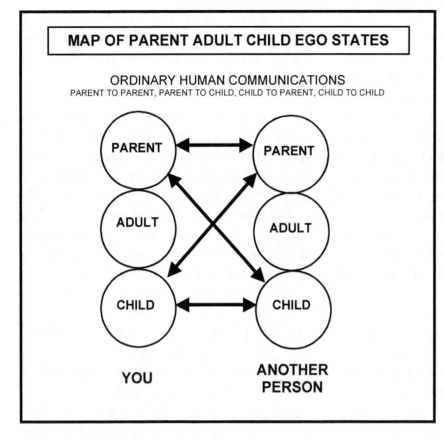

MAP OF PARENT ADULT CHILD EGO STATES

ORDINARY HUMAN COMMUNICATIONS
PARENT TO PARENT, PARENT TO CHILD, CHILD TO PARENT, CHILD TO CHILD

PARENT — PARENT

ADULT — ADULT

CHILD — CHILD

YOU — ANOTHER PERSON

In order to survive, you made their voices normal, no matter what they were telling you. When you left the source of these voices you maintained a sense of normalcy by keeping the voices going inside your own head. If you listen to those voices now, or grant them credibility, you are giving your power away to others. In contrast, in the Adult ego state you speak with your own voice – which may be completely neutral and silent in circumstances where the nurturing or critical Parent voices would be screaming their heads off. In using your own voice you have your own power.

Parent Ego State

The first thing to keep in mind as we investigate the Parent ego state is that, despite how things may feel, there is really no difference between praise and blame. Both are forms of conditioning, and both praise and blame are manipulations. If you say, "That is great," you are trying to condition somebody to keep doing what they have been doing. If you say, "That is horrible," you are trying to condition somebody to stop doing what they have been doing. In contrast to these Parental messages, the Adult ego state does not use praise or blame. Instead, the Adult says, "I like that. Please keep doing that," or "That hurts. Please stop doing that."

The other thing to know about the Parent ego state is that the voices that you may hear going on in your head are not *your* voices. The voices came from other people, perhaps from past authority figures such as your parents, grandparents, older siblings or teachers.

Child Ego State

The Child ego state includes both the "free natural Child" and the "scared needy adaptive Child." These names describe their behaviors exactly. The scared-needy-adaptive-Child ego state is one in which the worst thing that could ever happen to you has already happened, and you are feeling scared that it will happen again. Here is where ungraspable fear comes from. As children, we often had needs that were not met. Unmet childhood needs leave a hollow cold empty place in our guts. We try to fill that place when we stare into the open refrigerator. We want our partner to fill that profound emptiness with endless "I love you's." We try to fill that place with sex or drugs or rock-n-roll, and still it is not filled.

We might do anything to get that gaping pit of needs filled: give our self-respect away, be adaptive, get enmeshed, be co-dependent

– we would wait around as an invisible door-mat forever if there was a hope of filling that bottomless hole. We internally experience ourselves as forever lacking some unattainable thing that is crucial to our well-being. This unfulfilled sensation establishes our ordinary human relationship to the world as a weak and suffering victim just trying to survive.

Ego State Conversations

Ordinary human relationship is founded in Ordinary human communication – when the Parent or Child ego state in us speaks or gets spoken to by the Parent or Child ego state of another. The all-too-familiar dialogs go like this:

Parent to Parent: "Well, I don't like this. Too many freedoms for the children these days, don't you think? And your Johnny certainly is going to pay for his little attitude problem when it comes time for him to get a job! Everybody knows what happens around your dining table at night!"

Parent to Child: "Pick up your dirty clothes! Why do you always lose your eyeglasses? You are so forgetful. I always have to do it for you. Can't you figure out a way to be more organized? Don't sit there! Sit here! This will certainly be best for you."

Child to Parent: "I don't know how to do this. It is all so confusing. What should I do next? Is this right? You're always pestering me! Why can't they make things simpler? This is impossible for me. I am too tired. It's overwhelming for me. I can't do it."

Child to Child: "If you do that to me then I will do this to you! Asshole! Hey, I got you! That's mine! Not yours! That's my place. Your place is over here. He's on my team! I want to sit next to him! My dress is prettier than your dress! Get out of my way! I'm angry! You're ugly! I'm smarter than you are! I won! You lost! Haa-ha-haa-ha-haaaaa-ha!"

SECTION 2-C
Low Drama

Imagine being an ant that lives in a child's plastic ant farm. You might live out your entire life with every intention to live fully, but the result is that you fail to have many truly interesting options and you have no idea why not. The barrier that stands between you and the world is invisible to you because you are an ant and therefore do not have the capacity to understand the concept "acrylic plastic" or "ant farm." Lucky for us, you are not actually an ant! You do have the capacity to imagine an "ant farm." The concept of "ant farm" can be equated to an invisible barrier that captures the minds and hearts of most twenty-first-century human beings for their entire lives. That invisible barrier is "low drama." Low drama is any interaction designed to avoid responsibility. If we do not learn to detect and avoid low drama interactions, then we will live within an invisible "ant farm" that minimizes the quality of our relationships and we will have no idea why.

Dr. Stephen Karpman, a student of Dr. Eric Berne and Transactional Analysis, invented the model for low drama in San Francisco in 1965 and described it in an article in 1968. As the story goes, Dr. Karpman loved to diagram the action plays made during American football games. One Sunday afternoon he was watching a game on TV and his wife invited him to keep his promise of taking her to the movies. At the cinema Dr. Karpman still had his pencil and pad in hand. As the film began playing Dr. Karpman automatically started noting the interactions. In the first dramatic scene there was a bad guy persecuting a poor victim, and then along came a good guy for the rescue. Next scene there was a helpless victim being rescued and along comes a bad guy. Next scene there was a hero attacked by a villain and then rescued by his kids. On page after page Dr. Karpman diagrammed dramatic interactions and, to his great surprise, in each drama the roles being played out were identical. After thirty pages of diagrams, Dr.

Karpman had created his remarkable map that he named the "Drama Triangle."

Dr. Karpman's Drama Triangle reveals that many of our day-to-day human interactions are simply unconscious role-playing in one of three strategic characters: the victim, the persecutor or the rescuer. In this book I have renamed the Drama Triangle as "low drama" so as to incorporate it into a bigger map called the *Map of Possibility* which we will explore in depth much later.

Once you have integrated a thorough understanding of low drama you then have a chance of creating "high drama," which will be covered later when we look at The *Map of Possibility* in Section 13-F. First we start with low drama.

MAP OF LOW DRAMA

Any action designed to avoid responsibility is low drama.

PERSECUTOR   **RESCUER**

VICTIM

The most powerful player in a low drama is the victim. If there is no victim, there can be no low drama. A good victim can make a persecutor out of anyone! We believe low drama is real when we unconsciously change positions on the triangle. We can detect if we are playing low drama if we are blaming, resenting, justifying, being right, complaining, or making someone wrong. We go round and round in low dramas during our days and nights. The only thing that happens in low drama is we get older. (Note: This map is adapted directly from the original "Drama Triangle" created by Dr. Stephen Karpman in 1965, used in Transactional Analysis [TA] as taught by Dr. Eric Berne. I renamed it "low drama" to reveal its relationship to "high drama" on a bigger map called *The Map of Possibility*.)

Of the three roles, the victim is the most powerful. This is because a skilled victim can make a persecutor out of anyone. All the victim needs is one tiny shred of evidence to prove that "the persecutor is hurting me," and then the victim has the right to switch roles with the persecutor and go for revenge! Another way that the victim is the most powerful character in a low drama is that, if there is no victim, there can be no low drama.

When we first hear about victims and low drama we might be thinking, "oh, those poor people who get caught in low dramas! I would not want to be one of them!" Hey, baby! Wake up and smell the donuts. *Them* is *us*. Low drama is the most popular game played on Earth! You do it. I do it. We all do it. The only question is about details: When? Where? With whom? How often? And why?

Low drama is a survival game based on the perspective that there are not enough resources. Resources include such commodities as position, power, work time, space, energy, money, attention, love, fun, dessert, intimacy, and leisure. If there are not enough resources and the other person gets to have them, then we don't. They win and we lose. Low drama is played to win.

Low drama is *very* exciting: there are good guys, bad guys, even a poor damsel in distress. The good guy rides up on his white horse and says, "I'll pay the rent! I'll save the day!" (At least we are hoping some good guy comes to save us.) If a good guy comes and does a bad job of rescuing us, we spin the low drama around, shift from victim to persecutor, and we persecute the rescuer. If no good guy comes at all then we have to rescue ourselves. We *prove* that the persecutor is hurting us in some way, and then we are perfectly justified in persecuting the persecutor! Revenge at last. All this is very exciting. If we run out of low dramas in our own life then we can turn on the television, open a newspaper or go to a

movie. Low drama is so exciting it is almost like life. But low drama is not life. Low drama is only low drama. If we assume low drama is life we lock ourselves into the ant farm and throw away the key.

In trying to understand low drama as being a subset of life it is the rescuer who is most difficult to vilify. After all, the rescuer is trying to rescue somebody who needs their help, right? How could rescuing be bad?

First, nothing about low drama is bad. Nothing is good either, but also nothing is bad. Low drama is action designed to avoid responsibility, and these actions create certain results. It is easy to detect low drama by detecting the associated low drama behaviors: If there is blaming, resentment, justification, complaining, gossiping, being right, or making wrong, it is low drama. What low drama is, is ordinary. Very ordinary. Once we have clarity about what low drama is and how to detect low drama, then we have a choice. We can decide whether or not we want to continue creating low drama in our relationships.

Second, rescuing comes from the same emotionally charged position as persecuting. With arrogance and disrespect the persecutor says, "I'm okay. You are not okay. I must get rid of you." (Think of Adolf Hitler and the story of the "superior" Aryan race.) The rescuer says, "I'm okay. You are not okay. You are not good enough to do it yourself so I must do it for you." (Think of a mother who takes over her child's activity even if the child did not ask for help. This too is superior and disrespectful.) Notice how both the persecutor and the rescuer maintain the same viewpoint, that the victim is not okay. Rescuing is defined as offering help that is not wanted or asked for. Rescuing is just as much low drama as persecuting.

One particularly clever swindle is victims who act as if they are being responsible. They take out the garbage, vacuum the floor, take the kids to school, wash the dishes, go to work, all like a responsible person might. But they do it all as a victim, not really wanting to do it, not truly choosing to do it, and not fully committing to do it. They do it because no one else wants to do it, or because it should be done, or because it is the right or proper thing to do. They do it as a burden. They do it out of guilt or obligation rather than out of responsibility. Such a person is not being responsible. They are being a "responsible victim." The responsible victim is a low drama theatrical role with a very big payoff. After all, your complaints get to be truly *righteous*. Your woes are justified. When I first realized that I had been playing the responsible victim game for most of my adult life I sat through an entire Thai dinner crying into my pineapple shrimp curry while the rest of the people in the training went on happily eating. It was a dinner to remember.

The delusion of low drama is that by playing victim or by persecuting or rescuing something will change. This is a very expensive delusion. Low drama changes nothing. No matter how resentful we are, how perfectly justified we are, or how right we are, no matter how strongly we complain or attack with blame, nothing changes. The only thing that happens in low drama is that we get older. Change happens through responsibility, and low drama is about avoiding responsibility. Low drama is expensive because the time and energy we spend dramatically avoiding responsibility in low drama is time and energy that we will never get back.

Unfortunately, having intellectual clarity about low drama will not alter behavior. Behavior change occurs through responsibly experiencing what you are creating in each moment. The clarity in previous paragraphs about low drama may seem interesting, but don't kid yourself. You will change no words or actions until it gets too painful for you to keep doing what you do now. The purpose behind the following handbook is to increase the pain of your moment-to-moment awareness.

Handbook for Creating Ordinary Human Relationship

Here are 122 specific instructions and practices for how to start, grow and end ordinary human relationship. Study them carefully to improve your ordinary human relationship intelligence.

1. Complain to your partner about anything that does not suit you. Use a whining, victimy tone of voice when you complain. Respond negatively to any assurances given to you about anything. Make sure that the object of your complaints can never be resolved. You complain. Your partner tries to fix it. You create reasons why their solutions will not work. At least in this game you always have something to talk about.

2. Try to be right whenever issues arise. Argue your point. Do not give up until your partner concedes that you are right.

3. In order to supplement being right, also try to make your partner wrong whenever there is an opportunity to do so. After all, you are not making them wrong. They actually *are* wrong. You are just doing them the favor of pointing it out to them.

4. Take a rigid position about everything and anything ("I *have* to wash my face before I go to bed!"). Be fanatical about your positions. Go for the throat. Take no prisoners. Justify your position any way that you can. After all, everyone has a right to their own opinions.

5. Feel resentment about anything your partner ever did that offended or frightened or embarrassed you. Whenever you look at your partner, remember your resentments first. Never forget your resentments.

6. Feel resentment about your own childhood. Remember all of your old wounds. Assume that the people presently around you will wound you again. Project this onto your partner. Your partner then becomes your enemy with conscious or unconscious intentions to harm you. Stay little. Never grow up.

7. Feel resentment about your children, your boss, your colleagues. After all, resentment is a way to take care of yourself by feeling strong and righteous.

8. Have a never-ending competition with your partner about who has the worst life. Dedicate yourself to proving to your partner that your life is less fun than theirs. Even if life seems momentarily good, you have the shit end of the stick. Search for subtle evidence to demonstrate that your partner has it better than you. This gives you permission to go shopping.

9. If your partner does have a little bit of fun, make them feel guilty as hell. They should have been working on something. There is so much that needs to be done or that needs to be cleaned up. Who do they think they are having fun?

10. Confine your experience of love to the linear, personal, transient, conditional, minimized, localized, ordinary, verbal-reality of "I love you." As soon as the echo of the spoken words fades out of the room, so does your faith in your partner's love.

11. Give up about little things. Give up about life. Have no hope. Try to make your partner rescue you from hopelessness. If they fail to rescue you, blame them for not caring and assume they are having an affair.

12. Get a nice car and keep it clean. Get a hi-tech mobile phone and a slick computer. Live in your car, your phone and your computer. Look at your relationship and wonder why it is so messy compared to your car, your phone and your computer. Obviously, the mess must be your partner's fault.

13. Be strong, try hard, be perfect, always keep pushing yourself. Push yourself until you break down psychologically, emotionally or physically and then make your partner pick up the slack for you so they can finally value all the work you have been doing.

14. Do not be happy. Do not enjoy life. Do not be powerful. Have excuses that blame other people or your life circumstances for not being happy, powerful, and enjoying life.

15. Give away your authority so you do not have to make decisions about your life. Give your authority to any authority figure: doctors, plumbers, computer guys, the phone company, the car mechanics, the government, your children, the tax people, to anybody. Feel weak and used. Feel stupid. Complain about the bad service and high prices.

16. Stay in your head. Righteously value intellectual and rational considerations above

all else. Confine your life to your reasons. No matter what, do not feel. Feelings are irrational.

17. Stay in your bed. Sleep in. Try to keep dreaming. Sleeping and dreaming are better than what is happening in your life. If you are sleeping and dreaming maybe people will leave you alone. Maybe things will change by themselves.

18. Do not be glamorous and sexy for your partner. Instead, be glamorous and sexy for people who do not matter so that you maintain a good public image.

19. Conceive of "here" as very big, covering everywhere that you have ever been. Regard "now" as immense, extending far beyond this moment, back into the past and far into the distant future. Ignore the obvious fact that you can do nothing to change the past and little or nothing to predetermine the future, and nothing about what is not here. Include the past, the future, and everywhere into a gigantic "here and now." Then feel totally overwhelmed about how much you carry on your shoulders. Use this overwhelm as an excuse to eat chocolate.

20. Never say just "yes" or "no" in response to "yes or no" questions. Always go sideways instead, and make sure that you add in all the details.

21. Never answer the question that is asked. Always assume that *your* assumptions about the question and about the questioner are more correct than the questioner's. Then answer the question that you assume they are really asking.

22. Always be worried that the worst thing that ever happened to you is any minute going to happen to you again. Make it your partner's responsibility to protect you from this worry.

23. Limit your experience to your vocabulary. Have no experience that you do not have

a name for. Regard everything else as ridiculous and irrelevant. Teach this to your children.

24. Create and maintain the story in your mind that your partner is inferior to you or that your partner is an idiot. Consistently find little pieces of evidence to support that story. Whenever you look at your partner, see your stories about them instead of them.

25. To supplement the view that your partner is inferior to you, also create and maintain the story that you are superior to your partner. Find little ways to constantly remind your partner of this, especially when in the company of relatives, business associates, or mutual friends.

26. Have expectations about how your partner should act, about what they should feel, about where they should sit, about how they should dress, about how they should treat you, about what they should order to eat in the restaurant, about how they are driving, and so on. Get angry if their behavior ever fails to meet your expectations.

27. Feel afraid if your partner dares to express their feelings to you. As soon as they begin expressing their feelings to you, panic and express your feelings to them. After all, if they stop withholding their feelings it is only fair that you express your feelings too. Make sure that your feelings are bigger and stronger than their feelings.

28. Blame your partner for everything that is not handled, everything that goes wrong, everything that ever went wrong, and everything that could possibly ever go wrong. What else are they there for?

29. Attack your partner whenever you feel any kind of discomfort. This way they know you are there. If your partner ever thinks that you are comfortable, who knows, they might not give you any more attention.

30. Be a public doormat. Neurotically worry that you might cause a problem for somebody. Walk on eggshells around everyone. Keep imagining that you are being a problem for your partner or for others. Keep giving many excuses and reasons why it is not your fault, and also blame your partner for the unfairness of thinking that you are a problem.

31. Do not live your life. Feel resentment for having to be adaptive and not being able to be yourself and live your life. Never clear your resentments.

32. Make assumptions freely about whatever you want. Make your partner responsible for the effect of your assumptions.

33. Ignore the possibility of being an adult man or woman. Let your childhood thinking and feeling patterns take over and dominate your adult life. Create the popular fantasy of a scared needy adaptive inner child, and give more importance to this fantasy than to your mate.

34. Project your father onto your man. Find evidence to prove that he is your father because he is doing it to you again!

35. Project your mother onto your woman. Be in bed with your mother when you are in bed with your woman. Blame your woman for this.

36. Be scared about everything that you do not know and cannot control. Use your fear to control your partner.

37. Whenever your partner is willing to listen to you, complain about the mobbing at work, complain about projects being prematurely terminated, complain about the incredible laziness of your colleagues or employees or your boss, describe people dying in bizarre accidents, describe what is happening in the war, describe what is happening in politics, complain about the housework, complain about the kids always interrupting, complain about having too much to do and no time to complete anything. Keep talking about something. Above all do not be together in silence. Always keep the radio on.

38. Without making it obvious, distract your partner and yourself from entering the spaces where it would be possible to speak together about love or beauty or grace.

39. Be needy in such a way that your neediness can never be fulfilled. Make it your partner's responsibility to fulfill your neediness.

40. Be adaptive to the person who comes to your front door and asks for donations. Be adaptive at work. Be adaptive to the telephone salesperson. Be adaptive to your parents. Be angry with your partner for not protecting you from all the people with whom you are adaptive.

41. Let your parents' opinion about your life have more importance than your own opinion about your life. Let your parents' opinion about your partner's life have more importance than your own opinion about your partner's life.

42. Let your parents question and berate your decisions about childraising, vacations, housecleaning, and your job. Let your parents berate your mate. Give your parents controlling authority in your household. Decide that you will wait until your parents die before you start living your own life. Wait impatiently. Let the years go by.

43. Draw conclusions about whatever you want in life so as to sustain your present view of things. Believe your conclusions in the face of contradictory evidence. Especially ignore evidence offered by your partner.

44. Defend yourself from intimacy. Do not let anyone, especially your partner, get closer to you than your mask.

45. Do not trust your partner. Continuously collect evidence to prove that they are untrustworthy.

46. Defend yourself from evolution. Do not try to learn. Think that your habits are you. Try to stay solid in your habits and persevere with the set of behaviors that you established for yourself long ago. Always serve the same menu for Christmas dinner.

47. Become expert in avoiding responsibility. Procrastinate. Hesitate. Use your energy for creating excuses rather than creating results. Take no risks. Leave well enough alone. Do not rock the boat. Keep your hands clean. Relate to responsibility as if responsibility means fault, blame, guilt or a heavy burden. Do not play your life full out.

48. Do not make boundaries, or if you do make a boundary, make it too feebly or too late so that you get hurt first and are justified in making the boundary as a way to get revenge.

49. Do not ask for what you need. Expect that by now other people around you should already know exactly what you need.

50. If you do not get what you need, then use that as a good reason to cheat. Do not ask for what you want. Then, when you do not get it, live a double life and sneak to get what you want somewhere else.

51. Withhold sex to punish your mate for not giving you what you want. Lie about why you are withholding sex.

52. Make your own personal comfort and security the highest priority. Make other people dance around you to make you feel comfortable and secure. After all, you deserve basic comfort and security, don't you? Other people should know how to make you comfortable and secure. Be neurotic in ways that make it impossible to be comfortable or have security.

53. Attach yourself to your partner by getting into their private spaces. Look in their drawers, read papers on their desk, open their mail, cross-examine their friends and colleagues, check their receipts, listen to their phone messages, and snoop into their stuff. Know what they are going to do before *they* do. Be psychologically, emotionally, and energetically enmeshed with them. Think that fusion is closeness.

54. If your partner does not give you pleasure, if they do not cook you the right meal at the right time or the way you want it (without too much salt, eggs not too wet, salad torn rather than cut the way you like it), if they leave messes, if they do not touch you the right way, if they play the music too loudly, if they dress improperly, then feel insulted and close up your love for them. If they do not give you pleasure then obviously they do not love you. Why should you love them?

55. Try to make your partner change. If your partner will not change, then complain about them to their mother. Maybe she can make them change.

56. Try to change your parents, your boss, your colleagues, and your relatives. Hate them for not changing, or hate yourself for failing to change them, or hate both them and yourself.

57. Be involved in all the latest diet and health fads. Secretly think that your partner has no life if they do not get excited about your diet or health plan. Spend a lot of money. Change your plan when you get bored. Do not explain anything to your partner.

58. Blame the faults of your children on your partner. Your children obviously inherited their bad characteristics from your partner or your partner's family.

59. Guiltily buy expensive little things and put them away in your closet or in the garage.

Wait. When you finally wear them or use them and your partner notices, say, "Oh, I've had this a long time..."

60. Be a victim of time. Stay super busy. Chase after the clock. Be in a hurry. Rush around. Do not have enough time to feel or to be relaxed. Do not make time to really be present with anyone. Starve yourself from deep, nurturing, adult human contact, and go to bed exhausted each night.

61. Be late. Do not keep your time commitments. Never arrive on time. Make people wait for you. Always pack your things at the last minute and be completely wiped out or even sick before leaving on any trips with your partner.

62. Feel overwhelmed about all the details and responsibilities of life. Attack anyone who does not feel as overwhelmed as you for being irresponsible or unconscious.

63. Do sports. Use all your extra energy for athletic competition. Come home exhausted. Get hurt so your partner must respect your sport because it has the power to interfere with their life. Constantly talk about your sport whenever you get together with friends even if your partner does not participate. Use sore muscles and exhaustion as an excuse to avoid physical intimacy. Get up early and run seven days a week because it is inarguable that everyone needs cardiovascular exercise. Then you don't have to come up with another reason for not having sex in the morning.

64. Suddenly become holy. Read spiritual books and do whatever they say. Do breathing practices, yoga postures, Buddhist meditations, and shamanic rituals. Fill your house with crystals. Tell your partner what they should or should not do by quoting from your books. Bring over weird friends who are not really your friends but at least they are holy.

65. Surround yourself with persecutors and rescuers. Wake up in the morning and before you even get out of bed, count your enemies. Put on the day as if it has the same possibilities as yesterday, like wearing dirty clothes.

66. At parties, make jokes about your partner's personality quirks.

67. Be mean to your partner, but feel well justified that it is payback for all the times when they were mean to you. Accept disrespectful behavior from yourself toward your partner.

68. Expect your partner to be everything for you. Do not have friends. Do not let your partner have friends. Starve yourself from contact and make your partner starve themselves from contact so that you can prove that you have a "monogamous" relationship. Stay with your partner even if your relationship is no longer living so that you can have a relationship "'til death do you part." Sacrifice your aliveness to the customs of your culture and times.

69. Indulge yourself in addictive sentimentality, nostalgia, depression, and melancholy. Expect your partner not to react or to need you to be present for them.

70. Mix your emotions from the past with your feelings from the present to create confusion for yourself and others so that you never have to be accountable for what is happening right now.

71. Use your relationship to feed "psychological vampire-entities." Pretend that you don't know what I am talking about. Try to stay unconscious about the fact that you host psychological vampire-entities that feed on your partner as their main source of food. Let yourself be fed upon by your partner's psychological vampire-entities. Call this reciprocal vampire-feeding frenzy a "relationship."

72. Do not notice the predictable feeding patterns of the energetic vampire creatures that devour your life energy. Do not notice that you explode in rage and have an emotionally charged conflict once a month for five days, or once a week for a day and a night, or a few times a day. Do not notice that you have several identities within your psychology who do not know each other and who each think that they are the only one.

73. Live in the world of "me, me, me," as if you were separate from everyone else and they were all separate from you. If you do not take care of yourself, who will?

74. Stay in survival. Live a minimal life. Do not indulge your personal whims for adventure, extravagance, new experience, generosity, learning, discovery, exploration, or expansion. Instead, watch television night after night. Have no imagination. Be timid, linear and predictable. Let your fears stay bigger than you so that you can remain in a life of survival.

75. Engage in an ongoing power struggle with your partner. Struggle privately at home – about the children, about money, about making plans. Struggle publicly at meetings, at parties, at work, so that when you win, others can witness your great victory over your partner. Always make sure that your partner does not have more power or recognition than you do. If they do, figure out ways to undermine their power and destroy them. But not totally. If they were totally destroyed how could you continue enjoying the power struggle?

76. Be jealous of your partner's attractiveness or success. Resent them for it. Pull your appreciation away from them and minimize your love for them because they already get more than enough love and appreciation from other people.

77. Feel small. Feel weak. Feel like a failure. Feel unworthy. Feel unlovable. Find evidence to continuously prove the view that you are unlovable. This proves that your partner is stupid because they chose someone to love who is unlovable. This proves that life is bad. When life is proven to be bad then you can continue to live as you always have and not really care about anything.

78. Twist everything your partner says so that you are sure they are telling you, "You are wrong," "You are stupid," or "You are not good enough." Respond to your interpretation of what your partner says, not to what they actually say. Do not realize that you are twisting their communications around. Do not let them explain themselves.

79. Use your fear to limit your partner's radiant exuberance. Obviously there needs to be a balance. When your partner is effervescing beyond your permitted aliveness limit, then dump cold water on them. Keep your aliveness limit low so you get to dump cold water on your partner a lot. This way you have job security. Only be alive when your partner is not around to see.

80. Fight unfairly. Call your partner names (Know It All, Mr. Independent, Sad Sack, Mrs. Prudence). Use the words "never" and "always." Get violent, hit or throw things, or threaten violence. Think that the conflict is all their fault and that you are not equally responsible. Use the children or money or sex as weapons.

81. Think that you know who your partner is. Do not listen to your partner so that you can repeat back what you heard them say. Refuse to be-with your partner in the conflict. After the fight cut yourself off from your partner for days and sulk.

82. Use intimate time with your partner to "triangulate" (to speak about someone who is not there). Complain about people

to your partner rather than speaking only about that person to their face. Do not acknowledge that you again trivialized a moment that could have been profound.

83. Triangulate about your partner when they are not there. Gossip about your partner to your friends, to their friends, or to relatives when they are not there. Let the others lead you on until you share intimacies that would embarrass or hurt your partner.

84. Exaggerate when recounting stories about your partner to other people. Make your partner sound braver, stronger, and smarter, or weaker, slower and stupider than what actually happened. Exaggerate so often that you live in your own fantasy of what happened rather than in the simplicity of what really happened. If your partner exaggerates stories about you, assume they are doing so to hurt you. Make their transgression really important.

85. Use your partner as a garbage can for all the bad things that happen to you during your day. When you are finished unloading your psychic shit into their soul, then assume that your obligations for being intimate with them are over for the day.

86. Do not respect the natural inherent nobility, elegance and dignity of your partner as a man or a woman. Do not even see the possibility of such qualities in them or in their lives. Treat your partner as a child, or as a kind of monkey with the capacity for living only an ordinary low-grade animal life.

87. Do not let your partner have their own problems. Do things for your partner because you are afraid that they are incapable of doing those things for themselves. Think that you are helping your partner. If they ever complain, get offended because if they do not want your help then they obviously do not want your love.

88. Find evidence to support the story that your partner is a pig. Find a little piece of evidence each day. Even the tiniest piece of evidence is sufficient. After all, you have so much evidence already in the "evidence sack" that you carry around with you that you actually do not even need to find any more evidence at all. The new evidence just helps you to remember that your partner is a pig. You can also use the evidence to prove pigness to your partner so they do not forget it either.

89. Live as if you are your psychology. Live as if the reality that your psychology paints for you to live in is the one and only true and actual reality of the world. Believe it like the sun shines. Live as if your view is as solid as granite and your truth is as objective as God. Regard anyone who so much as hints that they doubt you as if they are an attacker.

90. Live as if your partner is their psychology. Assume they are always going to stay that way, and that they are completely inflexible and rigid. Take what they say as an absolute that you must either destroy or become the slave of. Do not assume that your partner is anything but their arguments and reasons. Do not let love or relationship or acceptance or healing be bigger than your psychological differences. Never simply rest in the psychology-free communion of being together.

91. Try not to know that you are going to die. Live as if you have all the time in the world. Do not appreciate those rare moments of simple companionship as if they could be the last moments. When nothing happens it is just wasted time. If one of you is sick, it is a problem. Something is wrong. It is a mistake in the program. Again, it is wasted time. If one of you dies or goes away, be shocked, but do not fundamentally learn anything about life.

92. Feed your addictions. Use part of your attention, even during the most intimate of times, to crave videos, foods, drinks; use it for self-gratification, for complaining, for being depressed; use it to judge, to stay in your head and think. Never learn to tolerate the ever-increasing intensity of being wholly with another human being. Get yourself a drink and turn down the volume of passionate love. Keep it normal. Only go where you already have been. Then you can be bored, and you do not have to be afraid of how magnificent and glorious life really is.

93. Do not speak about what really matters to you. Do not dare to risk sharing from the depths of your heart. Never trust so deeply as to open your soul and reveal your deepest, most tender, delicate, incomplete, uncertain desires to your partner, even alone in bed together. Assume that your partner would just laugh at you anyway, or use it to make fun of you in public. Instead of sharing your inner world, keep your desires secret. Do not allow life to be a creative playground in which you can unfold your being and create what really matters to you. Take your secrets with you to the grave.

94. Try to be a good boy. You know what a good boy is. Your mommy taught you to be a good boy. So did the teachers. If you are not a good boy, the teacher will tell mommy and mommy will tell daddy and daddy will whip you in the worst way. The rules for being a good boy are deeply imprinted and socially acceptable. Being a good boy is safe. If you keep being a good boy, even though the price is excruciating, gut-wrenching heartache about not being yourself, at least you are a good boy. Maybe a nice girl will approve of you like mommy and the teachers and then everything will be fine.

95. Dedicate yourself to being a nice girl. Give your authenticity over to the magazines and advertising media. Try to make yourself beautiful according to standards set by the makers of anti-aging creams, stylish clothing, and cellulite producing prepackaged cake mixes. Be a nice girl so deeply that you can no longer find the wickedly sensuous creature of whole-body orgasms skilled enough to keep a man at bay until she herself is satiated. Nice girls don't do that! At least your living room looks well ordered.

96. Permit yourself to be repeatedly disrespected and dishonored. Use this as permission to get revenge. If you save up enough "disgrace points" through silently eating disrespect and dishonor, perhaps you can cash them in for a wild spending binge, for an affair, or maybe even for a righteously justified divorce complete with lawyer-enforced alimony payments.

97. Decide that since you went to school you know everything there is to know about being a man or a woman, being in a human body, being in a long-term committed relationship, and being a parent besides. Do not go outside of your culture to learn things that your culture is incapable of teaching you. Do not admit to the necessity of change. Do not use your relationship as a way to create the necessity for evolutionary development. Act as if everything is okay. Act as if things are as they are and make it clear that you are not responsible for making them any different.

98. Surround yourself with "eggshells." Create a complex and sophisticated protective layer of ways that you can be offended. Maintain a hair trigger to threaten your partner with violent rage or other childish behavior so that you can control them.

99. Stay identified with the rules and views of your cultural, political or religious affiliation. (I am Italian. I drive only Fords. I am from the Big Apple. I am a Dodgers fan. I am Buddhist. I am Republican. I am vegetarian.) Hold on to your identification more strongly than to your partnership. Attend gatherings of your false identity circle to sustain your illusion of self-knowledge, belonging and being accepted. Never find an intimacy that is more subtle or profound than the intimacy of a cheering football crowd or a bar song.

100. Do not really care about the well-being of your partner. They are, after all, adult, and they should be able to take care of themselves. Use your partner as the butt of your jokes, feel glad when they lose, feel glad when they are not strong, feel glad when they are feeling pain. It is only fair that they too should suffer sometimes.

101. Worry about what the neighbors think. Make your highest priority to be seen and accepted as normal. Enter deep denial about your lack of connectedness in order to keep up the appearance of being in a happy relationship.

102. Worry about keeping up with the neighbors' possessions or vacations.

103. Complain about not having enough money. Buy things on credit. Live in subtle terror and deep confusion about not knowing how you are going to pay bills even if the bills are not due until far off in the future.

104. Keep around mementos and souvenirs of past relationships such as photos, letters, gifts and clothes. Keep putting attention on those objects as if they mean something. Do not give that attention to your partner.

105. Compare your partner to somebody else, such as their parents, past partners, their siblings, or movie stars. Find your partner lacking and point it out to them, more than once.

106. Do not apologize to your partner. Do not accept apologies from your partner. Never forget what has offended you, even if it was a long time ago. Never forgive your partner.

107. Listen to the critical voices in your head. Keep an internal dialog going in your mind about how stupid your partner is, what they are doing wrong, how they will never get it, how they are so self-centered and never think about the wants and needs of anybody else.

108. Get offended or scared if your partner is ever unpredictable. Allow no freedom for explorative expression, even in the privacy of your own home. Maintain your "kinkiness detector" on high, and reject your partner if they ever get weird beyond what you think your mother would accept. (Although, if you actually knew what your mother was doing ...) Declare yourself to be sane, and control your partner so they behave within your defined sanity limits, especially at parties.

109. Use your bed or your bedroom as a place to psychologically analyze or "process" your partner. Create no refuge. Protect no sanctuary. Permit no asylum free of your criticisms or complaints. Let there be no place in your home or no hour in the day that is a safe haven from the all-consuming considerations of Ordinary human relationship.

110. Assume that your partner's potential is limited. Assume that your relationship's potential is limited. Assume that you have already achieved the maximum of that potential, perhaps years ago. Relationship then becomes an endurance test. How long can you stand it? Whoever breaks first is the bad guy.

111. Assume that you have a problem child. Having a problem child distracts you from having a problem relationship. Focus all of your time and worries on managing the "proper education" and "proper socialization" of your "problem child" and let twenty years go by, *zippity doo-dah!* Use your children as the reason to postpone learning how to create anything but Ordinary human relationship until your learning faculty crystallizes into nonfunctionality. Then you don't have to think about it anymore because learning won't happen. (By the way, there is no such thing as a "problem child." However, this is the subject of a different book!)

112. Keep involved in conflicts in many areas of your life. Have fights with your boss and colleagues. Have fights with your partner's parents, siblings or relatives. Have fights with the labor union and the butcher. Have fights with the tax people, the government, the minister of the church, and the dog next door. By the time your day is over you are too worn out for anything else.

113. Repeat your parents' neurotic relationship patterns, whatever they are. Create a cult of pairs with your partner. Stay isolated and have no friends at all. Or have many superficial friends and be friends with your partner through being friends with everybody else.

114. Make sure that all of your life decisions are limited to good reasons and insist that your partner's decisions are too. Do not allow nonlinear or evolutionary influences to enter your life or the life of your partner. Protect your partner from questionable activities. Keep your lives squeaky clean and defensible. Read the newspaper.

115. Flirt, in subtle and overt ways, to make up for what you do not get from your partner. Flirt because you have no discipline with your gluttonous, greedy and insatiable appetite for sexual energy no matter where it comes from or how it contaminates you. Flirt with sexually overt billboards. Flirt through your computer. Flirt with singers on the radio. Flirt over the telephone. Flirt with the waitress, the postman or your tennis teacher. Flirt with total strangers and with your mother-in-law. Also flirt when your partner is around to make them afraid that you might leave so they shape up. Flirt to prove that at least somebody is sexually attracted to you.

116. Get worried if you start to feel something. Think that if you are having feelings then something must be wrong with you. Use addictive substances to stay away from your feelings. Use television, sugar, newspapers, alcohol, speeding, shopping, overwork, over-exercise, videos, the Internet, and so on, to keep you from being authentic about what is going on for you. Hide any feelings that leak out sideways, or find external reasons to legitimize your internal feelings.

117. Allow relatives, neighbors, babies, salesmen or friends to have priority over your partner when it comes to having your full admiring attention or expressing love and joy. For example, be vivacious and cheery while talking on the telephone with anyone who calls, and then when you hang up, go back to being dull and contracted. Forbid yourself to realize that your relationship is only an act of theater, and that you can shift roles in any moment with anyone.

118. Limit your concept of intimacy so that it only includes sex. Forget that you can explore and completely enjoy other physical intimacies such as cleaning out

the garage, dancing, gardening, hiking, filing finger- and toenails, washing hair, massage, singing, playing music, yoga, martial arts, cooking, eating, trying on clothes, painting the house, and so on. If opportunities for these other intimacies occur, stay in your head and consider them as merely chores.

119. Bring your work home so there is no time for intimacy. Stay late for work or have to travel so there is no time for intimacy. Use any way you can think of to avoid intimacy. Always have a good excuse. As a back door, be a hypochondriac. Always have some physical complaint. Make comments about your physical pains an important part of your daily conversations. Keep at least one illness alive so that you can use your illness if you ever run out of other excuses to avoid intimacy.

120. Assume that your partner has expectations of you. React to what you think your partner is expecting of you, even if they do not say that they have expectations. Get offended about what you think they expect of you. Let your emotional reaction destroy the possibility of communion.

121. Be a slave to your reactions. Create no gap between your internal emotional reactions and your consequent external actions. Definitely do not develop the discipline to observe your own behavior patterns by splitting your attention so that you can use part of your attention to become conscious of what you are doing with the rest of your attention. Instead, stay identified with your reactions as if you had no other choice. Be completely mechanical.

122. When you end your relationship, make it your partner's fault. (The asshole!) Live the rest of your life permanently scarred.

Find evidence to prove that you were horribly betrayed. Take no responsibility. Learn nothing. Hate your partner for eternity. Distrust all men (or all women). Use lawyers, relatives, and the children to get all you can out of your partner just for spite. Tell incriminating stories to mutual friends before your partner can, especially to their family, and whenever possible to the media. Take a pound of flesh. Hit them wherever it hurts. How could they dare to do this to you? Teach them a lesson they will never forget so that this will never happen to you again. Then, arrange for it to happen to you again.

To make best use of this list read it carefully and slowly once a week for three months. Each time you read the list new insights will reveal themselves. Let each insight bubble up slowly into your experience. Let each realization hit you with the full intensity of its shocking message. As we noted at the beginning, people do not change until it hurts too much to keep doing things the old way. It may feel counterintuitive, but if you want to change, then let it hurt.

The above list is valuable because it allows you to acquire an exact "x" for locating where you are on the *Map of Three Kinds of Relationship* (*see* page 29). When you are enacting to any degree even one of the above listed behaviors then you prove your commitment (no matter what else you might be thinking) to creating ordinary human relationship. This is your "x" on the map.

Gaining an experiential "x" on the map is the purpose for studying the list over and over again. Study this list until you are nauseated. As painful as it might be, studying the list of ways to create ordinary human relationship gives you intellectual and emotional reference points that you can use for the rest of your life. These guidelines and hints will help you detect what you are actually up to when your mind may be telling you that you are up to something else entirely. Knowing what you are actually up to is clarity. Clarity provides alternative options in the exact moment when you can take a different action. Such options are priceless. The point is, if you do not know with accuracy what you are doing in this moment then you will have little success trying to do something different in the next moment.

For example, if you think that you are appreciating and respecting and you are actually instead being superior and manipulating, then you do not have an accurate "x" on the map. You are in reality lost. Trying new actions will change nothing because trying to reconcile what you are doing with the way people are reacting to you won't make sense.

Think of it this way: If you have stopped your car at an intersection in a new city and you know where you want to go but you do not know where you are, then you will not know whether to go right, left, straight, backwards, or to park because you are already there. For finding where you are, you need landmarks that give you accurate feedback and a map that shows you where the landmarks are in relation to where you want to go. A map gets interesting when it also provides you with details that extend into new territory.

The next few chapters are about men and women; about the matriarchy and the patriarchy and how these contrasting worldviews continue to affect our lives today and influence our relationships. It will be important to consider how we got our ideas of what a man is, what a woman is. Exploring these issues builds the foundation for entering new territories of relationship.

CHAPTER 3

Ordinary Man and Ordinary Woman

Section 3-A

)(Matriarchy and Patriarchy

Previous to 6000 years ago, cultures of the world were matri-archal. (This whole idea about a matriarchal past is conjec-tural. There is evidence to support the matriarchy story. There is also evidence to support other stories. Whether the matriarchy story is true or not does not so much matter. What matters is that hearing stories of the matriarchy can set the stage for a wider view of relationship possibilities than the limited view dictated by the pervasive patriarchal story we live in today.) So, let us be-gin again. Previous to 6000 years ago, cultures of the world were matriarchal. We do not even know what the term "matriarchy" means anymore. We think matriarchy is simply a role reversal with women replacing men in patriarchal power positions. This is not so. Matriarchy functions through a completely different paradigm than patriarchy, not even on the same game board.

Matriarchy was the original successful design of human or-ganizations for 90,000 years. It was characterized by egalitari-anism, mutuality, and love of life. Most matriarchal viewpoints are wildly unfamiliar to us today, as our minds have been shaped by a patriarchal framework (for example, from the matriarchal perspective it is crippling insanity to think that a person can own land or claim legal rights to natural resources; for another example, the concept of "profit" is a bizarre intellectual disease). After you read this book, do the experiments, and feel the results in your relationships, then having a conversation about matriarchy might begin making sense. At this point it is enough to consider that the ways of humanity were probably not always like they are now.

Some historians think that 6000 years ago, after the last ice age, severe climatic changes forced matriarchal cultures into desperate survival. Out of the chaos arose patriarchal worldviews based on scarcity, competition, and the "I win, you lose" game plan. Patriarchal marauders seeking to irresponsibly benefit from the labors of others soon pillaged and subjugated any remaining matriarchies.

Patriarchy

If you do your own research you may be surprised to discover that the patriarchy has not made independent contributions to civilization. The patriarchy exists as the negation of matriarchy. The "original" inventions of patriarchy consist mainly of different forms of violence: the invention of domination as a universal rule within organizations, the invention of private property, the invention of war, the valuation of abstract linear thought, the invention of exploitation and profit, the replacement of sharing with competition, and the invention of mechanization and machinery.

This book has nothing to do with history, economics, science, politics or religion. This book is about you discovering greater possibilities for yourself and your relationships. Toward that end I invite you to consider the idea that what could be happening in the world right now is the last rampage and the predictable failure of patriarchy through the introduction of worldwide capitalism. Divide the resources by the population count and you discover that not everybody in the world gets to have an air-conditioned apartment and a gas-guzzling car. When you add up the numbers they cannot work out. At some point the house of cards falls down.

Identify the Patriarchy

As you think over what you are reading in this chapter and start identifying specific, detailed manifestations of the patriarchy in your daily life (like the fact that children play in the street, most buildings are angled instead of rounded and their design makes minimal or no use of an abundance of free solar energy) you may be surprised that a condition you either never noticed before or that you assumed was naturally true and ordinary could only exist in a patriarchy. It becomes even more astonishing when that thing is happening inside of you! For example, when you shut down your intuition, numb your feelings, and pass responsibility for conducting rituals of death, birth or transition over to priests and doctors instead of priestesses and midwives because of fears of reprisal from the culture. You can experience how deeply the patriarchy possesses you by wrestling to change a particular opinion, reaction, assumption or generalization and finding that it careens through your mind and emotions, forcibly driven by an unseen patriarchal engine.

Consciousness creates freedom from that possession.

Life in the Patriarchy (BLTLCH03.01)
A practice that awakens consciousness within you is to *name what is happening*. For example, you could say to yourself, "What is happening right now inside of me is a manifestation of the patriarchy. It is not authentically me." Unfettered by the patriarchal worldview you suddenly gain freedom of movement. You can

begin to take actions that are more authentically your own, even if they are not sanctioned by the patriarchy. Having options that are outside the boundaries of the patriarchy is essential for finding your way into something other than ordinary human relationship.

How Patriarchy Shapes Our Culture

Patriarchy shapes our culture like this:

- Our culture is dominated and controlled by men.
- Our culture is designed to serve the purposes of men. Men make the important decisions.
- Men design our government, police force, military, and our school systems.
- Men make and enforce the laws.
- Men specify and approve the design of our cities, streets, buildings, transportation systems, communication systems, entertainment, and clothes. Even kitchen appliances are designed and marketed by men, with unusable instructions written by technicians for technicians.
- Men define women's beauty ideals and "saturation bomb" the female mind with these definitions through multiple media channels.
- Men use the female body in advertisements as a sex object for manipulating other men's minds. What this does to women is not even considered.
- For men, women are just a market niche.
- Women are told they are free within the patriarchy but this is a false and ridiculous freedom more like having a prison cell enlarged. The freedom is without responsible consequence except to make monthly payments on the credit card bills. Women are free and disallowed to take responsibility.
- Women were recently given the right to vote in the patriarchy, but this is a total illusion of empowerment because voting itself is a masculine form of decision-making. Women do not make decisions by fifty-one percent vote. Women naturally make decisions through consensus. Men do not even know what consensus is.
- If women want power in the patriarchy they must first subvert their femininity and play the men's game. To gain power or recognition the women have to become better "men" than the men.
- To succeed in the patriarchy women give up their pride, self-confidence, dignity, and their direct connection to the source of the living Goddess.
- Women's culture is directed by men toward children, laundry, housekeeping, shopping, entertaining men, and so on; whatever the men do not want to do.
- Women are not empowered as top managers in trade and business. There is no women's management culture.
- Men dominate religion. Women's spiritual problems are "solved" by men, e.g. the pope.
- The patriarchy replicates itself by educating our children in the patriarchal context through all forms of media, and even, unconsciously, through women themselves.
- In the patriarchy there is no place for women to live their authentic power. So, they offer their bodies to get a little of what they want and to be accepted by men.
- Sexual abuse of women and children is understood as normal in the patriarchy and often unobstructed.
- Women compete with other women to survive in the patriarchy and for the love and acceptance of men. There is an ongoing war amongst women who could instead nourish and empower each other in a woman's culture.
- The patriarchy creates wars on the planet because the patriarchy is not round: love

is missing. Women know how to prevent war, but do not do it in order to demonstrate the little power that they do have, letting the boys go kill each other as a subtle form of feminine revenge.

- Women have forgotten that they ARE love.

It is important to remember that *there is nothing bad or wrong about the patriarchy.* The patriarchy works as a patriarchy works. Human beings live, work and play in virtual reality "gameworlds," life stories that we agree to create together. We could continue to live in a patriarchal gameworld for all of eternity and no one could blame us. It is just a patriarchy.

A New Solution

Patriarchy is not the only solution to life, just like steak and potatoes is not the only solution to what to have for dinner. The real question here is: how have we lost our personal ability to choose and live out a wider variety of alternatives than are allowed by standard Western culture?

You have the power to answer that question in an interesting way: by actually choosing attitudes and actions that are not offered by our present culture. You could do this in thousands of ways. You could, for example, love your wife and children more than anything else. You could define your neighborhood or your part of the apartment building as your village and hold village meetings once a week divided into men's culture, women's culture and children's culture, with village-wide festivals four times a year. You could start a school for children (or adults) that teaches from this or other non-belief-centered books. You could empower and organize men and women to provide rites of passage for your teenagers so they have a foundation that is broader and deeper than our culture can offer

them to use for the rest of their lives. You could give up trying to meet economic standards set for you by the culture and instead figure out who you are and how to make best use of your time while you are alive.

You could reclaim your power to take non-ordinary actions right here, right now, while reading this sentence, and then you could exercise that power again and again – every three seconds or so – from now on.

How do you actually reclaim your power to choose something that is not offered on the menu? It is an astonishing question, because such power is inalienable. Such power is not something that can be taken away from you. How you reclaim the power to choose from all options rather than only from the options presented is to specifically and exactly figure out how you are right now pretending that you do not have that power. This answer gives you the key to get through all patriarchal defenses.

Your Job

Your job is to personally rediscover and implement the knowledge of the interrelationship of all beings as the basis of your feeling, thinking and acting. Through your personal experimentation, matriarchal egalitarianism, mutuality and love of life can regain a foothold all over the world as viable alternatives to Western globalization. This cannot happen by decree. There will be no mass awakening. This is not theoretical. Evolution happens one person, one experiment, one insight at a time. Doing these experiments is your job.

Because matriarchal concepts are so shocking and foreign it is beyond the scope of this book to create an understanding in the reader about matriarchal values. You can learn more about matriarchy and matriarchal values from Riane Eisler's book *The Chalice and the Blade*. What is important is to know that although we do not presently see it, our patriarchal viewpoint completely imprisons our thinking through perceptual distortions. Your job is to start carefully observing the steel-bar certainties of the patriarchal story until the certainties go fuzzy around the edges and dissolve under the heat of your inquiry. Studying the patriarchal worldview and persistently asking "why?" reveals through experience that patriarchal boundaries are imaginary.

Objectively scrutinizing the patriarchy unfolds realizations in you that consciously and responsibly subvert the patriarchy. Subverting the patriarchy is different from overthrowing the patriarchy. For example, you subvert the patriarchy when you use the patriarchy itself for a purpose other than that for which it was originally intended. Rather than regarding patriarchal assumptions as barriers to your development, you can interact with patriarchal assumptions as your personal jungle gym for developing a fluidity of being. Then you are using the patriarchy rather than the patriarchy using you. As spiritual teacher Lee Lozowick puts it, "Be that which nothing can take root in." That is, through practice you can become that in which a rigid reaction to the patriarchy cannot take root. The patriarchy's grip on your personal convictions loosens because through practice your convictions evolve into something nongrippable.

This writing is *not* a call to revolution. This writing is a call to *evolution*. Your evolution. Overthrowing the patriarchy is completely irrelevant. What is relevant is you waking up to who you are.

Section 3-B
Getting Through Patriarchal Defenses

Questioning the patriarchy from within the patriarchy is not allowed by the rules of the patriarchy. Slipping outside the thought-control of those rules is not impossible, but also not very likely. It requires that you look at what you are looking with.

Your Way of Seeing (BLTLCH03.02). As a daily experiment you can begin simply noticing the ordinary details of your life with a different set of eyes. Shift your intention so that instead of observing things from the normal perspective as if you are the patriarchy, use the subversive perspective of noticing the insinuations of the patriarchy itself.

This experiment is simple and yet deceptively difficult. Self-ratifying patriarchal assumptions are the patriarchy's first defense. It is shocking to recognize how thoroughly our perceptions are captured when we are born into a worldview beyond which our parents cannot see. We receive the patriarchy's assumptions at the same time that we receive breast milk (or whatever the patriarchy is selling to mothers for baby food these days). Patriarchal attitudes come so early and are integrated so tightly into our identity that we forget our ability to seriously question the patriarchy. We have been hypnotized. Your experiment is to wake yourself up.

The practice of simply noticing holds within it the motionless and inescapable power of awareness, but only if the noticing is *neutral*, completely without judgment. Simply noticing the patriarchy's intimate influence in your life, step by step, loosens its personal grip on you. Over time you gain the sensitivity to distinguish between unconscious patriarchal habits and an abundance of alternative options. In the moment that you can actually take actions that are outside the patriarchal framework, the patriarchy becomes irrelevant.

The fact that questioning patriarchal assumptions is unlikely does not mean that you should not try to do it. To establish and maintain an extraordinary life and profound intimacy with your partner, some new ideas can be very helpful, including ideas that lie outside the reality boundaries of the patriarchy. But asking after such ideas may produce surprising consequences. For example, your inquiries may attract answers, and the answers are not guaranteed to be pain free. How has it come to pass that the patriarchy dominated our thinking? What other kinds of thinking are there? How has the patriarchy been allowed to continue? And why have we impoverished ourselves by handing our creative authority over to the patriarchy?

Misidentification

Similar questions are pondered in the field of exopsychology, the study of the origin and evolution of psychology in the universe. Don't conclude that psychology is unique to human beings! Any species of creature on any planet that identifies itself within a single body – i.e., not like an anthill – and that evolves a neurological system complex enough to sustain self-awareness will naturally start off with a psychology that functions just like ours.

How has the patriarchy been tolerated? One of the mechanisms is through misidentification. We adopt the classic rituals of the patriarchy, including scarcity-based competition and hierarchical structures, through two basic misidentifications – first with the body, next with the mind.

As babies we notice physical sensations. We feel warm, cold, pain, and pleasure. We see sights, hear sounds, smell smells, taste flavors, and feel textures. We wish to move and our body moves. We drink, eat, fart, pee and poop. Without question or doubt we make our first unconscious misidentification: "I am my body." Identifying with our body orients us toward fighting to compete for any resources that the body needs.

Months and years pass. Our certainty about who we are is not shaken. Then we notice that we also have thoughts and feelings. We acquire language. We take on opinions and start to figure things out. We give and ask for reasons and communication starts working. We get offended and our body responds emotionally. Experiencing our own thoughts, feelings and reactions catalyzes our second unconscious misidentification: "I am my mind." Identifying with our mind orients us toward rigid structures for organizational power, such as in hierarchies.

The purpose of the misidentification is originally noble: our own survival. Self-preservation. Using our mind to defend our body obviously helps to keep us alive. What is not so evident is that in order to accomplish its most obvious purpose – our physical survival – the misidentification must first accomplish its most fundamental purpose – its own continued survival. The unseen primary objective of misidentification is to continue our misidentification.

As a result of thinking that we are our body and our psychology, we conclude that consciousness comes from us. Extricating ourselves from this conclusion is not promoted by the patriarchy. In fact, the opposite is true. The patriarchy orients us toward fulfilling physical and psychological needs instead of opening to Archetypal realities that exist around us all of the time.

In the process of building Love that lasts

we will venture beyond patriarchal limitations. The journey may involve some struggle. That we do not gracefully extricate ourselves from our misidentifications confirms the power of the patriarchy.

And yet it is possible. The journey starts exactly where we are right now, face to face with some level of commitment to a defensiveness that regards the self that it is defending as a physical body and a psychological construct. Being thus occupied with defending our misidentifications we are distracted from the bigger possibilities of realizing our true abilities as a man or a woman.

A Special Appeal to Men

I hope that many men read this book. We men are handicapped by the patriarchy in profound ways that we do not realize. This chapter especially addresses our responsibilities and our possibilities. Fully discovering and enlivening our expansive birthright as men may include striving to make efforts beyond our fathers' reach. Reading this book is an effort we can make. I hope that many men read this book, do experiments and teach what they learn to their sons. We have so much to gain from starting over again. I hope many men read this book.

SECTION 3-C
Ordinary Man

Being Ordinary Man (BLTLCH03.03). Being a man in a patriarchy is like being a child in a daycare center, not knowing that just outside the nursery door lies a vast world waiting for you to grow up into.

This section addresses both men and women about the special circumstances of being a man raised in a patriarchy. Please understand that these ideas are not about Archetypal Man. Investigating what it is to become Archetypal Man will come later in this book and later in our evolution as men. We must first become a responsible adult man before we can begin exploring the delicacies of becoming Archetypal Man. Our present condition as so-called men in Western civilization is much worse than we think.

Men in a patriarchy do not have to grow up. Men in a patriarchy are not shown how to become authentically powerful by aligning themselves with the forces of evolution. In a patriarchy, men are protected (read that as imprisoned) in their infancy by the same arrogance that the patriarchy uses to protect itself. Even the men holding power positions in the government, the military, religion, education, science, or business (including the entertainment industry and the media) are handicapped with certain immaturities because the patriarchy does not initiate men into their own proper manhood. The patriarchy leaves men as intellectually educated, self-centered little boys with underdeveloped emotions and small-minded visions in adult male bodies.

This is a harsh generalization. If you are a man, see if you can let your heart rather than your mind digest the assessment to figure out if any parts of it are true. If you are a woman, ask yourself if you agree with the assessment or not.

Not so long ago, incomplete masculine development made little difference in the big-picture existence of humanity on planet Earth. These days the consequences have changed. For example, there is a gap between our present use of technology and the skills needed for living naturally on the Earth. That gap is now so big that without our technology we don't know how to live. Beneath our shallow bravado is a deep fear of losing the use of technology ("technopenuriaphobia" or TPP, *see* Section 7-C) that unconsciously but seriously constrains our behavior. We think that we own technology because we created it, but, because of our dependency on it, the technology owns us. We can't live without our technology, but we also can't live with it. Due to the toxicity of our technological byproducts, and the impact of modern weaponry, our immaturity as men threatens to annihilate the human race if not the entire planet.

Men in a patriarchy make an erroneous assumption. We assume that having an adult male body automatically makes us adults. Our culture tells us nothing different. But, in fact, there is a world of difference between having an adult male body and being an adult man. If you, as a man, some day wish to learn the difference, you can easily do so by asking fifteen or twenty strong, centered, clear-minded, vocal adult women to explain it to you personally, specifically and directly, en masse, for about an hour. You must promise to stand there and only listen. The avalanche of pure anguish, the torrent of feminine fury, the incisive clarity of the accusations, the simple beauty of what women desire, and the profound sorrow over unattained possibilities will bury you in self-reproach with no way to dig your way out while retaining any integrity. I strongly recommend that you do this for yourself (or come to one of my men's trainings). The impact of women's unrestricted voices speaking in harmony, the look in their eyes, the stoop of their weight-bearing shoulders and the cry of their still-aching hearts will be an experience you will never forget for the rest of your days.

Men Raised in a Patriarchy by Women

The situation of present day men is worse than simply being raised in a patriarchy. Men are raised in a patriarchy *by women*. We have no idea what this does to the possibility of becoming a man. In our neurotic, technological, time-stressed, entertainment-oriented, comfort-pandering culture men do not do the child raising. Men are "at work." Men are out of the house doing whatever men do in a patriarchy to stay out of the house. It is women who raise the children. Boys are raised by women who are living in a patriarchy. This is very bad news for any man hoping to authentically grow up.

Think for a moment. Consider the unconscious mechanisms that must be cooking in a familial stew pot. Women in any culture want (and deserve) to be respected as equal citizens without reason, just as the men want (and deserve). But in a patriarchy, feminine ways of being are seldom given the same respect as masculine viewpoints. This subtle imbalance insinuates women into a slave class, and rage over the degradation unconsciously infiltrates a mother's relationship with her boy children. Strong, withheld feelings and serpentine female thoughts cook together in the bowels of a patriarchy. Some of the twists do not even come from a woman's own experience – they are passed down from her mother.

A mother's womanly disgust as well as her hopes, her outrage as well as her justifications, produce two unrecognized strategies in her relationship to her son. Either she tries to sensitize (feminize) the boy so that he will not grow up to disrespect, hurt and abandon women the way she may have been treated by men in the patriarchy. Or, she dominates, invades and controls the boy so he can never acquire enough power to abuse. Either of these strategies may deform a boy's self-experience for a lifetime, and by making such privacies her business, the mother may end up feeling closer to the boy than she does to her own husband.

In addition to the mother's influence, most of a boy's teachers during twelve years of schooling are *also women*. What happens when a boy grows up with the vast majority of his instructors, authority figures and adult role models being women? A woman trying to feminize or dominate a boy generates deep distortions in his future relationships with women that are at least as disruptive as a woman being too distant. We would be naïve to think that these distortions are self-correcting.

Who Is Dad?

Boys do not know who Dad is. A modern dad is often not around. Modern life pulls him away from home and away from his children. He is out there somewhere, "working," leaving a vacuum where a child's role model for human manhood should be. To see our dad for an hour or so on Saturday afternoon, mowing the grass or reading the newspaper is pitifully insufficient. Boys need a man as a role model day in and day out for years – a man to stand with, to imitate, to wrestle with, to smell and to be confirmed by. And girls need to see a dad teaching the boys about manhood.

What boys learn about manhood in our present culture is how to be absent. We imitate our absent dads. We continue being absent when we avoid challenging responsibilities rather than grabbing them by the horns. We exhibit absenteeism when we ignore our profound desires to make our lives about what truly matters to us and to make the world a better place to live, and instead limit our creations to what is defined by the culture as normal and expected. This is how we are absent from ourselves. Then we pass on the tradition of absenteeism by being absent from our sons.

As a modern man lies alone on his sterile hospital deathbed, aching from some unfathomable disease, he wonders what life was supposed to be all about. Where did his life go? What was the purpose of all that?

Life was there. We weren't. We were obediently absent.

Why are we talking about all of this?

Because consciousness creates freedom.

By gaining additional perspectives about what transpires during the course of our lives we gain the possibility of creating something different. Since we are not trained to be conscious of the patriarchy in which we live, we are not free of the patriarchy. Without consciousness we have no freedom. In other words, without our realizing it, the patriarchy owns our body, mind, heart and soul, and dictates our destiny. When the patriarchy does not move, we men (and women) do not move. Where the patriarchy cannot go, we men (and women) cannot go. What men once created as a refuge has turned out to be our prison. We are indeed asleep with poop in our pants.

In order to grow up, we men are challenged to intelligently and effectively deal with the special condition of being a man raised in a patriarchy. Our culture does not train us how to grow into our true maturity. As a result, our culture is left largely without grown-up men, and almost no men realize the loss.

If as either man or woman you are moved to explore and expand into the possibilities inherent in the human form, then you are quite likely to be far more successful if you research outside of our Western culture to encounter those possibilities.

Ordinary Woman

Being a woman in a patriarchy is like being a black person in a white person's society. The white people have no idea…

As the subservient class, it is the women's responsibility to create a cultural game that is played by a more interesting set of rules, because the "white people" ain't a gonna do it for you. Responsibly creating a new game is far more complex and involved than the common practice of blaming men. No amount of blame, regardless of how true it seems, will make the slightest change. The world is not reinvented by complaining victims. The world is renewed by individuals responsibly changing their own behavior, one word at a time.

This section addresses both women and men about the special circumstances of being a woman raised in a patriarchy. Again, these ideas do not pertain to Archetypal Woman. One must first acquire the skills of becoming a responsible adult woman before she can begin exploring Archetypal Woman's radiant dimensions. Her handicaps may take more effort to abandon than she may at first imagine.

Women's handicap in a patriarchy is conflict with a lifelong enemy. The enemy of women raised in a patriarchy is men. The enemy is not a true enemy, but the circumstantial evidence supporting the story that the enemy exists is so pervasive, and the psycho-emotional payoff for being a victim of such an enemy is so big, that recognizing the "enemy" story as false is almost inconceivable. When women look to other women about this issue there is no dissension. Every woman subtly or overtly agrees, men are the unspoken enemy.

The way women relate to men in the patriarchy cannot be neutral or clean because men are perceived as the enemy. Just beneath the surface of her ordinary-looking interactions are each woman's perfected strategies for how to survive in a patriarchy where women have no overt power. The strategies are as varied as clothing styles. Here are a few standard strategies that women use. Compare them to yours. Women typically:

- Regard men as little boys. Everything you do for men you do with the attitude of being a resentful mother. Either coddle or scold men into doing what you want. When a man does something wrong, punish him by withholding sex or intimacy. Never respect him as an adult.
- Regard men as police. Represent yourself as a "good" housewife or worker and then behind the men's backs sneak out and do whatever you really want to do. If caught, deny everything, confuse the facts, and cover your tracks by creating a different problem, such as attacking the "police" man for the way he speaks to you.
- Regard men as a prize to win. Compete with other women to hypnotize men with your beauty, sexuality, intelligence or charm. Never actually deliver the beauty,

sexuality, intelligence or charm to the man. Instead keep it just out of reach so you can dangle your prized man in front of the other women to show off how powerful you are. Keep a couple of other men on the side, in reserve.

- Regard men as stupid animals. Communicate with men through commands; tell them what you want and what they should do about it. Continuously criticize men in public to prove to them they are stupid. Then you never have to take what they say seriously. Being disgusted about men's brutishness keeps you from feeling the pain of not being in the kind of relationship your heart aches for.

- Regard men as possessions, no different from your car or your house. The man needs maintenance now and then so you take him out to a few places, but since he cannot feel anything and is not really alive anyway, you leave him to take care of himself, including sexually. Use him whenever it suits you.

- Regard men as dangerous and abusive adversaries. Be proactively abusive toward men as a general policy, to make men keep their distance. Your unprovoked spitefulness protects you. Besides, men are the enemy, so expressing aggression toward men any way that you can is already justified.

- Regard men as rescuers and bank accounts. Play-act being a sweet victim and a sexy partner to your present sugar daddy so he keeps rescuing you and providing an abundance of cash. After he dies you will have time to be yourself. Through your sacrifice you have earned the right to inherit his money and the power of his name.

These are harsh generalizations. If you are a woman, see if you can let your heart rather than your mind digest these descriptions to figure out if any parts of them are true. If you are a man, review your experiences from these new perspectives to see what is accurate or not about these descriptions.

Establishing Another Way

Women in a patriarchy do not have to grow up because there are no men in the patriarchy to demand that of them. Men's attention is involved in power politics, money making, sports, and consumer sex (how many can I get?), so women do not receive the special attention required to shift into who they can potentially become as adult women. There is a deep brokenheartedness about this lack of opportunity to grow into the vastness of true womanhood. Rather than feeling the sorrow of this loss and using the wisdom of this pain to behave outside the restraints of the patriarchy, women tend to continue blaming men, and through this behavior prove themselves to be just as committed to supporting the patriarchy as the men are.

Both women and men may regularly play into one or more of the survival strategies mentioned above. Along your path of development there may come a time when you are ready to find another way of interacting that permits you to more intimately enter the delicate moments of life. Shifting strategy is possible but far more complex a process than just thinking about it.

Clarifying Survival Decisions (BLTLCH03.05). The complication comes from recognizing that your strategies were adopted long ago, perhaps even in childhood. And all the while – from then until now – you have found real examples in your life to serve as evidence to support the validity and necessity of maintaining your particular strategies. Your collection of evidence is so irrefutable that by now you have come to accept that your stories are not creative interpretations – rather, they are the truth. Unwinding your self-made puzzle involves your mind, body, heart and soul in a seven-step procedure that usually goes something like this:

Your first step is to experientially discover that just behind your strategy, and continuously propelling it forward, is an internal feeling such as anger, sadness or fear. When you detect which feeling it is that drives the words and actions of your strategy, shift your attention from focusing on the strategy to focusing on that feeling. Develop this as a habit.

Your second step is to decide to trust the feeling on its own merit, as if it had a message to deliver to you or a journey to take you on. The journey may be like a roller-coaster ride, but it is a true journey nonetheless, starting where you are now and ending at the place of origin of the strategy. Set aside time to trust the feeling and let it lead you to its source. This may occur stepwise over a period of weeks or months, or can occur more immediately in the company of a skilled guide. The way to let the feeling lead you will be to permit the feeling to get bigger and bigger until it is loud or tearful and brings you into contact with one or more of the times before now when you were experiencing this same feeling. Do not hurt yourself in this process and do not hurt anything else. When you arrive at a memory of a time, before now, where you experienced the same feeling that is driving your defense strategy, notice what was happening at that time. Decide if that is the first time you experienced this feeling or if there was another incident previous to then when you actually adopted your strategy. Keep following the feeling further and further back, until you arrive at the most dramatic memory of whatever was happening to you then. In that experience you made some decisions.

Your third step is to clarify the decision or decisions that you made in those dramatic moments. Often in such intense circumstances, the decision will feel and function more like a vow, something like, "I will *never* do

that again!" Or "I will always be good!" Or, "I will never trust men (or women) again!" Or, "No one is there to take care of me so I must forever take care of myself!" Or, "This was so unspeakably horrible that no matter what else happens I dedicate my life to getting revenge!" Extract from your experience the two or three core decisions you made. The decisions are about yourself, about other people, or about how you will survive in a world like this with people like them.

Your fourth step is to ask yourself if these old decisions are still influencing your life today. Not surprisingly, and, at the same time, surprisingly, the answer will be a definite and extensive, "Yes." Think of some specific examples of present day influence.

Your fifth step is to ask yourself if you would like to make a new decision? Have you been "good" long enough? Have you carried out your revenge long enough? Have you stayed alone and neurotically independent long enough? Are you ready to drop the certain warfare for a not so certain vulnerability that includes the possibility of more refined levels of relationship? Listen more to your body, your heart and your soul than to your mind. Whatever answer you get, respect it. The answer is not guaranteed to be, "Yes." You may not be quite ready yet. But if you have successfully derived this much clarity about what has been going on for you it is probably confirmation that, deep inside, you have already decided to make a shift. If your answer is "No," skip to step seven. If your answer is "Yes," you are at step six.

Your sixth step is to define what the new decision or decisions would be; what specific new decisions would empower you? For example, with regard to being good... one possible new decision could be, "I break the rules about being good and I take responsibility for the consequences of being myself." With regard to trust, "I trust myself to choose whom to trust, when, and how much, and I trust myself to take care of myself around them." With regard to staying isolated and doing things all by yourself, "I can ask for help and let the help in." Or, with regard to revenge, "I am finished with being a slave of revenge and violence. The contract is over. I take my life back and leave the past in the past."

Your seventh step is to write down your old and your new decisions.

Women Raised in a Patriarchy by Patriarchal Women

It is enlightening to wonder why a woman or man living in a patriarchy would voluntarily train their own children to constrict themselves to fit into the patriarchy when that distortion is not absolutely necessary anymore. There are enough subcultures and parallel cultures already thriving within and around the patriarchy these days that full subservience to the patriarchy is no longer enforced by threat of death as it has been in the past. But modern parents and teachers still continue to promote patriarchal survival strategies. Why is that? What happened to the natural manifestations of the deep feminine? Where did men and women's love of the Earth Mother go? How did such deep feminine roots get severed so permanently? A brief glance into history can provide quite an eye-opening if not downright chilling answer.

I am no historian so I suggest that you do your own research to confirm these stories, but from what I understand, during the era from roughly 1200 to 1800 the Christian church sponsored what have come to be called the Medieval, Spanish, Portuguese and Roman Inquisitions intended to rid European lands of so-called heretics. That is a 600-year period during which time several million "heretics" were killed and their money and property confiscated by the Church. In the middle of all this, from about 1450 to 1700, local governments created a similar opportunity to acquire land and wealth through implementing what became known as "witch hunts." Modern historians find that the originally estimated number of people tortured and killed during the "great hunt" was based on false records and was exaggerated. Today's historians estimate that the number of "witches" killed totaled between 60,000 and 100,000 individuals, 80 percent of whom were women, 10 percent children, and 10 percent men. The "burning times" lasted 250 years, and stretched from Ireland to Italy, from Scandinavia to Spain, and even to the Americas. All told, over 50,000 non-docile women were killed by the witch hunts, and an untold number but surprisingly high percentage of women were killed during the Holy Inquisitions.

These numbers boggle the mind, too massive to comprehend. But imagine for a moment what this must have been like. For a quarter millennium it was common knowledge and common practice that any woman who behaved in ways forbidden by the combined church and state patriarchies would be ripped from her home, tortured in the most obscene ways, and killed before the eyes of her own children, family and friends.

In those days people *knew* their neighbors. In those days, people did not move around in anonymity like we do now. Most people spent their entire lives within a ten-mile radius, in the company of relatives and neighbors who intimately knew the ins and outs of each other's lives. Today if the police arrest someone three houses down the street we don't even know who it is, and we certainly don't miss them. The whole thing is their problem. But back in the Middle Ages when the inquisitors and witch hunters came to town, everybody knew and were perhaps even related to the victims, and everybody was shown what behavior or attitudes resulted in a most hideous public death. Consistently, for ten generations, this memetic-weeding process continued unimpeded. What do you think the result is?

We are looking at the results today. The weeding process worked. Whoever survived got the message and passed it on to their children: if you offend the patriarchy you die. The possibility for women to become what adult and Archetypal Woman is capable of becoming has, in this graphically violent way, been eliminated from Western civilization. Women could not even think of enlivening the Great Mother in their daily lives anymore because three hundred years ago those thoughts were exterminated by the patriarchy.

Adult and Archetypal possibilities for men and women do not ever vanish. They have always been there and they will always remain, at least as a potential. Bringing the potential to life is a different story entirely. Since the late 1800s the feminine potential has been rumbling in women's souls. After long years of struggle women gradually gained the legal right to vote and hold office in patriarchal political systems. Although noteworthy and important, the right to vote does not bring life to what woman is. I am speaking about something else entirely.

Since the 1960s and 1970s the "women's liberation movement" has opened doors to women educating themselves and creating new dimensions for their lives in workshops, seminars, trainings and meetings. Contrary to the lack of coverage by popular media, the women's liberation movement never ended; it continues deepening and expanding itself further, bigger, and stronger than ever before. In comparison to the women's liberation movement, the "men's liberation movement" has not even begun. As truly noble-minded and magnificent as the human rights and human potential movements have been, they lack the level of ruthless clarity and brutal honesty necessary to bring psychological defense strategies into enough flux that they have a chance of coming back together in a more comprehensive and mature form. Our culture still arrogantly refuses to take responsibility for the messes it is creating.

One man, after years of personal development work, recently confessed, "I hate women. I used to think that I appreciated women, that I understood women, and that I could listen to women. The first thing I think when I meet a woman is how can I have sex with her? I thought this came from my love of women. Now I see that it all comes from one thing. I hate women. What can I do to get out of this?" I have heard the same sentiments from women regarding men. What we can do to get out of our hatred is to figure out exactly how we got into it. Therein lies the key.

A Rite of Passage

Our culture does not promote the idea of individuals going outside of the culture to learn things that the culture itself does not provide for us. Our culture is "synclastic." Synclastic means that our culture structurally turns in on itself, like a Möbius strip or a Klein bottle. Western culture has only one surface, and therefore has no way out. Through planet-wide media coverage and profit-oriented corporate strategies, the no-way-outness seeks to subsume all remaining outposts of diversity.

Western culture does not have to be designed this way. Western culture could be designed so as to promote its members going outside of the culture to learn more than the culture has to offer, and bringing what was learned back into the culture to enhance cultural diversity. Instead, Western culture is designed to be synclastic as a way of defending itself. You cannot get out. You may try going to the edges of our culture to get out, but by stepping over what you imagine to be the edge of our culture you will find yourself right back in its center.

Take, for example, army surplus clothing or faded blue jeans. Hippies used to wear army surplus clothing and tattered blue jeans as a way of being counter-culture. At first the hippie clothing was distinguishing and offensive. But our culture subsumes revolutions by transforming them into marketing trends. Army surplus clothes and stonewashed tattered jeans are now manufactured in third world sweathouses and accepted in the highest fashion circles worldwide. What was once a revolutionary idea has become an institution that defends itself against revolutionary ideas. We are trapped in ways far more perniciously than we can imagine.

This makes becoming authentically masculine (or feminine) within a patriarchy particularly tricky. The proposed method for accomplishing our aim will be nonlinear.

If you research the process of becoming a man or a woman in other cultures, in other ages, sooner or later you will encounter the idea of a "rite of passage." Traditional older cultures provided their people with a clearly defined and formidable, sometimes horrific (as is the case with scarification or female circumcision) rite of passage from childhood to adulthood. Our modern culture does not. (For a clear personal story of the conflict between the rite of passage tradition and Western civilization read Malidoma Patrice Somé's inspiring book *Of Water and the Spirit*.) The closest thing we have to a rite of passage in our culture is getting your ears pierced or getting your driver's license. And if you ever commute during rush hour you will observe that successfully obtaining a driver's license does nothing to increase a person's adult behavior.

What is a rite of passage? A rite of passage is the activation process for bringing a human being into the wisdom of responsibility and consequence. As children we are accustomed to making messes and not having to clean them up. Western civilization is significantly irresponsible. We are a culture of children because we make messes (for example, nuclear waste, depleted natural resources, the national debt, greenhouse gasses, children on Ritalin, plastic packaging materials, and so on) and think that somebody else will clean them up.

When human beings are approximately fifteen years of age we are structurally capable of taking responsibility. The child part of us wants to avoid responsibility and to keep making messes without facing the consequences. If nothing is done to change this, then the child part of us will remain in control for our entire lives. A rite of passage is the formal, irrevocable procedure through which the child part of us is permanently taken out of power. During this process a boy takes his balls back from his mother to become an adult man and a girl takes her center back from her father to become an adult woman. If a person survives the rite of passage, a newly formed adult steps back into the world as a force of "radical responsibility."

Radical responsibility is an Archetypal term that means to take responsibility for sourcing responsibility. You do not have to understand this right now. We will investigate radical responsibility in later chapters when we explore Archetypal domains. What you do need to know is that a true rite of passage is of necessity almost incomprehensibly formidable, *and*, without a formal rite of passage into adulthood, we are doomed to the neurotic mediocrity that is all too familiar in our modern world. For 40,000 years human beings knew that children do not become adult except through a formidable rite of passage. We seem to have forgotten.

I am *not* suggesting that we revert to tribal customs and start living like they did in the bad old days before telephones and running water. I have lived in pretechnical villages in Fiji, Indonesia, Thailand and the Philippines and I have seen first-hand what can go on there: nepotism, bigotry, inbreeding, adultery, jealousy, revenge – the worst kind of territorial terrorism. In contrast to the verbiage in travel agency brochures, it takes more than palm trees to make paradise. The demand is to create a new rite of passage that is effective for modern needs. Permanently forsaking modern amenities is not necessary.

A modern rite of passage differs from a traditional rite of passage through what is done with the "assemblage points." I borrow the term "assemblage points" from Carlos Castaneda's writings about Don Juan Matus' Yaqui Indian teachings. Assemblage points are core reference frames out of which a human mind and psychology constructs its worldview. During a rite of passage a person's assemblage points are brought into serious disorganization and then are resolidified into a new relationship to each other and to the energetic world.

In an ancient rite of passage the assemblage points are welded into complete identification with the village's traditional worldview and customs. This strategy constrains the young man or woman to think, feel and behave within strict norms of men or women of that tribe. When each new adult does things the way they have always been done, this assures the continued survival of the villagers.

Traditional rites of passage have duplicated this strategy for thousands of years and succeed marvelously in cultures that change only gradually if at all.

In Bali, for example, in the North Philippines, and in Southern China, probably all over Southeast Asia, there are gigantic cascades of emerald green rice terraces that have been painstakingly hacked out of the sides of mountains using only primitive hand tools. For 3000 years, these terraces have grown through careful planning in how the water flows from rice paddy to rice paddy so that all rice paddies are equally flooded. A different family owns each section of rice paddies. The man at the bottom rice paddy is in charge of water flow through all of the rice paddies. Because he is the last man in line for water he will make sure that, after everybody else gets water, he also gets water in his paddy. The culture must keep doing what it has always done so that villagers' long-proven terracing system continues to grow enough rice to eat. To slow down evolution, the village culture uses a rite of passage to lock new adults into the belief systems and worldviews of their traditional culture and times. For a village culture, this traditional form for a rite of passage makes good sense. For our culture it does not.

Initiating a boy or a girl into their fully functional adult potential in modern hyper-evolving Western civilization requires rites of passage with a different strategy. The modern rite of passage must be just as formidable as the traditional rite of passage because the shock of groundlessness is needed to loosen our assemblage points from their original childhood formations. But, rather than welding a young person's liquefied assemblage points back into the culture's traditional limits, the modern rite of passage establishes the new assemblage points in the evolutionary possibilities of Archetypal Man or Archetypal Woman. We only vaguely know what this means.

The difficulty of continuing this discussion is that any rite of passage created within a patriarchy will avoid providing irrefutable clarity that *the patriarchy is itself childish*. The patriarchy promotes the patriarchy, not the transformation of the patriarchy. We are in a delicate time in which the habits of present Western civilization are not sustainable. It is crucial for the world's survival that the patriarchy itself goes through a rite of passage into adulthood. That transformation happens only when you – an individual male or female member of the patriarchy – take personal responsibility and arrange for yourself to go through your rite of passage. The culture will not arrange this for you. Revolutions are not commonly started by the aristocracy.

So how are we men and women to grow up within the patriarchy? How do we arrange to embark on our own rite of passage?

Your Rite of Passage

Your Rite of Passage (BLTLCH03.06). Rather than initiating you into duplicating what has traditionally been done in the past, a modern rite of passage initiates you into the ability to redirect human cultures of the present into a sustainable future. The following are some hints and suggestions about what might be involved in a modern rite of passage.

One must keep in mind that there can be no guaranteed standard formula for a rite of passage that is also authentic. Authenticity is not standardizeable. Even with long-practiced and well-informed skills, the elders leading traditional rites of passage lose about ten percent of their candidates – yes, "lose" – meaning "dead." A rite of passage must be unique so as to ignite each individual's unquenchable inspiration for providing their unique contributions to humanity. At the same time, modern rites of passage have some common characteristics.

To begin with, this book that you have in your hands is a fairly decent map of what is involved in a rite of passage from childhood to adulthood. This is not a nice book. This book requires you to start where you are with a clear assessment of what you are up against if you are going to try to grow up. So, finish reading this book even if some parts of it make you angry, sad, or scared and you find a really good reason for putting the book down. You will see what I mean as you get into further chapters. After you finish reading this book, consider reading it again. The second time through seems to significantly help in digesting what was read the first time. You might even form a study group for discussing and implementing the ideas in this book.

- A rite of passage is a period of time during which you will undertake certain experiences or experiments to change your relationship to the world, to yourself, to your community, and to what is possible for you. The changes involved are not merely changes in intellectual understanding. The changes will include shifts of context, meaning shifts in *where* you come from, shifts in *what* you perceive with. These kinds of changes can take long periods of preparation and then occur quite suddenly. Although parts of your rite of passage will be minutes, hours, or days long, plan to spend at least two years seriously engaging the rite of passage process for yourself. What gets initiated during those two years could involve commitments or practices that continue for the rest of your life.
- A rite of passage from boyhood to manhood or from girlhood to womanhood is a journey. It is not a lone journey. A rite of passage is usually done in the company of peers and guided by older, more experienced men or women. Most of you reading this book may not even remember your fifteenth birthday party, yet we are structured for rite of passage work in

our mid-teens. I have had the honor of being-with fifteen-year-old males and females in training spaces where they make the leap to enliven particular Archetypal aspects in themselves and the experience can be unbelievable. The sudden transformations that can happen in properly conducted processes are clean and complete, far exceeding anything that we know of from our ordinary course of education and even what is shown in the most exciting and inspiring of films!

- But most of us are probably thirty to fifty years old, and unlike fifteen-year-olds we have some serious habits to contend with. Our thinking-joints do not flex as noiselessly or painlessly as they once did. There is more sludge built up in the system. We are slower and heavier than we once were. This is as it is. At times when contrary forces exert their resistance to your evolutionary steps try to remember this: It is never too late to begin a rite of passage. Galileo Galilee was fifty-one years old when he wrote *Dialogue Concerning the Two Chief World Systems*, the book that got him arrested for heresy, and it was his second book that reordered the world of science. Irina Tweedie was fifty-two years old when she first met her guide and started on her rite of passage that has helped so many people start on theirs. (See her book, *Daughter of Fire*, which exquisitely describes her journey.)

- To begin your rite of passage, declare that you are now beginning your rite of passage. You could be ridiculously bold and say that right now, out loud, before you read the next paragraph: "I (state your full name) hereby declare that I am beginning (or taking my next step in) my rite of passage into adulthood." It is best if you make no assumptions about already knowing what this could even mean.

- **Creating a Possibility Team (BLTLCH03.07).** Start regularly meeting with others in the name of your rite of passage. If you are a man, get together with a few other men, women gather with a few other women, and in your coming together try to discover what bonding is. These people do not need to be your friends. In fact it may need to be that most of the others are complete strangers to you. Your friends could well be in a completely different evolution swing from you, and perhaps you have used your feet-dragging friends as an excuse to procrastinate long enough.

Women have particular difficulty in bonding – a phenomenon that is easily dismissed in a patriarchy. Women don't trust each other enough to bond, being far more committed to competing against each other for power and favors from men. For women, getting through your deep-seated fear and hatred of your seductive sisters will involve breathtaking feats of trust. You will never encounter by accident the immense quantity of trust required, no matter how long you wait. Shadowy fears will always lurk in the dark recesses of your imagination – storing fears is what imagination is for. Bonding enough to go through your rite of passage together will involve trusting the other women in spite of your fears. Trust is a decision that you make. It can be particularly touching for women when your ritual of coming together includes speaking your trust out loud to each other. "Jane, I trust you. Petra, I trust you." Then keep dealing specifically with what comes up for each of you in this process. There will always be reasons to fear. Trust is the decision that something else – in this case your rite of passage to womanhood – is more important than fear. Take a breath. You can manage this.

We have only vague ideas what it might mean to bond with each other in our own gender cultures. Go ahead and bond anyway. This does not mean *go drinking*. Then again, neither does it mean *do not go drinking*. Just do not make your group *about drinking* or you will never have your rite of passage. These days, men's or women's groups are often confused with homosexual men's or women's groups. Making your group about being gay, touchy-feely flirting, and finding your next lover, will also not take you on your rite of passage. On the other hand, do not avoid being in a group just because someone is homosexual. For example, of the four men in my first men's group, one man was gay, one was alcoholic and gay, and the third man was confused, angry, punk, and occasionally gay. I met with these three men every week for three years and it changed my life in a profoundly sane way. Together these men helped build a foundation in me that I stand on to speak to you now, and for their work with me I will remain forever grateful. Create a team of two to four men or women, meet consistently every week or every other week *no matter what*, and go through your rite of passage together. Consider using this book as one of the study materials for supporting your group.

- Because a rite of passage involves upgrading ways that you think, feel, act and are, it is self-deceptive to think that you can design and manage a rite of passage for yourself by yourself. I do not like telling you that anything is impossible. Promoting impossibility is against my nature. And I have to say here that, based on my experience, when it comes to navigating your own unfolding it is far too easy to fool yourself. A central component of successful rite of passage work is persistent, clear, direct, and honest feedback from the

other members of your group. Thinking that you can give yourself accurate feedback would be like leaving a kleptomaniac to guard a jewelry store or a nymphomaniac to babysit your nine-year-old son. You might not get the results you hoped for.

In addition to exploring study materials, exchanging feedback, sharing stories and giving and receiving support with your team, the suggestion here is to also obtain the help of a rite of passage guide. A guide can be anyone who is more experienced and further advanced in their rite of passage than you are and who is responsible and clear enough to serve as a guide. Since rites of passage are not sponsored by our culture, your guide will need to be someone who already has gained access to a greater context than our culture. This does not mean that you should commit to the first Shaolin American-Indian Psychic Kabalistic Tibetan-Buddhist Tantric Sufi Shaman Kundalini Priest Healer from Africa who comes along. Stick a feather in your hat these days and advertise sweat lodges, vision quests, firewalking, outdoor drumming or meditation retreats and you can fill your pockets with gold from the gullible. Let the buyer beware. Being ripped off and betrayed a few times does not necessarily need to be part of your rite of passage. Then again, maybe it does.

- You will most likely end up with more than one guide along the way. But again beware. The tendency of mind to come up with reasonable arguments for jumping from guide to guide the instant before an important shift is about to happen is uncanny, irresistibly tempting, and classically predictable. Jumping from guide to guide will only make you good at jumping. The best way to find an authentic guide is to speak with other people who are already participating in what the guide is offering. Look for a guide whose participants tend to stick with him or her for a long time. Then, you plan to stick with that guide for just as long. A worthy guide will be surrounded by participants who are grounded, centered, balanced, healthy, vocal, interested, vibrant, kind, generous, informative, vulnerable, intelligent, patient, well-rounded, and not only able to speak about what they are doing with clarity and enthusiasm but also able to listen to what you are looking for with respectful attention. The way to have the guide commit to you is to commit to the guide first. Committing first is a little-known and extremely effective nonlinear action. Find out what the guide expects in practical terms as a commitment from the people he or she works with, and then commit in exactly those practical terms. The guide for a man's rite of passage into manhood will *not* be a woman. And vice versa. (Just being clear about this.)

- Preparing yourself for the various stages of a rite of passage involves developing internal disciplines, rigorous vigilance, various kinds of attention, consistency of practice, enduring various discomforts and challenges, perhaps feeling embarrassed or overwhelmed, an ability to persist in the face of unforeseen or unimaginable difficulties, paying certain participation fees, attending particularly nonattractive gatherings or work projects, accepting with equanimity your own and other people's lacks and insufficiencies, and so on. For a dignified rite of passage it helps when you decide from the start to do whatever it takes to proceed with sincerity and whole heartedness. Swâmi Prajnânpad, a little-known but skilled guide from India, was famous for telling his students, "It is not a joke. You will have to pay the full price."

Your guide will suggest specific practices that either prepare you for or actually take you a step forward on your journey. These practices could well include reading certain books, watching certain videos, listening to certain music, doing certain physical movements or exercises, making certain restrictions or enhancements to your daily diet, engaging some kind of meditative or sitting practice, attending certain talks, presentations, workshops or trainings, exposing yourself to certain environments, and developing specific inner faculties that allow you to perceive various energetic relationships and spaces. If your rite of passage does not challenge your cultural addictions or does not include most of the above listed practices, your rite of passage may not be strong enough to provide for you what you are looking for.

I was thirty-seven years old when I took my first step toward becoming a man. Even though I was graduated from the university, had traveled around the world for two-and-a-half years working in Australia and Japan, was happily married, had two wonderful children, owned a house and a car, and was running my own home-based electronic production company in northern California, I was still a boy. In 1989, at my wife's suggestion, I participated in a weekend training near Los Angeles. I had "some" resistance to attending this training because I was a scientist and I imagined that I already had everything figured out. How could I have any problems? Everything already worked – from my point of view.

This experience was not what one might typically imagine a seminar to be: a few days where you learn something new. This was a training: a few days where you *become* something new. This particular training originated in the bowels of the maximum-security federal penitentiary in Marion, Illinois, in the 1960s. It was developed through a creative collaboration between one of the prisoners,

Ken Windes, and the prison psychologist, Dr. Martin Groder. The style of the training was radical, transformational, guerilla street theater – quite confrontational and immune from manipulation, definitely originating far outside mainstream culture. Participating in this training formally started my rite of passage into adulthood. During the training I realized with serious dismay that, contrary to my previous self-concept, my highest priority and commitment in life was to be a "good boy." This shocking realization propelled me through a doorway into the expansive evolutionary journey that I am still on today. Perhaps you too will find that such a training contributes important ingredients to your rite of passage.

The Story of a Convalescence

The following is a personal letter written to me in August 2001. The author gave me permission to share his letter with you. The letter itself is only paper with handwritten marks on it. But this man's life is full of feelings, sensations, questions, and options. In his own words this is "the story of a convalescence." There is a rite of passage map in what he writes. You get a sense of what we are all up against in the patriarchy. Perhaps from this man's story you can breathe enough courage into your soul to make further steps in your own growing-up process, particularly in your man-woman relationships.

Dear Clinton,

This letter might come as a surprise to you. Well, I just felt the urge to send these lines to you and share some of my insights and experiences of the last few months.

But let me start from the beginning (which, looking back, was rather like an end). It was about two years ago. I participated in your training (it must have been my sixth or seventh training), and, maybe you remember, my process was about my stories going on with women and sex. It was my toughest and most persistent and lasting process so far. When after an eternity the training was finally over, it didn't feel like any "endings" I experienced before. Before, [after a training] there was always this relief, a new vision, a clarity, something got healed. This time I felt like I'd been annihilated. I felt so miserable that I wasn't even able to drive home. Fortunately another man stayed with me and took over the job of driving the car.

During the next 2-3 months, although still feeling miserable, I did as you suggested: I didn't connect in any way with women, neither women-friends I knew from before nor the unknown woman at the counter of a shop. No eye contact, nothing! It felt horrible, but I somehow knew that that was the only right thing to do. Somehow, that was the easy part, the logical understandable steps on the way. The difficult, frightening part of it was that this process scattered my whole life-plan, my whole story, a story about me, which I thought so far was true and more or less ok! This identity was gone, completely, only some fragments left here and there. I was in a big despair, in the middle of a nightmare: the old identity didn't work anymore, most of it wasn't even there anymore, and besides that, there was just this void. During these months I hated you. I was convinced that you had made a big mistake, that you had gone too far, that you lost all respect and in a sadistic way enjoyed "killing" me. As a result I decided to never do another training, to look for something nice and gentle. I quit my long-term training program and withdrew from my spiritual path.

So far this was a description of my internal emotional process. What happened on the outside is that I really was not able anymore to live the way I did before. During my process you said: "Mister, the game is over!" I didn't get it then, but I got it much, much later! The women / sex – game was (and still is) definitely over!

During the 18 months afterwards, it was like a pendulum had swung from one extreme to the opposite extreme. I didn't have any contact at all in the first few months, then slowly started to meet women once in awhile, but still staying very distanced and cautious. I really began to think that this was going to be my new style of life: the u-turn from the womanizer I used to be into a monk.

Now, in August 2001, things are different again. The pendulum found a balance! I'm in love with a wonderful woman. We met about 9 months ago for the first time, then met maybe every second week in the beginning, both being very cautious and respectful. By now we meet nearly daily, and, this really sounds incredible, since about a week or so we hold hands once in awhile. Two years ago this idea of a very slow, gentle approach was just not part of my imagination. It was about going to bed with a woman as fast as possible, and then (maybe) starting to get to know the person.

It's the complete opposite now. We talk and talk for hours, have wonderful walks in nature, and we just are both so fully nurtured with that. There's nothing missing! It's so beautiful. I feel like a 14-year-old adolescent, being in love with a girl for the first time.

Only now, looking back, I realize how fucked up in relation to relationship, women, and intimacy I was. I am so grateful that things have changed in such a positive way. And I must admit, it's thanks to you. You were the midwife of this much saner person I am now! No one else had the courage, the knowledge, the strength and the stubbornness to beat "me" with such a heavy club. With "me" I talk about all my destructive, egoistic, hurting, isolating mechanisms going on. I really feel like I am being healed on a very deep level. Like for the first time I can see what intimacy really means. I'm so grateful and happy you've shown up in my life and hit me so hard. It was absolutely necessary, and who knows, without your smack, I would probably still be on this very self-destructive track.

By the way, two months ago I finished my long-term training (with a little delay), I joined another training in spring, and I joined a men's group again! I am also much closer again to my spiritual path.

I am looking forward to seeing you again some day. With deepest respect,

Author's Note

A bit of explanation is called for here. By profession I am a trainer. There is a difference between educators and trainers. Educators share what they know so that you learn something new. Trainers do not depend on what they know. Trainers represent "Bright Principles," which are aspects of conscious responsibility. Trainers take actions in the service of Bright Principles during a training so that participants can become something new. Educators give you new knowledge. Trainers give you the possibility of new behavior. Sometimes to create this possibility the Principles show up as a "smack." There is a science to smacks. The man who wrote the letter above had participated in six or seven trainings. Many layers had already been healed and he had been well prepared. To be effective, a smack must come at exactly the right time, in exactly the right place, and in exactly the right way. This timing is too complicated for the mind to figure out. If a smack is to be delivered effectively it does not come from the trainer; it comes directly from the Principles. Trainings are not about smacks. But every now and then the Principles provide a smack that jumps the train of our thinking to a completely different set of tracks. I know of what I speak. Just a few weeks ago I received a big smack from my trainer. The smack he gave me will last the rest of my life.

Much of what men learn on the journey toward becoming an adult man our fathers never knew. Much of what women learn on the journey toward becoming an adult woman was clouded by a patriarchy that subjugated the intuitive intelligence of our mothers. Most of what we invest in and experience through our rite of passage will never appear on a job resume. However, when we lay down to die, much of the satisfaction from our life will have come from the risks that we took to fully step into the possibility of being a man or a woman in this world.

CHAPTER 4

Some Amazing Things About Having a Mind

Human beings live in solid, perfectly defended, little self-made mental prisons. Our mental prison is a personal and individual choice. Contrary to popular belief, the design of our mental prison is not something we inherit from our parents or society. We carefully choose and install each stone, bar and lock ourselves.

Some of us assume that our environment determines the way we think and perceive. But such a conclusion ignores the fact that each human being originates in the awesome force of his or her own free will. Free will is far stronger than environment – for that matter, free will is stronger than God! If free will were not stronger than environment, human beings would never invent anything new. We would only keep recreating what is already there. If free will were not stronger than God, human beings would be ecstatically creating relationships drenched in love and would be living lives of vibrant joy serving humanity through bringing our destiny to life. Instead, our conscious and unconscious purposes drive our free will to make other choices.

We invest a lot of effort into custom-designing our problems and our standard defense strategies. Consider that siblings (even identical twins) who are given exactly the same childhood treatment, the same opportunities and the same constraints, often form vastly different personality structures and make very different life decisions. Even if one child adopts the same habits and attitudes as the father, the sibling may adopt habits and attitudes that are the exact opposite.

We carefully construct our thought prisons ourselves, as a sculptor fabricates a piece of art. You are doing it right now reading this book: making little comparisons here, adding some finishing touches there. What is so amazing about our relationship to the mind is that we are its prisoners *and* we are the prison guards. After a Possibility Management training, one participant shared: "Time after time during the Laboratory I would desperately grip onto one of the bars of my prison as if to hold it in place as a solid piece of reality that I had always known and could count upon to persist, only to suddenly discover that I had nothing in my hands!"

We use our immense creative power not for disassembling our prison so that something new can occur for us and others in our life, but instead to repeatedly (every three seconds) reinvent an identical prison for ourselves so that everything remains exactly the same as the moment before. We commit ourselves to a life of solitary confinement with no chance of parole. We dedicate every effort to sustaining conditions as they are, because only then do we feel "safe." Only in this mental prison cell do we feel like we will survive.

Think about it: Each morning when we wake up we look in the mirror and start thinking the exact same series of thoughts that we think every morning: "I'm too fat. I should really exercise more. I'm getting old. I'm not pretty enough. Look at these wrinkles. What's wrong with my hair? I don't have enough money. Oh God! I have to get to work. I'll be late, and my boss is such a nitpicker! What am I going to cook for dinner tonight? What am I going to wear?"

SECTION 4-A
Creative Mind

Our mind is massively creative. Our mind is creative when we act and then identify ourselves with that action as if we are that action. For example, we say, "Good morning" to someone, we look both ways before we cross the street, we have a thought about a conflict that we had yesterday with one of our kids, we place our attention on the photo of a mostly nude woman on a billboard, we have fear about how the meeting will go today, and so on. These are all actions. Identification means that when we act we make no separation between ourselves and our action. We regard our actions as true, as if that one particular action were the only possible solution in response to the present circumstances. We generally have no idea of the purpose we are serving through executing that action, and we are usually blind or deaf to any feedback about our action. We think the action is isolated and independent. We think our action is not mechanical.

For example, we are massively creative when we ignore the fact that we restrict our conversation, day in and day out, to the same subjects. Our conversations are normally comments about the weather, complaints about politicians, secrets about where and how to get the best stuff for the best prices, complaints about our mates or children, stories from the latest movies, stories from the news, complaints about neighbors or relatives, complaints about our physical ailments, stories about sports, stories about our investments, or stories about our vacation. And that's it.

We know that *other* people have a limited repertoire of conversation topics. We think that we do not. But we do. An interesting experiment is to start carefully observing and making note of the conversations you start. Within one week you may be quite astonished about what you discover.

We tend to assume that our actions are authentic. Most remarkably, we pretend ignorance of the possibility that our action is merely a piece of dramatic theater that we produce. The unacknowledged purpose of our performance is to suck anyone around us into agreeing that we are victims of the circumstances in this situation. Our purpose is to get other people to agree that we have no alternatives but to act as we do.

If we get confronted about an action, we are extremely creative in generating an endless stream of reasons and excuses to justify our action. We ourselves believe that our reasons and excuses are the logical and reasonable cause for our action. For example, someone confronts us with breaking a time agreement and says, "You are late!" Without thinking, we avalanche them with our reasons, "I'm so sorry but the streets are not usually blocked up at this time of day. And just before I wanted to leave the house my mother called with the report from the doctor and she needed something from the pharmacy. You see, she can't drive there herself right now because she loaned her car to my brother who is looking for a job in the North," as if this were worth something; as if our reasons were true and valid. But reasons are not true and valid. Reasons are just reasons. You can have as many reasons as you want, ten cents the dozen.

We invoke these detailed, intricate, involved, emotionally charged and undeniably clever theatrical performances to attract our own attention away from paying attention to our own attention, so that we cannot self-observe and begin to notice our actual motivations and true intentions – which may not be as pretty or high-minded as we might like to think they are. Being thus identified, we prevent ourselves from realizing that what look like hard immutable circumstances forcing us to act a certain way are only solid looking when viewed from a certain specially chosen and unique perspective. We ignore the fact that we have carefully edited and formulated our perspective.

Our Show

Our perspective is a powerful editor; it includes certain views and excludes others. Our perspective frames up a set of interpretations which, when applied to the facts, twist them into enemies. This permits us to assess that we are "in" a situation, that we "have" a "problem," and that we are justified – no, *forced* – to act as we act to deal with the "problem." We think we are confined victims trapped "in" a situation, victims "of" a problem, rather than seeing that, moment to moment, we are generating and directing the "problem" and our "victimhood" as a theatrical performance. For example, when stopped by the police for speeding we might start the show: "I was speeding? Oh, my God! I'm so sorry! I just remembered that I have to iron my shirt before the speech I'm supposed to give at seven o'clock, at the children's hospital, about using magnets to cure hydrocephalus."

The truth is quite different from what we make out of the truth. The truth is not that we are victims of situations and problems but rather that we source our situations and problems through the interpretations we make. We spend our days (and nights) acting center stage in a show that we wrote the script for, set the stage for, and for which we have rehearsed and played one or more parts repeatedly for most of our lives. It is our favorite show. We arrange things so that we get to play out our best-loved characters. And, we don't want anyone to know that we are having this much fun, especially ourselves!

Part of the show is that we develop and profess some opinion of ourselves, some self-image that concludes that we are, perhaps, to some degree, creative; or maybe not very creative at all. We assume that some people are more creative than others. so we might even consider taking a class to improve our "creativity." Yet, every action we take is absolutely creative. Every word we speak, every thought we think, every energetic or physical gesture, every facial or tonal expression, every emotion we feel, the qualities of every experience, every place we put our attention or fail to put our attention, every condition we see or understand, or fail to see, or fail to understand, every interpretation we make, is an act of creation made to serve a purpose. We are either conscious of the purpose we serve (for example, "You are late." "Yes. I broke my commitment to be on time"), or we are serving unconscious purposes (for example, "You are late." "I am late? Oh, maybe so, but not by much! Maybe my watch is a little slow. You were late last time we met! Anyway, I had some important things to do").

Serving conscious or unconscious purposes is neither right nor wrong, neither good nor bad. Serving conscious or unconscious purposes simply produces different results in our relationships. In either case, we are just creating. It is all theater. All of our theatrical performances are overlaid onto a completely neutral universe. The universe does not care what we do with our time and energy.

Directing Free Will

It is amazing that we would submit the authority of our free will to the service of unconscious purposes. But we do it because directing our free will to serve unconscious purposes creates conditions that feel most familiar to us and seem to best guarantee our survival. These conditions feel most familiar because we are serving what we consider to be ourselves.

When unconscious purposes direct our free will we continue to put on the show we have always put on. This way we play out one role so thoroughly that no other roles are visible. We use our identification with that role (such as housewife) to forget that it is only a role and to exclude or minimize all of the other possible roles that are ours to play out and enjoy (such as lover, friend, partner, artist, woman, explorer, queen, sorceress, chef, business associate, author, warrioress, goddess, healer, and so on).

Directing our free will to serve *conscious* purposes does not feel safe because we have no role to hide within. Serving conscious purposes puts us at risk for being responsible for serving something greater than ourselves. We do not (cannot) know how to serve something greater than ourselves, so it is necessary to continuously reinvent ourselves in order to handle the jobs that get put on our bench.

We can always detect if we are serving a conscious or unconscious purpose by the quality of the results that are created. For example, if we said we would take out the garbage tonight and we fail to take out the garbage tonight, then even though we thought we were serving the conscious purpose of integrity, we were actually serving the unconscious purpose of betrayal. The results do not lie.

Being a Character

We think we have no other choice but to act as we do. We create this illusion for ourselves by thinking we have an identity that is real, permanent, solid and cannot shift, and which has a fixed set of "needs." But this is all internal politics! Whichever "identity" happens to be in power in this moment gets to determine which "needs" are "real" and must be met.

Your Various Identities (BLTLCH04.01). To wreck the Identification Game, do the experiment of "Naming the Identities." "Naming" is a powerful alchemical act. By giving a name to something that did not have a name before, you change the thing from invisible to visible, from subjective to objective, from unconscious to conscious, from background to foreground. By clearly naming an identity, you bring people's attention to the option of shifting to a different identity. By changing the identity of the moment, you change the "needs" of the moment. For example: You can name your own identities in order to catch yourself in the act. You may identify characters such as The Whiner, The Judge, The Complainer, The Victim, The Glutton, The Perfectionist, The Head Chopper, The Sneak, The Miser, and so on.

Or, you can use naming to open doorways through which you can then step, and thus shift your identity in that moment. One way to open a doorway is to say something that the new character might say, such as: "Enter The Dragon"; "May I present The Goddess"; "Jamison at your service, Madam"; "Which way to Kilimanjaro?"; "Choose your weapon!"; "What have we here, Sherlock?"; "Has anyone seen my Ferrari keys?"

You can also open doorways through which to shift identity without saying anything. For example, if you are going to bed with your partner at night and you feel the same old evening pattern arising, shift identity. For example, change the timing of your entry into the room. Take a different physical posture – crawl in, strut in, limp in, come in backwards, come in with your eyes closed. Use a different breathing pattern. Put on or take off different pieces of clothing. Change your mood. Beat up the teddy bear. Sing. If, while you are practicing shifting identities, your partner thinks that you have gone nuts, tell them that before now you were only pretending not to be nuts, and that you think they will get used to it.

Being Radically Honest (BLTLCH04.02). The idea is to reveal *yourself*, rather than waiting around for your partner to reveal themselves first. It is crucial to remember that revealing yourself does not involve complaining, gossiping, blaming, or talking about other people. Revealing yourself is about getting present and letting yourself be authentically known. You may not be able to manage this the first time you try it, so plan to keep experimenting.

SECTION 4-B
Playing the Victim

Your Victimhood (BLTLCH04.03). Recognizing that what you "have" is what you "want" opens a gateway to responsibility. Compare that to living in the fantasy that you are a victim of the circumstances. Which piece of theater gives you more power? Playing victim to the circumstances? Or taking responsibility for creating yourself into those circumstances?

It is curious that we could ever think that we would do something we don't want to do. Or the reverse; that we are not doing something we really want to do. Reality is that we only ever do just exactly what we want to do. If you want to know what you want, look at what you have. What you have is what you want. Period.

We continually create the illusion for ourselves of having no choice by failing to ask the question: "Who chooses to have no choice?" We train ourselves to ask no real questions, to not ask at all. Disallowing our awesome power to ask questions insures that we will not discover who operates the levers behind the curtain.

It is amazing that we would think that circumstances could dictate our actions. *Circumstances are absolutely powerless.* I repeat: Circumstances are absolutely powerless. It is *we* who make up the story about what the circumstances mean to us. It is *we* who consciously or unconsciously choose each and every action we make or do not make. It is *we* who formulate the reasons or justifications or explanations for what we do. And it is *we* who decide to give the power for our decisions to our reasons or to keep that power for ourselves for no reason.

We have the ability to make commitments and take responsibilities at a level that is greater than our preferences, our likes and dislikes, and our personal comfort. It is impossible to be a victim of any person or any thing. We only play-act being a victim to achieve an energetic or emotional payoff. For example, we justify complaining so that we get the payoff of a familiar, and therefore known and comfortable, although agitated, internal emotional state. We justify betraying someone's trust so as to have the payoff of taking revenge on them. If we have things arranged a certain way with people or things in our life it is only because we have arranged them to be that way and have *not* arranged them to be any other way. This insight opens the door to a large number of rather interesting experiments to do. For example, today, now, go change something either externally or internally that has been making you feel like a victim. Notice that in de-victimizing yourself (similar to de-worming a cat) you have

the option of changing external conditions or of changing the internal story that you have made about the conditions.

For example, this morning I woke up at 5:25 so I could sit for meditation at 6:00 and start working on this manuscript at 7:00. But, I live in Munich, and it is winter, and it snowed last night. Our duplex neighbor has this serious consideration that shoveling the snow out of our shared driveway should be an equal task, and a local ordinance says that residents must shovel off their sidewalk before 7:00 AM. Sometimes our neighbor shovels the snow before I am even out of my pajamas, and he does this for three days in a row. By that point I fear that he resents me for shirking my duty. As you could well imagine, here is a goldmine of potential victim stories! Previous occupants of our apartment used the opportunity in abundance. I am not interested is continuing the tradition. But how can I see this laptop keyboard begging for my dancing fingers and instead go out there in the cold dark morning and not feel like a victim? I cannot change the neighbor's habits. Nor can I, this moment, change the law.

What is left for me is to change my internal story about my morning, about what shoveling snow means to me. But what story could make it worthwhile to experience shoveling snow as exactly what I really want to do right now? What about this: I could then write about the experience in this book! *Voilà*. I am instantly transformed into a happy man enthusiastically shoveling snow.

The neighbor even came out to see what all the happy shoveling was about.

Avoiding Possibilities

Why is it that we think we don't have enough time when we have all the time there is: we have all the time that anyone else has, and we are choosing every moment what to do with that time. If we choose to do *anything* it is only because we have made time to do it. If we choose ever to not do something, we simply do not make the time to do that thing. We are time makers! Yet we try to blame other people or the circumstances for choosing what we make time for! This is truly amazing!

Many of us hand over our lives to some little voice from our mind that says, "I'm tired! I'm exhausted! I have to have one of those! I can't do this! I deserve a break today!" and then choose to go unconscious, thinking that things should be some way other than the way they are. It is amazing that we do not simply enjoy things as they are, or reinvent our experience of them if we want.

We typically glance over the dry, barren landscape of our life, looking for minimalized, mediocre opportunities, rather than realizing that we ourselves hold up the veil that makes the surrounding look dry and barren. We refuse to bathe in the ocean of possibilities spreading out in every direction in every moment. We make the wealth of options that are sitting at our feet invisible and inaccessible. Rather than creating noble, lively, juicy, dynamic, dignified, challenging opportunities for ourselves and others out of available materials, or better yet, out of nothing (a material which is readily at hand, anytime, anywhere, for no cost – if we have the space for it!), we go around like crippled elephants at a fashion show thinking there is no opportunity to be found, and that nobody loves us besides.

It is amazing that we have made ourselves afraid of the power of insanity. Without knowing it, one of our first considerations in making any decisions is whether or not we will appear to be sane. If the gap between our possible behavior and the appearance of sanity is too great, we will not do it. If the gap between the behavior of someone else and what is typically recognized as sane behavior is too great, we will call the police. By rejecting anything that even appears to be insane we simultaneously reject one of our greatest powers: the power of incongruity.

Being Loving (BLTLCH04.04). Insanity is where nonlinear possibilities and orthogonal moves come from. Relationship is ongoing nonlinear creation. If we do not have access to insanity, we cannot go nonlinear to create relationship. No wonder our relationships seem dead. We straightjacket ourselves so that we appear to be sane, but our pretended civility asphyxiates the aliveness of our interactions. In each moment relationship is sourced through invention. Love is invented. Right here, by us, with what we have right now. Life without inventing love is like finding an outdated coupon for thirty cents off a jar of mayonnaise, lying faded on a dirt road.

In the moment we commit to being the source of love in our life (or the source of love in someone else's life, or, if we are really insane, the source of love in life itself) even though we do not know how, life becomes simultaneously horrifying and exhilarating, the most fulfilling of endeavors. (We may think that we already know what this means, but consider the possibility that we do not. Consider the possibility that we do not even know that we do not know what this means. This is not new-age philosophy. This is consciousness expansion. There is a big difference. We can discover the difference.)

We have become experts in avoiding possibilities. You can prove this for yourself with the following experiment: If you really wanted to be Loving in *any* situation, find who stops you.

The Box

We usually forget that the number and variety of possible new actions that we could take in every moment and in every circumstance is practically unlimited. We forget that we always have direct access to all possible options. We forget that if someone backs their car into our car we could invite them to dinner or call our mother. We forget that if our child wants our attention we could stop talking on the telephone or teach them a new song to sing. We forget that when our partner doesn't hold our hand we can hold theirs.

Your Box (BLTLCH04.05). What causes us to behave the way we behave? What causes us to ignore the untold numbers of options that seem available to other people but not available to us? Why can we do something that another person cannot, and vice versa? In answering these questions we notice that differences between us and other people derive from specific factors: attitudes, assumptions, beliefs, expectations, reasons, perspectives, concepts, prejudices, meanings, conclusions, projections, opinions, stories, decisions, interpretations, strategies, and so on. These are the factors that establish and regulate our relationship to the infinite possibilities available to us in each moment.

These factors are the structural components of what we could call our "Box." Our Box stands like a firewall between us and the rest of the world. The Box has been recognized and called by other names, such as worldview, mind-set, belief system, psychological defense strategy, personality, mentality, self-image, comfort zone, ego structure, or identity. We will simply call it the Box.

What is the purpose of our Box? Through simple observations we can discover that the Box serves to buffer us from the unknown. What is in the Box is the known. What is outside of the Box is the unknown. The purpose of our Box is protection, comfort, self-definition, and security. When

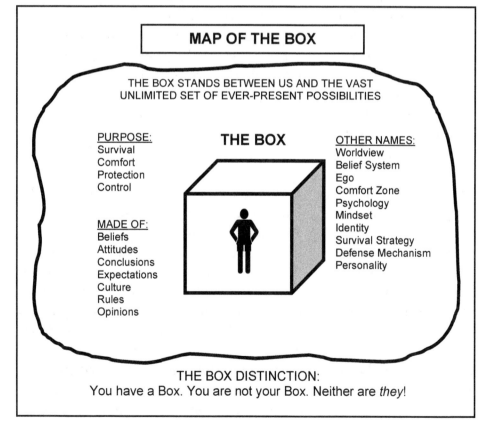

MAP OF THE BOX

THE BOX STANDS BETWEEN US AND THE VAST UNLIMITED SET OF EVER-PRESENT POSSIBILITIES

PURPOSE:
Survival
Comfort
Protection
Control

THE BOX

OTHER NAMES:
Worldview
Belief System
Ego
Comfort Zone
Psychology
Mindset
Identity
Survival Strategy
Defense Mechanism
Personality

MADE OF:
Beliefs
Attitudes
Conclusions
Expectations
Culture
Rules
Opinions

THE BOX DISTINCTION:
You have a Box. You are not your Box. Neither are *they*!

it comes to the bottom line, the purpose of our Box is to insure our survival.

How does the Box assure our survival? Through controlling our behavior with regard to our environment. The Box acts like a 360-degree filter, controlling everything that we can perceive and everything that we can express.

Who made our Box? There are two answers to this question. The first and by far the most common answer, the answer we use without thinking is, "They made my Box" – parents, society, culture, and the media. The second answer is less common: "I made my Box." These are the two choices. Since the experts are still arguing the "nature or nurture" question, we get to choose which answer we use.

What is the difference between the two answers? If we choose answer number one, that "they" made our Box, then if we want to change our Box we must wait around until "they" make up their minds to come and do whatever it takes to change our Box. How many of us are waiting around for Mom or Dad to come and hug us, to tell us that we are wonderful, that they love us, that they are proud of us. We are powerless victims waiting around for "them" to heal us and make it different for us.

If we choose answer number two, that "I" made my Box, then we are no longer victims. We do not have to wait around for anybody to do anything. We can make new decisions and redesign our Box any way we want, any time we want, for any reason we want, without asking permission from anyone. We are then fully responsible for our Box, for ourselves, and for what we make out of our lives. Making choice number two means we have no one else to blame about who we are and how things turn out for us. No one else to blame ever again for anything.

Leaving the domain of ordinary human relationship begins by making choice number two, "I made my Box." Welcome to responsibility.

From Protection to Imprisonment: The Mechanics of the Box

A bird's eggshell is designed to protect the baby bird until it can stand on its own two feet. A chrysalis is designed to protect a caterpillar's transformation into something that can fly. Likewise, the Box is designed to defend us until we are ready to shift from childhood to our life as a free and natural adult human being.

The transition from childhood to adulthood is intended to take place at around fifteen years of age. We are not structurally capable of taking responsibility before fifteen. But, tragically, our culture does not provide a rite of passage for us. If we do not go through the process that changes the purpose of our Box from its originally defensive and purely survival-based purpose to a mature, expansive, self-development, evolutionary purpose, our Box, which once protected us, then becomes our prison.

If your Box is dedicated to defending itself, then the purpose of your actions will be to protect your positions, blame or attack others, compete for resources, justify yourself, regard yourself as "right" and others as "wrong," feel resentment, and as a last resort destroy or isolate. These strategies are the foundation for creating Ordinary human relationship. If you change the purpose of your Box from defending itself to expanding itself, then your actions will have a completely different quality. A Box dedicated to expanding itself directs your actions toward exploring new territory, going beyond restrictive limits, self-development, discovery, trying new things, learning, growth, welcoming surprises, experimenting, and so on. Reading a book such as this and practicing with the suggested experiments is a Box-expanding action.

Our Box long ago concluded that if *it* can survive, then *we* can survive. That ancient decision still holds dominance until we radically change the game we are playing. We certainly have proof that if our Box can defend itself then we can continue to survive. But here are some striking examples of the opposite:

- A driver yells at another driver who offends him, even when the emotional outburst makes his lack of attention quite dangerous for himself.
- People buy things on credit even when they cannot afford to have those things. When debt becomes overwhelming, people feel nervous, lose self-respect and live miserable lives.
- Instead of being truly angry or truly sad, people mix the two feelings together and talk themselves into a depression that seems hopeless enough that they might even commit suicide.
- People get cosmetic surgeries and surgical implants to look "good." The procedures may make them unwell, permanently disfigured, or even dead from medical complications.
- A smoker can drown when ocean waves drag him into the sea because the smoker's highest habitual priority is to keep his cigarette from getting wet, even if it costs him his life.
- People continue to consume costly products and services that they do not actually need to live well. The heavy cash-flow demand forces them to work in cold, competitive, unsatisfactory jobs that cause high stress and a scarcity of nurturing that can take years off their life.
- Psychosomatic illnesses claim thousands of otherwise healthy human lives each year.
- Fanatical religious beliefs that promote an "I am right, you are wrong" positionality create deep hatred in people and result in wars where many people die.

- Individuals, businesses and governments imagine that there is a lack of resources and then conclude that the most effective solution is to fight against each other for control over those resources. This directs our immense ingenuity toward promoting lethal conflicts, rather than using this same ingenuity to work together and find collaborative solutions. And so on.

Our Box is extremely resilient, fast, clever, subtle, and justified in its self-defense. Without us making intelligent conscious efforts to create alternative options, our Box will minimize chances for intimacy and will control where we can go with relationship for the remainder of our days. The defensive Box dares let no one closer to us than the limits of our Box, because if someone gets nearer to us than the limits of our Box they could turn around and see that we have a Box. To avoid being discovered as a sham, the Box prevents us from experiencing true intimacy. Without the possibility of intimacy, new territories in relationship are never revealed.

The Gap Between You and Your Box (BLTLCH04.06). This Box model is world shaking: You *have* a Box; you *are not* your Box. If you understand and recontextualize your worldview to include this one idea, you will never have a conflict with another person again for the rest of your life. You will see that any conflict that arises is not your conflict. It is your Box's conflict. And your Box does not have a conflict with the other person. Your Box has a conflict with the other person's Box. Just because your Box has a conflict with another person's Box does not mean that you have a conflict with them. The distinction between you and your Box is a paper-thin sliver of light that creates freedom of movement between you and your Box. This frictionless gap means that you need never take an action dictated to you by your Box. It is just your Box doing the Box thing. This gives you tremendous freedom of movement – and, what is even more exhilarating, freedom of non-movement! You do not have to react anymore. Herein lies the value of thoroughly understanding "Box mechanics," the study of how Boxes work both internally and relationally.

Boxes Come in Layers

A first step in Box mechanics is to notice that Boxes come in layers. This means that our lives, our families, our professions and our cultures can be understood as an intertwined complex of nested Boxes.

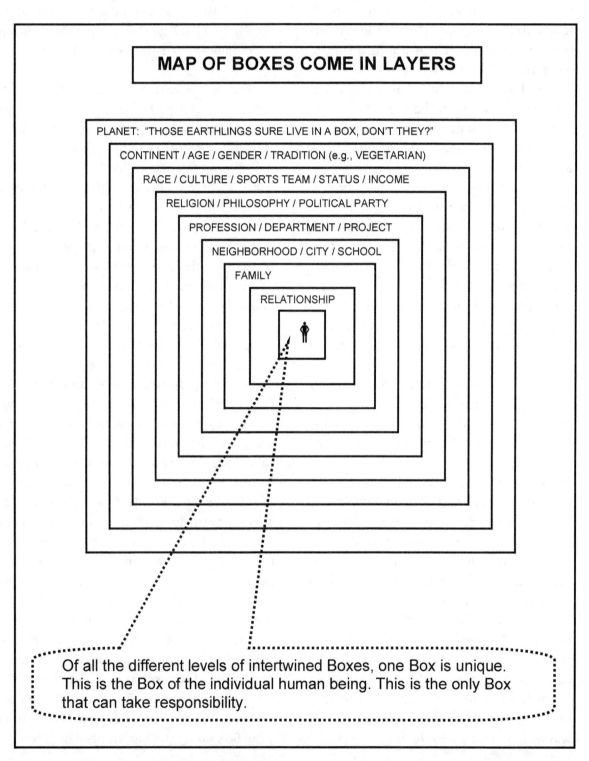

MAP OF BOXES COME IN LAYERS

PLANET: "THOSE EARTHLINGS SURE LIVE IN A BOX, DON'T THEY?"

CONTINENT / AGE / GENDER / TRADITION (e.g., VEGETARIAN)

RACE / CULTURE / SPORTS TEAM / STATUS / INCOME

RELIGION / PHILOSOPHY / POLITICAL PARTY

PROFESSION / DEPARTMENT / PROJECT

NEIGHBORHOOD / CITY / SCHOOL

FAMILY

RELATIONSHIP

Of all the different levels of intertwined Boxes, one Box is unique. This is the Box of the individual human being. This is the only Box that can take responsibility.

This diagram of layered Boxes is simplified to clearly indicate that we live in Boxes within Boxes. Interracial and intercultural issues become far easier to understand and approach when they are reduced to the laws of Box mechanics. Many conflicts become transparent when it is known that the first purpose of the Box is survival, and that a Box can have other purposes.

In reality, the relationships between nested Boxes are never so cleanly map-able as is suggested in this diagram. Neither are the Boxes themselves mere quadrangles as shown. Boxes have milliards of elegant and sophisticated interfacing surfaces and angles, as will be investigated later in Chapter 7, *Edgework*. Of importance is to recognize that no matter how twisted the relationship between Boxes is, no matter how irregularly shaped the Boxes are, they are still Boxes and subject to the laws of Box mechanics, the first law being: You have a Box. You are not your Box. And neither are they.

In the *Map of Boxes Come in Layers* there is one Box that is distinguishable from all the other Boxes. This is the Box of the individual person. This one Box is unique in all the world of Boxes because it is the only Box that can take responsibility. No other Box can take responsibility. For this reason when I refer to the term "Box" in this book I will be speaking only about the Box of the single individual human being. This is the Box that, like it or not, bears consequence. This is the Box that either sustains or chooses not to sustain any of the other Boxes at work in the world. Clarification about the one Box that can take responsibility is motivating towns in America such as Point Arena, California, to pass a "Resolution to End Corporate Personhood," meaning that the law no longer recognizes corporations as responsible entities. Then, directors of a corporation are held personally responsible for the actions of their organization instead of being able to hide behind a fictitious corporate identity.

18 Standard Boxes

Over the years of working with people we have come to recognize about eighteen standard Box defense strategies. All of them are effective. (*See* pp. 86-87) The list is not intended to be systematic or all inclusive. The value of this list is reading through it to recognize which defense strategies your Box uses. You may also recognize a number of your friends in this list.

None of these strategies is better or worse than any of the others. They are all very ordinary and all very human. The point is that consciousness creates freedom. As you become more and more aware of exactly how your Box defends itself and how your Box interacts with other Boxes, you gain a greater chance of being able to behave in ways not originating from your Box's defense strategy. What was once an imperative can become an option when your Box expands.

Expanding Your Box

Expanding your Box means acquiring real behavior possibilities that were not available before. Two methods have been discovered to effectively expand the Box, a push method and a pull method. The push method comes from Werner Heisenberg. The pull method comes from Santa Claus.

Werner Heisenberg (died 1976) was a world-class scientist who formulated many of the original mathematical models for quantum physics. The push method derives from what has come to be known as "The Heisenberg Uncertainty Principal." In layman's terminology, Heisenberg's principal says that details of a situation cannot be known without interfering in the situation. In other words, the closer we look at something the more we change it. This is a terrible consequence in quantum physics, but is fantastic for expanding the Box.

18 STANDARD BOXES

These are 18 standard Box defense strategies. We use them in their pure form, or hybridize them with two or more strategies blended in various proportions.

1) GOOD BOY, NICE GIRL Our highest purpose is to be recognized as being right and good. We are careful that our actions are justified. We are victims of responsibility, "responsible victims." We squirm in not-very-hidden resentment of the cost of having to be good rather than being ourselves.

2) GANGSTER, BLACK-WIDOW SPIDER WOMAN We either own you or we kill you. We trust no one. We use sex to manipulate. We pride ourselves in acting outside the law as if that were an expression of freedom. Our legendary badness keeps us safe. We feel glad when you feel pain. When we are done using you we fling you away like a used napkin. We fill our emptiness with sourceless rage.

3) GHOUL We appear non-threatening because we are not really here. We cannot be responsible because we keep leaving our bodies. We avoid nourishing ourselves. We mix terror and sadness to feel isolated. We call it "cool." We win by betraying your care for us. You cannot save us.

4) THINKER We live in verbal reality. We pride ourselves in arguing about everything and being right. We cannot be touched. We talk so as not to feel. We are a legend in our own mind.

5) BELIEVER We create a position-based belief system where we are right and special. Through being righteous we avoid the pain of being so alone. We use flexi-speak, talk in circles and conveniently forget what we say. We are self-effacing, but, for us, being proved wrong equals being killed.

6) HYSTERICAL We mix anger with fear. We defend ourselves by attacking everything, especially the opposite sex. This frazzles people's nerves. We are too crazy to be dangerous. We don't understand why everyone doesn't love us and why we are not in charge, because when we are not crazy we are "really nice people."

7) VICTIM We endlessly spin an airtight victim story. We can make a persecutor out of anyone. We hate whoever rescues us. We are committed to producing reasons and excuses instead of results. We blame others to avoid taking responsibility ourselves. We must be involved in a low drama or we do not have an identity. We are so sad.

8) CLOWN We cannot stop joking. We do not notice that the jokes kill everyone around us. We joke so as not to admit our terrible insecurity. We keep things superficial because then "everyone likes us." We cannot be responsible because for us nothing in the world is serious. We mix sadness with nostalgic joy to feel sentimental. Our heart is broken.

9) WEIRDO We can act weirder and tell sicker stories than anyone. We repel you to remain safe as the mysterious outsider, the artist, the science fiction buff. We know all the trivia and can recite it. We are too strange to be a threat. We derive status in our own private circle of friends. We long for recognition.

10) NEW AGE We have memorized all the psychobabble. We are workshop junkies. We are not a threat and cannot take responsibility because we see things from a politically or cosmically correct perspective, but we do not do anything about it really. We over-express with movement or voice so you see that we are free. We are really pissed off if you do not agree with us.

11) LOSER We send away our dignity. We mix sadness and anger to feel depressed that our dignity is missing. We do not take ourselves or the world seriously. We are bent on self-destruction. We sabotage anything that may become successful in our lives because we are unconsciously dedicated to revenging our parents by being an unhappy failure.

12) DOORMAT We feel everyone else's feelings. We have no boundaries and are totally adaptive. Our highest priority is to feel safe. We seek safety by giving our center away. Our personal life is minimized and we believe our brilliant justifications for this. We live in secret rage that sporadically leaks out and accidentally kills people.

13) CONFUSION We do not answer your questions directly, or else we answer a different question than you ask. If you get too close to us we can confuse you too. We live with repressed rage that comes out sideways and hurts people. We obtain your confidence, then fail to keep our commitments, thereby entangling you in our dramas where we feel most comfortable. We expertly hook rescuers into action but have no real relationships.

14) RICH AND BEAUTIFUL We do not have to listen to you because we are superior. Appearance is everything. We do not participate or take risks because we could lose status if we made a mistake. Losing status equals death. We are hollow and lonely because of our shallow connections to people. We dare not acknowledge our emptiness or our façade crumbles and we will not know who we are.

15) SNEAK We live secret lives. We tell lies and do not know it. We look nice on the outside and hide secrets on the inside. We experience shame and self-loathing. We feel most alive when we mix joy with fear and take risky gambles. We arrange our lives so that we are naïve and get repeatedly betrayed. This justifies our continued distrust of the world and our sneaking.

16) POWER HERO We are too tough to care. We cannot tolerate being unnoticed. We demand front-stage territory but cannot hold the responsibility. We surround ourselves with followers. We are terrified because if we cannot be the hero we are worthless. Then we sulk, go away cursing, and plot new ways to get power.

17) BOMB If you touch us you will die. We have a very short fuse. We threaten to blast you with unholy rage if we do not get our way. We lead with a loud mouth although our promises are worthless. We only make promises to stay safely in control, and then break our promises to create a distraction that keeps you angry at us because we cannot have friends. Our hearts are caged in barbed wire.

18) ACTOR We are always looking for a new identity and will enmesh with you just to try your identity on. We are too self-involved to be threatening. We are sexually ambiguous or homosexual and that keeps uncool people away. We are always looking for the next thing and use low drama to terminate anything normal or balanced. We constantly seek approval from others. There is nobody home in us to feel the pain.

The closer you investigate the structure, purpose and methodology of your Box, the more it unfolds into an expanding fluidity founded in clarity, love, possibility and evolution.

Santa Claus (still living) is a world-class sorcerer who delivers enticingly wrapped "gifts of unknown things" (to borrow the title of a great eye-opening book on cultural anthropology written by Lyall Watson) to "good" people on an especially auspicious occasion. The unanswerable mystery of unwrapped packages is so enticing that we are moved to take risky actions to reveal the mystery of what is inside the package. Gifts of new tools and techniques for creating extraordinary experience in relationship are too irresistible not to unwrap. The catch is that as soon as we try to use the new tools our Box expands.

The two methods of Box expansion, pushing and pulling, used simultaneously, open previously unseen doors and provide ways for us to take actions in new directions. We enter a natural process of individuation away from the collective unconscious. By expanding our Box we start unfolding into our vast potential as adult men and women for creating an extraordinary life and profound intimacy with our partners.

CHAPTER 5

Some Amazing Things About Having a Body

The person over there – the one you are interested in, for re-lationship – has a body. So do you. When the other person no longer has a body, they are dead. Same with you.

Sometimes, beings without bodies arrange to communicate to us – the beings with bodies. What the disembodied have to say can seem endlessly fascinating, but the relevancy of such information to our physical lives in the material world remains forever suspect. This is because no matter how well meaning or all knowing a disembodied being claims to be, it does not have a body. Period. Having a body is a rare condition that provides immediate feedback for evolutionary learning. Relationship is one of the most productive ways to make use of the learning opportunity of having a body.

SECTION 5-A
Four Bodies

The first amazing thing about having a body is the observation that we do not have just one body. In medicine and healing, the human body is divided up into various bodies for categorizing diagnosis and developing treatments. In the viewpoint of allopathic medicine, for example, we have a cardiovascular body, an endocrine body, a nervous system body, a skeletal muscular body, and so on. From the viewpoint of various other healing forms, we have an energetic body, an auric body, an etheric body, a soul body, a karmic body, a chakra body, a body of meridians, and others.

Many systems for working with the multidimensionality of the human mind-body-heart-soul complex have been developed. The approach of each system largely depends on the purpose for which it is to be used. Various healing systems or psychological typing systems distinguish three bodies, four bodies, seven bodies, nine bodies, twelve bodies, eighteen bodies, one-hundred-forty-four bodies.

The theme in our consideration about having a body is relationship. For relationship we need nothing esoteric or complicated, so we will use a thought-map that distinguishes four bodies. The *Map of Four Bodies* (created by Wolfgang Köhler, 2005) provides us with useful details for delightfully exploring in the domains of extraordinary human relationship and Archetypal Relationship.

The Four Bodies Are:

1. The physical body with tissues and organs that have sensations
2. The intellectual body with a mind that has thoughts
3. The emotional body with a heart that has feelings
4. And the energetic body with a being that has presence, purpose, and inspiration.

Without a map, we tend to regard all our sensations, thoughts, feelings and experiences as one mish-mash. The *Map of Four Bodies* gives us the clarity to distinguish among four unique domains in our relationships. This opens up four times the number of opportunities for experimentation, exploration and play.

Feeding Your Four Bodies (BLTLCH05.01). Each of the four bodies requires its own kind of food, has its own kind of pain, enjoys its own kind of ecstasy, and offers its own kind of intimacy. In this chapter we will unfold the foods, pains, and ecstasies of the four bodies. In a later chapter we will investigate the four kinds of intimacies.

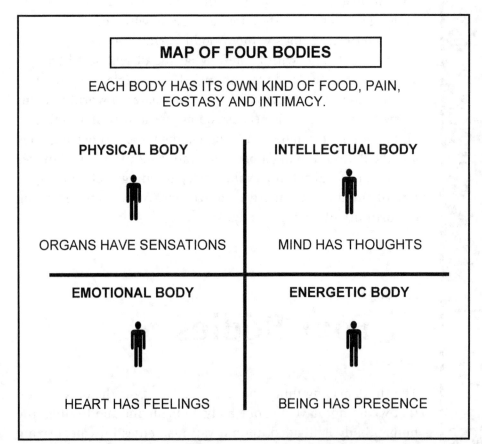

MAP OF FOUR BODIES

EACH BODY HAS ITS OWN KIND OF FOOD, PAIN, ECSTASY AND INTIMACY.

PHYSICAL BODY	INTELLECTUAL BODY
ORGANS HAVE SENSATIONS	MIND HAS THOUGHTS
EMOTIONAL BODY	ENERGETIC BODY
HEART HAS FEELINGS	BEING HAS PRESENCE

Physical food is vegetables, grains, proteins, water, air, sunlight, vitamins, minerals, or physical contact. Physical pain is hitting your finger with a hammer, having a fever, or being hungry. Physical ecstasy is sitting at a cozy café sipping *latté macchiato* while gazing at golden leaves on a bright crisp autumn morning.

Intellectual food is ideas, a good book, visiting an art exhibition, entertainment, information, instructions, or explanations. Intellectual pain is losing your keys, confusion, or doubt. Intellectual ecstasy is finding the keys again, solving a problem, gaining clarity, or inspiration.

Emotional food is communicating about feelings, appreciating and being appreciated. Emotional pain is holding feelings in, being rejected, or mixing feelings together such as with depression or jealousy. Emotional ecstasy is reasonless joy about responsibly using the wisdom and power of feelings to serve others.

Energetic food is certain books and teachings, radiations from sacred objects, shrines or temples, being in the presence of saints, being in the presence of transitions such as birth, death or transformation, or the experience of being-with – which does not involve doing anything in particular, but is rather an interaction previous to words in which the being of one person is in simple contact with the being of another person. Energetic pain is existential angst, not connecting to destiny, or the illusion of separation. Energetic ecstasy is accepting what is as it is, realization, insight, joy in groundlessness, selfless service.

The value of the *Map of Four Bodies* is that by incorporating the map into the structure of our Box we gain the possibility of consciously distinguishing and experiencing four kinds of relationship with each other: physical, intellectual, emotional, and energetic. Then we can create experiments to enter further into intimacy in each of these four bodies. We will go into more detail about intimacy experiments in Chapter 7, *Edgework*.

Pain

An amazing thing about having a physical body is that it delivers the experience of sensations. Sensations come in through a wide variety of sense organs and can range in intensity from undetectably low to overwhelmingly high. Contrary to what we might expect, some of the most intense sensations are those that are the most subtle, as expressed in the phrase "the unbearable lightness of being" (the title of Milan Kundera's 1984 novel).

Individually or mixed, sensations are usually classified into pleasure or pain. The boundary where pleasure changes into pain is subjective. That is, the boundary changes from person to person, from circumstance to circumstance, or from moment to moment. Whether something is pleasurable or painful is a matter of personal taste. And as the old Romans knew, "*de gustibus non disputandum est*," meaning, there is no arguing about taste.

Being a Story Maker (BLTLCH05.02). Where the consideration about pain gets interesting is in noticing that only human beings have the ability to transform pain into suffering. Pain is not suffering until the pain has been given meaning. By giving a particular sensation meaning, we human beings create our own suffering. Pain is experience. Experience is neutral. If pain were left completely neutral we would not suffer. We would just feel pain. But human beings do not leave things neutral. We are unceasingly creative. Our mind is a meaning-making machine. We create complex sophisticated stories about various sensations, and in this way we come to the category of sensations that we have named feelings.

Feelings

Identifying Your Four Feelings (BLTLCH05.03). It is amazing that our culture would not provide us with an education about feelings. Human beings have bodies. The human body is one of the most complex and sensitive structures in the universe. Human bodies are having feelings every moment about everything. This is not an exaggeration. You are having feelings right now. It is bizarre that our culture, which makes sure that we know how to do long division (When was the last time you did long division?), neither educates nor trains us about feelings, when we have feelings every day.

As we approach the territory of extraordinary human relationship and begin to observe in detail what is possible there, deep and long-repressed feelings could well arise. This is normal. If emotional reactions come, try to simply feel your feelings, and let them be there. Give your feelings permission to go though you. Feelings "hurt" only if you hold the feelings in. When you have clarity about what you are feeling in any moment, then the feeling no longer hurts. It just feels.

Your feelings are rocket fuel for change. If you repress your feelings (again), about how you have been creating relationship in the past, you will not have the fuel to break out of old tendencies and try new experiments. You can use the feeling as fuel for doing something different next time.

The Map of Four Feelings

Valerie Lankford studied with Dr. Eric Berne, the creator of Transactional Analysis. Valerie also went through an intense therapeutic process from 1971-1975 at the Cathexis Institute under the guidance of Jacqui Schiff and others who taught her to "think while feeling." Valerie's "thinking while feeling" resulted in creating a new thought-map for feelings that is presented to you here. The profound clarity of this little map has changed many people's lives, including mine.

The *Map of Four Feelings* proposes that all human feelings can be divided into four categories: anger, sadness, joy and fear. Using this map we suddenly have intellectual clarity about feelings. The map says: there are four feelings. The idea that there are only four feelings

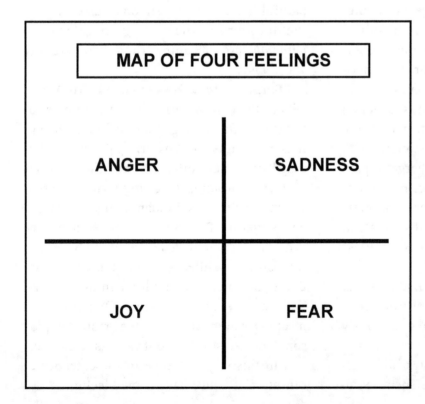

MAP OF FOUR FEELINGS

ANGER	SADNESS
JOY	FEAR

provides tremendous clarity in the area of feelings. (Especially for men! Only four feelings, guys. We can handle this.).

Our culture teaches us that three of these four feelings, namely anger, sadness and fear, are "negative," "dangerous" or "bad" feelings. When we feel any of the three "bad" feelings we conclude that something is wrong with us because we all know that "Indians feel no pain."

Not only are we taught that three of our feelings are bad, we are also taught that the one "positive" or "good" feeling – happiness – is actually dangerous. For instance, in Germany they say if a bird sings happily in the morning a cat eats it in the evening. Overall, our culture teaches us that it is not okay to feel. Our role models have shown us no differently.

If feelings are not okay and we experience feelings, then it is a short (and often unnoticed) leap to conclude that we ourselves are not okay. Perhaps many cases of crippling self-criticism or self-doubt actually come from our cultural confusion and misunderstandings about the okayness of feelings. We could make a new decision about the okayness of ourselves if we made a new decision about the okayness of feelings.

New Map for The Same Territory

Four hundred years ago, when people first started understanding and accepting the round-Earth map that Galileo Galilei and others proposed, do you think that people actually gained access to possibilities that they did not have before? The answer is, yes. People could take advantage of the new possibilities revealed on the new map.

For example, in the flat world map, if you sailed away from known territory you would fall off into the void and die a very unsettling death. In the round world map, you could sail as far away as you wanted from known territory in any direction and

it was impossible to fall off. On a spherical world you cannot fall off. The changed thought-map creates an entirely new game, a game that continues today with development, exploration and change advancing at a galloping rate in every field.

Here is another question for you. When the map of planet Earth changed, did the planet itself change? The answer is, no. The planet itself did not change at all. The planet is the planet.

These two questions reveal an astonishing attribute of the human mind. We acquired new possibilities and options when our map of the world changed even though the world itself did not change. That is because we do not relate directly to the world as it is. We relate to life through our thought-maps of the world. For us, if we get a new mental-map of the world we get a new world!

Let's use this powerful mapmaking phenomenon in another domain, the domain of feelings. Our old *Map of Feelings* says that it is not okay to feel. We specifically confirm that it is not okay to feel with evidence that we have collected repeatedly, for years. For example:

It is not okay to feel angry because anger is uncivilized, loud, destructive, unpredictable, impolite, might hurt someone, out of control, dangerous, insulting, immature, not taken seriously, embarrassing, makes others angry, creates chaos, and starts wars.

It is not okay to feel sad because sadness is weak, emotional, childish, pathetic, victimy, unprofessional, too soft, not fun, not creative, too vulnerable, makes you look ridiculous, ruins other people's day, is discouraging, not inspiring, lacks modern happy society life, and, no matter what, men do not cry.

It is not okay to feel scared because fear is weak, cowardly, "scared rabbit," irrational, impulsive, hysterical, incompetent, unstable, nerve wracking, paralyzing, powerless, stuck; it clouds decisions, is untrustworthy, childish, cannot protect, cannot lead, is an over reaction, can get out of control and can quickly cause general panic.

It is not okay to feel glad because joy is unrealistic, childish, giggly, not serious, pretentious, naïve, arrogant, temporary, means you are doing too well, not intellectual, not "real world," blind to the problems of life, makes other people jealous. What do you have to be glad about anyway – haven't you read the news? What goes up must come down! And besides, if you are sitting there smiling, people will think you are either on drugs or that you do not have enough work to do.

The conclusions we have collected to prove that it is not okay for us or anyone around us to feel, run deep in our hearts. But let's do an experiment, the "flat Earth / round Earth experiment." Let's take this territory of the four feelings and make a new map for it. Let the premise of the new map be that not only is it okay to feel, but the information and energy of feelings can actually serve us in creating relationship. How would this map look? For example:

What can we do with the energy and information called anger? We can say no, say yes (You cannot say yes unless it is okay for you to say no, otherwise the yes is a lie), start

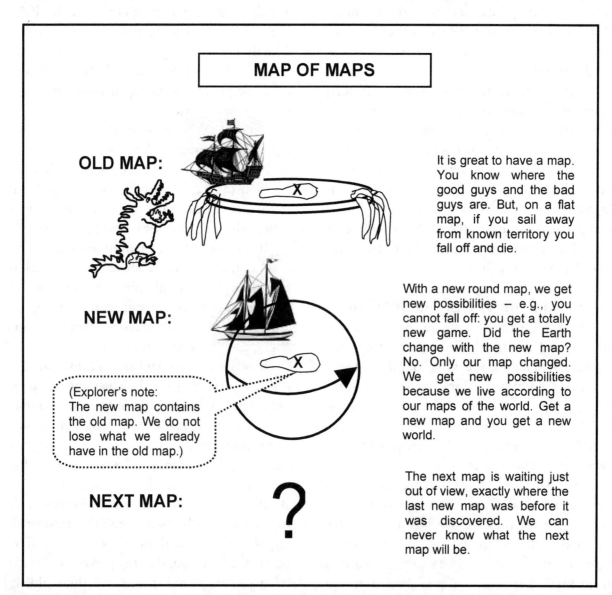

MAP OF MAPS

OLD MAP:

It is great to have a map. You know where the good guys and the bad guys are. But, on a flat map, if you sail away from known territory you fall off and die.

NEW MAP:

(Explorer's note:
The new map contains the old map. We do not lose what we already have in the old map.)

With a new round map, we get new possibilities – e.g., you cannot fall off: you get a totally new game. Did the Earth change with the new map? No. Only our map changed. We get new possibilities because we live according to our maps of the world. Get a new map and you get a new world.

NEXT MAP:

?

The next map is waiting just out of view, exactly where the last new map was before it was discovered. We can never know what the next map will be.

things, stop things, change things, clean out and get rid of things, create clarity, recognize unfairness, make boundaries, maintain integrity, show sincerity, make decisions, keep promises (for example: stay up all night to get a job finished on time), hold space, pay attention, self-observe, ask for what you want, take a stand for something or someone, or take actions, among other things.

What can we do with the energy and information called sadness? We can open up, share, be vulnerable, be still, accept things, let things go, grieve, give in, get healed, listen, contemplate, be spacious, connect, recognize pain, be authentic, finish things up, mourn, be wrong, be human, be silent, care, take a supportive position, be intimate, be invisible, and so on.

What can we do with the energy and information called fear? We can detect danger, measure risks, concentrate, focus, be curious, make plans, avoid disasters, stay balanced and centered, make agreements and contracts, handle details, be careful, be precise, ask dangerous questions, go beyond the known into the unknown, create something out of nothing, go nonlinear, stand there in the nothing and improvise, stay present, be alert, face the future, and so on.

What can we do with the energy and information called joy? We can be enthusiastic, motivate others, connect with our vision, go ahead, take risks, focus on possibilities, undertake adventures, explore, try new things, accept discomforts or hardships, dance through problems, be kind, be generous, build team spirit, make others alive, inspire people to keep going, lead, be playful, be easeful, and bless people for no reason.

The territory of feelings now has two maps. The old map where it is not okay to feel, and the new map where feelings serve your relationships. Which map do you choose?

A New Decision About Feelings

A new decision about feelings could go something like this: The feelings of anger, sadness, joy and fear are experiences. Experiences

---

MAP OF FOUR FEELINGS (OLD VERSION)
ASSUMPTION: IT IS NOT OKAY TO FEEL...

BECAUSE *ANGER* IS:
uncivilized, loud, destructive, unpredictable, impolite, might hurt someone, out of control, dangerous, insulting, immature, not taken seriously, chaotic, embarrassing, makes others angry, invites revenge, creates a mess, and starts wars.

BECAUSE *SADNESS* IS:
weak, emotional, childish, too soft, not fun, pathetic, victimy, unprofessional, not creative, too vulnerable, makes you look ridiculous, ruins other people's day, is discouraging, not inspiring, lacks modern happy society life, and, no matter what, men do not cry.

BECAUSE *JOY* IS:
unrealistic, childish, giggly, not serious, pretentious, naïve, arrogant, temporary, means you are doing too well, not intellectual, not real world, blind to the problems of life, makes other people jealous. What do you have to be glad about anyway? If you are smiling people will think you are on drugs or do not have enough work to do.

BECAUSE *FEAR* IS:
cowardly, irrational, unstable, "Chicken Little"-ish, impulsive, hysterical, nerve wracking, paralyzing, powerless, stuck, weak, incompetent, childish, untrustworthy and overreactive. It fogs decisions, cannot protect, cannot lead, can get out of control and can quickly cause general panic.

are completely neutral. An experience is experienced, and if you pay careful attention while you are experiencing the experience you will see that the experience arrives without a story attached to it. The experience is at first meaningless.

So where does the meaning of an experience come from? We know that two people in the same circumstance often give circumstances entirely different or even contradictory meanings. He says the garbage can needs to be emptied. She says the garbage can is not even half full! The relativity of the stories about an experience identifies human beings as the source of the stories. Human beings are meaning-making machines. Without a human being to add meaning, there would be no meaning.

If you focus your attention to a smaller more precise timeframe, you start noticing that there is a tiny gap after having an experience and before generating our story about that experience. In that gap you will discover neutrality, including the neutrality of experiencing feelings.

The new decision about feelings could be that the four feelings are as neutral as the four directions on a compass. Is north bad? Is east good? Is west negative? Is south positive? Silly questions. The same with anger, sadness, joy and fear. Feelings are neither good nor bad, neither positive nor negative. Feelings are feelings. Feelings are neutral experiences, and are as normal a part of being human as thinking, moving, sensing and being.

In the new map, feelings provide us with the information and energy we need to fulfill our "destiny," the three to five Bright Principles that most matter to us in life. To gain access to our information and energy we must leave our cultural education about feelings behind us and change our relationship to our feelings. In the old map, our feelings are bigger than us and our feelings own us. In the new map, we are bigger than our feelings. We have the feelings instead of the feelings having us. To genuinely implement this realization, however, you will need to go outside of the

---

MAP OF FOUR FEELINGS (NEW VERSION)

ASSUMPTION: FEELINGS SERVE US RELATIONALLY...

WITH **ANGER** YOU CAN:
say no, say yes, start things, stop things, change things, clean out and get rid of things, create clarity, recognize unfairness, make boundaries, maintain integrity, show intention, make decisions, keep promises, hold space, pay attention, self-observe, ask for what you want, take a stand for something or someone, protect, take actions.

WITH **SADNESS** YOU CAN:
open up, share, be vulnerable, be still, accept things, let things go, grieve, give in, get healed, listen, contemplate, be spacious, connect, recognize pain, be authentic, finish things up, mourn, be wrong, be human, be silent, care, take a supportive position, be intimate, be invisible.

WITH **JOY** YOU CAN:
be enthusiastic, motivate others, have vision, go ahead, enjoy possibilities, take adventures, experiment, discover, accept discomforts or hardships, dance through problems, be kind, be generous, support team spirit, inspire people to keep going, lead, be playful, be easeful, appreciate people for no reason.

WITH **FEAR** YOU CAN:
detect danger, measure risks, concentrate, be curious, make plans, avoid disasters, stay centered, make agreements, handle details, pay attention, be precise, ask dangerous questions, innovate, make mistakes, go nonlinear, stand there in the nothing and improvise, stay present, be alert, face the future.

limits of standard education and get further training. The ideas in this book can give you new perspectives and experiments to try. But actually changing your relationship to your feelings requires practice with real-time feedback from a living coach.

Inner Navigating

Feelings can be felt consciously or unconsciously. In order for the feelings to be felt consciously a person must learn "inner navigation." We develop inner navigation skills when we change our intellectual clarity about feelings into experiential clarity about feelings. Experiential clarity comes from learning the wordless feel of the feeling, its definition through the internal experience of its qualities rather than simply by its name. Each of the four feelings expresses itself with distinct sensations and physical manifestations. When we gain experiential clarity, our body becomes our compass. After learning the sensations internally, we know in any moment what we are feeling; and, therefore, where we are on the *Map of Feelings*.

When we know what *we* are feeling it becomes a simple matter to feel what *another person* is feeling. Knowing what we feel, and being able to listen to what our partner feels, adds precious dimensions for communication and intimacy with our partner.

Phase 1 Feelings Work (BLTLCH05.04). "Feeling consciously" includes experiencing and expressing our feelings at various levels of intensity, from 0 percent (numb), to 100 percent

(Archetypal). Feedback from an experienced coach permits us to calibrate our scale of how big 50 percent of Archetypal rage feels, for example. In a safe environment, such as in a training, we can experiment to allow ourselves to liberate 100 percent of each of the four feelings. "In a training" means: Do not try this at home. The reason is that, when we get our feelings back, they return at the same level of maturity they were at when we shut them down. For most of us this occurred when we were very young and very immature. During a training, the trainer can safely guide us to bring our feelings to maturity over a short period of time. Facilitating the maturation process is awkward to self-manage – like being handed a razor blade and a bottle of Scotch and being asked to take out your own appendix.

Reconnecting to our feelings involves experiencing things that we previously regarded as too painful to approach. Now we learn that what we blocked off as insurmountable pain is just one of the four feelings, and that adult men and women are designed to feel at an intensity far beyond what is tolerable for a child to endure. We shut the feelings down long ago when they overwhelmed us. Now we are getting our feelings back as adults. It is like returning to a long forgotten cave in which there is known to be a dragon. When we finally get enough courage to enter the cave and encounter the dragon, he turns out to be more the size of a fence lizard, and quite uncertain about himself.

SECTION 5-C
Mixing Feelings

Feelings are most useful when felt in their pure form. If you consciously or unconsciously experience your feelings in a mixed

form, that is, not distinctly experienced one from the other, then you are mixing feelings. Mixing feelings is not bad or wrong, but it tends to take your natural power and clarity away. Marion Lutz, who developed the *Map of Mixing Feelings* in 2003, found that people rapidly acquired clarity and enthusiasm as soon as they started experiencing their feelings clearly and distinctly. Separating mixed feelings, and feeling them in their pure form, uses inner navigation skills.

Your Depression (BLTLCH05.05). For example, mixing anger with sadness produces the sensation commonly known as depression. The result is automatic. What it *feels like* to mix anger with sadness is depression. These two feelings do not have to be mixed together. Even if you feel both anger and sadness about the same thing, the two feelings can be experienced each in its own measure, distinctly and clearly. You never need to mix your feelings.

Mixing anger with sadness is like mixing beer and cow poop together. Beer has its own uses. Cow poop has its own uses. If you mix the two of them together all you get is slime. The same is true of feelings. Mixing anger and sadness automatically produces the "feeling-slime" experience called "depression." To step out of depression, focus your intention to distinguish your anger from your sadness. Reach into your chest and pull the two feelings apart from each other with

your fingers. Pull your anger into your right hand and your sadness into your left hand. Put the sadness on a shelf so you can get to it later. Bring the anger back into your chest. Then you have your clarity and power back because you can experience and express pure anger. Next, you can put the anger on a shelf and pull the sadness back into your chest and experience and express your sadness. You feel anger in one moment, sadness in the next moment, and there is no more mixing so there will be no more depression.

Mixing sadness with fear produces isolation or desperation. Mixing sadness with joy produces sentimentality or nostalgia. Mixing anger and fear produces hysteria. Mixing fear

---

MAP OF MIXING FEELINGS

MIXING FEELINGS CAN CREATE DIS-EASE

DEPRESSION

S C H A D E N F R E U D E   **ANGER** | **SADNESS**   I S O L A T I O N

JOY | **FEAR**

CARELESS RISKS

ANGER + SADNESS = DEPRESSION
SADNESS + FEAR = ISOLATION
JOY + FEAR = CARELESS RISKS
ANGER + JOY = FEELING GLAD WHEN OTHERS HURT
ANGER + FEAR = HYSTERIA
JOY + SADNESS = SENTIMENTALITY, NOSTALGIA
MIXING 3 CAN CREATE STRONG JEALOUSY OR GUILT
MIXING 4 CAN CREATE PSYCHOLOGICAL BREAKDOWN

and joy produces careless risk, such as gambling or speeding. Mixing anger and joy produces "Ha-ha I got you! I win, you lose!" – feeling glad when someone else feels pain. In German there is a perfect word for this: *schadenfreude*, "damage joy."

Mixing three or four feelings all together can produce emotional or psychological breakdown. For example, jealousy is mixing rage, fear and sadness together. That is why jealousy can grab you with such force. When jealousy has its crusty hand wrapped around your heart, everything else fades into the background. Unwrap jealousy the same way you unwrap depression. Untangle all three feelings with clarity, one from the other, and bring them into their pure form. Then, experience and express each of the three feelings individually: no more jealousy.

The clarity about mixing feelings is not yet known in our culture. If you are a therapist or healer and you integrate the procedure of requiring your clients to separate their feelings distinctly one from the other while they communicate, you will be shocked by how effectively this procedure supports their development. Your results could bring you to ask a rather frightening question: How many people are prescribed with brain chemicals or actually locked away in institutions because our culture does not yet have this clarity about the four feelings and not mixing feelings together?

Human beings have the capacity to start learning about feelings when we are about seven years old. Our schools do not provide this clarity. To add such clarity to our schooling would require that teachers get trained to have the clarity first. The students can only go as far as the teachers can go. If you understand what I am saying, and you care about children and our schools, you have a job on your desk: Provide teachers with training in clarity about feelings.

SECTION 5-D
Our Fear of Fear

Following Signals from Evolution (BLTLCH05.06). We pretend to be afraid of fear. Every year, millions of people around the world swarm to amusement parks to feel the intense fear produced when dropping straight down on roller coasters, crashing into "solid barriers" on wild rides, or seeing ghosts and skeletons in the Haunted House. We crave fear and arrange to experience it on a daily basis by driving unsafely; eating and drinking unhealthily; flirting or having affairs in secret; breaking the law in little ways; exposing ourselves to terror in the news and on television; studying conspiracy theories, cataclysm scenarios or predictions of doomsday; meditating on WWII holocaust images or the techniques of serial killers; lying; engaging in gossip; playing in rough physical sports; and even by watching action films and reading gothic novels. Perhaps you have had the experience that no matter where your conversation starts with certain older people it inevitably leads to them recounting their horror experiences from the war (whatever war they happened to be in). The times they were most afraid were also the times they were most awake.

Clearly, we are not afraid of feeling fear. Rather, our Box strategically pretends to be afraid of feeling fear so as to avoid experiences that might change its established behaviors and attitudes. Pretending to be afraid of fear might protect our personal status quo, but sooner or later we might question the cost of continuing this self-deception. Those behaviors we protect from exposure to evolution easily harden into suits of armor that restrict our movement to predictable patterns. And the evolutionary forces we hide from may turn out to be those influences that are the most dear – our hearts, our inspiration, our passion and our love.

Feeling afraid of fear is the most common reason for avoiding intimacy, even with the people closest to us. I just witnessed a mother discover why she avoided physical, intellectual, emotional and spiritual intimacy with her own children. Deep in her heart she had an emotional scar that made her afraid of children in general, especially wild or loud children, especially boys. As a child she was teased at school for her fine clothes, for being neat and pretty, and for being smart. Half the children admired her and wanted to be her friend, but the other half hated her and tormented her constantly. They would pinch her and rip at her clothes. One time after school, some of the boys jumped out from behind the bushes and kicked her in the stomach. She was not able to take care of herself, and a fear of children entered her body with such force that it lasted into adulthood. Her fear of children prevented her from bonding with or even simply being-with her own children, all three of whom were boys. Her fear of boy children was unconscious, so she was making decisions based on fear without knowing that her decisions were based on fear. In her perception, the decisions seemed rational or practical. Her Box filled in the gap of cognitive dissonance with understandable reasons. Sadly, the decisions resulted in her keeping distance from her sons before she realized that she herself was creating the separation.

This woman's healing process began when she changed her mind about fear. Before, the experience of fear told her that something bad was about to happen. Feeling fear meant that she was about to be hurt or was actually in the process of being hurt. The connection between the feeling of fear and the experience of being physically hurt was established a long time ago in quite different circumstances from what she experienced now as an adult woman. With coaching, she made a new decision about fear. Fear no longer meant that she was about to be hurt. Fear became a neutral experience, without meaning. The wiring in her mind changed from "Fear equals being attacked" to "Fear equals fear. Fear is fear." The new wiring is true. The new wiring opens the door for her to use the wisdom and energy of fear to inform and empower her life.

After some practice with her new decision, this mother could freely feel fear, even maximum Archetypal fear. As fear became an acceptable and recognizable experience in her life, she noticed that she experienced fear around her sons, which was a complete surprise to her. The fear had been there all the while, but now she could experience the feeling consciously without automatically taking defensive or separative actions to protect herself. By letting the fear get larger and larger she suddenly saw that the fear was not actually about her children but rather about children in general. She could trace the fear of children back to its source in the incidents of her own childhood: While being badgered and attacked by her schoolmates she had made a life-shaping decision – "Children are dangerous." Seeing her old decision with clarity permitted her to reassess the situation and make a new decision: "I am no longer a child. I am an adult woman. As an adult woman I can easily take care of myself around children. Children are not dangerous. Children are children." As a result of her new decision she is not automatically afraid of children anymore, but neither is she naïve. She can open herself to children because she can take care of herself around children: she can use her voice, make boundaries, say "No," express her feelings, and ask for what she needs. Being close to her sons has now become a warm and safe experience.

Two Phases of Feeling Work

Reconnecting to our feelings involves two distinct phases. Phase 1 in feelings work is learning to feel. Phase 2 in feelings work is learning to use feelings responsibly. You cannot do Phase 2 without first doing Phase 1.

Knowing that there are two phases is important because thinking that we are in Phase 2 when we are actually in Phase 1 can be expensive in terms of the mistakes we might make. For example, going up to your boss and lambasting him with 100-percent righteous rage about the way he treats you, only later to realize that he is treating you appropriately but that you are projecting on him the ancient rage about your authoritarian father that has been stored in your guts since childhood, could cost you your next promotion. Here is how to pay attention to Phase 1 and Phase 2.

Phase 1 with feelings is simply to learn to feel the four feelings with clarity, from 0 to 100 percent, distinguishing one from the other. You should be warned that starting Phase 1 can be like blowing the top off a volcano. Long repressed resentments and grievances erupt in irresponsible abandon. It is important to start Phase 1 feelings work in an environment where no one will be harmed by the scatter blast. As you become more comfortable "erupting," you learn to start and stop on purpose. You can intentionally direct your feelings to a rage cushion or a wringing cloth in the privacy and safety of your own bedroom.

You may notice how childishly or irresponsibly you are behaving in Phase 1. This does not matter. What matters is that you *feel*, intensely and authentically. Learning to feel is so precious and important that the few weeks or months during which you are expressing your feelings irresponsibly as blame, resentment or a sense of betrayal are well worth the prize you are earning. Focus on going all the way – 100 percent big! – with clarity and full conscious power, in each of the four feelings. When you have succeeded you will enter Phase 2.

Phase 2 with feelings is to use the energy and information of your feelings as fuel and wisdom for creating responsible results in your life. The transition between Phase 1 and Phase 2 may take place at different times for each of the four different feelings. Such transitions do not happen by accident but rather through repeated conscious efforts. You will find yourself taking steps along the way, making mistakes and learning, trying again. You can detect Phase 2 happening when, for example, you start to feel scared that someone is doing something they should not be doing, the fear is followed by anger, and you notice your feelings instantly. Then you use the energy of the feelings to go directly and immediately to that person to see what they are actually doing. If needed, you ask that they do things differently. When the process is over, which may only take a few seconds, Phase 2 has happened, but only if you did not actually feel terrorized or volcanic during the process. Instead of your *feelings using you*, you were *using your feelings*. Upon observing your success you might find yourself in sudden ecstasy, ready for the next Phase-2 feeling experience. Great! Welcome to the high level fun of responsible creating with feelings. Welcome to Phase 2. Just remember, you cannot do Phase 2 without first doing Phase 1. Keep practicing.

Stellating Archetypes

Archetypal Feelings (BLTLCH05.07). We human beings have within us Archetypal structures, lying dormant, waiting to be brought to life. Purely expressing one of the four feelings with 100-percent intensity initializes an Archetypal structure. Each of the four feelings energizes one particular Archetype: anger the Doer (or Warrior/Warrioress), sadness the Communicator (or Lover), joy the Responsible Leader (or King/Queen), and fear the Creator (or Sorcerer/Sorceress). The Doer, the Communicator, and the Creator work in the service of the Responsible Leader. We hardly know what these Archetypes could mean for us in our relationships as men and women because we have few role models. Becoming an Archetypal force of nature is our birthright, is straightforward, and is necessary for entering the Archetypal realms of relationship. We will repeatedly return to this subject throughout the rest of this book.

Bringing an Archetype to life is a process comparable to changing a planet into a star, called "stellating." The difference between a planet and a star is that a planet absorbs more energy than it gives off. A star radiates more energy than it absorbs. Human beings are designed to live as stars (creators, producers), but our culture trains us to live as planets (consumers, judgers). As already mentioned, traditional cultures bring a fifteen-year-old child through a rite of passage into adulthood, stellating their four Archetypes into radiant, joyous, productive maturity. Our culture does not provide such a rite of passage for us. To stellate our Archetypes we must venture outside of our normal culture into certain environments that are designed specifically for the purpose of stellating Archetypes. To be safe and stable, the stellating process takes its own time, somewhere in the neighborhood of at least two years. (The *Map of Stellating Archetypes* is provided in Chapter 13, *Underworld*.)

SECTION 5-F

〉〉 Loving Your Body

Huge international corporations annually spend billions using high-tech psycho-emotional manipulations to hypnotize you into thinking that your body is not okay exactly the way it is. The reason companies want you to be forever dissatisfied with your face, your eyes, your hair, your skin, or your odors is so that they can forever keep you buying their products to rectify your deficiency. They want your money. The reason companies keep trying to hypnotize you into dissatisfaction is because it works. Corporate advertising budgets more than pay for themselves by the profit they generate from the cash you give them from your bank account.

Companies want you to try to make your body match the images they manufacture of what a man or woman should look like. (What is hilarious is that these marketing moguls do not even look like their images themselves!) And we get "hooked," meaning our free attention gets trapped and our emotions mechanically react. Year after year we read the magazines and pour through the catalogs and, at some point, we begin to believe that we are defective. We look at ourselves in a mirror and we are shocked. What we see does not match the computer-edited airbrushed photos in the media. "Magazine people" are obviously rich, successful and happy. We want to be rich, successful and happy like them. If we don't *look* like them, we cannot *be* like them. So, we examine ourselves in the mirror and reject our body as it is.

We judge that something is wrong, and then pick and pick at our body. To compensate for our imperfections we paint on a whole body mask. We color our body, curl it, tan it, muscle it, plump it, thin it, deodorize it, smooth it, shave it, tuck it, paint it, suck it, shake it, perfume it, cream it, and after all that, we cover it up with clothes. The goal of marketing teams is to make us incessantly unsatisfied so that we never stop buying. To a large extent in Western culture, the businesses have achieved their goal. Our culture does not promote well-being. Our culture promotes *trying to look good*. There is a huge difference between these two.

Advertising tells us that we will fail to attract a partner if we do not look good. Amazingly, we continue our neurotic body hatred even after we have been with our partner for five or ten years. This is where the false-image syndrome becomes malicious: If we are convinced of our physical unacceptability, then, when our partner expresses their authentic appreciation of our body, we hate them for being so naïve. We cannot accept their love of our body because we ourselves refuse to love our body. If we give our authority to marketing departments of large corporations, then, we conclude that our partner's love of our body must be manipulated as well. They cannot love our body when it is unpainted,

because the advertising says that our body is disgusting unpainted. But if our partner loves our body when it is painted, then they love what we know is a false image, a cheap fantasy. If our partner loves a cheap fantasy then they are cheap. We lose either way. Our partner loses too. The loss is devastating. In our culture the false-image syndrome is rampant.

Every bit of energy that we direct toward beautifying the little details of our mask is energy unavailable for nurturing our heart, feeding our soul, or building our being. Where our attention goes, our energy flows. Our energy goes only one way or the other. When it is used, it is used. You have to ask yourself what you want. Do you want a relationship that is heart to heart, soul to soul, and being to being? Or mask to mask?

Your Own Well-Being (BLTLCH05.08). The way out is for us to stand in our basic dignity, nobility and authority at a deeper level than cultural programming can undermine. This means taking back our authority and deciding that, for no reason and without evidence, our body *is* beautiful and lovable *exactly as it is*. Every part of it.

Our body is where we get to be. Our body is alive. If we fail to declare our body's "basic goodness" (Chögyam Trungpa), with a simplicity that is beyond the grasp of cultural prejudice, we will only create neurotic conditions in our relationship that no amount of makeup can disguise. So, get off it about your body. Your body is exactly what it is, with its bulges, pockmarks, scars, its lack of a tan, with its wrinkles, farts, hairs, moles, smells, aches and pains. Let your body be exactly the way it is through your unceasing and reasonless acceptance. There are other more interesting things to pay attention to than trying to meet someone else's fantasy-world expectations of what "sexy" looks like. You were born sexy. You still look sexy. Go do something else with your life than trying to fake a sexiness that is already there.

))(Brain Chemistry

Thoughts affect our feelings. Feelings affect our brain chemistry. Brain chemistry affects our thoughts and feelings. It is an amazing mess. Brain chemistry is a profitable field of play for researchers at the large pharmaceutical companies these days. They are trying to develop a pill that modifies brain chemistry to make us unconditionally happy. Unfortunately for them but fortunately for us, the human body is not unconditionally anything.

The human body is a skin sack wrapped around a saltwater-jelly computer. The gray slimy organ in our head is the most complicated structure yet discovered in this universe, and it is designed to evolve. Evolution is a state of flux, not a state of stasis! Most of our original models of the brain, life, physics and the universe start with the assumption of steady state conditions. Steady state conditions are purely theoretical because everything is in flux ("*Panta Rhei*," everything flows, Heraclitus, 500 B.C.). Humans are still generating theories and models for dealing with systems in flux. What we mostly end up with are estimations about how things should be, and the observation (along with a curse) that things are only seldom that way.

For example, in Western civilization we have somehow gotten the idea that our goal in life is to be happy. In other cultures such an idea is childish, shortsighted, and immature. Happiness is irrelevant because the context of life is *living life* rather than trying to limit the experience of life to only one of the four feelings. In other cultures the idea of trying to be happy is as silly as a dog trying to catch his own tail. Happiness is recognized as the basic condition and experience of human existence. We start out and remain in organic

joy. Why should we try to be what we already are without trying?

In many ways our Western culture is "crazymaking." Trying to be happy is one of the ways we drive ourselves crazy. The fact that three quarters of our daily feelings are classified as negative (fear, anger and sadness) leaves us in a quandary, somewhere between massive denial of what we undeniably feel in our physical body, and massive self-criticism, in which we worry deeply about trying to solve the "serious" problem of having a "negative" feeling that in actuality is not serious, not negative, and not a problem.

Perfect Mind (BLTLCH05.09). The invitation here is to simply let the brain do its thing. If we are on the path of evolution we can reasonably expect that our brain chemistry will periodically fluctuate all over the map, and we will encounter the feelings of anger, sadness, fear and joy several times every day. We can simply feel the feelings. Just because we are feeling depressed does not mean we have to blame our partner for causing our depression. Just because we are feeling angry does not mean we have to throw the dishes on the floor. Just because we are feeling ecstatic does not mean we have to quit our job and move to New Zealand. How ridiculous. No matter what mood you are in, no matter what feeling you are feeling, if you just wait a bit you can be sure it will change. By paying objective attention you will notice that nothing remains the same.

Another hint that will help create clarity about brain chemistry and relationship is to notice your use of the concepts of "never" or "always." "Never" or "always" are produced by a mind that can imagine perfection. When we use the concepts of "never" or "always" in regard to our life and relationships, these are very strong thoughts. Consistent use of strong hopeless thoughts like, "You never listen to me," "You always think of yourself first," "I never get to do what I want," "I always have to give in to your needs" and so on, definitely generate chemicals in our brain. With "never" or "always" thoughts you can talk yourself into depression in almost no time.

In reality, "never" or "always" do not exist. Life has more exceptions than rules. The Box uses impossibly perfect concepts like "never" or "always" as weapons for fortifying its own defenses. You should be extremely suspicious if you ever hear or use these words in your communications. Thoughts or mental sentences that include the words "never" or "always" are strategic Box lies, designed to support the internal politics of perception and Box-favorable positions. Learn to identify self-deceptive "always" and "never" thinking loops and make it a practice to exit those loops immediately.

Where does this leave you? Through accepting the tides of feelings and brain chemistry, you liberate your free attention and have greater permission to explore intimacies in your relationship. You will not stay stuck in having to behave in a certain way as a reaction to what you are experiencing. You no longer get trapped in "always" or "never" loops, yours or your partner's. These are big liberations.

The further we move along the path of evolution, the greater the depth of the reordering we go through. As surface layers are explored and healed, a greater freedom of movement is experienced. At the same time, more profound layers of the Box come to the surface for transformation. As we slowly work our way through the labyrinth of evolution, a capacity emerges for undertaking more complex and sophisticated experiments. Projects and relationships evolve away from mere personal survival into broader, more service-oriented, world-level games. With diligence we can prepare ourselves for surfing on or rolling with the vaster forces of evolution that will enter our lives. And, sooner or later along the way we will get interested in creating extraordinary human relationship.

PART III

The Extraordinary

CHAPTER 6

Extraordinary Human Relationship

The ideas in this book are not rules. Do not make these ideas into rules. If you make these ideas into rules then you will stop feeling and deciding, and you pass responsibility for your life over to the rules. Abdicating responsibility for your life is misusing this book. This book is about you taking *more* responsibility for your life, not less.

A distinction will be made here between ordinary human relationship and extraordinary human relationship. Without you making significant efforts to live each breath of your life in this distinction, creating extraordinary human relationship will only occur for you by accident.

With both the culture *and* your Box designed to prevent you from creating extraordinary human relationship, the chances are not very promising that you will have such an accident. You will have to do it on purpose. This chapter is about how to do it on purpose.

Before making a distinction between ordinary human relationship and extraordinary human relationship, you only had one category in which to place qualities of human relationship. There was but one criterion against which to measure and classify your behavior. Making a distinction between ordinary human relationship *and* extraordinary human relationship gives you greater resolution on your *Map of Relationship* (*see* p.110). The value of the *Map of Relationship* is that you can find out where you are on that map, and you can find out where else it is possible to go. As

EXTRAORDINARY HUMAN RELATIONSHIP 109

```
+--------------------------------------------------+
|  +--------------------------------------------+  |
|  |  MAP OF THREE KINDS OF RELATIONSHIP        |  |
|  +--------------------------------------------+  |
|                                                  |
|        +--------------------------------+        |
|        |                                |        |
|        |        ARCHETYPAL              |        |
|        |        RELATIONSHIP            |        |
|        |                                |        |
|        +--------------------------------+        |
|        |                                |        |
|        |      EXTRAORDINARY             |        |
|        |      HUMAN                     |        |
|        |      RELATIONSHIP              |        |
|        |                                |        |
|        +--------------------------------+        |
|        |                                |        |
|        |        ORDINARY                |        |
|        |        HUMAN                   |        |
|        |        RELATIONSHIP            |        |
|        |                                |        |
|        +--------------------------------+        |
|                                                  |
+--------------------------------------------------+
```

you will see there are some very interesting, previously unseen places to go.

We have all had experiences in extraordinary human relationship. These are moments when love seems to work. Our mind is empty of busy-ness and full of quiet respect, our heart overflows with joy, our body vibrates with passion, and our being is inspired with electric aliveness. We bathe in an abundant love that cannot be described, only felt, and it feels so right. Perhaps you have only dreamed about a love that hits on all four cylinders and hums smoothly and long, but I suspect it has been an actual experience for you – possibly long ago, perhaps only for a few moments. Still, I think that you already know deep in your bones that extraordinary human relationship exists and that you want to get back there … often.

There is no secret. Extraordinary human relationship is an automatic side effect of responsible Adult actions. For the most part, however, we have a fuzzy idea about what is meant by responsible Adult actions. That is

no fault of our own. Our lack of understanding and experience in Adult responsibility is also a characteristic of our general culture.

The tendency of our culture to avoid Adult responsibility creates a virtual boundary that we will have to approach and eventually step through if we want to enter and explore extraordinary human relationship. The virtual boundary restricts our perceptions, our thinking, our feeling, and our actions, and remains an effective barrier until we are ready to take responsibility for breaking the rules. Taking the situation into our own hands and finding our way to the other side of the "normal" barrier is a prerequisite for entering extraordinary human relationship.

Your Customized Graduate Degree Program (BLTLCH06.01). Gaining competencies for creating extraordinary human relationship is the equivalent of a university graduate degree program. Your success will come from committing to acquire extraordinary human relationship skills at that same level of discipline and professionalism that you would commit to obtaining an advanced degree. Along the way, large chunks of past understanding about reality and how the world works will fall away in the face of experiential clarifications about what it is to create and maintain extraordinary human relationship. This chapter opens possibility after possibility for finding your way into the domain of Adult responsibility. Because of how quickly the game can slide from extraordinary back to ordinary again, there is no time when your efforts are not important, even if in the moment they appear to have no success.

SECTION 6-A
Responsibility and Practice

Our education about responsibility has been thorough. We have been trained to *avoid* taking responsibility. We have been trained to be irresponsible about responsibility.

Instead of learning the ways of gripping responsibility cell by cell and nerve by nerve, so that the universe moves when we move and responds when we speak, we have learned the ways of cheating and getting away with the most for the least. If we can receive a benefit and avoid paying the full price, we call this profit. The game has become: Whoever has the most toys when he dies wins! Avoiding responsibility is the life plan we have inherited from our modern culture.

As children we innocently admitted full responsibility for anything we did. But then we found out that if we broke a vase and took responsibility we might get scolded. If we started a fight with our brother and admitted our motives we might get spanked. If we were late for school and revealed that we chose to come late because catching frogs in the stream was far more interesting than sitting in class, there would be serious consequences to contend with. We rapidly learned that creating excuses, blaming circumstances, finding scapegoats, lying and cheating were far less painful than taking responsibility. Over the years we perfected our techniques, until now; evading responsibility has become an automatic response that may form the basis of our relationship to life. We avoid responsibility because we have learned that:

- Responsibility has painful consequences.
- Responsibility makes us guilty.
- Responsibility means it is our fault.
- Responsibility means we are to blame.
- Responsibility means we are the one to get punished.
- Responsibility is a burden difficult to carry, even more difficult to put down.

Being Responsible for No Reason (BLTLCH06.02). There appears to be nothing attractive about responsibility. What we have not been shown is the *cost* of living life as a game of "Responsibility Dodge Ball." The price tag is so high because we live in a responsible, cause-and-consequence universe.

A responsible universe works like this: If you decide to do an experiment and walk through the woods and pick up litter, even if you hate picking up litter, even if you know that your picking up this litter is a theatrical act, if after the walk you *have* picked up litter then the litter *has actually been picked up*.

Avoiding responsibility brings us out of relationship with our fellow human beings, with nature, and with the practical realities of the universe. The opposite of maneuvering to avoid responsibility is taking responsibility for responsibility. Taking responsibility for responsibility means:

- Being at source for
- Being the cause of
- Being the creator of
- Being in relationship with
- Being the originator of
- Owning
- Taking care of
- Managing
- Representing
- Speaking for
- Taking a stand for
- Declaring
- Having the consequences of ... and so on

Taking responsibility is a delightful and honorable expression of caring for yourself, for others, and for the world. *Responsibility is extraordinary human love in action.* Entering the domain of extraordinary human relationship will depend on establishing a passionate relationship between yourself and responsibility.

Inquire about this: Is winning the lottery high up on your wish list? If yes, why? Why do we want to win the lottery? From the perspective of responsibility, winning the lottery is how we can cheat the world out of having to be responsible. Western culture teaches that the game of life is won by cheating. If we somehow feel left out or disappointed for having never won the lottery, this could only occur because we lack skills and practical experience in how the technology of responsibility works.

True responsibility is not a burden, despite what the culture tells us. It is a joy and a privilege. *Responsibility is intimate participation in a dance with the moment-to-moment causes and needs of the universe.* Through responsibility, your creative spirit exuberantly lives and expresses its passions in the world.

The process of establishing reciprocity with responsibility includes both internal and external changes. New parts of the Box get born, a few parts get ejected, and some parts get reengineered. Entering responsibility could be likened to being swallowed whole by a giant, and proceeding through his digestive system with no way out until the stinking end, at which time you have become useful to something greater than yourself. Being digested by a new relationship to responsibility occurs over time and through efforts. Efforts involve both starting new behaviors and diverting yourself from repeating other behaviors. Many experiments for developing responsibility-muscles are outlined in this book.

Meeting Your Gremlin (BLTLCH06.03). For starters, begin tracking the little ways that you habitually avoid responsibility in your day-to-day life. At the office, on the street, at home with the family, at parties, in private, wherever you go, whatever you do, simply notice the details. How are you trying to get away with things? Who do you specifically *not* listen to? What do you avoid noticing? Where do you make little messes without any consideration about cleaning them up? How do you avoid seeing the long-range picture? How do you numb yourself to feeling the consequences of what you do or don't do? Where do you leave responsibilities to someone unknown to you? Start keeping an "Irresponsibility Journal"; list whatever you discover. The exercise is not to blame yourself, but rather is meant to encourage you to be accountable and to discover how responsibility is avoided. The more precise your personal examples are, the more clearly you will grasp exactly how your Box works.

Ante Up

The most important ingredient in creating extraordinary human relationship is practice. You don't get practice by reading a book. *Practice you get only when you practice.*

You can practice alone. You can practice in the company of others. You can practice in trainings, in workshops, in weekly meetings, in men's or women's groups, and in many other different circumstances. Intellectual understanding is valuable and interesting, of course. But regardless of what you understand, long-term changes occur only through consistent practice.

We could have learned many of the skills related to creating extraordinary human relationship as children, but our culture did not provide these skills for us. If we want these skills now, it is within our power to search for them wherever they exist, and start regularly practicing them ourselves. When we speak differently or process our thoughts and feelings differently, the improved quality of our relationships will naturally radiate. Each more

---

MAP OF OVERWHELM

Overwhelm is one of the Box's favorite self-defense mechanisms:

STEP 1: Take on too much.

STEP 2: Feel overwhelmed.

STEP 3: Stop practicing.

STEP 4: Go back to normal.

Voilà! The Box wins. Very clever, Mr. Box.

---

those distinctions. It will present far more than you can reasonably be expected to absorb all at once. An individual can only manage to effectively advance one or two change-initiatives at any one time. Otherwise it is easy to feel overwhelmed and then to stop all efforts. If you stop all efforts, the Box wins. Overwhelm is one of the Box's favorite self-defense mechanisms.

Pace yourself. What this means will be different for each person. Perhaps you can best pace yourself by first reading all the way through this chapter while making notes about what most interests you. Then you can go back to those items and start working with them. Or perhaps while reading you will find one or two practices that inspire you to take immediate action. In that case, start experimenting with only those few things, but on a regular basis. Whatever your approach, make the decision now to take persistent baby steps. In terms of change, stable results are more likely to blossom through micro-experiments repeatedly practiced over the long run with consistency, rather than through dramatic but sporadic sudden moves.

responsible behavior improves our relationships over time.

Establishing responsible Adult attitudes and actions in our repertoire of behaviors is like paying the ante to get into a poker game. If we don't pay the ante we can't even start to play the game. Of course, paying the ante does not guarantee that we will win – it just gets us into the game. But if we don't pay the ante there's no chance *at all* of winning. The way to pay the ante in extraordinary human relationship is to practice relationship according to certain clear distinctions. The rest of this chapter is devoted to establishing

SECTION 6-B

Adult Ego State

Voices in Your Head

Identifying Your Ego States (BLTLCH06.04). The maps, clarifications and

experiments that follow are each aimed to get you into the "Adult ego state." As we've previously noted, Dr. Eric Berne labeled three "ego states" or Boxes that we use throughout our days and our nights: the "Parent," the "Adult," and the "Child." In Section 2-B we explored Parent and Child ego states. Here we will explore the Adult ego state.

Identifying Voices in Your Head (BLTLCH06.05). First let us review. When identified with the Parent ego state, in our mind we hear either "nurturing Parent" or "critical Parent" voices that give us affirming or denying opinions about our self, about other people, or about what to do to survive a situation like *this* with people like *them*. But our Parent ego state voices are not *our* voice. These voices came from other people, perhaps from past authority figures like parents, teachers, relatives, or TV commercials. The voices were so important that we made them normal. When we left the source of the voices, we maintained our sense of normal by keeping the voices going inside our head.

If we listen to those voices at all, or grant them any credibility in our life, we are giving our power away to the authority that was long ago imagined to be behind those voices. To create extraordinary human relationship we need to take our power back. We need our own voice.

Realizing that the praising or blaming Parent-ego-state voices are not *our* voice does not necessarily make those voices go away. The voices can persist senselessly for years, simply from the momentum of habit, like a broken CD-player mechanically repeating the same track over and over again without purpose. Quite boring – especially for anyone forced to listen to us repeating what we hear the voices say.

If you think those old voices are useful think again. Voices do not make you good or bad, responsible or irresponsible. Voices cannot protect you or harm you. You cannot hide behind the voices. You cannot justify yourself with voices. You cannot blame the voices. *Voices are completely irrelevant*. It is what you do or not do that matters. Results

are stark naked and voiceless. The results do not lie. The comments, judgments and opinions that come from the voices are not even ours, so we may as well get rid of the voices. But how? Dealing with voices becomes quite simple when you use your Voice Blaster®.

Voice Blaster

"They" probably never told you about your Voice Blaster. Every person is born with a Voice Blaster on their hip. Reach down; pull your Voice Blaster out of its holster and hold it in your hand. It looks like your hand pretending to be a pistol, but it is actually your own personal Voice Blaster.

Your Voice Blaster has always been there, ready for you to use. If you have never before used your Voice Blaster it is probably because it never occurred to you before. *Expanding what is possible to occur to you is the business of this book.* What you get here is the possibility that for the rest of your life it could occur to you to use your Voice Blaster.

The Voice Blaster (Mark IV) is an efficient modern weapon for vaporizing voices. The Blaster holds an infinite number of charges, so you never run out of ammunition, and a blast from the Voice Blaster never misses its target. Here are your Voice Blaster Operating Instructions: Shoot quickly in the direction of the voice and the "hunter seeker" function of the blast always finds its target. ("Hunter seeker" comes from Frank Herbert's incredible book *Dune*, and in A. E. Van Vogt's *The Weapon Shops of Isher*, guns protected the bearers by jumping into their hands and shooting whenever there was danger.) Please take note that voices that seem to be "in your head" are actually *not in your head*. Voices flutter around your head "out there" like a vampire bat flutters about its victim before it strikes for blood. The instant you sense a voice coming, whip out your Voice Blaster and "Bang!" Say it out loud, "Bang!" as you blast that voice right out of the sky.

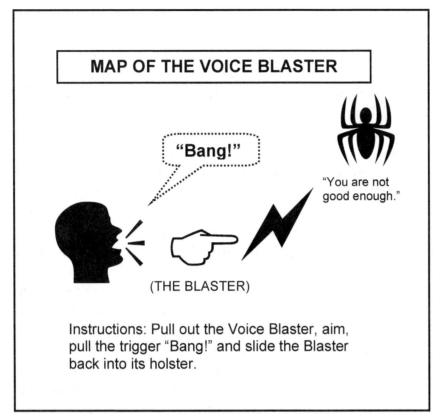

MAP OF THE VOICE BLASTER

"Bang!"

"You are not good enough."

(THE BLASTER)

Instructions: Pull out the Voice Blaster, aim, pull the trigger "Bang!" and slide the Blaster back into its holster.

The voice either falls dead "Blop!" on the floor in front of you, or it flutters raggedly off, trying to come around for a second attack. Any voice that returns "Bang!" ... dead again! "Bang! Bang! Bang!" Blast away, however many times it takes.

Sometimes voices present you with whiny little reasons why you should listen to them. They plead. They nag. They justify themselves. They pester. They tell you to be nice and obey the voice of reason from your elders. They tell you to be civilized and careful. They tell you that life without them would be terrible. If you listen and try to argue or reason with any voice at all, then you are already hooked and they've got you. The *only* conversation *ever* to have with a voice is "Bang!" End of conversation. Game over.

It may take a couple of months of repeated blasting before some of the more persistent voices decide they could probably get an easier blood-sucking meal with somebody for whom it does not yet occur to use their Voice Blaster.

Keep your Voice Blaster handy, even when you are in bed. You never know when you might be having sex with your partner and some little voices come around saying: "Remember what happened last time? That's probably going to happen again this time! You will never make it. For sure you have bad breath. You are a clumsy sex partner anyway. He / she is not really attracted to you. You are not beautiful enough. You are not sexy enough. You do not look like Brad Pitt. You are not..." "Bang! Bang! Bang!" (It took you long enough to remember your Voice Blaster! Man, shoot those suckers quicker, before they *even* get a chance to say *anything*. You are not a victim of your voices. Just blast 'em.) "Bang!" Then blow off your smoking pistol, spin it around your trigger finger, and drop it back into its holster ready for the next time. Welcome to the Adult ego state.

The Adult ego state speaks with your own authentic voice, and may be completely neutral and silent in circumstances where the nurturing or critical Parent voices are screaming their heads off. In using your own Adult voice you have your own power. Using your Voice Blaster is how to vanish pesky Parent-ego-state voices and anchor yourself into your Adult ego state.

Childhood Needs

The Child ego state includes both the "free natural" Child and the "scared needy adaptive" Child that originate with considerations from the past. Because it is childish, it communicates about being scared, needy and adaptive so as to avoid encountering uncomfortable things that have already happened to you, or to continue encountering "warm-fuzzy" experiences that are naively irrelevant.

The first thing to recognize about the Child ego state is that, no matter how real the feelings seem now, they *all* come from the past. Regardless of how present the fear or how strong the neediness seems to feel, everything from the past is merely a memory. The Adult knows that the present is the present, an always-evolving new set of unpredictable possibilities to create with. The Adult realizes that we have no power at all to change even the tiniest thing from the past.

Prove for yourself right now that you have no power to change the past. Do this experiment: Make it so that you did not just read this sentence. Can you do that? No. Why not? Because reading the sentence occurred in the past. Even though you read the sentence only a few seconds ago, you cannot alter the fact that it already happened. We have no power in the past. The only place we have the power to do anything is now.

Power is in the present. How much time and energy have you spent trying to make things different in your past? Trying to re-have a conversation in a better way? Wishing that you had made a different decision? Trying to find a solution to a problem that you had a long time ago? It is silly, actually, that we try to change the past. But we do. And what we get for our efforts is ordinary human relationship.

Your Inner Void (BLTLCH06.06). When we were children our parents were busy. Toward us, perhaps, they were being authoritarian, being anti-authoritarian, or trying out some other parenting fad. The results were that some of our childhood needs were not met. We sometimes can feel the void left from these unmet needs in our day-to-day life. We experience an aching space in our soul, deep, wide and unfulfilled. This aching emptiness comes from the Child ego state. We look to our partner to fill this void. But it is not his

or her job. No amount of chocolate-chocolate-chip ice cream can fill that void either. We seek for approval and acceptance, recognition and rewards, successes and glamorous attention to fill the hole, and none suffices. The emptiness remains.

Well, there is some bad news and some good news about this aching emptiness. The bad news is this: Your childhood needs will *never* be fulfilled. Your parents and teachers and brothers and sisters are never going to come to you and hug you and say, "You did a great job. We love you totally." It is never going to happen. That is the bad news.

Here is the good news about the aching emptiness: *Your childhood needs will never be fulfilled. You can finally stop waiting around with false expectations and faint hopes for something from the past to change.* You can stop waiting around and get on about living your Adult life. You can grow up! This is great news!

Relocate to the Adult Ego State

Adulthood (BLTLCH06.07). The Adult recognizes that you cannot change what happened to you. It happened exactly how it happened. It happened in the past so you cannot change what happened. But you *can* change your relationship to what happened. You can change the story that you subscribe to about what happened. You can change your subscription. That old story about the thing that happened to you is a stake in the ground that keeps you from flying. You can cut the rope. You can stop giving the old story your energy and let it be what it is: a memory. Then, you can get on with your life and put your energy into creating what really matters to you now.

Anchoring yourself into the short now-moment of the Adult ego state creates a startlingly clear perspective. All of a sudden a lot of extraneous psycho-emotional baggage from the Child ego state drifts effortlessly away from you. It is possible to graciously let this baggage go. All of those memories and conclusions are only *one* of your possible identities: your child identity. When you affirm that you are no longer a child, you let your child identity go back to where it belongs – in the past – and you step into your Adult identity. Sentimental nostalgia only interferes with the enjoyable lightness of being that characterizes the Adult state. There is a difference between reflecting on memories from time to time, and indulging in memories to try to relive them.

Memories are memories. You can experience memories in the present, but what happened in your memories is in the past. Whatever happened then, good or bad, cannot happen now. Only what is happening now can happen now, and we can only change what is happening now *now*. The Adult ego state includes only now.

Adults source responsibility; children do not. The free natural Child has a great time, but that great time is an illusion because the responsible Adult is the one who must clean up the mess.

The concept of "reclaiming the free natural Child ego" state has been frequently misunderstood. The concept has been somehow distorted to imply that the only real freedom of expression and joy in life comes through the free natural Child ego state. To finally experience freedom and fun, some people have desperately tried to drag that little guy or girl out of being abandoned in the basement of memory and then to place them into the driver's seat of their lives so they can go play with the other "kids"

MAP OF ADULT EGO STATE

EXTRAORDINARY HUMAN COMMUNICATIONS
COME FROM STAYING IN THE ADULT EGO STATE AND NOT GETTING HOOKED, EVEN IF IT IS NOT FAIR

PARENT   PARENT

ADULT   ADULT

CHILD   CHILD

YOU   ANOTHER PERSON

and eat ice cream. The embarrassing aspect of this distortion is that your life as an Adult is an Adult life, not a child's life. The Child neither knows how nor wants to take responsibility for your Adult life. Shirking responsibility and trying to live wisely and fully through the Child ego state is a choice that can be costly in terms of life decisions. Really, what Man wants to have sex with a little girl? What Woman is attracted and turned on when in bed with a little boy? Don't let years go by while you try to figure this out. Grow up now!

Childhood is the "bad old days" where we are born as functional victims and have no capacity to take responsibility. Authentic freedom, joy and high level fun happen through the free and natural Adult ego state. It is the Adult who can engage the world at the level of creative responsibility. The Adult starts "impossible" projects – and then completes them. The Adult builds cities, reinvents governments, changes company policy, creates organizational gameworlds, explores the fringe delicacies of intimacy, originates new languages, expands ways to express inner commitments, conquers fears, authenticates visions, transforms itself, launches new products, sources religions, creates and destroys universes before breakfast, *and cleans up the mess!* This is the Adult ego state.

To recap: In the Parent ego state you are at the effect of other people's voices *so you do not get to be you.* If you are mouthing words and feelings of someone else, you do not have your own power and intelligence. In the Child ego state you are hooked into the past, *so you do not get to be in the present.* If you are entangled with trying to change things that cannot be changed, you do not have your own power in the present. *The place where you have your own power and intelligence in the present is the Adult ego state.* So the Adult ego state is important. It is a key element in creating extraordinary human relationship.

How do you know that you are in the Adult ego state? Here is a big clue: In the Adult ego state there are no words. Reality is wordless. Words come from stories or interpretations that our Box makes up about what is happening. Stories occur in time. The present moment is only now. Now has no time. If the present moment has no time and stories occur in time, then the present moment can have no stories. If you are involved in stories, voices in your head, or words from the past, it indicates that you are not in the present moment and therefore not in the Adult ego state.

Another important clarification is that the Adult ego state is the gateway to the deep Masculine and deep Feminine Archetypal structures that are hardwired into your body and waiting for you to turn them on. You cannot get to the Archetypal Masculine or Archetypal Feminine except through the Adult ego state. This will be investigated later,

but it is helpful to start thinking about it now. Additional indicators for determining if you are in the Adult ego state include:

- Adult ego state respects people for creating the exact problems they need for taking themselves through their next step in evolution.
- Adult ego state lets other people have their own problems and takes responsibility for self-generated problems.
- Adult ego state does not rescue, persecute or play victim.
- Adult ego state keeps its center, is not hooked, stays present, makes contact, pays attention, holds space, and listens or speaks responsibly and with genius.

These conditions create extraordinary human relationship. The rest of the chapter unfolds these ideas. A short sample communication between Adult ego state and other ego states follows.

Parent addressing Adult: "Well, I don't like this. Too many freedoms for the children these days, don't you think? And your Johnny certainly is going to pay for his little attitude problem when it comes time for him to get a job! Everybody knows what happens around your dining table at night!"

Adult responding to Parent: "You don't like this."

Child addressing Adult: "I don't know how to do this. It is all so confusing. What should I do next? Is this right? Why can't they make things simpler? This is impossible for me. I am too tired. It's too hard for me. I can't do it."

Adult responding to Child: "You don't know how to do this."

Adult addressing and responding to Adult: "Hello."

Further explanations of Adult communication are given in a later section.

SECTION 6-C
Extraordinary Human Love

Our body, mind, heart and soul are designed to live in and be fed by extraordinary human love. But how do we get there from our familiar rounds in ordinary human love?

Ordinary human love originates in the irresponsible perspective of wanting to be loved. We focus on consuming love. We go around in love-scarcity, looking for someone to love us. We live in the childhood longing to have our unmet childhood needs finally fulfilled. When someone appears to be fulfilling our needs, and we say to them "I love you," what we actually mean is, "I need you to keep fulfilling my needs. I want to own you. I have to have you. I want to possess you and control you so that you keep taking care of me." We conclude that if someone is fulfilling our needs then they apparently love us and we apparently love them.

The ordinary definition of love, meaning "an exchange of need-fulfillment," gets shaky when we start asking what is meant by the term "need." Specifically, which aspect of our psychology, emotionality, personality, or habitual thinking patterns is speaking for us in the moment that we claim to have a need? What is really a need? Is it something that feels normal to us, like "I need you to put salt in the potatoes"? Is it something to make us comfortable, like "I need you to drive faster"? Is it a physical "need," like "I need to pee"? Or is it more of a preference, like "I need a hug"? Is it fulfilling an expectation? Agreeing with an opinion? Reacting from old fears? Love entangled with needs gets very messy.

Extraordinary human love is a different agreement with life than maneuvering to have other people take care of us and fulfill our needs. In extraordinary human relationship we are responsible Adults who take care of getting our own needs met.

Ordinary human love is like a paint-by-the-numbers kit that we got from our parents for a birthday gift. Extraordinary human love is a blank canvas with an easel, professional quality brushes, and a full set of colors that we have bought for ourselves. The empty canvas is a true laboratory for experimenting with extraordinary human love.

Ordinary human love depends on the evidence of love ("He says 'I love you' to me every night before he goes to sleep"), or the experience of love ("I feel overwhelming joy every time I see her"). Ordinary human love is conditional. In comparison, extraordinary human love has no conditions. Instead, extraordinary human love *is* the condition.

In extraordinary human love a person may have neither the evidence for love nor

---

MAP OF THREE KINDS OF LOVE

1. Ordinary Human Love, self referenced, neurotic, "I need you" love, dependent on certain expected circumstances and experiences.

2. Extraordinary Human Love, respectful, playful, adult, responsible, alive in the present, independent of circumstances because you create new love happening in each moment.

3.

the experience of being loved, and yet still be in love. An Adult man or woman takes responsibility for realizing that love does *not* come from somebody else. Love comes from you.

Extraordinary human love is like this: You experience love when you love. You no longer wait around for love to happen. You walk around in a self-caused field of love. There is no lack of love because no matter where you go love happens. Love is not scarce, something you look for or try to find. Love is abundantly there because *you* are there. Love is the playing field that you create and sustain for your relationships to unfold into. The whole twenty-four hours are about making love because you are a love maker. With your partner, your colleagues, your children or your friends you have love for no reason, love without cause. Your relationships happen not so you might *find* love; they happen because you are already in the space of love, and you are the "space holder" for this love happening. Love is not an ideal or a fantasy. Love is the way. "I love you" is a declaration. Love exists because you say it exists.

In extraordinary human relationship if you are not happy it is not the other person's fault. If you are not happy it is because you have not taken care of yourself to be happy. Taking care of yourself to be happy is Adult responsibility. In extraordinary human relationship your own happiness is a gift that you make and bring to your partner to share with them.

SECTION 6-D
The Soft Skills of Extraordinary Human Relationship

We might have assumed that since we are human beings we already know about love and relationship. But think about sex. Did you already know about sex when you began your first sexual encounters? If so, it was sex in its most rudimentary form. The same is true of love and relationship. There are so many levels to discover and explore. Gaining skills in love and relationship is a different procedure from gaining skills in mathematics or sewing. There is a considerable difference between learning "soft skills" and learning "hard skills."

"Hard skills" are skills that produce an immediately visible result. If someone teaches you how to fry a sunny-side-up egg, it is easy to confirm that you have acquired the skill. The same is true of mowing the grass, paying the bills, ironing shirts, setting the table, cleaning the toilet, and so on. The results of learning a hard skill are visible, well defined, directly obvious, and usually involve a human being manipulating inanimate objects.

"Soft skills," in contrast, usually involve interactions with other human beings. Suddenly the equation takes on a very wiggly character. Human beings are not inanimate objects. They have a will of their own; suffer from short attention spans; are prone to reacting irrationally with strong emotions; and possess agendas not always obvious even to themselves. In short, soft skills are complex! Hard skills are simple in comparison.

Learning a hard skill is usually a matter of figuring out how things work and then doing it that way. Not so with soft skills. Acquiring a new soft skill means modifying your already existing habitual behavior. Even if your present behavior is to go numb, avoid contact, avert the eyes, stay silent, or do nothing, it is still a behavior. Doing something different from that requires behavior change. Behavior does not often change by simply figuring it out. How often have you figured out that a certain behavior produced unwanted results and yet you still continued with the same behavior? Behavior change requires constant, careful self-observation and continued involvement with other people who are willing and able to give you feedback, coaching, encouragement and attention. Even with abundant support the results are not guaranteed.

The sobering news is that the difference between ordinary human relationship and extraordinary human relationship has almost nothing to do with your ability to deal with inanimate objects, and everything to do with your ability to navigate interactions between subtle and fickle human beings. You will need to learn new soft skills.

Soft Skills Cannot Be Taught

The actions that shift you from ordinary human relationship into extraordinary human relationship are soft skills. Acquiring new soft skills requires a more complex holistic learning than hard skills. Learning soft skills is not restricted to the intellect or physical body. Soft skills are learned in all four bodies, including the heart and the energetic body. Four-body learning encompasses a much broader range of experiences than we might be accustomed to experiencing during our usual intellectual or physical learning.

As shown in the *Map of Learning Soft Skills* (*see* page 122), the development of soft skill competence comes as a result of engaging four subtle but powerful learning forces. Engaging these learning forces is volitional. In other words, we have the power to choose

whether or not we will engage these learning forces. Our present set of soft skills are so deeply ingrained in our behavior that we stay in Unconscious Incompetence, where almost nothing changes until such time as we start making conscious efforts. But, making conscious efforts rubs against our ordinary nature – gaining consciousness and making efforts can both feel highly uncomfortable.

For example, the first step in learning soft skills is moving from our original "ignorance is bliss" condition in Unconscious Incompetence (quadrant 1 in the map) to Conscious Incompetence (quadrant 2). This shift is like being awakened from a fabulous dream with a bucket of cold water, and then seeing that while we were sleeping our house burned down.

The cold water in the process of learning soft skills comes in the form of feedback, either verbal feedback from somebody we are forced to respect or someone who cares enough about us to speak in the face of our obstinacy, or physical feedback like how much money is in our account, the level of our blood cholesterol, or our car's tire rolling ahead of us on the highway. The world is generous with its feedback. Subtle and obvious signs are constantly mirroring back to us the consequences of what we are creating. But, until the cold water wakes us up, we are fast asleep and not able to consciously perceive the feedback.

What makes us able to hear feedback is the growth of a bigger and more sophisticated matrix able to support our expanded consciousness, as shown on the *Map of Learning Soft Skills*. With the expanded matrix to catch and integrate new feedback we leave area (1.) Unconscious Incompetence and enter area (2.) Conscious Incompetence.

The two qualities of feedback that make it useful for learning are clarity and possibility. *Clarity* comes from distinctions that show exactly where, how and why our present level

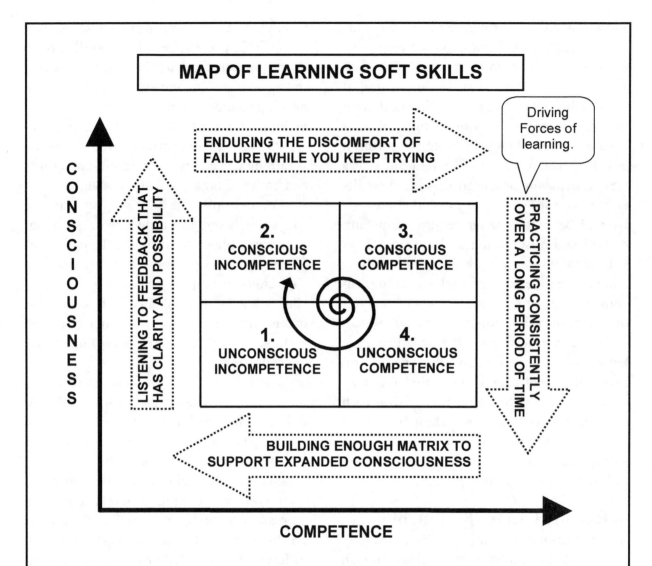

MAP OF LEARNING SOFT SKILLS

CONSCIOUSNESS

LISTENING TO FEEDBACK THAT HAS CLARITY AND POSSIBILITY

ENDURING THE DISCOMFORT OF FAILURE WHILE YOU KEEP TRYING

Driving Forces of learning.

PRACTICING CONSISTENTLY OVER A LONG PERIOD OF TIME

2.
CONSCIOUS
INCOMPETENCE

3.
CONSCIOUS
COMPETENCE

1.
UNCONSCIOUS
INCOMPETENCE

4.
UNCONSCIOUS
COMPETENCE

BUILDING ENOUGH MATRIX TO SUPPORT EXPANDED CONSCIOUSNESS

COMPETENCE

Learning happens when any of the four driving forces actively take you to the next level. The map shows a spiral going clockwise round and round coming straight up out of the page. This means that although you can learn by making different kinds of efforts, completing the learning cycle must include a balance of all four forces and go through all four stages. The step from Unconscious Incompetence to Conscious Incompetence feels awful because everyone sees that you do not already know. This step cannot be avoided. Decide now to go ahead and learn even if you look bad. Feedback guides you to the treasure of gaining new competence. Fierce learners do not hang out in Unconscious Competence for more than about 15 seconds before seeking consciousness about a new incompetence. (The original source of this map is disputed, possibly D. L. Kirkpatrick 1971, W. C. Howell 1977, or T. Gordon in the 1970s. This map is also similar to the famous Johari Window. The driving forces of learning were added to the map by Clinton Callahan in 2006.)

of competence is lacking and what that causes for us. *Possibility* comes from new perspectives that spotlight previously unseen behavior options. Both the clarity and the possibility are already there – but we cannot see them before we acquire enough matrix.

Recognizing deficiencies can be reason enough for us to react with embarrassment, shame, guilt, hopelessness, self-reproach or rage. The pain of seeing that there is a soft skill we don't know is only made bearable by contrasting it to the pain of seeing how much difficulty we cause *without* the new soft skill. When the clarity and possibility from feedback cause us too much pain, we are finally motivated to try to do something differently. At first, however, all we understand is that we are incompetent. We do not know how to behave competently. Even though we don't know *how* to change we still *want* to change, so we keep trying. But our trying is imperfect. So with each new try we also keep failing. Enduring the discomfort of repeated failures as we keep trying to behave in more effective ways is actually two things occupying the same place at the same time. Holding both experiences within us creates an uncomfortable conflict. Willing ourselves to contain this conflict rather than giving up in the face of repeated failings builds an energetic learning force. By remaining convincingly cheery while repeatedly trying and repeatedly failing we give the force a useful direction that slowly develops incompetence into competence. Eventually, we enter the domain of Conscious Competence (3.), to some degree.

Practicing our new competence over a long period of time builds a new learning force. The new force is momentum. The Box becomes accustomed to experiencing its new shape and therefore its new patterns of behavior. The new responses to external conditions become more normal, familiar and automatic until the Box fails to identify the new behaviors as new anymore. They have simply become the Box's natural way of behaving. Our Conscious Competence (3.) drifts into Unconscious Competence (4.) succumbing to the learning force of momentum. What we may not realize is that Unconscious Competence is a learning force of its own.

Unconscious Competence continues to build matrix at its new level. Even though we may start feeling bored or unchallenged at this stage, if we responsibly continue, then matrix is still being built. Often, when we least expect it, the floor suddenly drops out from under our feet. Where we thought we had everything under control we suddenly find ourselves in internal or external chaos, bigger than ever. Our peak performance of Unconscious Competence (4.) spirals up to the next level of Unconscious Incompetence (1.), ready for the next adventure in learning. To watch this cycle of learning occur over and over again gives us new respect for a force of evolution full of elegance, beauty and grace.

After a few times around the cycle we may conclude that we are merely going in circles. Here we are, back again being conscious of our incompetence. While it may feel the same each time, it can be useful to notice that we are actually moving along in a spiral and the one who *has* the feeling has changed. Not *everything* is still the same. Yet, overall, we may well imagine it being better to stay in denial about our inabilities, because recognizing our incompetence mercilessly annihilates our present self-image. Learning may be hindered through consciously or unconsciously deciding that, all in all, it is better not to know. Why should we choose the pain of disambiguation over the bliss of our ignorance? Such a decision is a personal preference and therefore inarguable. The inarguability inhibits learning soft skills.

We make a private decision as to what extent we are willing to experience the pain of increased awareness. The subjectivity of this decision creates a "soft-skills learning paradox": *Soft skills cannot be taught; they can only be learned.* You cannot force anybody to learn a new soft skill. Learning soft skills is a personal choice and is accomplished only through diligent personal efforts. Personal efforts means repeated practice in a safe environment where mistakes do not cost too much. In such an environment you can begin your soft-skill learning journey into the extraordinary.

SECTION 6-E

New Results Come From New Actions

Light reflected from the ink patterns on this paper enters your eyes. You have trained your mind to take nerve impulses from your eyes and recognize the twenty-six familiar letter shapes of the English alphabet. Your mind further assembles patterns of letters into individual words. Then your mind does an amazing thing. It takes groups of words and melds them together into ideas. The jump from bunches of words to meaningful concepts is nothing less than miraculous. And you are doing that right now.

I bring your attention to the phenomena of your mind making concepts out of ink marks on paper because, as remarkable as is it, I am interested in more than that from you. I am interested in you taking these ink marks and creating new behavior patterns in your life. I want you to actually be able to enter the experiential territory of extraordinary human relationship. Having new electrical patterns in your brain from new thinking patterns may be a necessary first step. But I want real results! New results only come from you taking new actions.

Did you ever think that you could create new results from taking the same actions? Most of us do. Such thinking is a kind of insanity. New results cannot come from taking the same actions. New results only come from taking *new* actions. The question is precisely this: How do you get new concepts into your mind to produce new actions from your body? The answer is: Some kind of leap, some new connections have to be made. The actions we take now come easily for us. Most of our daily actions are produced by reflexive habit patterns; they are unconscious. New actions require conscious decisions. Your willpower must be involved – your conscious motivational volition.

What do you really want? Do you want to keep experiencing what you have always been experiencing in relationship? Yes or no? Answer now.

If your answer is no, then you are going to have to enter the unusual. You are going to have to break out of your own pigpen. You are going to have to try some unfamiliar and perhaps, at first, uncomfortable things.

For starters, try something new right now. Raise your right hand and say out loud, no matter where you are and no matter who else is there, "I am willing to take new actions."

I am waiting. Did you do it?

If you don't do it this instant you will never do it.

C'mon! Who really has control over your ability to decide? Who really has control over your voice? Who really has control over the part in you who chooses what you do? Is it you? Or is it the rules that were hammered into you by parents, normalcy, or other authority figures? Who has authority over your actions right this moment? If you think that you have the authority, *then prove it*. Prove it to me. Prove it to yourself. Raise up your hand and say out loud, "I am willing to take new actions."

C'mon! I just did it myself, sitting in front of my old Dell Inspiron 4000 laptop computer at 6:08 PM on a Sunday night in December in the Callahan Academy office on Gistlstrasse in Pullach, Germany. I am alone here but someone could have seen me through the window. I did it anyway. You can do it too.

Last chance. Low risk here. This is just an experiment. Go ahead. If you are not willing to risk such a simple new action as raising your hand and saying a few unusual words like, "I am willing to take new actions," how can I expect you to responsibly decode an irresponsibly encoded message from your partner late some night when it is really difficult and it really matters?

Thank you. I assume that you did the experiment. I first did such an experiment some twenty-five years ago sitting alone in a doublewide trailer near a cotton field in Phoenix, Arizona, and I still remember that experience. It shocked me that it was so difficult to make such a simple new action. It surprised me to hear my own voice in an empty room. It woke me up to the just-proved and now undeniable fact that I do have enough courage to actually take new actions. The unusual action created a waking moment for me that I still remember. Your life can be filled with waking moments if you start taking more new actions.

Like to Learn

The fact that we do not know already about extraordinary human relationship is not bad. The fact that we do not already know means that the universe is vast, elegant, multi-dimensional and sophisticated. The fact that there is a lot that we do not know is actually a blessing – that is, it is a blessing if you like to learn. If you think that you do *not* like to learn it may be worth investigating why you think that.

The way to investigate why you do not like to learn begins with trusting the internal sensation that you do not like learning. Once you decide to trust that sensation, take a deep breath, let it out, relax, and allow yourself to drift back along the sensation to recall your feeling's place of origin. You may recall one or more events, self-reinforcing moments in which you came to the conclusion that you did not like to learn.

The "I can't learn" or "I hate to learn" stories build on and reinforce each other. For example, there may have been a promotion available for you at work, but being promoted depended on you learning how to operate a new computer-software program. You may have tried a few times and gotten frustrated. Then, every time you thought of the promotion you remembered how much you hate to learn new computer programs, so you didn't do anything to get that promotion. You developed an automatic story that replays in your thoughts about not being able to learn. Then that story sought ongoing evidence to keep itself alive.

This is only one example. You probably have several other examples from earlier in your life. Bring back the memory of one of those earlier "I can't learn" incidents and let the feelings get bigger. Watch any pictures that go by. Recall the exact moments in which you made the decision that you do not like to learn. Say out loud the exact words of your decision about not liking to learn. When you have said the sentence, take another deep breath and write down your old decision.

As babies and children we were subject to various forms of abuse, neglect and betrayal by those people who were theoretically being responsible for taking care of us and educating us. Even small or momentary abuses can be the cause of lifelong high-impact decisions.

The people who created the circumstances in which the abuses occurred were probably not aware that they were being abusive and causing scars. They probably had no idea what we felt like and what kinds of life-shaping decisions we were making. Perhaps we did not even know it ourselves. The people who were taking care of us probably thought that they were creating the best possible circumstances for our survival. For sure, they were doing the best they could do, given their own life experiences and upbringing.

You may have made a rational and expedient decision to avoid learning. But before you made that decision *you loved to learn*. In fact, you probably decided to be born for the sole purpose of learning. Even if you think that you are what in esoteric circles is referred to as a "walk-on" – someone who is an "old soul" who has already been around "many times," who has already "been enlightened" and who

has come back for the altruistic purpose of "serving others less fortunate than themselves" – you still came here to learn how to serve better. There are no "walk-ons."

Esoteric labels have the power to block you from being vulnerable; the same as everyone else. The idea that you are here to "teach" rather than to learn may simply turn out to be a clever ruse created by your Box for avoiding the inevitable discomforts that occur during learning. Without irrevocably acknowledging that you do not already know what is next for you to learn about, learning stops.

Your mind is yours to play with and to make into whatever you want. You made up your mind once about learning. Using the same procedure, you can make up your mind *a different way* about learning now.

Without permission from anyone, without warning, you can change your old decision about learning and in this moment make a new decision.

No matter what you decided before, about you and learning, regardless of what happened in the past, you could make a new decision now. Are you ready for your next experiment? Here it is. Put up your right hand again and say out loud, "I am changing my mind. I have decided that I like to learn." Now, grab a scrap of paper and write down the exact words of your new decision.

)(Entering the Liquid State

We can't modify our behavior and create extraordinary human relationship without first modifying the thing that *decides* what we do – our Box. The Box is one of the hardest substances in the universe, far harder than diamonds. Not only is the Box resilient, it also

has the uncanny ability to repair itself. Given these challenges, what procedure could actually cause the Box to change shape?

We are asking how to change a solid with one shape into a solid of a different shape. This would be like having a handful of gold coins and deciding to use the gold to form a statue of an angel. How do you do that? First you must melt the gold coins. As the coins melt, the gold is released from its disk shape and flows into shapeless liquid. The liquid is then poured into an angel mold. After pouring the hot liquid gold you do nothing. The gold cools down all by itself. You peel off the mold, and there you have it– an angel! Same gold. Different form. Since the gold has a different form it has a different functionality. Function follows form. Previously the gold functioned as money. Now the gold functions as sacred art.

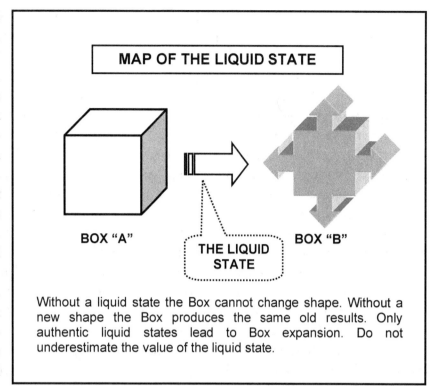

MAP OF THE LIQUID STATE

BOX "A"

THE LIQUID STATE

BOX "B"

Without a liquid state the Box cannot change shape. Without a new shape the Box produces the same old results. Only authentic liquid states lead to Box expansion. Do not underestimate the value of the liquid state.

This same method is used on the Box. The Box is made out of solid beliefs, opinions, attitudes, assumptions, expectations, and so on. These components can find a new relationship to each other while the Box is in the "liquid state." When the Box solidifies again its new form – *you* – gets a new functionality. This is how to make behavior changes and gain abilities that help you to create extraordinary human relationship.

You already know the value of changed functionality or you would not be reading a book about improving relationship competence. What you may not yet recognize is the value of the liquid stage between one solid shape and the next. If you don't go through some kind of liquid state you get no new shapes in your Box, and therefore no new behaviors.

Entering the Liquid State (BLTLCH06.08). The secret for changing behavior is to navigate to the liquid state. Whether the liquid state lasts for three seconds or three days, it is the way to experience

sustainable change. For example, your organic comprehension of any of the ideas in this book occurs through releasing previously solid perspectives and passing through the liquid state of "not knowing" until a new understanding solidifies.

What does the liquid state feel like? Each of the four bodies has its own particular liquid state sensations. For example, physical-body liquid states can range from 100-percent "on" – like being in the "flow" or the "zone"– with exhilarating power and no resistance to movement; all the way to 100-percent "off" – like feeling nauseous and being sick in bed for three days with a "flu." Intellectual-body liquid states can range from unendingly brilliant clarity to confused blankness or stubborn disagreement. Emotional-body liquid states can range from tears of ecstatic joyousness to tears of despair, outrage, vengefulness or hysteria. And energetic-body liquid states can range from groundless spaciousness, total freedom and oneness with all beings everywhere, to meaningless angst and existential chaos. The liquid state experience, like all experience, is *completely neutral*. The experience has no built-in implications – it simply is what it is and feels exactly like it feels. The liquid state experience, like all experience, is also temporary. Any stories that get attached to the liquid state experience are produced and sponsored by the creative genius of your Box. Pay attention to the editorial slant behind the stories your Box generates for you. The test is to discover their purpose.

Sudden reordering applies to individuals, to relationships, and to organizations. All three configurations are able to stay in denial and resist an opportunity to evolve with extreme ferocity. When you are in any of these three configurations and evolution is knocking on your door in the form of potential chaos, although you were taught that "the show must go on," you can also use the opposite strategy: let the show fall apart. Stay present, stay involved, keep breathing, and take the whole system into breakdown. By intentionally navigating directly into the liquid state instead of away from it, you can save yourself a lot of grief caused by waiting for "accidental" circumstances to build up and force an even bigger breakdown.

When doing the experiment of heading for the liquid state remember that it is the Box that goes into the liquid state, not you. You have a Box. You are not your Box. What you actually *are* cannot go into the liquid state.

If you include the liquid state in your concept of the experience of being human, of being in relationship, or of being in an organization like a family or a neighborhood or a company, then nothing is wrong or bad about the liquid state. The liquid state is *the way* of relationship. The purpose of relationship is evolution, so when *authentic* liquid state arises it is just a sign that you have an opportunity to evolve.

Liquid states can be authentic or inauthentic. How many times have you gone through what you hoped was a transformational learning process only to find that nothing changed? Perhaps the reason there was no sustained change is that the process did not take you through an *authentic* liquid state. Crying or rage, chaos or confusion, conflict or breakdown, these may or may not be signs of an authentic liquid state. On the surface, many signs of irresponsible interaction can look as if they are authentic liquid states, but they are not. Determining the authenticity of a liquid state requires looking at the total end results. If evolution has occurred after the interaction or the meeting and responsible changes resulted, then the liquid state was authentic. If nothing changed, if time and energy were wasted, or if the "liquid state" simply repeated itself at a later date, the liquid state was not authentic.

Knowing the distinction between authentic and inauthentic liquid states, the next time you are involved in a liquid state situation you can start sensing into the intention vector of the liquid state to determine instantly, at its beginning, if the liquid state is authentic or not. You can sense along the lines of peoples' intention. You can feel out along the purpose of subtle actions and detect the responsibility in tones of voice, in feelings, and in the momentum of actions. These things are easy to sense. After awhile you can learn to detect the authenticity of a liquid state even before it starts. The ability to detect such authenticity grows out of becoming authentic yourself.

SECTION 6-G
Authenticity

The gateway from ordinary human relationship to extraordinary human relationship is through the Bright Principle of authenticity. "Authenticity" is one of those weighty words we might unknowingly avoid in our casual vocabulary, along with words like commitment, integrity, or accountability. There is no way to wrap our mind around authenticity. We are not trained to endure the intensity of authenticity in our relationships because with authenticity the edges of our Box are in our face. authentic experience is typically too raw. We feel embarrassed, or uncertain. We do not know what to say. Unmitigated presence is not our usual abode. So, we tend to let authenticity slide by when being together, just like we let time slide by when watching television.

The way we tolerate abandoning authenticity is by not cherishing the true value that authenticity creates. The difficulty arises when we observe that appreciating relational authenticity often involves experiencing what is commonly regarded as pain. In ordinary human relationship pain is problematical, but in extraordinary human relationship pain liberates the wisdom and power of feelings.

Authenticity can be explored by examining how we regard the actions of our partner. Some of our partner's actions are acceptable to us. Others are not. We assume that we live out our relationship on the basis of accepting or not accepting the actions of our partner.

False Acceptance (BLTLCH06.09). The truth of the matter may not be so simple. Most probably there is a third category of ways we regard our partner's behavior. In the third category we act *as if* we accept our partner's actions but *in reality we do not*. This new category is called "false acceptance." In the area of false acceptance we are being inauthentic.

If you are not authentic about how things are for you, if you withhold your own truth, then you start to live a double life. One life you show. One life is secret, perhaps secret even from yourself.

I know a man who was inauthentic in his marriage for twenty-five years. Why would someone be inauthentic? Why would this man

---

MAP OF AUTHENTICITY

ACCEPTABLE BEHAVIORS	**AUTHENTICITY**
FALSE ACCEPTANCE OF BEHAVIORS	**INAUTHENTICITY** Experiment: To become more authentic start telling the truth about your inauthenticity.
UNACCEPTABLE BEHAVIORS	**AUTHENTICITY**

(This Map is in part derived from Thomas Gordon's Effectiveness Trainings. For more information see www.gordontraining.com.)

go along for a quarter-century pretending to accept things that in fact he did not accept? Such behavior is crazy. Such behavior would indicate a tendency toward pathological lying. What reasons would a man use to justify misrepresenting himself to such a great degree? For that matter, why do some women stay with husbands who beat them or husbands who flirt with other women? Why do some men stay with wives who psychologically torment them?

The answer is simple and also frighteningly common: We continue the patterns of our childhood. To endure the circumstances of our childhood we often became inauthentic by continuously accepting the unacceptable behaviors of our parents. Our inauthentic acceptance became deeply habitual, even unconscious. If we marry someone who is like our mother or father (and who doesn't?), then it is likely that to some degree our partnership will invisibly include the same inauthentic acceptance that we have performed our whole life. Until we gain a bigger perspective about what we are doing, we may habitually continue our false acceptance of our partner's behaviors. We may have, to some degree, hated how our parents related, but we may be duplicating that behavior ourselves.

SECTION 6-H

About Denial and Drivers

Obtaining a Ph.D. in psychology will not guarantee that you have a working relationship. Yet still, some clarity is revealed about how a person could accept unacceptable behaviors for twenty-five years when we investigate two particular Box mechanisms: denial and drivers.

What is denial? Denial is a Box-generated defense strategy for refusing to acknowledge the existence or the severity of unpleasant external realities, conflicting thoughts, or disturbing feelings.

Denial can continue indefinitely because we have no idea at all what we are in denial about until we suddenly come out of denial about it. Like a dream, we may have no idea that, in fact, we are dreaming, until we awaken from the dream. Like with dreams, the awakening from denial can be sudden and rude.

The wide variety of ways our Box goes into denial exhibit the Box's vast resources of creativity. Mechanisms for creating denial are

rich and dynamic. One typical mechanism for entering and staying in denial was described by Dr. Eric Berne as a "driver."

Drivers are behavior engines. The Box's idea is that if we fulfill the imperative of the driver then we will survive. Berne labeled five drivers: Be perfect! Please authorities! Try hard! Be strong! And hurry up! These are "positive" drivers that deliver the appearance of "responsibility." Berne neglected to name the equal number of frequently used "negative" or "irresponsible" drivers: Make a mess! Attack authorities! Don't try at all! Fail! And be late! Contemplate these drivers for a moment. Which three drivers motivate you the most in your life?

Drivers are not actually responsible or irresponsible. They are simply our Box's preferred survival mechanisms. ("Merely surviving" is in itself irresponsible. Being responsible involves "really living." There is a big difference between merely surviving and really living.)

The behaviors produced by our particular drivers are automatically driven. It is the *mechanicality* that makes our behaviors inauthentic. We are unable to *not* do what our driver is telling us to do. That is why it is called a *driver*. If we cannot disobey the driver then we are inauthentic slaves to a psychological machine.

You just found the key to starting a very important series of experiments for yourself. Select one each of the "responsible" and "irresponsible" drivers that your Box uses and stop doing them. For example, select "Be perfect!" and "Attack authorities!" and no matter what happens to you, fulfill neither of them. Period. This will keep you busy for a couple of years.

The responsible drivers are the more difficult to unravel. First of all, the responsible drivers are not truly responsible because they lack consciousness. Drivers are automatic Box responses to circumstances. For example, being perfect is not responsible if we are unable to be *imperfect*. In this same way, the irresponsible drivers are not actually irresponsible either, because they too are mechanical, unconscious Box responses to circumstances. Following the impulses of responsible drivers can make you the CEO of a company or the mayor of a town. Following the impulses of irresponsible drivers can land you behind bars with a life sentence. That is because we live in a responsible universe, where irresponsibility is an illusion. In this universe it is impossible to avoid responsibility.

The responsible drivers are also difficult to unravel because they are associated with being good: a good person, a good man, a good woman, a good boy, a good girl, a good father, a good mother, a good wife, a good husband, a good employee, a good citizen, a good leader, and so on. In our dichotomized mind, being good is the equivalent of being right. Being right can justify our particular position or decision, but being right still keeps us in denial and inauthenticity.

It is possible to suffer decades of inauthenticity under the guise of "being good" or thinking "I am right." The opposite of being good is not being bad; it is rather being yourself.

Strategically playing the role of being good can show up in a multitude of variations. Instead of being authentic, the man in our example above elected to *tough things out* and be a hero. This man made it more important to be a hero and a nice guy than to be himself. Without awareness he could well have been thinking, "I don't want to cause a problem. I don't want to stand out and be visible. I don't want to look like a failure. I don't want to break society's rules. I want to keep my promises. I don't want to abandon or betray my children. I don't want to upset anyone. I don't see anyone else in a better relationship than me anyway, so why should I bother trying to make mine better? I have other things to do besides trying to fix my relationship. I don't want to go to some therapist. I want to be normal and happy, like everyone else. I want everything to be fine. I don't want to cause myself or my partner to have bad feelings. I don't want to hurt *anybody's* feelings. If I leave her or she leaves me I will be alone and I don't want to be alone. And if we start in on all this, what will my parents think?"

Deciding to be a hero or a nice guy is a formatory decision that can, contrary to what you might have expected, support a relationship full of emotional, psychological, physical or sexual abuse. It is not necessarily a smooth road from being good to being authentic.

Take Possession of Your Attention

To stop being a slave of denial and unconscious drivers you will need to take possession of your attention. We do not normally think much about our attention. Perhaps this is because our attention is so close to us. Like glasses on our nose, we sometimes forget that our attention is there. But our attention is there. And neither our culture nor our education inform us about how extremely important our attention is in our daily life, and in particular, how extremely important our attention is in the quality of the relationships that we create.

Relationship is about "being" together. "Being" has two components: our attention and our presence. A person's presence grows in direct proportion to the growth of the matrix structure upon which consciousness can grow. Since matrix only grows slowly and under certain conditions, presence also grows slowly over time. Watching presence grow would be like trying to watch hair grow. Rather uninteresting. We cannot really *do anything* with our presence.

Not so with attention. Our attention is mobile and flutters about like a butterfly in a daisy field. When we turn on the television, our attention flutters about like a butterfly in a tornado (the tornado being the television). *Attention is our main tool in relationship.* We can actually work with our attention.

Learning to possess your attention is as crucial to extraordinary human relationship as learning to turn the steering wheel is to driving.

Mostly, during the day our attention is not our own. Mostly, during the day our attention is owned by the biggest sound, the strongest urge, the brightest flash, or the most dangerous threat in our environment. If there is any passing billboard that shows skin from a half-naked woman our attention is gone. Gone.

Taking possession of your attention is not easy. For one thing, you face cutthroat competition from professional attention predators. Huge corporations spend billions every year in order to get your attention. Corporate marketing departments receive immense budgets for hijacking your attention for two reasons. The first reason is because it works – they *can* hijack your attention. Your untrained attention is *easy* to get. The second reason is because getting your attention more than pays for itself. If they have your attention, they have your wallet.

The reason to learn to work with your attention is because where your attention goes, your energy flows. If you do not know where your attention is at any moment, then that is where your energy goes – into the unknown. If you are not consciously placing your attention somewhere, then you are unconsciously placing your attention somewhere else. And that is where your energy is disappearing.

Each person wakes up in the morning with the same amount of energy as everybody else. The difference between the results that one person or another person creates is precisely what they do with their attention. Do you think that Mother Teresa had special solar bio-energy collectors that gave her the inspiration to create and manage a worldwide service program? No, she did not. She succeeded because she learned to discipline her attention. Do you think Nelson Mandela stayed sane in prison for twenty-seven years by luck? No. He paid careful attention to his attention.

Paying Attention to Your Attention (BLTLCH06.10). You can learn to pay attention to your attention by consciously practicing to move your attention from one thing to another. You can place your attention on an object, an image, a sensation or an idea. You can move your attention from one object to another. You can lose your attention. You can give your attention away. You can steal someone's attention. You can split your attention, paying attention to more than one thing at a time. For example, you can drive a car, chew gum, listen to the radio, watch interesting people on the sidewalk, scratch your nose and make plans for your day all.

Experiment. Start to notice what you do with your attention minute by minute during the day. Where is your attention right now, for example? The instructions are simple:

- Pay attention to your attention.
- Be aware of what you are aware of.
- Think about what you are thinking with.
- Perceive the perceiver.
- Look at what you are looking *with*.
- Role-play yourself.

- Notice what you are noticing.
- Be conscious of what you are conscious of.
- Sense the way you are sensing.
- Observe the observer, and so on.

You can adjust the focus of your attention from narrow to broad. Narrow focus is called "point attention" and is useful for reading, sawing wood along a marked line, threading a needle, adding numbers, and listening to what someone is saying. A broad focus of attention is called "field attention" and is good for scanning, for "navigating" (that is, guiding or steering) meetings to hold to a certain purpose, for managing meaning during a conversation, for planning, multitasking, and so on. Learning to use your attention is like learning to ride a bike. At first it feels strange; after awhile you get the knack of it. No one else can manage your attention for you. If you don't do it, it doesn't happen. The instructions for developing conscious attention may seem simple, but carrying them out can take effort. Becoming aware of what you are aware of has a side effect: it builds matrix, and it can allow you to discover and enter the waking state.

SECTION 6-J
Heal Yourself of Beliefs

Your Beliefs (BLTLCH06.11). Beliefs act with powerful force in ordinary human relationship because in ordinary human relationship beliefs are regarded as having validity. The usual, although often unspoken, justification for beliefs is that they can serve as a crutch to supply "weak" minds with at least something to hold onto. But beliefs do not actually provide anything to hold onto because any person can believe anything about anything!

For instance, villagers on one side of a mountain can believe that the most sacred and holy thing in the world is a hotdog, and that the proper way to pay respects to this most holy of objects is to sing daily prayers of praise to it. For them, the greatest sin is to eat a hotdog. The villagers on the other side of the mountain might believe that the most sacred and holy thing in the world is also a hotdog, but that the true and righteous way to honor the sacred hotdog is to eat it, in the company of friends, with relish.

The greatest sin is to waste the hotdog by not eating it. Which belief is true? How could one belief be true if a contradictory belief is also true? This is the insanity of beliefs. Beliefs justify their irrationality by including in the fine print the following stipulation: "And any contradictory belief is wrong." Each belief guards its own validity by disenfranchising all other beliefs. This is all fine and dandy as long as the two kinds of villagers stay away from each other. But when villagers who consider their beliefs to be the "one true way" encounter villagers of a different persuasion, they must regard the others as infidels, blasphemers and enemies of the faith! The almost unavoidable result of a meeting between villagers who regard their beliefs as reality is war. Look at human history.

In a world that is actually as wide and free as the sky, beliefs act like bumpers and clappers in a closed-in pinball game. *Boing!* Men cannot feel. *Pang! Pang!* Children should be seen and not heard. *Tock! Tock! Tock!* Fords are better than Chevys. *Rrrrrrrrrrrrrr!* East is east and west is west and never the twain shall meet. *Ding! Ding! Ding! Ding! Ding!* Women are unstable and should only work in the back office. *Boing! Boing!* I am not allowed to do that. *Clang!* Our way is right. Their way is wrong. *Tilt!* And so on.

Any phrase you speak or think that begins with, "We have to...," or "I can't...," or "You must...," or "We never..." is a positional stance that may be coming directly from a belief.

There is a big difference between a belief and a way that we think. We may say, "I believe," when what we really mean to say is, "I think..." or "my best guess is..." or "based on my experience I conclude that..." An important experiment is to check your use of the word "belief."

We may regard a "belief" as if it causes a reality to come into existence. Actually the opposite is true. Beliefs block us from being able to use the parts of reality that lay on the other side of our beliefs.

A belief is a scab on the mind that provides us with a readymade answer when there actually is none. The Box thrives on readymade answers. Take for example death. We have no answer to the question, "What happens after we die?" The Box feels out of order when it has no answer, and would rather have any answer than no answer. Having no answer leaves an unprotected gap in the Box's defenses. That is why myriads of beliefs about what happens after we die have been fabricated. If we use a belief to answer the question about death, for example, either a standard off-the-shelf belief or something more customized, then whenever we come around to questions about death, we do not have to stand in a doorway open to freezing cold answerlessness. The Box pulls out the appropriate belief and slaps it over the opening. Case closed. Next question please.

If the belief is torn off it reveals a wound. The wound is a rejection of the raw experience of being faced with not knowing. The wound occurred in some previous circumstance when the Box decided that it was not okay to not know. The difficulty with using a belief to avoid experiencing that you do not know is that sometimes it is irrefutably the case that *you do not know!* Healing yourself of beliefs involves modifying the design of your Box so as to be okay with the experience of not knowing.

One of the first blockades to entering extraordinary human relationship is your personal internal jungle of beliefs. Each person's belief jungle includes different species of beliefs, different densities of beliefs, different ages of beliefs – ancient hardened beliefs and new young tender beliefs. On your way toward extraordinary human relationship you have a preparatory job to do: to examine each and every one of your beliefs under the clear light of the new perspective that beliefs block reality.

Each belief has its own unique purpose, causes its own kind of seeing and thinking,

MAP OF THE TECHNOLOGY OF BELIEFS

Here is a little list of observations about beliefs. Nothing in this list is to be believed. The list is offered here as a map to use while making experiments to find out how beliefs actually work.

1. Beliefs are a Band-Aid placed over a hole on the inside of your Box so you do not have to experience not knowing.
2. Beliefs have no relationship to reality.
3. Any person can have any belief about anything.
4. There is no objective hierarchy of beliefs so no one belief takes priority over another.
5. If you make beliefs valid in your world then you will unavoidably have a war between your belief — that says, "this is right and that is wrong" — and another person's belief that declares, with equal fervor, the exact opposite.

looks for other people with whom to find safety in belief affinity, and avoids or attacks enemies of belief. Take out and inspect the beliefs that you got from your mother. Examine the beliefs that you got from your father. Scrutinize the beliefs you got from schoolteachers, from religion, from science, from society, from the media. Take each belief out separately and ask yourself questions. Do you need to have this belief? What does this belief do for you? How have you been using this belief? What is the belief's purpose? What does this belief block you from experiencing? What would your life be like if you decided to let this belief dissolve and be washed away downstream? Whose friendship would you lose? What might you gain?

You may already know about your belief jungle. You might have already spent years hacking away at belief brambles to clear the landscape for other possibilities. Or this may be your first introduction to the idea that beliefs block reality. If this is your first encounter with the idea of beliefs blocking reality, try not to get offended, and try not to get overwhelmed by the huge number of beliefs and the amount of time such investigation takes. The process takes time and cannot be hurried. Give yourself the time, and ask lots of people lots of questions along the way. Try to avoid looking for simple answers.

Taking responsibility for the fact that you have fortified the weaker parts of your Box with beliefs may require some months or years of work, but is worth the effort. The fewer beliefs that you support, the fewer shipwrecked intimacies you will experience. You may need to have some rather intense conversations with people who have already been disassembling their beliefs for some time. Your Box may have prevented such "dangerous" characters from being included in your usual circle of friends, but these people are never far off. When you are clear about wanting to floss your mind of beliefs, helpers will pop out of the woodwork. Your intention in these conversations can be to take apart your own beliefs before they take apart your chances to be in extraordinary human relationship.

Discover The Part That Is Not An Animal

Just like animals, we humans eat, we shit, we mate, we play around, we get sick, and we die. Physically we *are* animals. Physicality dominates much of our experience. And, there are more levels to being human than just the animal part. Practice is a way of discovering those aspects of ourselves that are *not* animal.

Here is an experiment to do several times that will help you to discover and clarify the difference between the animal part and the conscious human part. Sit cross-legged on the floor or upright in straight-backed chair. Carefully stretch your arms straight out sideways with your fingers pointing toward the sky and palms facing away from you. Take a deep breath and relax into that position. Stay in that position for twenty minutes.

Within a short time you will be intimately involved with distinguishing the difference between animal and spirit. The animal part will be feeling pain in the shoulders, back, arms and neck. Soon the pain is compounded by shaking, sweating, moans, contortions, nausea, and so on. The animal part starts screaming at you, "What? Are you crazy? This hurts! You are hurting me! You idiot! Ow! Ouch! Ohhhhhhh! Arrrgh! Stop this! Hey! It's hurting! I am going to die!"

Contrary to your animalistic certainty of impending doom, you will not die. Not from this. No matter what it feels like, no matter what the animal says to you, you will not die from holding your arms out. You may have sore muscles for a few days, but there will be no permanent damage.

In this experiment you will notice that the animal tells you to put your arms down as soon as it gets uncomfortable. Your spirit or volition has the ability to not obey the commands of the animal. Your spirit can keep your arms out for twenty minutes or longer even though keeping your arms out can be excruciatingly uncomfortable for the animal. If you do this experiment, plan to do it more than once. The second time you do it you will have a better idea of what was happening the first time. Learning to not obey the animal's every whim is a step in the direction of developing discipline. Developing discipline lets you differentiate your spiritual body from your physical animal body.

SECTION 6-K
☀ Hooked or Not-Hooked

Being Unhookable (BLTLCH06.12). Extraordinary human relationship depends on you staying "unhookable." Being unhookable means having the capacity to act independently from the circumstances, no matter what the circumstances are. A "hook" is any stimulus that might cause an automatic emotional reaction. The list of potential hooks is endless. It can drive people instantly nuts if you chew with your mouth open, ring the doorbell twice, insinuate that someone is stupid, criticize someone's religion, brag about your kids' grades, give problem solutions unasked for, continuously talk, make house decoration suggestions, refuse to tell your birthday, give away a movie plot before someone has seen it, and so on.

Obviously it is not *you* that gets hooked; it is your Box that gets hooked. You can prove this because different hooks catch different kinds of "fish," meaning what hooks one person's Box may be invisible to another's. The instant you are hooked you lose access to any possibilities other than your Box's mechanical reactions – you forget what extraordinary and Archetypal Possibilities are and how to go there. You are stuck in ordinary human relationship. The brain dumps a truckload of hormones into your system and your adrenaline shoots through the roof. You can't hide being hooked because everybody around you sees and feels the side effects. It takes a minimum of fifteen minutes to metabolize the chemicals out of your system and return to normal again – fifteen minutes you will never get back again.

Each of us contains a variety of internal characters or parts, one of which – known as the "Gremlin"– derives great joy by hooking other people. Some Gremlins entertain themselves by seeing how many people they can hook in a day, because once a person is hooked, the Gremlin has won. Hooking others is also a strong defensive strategy for the Box, because once you have hooked someone else they have no power to create unpredictable behaviors.

Human beings are *so easily hooked* that if you actually succeed at becoming even partly unhookable you almost seem inhuman. Staying unhookable, while still remaining human, is an art form.

Staying unhookable does not mean unfeeling, isolated, shut down or numb. On the contrary, staying unhookable means that you perceive the hooks with great sensitivity and precision, and while still being compassionate, you shift slightly into a different space before the hooks have a chance to set into the psychological flesh of your Box.

Staying unhookable is not so different from bullfighting. The toreador knows that a bull performs certain predictable movements, which are neither good nor bad; they are simply the movements that bulls make. To interact with the bull the toreador stands with his red cloth to his side, not in front of him. The bull automatically goes for the red cloth. With the cloth held to the side, the bull runs past while doing no harm. The toreador stays in contact with the bull but does not get hit. If the toreador held his cloth in front of him he would bullfight no longer. He would be hooked.

Hooks can be anything – looks, gestures, sounds, physical objects – so you cannot stay unhookable by simply trying to avoid hooks. A true capacity for staying unhookable emerges through first admitting that you are indeed hooked when you realize you are hooked. Start by naming your condition. Say, "I am hooked." Notice what it feels like, how often it occurs, how long it lasts, and what your hooked – reaction – patterns tend to be. Consciousness creates freedom. Your ability to stay unhookable matures through increased awareness of your Box's hookability. Here are some common symptoms of being hooked.

Symptoms of Being Hooked
- Feeling offended or insulted, being stressed, worrying, disapproving
- Swearing, striking out at someone, destroying, attacking, taking revenge
- Making physical gestures or faces (giving the finger, sticking out the tongue, etc.)
- Emotional reactions, uncontrolled rage, childish fears or sadness

- Expressing violent temper, feeling glad when someone else feels pain
- Feeling as a victim, sacrificing yourself, thinking "I have to," being disgusted
- Resenting, judging, criticizing, blaming, threatening
- Trying to be right, defending yourself, justifying yourself
- Role-playing a character, being inauthentic, overdoing it, underdoing it
- Being numb, being indifferent (as opposed to being neutral)
- Pouting, sulking, making excuses, giving up hope, resignation
- Being cynical, ironical, being self–important, bragging, exaggerating
- Being stuck in linear thinking, trying to be prepared for anything
- Competing, challenging, comparing with others, envy, jealousy
- Excluding others, feeling superior, trying to look good, being arrogant
- Thinking that you have lost, feeling like a failure, isolating from others, feeling depressed
- Defending your position, arguing, giving reasons, saying, "Yes, but…"
- Being adaptive, "kissing ass," giving your center away, trying to be nice
- Manipulating, blackmailing, forcing your way, trying to make order
- Complaining, feeling "sour grapes"; saying "So what!"; ignoring someone
- Backbiting, gossiping, triangulating, having arguments in your mind
- Forgetting your destiny or your Principles
- Panicking, compulsive behavior, addictive behavior, mechanical behavior
- Being embarrassed, saying, "I cannot," feeling stage fright, being stuck at GO
- Losing your attention, being distracted by advertising, snooping, voyeurism
- Hesitating, being speechless, stalling, delaying, oversleeping, daydreaming
- Answering questions with questions, saying, "Of course!"
- Name calling, making fun of someone, imitating someone else's mannerisms
- Interrupting conversations, having to tell your opinion, having to do something
- Saying, "Always," or, "Never," trying to be perfect, trying to be the best
- Thinking that you can win, trying to profit, trying to have power over others
- Trying to hook someone back, trying to piss someone else off
- Pretending to be unhookable… and so on.

The above guide is a map that you can use to find out where you are. The moment you have any of the above behaviors, attitudes or experiences, you are hooked! (Go directly to jail – do not pass GO. Do not collect $200.) It does not work to try to be unhookable once you are already hooked.

The paradox of staying unhookable is that you will always have a Box. If you have a Box, there will always be something that can be hooked into. Clearly, finding unhookability will have to involve numerous nonlinear approaches, because there is no obvious linear approach. Here are twenty-five experiments for staying unhookable. Most of these approaches for staying unhookable are indirectly explained in this book and the terms are defined in the Glossary. Do not expect to already understand them. Rather than looking for a detailed explanation of each one, unzip your imagination and try a few experiments, using whatever you would guess they *might be*, to stay unhookable.

How To Stay Unhookable

1. Place 100 percent of your attention on noticing what is, as it is, right here and now.
2. Put your "being center" on your physical center.

3. Put your attention on your attention; look at what you are looking with.
4. Make no assumptions, make no conclusions, have no expectations.
5. Practice being-with.
6. Listen as a space; be of service to the person speaking, not yourself.
7. Be neutral, without any story at all.
8. Be in complete acceptance.
9. Be the most radiant being in the space.
10. Be yes, be touched by everything and give it no meaning.
11. Make a decision, get off the fence, stand in your own simple clarity.
12. Put your Gremlin's expertise to use in some of these ways:
    - Gremlin sees hooks coming from other Gremlins so if Gremlin is alert he can give you an early warning and you can step sideways out of the line of fire.
    - Keep one of Gremlin's feet outside of every space so you always retain the option to exit any space you are in at any time.
    - Gremlin can stay unhypnotized, so Gremlin can keep you from being duped into smaller perspectives and limiting circumstances.
    - Gremlin can add dimensions to what is possible by going nonlinear.
    - To Gremlin everything is bullshit, meaningless, respectless, and beliefless, so Gremlin has the freedom to offer unpopular opinions, venture into sacred territory, or ask for help from millionaires.
    - Gremlin does not care so can be neither attracted nor repelled, giving Gremlin the ability to be completely steady where other people are reactive and hooked.
    - Gremlin sees every action as theatrical, even his own, so Gremlin can play with alternatives when everyone else is overly serious.

13. Be in the space gap between the inner world and the outer world.
14. Shift your identity so you become a less hookable character and can see the situation through new eyes. For example, replicate the attitude of "Make my day" Harry Callahan, or "Since when do people die from being wet?" Pippi Longstocking. Relate to the situation in accordance with the qualities of the new character.
15. If the interaction is emotionally charged, extract the information from the conversation while putting the energy into a black hole in the ground.
16. Use a "possibility wand" of nonlinearity to declare: "Something completely different from this is possible right now."
17. Use your "sword of clarity" to make distinctions even if there are none in sight.
18. Avoid discussion, defend no position; agree and be on their side.
19. Build and use your low drama detector from 100-yard range.
20. Vanish your Box's baggage, old decisions, incomplete emotions.
21. Use a responsible decoder for receiving communications.
22. Play the game of "Winning Happening," where you win when they win. This means serving Bright Principles.
23. Clean all spaces wherever you are every three seconds.
24. Use a Disk of Nothing (see Glossary).
25. Use a Springscreen (see Glossary).

The intention throughout is not to supply you with techniques or methods. The subjects covered here are too important and complex to be methodologized. Methods and techniques tend to be usurped by the Box's intellect and are then kept on special reserve for cogitation in those moments when you do not really need them. Do what you can *now* with what you have *now*. That means, start observing when and in what ways you are hooked. Out of your careful observations will come your own ways for staying unhookable.

)))(Holding and Navigating Space

A man or woman who establishes themselves in the Adult ego state and does experiments there will sooner or later discover that there are two kinds of space that they are dealing with on a daily basis. First, common ordinary physical space, defined by walls, floor, ceiling, furniture, decorations, sounds, smells and so on. Before now, when we would think of the concept of "space," physical space is all that we would normally think of. The second kind of space is energetic space, defined by attention, intention, quality, tone, mood, purpose, timing, and so on.

Physical space is solid and relatively permanent, compared to energetic space, which is mobile and flexible, having the capacity to change shape, purpose, direction and speed almost instantaneously. Energetic space can have the same dimensions as the surrounding physical space. Energetic space can also have larger or smaller dimensions than the physical space. For example, the space of a conversation between two people in a noisy restaurant is smaller than the physical space of the whole restaurant. The space of the conversation might be a small amorphous bubble enclosing only the two people, making them oblivious to the general noise in the restaurant as a whole.

We are either conscious of these two kinds of spaces or we are not. If we are not conscious that we are, in each moment of every day, involved in both physical spaces *and* subtle energetic spaces, this does not make us immune to the effect of the qualities of energetic spaces. We *are* affected. But, without energetic space-navigation skills, we are powerless to create any difference in what is going on. Simply by adopting the new thought-map that "there is physical space, and right along with it, perhaps even with the same physical dimensions, energetic space," we gain the possibility of making changes that were previously

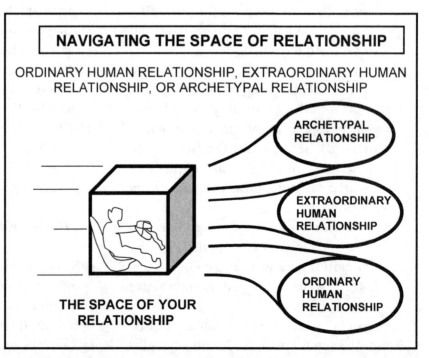

NAVIGATING THE SPACE OF RELATIONSHIP

ORDINARY HUMAN RELATIONSHIP, EXTRAORDINARY HUMAN RELATIONSHIP, OR ARCHETYPAL RELATIONSHIP

ARCHETYPAL RELATIONSHIP

EXTRAORDINARY HUMAN RELATIONSHIP

ORDINARY HUMAN RELATIONSHIP

THE SPACE OF YOUR RELATIONSHIP

too subtle and out of our reach. Navigating energetic space lets us create profound effects at the quick, subtle and complex levels where relationship takes place.

Extending our responsibility to include energetic spaces gives us the possibility to navigate energetic spaces. Navigating space is not much different from driving a car or playing a video game. By navigating space we can choose which direction the space goes, or when and how to leave one space and enter another.

It is worth looking again at the *Map of Navigating the Space of Relationship*. The awareness to develop is that we are choosing every moment where we will go with the space of our relationship: ordinary human relationship, extraordinary human relationship, or Archetypal Relationship. We choose which quality of relationship space to enter through holding and navigating energetic space.

"Holding space" means taking responsibility at the level of energetic space. When I first started learning about holding space I thought holding space meant controlling the space. I became a fanatic for details. I would grip a space so tightly that I would not let anybody move or create anything at all. In that way the space would not get out of my control. But, after awhile, I started noticing that nothing happened in such a petrified space. It was cold, dead, and stiff with rigor mortis. Somehow I had to loosen up and still hold space at the same time. I had to relax and find some way to allow movement without taking my hands off the wheel.

About six months later I found that I could fill a space knee-deep with a kind of energetic mud, a sleepiness from the waist down induced by my own fear of chaos. People were permitted to think and talk, but they were strictly not allowed to feel or take any surprising actions. I thought I had found the solution to holding space because there was a greater freedom of movement and yet the space would not be out

of my control. Unfortunately, the movements were tedious and inauthentic, like trying to dance while carrying a bag of cement. There was no real aliveness, nonlinearity or flow.

During the next six months I experimented with letting myself be more and more afraid and still staying functional. I was terrified of the freedom I gave people to create anything they were moved to create in each next moment, while I still retained responsibility for what happened. Me being afraid but not paralyzed permitted the others to safely erupt with joyous nonlinear creation. Far deeper conversations and interactions could take place than I had ever before suspected. My fear became an ally that gave me a sensitivity to more and more influences. I discovered that spaces had wings like an airplane and, if I could permit a space to zoom fast enough along the ground, I could pull back on the "steering wheel" with my attention and we could lift off into completely unsuspected angles and dimensions, using both Bright and Shadow Principles as fuel for accomplishing the creative tasks set before the group.

The next level of space holding came as a major Box-expansion for me. The expansion occurred when I allowed the Clinton-personality-Box who was holding the space to be replaced by a more expanded set of possibilities, namely, the space-holder-Box. As the specific tendencies of the "Clinton show" relaxed, a more neutral space holder took its place. This not-pre-programmed space holder could shift character according to what was wanted and needed, and in various circumstances could be the father, the man, the husband, the sexual partner, the friend, the enemy, the whining victim, the trainer, the clown, the research scientist, the meeting leader, the artist, the theater performer, or others. The space holder was no longer representing the usual "Clinton" channels with habits and restrictions that I knew. Instead, I created and held a space through which the Principles that I served could do their work, and I was continuously surprised – sometimes even shocked – by the words, attitudes, speech patterns, behavior strategies, opinions and expanded character traits that I exhibited. I shifted from controlling the energetics of a space to navigating the energetics of a space because I was moved by a different purpose. No longer was it "Clinton's" purpose; it was the purpose of the Principles. Suddenly, the relationships I was in and the projects I was doing became far more freed up, interesting and productive than before.

Holding Space (BLTLCH06.13). If you place your expanded "field attention" on the whole of the space you are holding – for example, the entire room you are in with people, or just the two of you at a café table, or even you and the other person not in the same room but in the space of a telephone conversation – and you declare that space as distinct from all other spaces, then you gain the ability to name the Principles that the space itself is called into existence to serve. While you proceed from one space to another space as part of your work together, then, as you enter a space, your first action is to recognize and pay respects to the "presiding deity of the space" – the Bright (or Shadow) character concocted out of the Principles that work through that space. Recognizing and greeting the presiding deity of a space establishes a connection between you as the space navigator and the deity, in such a way that a profitable exchange can occur, a "reciprocal feeding," resulting in a flow of blessings for everyone in the space.

Don't worry if the previous few paragraphs do not make sense to you right now. The concepts come from outside ordinary Western culture and will only become interesting and useful as you develop your space-holding skills. In the meantime, make a mental note that the information is here so you can return to it as needed while experimenting further.

What is crucial for you to know right now is that what happens and what is possible in each conversation or each moment in your relationship does not happen or become possible by "accident." It happens or becomes possible according to what space *you* are holding. The quality of the space is the determining factor. If what is happening right now does not match what you want or need in your relationship, you can simply stay in contact with your partner or with whoever is in the space, then lean your shoulder up against the wall of the space and direct your attention so as to make an energetic sucking gesture. Suddenly you will be in the next space, and whoever was in contact with you will be in the new space with you. Since every space is connected to every other space, you can get to anywhere from here. Again, do not worry about figuring this all out right now. It will come to you through experience.

Bright Principles are aspects of responsibility. Shadow Principles are aspects of irresponsibility. Each space has its own mix of Principles. As you create or enter a space it is helpful to know which Principles are at work and which Principles you can call into that space.

The easiest way to detect what Principles are at work in an energetic space is to continuously ask yourself the experiential questions, "What is the purpose here? What is really going on here?" The answer to your questions will be a whole-body sensing of the set of Bright or Shadow Principles being fulfilled by what is present or what is happening in that space. This way, you will continue to refine your space holding and space navigating skills. It is like learning to read road signs while you are driving so that you can tell what country you are in: ordinary human relationship, extraordinary human relationship, or Archetypal Relationship. With your new driving skills and a few maps you can drive wherever you like.

SECTION 6-M
XNIT Education

The Impact of Nits (BLTLCH06.14). Nits are the tiny, nearly indestructible eggs that lice lay on your hairs. If you don't destroy the nits, they hatch into insects that quickly lay even more eggs and start an entire infestation. The phrase "nit picking" derives from the zealous efforts needed to pick the nits off of your hairs before they hatch. The term nit picking accurately names a hypercritical, finicky, faultfinding behavior that eats away at the foundation of relationships. Nit picking is a specialty of the Box.

Nits are idiosyncratic persnickety opinions, preferences and prejudices that form integral components of every Box. Our Box is so comfortable with *its own* nits that they become invisible, like bad breath to the one who has it. People with similar nits become friends. If we find someone with many nits that match our own, we may marry them. From inside of our Box our own nits look and feel completely normal. But, being near a Box with nits that differ from ours drives us crazy. Since no two Boxes are identical, the potential for nit picking to drive us crazy exists in every relationship.

A sobering consideration is to recognize that, over a period of time, Boxes can become "crystallized." If we forget or ignore the fact that the nits out of which we construct our Box are completely arbitrary and have no true or "God-given" validity, then by our late forties or early fifties our nits can solidify into a self-defending structure. It is like not exercising enough. The less we stretch the less we are able to stretch. Crystallization sneaks up on us and suddenly we can't move at all. Once a Box is crystallized it can be extremely difficult, and perhaps even unwise, to attempt Box expansion – the nits could "break." Better to

remember this idea and make it a practice to flex your nits, mix them up, keep studying and learning, upgrade your nits over the long term. You could probably scan your family, friends and acquaintances, and without much trouble detect a few people with crystallized Boxes: repeating the same stories and complaints over and over again, refusing to try new experiences, blind to physical or verbal feedback, and defending with baseless reasons and excuses. Be careful or "them" becomes us. The older you get the more seriously this applies.

The most confrontational condition for our Box turns out to be the most nurturing condition for our being: relationship. Put any two people together and within a short time, often less than a second, each Box reacts to whatever is different or identical in the design of the other Box. The differences can be miniscule, but the reactions can be enormous. Such reactivity toward an inanimate Box (yours or the other person's) is as insane as cursing ragefully at a chair because you smashed your knee on it. Insane reactivity is the basis of ordinary human relationship.

To enter extraordinary human relationship requires complete clarity about nits. Without a pre-knowledge about the fact that nits exist, and the kinds of nits that exist, your Box instantly absorbs itself with picking at the nits of your partner. Avoiding nit picking comes through understanding how your Box concretizes its own nits into rules. Watch in horror as your Box initiates "I'm right! You're wrong!" battles with your loved ones, even though such a polarity is ridiculous because all nits are subjective and fictional. Even when you have the discipline to restrain your nit-picking monster, your Box can still get hooked and explode in reaction to the insidious nit picking of other peoples' Boxes.

Although not a pretty sight, having clarity about nit picking is a catalyst that inserts a gap in your Box's reaction mechanism. With a gap in the works, the reaction gears cannot mesh and the emotional force of the reaction has nothing to grab onto. As if you coated your tires with grease, the reaction freewheels without effect and eventually stalls out, going back to neutrality. With a little practice, the time from reaction to stall-out can shrink down to three seconds. When your internal nit reactions do not get to cause any external actions (such as words or gestures), then your being gets to stay centered, present, respectful, and attentive. Nit reactions that previously may have blown you out of kilter for days or weeks can now pass in a few moments. All the energy you conserve can then be directed toward more interesting experiments.

All Boxes have nits because Boxes are made out of nits. Box reactions to nit conflicts are completely unavoidable. What is avoidable is being identified or hooked into fully participating in your Box's reaction. Staying unhookable comes from the clarity that nits are nothing more than nits.

List of Common Nits

Nits vary from subculture to subculture, from status to status, from age to age. Here are 100 typical nits from early twenty-first century Western civilization.

1. When to empty the trashcan (e.g., For one Box the trashcan must be emptied if it has anything in it at all. For another Box the trashcan is regretfully emptied only when not another thing can be stuffed into it and pieces overflow onto the floor. Neither is right. Neither is wrong. The perceptions and the associated thoughts and feelings are all propelled by nits!)
2. How to hang the laundry
3. Where to put things in the refrigerator
4. How to know when the spaghetti is ready
5. How much salt to put in the potatoes
6. How loud is loud (music, arguing kids, television)
7. How much is enough light to read by
8. How strong is good coffee
9. How to fold the sheets while making the bed
10. Which boundaries are necessary for healthy children
11. How to parallel park the car
12. The best procedure for drying the dishes
13. The proper way to squeeze toothpaste out of the tube
14. When is the toothpaste tube actually empty
15. When do the windows or mirrors actually need cleaning

---

16. Whose job is it to pay the bills, maintain the cars, get rid of bugs or rodents, change the light bulbs
17. How friendly to be with the neighbors
18. How much time with the relatives is too much time with the relatives
19. What words to use when answering the telephone
20. How to clean the toilet when it is dirty
21. Who cleans the toilet when it is dirty
22. Do toilets even get dirty?
23. When to use credit cards; how much cash to carry
24. How much suntan a person needs to be healthy or beautiful
25. How to dress appropriately for each occasion
26. How long is needed in the bathroom
27. When to arrive: early, exactly on time, five minutes late, twenty minutes late
28. What constitutes a good breakfast
29. When to eat lunch or dinner
30. How much fat around the middle is too much fat
31. The importance of self-improvement or spiritual work
32. The value of art; what to hang in the hallway
33. How many knick-knacks to have around the house
34. The importance of knowing the news
35. The entertainment value of sports
36. How to load the dishwasher
37. When does the car need cleaning
38. How much is the dog a member of the family; where does the dog sleep
39. How to play tennis together: to win or to enjoy the exercise and the company?
40. How to pull the weeds, cut the hedges, plant the flowers; are there weeds?
41. How badly cat piss smells
42. How much is enough ice cream
43. How much is too much sugar for the kids
44. How to decorate the living room
45. What books or magazines are worth keeping around the house
46. How many extra plastic bags or empty cardboard boxes do we need
47. How many rubber bands to keep and where
48. What should go on the refrigerator
49. Who are our friends
50. What constitutes fun
51. How much time off equates to a vacation
52. How important is politics

53. How much effort to use recycling
54. Where to go for a good restaurant meal
55. What makes a good melon
56. What makes a good man
57. What should a functional desk look like
58. How to organize the tax papers
59. What to do about writing Christmas thank-you cards
60. What about the children's school grades
61. When is something dusty enough to require dusting or vacuuming
62. Who to call to personally wish them a Happy Birthday
63. Do we say a prayer or not say a prayer before meals
64. Do we get married; what last name does the wife take; wedding rings
65. What is a good movie
66. How late is too late to stay up
67. What is a funny joke
68. What is good sex
69. What is too much or not enough sex
70. How much is too much television; how many televisions to have
71. Who decides how we drive there; who reads the map
72. When to shovel the snow; how perfectly should it be shoveled
73. What to keep in the freezer
74. Where to clean the fish
75. How many packages of chips to buy
76. Where to shop for the best grocery deals
77. Floss teeth before or after brushing; floss teeth at all
78. Where to put the dirty clothes; when are clothes actually dirty
79. When to fill the car up with gas; where; who checks the oil
80. How many pairs of shoes to own
81. How many movies are too many movies; buy or rent
82. Where to keep notepaper and pens
83. Where to keep the keys
84. To color or not color the hair; makeup or no makeup; how long hair
85. Sexual apparatus or not; sexual stimulants or not
86. How much sleep is really needed
87. To go to church or not; to belong to a church or not
88. How many vitamins to take
89. How much time to spend exercising
90. How long to stay on the telephone
91. How late should the kids stay out

92. Should our daughter have an older boyfriend
93. What clothes are decent for a teenager
94. How much money to owe to banks or other people
95. How much is too much alcohol, gambling, or drugs
96. How much emergency food or supplies to keep around the house
97. How much insurance to have
98. When to mow the lawn; when to cut the shrubbery
99. Are potatoes and carrots better peeled or with the skins on
100. What constitutes flirting

Once you know that nits are nits and "there ain't no arguin' about nits," you can start using your Box's sensitivity to nits as an irresponsibility detector. If you find yourself overreacting to nits it can indicate that you are low on tolerance because you are not taking care of yourself. *It is your responsibility to take care of yourself.* If you do not take care of yourself you become overly sensitive to nits and a needy burden to the other people around you. Your Gremlin may get a big "kick" out of being needy, because then he or she can manipulate all the rescuers and nice people around you; but being needy is not a basis of extraordinary human relationship.

Take Care of Yourself

A clarification is necessary here. *Taking care of yourself* does not mean always making sure that you are comfortable. Taking care of yourself means making sure that your decisions and actions are resonant to your true purposes. Being resonant to your true purposes is not stress free. The stress that arises through being resonant to your true purposes provides useful nutrients needed for building matrix.

In this section I am not talking about this kind of stress. I am talking about the kind of stress that results from deceiving yourself and trying to look good instead of taking responsible care of yourself. Ignoring your true purposes throws you into a self-perpetuating stress cycle: try to look good – behave out of alignment with yourself – feel stressed out – try to look good. This cycle is a direct highway to ordinary human relationship.

Start using stress as an irresponsibility detector. Instead of denying stress, numbing out to stress, or complaining about stress, recognize and accept your stress with gratitude as useful information. Signs of stress such as crankiness, sleeplessness, overreacting, nervousness, illness, accidents, or psychological breakdown are signals pointing to exactly where you are being irresponsible. Follow the signal back to its source. Where you are being irresponsible is where you can start taking care of yourself.

To experiment with responsibly taking care of yourself, try this. Creatively change your circumstances to alleviate stress rather than playing out the role of being a victim of the circumstances. Be proactive. You can feel stress coming long before it arrives. Take action immediately, before you are forced to act. Lower your sensitivity bar so that you become more perceptive of your environment and its impact on your body, mind, heart, and soul. Say yes or say no to make decisions and boundaries before the stress gets so high that your nervous system goes into breakdown and makes the decisions for you. For example: Take a nap. Turn off the cell phone. Take another nap. Drink water. Draw pictures for no purpose. Lie in the sun. Have a carrot juice for lunch. Say no to houseguests. Take a long bath. Go to bed at nine o'clock. Get rid of the dog. Walk barefoot in the grass. Do twenty-five pushups. Talk with a trusted friend and ask them to give you a stress interview where they repeatedly ask you what causes stress in your life and you write down the answers. Immediately change the top three items on your list by vanishing the stressful circumstances, or creating a more responsible story for yourself about why you have involved yourself in these circumstances. For example, if you are stressed out about your husband watching too much television, either throw out the television or decide that you love your husband more than the television, and insert your ear plugs, sit down next to your husband, put your feet in his lap and read a book.

Extraordinary human relationship does not come from finding someone who has nits that harmonize with your own. Finding the perfect man or woman is a mental-fantasy construct that has no relationship to reality. You can count on your Box persistently reacting to some of your partner's nits no matter how profoundly you love them. Extraordinary human relationship comes from familiarity with your Box's nit-picking habits, and letting the Box do its own thing without believing your Box's propaganda about what it is doing. Instead, you notice your Box's reaction and think to yourself, "Ah, the Box is nit picking again. Fascinating." And then go on about your business of navigating to extraordinary human relationship.

Consider Forgetting Your Rules

Through your every thought, feeling, word and action you choose which quality of relationship to establish in any moment, ordinary or extraordinary. Many formative actions are so subtle that you might not even regard them as actions. For example, presenting logical thinking to explain your point of view may seem irreducibly necessary in your interactions. It may take some time before you would grant that logic is not particularly suited for creating extraordinary human relationship. If you have developed the most inarguable sequence of logic to explain why something should be done a certain way and why your nits are right, you may consistently win in a battle of nits. But, when you win, your partner loses. And when your partner loses, what have you really won? Rationality has its uses but not necessarily in building extraordinary relationship.

Those times when a nit is screaming logical arguments in your head are good times to remember your priorities about what kind of relationship space you want to navigate into (and also good times to remember your Voice Blaster!). You declare your priorities through your actions. What you say and do will declare whether you have chosen to be right or to be in relationship. You choose either the Box's survival purpose or your soul's life-enhancing purpose. Logic will not help you make that choice.

One day, as my partner was washing the breakfast dishes, I picked up a towel to dry them. She had just rinsed the frying pan and I intercepted it on its way to the drying rack. "No, no, no, no, *no!*" she said, refusing to let me take the frying pan from her hand. I said, "Okay," and started drying the other dishes. She realized that her Box had freaked out about me wanting to dry the frying pan and she started inquiring internally as to what it was about. She discovered a nit, a logically supported preference that was self-made into a rule about how to dry the dishes. Probably she copied it from her mother. Finally she said, "So what do I *do*? For me, after years of experience, I have found the *best* method for drying the dishes. Let me explain it to you. Start with the glasses and silverware. This way the towel is driest, absorbs water more efficiently, and leaves no streaks or water spots on the glasses or silverware. Next, dry the dishes. Then, afterward, dry the pots and pans. It is very simple. I always use this method."

As we discussed the circumstance, we started to realize how pervasively nits rule our lives and kill with logic the possibility of other possibilities. Nits that we have hardened into rules prevent us from navigating into spaces that serve purposes other than logical expediency. In the case with the dish drying, only two people ate breakfast. There were so few dishes that the dish towel could not possibly have gotten wet enough to leave streaks or water spots, no matter what order the dishes were dried in. Using the dish-drying method as a rule, killed the tender physical intimacy of passing the frying pan from her to me. What was killed was the opportunity for a direct experience of nearness in a space that was not exclusively dedicated to intimacy. With her sharp degrading, "No, no, no, no, *no!*" I was treated like a little boy being scolded by his all-knowing mommy for doing something wrong. The rule killed

the possibility of extraordinary human relationship. That is, until we started honestly investigating what was going on. The conversation *about* the conversation opened up intimacies that took us directly back into the extraordinary.

The point is that the Box has nits. The Box having nits is unavoidable. The Box is made out of nits. But you have the choice of deciding whether or not a nit is treated as a rule. When a nit gets triggered, all the Box's defenses react. Now that you know that the Box is reacting to an internal self-created nit, you know your reaction is not caused by the other person. Your feelings of rage or fear or sorrow come from the Box's *story* about what is happening, not from what is happening. This clarity gives you the chance to notice your nit's rule with objective neutrality and the possibility of letting the whole reaction bypass you in three seconds while taking no actions. You stay in the present. The reaction fades into the past. Then, you can start over, unhooked.

Notice your nits. Regard them as just nits. Consciousness creates freedom. Nits are neither right nor wrong. They are nits. Just nits. You do not have to make your nits into rules that cement you into certain rigid, logically-defendable patterns of behavior. Instead, you can live. You can float in a luscious, fluidic, reciprocal, responsive relationship to what is needed and wanted in the abundant life happening around you.

Meta-Conversations

Creating Meta-Conversations (BLTLCH06.15). One way to create greater authenticity for yourself, your relationship or your organization is to navigate into a liquid state through having a conversation about the conversation, as was described in the dish-drying example above. Having a conversation about the conversation is called a "meta-conversation."

The way to enter a meta-conversation is to place your attention outside the limits of the original conversation, turn around and look back where you came from, and then speak from *outside* the conversation about what you observe happening *inside* the conversation. Start speaking together about the way the speaking is happening. Talk about how the talking is going. Change the topic of the conversation to the conversation itself. Find the purpose behind the original conversation.

Developing the ability to create meta-conversations takes practice. The first step is the most difficult: placing your attention outside the limits of the original conversation. We are so easily hypnotized into the present story that we occlude our responsible ability to extemporize alternative and perhaps more productive stories, which are possible in every circumstance. When the kids are screaming at each other, or the husband is complaining, we tend to believe the reality of their feelings,

their reasons and their perceived behavior options. The "possibility wand" that gives you the power to go nonlinearly outside of the limits of the present conversation is a declaration that you make. The declaration is: "Something completely different from this is possible right now." In both the ordinary and extraordinary human domains this declaration is always true. (In the Archetypal domains this declaration is not always true, but we will get to that later.)

It requires a samurai's relaxed alertness, and a pirate's "Rules? What rules?" attitude to extend what is possible for you personally beyond any conversation limits that are proposed. A conversation limit is only an offer. You don't have to accept that offer unconditionally. Ever.

Having a meta-conversation lets you ask questions that are not permitted from within the original conversation. Your extracurricular inquiry generates clarity and possibility that were not previously visible or allowed. It is the new clarity itself that initiates the liquid state. Clearly seeing the organizational force

---

MAP OF CREATING A META-CONVERSATION

A three-step procedure for navigating to the liquid state where change can happen.

1. Place your attention outside the limits of the original conversation.
2. Turn around and look back where you just came from.
3. Start speaking from outside the conversation about what you observe happening inside the conversation. This is a meta-conversation.

Step 1 is the most difficult because we are so easily hypnotized into the present story that we block our responsible ability to shift to a different story. The idea is that totally new and perhaps more productive stories can be extemporized in every circumstance.

field behind the Box's perspective disorganizes the force field. The perceptual prison is left behind and suddenly we can see from a new perspective.

Starting a meta-conversation can change the purpose or the context of the original conversation into a purpose or a context that would never have otherwise been reached.

Meta-Conversation Starters

- Why is this thing that you are talking about so important to you?
- Why are we talking about this anyway?
- Twice now you have failed to answer my question. What is going on for you about this?
- My Box is freaking out about what you just did. Did you notice that too? I must have an expectation or a belief about this. Could you help me track it down?
- What is your purpose in saying that? What is it that you are trying to accomplish?
- I notice an undertone of some feeling in your voice. Can you say more about that?
- It seems like you are trying to create an argument with me. I am not interested in arguing. Can you say what you want to say in another way?
- Do you realize that you have interrupted me three times in the last few minutes? Is there something you do not want to hear from me?
- Where are you trying to go with this? Is there another way we could get there?
- I noticed your jaw muscles clenching. Are you feeling something?
- You have just changed the subject of the conversation. I am not ready to change the subject of this conversation yet. Are you willing to complete the original conversation with me?
- Could it be that you are trying to prove yourself right? Would you be willing to have another purpose in this conversation?
- Could there be something in this that frightens you?
- What is it that you really want to say to me? Where are you going with this?
- What if we stepped back a bit and checked in about our individual desires?
- It seems that you are saying two things at once. Could you please say them separately?
- We seem to be having an intellectual discussion about what we already know and I am more interested in exploring something that we don't know. What would you say to that?
- I hear what you are *thinking*. I would also like to know what you are *feeling*.
- I think you might be using an assumption that is not true. What do you think?
- Could it be that you are claiming to be a victim of these circumstances?
- Perhaps you do not realize that I agree with you.
- I am grateful for the passion with which you speak about what really matters to you.
- It seems to me like what you just said is a manipulation and disrespects our relationship as partners. Could you share about how that was for you?
- Tell me something that would help me to understand you better.

This makes meta-conversations an excellent tool for shifting ordinary human relationship into extraordinary human relationship.

Meta-conversations are started with meta-conversation starters. That sounds simple enough, except that the Box has a strong bias against us having meta-conversation starters in our common vocabulary. I personally have had to make specific efforts to memorize meta-conversation starter-phrases so that they were available in the moments when they would be most useful. Without memorizing them, I would have completely forgotten that meta-conversations existed. What is astonishing is that, if you can remember to use meta-conversation starters, they do their job very well. The resultant intimacies and authenticities can be well worth the risk you take by asking such questions.

Many of the meta-conversation starters listed are completely foreign to our ordinary ways of speaking. For an experiment, choose three of these sentences and memorize them so they are on the tip of your tongue at all times. Then, use your selected meta-conversation starters during the next few days and see what happens.

Having a conversation about the conversation creates the possibility of possibility. This makes meta-conversations a central tool for navigating into extraordinary human relationship where possibility is abundant. The keys to being able to start a meta-conversation are: 1. possessing your attention so that you can move your attention about freely, 2. being centered so that you are not giving your authority away, and 3. *going nonlinear* so that you are not limited by the apparent reality barriers offered by the space of a conversation.

Meta-Conversations with Children

In just a few moments, having a meta-conversation with your child can create wonders that you may have already concluded could never occur. In general, children less than fifteen years old are still in the testing and formatory stages of Box building. The structure of their Box is still being determined. After fifteen years of age, the Box tends to stop evolving and start crystallizing, unless a person is brought through some kind of rite of passage where they become cognizant of and take responsibility for having a Box. A child has more flexible habits than an adult. When you, as an adult, initiate a conversation about the conversation with a child, the child will usually slip right into the new conditions with an easefulness that would startle most adults.

The reason adults fail to create meta-conversations with children is not that the children cannot go there with them; it is that the adults avoid functioning from the perspective that the conversation that is happening right now is *not* the only possible conversation that could be happening right now. We adults tend to defend the original options that our Box allows us to see, as if these were the only options that could be seen. So, when a child-adult conflict arises, the adults shift into a power struggle using physical size, physical strength, age, position, role, education, or financial status as weapons to overpower the child into submission.

Isaac Asimov used to say, "Violence is the last refuge of the incompetent." The adult's particular incompetence in this case is the inability to "go nonlinear" – that is, to not assume that the present conversation or struggle that you are having right now with your child is the only possible conversation that could be happening. In fact, many other kinds of conversations are available, and waiting for you to enter. All that you as the adult need to do to get there is to start a meta-conversation. If you start a meta-conversation, the child will tend to join

Meta-Conversations You Could Have With Your Children

- This living room is not a jungle gym. How can you do what you want to do without using this room like a jungle gym?
- A relationship between brothers / sisters is an honor and a privilege. Through teasing or physical violence you lose the privilege of being together. Each of you please go into a different room for the next two hours. Then we can speak about what you are asking for that is expressed in fighting.
- I notice that you are talking a lot just to fill up the space with your voice. What is really going on for you behind all this talking?
- It looks like you are having a feeling. What feeling is that?
- Is there a problem? Whose problem is this?
- How do you like how it is going so far?
- Did I hear you well? Could you give me another chance to hear what you are saying?
- What are your biggest complaints about being a child in this family?
- It seems that you disagree. Can you propose some other options?
- How was that for you?
- I hear your reasoning. What I said is a boundary. I will not argue reasons about this. But I would like to know more about what you need. Then perhaps we can find a different way to get there together.
- What is really going on here?
- This choice is up to you. No matter what you choose I love you and I respect you.
- This is what I want to do. What do you want to do?
- What could you tell me so that I could get to know you better?

you immediately in the new world opened up by the meta-conversation. Not only that, but the child will learn how to go nonlinear and make meta-conversations themselves in their lives. I still remember when my daughters, in their early teens, first started using meta-conversations on me and their mother to create what they really wanted for themselves instead of being trapped by the limits of what their mother and I could imagine was best for them. The children will use this ability for the rest of their lives.

An important element in successful communication with children is your ability to listen. The adage, "Children are to be seen and not heard," runs deep in our culture. When children are not heard and are also not given boundaries to work with, they will take over spaces and do anything to get adult attention, even if all they get is negative attention. When we make our cursory attempts to listen to children and find them speaking nonsense, we only strengthen our commitment to the adage. You can discover richness and depth in your communications with children (and with adults) when you use meta-conversations to distinguish between babble and authentic sharing.

Using Adult Communication

Love, they say, is a function of communication. When you think about it, this makes sense. When you look from the Adult perspective, what is the purpose behind communication? What is the central message behind every communication? Why do people communicate with each other? Why do people talk to you? When someone talks to you what is the core energetic of every communication?

We do not often recognize, consciously, that the core message in every communication, no matter what the communication is, is "I love you." Even when a person says, "I hate you," the core message in that communication is, "I love you," *or they would not bother telling you that they hate you.* They would just not bother to communicate with you at all. Let this idea sink in for awhile. The prime motivator that transports every communication is deep caring love.

Now you have an important experiment to do. Use the proposal that "I love you" is the underlying message in every communication you receive and see what happens. To do the experiment, split your attention. Use 50 percent of your attention to listen to what a person is saying to you, to read their note, their letter, their email, etc. And at the same time use the other 50 percent of your attention to remember that what is moving them to communicate to you is their love for you. Beneath all the layers, even within complaints, blaming, ridicule, or negative feedback, the motivating force of the communication is love. What they are really saying in so many words is, "I love you." With this Adult perspective in place, notice what happens to the quality of your relating. Spend time enjoying what you notice.

As explained on the *Map of Communication*, the purpose of Adult communication is to complete communications. The underlying principle of Adult communication is that a communication persists until it is received. Receiving communications completes them. When a communication is completed, that communication vanishes with a "Bing!" and you sink to the next subtler layer in the communication.

Communications often have many layers. Through receiving communications, we complete layer after layer and move ever closer to the central message, which is "I love you." If we do not receive the first layer of a communication, in whatever way it is offered to us, then the further and perhaps more important layers will never be revealed. If a communication is not completed, the communicator is frustrated and must try again later, in some other way. By blocking communications we are saying *no* to love.

As it is, we do not know how to receive and complete communications. We have not been trained. In fact, we have been trained in the opposite, how to avoid receiving and completing communications. The avoidance of receiving and completing communications is a characteristic of ordinary human relationship. Again, if we wish to enter extraordinary human relationship, we have to learn new skills. In this case, we need to learn and practice receiving and completing communications.

Communication originates in the conscious and unconscious intentions of the sender. The sender experiences an urge to communicate and then does the best they can to encode the communication into a form that can be transmitted to the receiver. Most often

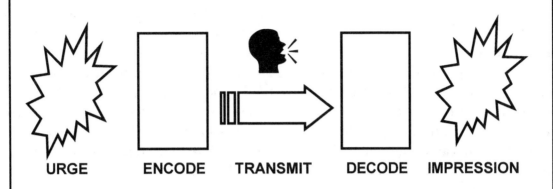

MAP OF COMMUNICATION (partial)

A communication persists until it is received.

URGE   ENCODE   TRANSMIT   DECODE   IMPRESSION

We think this is how communication works. However this map is incomplete. *Half of the process is missing!* Without including the other half of the process our communications fail because they are not completed.

the encoding is spoken language, either directly in person, over the phone, or through some other media. Encoding can also include written or typed words, drawings, musical notes, schematic diagrams, designs, shapes, or constructed objects. In whatever form the message is encoded and transmitted, the receiver must then decode the message to receive the communication, as shown on the map.

As you know from experience, this urge-encode-transmit-decode-impression process is lightening fast, delicate, complicated, and quite susceptible to glitches, assumptions, errors, expectations, misinterpretations, mixed messages, projections, crossed communications and so on.

In addition, we *assume* that this diagram of the communication process is complete, and *it is not complete!* We do not realize the consequences of using this incomplete communication model. Our fractional understanding of communication causes failure and breakdown in most of our relationships, and traps us in the ordinary no matter what else we try.

The missing component of our communication process is the "completion loop" where the listener repeats back to the speaker what they heard the speaker say. If what the listener repeats accurately reflects what the speaker said, the speaker almost involuntarily says, "Yes." When the speaker hears himself saying "Yes," he confirms that the listener has indeed heard his original message and something relaxes. You can see the relaxation happen. The speaker's original intention is satisfied because the communication comes back to where it started. The completion loop consumes the original urge and the whole communication vanishes into itself. Acceptance has occurred. With the first communication fulfilled, a completely new communication can begin. But, until the first communication has been completed, no new communication can start.

Thousands of intelligent people in trainings have consistently demonstrated that they do not know how to generate a completion loop. Few of us have ever had a communications class. We learned to communicate by imitating the communications delivered to us. Few of our parents ever had a communications class either. Largely by imitating our parents, we learned to generate communication roadblocks instead of completion loops.

Roadblocks to Adult Communication

Dr. Thomas Gordon described twelve communication "roadblocks" in his groundbreaking book *Parent Effectiveness Training*. When I first read this list it shattered my world. I had to copy the list and carry it around with me, and read it whenever I was communicating with someone. I had no idea how to communicate without killing communications with roadblocks. A roadblock is whatever you say – no matter what it is – that does not repeat back and prove you heard what was said. My habit to deliver roadblocks was so deep that I had to start all over with my communications. Probably you do too. (Sorry...)

Plan on being consciously (meaning painfully) incompetent for three to six months, as it takes about that long to make a shift in communication habits. But do it. Make the effort, now, before more time goes by. Whole new worlds of trust and intimacy can open up as

---

Twelve Roadblocks

Communication	Response
1) "I hate you."	"Shut your mouth. Do not say things like that to me!"

Roadblock #1: ORDERING / DIRECTING / COMMANDING

2) "I hate you."	"Say that again and I will walk out this door!"

Roadblock #2: WARNING / ADMONISHING / THREATENING

3) "I hate you."	"Good people do not hate. If you hate it comes back to you."

Roadblock #3: MORALIZING / PREACHING / PHILOSOPHIZING

4) "I hate you."	"Maybe you should do rage work or see a psychologist."

Roadblock #4: ADVISING / GIVING SOLUTIONS / GIVING SUGGESTIONS

5) "I hate you."	"Hate comes from misunderstandings or sloppy thinking."

Roadblock #5: LECTURING / TEACHING / GIVING LOGICAL ARGUMENTS

6) "I hate you."	"It is stupid to say that. You caused this argument anyway!"

Roadblock #6: JUDGING / CRITICISING / DISAGREEING / BLAMING

7) "I hate you."	"You are so brave to express yourself. I understand."

Roadblock #7: PRAISING / AGREEING

8) "I hate you."	"You are overreacting again! Look how red your face is!"

Roadblock #8: NAME CALLING / RIDICULING / SHAMING

9) "I hate you."	"Probably you are just tired and your blood sugar is low."

Roadblock #9: INTERPRETING / ANALYZING / DIAGNOSING

10) "I hate you."	"It's alright honey. I'll help do things and you will feel better."

Roadblock #10: REASSURING / SYMPATHIZING / CONSOLING / SUPPORTING

11) "I hate you."	"What's wrong? When did you start feeling this way?"

Roadblock #11: PROBING / QUESTIONING / INTERROGATING

12) "I hate you."	"Just when I was thinking of getting ice cream. Want to go?"

Roadblock #12: WITHDRAWING / DISTRACTING / HUMORING / DIVERTING

---

a result of you learning to stop making roadblocks and start making completion loops.

Even giving intelligent suggestions or providing sincere sympathy destroys the completion loop and therefore kills the relationship simply because *what you say does not complete the communication*. The speaker cannot experience being heard by you if you do not repeat back what you heard them say. When you seriously consider this list of roadblocks most people come away thinking, "My God! What else is there? This is all I ever say in my communications."

The Completion Loop

Completion Loops (BLTLCH06.16). Using the completion loop can feel remarkably strange at first. All you are doing is repeating back what you heard the person say. Repeating back what a person says is not a normal part of our typical speech patterns because we already know what we want to say before the other person has even finished with their sentence. We are not really listening to them with our heart and soul; we are dueling with them with our mind. As a result most of our conversations occur between intellect and intellect, rather than between the whole complex of four bodies.

Mind chatter is like Ping Pong: *Ka-ping ka-pong ka-ping ka-pong ka-ping ka-pong*, the communication zips back and forth between intellects, never really landing in our souls. We give each other ideas, but walk away feeling a kind of emptiness, because we have not really connected and shared ourselves. We have not let ourselves be known. True, head-to-head communication feels safer (to Westerners). But what is so great about feeling safe anyway? Communicating from heart to heart may well be the exciting adventure that provides the energetic food our soul has been hungering for. The adventure starts with you learning Adult communication that includes completion loops. When using completion loops our communications quickly get to the heart of the matter. Sit for awhile with this next example of how communication can be when you finally use the completion loop.

Communication	Response
1) "I hate you."	"You hate me."

Completion Loop: REPEATING BACK WHAT YOU HEARD THEM SAY

2) "Yes."   BING! (The "yes" is the "Bing!" the sound of a completed communication. You have finally listened. The speaker has the experience that you have actually heard what they said to you. Now their next deeper message can *finally* be communicated to you!)

3) "I hate you because you never listen to me when I tell you that I love you."

Completion loops also work when communicating with children. So often we adults assume that we already know about children (after all, we were one once), that we already know about our children (after all, we have been living with them since they were born), and that we already know what the children are communicating to us (after all, we have already heard it a million times from them). We consistently react with one of the twelve roadblocks because we think this is the most expedient way to handle the kids (after all, kids are problems that are *our* job to handle…). *So much is missed.*

Listen to this sample conversation between twelve-year-old Johnny and his Dad:

Johnny: "Dad, I hate school."
Typical answer with roadblocks: "You can't hate school. Everybody has to go to school. I had to go to school and for me it was a privilege. If you don't go to school you won't learn what you need to get a good job. Then you will be out there on the streets picking up garbage

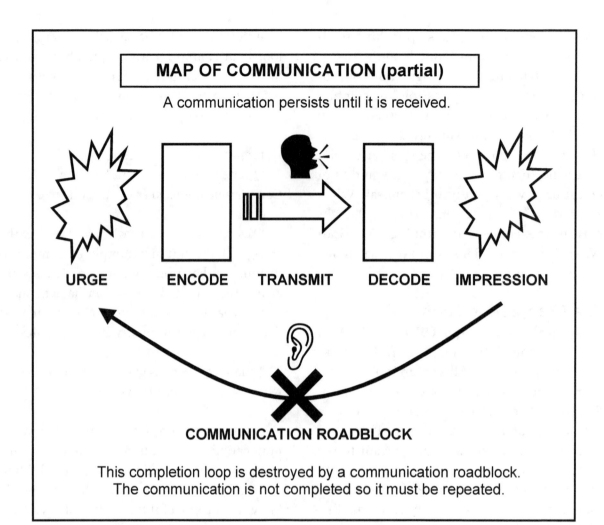

MAP OF COMMUNICATION (partial)

A communication persists until it is received.

URGE   ENCODE   TRANSMIT   DECODE   IMPRESSION

COMMUNICATION ROADBLOCK

This completion loop is destroyed by a communication roadblock.
The communication is not completed so it must be repeated.

for a living. Do you want that? Just buckle down and do your homework. Only eight more years to go. Say, do you want to help me remodel grandpa's living room this weekend?"

Now this time, the same communication but with completion loops:

Johnny: "Dad, I hate school."

Dad: "You hate school."

Johnny: "Yes." (That "yes" is the automatic *Bing!* of a received and completed communication. You have just won the battle against your Box jumping in with what it wants to say. Instead *you* are listening, not your Box. Your goal is to complete as many communication loops as you can, knowing that at the heart of each communication is the

message "I love you." You just used a completion loop. Can you do it again? And again?) "Yes. I really hate school. Especially my teacher Mr. Dandy."

Dad: "You hate Mr. Dandy." (Make sure that you are not asking a question. You are simply repeating back what you heard him say. Add no spin.)

Johnny: "Yes." (*Bing #2!*) "He is such a jerk! He yelled at me in math class today."

Dad: "Mr. Dandy yelled at you in math class."

Johnny: "Yes, and all the kids laughed at me."

Dad: "All the kids laughed at you."

Johnny: "He didn't have to yell at me. All I was doing was passing a note."

Dad: "You were just passing a note."
Johnny: "Yeah, to Priscilla."
Dad: "To Priscilla."
Johnny: "Yeah, she's this new girl. I was thinking of inviting her to the pool this weekend."
Dad: "You want to invite Priscilla to the pool this weekend."
Johnny: "Yeah. Dad, could you take me and Priscilla to the pool this weekend? She's really great."
Dad: "You want me to take you and Priscilla to the pool this weekend?"
Johnny: "Yeah."

The final "Yeah," without further explanations from the child, means that you have come to the central communication, the message that was buried under the original communication "I hate school." Notice that the central communication had *nothing at all* to do with hating school. By listening with completion loops, you were able to make it safe enough to hear the deeper message, a delicate and precious communication about love. Notice that you would *never* have gotten to hear the real communication if you had reacted with roadblocks to the surface communication. How many opportunities for deeply connecting have you destroyed with your habitual roadblocks?

Was using completion loops difficult for Dad? No. Was it great for Johnny? Yes. Was it great for Dad even though he did not get to do his ordinary thing? You have to answer that question yourself.

How many times have you wished that your parents or other people would listen to you like this? Your children can have deep communication with their future children if you start communicating with them with completion loops. It starts with you. Your struggle to change can make a difference for many generations into the future.

Notice in the above example that the end of communication leaves a question in Dad's lap. The question is a real question and requires a real yes or no answer, not a vague procrastination, not a "We'll see." Communications with children often end with a problem in the parent's lap. This is a common reason why parents avoid conversations with their children; they do not want to have to commit to the time and energy required of a "yes" answer, or to deal with the child's reaction to a "no" answer. The parent wants to avoid responsibility.

You have just discovered the reason why your Box so persistently uses roadblocks in your communications. Using a roadblock instead of a completion loop is the Box's technology for avoiding responsibility. Every roadblock causes a breakdown in the heart of your relationship. Your Box prefers to create a breakdown in the heart of your relationship rather than having to take responsibility itself for shifting or for dealing with the emotional recoil of the other person's Box when it must shift or expand.

Problem Ownership (BLTLCH06.17). To deepen authenticity in your relationships your practice is to stop trying to avoid responsibility. Look at what you are demonstrating to your children. Again, boundaries are the jungle gym upon which children develop their muscles of responsibility. Pull out your "sword of clarity." Say yes or say no, and then be responsible about your decision. The *Map of Problem Ownership* creates distinctions for you that give you tremendous clarity about how to deal with these kinds of problems.

The question clarified by the *Map of Problem Ownership* is: Whose problem is it? Without knowing how or why, we often act in confusion about who owns a problem. It is common to conclude that if someone else has a problem – our child, parent, spouse or boss – then automatically we have a problem. This is especially true if we tend to be adaptive and

```
┌─────────────────────────────────────────────────────────┐
│        ┌─────────────────────────────────────┐           │
│        │     MAP OF PROBLEM OWNERSHIP         │           │
│        └─────────────────────────────────────┘           │
│                                                           │
│                 WHOSE PROBLEM IS IT?                      │
│                                                           │
│                          ┌──────────────────────────────┐│
│                          │                              ││
│    ACCEPTABLE            │   THEY HAVE A PROBLEM         ││
│    SITUATION             │                              ││
│    (my needs are met)    ├──────────────────────────────┤│
│                          │                              ││
│                          │   THERE IS NO PROBLEM        ││
│                          │                              ││
│                          ├──────────────────────────────┤│
│    UNACCEPTABLE          │                              ││
│    SITUATION             │   I HAVE A PROBLEM           ││
│    (my needs are not     │                              ││
│    met, and perhaps      ├──────────────────────────────┤│
│    theirs aren't either) │   WE HAVE A PROBLEM          ││
│                          │                              ││
│                          └──────────────────────────────┘│
└───────────────────────────────────────────────────────────┘
```

Me having a problem does not mean *they* have a problem. *Them* having a problem does not mean *I* have a problem. Let them have their own problems – they worked hard for them. Take responsibility for your own problems. Dealing with a problem is evolution's way for you to learn what you need to learn. Through being clear about whose problem it is you discover an interesting condition of having no problem. This place may be bigger than you think. Clarifying which of the four problem conditions you have empowers you to apply the most appropriate skills. (This map is adapted from the "Behavior Window" originated by Dr. Thomas Gordon in the 1960s and further developed by his wife Linda Adams in her book *Be Your Best*. www.gordontraining.com)

give our center away. If the authority figure has a problem (and it is shocking how many people regard their children as authority figures), then we better watch out. As a survival strategy, we extend our feelings into the lives of others and walk on eggshells around them to try to arrange it so that they never have a problem. They probably like it when we are adaptive around them, accept their invitation and give them our center, but such behavior is ordinary human relationship and can drive us into being a nervous wreck.

Using the *Map of Problem Ownership* vastly simplifies things. The idea is to respect people for their creativity. If someone else has a problem it does not mean that you have a problem. They worked hard for their problem. They created their problem. Let them have their own problem. If you have made a boundary for your child, the decision is made – the question of whether or not to have ice cream, to see another movie, or to stay up past bedtime has been decided; it is no longer *your* problem. It is your *child's* problem. Let them have their problem. And let them work it out for themselves and go through dealing with the boundary without being able to use whining, shunning, name-calling, or tantrums to manipulate you into deciding differently. They will get over it.

On the other hand, if you have a problem, get it that it is *your* problem. You having a problem is not a problem for anybody else. Take responsibility for having created the problem as a custom-designed learning environment for yourself. Dealing with problems is how we learn what we need to learn.

Once you extract yourself from imagining that you are responsible for someone else's problems, you suddenly have all that energy back to use for other things. Being clear about whose problem it is opens up the possibility of discovering an interesting new territory – one in which you are alive and in relationship, and *there is no problem.* This territory may be bigger than you think. You could use the energy you conserve through clarity about problem ownership to create interesting nonlinear alternatives for relating with people where there is no problem. These alternatives could soon become the central preoccupation of your life, and could inspire and nurture your relationships into extraordinary experiences that you never experienced before.

In the example above with Johnny and his father, when Johnny asks, "Dad, could you take me and Priscilla to the pool this weekend?" and Dad repeats back, "You want me to take you and Priscilla to the pool this weekend?" and Johnny confirms, "Yeah," then, in that moment, Dad has a problem. Dad is on the spot. Dad is required to make a yes or no decision. Dad's typical response may be to try to wriggle out of being on the spot, but even effective wriggling does not change the fact that Dad is on the spot. Dad's avoidance strategy only establishes the relationship with his son as ordinary human relationship. To continue in extraordinary human relationship, Dad would make the yes or no decision then and there. "Just a second. I need to look in my calendar book before I can answer your question. Let me see here. Uh, yes, Saturday morning I have tennis, but Saturday afternoon

after one o'clock I can take you to the pool. Tomorrow you ask Priscilla to ask her parents if she can come with us and then tell me what they say by Thursday night. We will pick her up at one fifteen and bring her home by five. It works for me. Does that work for you?" Or, "No, sorry, I am all weekend over at my parents helping with their remodel. We could ask Mom if she can take you this weekend, or I can take you next weekend. Which would you prefer?" Now the problem is back to being Johnny's.

Especially with younger children, when, for example, their request is about sugar foods or videos or bedtime, and your answer is *no* (which will be the answer more often than *yes*), be sure to energetically disconnect from the problem. After you have given your answer it is no longer your problem. You need not be swayed by any amount of whining, reasoning, or aggressive behavior. Those responses from the child are just testing the stability of your boundary. Let them do their testing. A boundary is a boundary. You already made your decision. It is not your problem anymore. This is the value and use of the *Map of Problem Ownership.* You have certainty about whose problem it is.

Now, back to Adult communication.

We discover a truly astonishing possibility for consistently creating extraordinary human relationship by adding one more element to our *Map of Communication*: the distinction of consciously choosing between *responsibly* or *irresponsibly* encoding messages, and *responsibly* or *irresponsibly* decoding messages. In the map we use two triangles divided by a vertical line to represent this choice. Responsibly encoding or decoding is called "high drama," consciously serving responsible Principles. Irresponsibly encoding or decoding is called "low drama." Neither choice is right or wrong, good or bad. Each choice produces quite different results. If you do not consciously

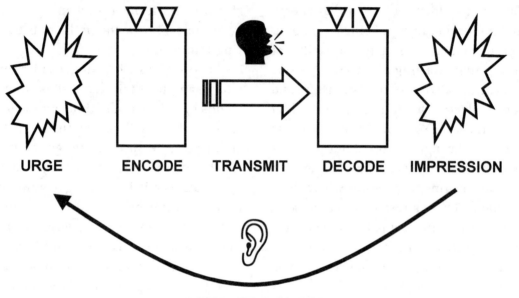

MAP OF COMMUNICATION

A communication persists until it is received. The purpose of Adult communication is to complete communications through receiving them. When we complete a communication then we end the "doing" of communication and go back to the original background state of "being" in love together.

URGE   ENCODE   TRANSMIT   DECODE   IMPRESSION

COMPLETION LOOP

Repeat back what you heard them say. When they confirm the accuracy of what you repeated with a "Yes" it signals that this communication has been completed. Then you can go to the next deeper level together.

In the Adult ego state you have the power to responsibly decode an irresponsibly encoded message. This is nothing less than miraculous.

---

choose "responsible," then you will unconsciously choose "irresponsible." This is how the Box works.

For example, let us say the original urge in a communication is hunger. If the wife comes home hungry and tired after a long hard day at work and she *irresponsibly* encodes her communication, she might say, "Why is dinner so late?"

If the husband is not familiar with the *Map of Communication* he might irresponsibly decode the question from his wife to mean that

he is incompetent for not already having dinner on the table. The impression he receives could be that she does not love him or she does not appreciate his efforts. He might respond with, "Fix your own meal then!" Have you ever had a communication like this? If so, you now know exactly what was happening.

Let us try another possibility. Let us say the wife comes home hungry and tired but *responsibly* encodes her urge as, "Wow, that smells great! I can't wait to eat!" Sadly, the husband might still *irresponsibly* decode this responsibly encoded message to mean that she is trying to manipulate him into doing it faster. His impression might be that she is never happy with him. And he might say back, "I am going as fast as I can. Maybe *I* should mow the lawn and *you* can do the cooking."

Where the *Map of Communication* lets you move beyond all ordinary possibilities is when you are the receiver of an irresponsibly encoded message and you decode it responsibly. In our example, the wife would come home tired and hungry and say, "Why is dinner so late?" – an irresponsibly encoded message. The husband would responsibly decode this to mean that she is tired and hungry. His impression is that she trusts his compassionate understanding enough not to put on a false smiley face, but instead, to authentically reveal her intimate personal state. His completion loop would then be, "I am so glad that you are home and feeling hungry enough for the delicious meal I am preparing for you. Would you like apple juice or tea to drink with your dinner?" He has the ability to stay unhooked. Responsibly decoding irresponsibly encoded messages is nothing less than magical. Any low drama can end with the receiver.

Four Kinds of Listening

Leaving the skills of listening and speaking out of considerations about relationship would be like leaving the steak out of a steak dinner. We are tempted to disregard the influence of our listening and speaking because we think that we already know how to do it. Questioning our ability to listen and speak seems ridiculous because our mind says that if we are not deaf or dumb then we obviously can already listen and speak. We assume that our hearing and speech *are* normal. That is the point – our listening and speaking are *normal*. What we are interested in here is making changes that let our listening and speaking become *extraordinary*.

Concluding that we already know *how*, fails to recognize the world we live in as a richly textured, subtle, multi-dimensional, flowing and vibrating environment with far more possibilities immediately available to us than our Box will allow us to perceive. Listening and speaking are fundamental modes for relating to and being creative in this wild world. By improving our practical abilities of listening and speaking we expand our senses into qualitatively new realms. To learn more about the subtleties of listening read *The Conscious Ear – My Life of Transformation through Listening* by Alfred A. Tomatis.

In this section we will distinguish four kinds of listening. In the next section we will distinguish five kinds of speaking. These few distinctions are enough to start you behaving in ways that open up whole new patterns of relationship. Keep in mind that since soft skills are applied in relationship with another person, they are learned the same way. Find someone with whom you can practice listening and speaking exercises, and practice them again and again until they naturally settle into your behavior repertoire.

Extraordinary human relationship is supported by four kinds of listening: 1) normal neurotic listening, 2) adult listening,

3) possibility listening, and 4) discovery listening. Distinguishing and consciously implementing which kind of listening we use in each circumstance changes listening from an unconscious habit pattern to a set of consciously applied tools. The four kinds of listening are neither good nor bad. They each produce certain results. It is most useful to be skilled in all four kinds of listening so you can create the most beneficial results in each situation. Using the wrong tool for the wrong job tends to lead to the standard and familiar difficulties of ordinary human relationship.

1) Normal Neurotic Listening is by far the most common sort of listening that we encounter and produce during our usual day. It is named "neurotic" because it is behavior that is self-referenced, self-serving and does not often accomplish what it promises, namely listening. In normal neurotic listening there is almost no correlation between what is spoken and what is heard. If the speaker says something important to them, and we use normal neurotic listening, we might interpret what they said as a personal attack. We could feel either challenged or stimulated, and before the speaker even finishes we could start formulating in our mind what we are going to say to them. We allow no time for what they said to land in our heart. Our mind keeps running, and words burst out of our mouth, like horses out of a starting gate. If the speaker communicates with anger or sadness or fear, we take it as our problem and try to avoid it or try to solve it. Many things the speaker wants to share are things we do not want to hear about, so we cleverly ask diagonal questions, change the subject, make a joke, or look at our watch and whip up some excuse for leaving. Normal neurotic listening is not about listening to the other person at all. It is about listening to ourselves. Neurotic listening is listening that serves "me." It is this type of listening that

was demonstrated to us so often that we still imitate it today. Remember, normal neurotic listening is neither good nor bad. It produces certain results. Some results of normal neurotic listening can be extremely useful, such as interrupting a normal neurotic speaker in order to start a meta-conversation, or at least for sending away obnoxious vacuum-cleaner salespeople. Some of us cannot do normal neurotic listening so we do not have the tool available when we need it. We end up with more vacuum cleaners than we need.

2) Adult Listening follows the *Map of Communication* with the intention to complete communications and navigate toward extraordinary human love. Adult listening is rare and extraordinary; it leads to extraordinary human relationship. In adult listening there are consequences to receiving a communication: something changes; something stops or starts; something happens. With adult listening you look into the eyes of the speaker, maintain an open body posture (with uncrossed legs, arms and fingers), or you mirror the posture of the speaker. Your purpose is to understand what the speaker is saying. Sometimes a question is needed for you to clarify your understanding of what the speaker is saying, but be careful. Questions are the most powerful way to dominate a conversation. Questions easily let you guide the speaker into talking about what you want to hear rather than what the speaker wants to say. Also remember that, if you are repeating back what a person says with your own comments attached, or if you are asking elaborate questions, *you* are talking. If you are talking, you are not listening. Adult listening serves both the listener and the speaker. It is listening for "us."

3) Possibility Listening (BLTLCH06.18) is something you probably have done before, but now you will have a name for it and an energetic diagram of what is happening. In possibility listening the listener takes on the Archetypal King or Queen posture sitting on

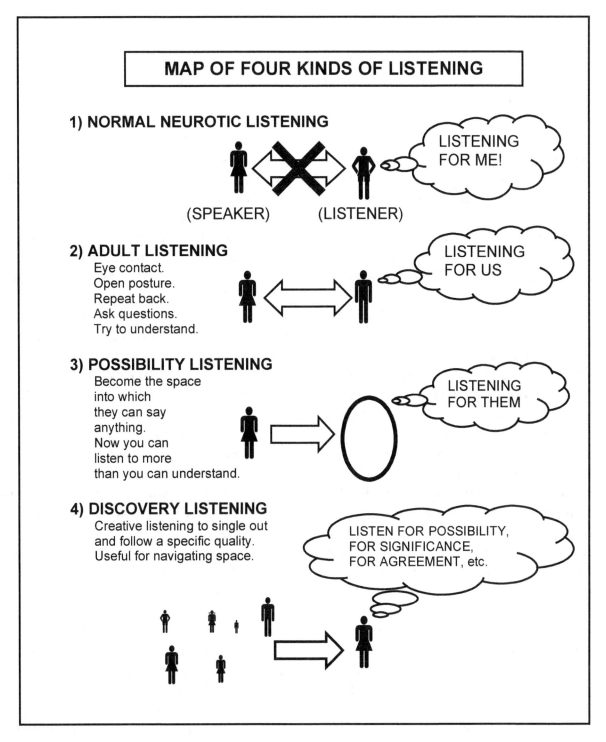

MAP OF FOUR KINDS OF LISTENING

1) NORMAL NEUROTIC LISTENING

(SPEAKER)   (LISTENER)

LISTENING FOR ME!

2) ADULT LISTENING
Eye contact.
Open posture.
Repeat back.
Ask questions.
Try to understand.

LISTENING FOR US

3) POSSIBILITY LISTENING
Become the space
into which
they can say
anything.
Now you can
listen to more
than you can understand.

LISTENING FOR THEM

4) DISCOVERY LISTENING
Creative listening to single out
and follow a specific quality.
Useful for navigating space.

LISTEN FOR POSSIBILITY,
FOR SIGNIFICANCE,
FOR AGREEMENT, etc.

a throne. The head is straight. Feet are flat on the floor. Shoulders are relaxed. Hands are palm down on the lap. (If palms face upward then it is likely you will unground yourself and therefore be less present to difficult communications.) No expression crosses your face, not even a smile (even if you have practiced a "plastic," nice-person, smiley mask for years). You do not nod your head. (Nodding, like smiling, can be a subtle form of conditioning. If the speaker sees you smile or nod they will unconsciously try to repeat whatever behavior provoked the smile or the nod. Smiling or nodding then serves to manipulate the speaker.)

You look directly into their eyes, silently snap your fingers once, to declare that you are a space, and just listen. You do not speak. Every now and then you might say, "Hmmmm," just so they know you are not dead. Your job is to be the space into which the other person can say anything. In contrast to adult listening in which your intention is to understand the speaker, in possibility listening you can listen to more than you can understand. Your listening serves the other person as a workbench for them to work things out on. You offer zero resistance to the flow of their speaking: no reaction, no nodding, no smiling, no questions, no comments. You are simply being a yes for them, being "there" for them. Possibility listening is not intended to serve you; it is a service for the speaker.

Possibility listening is not to be used indiscriminately. In particular, it does not mean that you become a doormat for complaints or a garbage can for emotional catharsis. Possibility listening is a powerful experience both for the listener and for the speaker. For example, listeners often report experiencing an unexpectedly intense compassion for the speaker and empathy with their feelings and desires. Tremendous elegance and respect can be created in relationship through possibility listening. We are so accustomed to fighting in order to be heard that many people need practice-time to learn how to speak into and make use of such a profound listening space.

When you make the gesture of possibility listening, you can detect if the speaker hesitates. Rather than making your speaker uncomfortable, you might try doing possibility listening for short five-second bursts between streams of adult listening. On the other hand, one manager told me that he used possibility listening for six hours straight with a client who was ready to fire him and he instead came away with two additional jobs. Given a possibility-listening space to speak into,

people often report that they say things out loud that they have never dared to say before; things they did not even know were in them. What they say becomes more clear and solid for them while speaking it; plans and visions become more real. Possibility listening is a precious and astonishing service to provide.

4) Discovery Listening is a consciously directed "listening for" where you pay specific attention to hearing certain signals that align to an intention you have in mind, as you mostly ignore the rest. In ordinary human relationship we use discovery listening unconsciously as "having a chip on your shoulder," "having an attitude," or "having a one track mind." We listen only to hear what will "push our buttons," make us angry, make the job impossible, make us feel excluded from the group, make us miserable, make us depressed, make us superior, make us offended and permit us to get revenge, and so on. We might also habitually use "listening for" to push "positive" but equally mechanical buttons that trigger false emotional happiness in us, such as listening for people who also graduated from Yale, for people who also collect coins, or for people who also love Hawaii. Discovery listening consciously directs your "listening for" to detect and amplify a particular quality in the speaker the same way a miner sifts through sand to find flakes of pure gold. For example, you might use discovery listening to listen for a person's commitment, meaning to tune your listening so as to detect what really matters to that person. The moment you detect their commitment you can "commit to their commitment," thereby strengthening your relationship bond with them. With discovery listening you could also listen for significance, meaning that you scan for what triggers a physical reaction in the person's nervous system the same way a galvanic skin response (GSR) "lie detector" responds to a certain physical reaction. For example, when you are suggesting what to have for dinner or where to go on holiday or which dress to wear, the person's whole body will react when you have made the right suggestion. Or, when listening to children (or adults) about their day and you know that something is wrong but they have not shared it, you use discovery listening to hone in on what is bothering them and causing the feeling they have but are not expressing. Discovery listening is thus a useful parenting or healing tool.

You can use discovery listening for navigating space with individuals or groups – for example, to listen for love so as to detect if a person loves you or not; to listen for possibility to detect if a group considers your offer to be possible or not; to listen for agreement or disagreement; to listen for understanding or the lack of it; or to listen for dignity and respect. Listening for dignity and respect is a creative way to only hear and notice those qualities about a person that make them noble. If you only hear and see what is noble, intelligent and beautiful about a person and ignore the rest soon they will start to notice those same things about themselves. (*See* Section 14-A, The Nine Cow Story.)

These four kinds of listening have unique applications and should be used appropriately when they are needed. As, for example, with hand tools, it is possible to separate a piece of wood into two parts with a hammer, and it is possible to pound in a nail with a saw, but using the right tool for the right job proves to be far more rewarding.

A few years ago I was with about twenty people who had the opportunity to attend a private dinner party with a venerated spiritual teacher. It was proposed that after dinner we get a chance to ask this teacher questions, a rare opportunity. On this occasion the teacher said yes. While the summer sky faded into dusk we carefully seated ourselves around his feet on an outdoor patio. I planted myself in the center

of the group, directly in front of the teacher. I grounded myself, found my center, went into the open-body posture that characterizes possibility listening, and placed my attention on my attention, trying to be as present as I could. As the group settled into silence he said, "Are there any questions?" My hand shot up unwaveringly before I had a chance to think about it. Out of my mouth came an open question, one that reflected great personal need but no personal agenda, one that could receive an unlimited amount of information. I said, "Could you tell us about your lineage and your teacher?" Then I shifted into being a space.

At first, the teacher tested the connection to determine what level of current I could handle. His eyes bored into my soul with an unwavering intensity for several long moments. There was absolute stillness and silence. When he saw that my intention remained solid and that I was not resisting, he went straight to full power. It was like having all filters removed and being directly exposed to the sun's maximum radiation; only instead of light and heat, what poured out of his heart was pure love for his teacher and his path. It felt like a constant bolt of lightening, 10,000 volts roaring through my body.

I tried to keep breathing, and every few seconds I "cleaned out" my listening space so it was fresh again for him to continue speaking into. Forty-five minutes went by before he stopped. I hardly understood a word he said. I was counting on the others to understand and remember. My job was to be the listening into which he could speak for as long as he wanted. I intended the listening to be without obstruction, and to be unfillable. Even though it was years ago, people who attended that talk still remember it today as extraordinary. The teacher shared with such vulnerability, tenderness and candor. Only with possibility listening was I was able to serve the teacher and the group by making optimal use of an occasion that could have easily been sidetracked and minimalized through the reduced listening of the intellect. In such an opportunity, this is what I would wish for you.

Listening in Four Bodies

In Section 5-A we mapped out four distinct aspects of the human body: physical, intellectual, emotional and energetic. Now that you have some new clarity and possibilities about listening, it can be useful and interesting to distinguish, in each communication being made, which of the four bodies is speaking.

Your Four-Body Stethoscope (BLTLCH06.19). Start by sensing which of your own four bodies wants to say something. Imagine that you are using an internal stethoscope, just like a doctor. Probe and listen for where your communication urge is coming from. Which of your four bodies wants to express itself? Physical? Intellectual? Emotional? Energetic? When you can sense what kind of urge is moving you to communicate, you will easily be able to sense which of another person's four bodies wants to speak to you. The four bodies each have their own unique urges for communication.

Four Urges to Communicate

- The physical body communicates needs.
- The intellectual body communicates either objective ideas or subjective opinions.
- The emotional body communicates feelings.
- The energetic body communicates imaginings, dreams, wishes, visions or wants.

MAP OF DETECTING MESSAGES

Which body is talking to you? Body? Mind? Heart? Or Soul? After you know this then you know what language to respond in – the language of actions, ideas, feelings, or aspirations. You can detect which body is speaking to you with your internal scanner.

Each urge to communicate has a different experiential quality. Your internal stethoscope can amplify the intensity of your experience so you can sense the experience clearly.

The urge to communicate reflects an imbalance, i.e., an excess or a lack. Communicating from an excess attempts to relieve a pressure. Communicating from a lack attempts to relieve a vacuum. Successful communication reestablishes equilibrium.

As soon as you become sensitive to which of your four bodies wants to communicate to someone else you are already resonant to

```
┌─────────────────────────────────────────────────────┐
│           ┌───────────────────────────────┐          │
│           │  MAP OF FOUR KINDS OF MESSAGES │          │
│           └───────────────────────────────┘          │
│                                                        │
│  THE URGE TO COMMUNICATE COMES FROM AN EXCESS OR LACK. │
│                                                        │
│  1) PHYSICAL MESSAGES EXPRESS NEEDS                    │
└─────────────────────────────────────────────────────┘
```

MAP OF FOUR KINDS OF MESSAGES

THE URGE TO COMMUNICATE COMES FROM AN EXCESS OR LACK.

1) PHYSICAL MESSAGES EXPRESS NEEDS

EXCESS NEEDS: to go play, to exercise, to move, to cool off, to go out, to use the toilet	LACK NEEDS: tired, hungry, thirsty, sick, need physical contact, feeling cold

2) INTELLECTUAL MESSAGES EXPRESS INFORMATION

EXCESS OF OBJECTIVE INFORMATION: facts, details, maps, clarity, rules, costs, times	LACK OF OBJECTIVE INFORMATION: requests, inquiry, questions, confusion
EXCESS OF SUBJECTIVE INFORMATION: opinions, reasons, assumptions, projections, beliefs, complaints	LACK OF SUBJECTIVE INFORMATION: being adaptive, insecurity, withhold, following, expectations

3) EMOTIONAL MESSAGES EXPRESS FEELINGS

EXCESS FEELINGS: such as anger or joy	LACK FEELINGS: such as sadness or fear

4) ENERGETIC MESSAGES EXPRESS WANTS

EXCESS OF SPIRIT: vision, inspiration, discovery, design, leading, creativity, curiosity, innovation, experimentation	LACK OF SPIRIT: existential angst, seeking, boredom, lethargy, hopelessness, waiting, following, depression

detecting which of another person's four bodies wants to communicate to you. With this new sensitivity your completion loops can include an additional dimension of understanding. You can respond to the speaker not only with the same information but also in the same language they have used to speak to you. For example:

- When a message comes from the speaker's physical body and communicates, "I need..." then your completion loop repeats back, "You need..."

- When a message comes from the speaker's *objective* intellect and says, "I know that…" then your completion loop mirrors back, "You know that…"
- When a message comes from the speaker's *subjective* intellect and says, "My opinion is…" then you would repeat back, "Your opinion is…"
- When a message comes from the speaker's emotional body and says, "I feel… because…" then your completion loop repeats back, "You feel… because…"
- And when a message comes from the speaker's energetic body and says, "I wish…", "I imagine…", "I dream…" or, "If only…" then your completion loop confirms that you heard their inspiration speaking. You then repeat what you heard them say, in a way that reflects their same mood.

This added dimension, of confirming what you heard the speaker say using a completion loop formulated in the language of the body from which they spoke to you, instantly builds a contact bridge between you. Trust immediately walks across this bridge, confidently encouraging each of you to take further risks in letting yourselves be known. The clarity and joy of communication in extraordinary human relationship is an ecstatic dance that can lighten the delivery or reception of even weighty messages. However, no matter how majestic and marvelous this communication model is, nothing will change without you practicing it over and over and endlessly over again. The futility of hoping to change something without disciplined practice cannot be overstressed. Ask anyone who plays the violin well.

SECTION 6-Q

Five Kinds of Speaking

The five speaking distinctions that support Extraordinary human relationship are 1) normal neurotic speaking, 2) discussion, 3) adult speaking, 4) possibility speaking, and 5) discovery speaking.

1) Normal Neurotic Speaking is babble, gossip, chatter, word salad, stream of consciousness, speaking for the sake of speaking, getting attention by speaking, dominating spaces by speaking, opinions about sports, politics, the weather, and so on … not much different from background TV noise. It is called "neurotic" because if done unconsciously it is self-referenced and self-serving. Being involved in making normal neurotic speaking is not wrong, bad or dangerous. It simply produces certain results. Before this moment you

may not have had the term "normal neurotic speaking" to describe such behavior. Now the "x" is on the map and you can identify what you are creating. If you are doing it unconsciously you do not know what purpose you serve. Knowing what purpose you serve is the first step in creating Extraordinary human relationship.

2) Discussion Speaking can be either irresponsible or responsible, neurotic or adult, defensive or expansive, depending on what purpose is being served. Your job is to viscerally detect the difference between a discussion moderated by Shadow Principles and a discussion moderated by Bright Principles. Many efforts to discuss something – either as a couple or in meetings – end up as mere power

MAP OF FIVE KINDS OF SPEAKING

(SPEAKER)   (LISTENER)

1) NORMAL NEUROTIC SPEAKING

Babble, gossip, arguing, complaining, excuses, chatter, background noise.

2) DISCUSSION (could be irresponsible or responsible)

Depends on the purpose, can be neurotic or adult, power struggle or collaboration. Discussion may be a battle of opinions or sharing valuable information and insights.

3) ADULT SPEAKING

Authentic communication, sharing, agreements, instructions, information, plans.

4) POSSIBILITY SPEAKING

Speaking as a space. Commit first to the other person's necessity then speak from not knowing. Includes distinctions, new perspectives, and linear or nonlinear possibilities.

5) DISCOVERY SPEAKING

Space holder navigates one team into new territory to discover whatever is needed.

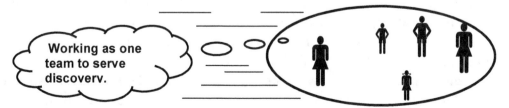

struggles rather than useful collaborations. By remembering Box mechanics it becomes quite understandable why the default mode of discussions serves unconscious purposes. The Box wants to survive and strives to do so by asserting that its opinions are right. Having its opinions challenged feels life-threatening to the Box, and in this case the Box enters discussions with normal neurotic speaking. So discussion can be either a verbal "I win, you lose" combat, or a creative collaboration serving the Bright Principle of "Winning Happening." The deciding factor is you, the space holder. If cared for with attention, discussions can be highly effective and responsible ways to come together and share valuable information and insights. Participating in discussions without carefully navigating the purpose can also be a big waste of time.

3) Adult Speaking includes all of the responsible communication tools and considerations already outlined in this chapter. Adult speaking creates a foundation of integrity and respect, and consistently communicates only one background message: extraordinary human love. Adult speaking follows the *Map of Communication* and ranges all the way from simply relating information, such as, "Dinner is at six o'clock in the backyard. Alexander is not coming," to more complex speech actions such as sharing feelings, making distinctions, creating agreements, making promises, making requests, or establishing boundaries. Adult speaking is best used for speaking about what is known. When wishing to speak about what is unknown, there are two additional forms of speaking: possibility speaking and discovery speaking.

4) Possibility Speaking (BLTLCH06.20) is how to respond to true necessity even without previous expertise in what is needed or wanted. Possibility speaking begins when the listener says, "Please give me possibility." The request can be specific or open. For example,

one partner says, "Please give me possibility about how to be more intimate with you," or, "Please give me possibility about dealing better with our teenage daughter's aloofness," or, "Please give me possibility about coming home from work unstressed," or, in general, "Please give me possibility." Then the listener stops questioning and just listens. The possibility speaker immediately commits to the authentic necessity of the questioner. The commitment comes first. After the commitment to provide value, the possibility speaker snaps themselves into a space and begins talking before they begin thinking. Possibility speaking happens when a speaker is bold, firm, demanding, fiercely honest, and speaks before he thinks – directly the opposite of adult speaking where you think before you speak. The possibility speaker speaks as a space. This lets them speak about more than they know about in their conscious mind. The question arises, *"What speaks* if the speaker is a space and is speaking from not knowing?" *What speaks* is a combination of the Bright Principles from the speaker's destiny and / or the Archetypes that the speaker has already stellated (ignited) through deep emotional work. The questioner has asked for possibility – for whatever will allow them to create new results in their life. True possibility will create a change in their Box design, and will come in the form of clarifications, distinctions, dangerous questions that can only be answered by opening up new perspectives, or previously invisible linear or nonlinear options for actions.

5) Discovery Speaking is a rare and delightful experience both for the speaker and for the listener or listeners. Discovery speaking runs on a different energy than normal or adult interactions: the energy is purely electric – you feel it in your bones and the space sings. The discovery speaker acts as a space holder, a navigator, and a lightening rod in service to the other participants in the conversation. The discovery speaker is in charge of the conversation but does not know what they are talking about. This leaves the field for discovery wide open for explorative questions, careful observations, and sharing of experiences by all participants, including the space holder. Working together, the group casts unanswered or unanswerable questions into unknown territory at the edge of what is already known. If a question hooks onto solid ground, participants work as one team to pull themselves toward the question and therefore into unexplored domains. If you document what you find and share it with others, you become reliable to again be admitted to undiscovered territory. There is no end to the undiscovered.

Don't expect to suddenly be able to do possibility speaking or discovery speaking based on what you just read. Developing these skills usually requires demonstration and guided practice (such as in "Expand the Box" training and Possibility Laboratories; *see* Contact Information at the end of this book).

But go ahead and start experimenting without requiring yourself to understand it entirely, without demanding that you do it perfectly. Adult speaking, discovery speaking and possibility speaking are all natural human capabilities. It can be inspiring to recognize that there are levels of relationship and communication that can be explained or engaged in but that you cannot yet wrap your mind around. Then, you realize that there are greater subtleties, levels and dimensions of communication to experiment with than you may have suspected. As with the four kinds of listening, each of the five kinds of speaking becomes a tool for you in the moment that you name them clearly and use them on purpose. Your competence will come through attentive, persistent practice.

Centering

Being Centered (BLTLCH06.21). We have two kinds of "center." We have a physical center, which is our center of balance, located directly between our hipbones and halfway back in our body. The location of this center is relatively fixed.

We also have a "center of being," which starts out about the size of a grapefruit, and which is mobile. We in Western civilization tend to keep our center of being located in one particular place in our body. Where is that?

Yes. In our heads. For the most part we are not aware of what we are doing with our center of being. However, outside of our awareness, we still move our being center around for various purposes. One particularly effective yet insidious use of moving our being center is as a Box survival strategy. We can energetically disempower ourselves around whomever we perceive as an authority figure by giving our center to them. If we give our center away to an authority figure we are no longer a threat to them. When we give our center away we arrange to be no longer responsible, no longer capable of creating, no longer able to make decisions, no longer able to ask dangerous questions, and no longer able to take the initiative to change things. We put the authority figure on an untouchable pedestal and establish ourselves as their follower. Wherever or whenever we give our center away, we then act out with typically adaptive behavior and thus inescapably create ordinary human relationship. It is important to learn about your center because, in any case where you wish to enliven extraordinary human relationship, you cannot be giving your center away.

Please note that no one can take your center away. There are people in professions of authority who may have slipped into the habit of providing you with a strong invitation to give them your center, for example, a doctor, a lawyer, a politician, a policeman, a competitor, a boss, a condo-salesperson, a mother-in-law, or a child. Certain people might surround themselves with "eggshells," or have too much fear of being present to enter spaces without dominating them with their loud commanding voice, implied threats, or hysterical rants about unsolvable problems. They might smother spaces with normal neurotic babbling and try to force you to abandon your center to them. You might indeed give them your center, but *no one can take your center away.*

If no one can take your center away, why would you give your center away? Basically

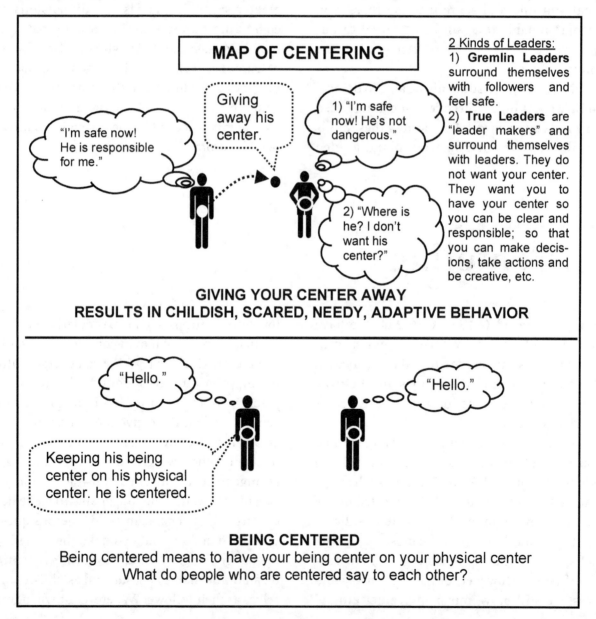

MAP OF CENTERING

"I'm safe now! He is responsible for me."

Giving away his center.

1) "I'm safe now! He's not dangerous."

2) "Where is he? I don't want his center?"

2 Kinds of Leaders:
1) **Gremlin Leaders** surround themselves with followers and feel safe.
2) **True Leaders** are "leader makers" and surround themselves with leaders. They do not want your center. They want you to have your center so you can be clear and responsible; so that you can make decisions, take actions and be creative, etc.

GIVING YOUR CENTER AWAY
RESULTS IN CHILDISH, SCARED, NEEDY, ADAPTIVE BEHAVIOR

"Hello."

"Hello."

Keeping his being center on his physical center. he is centered.

BEING CENTERED
Being centered means to have your being center on your physical center
What do people who are centered say to each other?

to feel safe – so someone else will take care of you; to avoid responsibility; to avoid making decisions and facing the consequences; to protect yourself from blame if something goes wrong; to avoid the "horrible" consequences of a confrontation. If you give the "authority figure" your center you are no longer "dangerous" and they do not have to "kill" you (fire you, demote you, belittle you, blackball you, tease you). The Box then assures you that you are safe.

Why would someone else want you to give them your center? Interestingly enough for the same reason – safety. When someone collects people's centers, he or she surrounds themselves with followers. With only followers around, no one represents a serious threat. The authority figure then feels safe. The only price the authority figure pays is enduring day-in and day-out ordinary human relationship. If they know of no alternative, if they long for nothing deeper, ordinary human relationship is not too high a price to pay for the illusion of feeling safe.

But you ... you may be longing for extraordinary human relationship or even Archetypal Relationship. This means there is no way around learning what you are doing with your center. Extraordinary human relationship only becomes possible when you place your being center on your physical center to "be centered." Being centered you can then "ground yourself" with two feet flat on the floor and a direct connection from your centered being to the center of the Earth. You are now "on the spot," as Tibetan Master Chögyam Trungpa used to say, committed, at risk, participating, capable of being present and attentive, making contact, and actually saying "Hello" to whomever you are being-with. By placing your being center on your physical center you may interact with conditions and situations more productively than when you are not centered.

The entirety of being centered includes positioning your being center on your physical center, minimizing your *now* so that your experience of now is very small, and minimizing your *here* so that it includes only the present conditions. For most of us, being centered is a rare to nonexistent experience. When centered, we enter a state of calm receptivity and equilibrium in which our attention is no longer directed to meet the expectations that other people have about us. It is a condition of being simply ourselves. If we ever *do* have this experience, it feels like we enter a completely new world. The new world is extraordinary human relationship, and being centered is a gateway for entering that world.

How do you learn to put your center of being on your physical center? First you must be able to place your attention on your being center to find out where it is. Then you move your being center to your physical center and split your attention enough to monitor your being center so that it stays on your physical center, even when your husband or boss or child bursts into your room demanding your attention. Finding your center is one thing. Keeping your center is another level entirely. Finding your center and keeping your center both require, or at least deserve, years of practice.

Keeping your center does not mean being belligerent, stubborn, heavy or inattentive, although it may sometimes appear this way. Keeping your center does not mean not getting out of the way, being resistant to, or ignoring signs, although it may sometimes involve these things. Keeping your center means that when you respond, you respond by choice, not by being adaptive.

A Centering Experiment

You are left with the sophisticated and utterly simple task of discovering how to be yourself and still be in relationship, how to be in relationship and not give your center away. You now have all the intellectual clarity you can possibly get, and this is as far as a book can take you with learning to be centered. From here on it is your job to proceed, beyond merely thinking about the practice of centering. It is time to put your body on the line.

Many of the Asian martial arts include centering as one of their core skills. I suggest that you find yourself a local Aikido class with a teacher who practices in the original form as delivered by Morihei Ueshiba Sensei. Some "teachers" have taken it upon themselves to "modernize" the traditional form of Aikido – I suggest that you try to avoid working with these teachers. Attend one or two Aikido classes each week for a year. Be sure to get yourself a wooden practice sword, the *Bokken*, and attend Aikido sword work and *Jo* (wooden stick) classes as part of your centering lessons. The sword work is elegant food for your Archetypal Warrior or Warrioress, and an exact metaphor for the clarity "sword work" that is naturally required in establishing and navigating extraordinary human and Archetypal Relationships. And while you are at it, watch *The Last Samurai* film with Ken Watanabe (what a King!), Koyuki (what a Lover!), and Tom Cruise (what a Warrior!). Learning to center is magnificent relationship training.

SECTION 6-S

Feeling Communication

The *Map of Four Feelings* and the *Map of Mixing Feelings* were shown in Chapter 5, *Some Amazing Things About Having A Body*. These two maps can provide marvelous clarity for navigating your way within extraordinary human relationship and Archetypal Relationships. However, having clarity about feelings is not nearly enough. *You also must learn to feel.* We do not know what this means – "learn to feel" – because such knowledge is outside the experience of our culture. To get this experiential knowledge you will need to take yourself beyond our cultural limits.

Back around 1985 I had returned to California from world travels and thought that by then I had certainly collected enough new and interesting ideas to start writing useful books. One evening I ended up in someone's private home at a meeting with a psychic-reader. She was a middle-aged woman with a matter-of-fact, no-nonsense attitude as she looked over her fifteen guests. Individuals started asking their personal questions. I waited, listening to what she told them and watching their reactions. It seemed that each of her answers was precise and, as far as I could detect, accurate. Near the end of the meeting I finally risked being vulnerable enough to ask my question. "Is it time for me to start writing books?" I asked. She looked at me for a moment and then without a word she started laughing. It was not a cynical laugh. The laughter erupted out of her like a swarm of disturbed wasps. She could not help laughing at the ridiculous implications of my question. She had not laughed like this at anyone else. In fact, she had taken their questions quite seriously. To me the question could not possibly warrant such a response. So I sat there with a puzzled expression on my face, waiting. When she could finally get control of herself, she rhetorically asked, "How could you expect to write useful books when you do not even know how to feel?" Four years later I attended my first training and finally began my journey into feelings. In 2003, after fourteen years of feelings-work and eighteen years after I thought I was ready to write, my spiritual teacher told me to start writing books.

There is a significant connection between being centered and learning to feel. Being centered gives us back our power, our ability to take action, our ability to be responsible, to create, to choose, and to fully enjoy our moment-to-moment present experience. With all these benefits you would think we would naturally want to enter the state of being centered. But a big part of us does not want to be centered because we are not prepared for the impact of the emotion-rich "being centered" experience. Our Box automatically – oftentimes more quickly than we are aware – avoids being centered to avoid the accompanying feeling reactions that are triggered.

It turns out that when we center here and now in our body we automatically start experiencing feelings that were locked away ever since childhood, or perhaps even before. Back then we were unwilling or unable to experience the feelings because they were too intense, too big for us, too "dangerous," or too overwhelming. The unexpressed feelings gradually locked into our muscular system and have been there ever since. The sum total of accumulated unprocessed feelings turns out to be quite massive for most of us – like an immense mountain materializing out of the fog of our denial. We semi-consciously know the feelings are in there. From time to time they rumble around in us, an ancient grumpy dragon knocking around in our dungeon. We semi-consciously decide to maintain our strategy – ignoring the dragon, hoping that it will go away all by itself. But the dragon does not go away all by itself. It waits for you to build up enough pain or enough courage to come to the dungeon and learn what it has to say.

If you wait much past fifty years of age before you undertake the journey to learn from your dragon, then your Box's structure may get brittle hard. Your beliefs, attitudes and assumptions can solidify into a high-security prison that will not likely be breached before the end of your life. You know people who are crystallized in this way. They might even be your parents. The invitation here is to avoid getting caught in the trap of ignoring your feelings-work until you cannot do it anymore. By the time you read and understand the implications of what I have just said, you will already have barely enough time to do the work needed to free yourself of enough psycho-emotional baggage to enter extraordinary human relationship and Archetypal Relationship domains. You have no time to waste.

Learning "inner navigation" skills for exploring the territory of feelings can be greatly enhanced through the direct assistance of a coach, trainer or guide. At a certain phase of your development there is no substitute for getting your butt into a chair in an environment that is safe enough, clear enough and authentic enough to provide you with experiential feelings training. I strongly advise arranging some single coaching sessions or, better yet, participating in specific kinds of trainings. Such trainings are founded in the possibility of transformation, in making sudden shifts. The possibility context is very different from the therapeutic or psychological contexts that are generally more acceptable in Western culture and therefore more readily available. Possibility trainings can indeed be found if you search more on the cultural fringe. Make the time to meet the trainer and ask questions of other participants before you jump into something you have never heard of before. There are definitely a range of offerings to choose from. Make sure you choose something that you feel comfortable with and excited about.

Feelings do not occur in your mind as thoughts. Feelings do not occur as intellectual concepts. Feelings do not occur as words or diagrams on paper. Feelings only occur in your body, personally, immediately, as experience. Learning to navigate your way through feelings is a set of skills that we could have started learning when we were seven years old (or perhaps even earlier). But neither our parents nor our teachers had that clarity themselves. They could not pass it on to us.

Wanting to learn how to feel is like wanting to walk barefoot on fire. You were probably not taught firewalking in school. To obtain the experience and knowledge of firewalking you would need to inquire into a fringe information source such as the bulletin board at a health food store, the advertisements in a new-age magazine, by talking to friends who have friends who already did it, or by searching for firewalking websites on the Internet. You would locate an extracultural association, contact the organizers, choose a date, register, pay the tuition, and go to the firewalking training. Each step in this procedure is a potential barricade for your Box. Internal and external resistances mysteriously appear. Each hurdle could stop or delay the whole process because there are parts of your Box that do not want you to learn something beyond your Box's present possibilities. There are also people in your

life whose Boxes do not want you to change, because if your Box changes, then their Box must accommodate to your Box's new size and shape.

In 1986 I was driving down the highway and realized that I wanted to walk barefoot on fire. I made inquiring phone calls, found a firewalking instructor (...this was before the Internet. Can you imagine that there was a time before the Internet?), selected a date, registered, and paid the tuition. As I got into my car to drive to the firewalking site my two closest friends stopped me and said, "Don't go!" It was not a request they made; they *demanded* that I not go. Apparently, whatever I was about to learn would change me, and if I changed, then my friends would have to change too. My friends were afraid of those changes so they set up barriers to try to keep me from changing.

If you decide to undertake additional training in feelings-work, negotiating your way through the many powerful barriers will take serious intention on your part. It is possible to succeed. But while you are trying to attain enough momentum to actually dial the number and register, the people in your life might regard you as seriously, maybe even dangerously demented. If you make it through your Box's resistances and their Box's resistances and our culture's Box's resistances, the courage to participate in the processes becomes almost insignificant by comparison. It is "feelings-work" just to get to the feelings-work. Once you succeed, a wide range of impressions and new experiences enter your world. You go through the liquid state, your Box's structure evolves, and the expanded reference points serve you for the rest of your life.

All learning involves change. Change involves inner questioning, doubts, fears, ecstasies – in short, it hurts. You cannot avoid the pain included in learning, and this applies to feelings-work in particular. Pain is not bad. As

Westley says in the film *Princess Bride*, "Life is pain. Anybody who says different is trying to sell you something."

Pain is neutral experience and has no meaning whatsoever. But we are human beings. We have a Box and our Box is a meaning-making machine. Our Box gives pain meaning (both our pain and other people's pain). Our Box changes pain into suffering.

I think that the Buddha is often misquoted as saying, "All life is suffering." What I think he actually said is, "All life is pain," meaning, "If you are alive you will feel things." But we did not get the transmission. That is because for us human beings, until we do the clarity work of separating them, pain and suffering are glued together as one thing. But pain and suffering are *not* the same thing. The difference between pain and suffering is that pain is neutral and suffering has implications. Human beings have the ability (and the tendency) to change pain into suffering. We are the only animals that can do this.

If the Buddha ever said that all life is pain, he understood that there are four kinds of pain: anger, sadness, joy and fear, and he understood that pain is valuable. (Obviously the Buddha visited France, where if you drive down the road you can see signs everywhere advertising fresh hot *pain* for sale.) Pain is valuable because neutral pain contains neutral energy and neutral information that are rich resources for life. Energy and information are "building blocks" for evolution. The building blocks are far more available and effective if we avoid the temptation to give our pain meaning, such as "this pain is good" or "this pain is bad;" "this pain is right," or "this pain is wrong." If you want to avoid evolution all you need to do is keep pain equivalent to suffering in your mind. If you want to enter extraordinary human relationship, learn to intelligently and maturely feel pain without suffering over it.

Emotions Are Not Feelings

Separating Emotions from Feelings (BLTLCH06.22). Without understanding the difference between emotions and feelings we may struggle in relationship thinking that emotions and feelings are the same thing. Emotions and feelings are not the same thing. One of the steps in establishing yourself in the Adult ego state and entering extraordinary human relationship is to live in the distinction between emotions and feelings. Without having this distinction on the pads of your fingers and the tip of your tongue, you will keep being confused thinking that emotions are feelings when, in fact, emotions are not feelings. For our purposes: *Emotions are incomplete feelings from the past or from someone else that feel present only because they are still locked in your body unexpressed.*

Emotions from the past are triggered through present association. That is, some detail in the present situation resonates with an uncompleted feeling that is stuck in your tissues from the recent or distant past. The resonance between the unprocessed emotion and the present situation awakens the unexpressed emotion as if it were a present experience.

In actuality, this is the healing opportunity that you have been waiting for. The emotion is a signal announcing to your consciousness that there is an unexpressed feeling locked in your muscles that, in this moment, has a chance to be healed. The healing occurs through recognizing and understanding the emotion from the Adult perspective. The redeeming value of emotional pain is when the pain becomes conscious. Gaining clarity about the validity of the emotion and the cause of the emotion, in other words, by hearing the emotion's personal painful story, completes the communication and vanishes the emotion forever. But since we are not trained or practiced at going through the process of completing communications, *we instead think that the emotion is a real feeling.* We assume that, since we are feeling anger, fear, sadness or joy, the emotion must be a true and justified reaction to the person standing in front of us, or to our present circumstances that "caused" the emotion. Lacking clarity about what is really happening, we project our emotion onto the person or circumstance. We blame the other person, we react with fear and anger toward the circumstance, we feel sad or depressed, and this is how we create spending our days and our nights in ordinary human relationship. I tell you, the moment I realized that all the joy I had been feeling fairly consistently since my childhood was actually emotional joy and not a real feeling at all, it ruined my day.

Although both feelings and emotions at first feel the same and fall into one of the four categories of anger, sadness, joy or fear, it is very easy to experientially distinguish emotions from feelings. Here is how: Feelings are triggered, they arise, the energy and information gets used, and then, within a minute or so, they are completely gone from your body. Emotions on the other hand, are triggered, they arise, and then no matter how you seem to express them, *they persist in your experience.*

Did you every feel scared and then an hour later you were still scared? That is emotional fear. Did you ever feel angry and then a day later you were still angry? That is emotional anger. Did you ever feel sad and then a week later you were still sad? That is emotional sadness. If you feel a feeling and five minutes later you are still feeling that feeling, it is not a feeling at all. It is an emotion. By paying attention you will soon learn to backtrack along the course of the feeling to its point of origin. If the point of origin of the feeling experience is in the wordless present, it is a feeling. If the point of origin of the feeling experience is a sentence or a picture in your mind's eye, it is an emotion.

I still remember the moment when at thirty-eight years old I experienced my first Adult feeling. My anger arose to 100-percent intensity, was used to make a boundary communication with a petty tyrant, completed itself and vanished from my body in less than a minute. In the next moment I was talking with a different person about something else entirely, freely laughing as if nothing had occurred just a moment before. This was so new and strange that at first I thought perhaps I was going insane. But then I realized, "This is what it feels like to have a real feeling."

To avoid letting emotions run their automatic and often obnoxiously disruptive course in your relationships, you need only open the smallest gap between the picture or thought that triggers the emotion and the Box's automatic reactionary machinery. You have about one instant of time to open this gap. Opening the gap will stall out the mechanical process. Like with an orgasm, once the Box's machinery starts chugging away there is no stopping it until it runs its full course – you must ride it out, and precious time and energy are lost in the meantime. But, if you blast a little gap between the origin of the emotion and the Box's reaction mechanism, then the machine never starts going. Sense the trigger being stimulated; throw in the gap; hold the gap in place; wait a few seconds, and in those few seconds the triggering momentum will die out. Let the train come into the station but do not get on the train. Wait. Wait. Make no sudden moves. Soon the train will proceed on its way, not taking you with it. Then you can stay in the blissful present.

A straightforward way to blast the gap between the triggering thought or picture and the emotional reaction mechanism is by naming the emotion as an emotion. In your mind, or out loud if you like, you distinguish the experience by giving it a name: "This trigger is only an emotion." Hold that thought. Tag the incident for later work if you want, but do the work at some other time … and away from the person or the circumstance with whom you are presently involved. The emotion has nothing at all to do with the person standing in front of you. They simply provide the triggering-association stimulus. Be grateful for the learning opportunity they have provided. Then drastically change the subject of your conversation.

An emotional reaction reveals a wound that still needs healing. If you make a practice of inserting gaps between the triggering circumstances and the ensuing emotional reaction, then the healing will tend to take care of itself. Growing up involves learning that you do indeed have unhealed wounds, and also realizing, "So what?" You can never heal all the old wounds anyway. Say thanks to the triggering experience, thanks to any other people involved, thanks to your own discipline to not get on the emotional-machinery train, thanks to the gap, then go on creating for yourself and other people experiments in extraordinary human relationship overflowing with extraordinary human love.

Communicate About Feelings

Communications are a combination of energy and information. The energy serves as a "carrier wave" that transports the information. We do not usually realize this. Our ordinary communications are often incomplete. Ordinary communications deliver information but fail to acknowledge and deliver the associated energy. This incompleteness can make the communication inauthentic, confusing and shallow.

The impulse for communication comes from the energy of feelings. To deliver a whole communication you would then express both the energy and the information of the communication, both the feeling and the data. This is a new skill.

When you do not recognize that there is a carrier wave of feelings supporting your message, the feeling doing the carrying is often joy. (It could also be fear because fear often manifests itself as paralysis or numbness, so you do not at first recognize that it is fear. But most often the carrier is joy.) Joy is the natural-background, steady-state feeling in every human being. Joy is so abundant and familiar that it is often not recognized. To admit that we are mostly happy in our lives is a shock that contradicts our habitual problem-oriented "life is hard and then you die" perspective. To admit that you are considerably happier than you realized begins by admitting that you feel happy even in those moments when the happiness only lasts for two seconds. With Adult feelings you may begin noticing that you can even feel glad about feeling angry. You feel glad about feeling sad or scared. No, you are not going crazy! This is how it actually is being alive with mature Adult feelings. If you take responsibility for feeling happy in those two seconds, even if the happiness is about feeling angry, sad or scared, then you begin noticing how many of those two seconds of happiness there are in your day. Suddenly you start feeling happy about feeling happy.

Learning to communicate about feelings is simple. You only have to memorize one sentence. The feeling communication sentence goes like this:

"I feel (mad, sad, glad or scared) because _____."

You fill in the blanks. Experiment by using this sentence three times a day.

For example, when you say to someone, "Hello," if you were to deliver both the energy and the information of the communication verbally you would say, "I feel glad to say hello." When you say, "I'd like coffee and a donut," you would say, "I feel glad to ask you to bring me coffee and a donut."

Next, start doing experiments that are a little more risky. Remember that feelings-work starts with Phase 1 (*See* Section 5-E), which is simply being able to clearly identify and feel your feelings from 0 to 100-percent intensity. Feelings are not thoughts. Feelings are not emotions. Feelings are not mixed. Feelings are mad, sad, glad or scared. Phase 2 of feelings-work is responsibly applying the energy and information of feelings toward fulfilling your destiny. In Phase 2 of feelings-work there is no final mastery. It is a no-top-end, ongoing evolutionary process of continuing to develop your art.

To begin, we start where we are. Start slowly and simply. Go to the post office and say, "I feel scared that there are not enough stamps on this letter." Go to the café and say, "I feel angry because I am already full and I want to eat more cake." Call your friend and say, "I feel sad because we have not talked in two weeks and I miss talking to you."

Then you can start communicating feelings with your partner. The form for communicating feelings is precise. Feelings are personal and inarguable. Your experience of feelings is subjective, not objective. There are no right feelings or wrong feelings. Give two people identical experiences and they will invariably have wildly different feeling responses. Tell two people, "Your dog just died," and one will feel sad to have lost a friend and the other will feel glad that the dog's suffering is over. Tell two people, "We only have vanilla ice cream," and one will feel scared not to ever taste spumoni again while the other will feel angry that it was vanilla ice cream last week. Sharing about feelings is a courageous act of letting yourself be known. The following communication example respects the vulnerability of revealing your inner experience. It demonstrates the expression of feelings using a completion loop:

Jane: "I feel scared to look you in the eyes because I think that you will see right through me and that you won't like what you see."
Bob: "What I heard you say is that you hate it when I act superior to you."
Jane: "No. That is not what I said. What I said is that I feel scared to look you in the eyes because I feel naked and judged by you and I think that your are disgusted by me."
Bob: "What I heard you say is that you won't look me in the eyes because I internally criticize you."
Jane: "No. That is not what I said. What I said is that I feel scared to look you directly in the eyes because I feel totally exposed and you will see that I am not perfect."
Bob: "What I heard you say is that you feel afraid to look into my eyes because you think I will see that you are not perfect."
Jane: "Yes. Thank you. Your turn."
Bob: "I feel angry because nobody is perfect. I am not perfect. And I don't care that you are not perfect. I need you to be imperfect. And when you do not let me look into your eyes – when you feel scared when I look into your eyes and you look away – then I feel rejected and I do not get to be close to you in a way that I want to be close to you."
Jane: "What I heard you say is that you feel angry if I do not look into your eyes because you feel rejected. You do not care that I am not perfect. You just want to be close to me."
Bob: "Yes. Thank you. Your turn."
Jane: "I feel sad because..." and so on.

Notice that at first Bob was listening more to himself than to Jane. He listened to his own projections and did not hear Jane's feelings. Bob heard the information but he did not hear the carrier impulse. After a couple of rounds, using a completion loop, Bob got enough feedback to shift his listening. As soon as he received Jane's whole message, both the information *and* the carrier impulse, then the message was completed and it became Bob's turn.

The purpose of communicating about feelings is to be in love together. You can successfully include both delicate and intense feelings in your communications if you use a completion loop to confirm what was heard. Your daily communications will not always follow this exact form, but to be effective they will in some way repeat back both the information and the energy of the communication.

Adult responsible feelings are not used to blame, justify, resent, complain, be right or make someone else wrong. This would be using feelings to create low drama. To avoid using feelings for fueling low drama you will need to build and use a low drama detector.

Build and Use A Low Drama Detector

In Section 2-C the *Map of Low Drama* introduced what low drama is, how it works, and how pervasively low drama is woven into our ordinary human relationships. In fact, low drama is the main characteristic of ordinary human relationship. The point here is: "If low drama is happening, nothing else can." You would not be reading this book unless you wanted something else to happen. What are we then to do? If we start seeing how committed we are to creating low drama at home, at work, and maybe even at church, what can we do to change? Clearly we need some ways to avoid creating low drama ourselves, to exit low drama once we are in it, and especially not to enter low drama even when we are so temptingly invited.

The first thing we will need is a foolproof way to identify and distinguish low drama from other actions in our life. What we seek is a low drama detector. When we sincerely and from the depth of our souls and the bottom of our hearts insistently ask with intense self-reflective anguish: "How do I avoid making low drama? How do I exit low drama once I am in it? Better yet, how do I avoid entering low drama in the first place?" there may be some possibility. The secret alchemical ingredient in these questions is the "I." The "I" indicates you taking inescapable responsibility for creating your involvement in any low drama. It can never be anyone else's fault that you are in low drama, even to the smallest degree. No one else can ever bring you into even the tiniest role in a low drama. It is always and only you who get yourself there. From this realization you can start building yourself a low drama detector.

You will find plans for building your low drama detector by seeing the responsible adult view of low drama. The responsible Adult view of low drama is nearly incomprehensible to the ordinary human view as given to us by our culture. Attaining a responsible Adult view of low drama requires that we start over again, understanding low drama from the beginning without any assumptions. From the responsible Adult perspective, *low drama is an unconscious theatrical performance* through which the Shadow Principles can do their work in the world. Low drama is the arrangement to have a few winners and lots of losers, to have aggression, hopelessness, jealousy, scarcity and survival. The objective in low drama is to gain power over others, where the highest reward you can ever achieve is proving yourself to be right. Nothing ever changes in low drama. What you produce after successful low drama is more low drama, because losers want revenge. After one low drama the ever-present question remains, "When is the rematch?" The Box loves action as distraction, like Roman citizens loved Circus Maximus. Low drama is a perpetual action machine – the motor for turning the wheels of ordinary human relationship.

Becoming a Low Drama Detector (BLTLCH06.23). Begin building your low drama detector by remembering the three roles played out in low drama: victim, persecutor, and rescuer. The three roles of low drama are excruciatingly obvious to detect. Ordinarily we do not see the roles because before now we did not have the *Map of Low Drama* to refer to. We thought that real things were happening and that this was just how life is. Now that we have the *Map of Low Drama* we can observe low dramas from the outside.

Construct your low drama detector by wiring in a whole-body sensor connected to a large warning lamp mounted onto your chest. The sensor glows red and screams "Beep! Beep! Beep!" whenever it detects a low drama. An approaching low drama is simple to detect. If there is resentment, victimhood, blaming, complaining, justifying, proving yourself right, or making someone else wrong, it is low drama. If a person thinks there is a problem and the problem is someone else's fault or the fault of circumstances, then it is guaranteed to be low drama.

Initially your low drama detector is not fine-tuned. Three days after you make a low drama your low drama detector will trigger for the first time, "Beep! Beep! Beep!" and announce, "You have

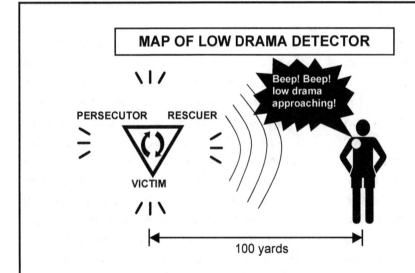

MAP OF LOW DRAMA DETECTOR

PERSECUTOR   RESCUER

VICTIM

Beep! Beep! low drama approaching!

100 yards

It is simple but not easy to detect an approaching low drama. If there is resentment, blaming, complaining, justifying, proving yourself right, or making someone else wrong, it is low drama. The "not easy" part is that low drama is tempting Gremlin food. If anyone thinks there is a problem and it is someone else's fault, or the fault of circumstances, then it is low drama. Your low drama detector can sense a low drama 100 yards away, and will warn you with a red flashing light on your right shoulder: "Beep! Beep! Beep! Low drama approaching! Proceed with extreme caution! Do not get hooked! Use your "sword of clarity" to make distinctions so you can take responsible actions!"

been sleeping for three days! Three days ago you were in a low drama!" And you think, "Oh, yeah! That's what that was! Sure! Three days ago I whipped up a low drama. Hmmmm."

If you increase detection sensitivity then soon your low drama detector will go off again, "Beep! Beep! Beep! This morning you were in a low drama!" And you think, "Oh my God! Yes! That is what this glum residue is around here! I had a low drama this morning. Hmmmm."

If you increase the sensitivity even further, then almost before you know it your low drama detector will go, "Beep! Beep! Beep! Hey buddy! That was just now a low drama that you did!" And you think, "No! No! Really? *That* was a low drama? But I was right! I was justified! They were wrong! They were hurting me! I had to take action... Whoa! That's right! That *was* a low drama! This is amazing! I was just then doing low drama and I did not even realize it. I did it again. Inconceivable!"

This tuning procedure may take weeks, or even months. With further careful adjustments to increase sensitivity your low drama detector will go, "*Beep! Beep! Beep! This here right now is a low drama. You are in a low drama now. This is it. Happening right now.*" There won't be anything that you can do about it right then. It is too late. You are already in it. But from inside the low drama you can observe it happening. You can observe your part, your payoff, your Gremlin in ecstasy devouring the possibility of love happening and replacing it with grief, separation, and the temporary satisfaction of conquering your enemy through subterfuge. At this point clarity is your key. Do not shy away from seeing what you are really doing to other people, to your children, to your mate. The details of your Shadow World pleasures instruct you exactly where to make your next detector refinements.

Finally, one day, after months of effort to avoid getting hit on the side of the head and

knocked unconscious by low drama, your detector does its true job, "Beep! Beep! Beep! Beep! Wake up! Wake up! That right there in front of you is *about to be* a low drama. You are now being seriously invited to do low drama. *That* is it! Right *there! That!* Do you see it coming? It is the tone of voice. That 'hidden purpose' – the Shadow Principles of Gremlin. It is those vectors of intention. The spin on the words. The attitude. You can feel them coming and you are about ready to dish them out yourself. Do you want to play or not?"

In that instant you get your first chance to do something other than low drama. Before then, for your entire life, you never had that choice; the Box's whole low drama operation was mechanical and automatic. You were unavoidably sucked into each low drama and your life juice was inexorably consumed. Now the precious blessing of your low drama detector becomes more obvious. After months of gaining more and more awareness about your particular style of suffering you finally have a choice about whether or not do create low drama. That choice gives you your life juice back. Now – what are you going to do about it?

"Don't Go There"

One possibility for taking action in the instant that you recognize low drama is to reflexively reach into your tool belt and grab a little wooden picket sign that says: *don't go there!* Lean forward and ram that sign into the road directly between you and the low drama. Then obey the sign. Do not go there. Go somewhere else. Completely avoid considering anything more about the low drama. Put your intention and your attention on something else entirely, on something that you would prefer to use your energy to create. Put your body in motion on another road. Go toward your writing project; or remember the love you have for your children; imagine tending the vegetables in your garden, or cooking a fine meal for your mate; focus on developing your self-respect; on breathing fine radiant joy; on something else, anything else, and then go there instead. There, you have just bypassed your first low drama! Good. Now, can you do it again in five minutes? And once more this afternoon?

Most of us arrange a steady diet of low drama for our Gremlin, who has its own particular feeding schedule. Some Gremlins need one big feeding frenzy each month for four or five days. Some Gremlins need one low drama a week for a whole day. Some Gremlins are snackers, nibbling here and there all day long, trading little nasty jokes and hurtful comments with other Gremlins to keep their appetites satisfied. Low drama is about feeding Gremlins – not about solving problems, resolving conflicts or changing *anything*. Low drama is not about change. If you want something to change the key is you taking responsibility. As Ken Windes, the leader of my first training used to say, "Responsibility is the procedure for change."

You should be warned that, if you succeed in initializing your low drama detector so that it can sniff out low dramas approaching from 100 yards away, you will be avoiding Low dramas that used to be normal for you. If you avoid even one low drama, the energy that would have been consumed during that low drama is conserved in your body. It will not take long before the conserved energy builds up an uncomfortable charge of reserve energy that must be dealt with in ways you are not accustomed to. You used to consume that energy in low dramas. Now you must figure out

something else to do with it. Having more energy in your system than the Box is structured to tolerate can feel quite intense. If you start doing experiments that permit you to avoid low drama you should be prepared to do *simultaneous* experiments in tolerating the intensity of having more energy in your system than your Box considers to be normal.

The Box has little tolerance for managing more than its usual amount of energy. The added intensity is extremely irritating and our Box makes immediate efforts to go back to its familiar state. The Box has many creative ways to instantly burn off excess energy. Sneaking a few low dramas here and there is especially effective, but the Box has other favorites. You know them: over-indulging in alcohol, caffeine, nicotine, sugary greasy junk food, drugs, chocolate, Internet sex, gambling, flirting, videos, exercise, work, shopping, or, at the other extreme, insufficient sleep, insufficient water, lack of exercise, lack of good food, lack of good company, and so on. Learning to hold greater levels of energy may involve lifestyle changes that you never expected to have the discipline to make. Now, all of a sudden, discipline is easier than suffering the familiar but painful consequences of unconscious Box mechanisms. Isn't life fascinating?

In practical terms, the energy conserved by sidestepping low dramas is then available for making responsible moves toward being your destiny Principles in action. This answers the question, "What do I do instead of creating low drama?" Three options will be explored in the next sections: 1. Say yes or say no, 2. Ask for what you want, and 3. Make boundaries.

Say Yes or Say No

Ordinary human relationship is rife with fuzziness, confusion, loopholes, delays, excuses, misdirection, miscommunication, withhold, sloppiness and a clear commitment to non-commitment. Having myriads of non-strict flexi-rules is neither good nor bad; it is how it is in ordinary human relationship. The further you refine the quality of relationship – from ordinary to extraordinary to Archetypal – the fewer the rules and the more strictly they apply. But, at the level of ordinary human relationship, forgetfulness, gray zones, and deception are the norms.

Fuzziness and non-commitment are easily created by never finally deciding yes or no. Without making decisions you cannot be blamed. You are not at risk. You never really fail, nor do you ever really succeed. Mediocrity prevails. This is ordinary human relationship. The kids say, "Dad can I have an ice cream?" and your answer is, "Let me check with your mother. We'll see. I don't know how soon dinner will be ready. When was the last time you had ice cream? What about having some fruit? I think the ice cream store might even be closed already." And so on. Without a yes or no decision the consequences are more vague than the known consequences of a clear decision. We imagine that by not deciding we avoid suffering, when, in fact, not deciding is its own form of suffering.

Simply making up your mind to make up your mind is not going to help you make yes or no decisions and permit you to enter extraordinary human relationship. The hesitation to make yes or no decisions does not come from the mind floundering in a lack of information or too much information. The hindrance to making yes or no decisions comes from the heart and has to do with our reticence to feel. Decisions intimately involve feelings in ways that we may not have studied before.

On the surface, making a yes or no decision appears to involve making distinctions, creating clarity, and then taking action. Distinguishing, clarifying and acting all involve energetic "sword work" that is empowered by feeling angry. Not that expressing the distinction, clarity or action must be with anger, but that by their nature making distinctions, creating clarity and taking action are motivated by Archetypal anger energy. What this means is that if it is not viscerally okay for you to feel and use the energy of anger because of old childhood survival decisions to disempower yourself, then distinguishing, discernment, clarification and action are not going to happen naturally for you.

But, a deeper level of feelings – a confrontation with grief – is involved with the consequences of decision-making. This is because in every circumstance there are practically an unlimited number of options available to choose from. If you decide for one of those options you are simultaneously deciding against ninety-nine million other options. That is, if you choose to give life to one possibility you are at the same time killing ninety-nine million other possibilities, forever, for all time. These unmade choices are now *really* dead. It is not possible to choose them anymore. The passing of the ninety-nine million possibilities into irretrievable oblivion must be grieved. So, if it is not perfectly okay for you to feel deep authentic sadness over the death of all the options you've decided against whenever you've make a decision, then you will unconsciously avoid making decisions about anything just to avoid feeling sad.

Start with making a decision to grant yourself permission to let anger course through your veins for the rest of your life no matter what the consequences. We are so conditioned to regard anger as bad or destructive or hurtful that it takes some experimenting to realize that anger is simply energy for moving us forward to accomplish things. Experiment with feeling angry and using the anger to empower your discernment, insight, speaking and gestures with passion. Use anger energy to practice responding immediately to yes or no questions with a simple, unexplained, unjustified, undefended *yes* or *no*. Then do not waver, regardless of what additional considerations the Box supplies you with. No wiggling.

At the same time make an additional decision to grant yourself permission to let the feeling of sadness flow through your veins, again, for the rest of your life, no matter what the consequences. Be careful not to mix your sadness with your anger. As shown in the *Map of Mixing Feelings*, integrating your sadness with your anger will automatically produce the experience of depression. To avoid feeling depressed, or to exit depression, just be clear about what you are feeling. First feel anger, then feel sadness, then feel anger again if you want, never mixing the two together. Quantize your feelings. You are angry about some things, and also sad about the same things or sad about different things. Anger and sadness come from completely different Archetypal domains. Experientially mixing them together confuses and disempowers one of your primary resources of energy and wisdom. No wonder you feel depressed! Just do not mix the two feelings together. Your new willingness to feel sad gives you the ability to let unchosen alternatives pass you by with respectfulness and without drowning in nostalgia. Daily life in the flesh involves life and death consequences. When you choose the veal parmesan, you pass up the chicken cacciatore *and* the spinach lasagna. You cause many possibilities to die by choosing one possibility to enliven. That is how it is. Letting the waiter or your wife choose for you does not change the consequences of your decision one iota.

When the man asks his woman a yes or no question, like, "Do you want to go to the beach this weekend?" and she takes off on a tangent, like, "We only have three hundred in the bank and your mother wants to come over for lunch on Sunday," he can avoid getting hooked if he does not go into automatic reaction mode. After all, it is just the Box speaking. He can keep listening and not say anything until there is a slight pause. Then he can say, "Those are answers to the questions, 'How much money do we have in the bank?' and 'What does my mother want to do on Sunday?' I did not ask those questions. I asked, 'Do you want to go to the beach this weekend?'" If she says yes then he can say, "I have a hundred and fifty in my wallet, enough for gas for the camper and a splendid two day picnic. I will call my mother and explain that we won't be here this weekend. Are there any other details to handle?" All of a sudden, almost miraculously, this couple is in extraordinary human relationship.

Ask For What You Want

It is true that all human beings are psychic. It is also true that in our modern world we are trained to ignore our nonlinear magical knacks because they do not fit into scientific linear explanations. Although we are modern and scientific, we continue to assume that our partner, our children, our neighbors or our colleagues know what we want of them without our having to ask for it. We somehow expect people to know what we like or don't like, what we need or don't need, what we want or don't want. We don't even stop to consider how absurd this is.

For example, if as your husband rubs your back he moves his hand round and round in the same place, it may quickly irritate you to the point of anger. You can pull away, go to sleep, and avoid letting him ever rub your back again, because, you conclude, he obviously does not know how to rub backs! Do that with cooking the eggs, dressing the kids, wrapping birthday presents, and singing Christmas carols, and you have successfully erased five areas in which you could instead experience wonderful and stimulating intimacies with your husband.

Relationships do not die from lack of love; relationships die from a lack of intimacy. The basis of intimacy is letting yourself be known. But we are Westerners. We are individualists whose identity includes being independent and wanting to accomplish our life on our own. We are not familiar with revealing and communicating about intimacies. It is too frightening to reveal who we really are, what we really want, what is working for us or not working for us. It is too frightening to reveal such intimacies about ourselves because even if we take the risk of exposing ourselves

so heartfully, there is no guarantee that we will be accepted as we are. We have so much experience being rejected, or worse yet being ridiculed, teased or taken advantage of, that we decided long ago to never again be so naïve as to reveal ourselves to such a degree. Instead, we develop stealth skills for manipulating, strategizing, bargaining, sneaking roundabout, or whining to get what we want, or forgetting all niceties and just taking what we want by force. Our automatic strategies leap into action whenever they are triggered and we do not understand why we do not get closer to our partners and friends.

If it is not okay for us to feel fear, it will never be okay for us to reveal who we are by asking directly for what we want. Revealing ourselves is always risky. Fear of being hurt again is natural. If we cannot allow ourselves to experience fear, then we can never be so direct as to simply ask for what we want.

Asking for What You Want (BLTLCH06.24). Let's return to the back-rubbing example. Why is the man rubbing the woman's back in the first place? The greatest pleasure for a man is pleasing a woman. If the woman can help her man please her, then he will be pleased even more, and so will she. This is a "Winning Happening" game. He is pleased when she is pleased. She is pleased when he is pleased. It all revolves around the woman being okay with feeling afraid while she gives feedback, "Slower and down to the right, James. Ah, that's better. A little farther left. Use your fingernails just a little. Ah, yes. Like that. Not too rough. Up more now. Slower. Mmmmmm." He might say no. He might feel insulted about being told what to do. He might not be able to understand or change for awhile. He might reject her vulnerable request and there is a chance that she will not get what she wants. Yes, that is a risk. But if she does not ask then it is almost certain that she will not get it.

Learning to ask for what we want is central to self-knowledge. We might be assuming that first we have to *know* what we want before we ask for what we want. Then, instead of saying "I want to have a clearer picture of what I want, can you help me?," we try to figure out what we want by ourselves and we ask nothing. This may satisfy the Box just fine because the Box may not be so interested in having us know what we want. If we know what we want we might ask for it and get it. But what we want might not be the same as what the Box wants. If we drop the requirement that we must *know* before we ask, we can simply start by asking for what we want, ignoring the Box's sense of confusion, doubt, or insecurity that it uses as a defense against change. We can ask for what we want on our way to getting clear about what we want: "I want to find out what I want." "I want to find out who I am." "I want to be more effective without focusing on Box-centric goals to achieve." "I want a sense of the mysterious in every day life." Through rapid learning we will quickly learn what we *really* want.

The point is that we want what we want and we don't want what we don't want. End of story. There is no reason, no explanation, and no justification necessary. Certain things matter to us because they matter to us. Period. What matters to us is built into our destiny at birth. I want world peace. I want to make a film of two guys discovering Possibility Management. I want a Soft-Skills Invention Think Tank designed like a galaxy instead of a hierarchy. I want an international conflict resolution team trained in Possibility Management. I want a Possibility Mediator certification program. I want to write and publish five more books. I want to write and make three films. I want the third biggest building in every village (after the church and the town hall) to be a Temple of Evolution. I want no country to be bigger than 1500 people so that human diversity explodes on planet Earth and no more big wars can happen. I want to outlaw franchises and television stations that can broadcast farther than twenty-five miles. I want to reinvent schooling by certifying Possibility Trainers to transform teachers into trainers who provide children with expanding Boxes rather than staying educators who merely cram more contents into children's Boxes. I want to enliven a truly confrontive and dangerous rite of passage from childhood to adulthood in Western cultures so men and women can grow up and take responsibility for creating what truly matters to them and therefore have a better chance to enter the domains of extraordinary human relationship and Archetypal Relationship.

What difference does it make that I want these things? If we do not acknowledge to ourselves specifically what we want, then we manipulate ourselves into not wanting what we want, or perhaps we manipulate ourselves into wanting what society wants for us, what our parents want for us, or what some company's marketing department wants for us. There are enough forces out there trying to manipulate us already. We do not need to manipulate ourselves too. Amazingly, we are so accustomed to being manipulated that some of us put energy into manipulating ourselves into doing what we really want to do! Like we want to take a world trip and travel with a backpack through Southeast Asia, so we manipulate ourselves to get up each morning and drudge off to work to earn the money for plane tickets, instead of working in the present delight of already fulfilling our dream by earning the money, or taking off with almost no money and creating legal and fun ways to make the money we need along the way.

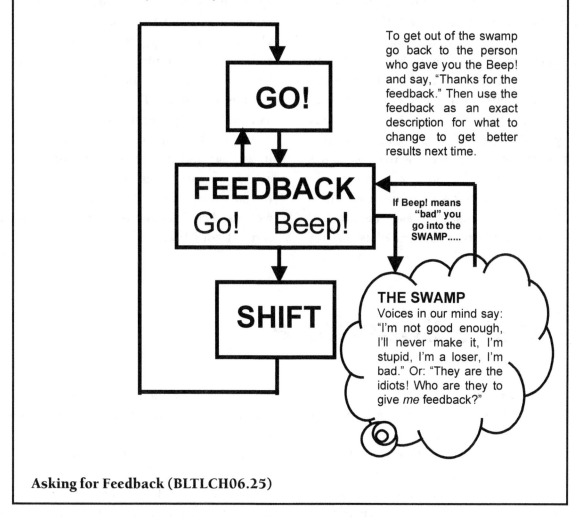

MAP OF RAPID LEARNING

Rapid learning is a four-step process that incorporates feedback from your environment as exact instructions for what to change in order to get better results. In rapid learning, feedback is neutral, and there are only two kinds of feedback you can receive: Go! or Beep! Go! means keep going. Beep! means stop; it is not working. Shift means change something and then try again. In rapid learning, feedback is gold. The problem is that we went to school and learned that Beeps! are bad. If we still think Beeps! are bad then we avoid taking risks. If we do receive a Beep! we go directly into the swamp where voices suck away our ability to learn.

GO!

FEEDBACK
Go!   Beep!

SHIFT

To get out of the swamp go back to the person who gave you the Beep! and say, "Thanks for the feedback." Then use the feedback as an exact description for what to change to get better results next time.

If Beep! means "bad" you go into the SWAMP.....

THE SWAMP
Voices in our mind say: "I'm not good enough, I'll never make it, I'm stupid, I'm a loser, I'm bad." Or: "They are the idiots! Who are they to give *me* feedback?"

Asking for Feedback (BLTLCH06.25)

Even if we cannot *now* have what we want, even if what we want is impossible and we can *never* have what we want, we can still admit to ourselves what we want and stop lying to ourselves about it. We may know that because of our discipline or because of our practice we would never choose to go back to college and earn a Ph.D., for example, but to not *acknowledge* that there is a part of ourselves that wants to do that is self-deception. There is enough deception from outside sources working on us already; we do not need to deceive ourselves in addition. We also don't have to be reasonable about what we want. After all, asking for what you want may change the circumstances so that you can actually *get* what you want!

A friend of mine heard of an exciting conference that he wanted to attend in Johannesburg. He told his office colleagues about the conference and they all wanted to go too. The problem, they all lamented, was that the company had no budget to pay for travel costs. My friend suddenly picked up the phone and dialed another colleague in the sales department. "Hey Jack!" he said. "There is this conference in Johannesburg that I want to attend. It would be great for our company. Could I use your extra frequent flyer miles to go?" My friend asked for what he wanted. Jack said yes. The call took less than one minute. He went to the conference. His two colleagues did not. Ask for what you want.

One of the things we are most afraid to ask for is help. Consider these questions. If we could avoid letting the fear of asking for help stop us from asking for help, is there any problem we could not face? If all the help of everybody around us were available just for the asking, is there anything we could not accomplish? Try this experiment: without hesitating, for no reason, ask for the help that you want.

Appropriately asking for help – meaning, the asking of help that is inspired by true necessity, not for manipulative, attention-getting or low drama purposes – places you as a "job" on someone else's workbench. Someone who is in the position of being able to provide objective help benefits from helping. If a trainer had no one to train, how could the trainer fulfill his or her destiny? One hand washes the other. Do not get the idea that asking for help implies that you are weak. Think of the last time you helped someone in a meaningful way. A friend of mine was asked by a movie star to be-with her alone in her last days as she died from cancer. Being well-used could make any experience the best time of your life.

SECTION 6-W

Make Boundaries

Making Boundaries (BLTLCH06.26). Your body instantly tells you when a boundary needs to be made, exactly where, exactly with whom, and exactly about what. Your body knows. The conflict that interferes with hearing your body's boundary messages is that the carrier wave of boundary information is the feeling of anger. If it is not okay for you to consciously experience feeling angry, then all your body's boundary messages will be repressed right along with the anger.

The natural response to anger is to stop the circumstances causing the anger. Instead, we have been trained to stop the anger. As an experiment, consider this question: If it were okay for you to feel angry and to use your anger to make decisions, make boundaries, and make changes, what decisions, boundaries and changes would you make? Seriously engaging this question would produce answers in writing.

There are two ways to use the energy and information of anger to make changes. One changes conditions outside of yourself and involves making boundaries. The other uses anger to change conditions inside of yourself and involves making distinctions. Making distinctions is a higher technology than making boundaries. Distinctions are smoother, less confrontive, more elegant, and conserve more energy than boundaries. But making distinctions is also subtler, more delicate, and less obvious. Let's start with the work of making boundaries.

A boundary functions like an energetic wall. Examples of boundaries include: No! Stop! Stay away! Yes! I want that! We made an agreement already about this and I want you to keep the agreement! This arrangement is not okay! Never do that behavior again! Only do it this way! That is none of your business! This is my life! I will not do that! Leave me alone! And so on. As simple as they may seem, it may be a surprise to learn how inadequate most of us are when it comes to making boundaries. In training after training I observe that most people cannot even effectively say, "No!"

Trusting (BLTLCH06.28). Boundaries supplement our ability to trust – an important contribution to the functional life of an adult man or woman. If you do not yet have the skill of making boundaries, it will be helpful to develop and exercise that skill. *Not trusting another person is actually you not trusting your own ability to take care of yourself around that person.* It does not have to do with them. It has to do with you. You could find valid reasons to distrust anyone. With instant access to your ability to make boundaries, however, you can take care of yourself without having to depend on the separation created by distrusting your ability to take care of yourself. Enlivening your ability to make boundaries lets you expand the group of people you consider to be your friends. You don't have to remain so guarded when you realize that a wider variety of characters could enrich your life experience. You could be friends with Harley Davidson bikers, with that gossipy neighbor woman, with those arrogant colleagues in the other department, with the lonely kid next door, with

your own kids for that matter. As you begin making boundaries with your own children you will feel the separation between you and them decreasing, which is the *opposite* of what we would expect. We separate ourselves from our children as a way to protect ourselves, but then we are separate from our own children. When we can take care of ourselves by making boundaries, when our "sword of clarity" is always at the ready, then we can get quite close to people and still feel safe.

Because boundaries ride on the energy of anger, and because we tend to block consciously feeling our anger, we may not sense the need to make a boundary until the "enemy" is at our castle gates. You may be surprised to know that you have the capacity to detect your anger when it arises in your body at only 1-3 percent of its maximum Archetypal intensity. Such a small amount of anger is still anger. Even at 1-3 percent, anger can still inform us of the need for attention toward a specific concern, or perhaps even alert us to the possibility of making a pre-emptive boundary. If we do not detect that we are angry until it surpasses 80-percent intensity, we could suddenly go from 0 to 80 percent and be ready to explode! The condition has gone from green to red without any noticeable yellow in between. Then we may be shocked and leap into full-attack mode instead of maturely and wisely taking care of ourselves when our anger was first awakened. In this case we simply waited too long to make the boundary. Waiting is naïve. Letting the enemy cross our entire yard and enter our foyer before we even notice that they are there is a result of self-induced sleep. To make a shift, experiment with lowering your anger sensitivity bar. Practice becoming conscious of what you are feeling when the feeling intensity level rises up to only about 3 percent. Such experiments may reveal that you feel more often and feel more deeply than you previously realized. Lowering your sensitivity limit gives you earlier warnings so that you can make boundaries at the border of your frontier, at the white picket fence on the street rather than at your bedroom door where a boundary would be far less believable and effective. By increasing your sensitivity toward your feeling you can be more intelligent, relational and compassionate with your boundaries because you do not have to enter full-attack mode before making them.

The evolution of your boundary making relates to Phase 1 and Phase 2 of feelings-work. As you recall, Phase 1 is simply to feel. Learning to consciously feel is a huge step. In the beginning of feelings-work you may find that some of your first long-overdue boundaries are accompanied by hollering at the top of your lungs in 100-percent rage. The results may be somewhat embarrassing if you make a boundary with 100-percent rage where only 30 percent would have been sufficient. But don't worry. It only takes a few months of use to develop your feelings from the immature stage to the mature stage, where you need them as an Adult. Making a few sloppy boundaries along the way is far more important than continuing to make no boundaries at all. Other people will get over it. You will be forgiven.

In Phase 2 of feelings-work when you have your feelings back and your voice back, then you can be more precise about the ways in which you establish boundaries. In Phase 2 the feeling tells you that a boundary is needed, but no shouting or screaming is necessary. Merely stating a boundary in all four of your bodies with full clarity about what is happening and what you are doing is sufficient. Even though you are not shouting you still represent the potential to shout, or scream, or cry, in any necessary instant. Your potential to instantly escalate, if needed, is enough to make and hold almost any boundary.

Shifting Boundaries to Distinctions (BLTLCH06.29). Your first boundaries may establish a full barrier: a thick impenetrable concrete wall, 30-feet tall, topped with broken glass and barbed wire, spotlights and machine guns, and electrified with 10,000 volts. Nobody could get through such a boundary, so you are definitely protected. As you continue to practice making boundaries with Phase 2 you may observe that while boundaries do form a barrier, that barrier also blocks relationship. You do not get much communication through a concrete wall. Over time you might experiment with making finer boundaries – less solid barriers. Your new boundaries prove to be just as effective but will require fewer energetic materials in their construction, and less attention to maintain. Continue making subtle boundaries and you will soon discover the second way to make changes: clarity. Clarity often protects you from harm even better than a boundary.

Clarity

Clarity is produced by making distinctions. Distinction-making causes changes in your own Box. Creating solutions and possibilities by making changes in your own Box has a distinctly different effect than trying to make changes in the Boxes of others. Distinctions let you perceive the set-up of things so that you can work with them or move around them on purpose. Without clarity you can't help but clumsily smash around.

When a distinction rearranges your Box to create clarity, it is like having been severely nearsighted and suddenly putting on corrective eyeglasses. What a difference! Just a moment before the area spread out in front of you was a smear of colored fuzziness. Now, with the glasses on, you can distinguish tables, chairs, sleeping dogs, kids' roller-skates and all sorts of obstacles to be avoided. If a person who could naturally see watched their friend "deliberately" kick the sleeping dog and get bitten day after day, they might not comprehend their friend's crazy behavior. As soon as the seeing person understood that it is possible for a person to be shortsighted, they might stop scolding their friend and instead help them get to the eye doctor.

The same is true in relationship. The first step in correcting bothersome communication and relationship experiences is to imagine that you may be encountering obstacles that you cannot yet see.

Ordinary human relationship is the *automatic result* of bumbling around with immature or uneducated perceptions about what is going on in your relationships. Extraordinary human relationship is the *automatic result* of relating to human beings through clarity about feelings, listening, speaking, communications, centers, ego states, problem ownership, low dramas, making boundaries, and so on.

Using clarity produces different results from using boundaries. For example, if you go to a dance party and want to protect yourself you can sit in a corner behind a boundary of chairs or refuse to dance so no one can cut in and flirt with your partner. Or, you can make *distinctions* to gain *clarity* about what is going on at the party. Then, with clarity, you can go ahead and dance, move your own feet out of the way, flirt with beautiful and ugly strangers, explore different dimensions of conversation, and in general take care of yourself while still interacting. Clarity does not guarantee that no one will step on your toes. But neither does sitting in the corner behind a wall of chairs.

A boundary at its most basic level specifies limits and blocks energy flow. A distinction, on the other hand, specifies limits yet still allows energy to flow. A boundary is like a wall between neighbors. A distinction is more like a picket fence between neighbors that defines the property line but still permits you to chat with each other on Saturday mornings.

To evolve your boundary-defined relationships into distinction-defined relationships, start by examining the boundaries you are holding. Sense into your connections with other people and determine: Who are you holding boundaries with? Why do you feel the need to maintain these boundaries? Who are you thinking the other person is? Are you assuming that they are their Box or that they are an unknowable mystery? Why are you granting sentience to the mechanical actions of their Box? How could you evolve your boundaries into distinctions that give you and your relationships more possibility? How could you stay in relationship with a person and not get hit by the mechanical manifestations of their Box? Sense into any boundaries that other people are holding with you. *Who holds them?* Why are other people feeling like they must keep boundaries up with you? Ask yourself (or them) how they could gain the clarity that frees them from their boundaries with you and gives them distinctions instead?

Make Boundaries with Children

Making Boundaries with Children (BLTLCH06.27). When a mother and father build a family culture for their children to live in, the parents' model for what a family culture should look like comes from their own childhood family experiences. The process of inventing family culture is, in general, unconscious and automatic. Parents do not often consider, "Hmmm, do you think we should have Hanukkah / Christmas / Ramadan / Chinese New Year, or not? What about not having television or newspapers in our house? Should the kids be born at home and sleep in our bed with us for their first five or six years? How many rooms do the children need anyway? Let's skip the 'big house with everybody in their own room' fantasy and spend our time and money traveling more and being together in nature, shall we?" Although these are *real* options

More Box Mechanics

The following distinctions about Boxes create a level of clarity in human relationship that has been, for the most part, unknown in the history of humanity. The quality of communication and relationship that comes from applying this clarity from moment to moment in your daily life is truly extraordinary. It is yours whenever you wish to use it.

- You have a Box. You are not your Box. You are a vast awesome potential. The same is true of everyone else.
- Boxes are neither alive nor volitional. Boxes are unconscious mechanical machines dedicated to defending themselves. Machines can be counted upon to mechanically do exactly what they are designed to do, to fulfill their unconscious purposes. For example, one job of your Box is to produce an endless stream of meaningless thoughts. It does this job marvelously.
- With this clarity you need never have a conflict again. If you feel like you are having a conflict with another person it is not you that is having the conflict with them. It is your Box having a conflict with their Box.
- Playing the role of victim to a machine is always strategic. If you are in a conflict with someone else's Box *you* are deriving a payoff. To step out of the conflict get conscious about your payoff.
- It is impossible to be offended by anyone or anything. If you ever feel offended you have offended yourself. Any circumstances can be used as a reason to offend yourself. Any perceived insult is self-manufactured to serve your own Shadow Principles. This is obvious because anyone could feel offended about anything, and anyone could also feel unoffended about anything. Feeling offended or unoffended is a personal preference of your Box.
- Being offended by a Box (yours or someone else's) is no different from hitting your finger with a hammer and being angry at the hammer. The Box did not do anything to you. You used the Box to do it to yourself.
- No one else can "hurt" your feelings. You "hurt" your own feelings. The way you "hurt" your own feelings is by creating low drama victim stories about the circumstances that are happening around you. You also cannot "hurt" other people's feelings. You may have been manipulated by someone who surrounds themselves with "eggshells." They hold it over your head that if you behave a certain way they will feel a certain way. Since the way they feel is "bad" (meaning angry, scared or sad), then you are "bad" for "making" them feel this way. Allowing yourself to be manipulated is just as much a Shadow Principle as manipulating.
- The clarity that your Box is mechanical and unconscious is exactly the same clarity that a mature driver has about his car. The driver does not expect that his car will automatically take him wherever he wants to go and stop at red lights along the way. No policeman would accept the excuse, "Well officer, the car decided not to stop." The driver knows that his car is not sentient and that the car's mechanical operations

follow physical laws determined by the car's design. The driver is not a victim of his car's insentience. The driver gets behind the wheel and drives the car where he wants it to go. Relate to Boxes like an intelligent driver relates to cars.

- If you relate to someone as if you know who they are, you are wrong. If someone else relates to you like they know who you are, they are wrong too. All that we can know about another person is their Box. Who they truly are is unknowable mystery.
- Relationship to a Box is boring. Relationship to unknowable mystery is forever exciting. In each moment of your relationship you choose to whom you are relating.

available for *every* parent to choose from, for the most part we abandon our creative freedom to the machinations of mass media and predominant cultural precedents. We then suffer the broad consequences of passively choosing without recognizing our responsibility for having made a choice in the first place.

Compared to other cultures in the world, our modern Western culture is completely bereft of ritual. In comparison to the family culture of an African tribal village, modern Western family culture is like a featureless desert. Indeed, in our ritual-free environments we gain tremendous freedom for lateral thinking, that is, for thinking our way off the page, but at what cost? Without a webwork of ritual to contextualize our perspectives we lose our ability to make natural and necessary boundaries and distinctions for our children.

For example, there is nothing to stop parents from teaching their children the ritual boundaries and distinctions for obtaining, preserving and preparing food; rituals for differentiating between the sexes; rituals for celebrating the changing seasons of the year; rituals around festival days and celebrations; rituals for courting partners; rituals for honoring the wisdom of elders and the dead; rituals for relating to spiritual teachers, sacred objects, sacred spaces, and sacred teachings; rituals for healing and transitioning through different stages in life. But Western civilization has shrugged

them all away. Without ritual, the depth of our family culture decreases drastically to the point where parents have almost nothing to teach the children, forcing children to absorb cultural norms from their peers rather than from their parents. (To learn more about how to counteract the destructive consequences of peer bonding through attachment parenting read Gordon Neufeld's book *Hold On To Your Kids*.) Modern children regard boundaries and distinctions coming from parents as some kind of archaic neurosis, and parents have little chance of changing this without seriously reshaping their personal behavior habits.

Begin by realizing that many attention-seeking maneuvers by children are actually last-resort, unconscious, survival attempts to get "food." What is it that our children starve for? In our busy-busy Western culture where media, time and money devour more than 100 percent of our adult attention, our children often starve for lack of parental love. Where our attention goes our energy flows. When from time to time we do not place 100-percent loving attention on our children they starve for lack of authentic intimacy. (*See* the sub-section *Being-With Children*, below.)

Any food is better than no food to a child. Getting negative attention from parents such as scolding, yelling, complaining, resentment about being manipulated, fear of being made to look bad in public, and so on is at least some recognition from the parents that they exist. I have seen children manipulate parents into giving them attention by getting hurt over and over again on purpose – actually falling down on purpose, or banging their head on a wall, or starting a fight with an older sibling knowing they are going to get thrashed – and then can come crying to mommy or daddy for attention. I have seen children try to get attention by becoming sick, by adopting unprovoked neurotic or nerve-wracking behaviors, by playing weak or aggressive, by asking incessant questions, by having "accidents," by creating false problems, or by breaking the law. The same mechanism can manifest in many other ways, including bringing home straight A's or straight F's from school.

Children do not want boundaries, but children need boundaries. When parents have no experience with their own feelings, they cannot tolerate their children screaming with rage in response to finding a boundary. At the sound of screaming many parents relax all boundaries thinking they are doing their children a favor. They think that withholding boundaries is how a parent must sacrifice their life for the sake of their children. This is utter and horrifying nonsense, and frighteningly normal in our modern culture.

If there is a problem between you and a child, it has nothing to do with the child. It has to do with you not providing boundaries and clarity for the child. For a big person to solve their problem with a little person by being violent with the little person is an act of insanity.

Children desperately need boundaries for developing their physical, mental, emotional, and energetic bodies. If children do not experience durable, persistent boundaries in their home environment, then children flail about frantically in a desperate state of survival terror where they must inappropriately try to hold space for themselves. I have seen

small children (less than two years old) seeking solid boundaries to wrestle with in their environment and not getting them because the parents wanted to be "good parents." The parents wanted the children to experience having a "good childhood," so they avoided providing the children with a framework of boundaries. Without clear solid boundaries around them the children felt abandoned, which is the *opposite* of what the parents thought they were creating for their children.

Not making boundaries starts off harmlessly enough, at the breakfast table, with the child choosing Cheerios and then screaming for corn flakes when they see the parent choosing corn flakes. If the parent is manipulated even in the slightest way by the screaming to replace the child's Cheerios with corn flakes, even to think about exchanging the cereals, even to give defensive reasons as to why they are not exchanging the cereals, then the parent's boundary fails the screaming test. *When screaming can destroy a boundary, there is no boundary.* When there is no boundary the child loses respect for reality and goes berserk. This berserkness and disrespect for reality stays with the child for their entire lives and, indeed, could be a contributing factor to the drastically increasing number of child suicides, drug addictions, school massacres, and other horrific occurrences. Living with children in a self-made boundaryless environment is an all-too-common modern nightmare. It does not have to be this way.

Being-With Children

Being-with your children is *not* about letting the children control and dominate the spaces in your life together, or giving your center away to your children, or forsaking your Adult responsibilities and trying to become a child yourself. These all too common behaviors actually drive children crazy. The boundaries and clarifications that you as the

Adult create in the life of your child establish bars on a jungle-gym upon which your child can develop their muscles of responsibility. Not fulfilling your role as an Adult parent is like giving your child a jungle-gym with no bars and wondering why they develop no stamina, no presence, no fortitude, and no intelligent abilities to relate.

Being-With Your Children (BLTLCH06.30). To nurture extraordinary human relationship with your children (or with anybody's children, for that matter) try the experiment of being-with children. The experiment goes like this. Reserve and make sacred a priority for spending twenty minutes of being-with time once or twice a week with each child individually.

Knock on their door and ask, "May I come in and be-with you?" If they say, "No, not now," then you say, "Okay," and walk away. If they say, "Yes," then you inconspicuously walk into their room and immediately lie down on their floor. Lie on your side, with your head propped up on your hand. Do not stand there. Do not sit in a chair. Do not lie on their bed or couch. Lie down on the side of their room on their floor. The bed, chair, couch and center of the floor are power positions in their room. Do not take a power position. Lying on your side on the floor puts you in a weaker and therefore less protected position, making you more available and vulnerable for relationship with your child. These details are critical, so after you have tried this experiment once then come back and re-read these lines to check that you understood them correctly.

When you are lying on the floor you do nothing and say nothing. You are now "being." The "with" part of the "being-with" is up to the child. If this is the first time that you try the experiment the response will be different according to the child's age. An older child will look at you and say, "What's wrong? Are you sick?" You say, "No. I just wanted to come in and be-with you." Then say nothing else. Particularly do not say, "I am reading a book that says to try this experiment in being-with children…" You might be surprised how difficult it can be to refrain from vomiting your mind into the space as a Box-reassuring monologue that shatters the silence. Resist the temptation. Contain your radioactive waste dump. Let it fall into fathomless stillness. The child is testing to see if you are going to do your usual thing. Just keep breathing and be there.

If the child is younger, it takes but a moment before they realize that mom or dad is finally offering them just exactly what they have been waiting for: being together with them for no reason; sharing your company. A younger child may come over and jump on you to wrestle. They might come with a broken doll and say, "Daddy, can you fix this?" Or with a storybook and say, "Let's read." They may come with coloring pencils, a puzzle, or a video game. If the child is older they may ask for help with an algebra problem or complain about what happened at school. They might tell stories about their friends, share plans for the weekend, or show you a catalog of what they want to buy. Whatever they bring or offer to you, be a yes for that. Use none of the twelve roadblocks. Do not offer solutions. Do not correct their attitude. Do not be positive. Do not praise. Do not rationalize or explain that this is how life is. Simply be there, and enjoy listening.

This is an exercise in being-with. That means do not look under their bed and say, "Oh my god! That's where the other socks go! Jeez! Look at all that dust! Don't you ever vacuum in here? How can you live in such a mess? Isn't this the toy from grandpa? And it's broken already? I asked you to put your clothes away last week and they are still sitting here! Have you finished your homework yet? It is almost time for dinner – have you washed your hands yet? It is almost bedtime – have you brushed your teeth yet?" *None of that shit!* These twenty minutes are a parenting-babble free zone. This is about two people being-with each other – human to human. That is all.

This is also not the time to go eat ice cream together. It is not time for movies or TV. It is not time to put on a sticky-sweet attitude of false niceness. It is time to be-with. And it is time for your child, *not time for you.* Do not fill up the space with your troubles and make your child listen to you, comfort you or psychoanalyze you. You are the adult. Be-with your child. After the twenty minutes, slowly get up and say, "Thanks. It was great to be-with you. See you later," and walk out of the room. If you have more than one child, try to arrange to be-with them individually. It does not work so well trying to be-with more than one child at the same time in this way. If done consistently, this little experiment can completely transform your relationship with your children.

))(Going Nonlinear

Extraordinary human relationship is alive because of its continuous ongoing re-creation. Interactions are dynamic, surprising, unexpected and nonlinear. In general we do not have access to nonlinear creating because we have been cut off from our imaginations and nailed into modern linear viewpoints. In our civilization, mind is at war with imagination, and mind has decidedly won. Regaining access to our powers of nonlinear creating requires locating and reconnecting to our imagination.

Linear relationship goes like this. On the first evening after their honeymoon the man returns from work and announces, "Honey, I'm home! I love you!" His starry-eyed woman arrives breathless and wraps herself into his arms saying, "Oh darling! I love you too! I missed you so much! Dinner is waiting for you on the table." The next evening the man opens the front door and announces, "Honey, I'm home! I love you!" The wife comes wearing a smile, and says, "Oh good. Right on time. Did you have a nice day?" The next evening the man opens the front door and announces, "Honey, I'm home! I love you!" The wife says, "I'll be right there. I love you too." The next evening the man opens the front door and announces, "Honey, I'm home! I love you!" The wife says, "I'm in the kitchen! What did you say?" "Honey, I'm home! I love you!" he repeats. "Yes, great," she says. "You love me. I love you. Great! And, what else have you got?"

That extraordinary human love is alive and requires similar attentive care to a pet or a vegetable garden keeps us on our toes. Without feeding our relationship with a steady diet of authentic actions moved by unpredictable originality, the aliveness of our relating fades into a habitual rut. And, as the saying goes, the only difference between a rut and a grave is their length.

Reclaiming Your Nonlinear Imagination (BLTLCH06.31). The challenge of extraordinary human relationship is learning to create something that you have never created before, differently each time, and over and over again. Nonlinear imagination easily fulfills that challenge. But connecting to nonlinear imagination can feel like filling your belly with hot coals and endlessly burning inside. Only one person can make the efforts to authentically reconnect you to nonlinear imagination. Guess who? Even the *Kama Sutra* runs out of positions sooner or later. Then you are back on your own.

Learning to be okay even if you cannot predict what you are going to do next plugs you into a new form of electricity. Suddenly you can start the "same" conversation differently, and each time feel its uniquely radiant possibilities. What comes after that is a mystery. Back in Shakespeare's day it was a common pastime to converse only in rhyming pentameter, or to sing rhyming pentameter, or to sing and dance rhyming pentameter. The human being has a far greater capacity to be endlessly nonlinear than we are ever led to believe. It is up to you to explore that potential and to make use of it.

Your actions should not be intended to frighten or offend people. Your actions do not have to be drastic, even subtle creations can open new worlds of relationship. Maybe you never thought of possibilities such as these: You come home dragging a new fruit tree in the front door and explain that since you do not live out on a farm you are going to bring the farm home. You stand outside the door beating your chest and doing the Tarzan jungle call until your woman comes to get you. You take off your shirt in the snow outside and come in freezing cold needing desperately to be warmed up. You bring three friends for dinner, unannounced. You come in saying nothing and speak only in a whisper. You lay on the floor and cry for being so glad to come home again. You enter through the side door and go straight to the kids and listen to them about their day. You climb up the gutter and come in over the bedroom balcony like Romeo. You say nothing until after you flawlessly recite from memory Edgar Allen Poe's *The Raven* in its entirety. You bring home Chinese take-out food, consisting of the chef's favorite delicacies. You enter singing Broadway show tunes and refuse to be interrupted until the grand finale. You cut out paper dolls and wear them around your shoulders like a lace shawl. You speak in the accent of Count Dracula and are only attracted to your woman's neck. You come in with your eyes closed saying that you are doing a science experiment and could your woman please lead you through the rest of your evening together. You have an unlit cigar in your mouth and keep it there all through dinner. You walk in backwards telling jokes to an invisible friend. You only look straight into the eyes of your woman with an intense unwavering gaze not being attracted to look anywhere else. You take her hand and proceed to give her a detailed hour-long palm reading about her exotic past and her wild possible futures. You hand your woman the cell phone – an old best friend (whom you have called on your woman's behalf) is on the line; someone your woman loves but hasn't spoken to in a long while.

I could keep going, but it's your turn. You have a feeling for it now. The source that these come from is truly endless.

Compare these examples to walking in with flowers or chocolates. At the same time, realize that avoiding linearity is not a rule. Flowers or chocolates *now and then* add spice to nonlinearity.

Reconnecting to your imagination will take intentional efforts. It does not happen all by itself or just by thinking about it. Participating in improvisational theater workshops could get you started. Not improvisational dance, but improvisational theater where you feel and express emotions not by acting but rather by re-experiencing them and sharing the experience out loud. Look for a workshop leader who uses warm-up exercises from Keith Johnstone and his book *Impro* – exercises which require you to go up on stage with a partner and use face, voice and posture to start something out of nothing and for no reason; exercises that require you to tell nonlinear imagination stories that you never heard before, one after the other in rapid succession, being interrupted at short random intervals and required to change stories mid-sentence. These are steps along the path of rediscovering the whereabouts of your nonlinear imagination. Once you find your imagination and see that it still functions after all these years, you can plug your heart back into its richly abundant resources.

Mind Your Own Business

After all this talk of saying yes or no, asking for what you want, making boundaries, and so on, it is still necessary to directly examine a particularly pernicious mechanicality of the Box that undermines even noble efforts to establish extraordinary human relationship. The mechanicality comes from the Box's basic assertion that its own solutions to the problems of life are the *best* solutions to the problems of life. Since your Box assumes it has the best answers, whenever there is a conflict between your Box and anyone else's Box the obvious solution is for the other person to change so they are using *your* better solutions. Our Box is absolutely committed to the viewpoint that the other person is wrong and stupid if they do not change in the ways we see they could so easily change.

Despite all your efforts have you ever

succeeded in changing anyone? Has anyone ever succeeded in changing you? No. Change of behavior is not so simple. For example, change of behavior does not result from changing your behavior. Change of behavior results from changing the design of the Box – which does not change except through building new matrix to hold expanded consciousness. This expanded consciousness reshapes the Box by taking it through the liquid state into a new form. Yet, astonishing as it is, we still listen to our Box insist that the solution to our problems would be so easy if only the other person would change. The fact that they do not change is the source of our irritation. The view that our problems are the other person's fault grips our thinking like Velcro gloves grip the back of a sheep.

Our partnership problems do not come from our partner not changing. Our problems with our partner come from our own rigidity

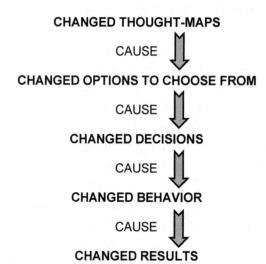

MAP OF CHANGED RESULTS

CHANGED RESULTS DO NOT COME FROM TRYING TO CHANGE YOUR BEHAVIOR. CHANGED RESULTS COME FROM CHANGING THE THOUGHT-MAPS OF YOUR BOX.

CHANGED THOUGHT-MAPS

CAUSE

CHANGED OPTIONS TO CHOOSE FROM

CAUSE

CHANGED DECISIONS

CAUSE

CHANGED BEHAVIOR

CAUSE

CHANGED RESULTS

Ordinary thinking assumes that we can get new results without changing our behavior, or that we can change our behaviors without changing the thought-maps of our Box that produced these particular behaviors. Our real challenge is the rigidity of our Box's assumptions!

about how things should be. It takes ruthless self-honesty to admit that our real challenge is the rigidity of our Box's expectations. Our Box's self-defending structure provides us with rigid criteria to measure our circumstances against. If a circumstance does not meet our Box's expectation then it tells us that the circumstance (our partner) is wrong. If the circumstance does not change, this proves that the circumstance (our partner) is committed to being our enemy. Obviously, if our partner loved us they would not attack us by doing things that are so infuriating.

Wishing for someone else to change is the equivalent of wanting someone else to vote Republican or to become Buddhist. It is not up to you what they choose to do. If you vote Republican or become Buddhist is that anyone else's business? What someone else does is out of your hands. If you think the problem with your horrible neighbor will be resolved by them moving out, just wait until they move out and the next horrible neighbor moves in. In most cases the conflicts you have are not externally sourced by the circumstances; your conflicts are internally sourced by your own Box.

For example, have you ever been kept awake by someone else's party noise? Midnight construction workers? Someone snoring? The linear solutions presented by the Box for solving these problems seem so obvious: Go tell the neighbors to turn down the music. (After all, don't they know what time it is?) Complain to the city about the construction noise. Shove a sock into the snorer's mouth. These are linear solutions. What about nonlinear solutions? What if instead of trying to force external conditions to change so that they match the rigid requirements specified by your Box, you instead took your Box into the liquid state where it could no longer hold rigid requirements? What if you applied the nonlinear possibilities of extraordinary human love? What if you decided that the local party animals are your best friends and you truly enjoy hearing them have such a great time together? What if you loved the workers for sacrificing their night to repair things so you could live in a better city? What if you loved that person snoring next to you so much that their snores wrapped you in a warm blanket and rocked you to sleep?

The Box leads us to think that we can be happy by changing what we have. The Box says that what we *have* determines what we can *do*. Then what we do determines whether or not we can be happy, or satisfied, or pleased, or fulfilled. The way the Box sees things, if we had a great job then we could do what we really love to do and then we could finally be happy. The problem, in the Box's view, is that *we do not have* the right job (the right partner, the right dress). So then we spend all our efforts trying to get a new job, have more money in the bank, own the Z4 convertible, and dust the souvenirs from our Egyptian vacation, but has anything changed for us? No. We still make the same decisions to make the same actions as we did before, because the place where our decisions and our actions come from has not changed. As Buckaroo Banzai said in the film of the same name, "Wherever you go, there you are." The place where our decisions and our actions come from is our being. They come from who we are.

Thinking about who you are before you think about what to *do* or what you *have* is not the Box's strategy. The Box's original commitment is to keep you the same, not to change who you are. The Box has ulterior motives behind its strategy. Keeping you the same is how the Box thinks it can guarantee your survival. The Box's motivation to assure survival is exactly what it is supposed to do for you until age fifteen. But after that, limiting you to merely surviving is a pitiable outcome compared to what is possible if you are really living. In fact, the formula may not work at all like the Box markets it. Things may actually be exactly the opposite.

Being Happy (BLTLCH06.32). If being happy, for example, depended on what you *did* and you found that raking leaves made you happy, then it would be a certain and repeatable way to stay happy if you raked leaves all day every day. But, of course, this is nonsense. You already know by experience that even if raking leaves all day made you happy one day, there is no guarantee how you might feel raking leaves the next day, or even the next minute.

Being happy is a Bright Principle. So is being satisfied, fulfilled, challenged, engaged, excited, loving, generous, accepting, kind, grateful, communicative, spontaneous and appreciative. Bright Principles are forces of nature that move you to do what is necessary to do in each moment during your day. The Bright Principles you represent determine the qualities of who you are being. Out of the doing that flows from the Bright Principles that you are being come the results of what you *have*. What you *have* turns out to be totally satisfying, no matter what it is, because what you have comes directly from who you are. And who you are is your own business.

Be Responsible for Who You Talk To in Your Partner

Changing what you have or what you do starts with changing who you are. How do you change who you are? Like ordering lunch at a restaurant, how do you "order up" which Principles to serve? If you do not place your order consciously in each moment for particular Bright Principles to serve, then what you get is the "special of the day," usually some slop from the underworld that your Gremlin ordered while you were napping.

Ordering from the menu also applies to ordering what you want from your partner. Imagine that you are going to a fine restaurant, sitting at the perfect table, looking carefully through the elegant menu and ordering exactly those things that you hate to eat. Doesn't this sound crazy? You would be torturing yourself. But this is exactly what we do in ordinary human relationship. We look at our partner and what we focus on is what we do not like about them. By focusing our attention on what we *don't like,* we feed those qualities with our energy and cause them to show up more intensely. We arrange to order from our partner what we hate about them, and then we blame our partner for what we just ordered.

Conscious Schizophrenia (BLTLCH06.33). Here is an experiment to try. If there are some behaviors of your partner that particularly irritate your Box, stop placing an order for those behaviors. A human being is not a single, solid, and unchanging personality. A human being is a whole neighborhood of personalities. Your partner is a human being. So, just like every other human being, your partner experiences and expresses a vast array of characteristic qualities during their day. Why are you consistently dialing up Grumpy or Ditzy when who you really want to be-with is Captain Jack Sparrow? Cross the old characters out of your phone book. Dial up the characters you want to enjoy.

If you accidentally dial the wrong number, apologize. Hang up and try again. Say, "Not that one. I am not speaking to that one. I want to speak with the other guy." When your partner says, "He's busy. He's out to lunch. He is not available right now," then you say, "I'd like to make an appointment for when he returns. I am only interested in speaking with him directly. I'll call back later." And then do exactly that.

The Box is what the Box is. The characters of the Box are the characters of the Box. There are characters in your partner's-neighborhood Box whom you truly love, admire and appreciate. Call them up and enjoy the hell out of them. The rest? Let them do their thing. None of those characters are any of your business or any of your responsibility. Spend your time visiting with your favorites. Why not?

Meeting Your Evolutionary Needs (BLTLCH06.34). Every human being is involved in their own unique process of development, dealing with their own particular issues in their own unique time. Our evolutionary process is no one else's business. It is private. This means that it is *not* your job to educate your partner, to heal your partner, or to change your partner. If their mother could not change them, why do you think that you can? It is your job to respect your partner, enjoy your partner, and accept them exactly how they are. And. It is your job to take care of your own evolutionary needs. If that means reading books, attending talks, being in trainings, meeting with your men's or women's circle, doing meditation or martial arts practices, whatever you need, take care of getting it for yourself. Do not wait around thinking that your partner can provide you with all the energetic vitamins and minerals necessary to maintain your four bodies in good health. The fallacy of thinking that both partners in a relationship will evolve at the same rate and have the same requirements at the same time will only lead to frustration and deep resentments. Extraordinary human relationship is not about holding yourself back for the comfort of your partner. The relationship itself is part of what moves you forward. It is up to you to make use of it that way.

Do the Italian Thing

In many cultures of the world arguing with your mate immediately, up front, and out loud is offensive and unacceptable. Particularly in modern Western cultures where we have been civilized. The storm rider in us has been anaesthetized. What we forget is that our concept of "being civilized" is totally relative, depending completely on which civilization raises us. Travel to Greece sometime, or Italy. Hang around small shops and back street neighborhoods. Soak in the way people talk to each other. Before long you will notice how "hot" the conversations are. People do not talk to each other, they shout at each other. They argue, rant, and rail each other about every incident or question. Their interactions are consistently and repeatedly intense. And this behavior is completely normal in that culture. In fact, they do not even notice what they are doing, until such time as they travel to another country where the conversation habits are different. An Italian in Germany cannot understand why the German people are so cold and aloof with each other. It feels distant and makes no sense.

Doing the Italian Thing (BLTLCH06.35). Arguing hotly with your mate is not necessarily bad or wrong. It is not necessarily immature or irresponsible. It could be an experiment, interacting in a different style, portraying a different character. It could be giving yourself more permission to be publicly passionate about what you are already privately passionate about. The point here is to not always stick to monotone and logic in your interactions. Try doing the "Italian thing." Exploding with passion now and then gets the juices flowing in ways and in places where maybe the juices have been stagnating for far too long. Rant, rave, and whip up a little chaos now and then. Stir the soup. Shake the scorpions. To paraphrase Emile Zola, "Life is meant to be lived out loud."

Breaking out of the somnambulant, smiling "nice girl" or "nice guy" mask – plastered on us by well-meaning parents, relatives and schoolteachers in modern civilization – can be nearly impossible. Extracting ourselves from this glutinous sweetness will not happen by itself. You either make efforts to break the mold or you continue to get make efforts to break the mold or you continue to get moldy.

Do Not Date to Find a Mate

Not Dating (BLTLCH06.36). Looking for a partner while using what we typically understand to be "dating" includes so many problem offspring that you will spend most of your energy running in circles trying to undo the difficulties they create. The conventional idea of dating is to present yourself attractively so as to make a fine catch of a partner. The joke becomes apparent when you realize that you are falsely representing yourself so as to find a "perfect match" who turns out to also be falsely representing *them*selves! No wonder you get disappointed. It's an old joke – but with the popularity of silicon implants, liposuction, hair waxing and Botox injections – the joke is eminently worth retelling: One man on his wedding night waited for his new bride to get undressed for bed. She went into the bathroom and took off her wig, her girdle, her padded bra, her false eyelashes, her makeup, and her colored contact lenses. When she re-entered the bedroom her husband screamed in fright because he did not recognize her at all. He thought he was in the wrong hotel room!

Dating is a way to try to outsmart Mother Nature. We think we can make a better choice about our partner than She can. We have all heard stories of computer dating agencies producing life long relationships. We have also heard stories of people winning the lottery. The point is that if you focus all your efforts on finding a mate, once you have one, then what? Then you can finally start living?

I strongly suggest that you live first. Go get on your way. Find out where you are going before you try to find someone to go with you. First finding out who you and where you are going allows the laws of precession can come into play. "Precession" is a term from physics, meaning that when certain objects are in motion then sideways forces come from "out of nowhere" and influence how the object moves. This is how boomerangs turn around and come back when you throw them. The thing to remember about boomerangs is that they do not come back *if you do not throw them first*. An object has to be moving before the laws of precession take effect.

For example, if you decide that you want to find a partner, a mate, and you go to a party for *that* purpose, you probably won't have much luck. But if you get seriously into your life and take actions toward creating what really matters to you, then when you need some lettuce you, of course, go to the grocery store to buy lettuce. The man next to you says, "Sniff the stem." You say, "Huh?" He says, "Try sniffing the cut stem. If it smells bitter try another one. If it smells sweet it's a tasty head of lettuce." You get to talking. It turns out he hires you to help with a project that is exactly in your field of expertise. While doing your work you represent the project at a trade fair and there working across from you in a competing booth is a woman. She becomes your partner. This is how the laws of precession work. When you are in authentic motion, serving your destiny, then sideways forces can create "coincidences" that support your evolution. If you are not propelled into motion, being moved by the force of your destiny, then Mother Nature does not have the elbowroom to work with you. False motion is not good enough. Being busy with dating so as to find the perfect "10" to fulfill your fantasy image is false motion.

Experimenting with the Italian thing may feel like you are going a little bit crazy. Great! We get so worried sometimes about losing control, going out of our mind, stepping over the limit, being impolite, "hurting other people's feelings," coming unglued, losing our marbles, and so on. We are so habitually flaccid that our vitality dribbles away like an old man's piss. Spunk can instantaneously reignite itself as soon as you unlock your own handcuffs, waken the storm rider, or pull the rubber pacifier out of your mouth that they shoved in there so long ago to keep you quiet. Pirates do not wear pacifiers. Go knock on some doors after midnight. Wake yourself up. The Italian thing: it comes and it goes. Afterward you can share cappuccinos and cantuccine, and laugh together.

Be Wrong

Being Wrong (BLTLCH06.37). You have to choose what is more important to you, being right or being in extraordinary human relationship. For your Box the choice is obvious: being right is much more important. Making the other person wrong – your mate, your boss, your kids, your parents – is much more important; winning is much more important. But, if you have a different set of priorities than your Box, if experimenting with extraordinary human relationship is more important to you than being right, then focus on

being in relationship and let the "facts" fall where they may. What is so important about details anyway when what you have here is a genuine opportunity to be in extraordinary human relationship with *him* or *her*?

Making Do-Overs (BLTLCH06.38). "Do-overs" are possible. If by habit you have created the conversation to result in you being right, whether your position is obnoxiously superior or not, quickly apologize and get off it. Say, "Whoops! Excuse me! I did not mean it that way. Let me try that again." And, without waiting for a comment, immediately start over, all the way from the "Hello" at the beginning of the conversation, creating a different result than you being right. For an extra credit experiment, arrange the conversation so that you end up being wrong. If you are wrong, then you can ask for help or for feedback and coaching. If you are right the game is over. You win. They lose. If you are wrong, then there are myriads of options still open to both of you for continued exploration. By making yourself wrong I do not mean to actually cause destruction, waste, pain or confusion. To be wrong is a way to be in relationship where you do not automatically fulfill the Box's desires to know, to feel safe, to be in control, to be right. The experiment is to come from the perspective of not knowing, and to make being-with in extraordinary human relationship a higher priority than security for the Box.

Feed Your Heart and Feed Your Soul

Nurturing Your Heart and Your Soul (BLTLCH06.39). The practical understanding of the difference between feeding your heart and feeding your soul is not distinguished by our culture, so we live our lives

without having that clarity to work with. Gaining this knowledge can make a tremendous difference in your ongoing ability to navigate into extraordinary human relationship.

I first learned of the difference between heart and soul from the words of a song:

> *A man gives his heart*
> *to the woman who he loves,*
> *but a man gives his soul to his destiny.*
> *If you try to make him choose*
> *you might just end up with*
> *a man who's not man, can't you see?*

Lyrics by Lee Lozowick
(© 1986, Bad Poet Productions, used with permission.)

It goes without saying that this clarification for a man: heart – to love, soul – to destiny, applies equally in reverse. That is, it applies to a man trying to force his wife to choose either nurturing her heart or nurturing her soul, instead of encouraging her to nurture both distinctly in her life. (Since it needed saying here, perhaps it does *not* go without saying.)

The closest we come to considering ways to care for our heart and our soul is through the modern consideration about establishing some kind of "work life balance," which is only a weak approximation of what the lyrics are talking about.

Our heart and soul are centered in different bodies, and therefore have need of different kinds of food (as was briefly considered in the discussion about the *Map of Four Bodies* in Section 5-A). Without caring for our heart differently from the way that we care for our soul, we may be mixing foods, or starving a part of ourselves while overfeeding another with something it does not need. By distinguishing between heart and soul, and by intentionally nourishing both your heart and your soul, each with its appropriate nutrition, it becomes immediately clear how important this is for building and maintaining extraordinary human relationship.

For example, some women try to lasso their man's destiny-driven, soul-food-seeking attention and focus it onto themselves, the children, the family, the house, the dog, and so on. Because the woman is not creating food for her own soul, she consciously or unconsciously feels that it is not fair that she "stays at home with the kids" while the man goes out to "play" where he gets food for his soul. She may force the man into an either/or decision, "Either me or your job! Either me or your art! Either me or whatever it is you are doing out there!" She does not realize that her man needs both her heart food *and* his destiny food, just like she does. If she tries to make her man choose, she might end up with a man with no balls, a man not challenging himself to go beyond his own limits, a man with no adventure stories to tell around the fire at night. This would be "a man who's not man," as the lyrics above explain.

Garth, a highly creative and self-motivated man, had arranged for his work to be in alignment with his destiny. As a result, his work-life was rich to overflowing with soul food and his soul was well nourished. He had always been active with explorative adventures, and ever since childhood his abundance of soul food had also flowed to his heart, without his awareness. His heart was then filled to overflowing with soul food, not with heart food. Since his heart was already full, it was neither interested nor able to receive proper heart food, such as the direct heart to heart extraordinary human love from his woman.

The heart/soul food imbalance causes diseases equivalent to imbalances in ordinary food. For example, you cannot only live on protein. Your body also needs carbohydrates. It is rumored that a widow had enough money when her husband died that every day she could finally eat what she had always wanted to eat: fried chicken. After a few years she died of starvation. Fortunately for Garth, when he understood what he was doing it was not too late. He immediately made changes in his inner navigating. Garth had to learn how to "flow" the soul food from his destiny only into his soul, and then to hold open the channel for receiving heart food from his woman into his heart. Many things in Garth's life changed for the better soon after that, with his children, with work associates, and with his woman.

Another man, let's call him Sid, followed the normal cultural program and never took strong steps to align his work with his destiny. His work put food on the table and paid the bills, but it did not feed his soul. Sid had graduated from college and accepted a small "safe" position in a large company doing technical work on various projects. Then, after years of dedicated work, he was unceremoniously laid off. His soul would have been starving except that he had a strong heart connection to his wife and to his adopted children. After being fired, Sid spent more than a year "looking for work," hanging around his wife and kids at the house, driving himself and them totally crazy by trying to feed his soul with heart food from them. (You cannot survive on just carbohydrates either. You also need protein.) As Sid's severance pay ran out, he finally took courage and followed his destiny, getting certified and starting his own business leading workshops and coaching other families who wanted to adopt children. His new work generated food for his soul, and the resulting balance provided sanity in his roles as husband and father.

Many modern women avoid starting a family, and may keep relationship to a sterile minimum, so as to follow a momentous career path that may or may not be in alignment with their destiny. These women may suffer from starving hearts *and* starving souls, because most corporate work does not provide food suitable for feeding feminine souls. Other women avoid applying their education, and "sacrifice" a potential career in order to build families and nurture children. They may have plenty of heart food, but try to get their soul food vicariously from meddling in their husband's work. He in turn may be trying to feed his heart vicariously from enmeshing himself with her relationship to the children. These things may be happening to you and will definitely trap you in ordinary human relationship.

Taking care to feed your heart and your soul abundant meals, with their appropriate kinds of experiential and energetic foods, will go a long way toward establishing a foundation upon which you can experiment in extraordinary human relationship.

27 Experiments for Creating Extraordinary Human Relationship

These twenty-seven experiments help build a foundation for Adult responsibility and extraordinary human relationship. The difficulty here is that extraordinary human relationship is generated through ongoing *nonlinear creation,* for which there can never be a methodical system. Nonlinear creation means: Something that works once will not necessarily ever work again in the history of the universe. Then again, maybe it will. There are no guaranteed formulas. Extraordinary human relationship demands that you take fierce, reasonless responsibility for ongoingly creating the possibility of extraordinary human love. There are no rules for making this happen. You just need to keep trying. (Watch the movie *Groundhog Day* with Bill Murray to see what is meant by *keep trying.*) Remember, these are experiments. Some of the experiments are simple actions that take only a few moments and are repeated over and over again. Some are subtle or fundamental attitude shifts that show up as a totally new tactical approach to problems or potential conflicts. Other experiments may take days or weeks to try, but might be done only once in a lifetime.

While experimenting it can be both wise and practical to adopt the perspective of Old Lodge Skins in the film *Little Big Man,* "Sometimes the magic works. Sometimes it does not." Each experiment works in its own dimensions, so the results of one experiment may or may not have a connection to the performance of another experiment.

You can conduct your experiments like the conductor of an orchestra, choosing which experiments to try when, how intensely, and deciding how to harmonize the mood of each experiment with the others when you are doing more than one experiment at a time. As you conduct your life's concerto, consider this: How would your relationships be if moment to moment you consciously knew that every move you made while being together was a living improvised experiment and that this is how it is supposed to be? **Doing Experiments (BLTLCH06.40).**

1. Do not complain to your partner. No matter what is happening make zero derogatory comments about *anything,* even under your breath. Notice whatever you notice.

Decide whatever you decide. Do what you do. But along the way, do not complain. Not even one little squeak. Complaining places you in the victim position of low drama – you become adaptive and manipulating. Life is not low drama. If there is something to complain about, then change it. If you decide not to change it, then be happy with how it is.

2. Be radiantly happy. Most of us have squelched our happiness down to that level of happiness tolerated in a bank lobby. It is far more acceptable these days to be cool than it is to be happy. Unsquelch your happiness. Discover and connect into the source of being happy for no reason. Watch children under the age of three. If their innocence has not yet been shattered, then their actions are fueled by pure joy. That joy is still in you somewhere. Find it. Let it shine, out loud, with your voice and body and facial expressions attached.

3. If the waiter brings you something different from what you ordered, do not explain that a mistake was made. Calling it a mistake is questioning the intelligence of the universe. Who knows? Maybe your body needs vitamins or proteins that were not contained in your original order. Instead of sending your order back to the kitchen, change your mind. Decide, "Yes, wow! A surprise from the universe! This is so much better than what I ordered." *Choose* what was served, and make your choosing invisible to others. You are not a victim if you have changed your mind. It builds matrix to eat what was served rather than what you ordered. This also applies to life at large.

4. Repeatedly experiment with not knowing your partner. Have no history with them. Dwell on no memories. See them now as if it is the first time you are seeing them, perhaps even the first time you are seeing another human being. Make it be the first

time you are holding their hand, the first time you are holding any hand. What a wonderfully fulfilling experience it is to hold this incredible being's hand.

5. Do not remember any pre-existing story that your partner has told about themselves. Listen instead to whatever story they are creating about themselves in that moment and repeat it back to them so that they know you heard their story. Know that the story they are telling now, no matter what that story is, once it is heard can completely vanish, as if it never existed. Then, an entirely new and different story can take its place.

6. Make surprises. Surprises do not involve money or gifts. Surprises do not involve physical objects or props. Surprises are delightful theater pieces created through wrapping you and your partner into unexpected qualities of space. Surprises are not practical jokes or gags. No one is insulted. No one looks bad. Surprises come from you going nonlinear into a possibility that was invisible just a moment ago and did not occur to anyone else. Learn to shift identity, to speak in different accents, take on a wide variety of characters, go sideways into parallel conversations, adopt extraordinary viewpoints and consider staying there and going back there often.

7. Be early. Do not make your partner wait for you. Think ahead and be proactive. Learn to move faster than the speed of time. That means do whatever it takes, without rushing, to arrive where you intended to be before the clock gets there. Get present before your partner arrives. Truly enjoy yourself while waiting for your partner to join you.

8. Ordinary human relationships involve a kind of mutual vampire feeding, "I'll do this for you if you do that for me." These relationships will never rise above the ordinary. Whatever you provide for your partner do *not* make them pay. Provide extraordinary love *for free*, as if you had an infinitely inexhaustible supply.

9. Take care of your energetic body. Make it so that you have a surplus of energy for your partner rather than being a drag on them. Flow energy to your partner rather than wanting them to flow energy to you. There may be times when you ask your partner to listen to your pain, but do not make their listening to your pain the main meal of your relationship. Your partner is not mommy or daddy. When you need them to listen to your pain, ask if you can share something with them; say that you do not expect them to do anything about it, but to be-with you. If you do want them to do something, then be specific and ask them directly: "Would you hold me please?" "Would you get the kids in bed tonight?" Do not expect your partner to be manipulated into action by your victim story.

10. Take care of your physical body. Your physical body is probably the only physical body that your partner gets to play with. Keep it clean, pretty, strong, and in tip-top shape for being played with rigorously. *This particularly does* not *mean preoccupation with trying to make your body like the computer augmented magazine photos!* Your partner is not attracted to you because of your tan, your eye makeup, or the size of your penis or breasts. They are attracted to you because you enjoy being yourself, exactly as you are. Your physical body has its own unique state of wellness and radiant health. Take care to have that.

11. Take care of your intellectual body by studying, engaging in stimulating conversation, attending talks and workshops and seminars that interest you. Feed yourself a steady diet of nonlinear high-meme-content intellectual foods. Do not depend

only on your partner for your intellectual nourishment.

12. Take care of your emotional body by continuously knowing the difference between feelings and emotions. Seek the immediacy of your feelings. Clean up the contaminating residue of your emotions. *Your emotional healing process is none of your partner's business.* Handle it maturely yourself. Do not use your partner as surrogate therapist, psychologist, doctor, healer, nurse, teacher, or parent. It is not your partner's job to heal you. It is your partner's job to enjoy your company. So, be good company.

13. Clean up messes. Messes get in the way of perceiving subtle joys of life like dog poop gets in the way of rolling in fresh green grass. A little dog poop can stink up a whole room. A dirty dish or kid's toy can destroy the elegant sanctuary of your home like a cigarette butt destroys the *wa* (meaning *harmony*) of a Japanese garden. Consistently scan with an "eagle eye" for messes that you can put into order. (There is a difference between an "eagle eye" and a "neurotically critical eye." Use the former. Avoid the latter.) There are little messes everywhere. Even if it is not your mess, you can clean it up as a matter of course with almost no effort. Be careful though. One person's mess is another person's museum. Respect the idiosyncratic needs of your partner's Box. For example, *Do not touch their desk!* Do not put anything on their desk except at a designated in-box.

14. Make elegance. Elegance effervesces from revealed details. If you do not have an organic experience of what elegance is, learn. Elegance can radiate from a cleaned room. Elegance can radiate from simple furniture, fine art, carefully prepared food, well-spoken words. Elegance can radiate from the way you move your attention in empty space, how you say, "Good morning," how you open a door, or how you enjoy your partner's smile.

15. Unstress yourself. Arranging to be stressed is your Box's strategy for avoiding intimacy, and our culture's principal distraction from authenticity. Here is how to unstress: Get enough sleep – take naps. Drink enough water – not just coffee, tea, soda, or alcohol. Take a warm bath. Eat well – not too much or too little. Avoid overstimulating yourself – manage your energy. Exercise. Stay healthy – do not catch colds. Renegotiate overwork and overwhelm. Do not have accidents – get nurtured through intentional physical intimacy instead.

16. Move instantaneously without procrastination. There is often no need to think about or discuss things. What if your instinctual intuition was God giving you direct instructions as to exactly what to do now? *And then you decide to think about it?* Stop looking for triple confirmation. Skip the explanations – they are intellectual superfluosity. Just move.

17. Be yes. When your partner or child says no, be yes for their no, meaning support their no. Say, "I love you and I respect you whatever you choose." Then honor their choice without further discussion. Carry no emotional baggage about it. "Yes, but…" is negation. Do not say, "Yes, but…" Instead learn to say, "Yes, and…" When someone offers you an idea to try out, accept their offer through being a yes for their offer. "Accepting offers" is an important piece of improvisational theater. (For more on this see Keith Johnstone's great book *Improv*.) We so often reject what we are offered because it is not in our original plans. Who do you think made the plans anyway? Are you bending

your life around, forcing other people as well as your endless self to fit into your Box's plans? Try this experiment: Do not reject whatever your partner offers you. Surprise them with your utter lack of resistance. Provide pleasurable accompaniment. Even if you are holding hands at a football game you are still holding hands. Pay attention to what you are yes about. In this case, be yes about the experience of the hand you are holding.

18. Commit to what your partner is committed to. This means developing possibility listening. Listen for what your partner is committed to and then commit to that. Most of us do not really know what our partner, our children, or our boss are committed to. It may be to finish knitting a sweater by Christmas, or to do 500 push-ups, or to open a successful restaurant, or to spend some weekend hours totally relaxing. We all have both conscious and unconscious commitments. Many of the unconscious commitments that we are most fiercely committed to fulfilling are irresponsible. This experiment is not like Bonnie's commitment to Clyde's irresponsible habit of bank robbing. This experiment is about listening for and committing to your partner's responsible commitments.

19. If you ever get sick or hurt yourself in an accident, even in a minor way like bumping your head or cutting your finger while slicing carrots, develop the immediate habit of saying "Thank you" to the universe. You can either trust or distrust the universe; it can be your friend or your enemy. If you establish a trusting relationship to the universe, that trust includes *everything*, even things that at first seem "bad" or "negative." Having an accident sends a shock to your attention. Most often, accidents occur in a moment when we are unconscious or "asleep," not paying attention to our attention. In the moment of the accident we are shocked into the "waking state" and are aware of what we are aware of. If you reject the value of the accident you also reject the waking state. If you do not wake up immediately and fully in response to each little bug bite, intestinal pain, itch or ache, then the universe has to resort to bigger shocks to wake you up, and it will. A headache does not mean a lack of aspirin. Figure it out. The universe wants you awake and evolving. When you are not, the universe will do whatever it can to get through to you. If you have already decided to trust the universe, then if you smash your toe it is "cosmic acupuncture" at work on you. Be grateful. If you are sick in bed there is some use to that, even if you don't see it at first. Write poetry. Get rested. Grieve the loss of a loved one. Paint. Let the puzzlement of it work you into a new shape. This does not mean that anything "bad" is actually punishment for some past "sin." It means, "Who are you to judge something as bad?" Life is not pain free. "Life is hard and then you die." Dying from some horrible disease does not necessarily mean anything at all. The world is so full of toxins and contaminants that your body will eventually succumb to something – it does not mean you did something wrong. When you refuse to be a victim and you trust the universe, even in the midst of pain, illness and accidents, you can stay open to receiving the benefits. Doing so is a huge blessing for your partner, even if your "partner" is the temporary cohabitant of a hospital room.

20. Avoid saying, "Obviously...." As in, "Would you like me to take your coat?" "Obviously." Or, "Did you enjoy your meal?" "Obviously." Instead say yes or no.

And Above All, Never Ignore Your Ignorance

Being Responsible for Your Ignorance (BLTLCH06.41). Do not forget that you are truly an *expert* at creating ordinary human relationship. Do not forget your ignorance. Ignorance and knowledge, darkness and light, scarcity and abundance, all the contrasting opposites come hand in hand. You do not get one without the other. Do not live in the fantasy expectation that you can only be the source of extraordinary human relationship and that ordinary human relationship is a thing of the past. Can a horse outrun its own tail? Can you dine in five-star restaurants without making shit? Even if you do not consciously choose actions that create ordinary human relationship, they are always at hand. The ignorance never leaves you.

Even if you do the experiments from this book and you succeed at entering extraordinary or Archetypal domains of relationship, you can never ignore your well-oiled mechanisms for enlivening Shadow Principles, lest they sneak out and stealthily devour your hard-earned treasures.

Ignorance is like a rabid dog. As soon as you stop guarding against a rabid dog it will jump up and bite your ass. Trying to forget your previous and still readily-available incompetences can be a rabid dog biting your ass if you turn arrogant or proud about the new soft skills you have learned. Becoming aware of what you were not aware of before can produce a superiority that the Tibetan Buddhist Vajrayana Master Chögyam Trungpa called "spiritual materialism" in his book of the same title. Your hard-earned soft skills can be a justification used by your Box for regarding yourself as someone who really knows something. You take a secretly haughty position, from which you can look down over your nose, disgustedly, at all the poor ignorant peasants around you. Before you know it, you will be mentally competing against others to find who is the better practitioner! Spiritual materialism is a seriously debilitating affliction and should be treated with full strength anti-memes the moment it is detected (like, now).

Another way your ignorance can bite you in the ass is if you judge your previous incompetence as "bad." Judging the behaviors that produce ordinary human relationship as "bad" and banishing them into forgetfulness is fanaticism. Fanaticism is the fantasy that: "I never do this anymore [forgetting that just a short while ago you *did* do *exactly* this]; if *you* do it then you need to be fixed." Fanaticism will not protect you from your own ignorance.

The only thing that protects you from your own ignorance is diamond-sharp clarity that behaviors are neither good nor bad, but that each behavior produces a different kind of result. Vigilant consciousness means holding a sword of persistent awakeness about what behaviors you enact and why. The sword is presence of mind, paying relaxed but precise attention to your purpose; staying at the edge, able to move in any direction. Vigilant consciousness is at the core of the term "practice." The only thing that protects you in each moment from falling back into being a slave to the purposes of ordinary human relationship is your practice.

It is not like you can practice for a number of months or years and then achieve some kind of steady-state safety zone of "mastery." Such "mastery" is an illusion presented by the Box. The illusion is that the Box can sacrifice to make a flurry of efforts and achieve a certificate of "mastery," after which you can kick back and relax, assured that you are a responsible Adult and will only create extraordinary human relationship. It does not work that way. Ask any true master. Their answer will be the same: "You will need to practice until your last breath."

When decoded, what "obviously" really means is, "you idiot!"

21. Take care of the kids. You have kids. Take care of them. This is an eighteen- or twenty-year commitment of time, energy, money and attention. Such an investment was made in you. Do it for them. It is easy to take care of children because their problems amount to one of five things: They are 1) hungry, 2) tired, 3) physically hurt, 4) sick, 5) unheard. This number "5" is the most problematical for parents, and the most easily resolved by engaging the completion loop (*See* Section 6-O) with your child. Recall that a communication persists until it is received. Holding unreceived communications is painful for the child. Receiving communications is healing. Listen directly to what your child or partner says. Repeat back what you heard them say until they confirm that you got it by saying yes. The yes signifies that you have received their communication accurately. As soon as you get a yes, the communication drops into the next deeper level of communion and a new communication begins.

22. Make boundaries with the kids instantly and without effort. Being a family is like singing a familiar song together. You already know how the song goes. You already know the melody and the words. When one note or one word is even slightly off, in timing or tone, you recognize it instantly in your whole body. *This is the key to making boundaries.* You detect when a correction needs to be made the millisecond the mood is off. Act then. Do not even think. Handle it. Move. Take responsibility for being the parent and make the changes during the singing so that the singing can continue in its beautiful harmony. There are two ways to conduct the orchestration of your family: neurotic control or responsible navigating. Neurotic control serves the comfort of your Box. Responsible navigating serves the Principles of family, communication, and extraordinary human love. Do not confuse the two.

23. Whining is manipulation that a person (child or adult) does rather than being in relationship. Tolerate no whining. Period. When there is whining, start a meta-conversation: "I notice that you are whining. Whining is its own payoff. Are you willing to switch to a different kind of conversation? If not I will talk with you later." Make a boundary: "No whining. I will not participate in a whining conversation." Create clarity: "That specific behavior is whining. I am not a garbage can for whining." Create possibility: "Is there some feeling that you want to share? Do you have a need? Do you have a different opinion? Is there something moving in you?" Then listen. But, if whining continues, go somewhere else or have the person whine somewhere else, not into you. This is not about them; it is simple clarity about the quality of communication that you support in your

relationship. Whining yourself or permitting your mate, children, employees or boss to whine around you is beneath the dignity of an Adult relationship. Make clear distinctions about exactly what constitutes whining, including tone of voice, mood, and the intention of the message. Whining happening around you is feedback that *you* are creating ordinary human relationship. When whining stops, then talk together.

24. Feed your soul. It is not your partner's job to feed your soul. In rare instances both people in a relationship require the same soul food at the same time and can lead projects together, or can live in praise of the same spiritual master. But don't fool yourself about this! Having projects together does not necessarily solve more problems than it causes. Your partner may need totally different soul food than you do. Respect the different need like you would respect your partner ordering liver and onions even when you want to eat Caesar salad. Encourage them to get their soul fed, and take care to feed yours.

25. Live integrity. Most of us freak out just hearing the word "integrity." Our nervous system sends lie detectors off the scale just seeing words like "accountable," "impeccable," or "responsible" written on a piece of paper. "Integrity" simply means doing what you say you are going to do. "I will put a new light bulb in," is not an empty phrase. It is a measurable promise. People to whom you say such things, even offhandedly, take note. They cannot help it. Promises go into the soul, and then the soul starts waiting for the promise to be kept through your actions. If you do not do what you say you are going to do, what you say and what you do are not one, they are not integral. With enough incomplete promises, your partner's being-to-being connection to you will break down in confusion and resentment. This is totally predictable and totally avoidable. Being "integrity in action" builds more and more connection.

26. "Rub her feet." This is an amazing experiment to be done almost anywhere and any time for no reason. This extraordinary idea comes from Lazarus Long, the character from Robert Heinlein's novel, *Time Enough for Love*, who lived 3500 years often in the company of women – obvious proof that he knew what he was talking about!

27. Try again. You have probably tried any number of things with your partner that did not seem to work. Maybe you tried to have them tell you about their fears, or tried to relax yourself more and be happy while visiting with the in-laws, or tried to be more appreciative of the children. When at first our trials do not work, we tend to not try again. The experiment here is to go ahead and try again. In extraordinary human relationship, do-overs are allowed. Try again, even if the first time that you tried was only a few seconds ago. You might be surprised to find how many possibilities are available in each next three seconds.

Ending An Extraordinary Human Relationship

Ending or Not

There are three sensible reasons for a relationship to end: violence, drugs, or lack of intimacy. None of these circumstances provides an absolute reason to end a relationship. Nobody can decide *for you* to end a relationship, just as nobody can decide for you to start one. And besides all that, there is nothing in the rulebook that says you have to make sense.

Violence in a relationship may be physical, psychological or emotional. The drugs in use may be legal or illegal drugs. Using violence or drugs as a reason to end a relationship is completely understandable. *But*, no matter how understandable a *reason* is, using a reason to end your relationship gives the *reason* the responsibility for your decision. If the reason has the responsibility, then the *reason* has the power, not you. Giving the power of your decision to a reason is an attempt to avoid responsibility for making a choice.

It is quite understandable and acceptable to use violence or drugs as a reason to end a relationship. But when it comes to using "lack of intimacy" as the reason for ending a relationship, the reason itself becomes questionable. Without a complete education and training in extraordinary human relationship, it is quite predictable that the only kind of relationship you can create is ordinary human relationship. Ordinary human relationship is contexted in low drama enacted through blame, resentment, withhold, justification, complaining, being right or making wrong. It just so happens that these are exactly the same behaviors that avoid intimacy! Until you have practiced creating extraordinary human relationship with feedback and coaching for some time, you will most likely continue creating only ordinary human relationship. Having no ability to create intimacy and then using "lack of intimacy" as a reason to end a relationship, as common as this is, approaches the absurd.

Withdrawing Your Resentments (BLTLCH06.42). But it can get even more complex and absurd. Take for example resentment. Once we have buried a resentment about our partner into our heart, that resentment will stay there and continue causing pain until such time as we consciously and intentionally take that particular resentment out of our heart. The pain of having that resentment provides us with a justifiable, experiential reason for behaving with disrespect toward our partner, and, oh, by the way, fulfilling our Shadow Principles and abundantly feeding our Gremlin at our partner's expense. We may therefore set up a complex, mostly unconscious ordinary-human-relationship game with our partner, based on reasons that are empowered by resentments about things that happened between us long ago. Taking away even one resentment would destabilize our game. Without the heart-torturing resentment we might lose motivation for our revengeful behavior, and then our Gremlin would have to go hungry.

Resentment-empowered reasons justifying subtle and overt Gremlin-feeding interactions is how most of us live out our ordinary human relationships. From this perspective it may seem easier *to not learn anything* about all this stuff and to let things stay how they are. But, if things how they are become too

Decisions vs. Reasons

Separating Decisions from Reasons (BLTLCH06.43). Regardless of how good your reason is for making a decision, every conscious or unconscious decision you make is *unavoidably* your responsibility. Since you already *have* responsibility for your decisions, you may as well also have the power that naturally accompanies responsibility. If you take back the power for making your decision, then you no longer need to hide your decision behind a reason. This means you are making your decisions for no reason. Taking responsibility for making decisions for *no* reason is an astonishing change of perspective (a change that you would do best to keep in the privacy of your own mind, heart, soul and body).

In the public's eye, you are more socially acceptable if you provide understandable reasons for what you decide. The point is, decide first. Make reasons later. If you use reasons, do your reason-making as an act of "conscious theater," that is, know that the reasons you present are a fabrication and do not actually have any power in your decision. Use reasons like PR to make your decision understandable and acceptable to others, but not as a basis for actually making the decision.

Trying to make a decision the other way around – by collecting reasons first and then making a decision based on the impetus or the logic of the reasons – is maddening. Even a mountain of good reasons does not contain enough responsibility to make one little decision. *You* are the one with all the responsibility. Acknowledging your natural responsibility for making your own decisions makes it easier to trust yourself to make your own decisions, even if the decisions are massively life-changing.

Relationships end nastily when either or both partners try to avoid being responsible for deciding to end the relationship. The illusion is, if you can present enough evidence to prove to the world that the other person (is a jerk and) is the reason the relationship has to end, the relationship ending is not your fault. "I was forced by the horrendous circumstances to decide to end it." However, since you are *unavoidably* responsible for *every* decision that you make, trying to avoid responsibility for the decision to separate results in a blame war, fabulous for Gremlin, not so fabulous for Adult men and women. The only one who profits in the case of Decisions vs. Reasons is the lawyer.

---

painful to continue, ending our relationship looks easier than the even *more* painful process of taking the hooks of resentment out of our heart and starting over again with the same person.

Succeeding or Not

Why You are in Relationship (BLTLCH06.44). A wedding vow is a fixed thing. Human beings are not. It is improbable that even on their wedding day two people have the same conscious and unconscious intentions, the same size of being, and the same interest in personal development. Do we expect ourselves to? As we live, we learn. As we learn, we grow. As we grow, we change. It is quite improbable that two individuals will live, learn, grow and change at the same speed or in the same ways. Do we expect that we should? Needs change. Priorities change. Sensitivities change. What is to happen if the one in us who made our wedding vows "dies" and a new configuration grows out of the ashes? What causes a relationship to continue? What is the purpose of relationship anyway?

After some years of natural development and growth, we may find that our relationship no longer nurtures our development. Then what? We may sense that we have to choose between the least of two evils: sacrificing our aliveness to maintain our marriage, or sacrificing our marriage vows to keep growing. That the vows are powerful is evidenced by the percentage of married people who, rather than ending their relationship, act as if their vows are true but work out "creative" ways to try to stay alive. Even though a dual life is excruciatingly destructive, we may come to the conclusion that feeding ourselves extramaritally is better than quitting the relationship and seeing ourselves as a failure.

If our relationship does end, the common tendency is to conclude that our relationship was a failure overall, perhaps even from the very beginning. We studiously think back and try to find the root causes of our split-up. We may even conclude that to have integrity we should never have made a commitment to relationship in the first place.

Looking at our situation, we assess the "alternatives":

1. Use denial, belief systems, or drugs to imprison ourselves within the original boundaries of a now dead relationship to keep up the appearances of being successful.
2. Find extramarital intimacies, yet still maintain the appearance of being in a working relationship.
3. Acknowledge that we have failed and end the relationship in disgrace.

There is an additional alternative to consider. The other alternative is not common but it is imminently possible. The possibility is to use the pressing necessity in your relationship to commit to an intense experiment in radical honesty. You begin the experiment suddenly and for no reason, by taking every risk to bring your relationship moment by moment into the Adult responsibility of extraordinary human relationship. With a fierce, irrevocable commitment, you pay attention, stay alert and hold it there – in the extraordinary – wielding the sword of clarity in your one hand and your vulnerable heart in the other, never allowing behaviors that might drop you back into ordinary human relationship. Keep your center, express what you feel, ask for what you need, make boundaries, make decisions, go nonlinear, ask for help from the best help available (not just your usual friends) and let the cards fall where they may. If the relationship is already on the line, what do you actually risk by finally and extensively letting your authentic self be known?

If, after some months of maximum efforts to maintain extraordinary human relationship, the relationship still ends, then *decide* that the relationship ended because *it was successful*. From the perspective of extraordinary human relationship, the relationship has gone through its life cycle and has accomplished the evolution that it was originated to accomplish. By taking your relationship beyond your ordinary world of habits, and simultaneously bringing in contributions from all available resources, you wring out of your relationship every last shred of learning. That learning then stands as a foundation so that your next "relationship laboratory" can unfold with dignity for each of you.

Although you made mistakes, although you caused pain or felt pain, although someone else "could have done it better," you could have faith that you *both* did the best you could.

You could decide to forgive yourself and your partner, and accept yourself and your partner, by having faith that actually you both did the best that *could be done*, because you were the only ones there to try.

You could also have faith that what you are doing right now is also the best that you can do. Certainly you might learn something later that will allow you to do better. But whatever you do better later will be done by a different "you" in different circumstances.

Dangerous complexities do not stop people from wanting to come together as couples. It has not stopped you. Think of that. Even after all that has happened to you so far, you still want to come together with someone, with a partner. It is the purity and innocence of your simple wish to come together with someone that you can trust. Coupling is an Archetypal form that we are deeply attracted to living into. Every moment enlivened by extraordinary human love brings benefit to the world. Let your inner wish to come together move you to learn and grow and do experiments that bring you more fully into living as an expression of your inner wish.

CHAPTER 7

Edgework

The term "Edgework" is extrapolated from a discussion in Seth Godin's energetic and wise little marketing book called *Free Prize Inside*. Seth explores ways to expand a market. We explore ways to expand the Box – in this case, expanding the Box of relationship possibilities. One effective and interesting way to expand the Box is through Edgework. Edgework is about responsibly opening up fresh opportunities in several dimensions of your Box at the same time. Fresh opportunities are most abundant at the edges of your Box where there can be intersections with the unknown.

Through doing Edgework you take responsibility for creating what is important for you in your own life. Nobody can do Edgework for you. If you succeed in taking actions with enough momentum to break free of the culture's gravitational field that incessantly pulls you back toward its definition of "normal," you are creating in a way that can potentially transform the culture. True creating is accompanied by a joyous edginess, an "invention stress," caused by being at risk for producing from the unknown something that did not exist before. Responsible invention stress builds matrix for extraordinary human relationship.

These ideas may at first seem unusual. But as soon as you begin seeking extraordinary human relationship they immediately fall into place and start making sense. Edgework is not ready-made, and not something that you do once. In extraordinary human relationship, Edgework becomes your way of life.

The Contest Between You and Your Box

As discussed earlier, each of us has created a Box. The Box acts as a giant multidimensional filter between you and the world. The Box determines everything that you can perceive and everything that you can express. The purpose of the Box is to ensure your survival. From the Box's perspective, its present design has been successful because you *have* survived. Therefore, the Box concludes that if it can continue to protect itself *first,* then it can continue to protect you. The Box is therefore justified in defending *itself* at all costs.

Bringing Your Life to Life (BLTLCH07.01). Over time, you may find that you are unwilling to pay some of the costs that your Box is still willing to pay. This difference of opinion begins a contest between you and your Box. The Box may want to continue spending your energy and attention on actions like trying to be perfect, keeping resentments, staying in isolation, putting on the "show," constantly competing to be the best, not letting others know about your true inner experience, constantly struggling for survival, being secretly hypercritical of others, hiding your inadequacies or your superiority, or questioning the value of life itself. From the Box's perspective, these actions are how you survive. From your new perspective,

these actions produce unnecessary suffering. Some of the suffering the Box is willing to endure are no longer worth the false security attained by remaining in such a well-defended Box. The question is: Who will win? You or your Box? If you do not engage in this contest with focused intention and with all efforts, then your Box will continue creating what it has designed itself to create – ordinary human relationship. To create extraordinary human relationship you face the challenge of expanding your Box. Exactly here is where we apply Edgework.

Edgework is a way for loosening the grip of your Box on your limitations. With certain restrictions eased, you will be able to start taking what were previously forbidden actions. Your new actions, small though they might seem, will permit you to enter previously inaccessible areas of extraordinary human relationship. The procedure for Edgework is to go to an interesting "edge" of your Box, to stay at that edge, and while staying there do Edgework experiments. Edgework brings your life to life.

The Marshmallow Zone

Stepping Out of Your Marshmallow Zone (BLTLCH07.02). Contrary to what we might assume, we do not live in our whole Box. We live toward the center of our Box, well away from its edges, in the warm, soft, familiar, and sweet "marshmallow zone." Life in the marshmallow zone is secure, predictable, controllable and safe. If we are honest we must also admit that the marshmallow zone is restrictive, boring, lifeless, frustrating, and in some ways dead.

You have wrapped yourself into the comforts of the marshmallow zone because you

know what it feels like to get too close to an edge. Just thinking about going to the edge of your Box sends a cold chill running down your spine. Try to remember the last time this happened to you. Perhaps you accidentally found yourself in a homosexual apparatus shop. Or your boss asked you to give a speech to the board of directors. Or your partner accused you of having an affair. Or an ill friend asked you to accompany her as she approached death. Or you turned a corner and were suddenly face to face with

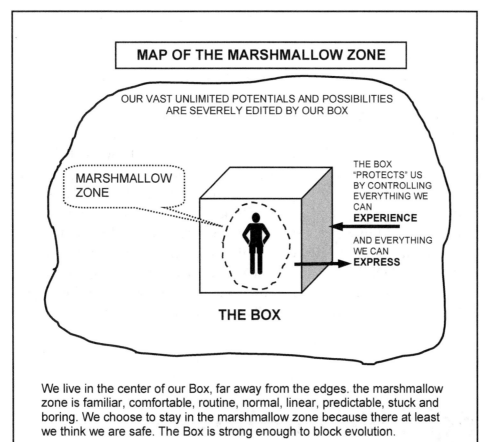

MAP OF THE MARSHMALLOW ZONE

OUR VAST UNLIMITED POTENTIALS AND POSSIBILITIES
ARE SEVERELY EDITED BY OUR BOX

MARSHMALLOW
ZONE

THE BOX
"PROTECTS" US
BY CONTROLLING
EVERYTHING WE
CAN
EXPERIENCE

AND EVERYTHING
WE CAN
EXPRESS

THE BOX

We live in the center of our Box, far away from the edges. the marshmallow zone is familiar, comfortable, routine, normal, linear, predictable, stuck and boring. We choose to stay in the marshmallow zone because there at least we think we are safe. The Box is strong enough to block evolution.

a rough looking gang of teenagers. Or you clicked on the wrong icon and found yourself in a triple-X sex website. Or you got a tax bill from the government for several zeros more than the balance of your bank account. Or you got a flat tire in a ghetto neighborhood alone at night. Or someone misinterpreted what you said, considering it to be seriously flirting. Or you thought your lottery ticket contained winning numbers. Or someone at the train station tried to sell you heroin.

Over "there," as in the examples cited above, beyond the edge, is the scary unknown. Being at the edge is risky! Control slips through your fingers, and mysterious and unending, although nameless, dangers wait for you. Long ago, perhaps out of your awareness, you decided that the best place to be was far away from those scary edges, in the safety of the marshmallow zone, no matter what it cost you.

The marshmallow zone is protection against life's greatest paradox: death. The marshmallow zone gives us the illusion that death does not exist, or at least "does not apply to me." It is exactly here that the paradox reveals its necessity. Unless you are aware that at some point all life inevitably comes to an end, you are not really living. Life thrives at the edge where the old dies and the new is born, the intersection between what is and what could be. In other words, life thrives through evolution. The paradox is that evolution does not occur in the overprotected marshmallow zone. Our difficulty is that evolution is the catalyst for sustaining extraordinary human relationship.

In the conflict between the Box and evolution, nothing is automatically decided. It is completely your privilege and your responsibility to choose whether or not you use the force of your free will to defend yourself from the influences of evolution. It is clear that if you are single and live alone in the marshmallow zone, years can go by unnoticed because you have chosen to not let anyone near enough to press you with alternatives to your Box's view of reality. If you choose relationship, but you still intend to stay in your marshmallow zone, then it is guaranteed that you will generate only ordinary human relationship. Locked in your marshmallow zone your partner does not get to be in contact with you. The closest they can come to you is the periphery. Relationship itself soon turns stale and dry, suffocated by lack of possibility. Interactions are theoretical and do not feed you or your partner. Conflicts arise because your heart and your soul are struggling for their lives. Your partner's are too.

The marshmallow zone is like a bath. No matter how warm, safe, soft and familiar it feels, sooner or later you have to get out of it. Especially if you (as a man) intend to engage in "parley" with a Pirate Sorceress Warrioress Queen Goddess Woman! Or if you (as a woman) wish to join adventures with a Pirate Magician King Spiritual Warrior Man!

(We'll discuss these possibilities in depth in Part IV, Chapters 10 and 11.)

Happiness and a fulfilled relationship are never permanent and achievable objectives. Joy is dynamic and fluid, discovered over and over again, each time in a new way. Such exploring demands that you have access to a robust set of resources. A baby chick does not fulfill its destiny except by cracking out of its protective shell. A butterfly does not stretch into its beauty except by splitting its chrysalis and taking flight. You will not unfold into extraordinary human relationship except by pulling the stopper and draining your marshmallow zone dry, then going to the edge of your Box and stretching outward.

SECTION 7-B
))(The Edges of Your Box

Edgework involves three steps. The first step in Edgework is to find an edge. The second step involves staying exactly on that edge. The third step is doing Edgework experiments at that edge. Clearly, a strong understanding of edges is crucial to the success of Edgework.

Imagine your Box. The Box portrayed on page 223 is a simple six-sided cube. Your actual Box is far more complex and sophisticated than a simple cube. Each surface of your Box is assembled out of basic mental and psychological components: beliefs, attitudes, assumptions, interpretations, conclusions, opinions, projections, and stories. Everyone's Box is built of the same structural components, but each Box is constructed in its own unique design, with edges that are short or long, straight or curvy, dull or sharp. Each edge is our personal declaration about what we are committed to hold as real. All edges are arbitrary. For example, one person

may believe that making one or two mistakes is a sign of total incompetence, whereas another might completely accept three or four mistakes as a sign of being a truly creative artist. One person may have an edge that assesses eating cake and coffee as, "I have no self-discipline," whereas another might assess the exact same behavior as, "I passionately love to experience the abundance that life has to offer!"

Evolution occurs most dynamically at the intersection between two media. Think of the intertidal zones between ocean and land. This is where creatures first learned to breathe and crawl and eventually fly. Think of the interface between the fields of biology and physics. This is where biophysics and biotechnology develop medicines and diagnostics like x-ray, ultrasound and brain scan. Evolution is most rambunctious at the edges, so for extraordinary human relationship, it is to the edges we go.

Since we live within the perceptual limits of our Box and the Box confidently reassures us, "This is all there is," we sometimes forget that there are vast domains just beyond the edges of our Box – full of what we do not know that we do not know. The interface between the known and the unknown is where we have the greatest opportunity to gain new perspective and make unrestricted actions. At the edge, traditional systems break down, thus creating real necessity for new possibilities to be discovered. To get to the edge we exchange security for adventure. Suddenly, there is a rich source of riskiness and aliveness, both of which are foods that nurture extraordinary human relationship. Nonlinear nutrition is not available in the marshmallow zone.

The view at the edge is exhilarating, inspiring, enlightening, and also a bit confusing or scary. You can tell that you are at an edge because you will have two simultaneous perspectives: the familiar view of what used to be considered normal, and an additional view completely at odds with the traditional view. Holding both views long enough to realize that you have two views is the beginning of Edgework. Sustaining two views demands the same kind of practice it takes to learn tightrope walking. While practicing, you will find that it is far easier to fall into one view or the other than it is to balance on the razor's edge experiencing both realities together.

Cracking Your Certainty (BLTLCH07.03). The double perspective produces a crack in your certainty that causes your familiar perspective to lose its omnipotence. Given the Box's voracious commitment to defending its views as irreproachable and almost holy, having a way to change solid to liquid verges on the miraculous.

The original vice-grip thinking about what is possible or what is important dissolves, revealing a freedom *and* a groundlessness that feel both refreshing and threatening. As your old world disintegrates, there may arise some fear, but the fear is exciting because you are reaping the reward of what could be years of hard work integrating this new double perspective. Suddenly, you take action in ways that surprise the old you. For instance, you may find yourself able to disagree with the general consensus at meetings and to voice your own opinions in a calm and convincing manner; you may easefully gather a team of people and resources together and start a project that you have long been wanting to start; you may clean out the attic or garage of extraneous objects; or you may arrange to meet with someone you admire, but were too self-conscious to connect with. These are actions that you may have instinctively felt to be possible, but for which you previously had no access. The chaos of the edge's two perspectives opens the access.

When doing Edgework avoid the temptation to dive into the new perspective with as much fanatical fervor as you had committed to staying in the original perspective. Returning to certainty, regardless of where the certainty is, turns out to be more of a handicap than a benefit. With certainty, many options are lost. Fluidity is replaced by rigidity. Available

---

MAP OF EDGEWORK

1) Find an exciting edge.

2) Go all the way to the edge and stay there.

3) Do Edgework experiments.

resources are ignored – we can't see them because we are blinded by our certainty that no more resources are available.

Even with the handicaps of certainty being so clearly spelled out, it is not as easy to abandon certainty as one might imagine. For example, one religious fundamentalist miraculously freed from the thought-prison of her original beliefs found that she had the strong tendency to establish herself in new beliefs with equal extremism. Recovering fundamentalists may take on vegetarianism or ecology as replacement fanatical belief systems, because the uncertainty of having no belief system feels so unsolid. Uncertainty *is* unsolid. However, consistent experimentation with Edgework reveals that certainty is an illusionary safe harbor, not sponsored in a universe that flows. The groundless experience is a hard earned and hard kept treasure for the Edgeworker. That treasure, once found, can be well put to use.

Find an Edge

Finding Your Edges (BLTLCH07.04). Start experimenting with sliding out of your marshmallow zone and moving toward edges in unexpected or unusual ways. You will discover that your Box is constructed with myriads of fine to rough edges. Examine each edge, long enough to get a sense of how strongly that particular edge shapes the way the world looks to you.

Edges reveal themselves when you internally ask certain rare questions. If you listen openly to your answers, you may find that the universe has been asking you such questions for quite some time: How honest can I be? (Notice if your body has an immediate contraction away from the edge that such a question reveals.) How much fun am I allowed to have? For how long? How long can I stay unhookable when talking to the opposite sex? How totally can I accept my okayness? In what circumstances? How much discipline can I practice? How much can I ask for help?

How few beliefs can I have? How much of a problem can I be? How exciting can I let my Edgework experiments get? How insane can I appear? In front of whom? How intensely can I love someone? For how long? How long can I work without needing to be successful? How much sorrow can I experience and share? How close can I come to my soul? How long can I go without a fight, an argument, or a rage outburst? How persistently can I align my actions to creating what really matters to me? Questions like these bring us immediately into the "edgy" sensation of being at an edge. Finding an edge is not necessarily comforting, but it is definitely out of the marshmallow zone! Take note of any edges that would excite you to explore in Edgework experiments.

Stay At the Edge

Staying at an Edge (BLTLCH07.05). Recall that the second step of Edgework is figuring out how to *stay* at the edge, not to simply touch the edge and go back. We touch edges of our Box and go back to our marshmallow zone ten times a day.

And, don't think that the goal is to go over the edge and "get out of the Box" – *you cannot get out of the Box!* Did you ever meet anybody without a Box? Neither did I. The image of getting out of the Box is linguistic sleight-of-mind. You may have met someone with an expanded Box, bigger than your own, yes. But we all have a Box. To successfully engage in Edgework it is enough to go to the edge of the Box, and then stay there. Developing an ability to stay at the edge of your Box will take significant work. It helps to observe and gain familiarity with your Box's particular strategies for avoiding the intensity of staying at an edge. Strategies can involve creating physical, intellectual, emotional or energetic complaints, even combinations of several mixed together. Let the seconds tick by while you continue to tolerate the intensity of staying at an edge. Every second counts.

SECTION 7-C
Edgework Experiments

Discovery and Adventure (BLTLCH07.06). We have already been considering edges. Let us now consider experiments. To experiment means to try something about which you cannot, with certainty, predict the outcome. Experimenting is making actions or non-actions on purpose. As the experimenter, you apply your *conscious intention* to serve a *conscious purpose*. For example, you could apply your *conscious intention* to read no further beyond the following list of Edgework experiments until you have actually done three of the listed Edgework experiments yourself. Your *conscious purpose* would be to avoid a common tendency to marvel at cool ideas in your mind, rather than actually integrating them into your life. That would be an Edgework experiment.

Since the exact structure and outcome of such an experiment is not already known, the environs of an experiment are alive and flowing with options. This experiment will live through your committed participation as the experimenter. From start to finish, you will make subtle and instant choices as to the direction and mood of the experiment. You will do this with the tone of your voice, where you place your attention, the timing and intention vector of your moves and gestures, and so on. If you decide to set a romantic mood, for example, you might take your partner to a more elegant restaurant rather than to a fast-food drive-in. If the experiment involves increasing intimacy with your partner and you already know that there are some fears about this for you, you might take an acting workshop or a therapeutic coaching session to shift your ability to experience and express fear, before beginning your intimacy experiment. Then your

explorations and sharing will have a greater range of movement.

The experiment would not be happening except for you doing the experiment. Experimenting makes you inarguably responsible for the existence of the experiment, which puts you at risk. This risk is authentic and serious because your actions have consequence; for example, your partner could take offense at the unexpected doors to new experience that get opened up during one of your experiments. Since the culture does not teach you to experiment, the culture does not protect you from the consequences of your experimental actions. The actions you take will be yours alone. You are the epicenter of the experiment, so all repercussions bounce back to you. There will be no buffer zone.

Doing Edgework experiments involves an extreme level of risk from the Box's point of view. The Box's perception of risk automatically keeps most people from experimenting. Deciding to experiment, even in situations beyond the limits of cultural awareness, makes *you* the source of the experiment, rather than the *culture* being the source. There is no more hiding for you behind the traditions and standards of the culture, which itself may subtly or overtly be telling you to "leave things alone." When experimenting, you go to the limits of the reaches of your Box, but external to the reaches of your culture's Box. In other words, your mother never did such experiments. (Or did she? It is an interesting experiment in itself to spend time making it safe enough for your mother to tell stories about some of the private experiments she has done in her life so far. After all, you gained the confidence to experiment beyond

> ## MAP OF THE 4 SECRETS OF BRINGING YOUR LIFE TO LIFE
>
> **SECRET #1:** This is the greatest secret of bringing your life to life. **The edges of your Box are not permanent.** From the center of your Box the edges look as solid as a brick wall. But when you get up close you can see that the edges are only as solid as a brick wall painted on tissue paper. You can push your finger right through the edge. Key question: *Who is the artist?*
>
> **SECRET #2: As soon as you see an edge you are at the edge.** Just seeing the edge makes it possible to go there and experiment. Whenever someone or something causes you to recognize an edge of your Box, feel grateful. The more unexpected the edge, the more raw opportunity it represents. Key question: *Even here at the edge, am I okay?*
>
> **SECRET #3: There are no special qualifications for doing Edgework experiments.** You do not have to be licensed, rich, sexy, lucky, Italian, spiritually enlightened, or have a certain I.Q. Go ahead and do whatever responsible Edgework experiments turn you on. Key question: *Who should give me permission?*
>
> **SECRET #4:** Edgework is personal and not ready-made. You must do it yourself. Here is the secret: **You already have everything that you need to do Edgework.** You have had it for a long time. You just need to remember that you are an Edgeworker and then keep practicing. Key question: *If not me, then who?*

the culture from somewhere. Perhaps it was from your own mother!)

Being involved with originating an experiment means that you are creating in the pure form. You are creating as the source of the creating. By placing yourself in the driver's seat of an experiment, you are solely responsible for the outcome. Creators who take this level of responsibility often report that creating feels like being in extraordinary human love.

The tactile presence of love establishes the connection between creating and relationship: relationship is ongoing nonlinear creation. Relationship is ongoing experiment: You choose a partner with whom to do experiments and you learn to do experiments together. Then, relationship is no longer a static thing, but a continuous dance of discovery and adventure – not as a fantasy, but as a never-ending series of multidimensional experiments investigating the nature of love and what is possible as a human being. Edgework experiments bring extraordinary human relationship to life.

Edgework Experiments

Empowering Your Curiosity (BLTLCH07.07). Now that you have a clear idea about what edges are and what experimenting is, remember that to do Edgework you simply: 1. Choose an *exciting* edge. 2. Go *all* the way to the edge and stay there, and 3. *Do* Edgework experiments.

While doing your experiments, keep in mind that the immediate, natural feeling response to entering the unknown is fear. As a child, that fear was interpreted as curiosity and excitement. Try interpreting it the same way now as an adult. Feeling the fear of not

Experiments for Four Bodies

Four-Body Edgework (BLTLCH07.08). Because we live quadraphonically – through four bodies: physical body, intellectual body, emotional body, and energetic body (as noted in Section 5-A) – we can do Edgework experiments in these same four domains. While designing and engaging in your Edgework experiments, direct part of your attention to noticing the balance in your experimental diet. It is a common tendency to overdo one kind of Edgework, not realizing that we are completely ignoring one or more of the other three kinds. In the same way that a balance of food nutrients nurture extraordinary physical health, a balance of four kinds of Edgework experiments are needed to nurture extraordinary human relationship.

Physical Edgework experiments include diet, exercise, how you groom yourself, how you move, how you stand or sit, the timing of your actions, how you breathe, learning physical skills such as balancing, centering, using tools and equipment, engaging in new physical intimacies such as travel to different cultures, wearing different clothing, dancing, swimming, sporting skills, gardening, hiking, health treatments, fasting, and meditation.

Intellectual Edgework experiments include studying wildly new topics, researching areas not explored before, expanding your vocabulary or languages, experiencing new levels of clarity or confusion, expressing yourself in words, sharing of core understandings, playing games, exploring entertainment and media, creating poetry or theatrical pieces, expanding your abilities to improvise, going beyond knowing into being okay with not knowing and still taking responsibility and being able to commit to producing an outcome, mixing with others of widely differing professions or backgrounds, extending your abilities to ask dangerous questions, and letting others ask you dangerous questions.

Emotional Edgework experiments include explorations of what makes you afraid, angry, sad or glad – from the past, the present or the future – whether alone or with somebody else – male or female, young or old; consciously experiencing and expressing zero (0) to 100-percent feeling intensity, compared to unconsciously experiencing and expressing low dramas; learning the distinctions of feelings vs. thoughts, feelings vs. emotions, starting and stopping feelings, where you are mixing feelings and thus creating depression, despair, sentimentality, hysteria, *schadenfreude*, or adrenalin rushes.

And Energetic Edgework experiments include speaking, creating alone or with groups – such as artistic or practical (or combined) design and construction; teamwork; management skills; communication skills; experiencing and expressing your destiny Principles; practices that build matrix; examination of where you are placing your attention and for what purpose; observing where you are flowing your energy or absorbing energy and for what purpose; seeing how responsible you can be and with what new area; accessing how accountable, how much integrity, which of your possessions consume your energy and which of them give you energy; examining the placement of your possessions in your living and working spaces; creating art, appreciating art; noting what spaces you can enter; seeing what spaces you can create and then destroy or can destroy and then can recreate; involvement in evolutionary environments such as talks, workshops, and trainings.

knowing is a reliable indicator that you are in the unknown. Do not put the fear away or numb the fear. Welcoming your feelings will help you use the feelings to effectively navigate through unknown territories.

Mix things up and tell yourself, "It is okay to not know how to do it." Then, while not knowing, just see what you see, and feel what you feel, without trying to fit it in anywhere. This means that you might not know what it is that you are experiencing at first, how it works, or how it all fits together, but it also makes even ordinary experiences remarkably fresh and invigorating. Hold a grape in your hand for a moment without giving it the name "grape" before you eat it, and then instead of having a known object, you see this green or purple blob and think, "Wow. What is this amazing thing?" It is exciting to perceive things raw, even if you do not know what they are. Noticing new unnamed things builds matrix and expands your Box. There is a refreshing excitement in beholding an unnamed thing; the experience of not knowing signals the chance to explore new possibilities.

Edgework experiments are utterly simple, the simpler the better. For example, it can be significant Edgework to cook rice instead of potatoes, let your phone ring unanswered, wash your windows inside and out, listen without one word of comment or argument, pet your neighbor's dog with true affection, randomly walk into a stranger's office cubicle unannounced and meet with them, not eat all the food on your plate, wear clothes to work that don't match, wake up at 4:00 A.M. to walk to work instead of taking the bus, on and on. We have so many edges and we can reach them so quickly. You know best how. Keep your Edgework experiments simple, but most importantly, keep staying on the edge.

After an experiment, take time to write a journal entry or a few paragraphs about your experience. What happened? What did you notice? Agree at the outset that your writing does not have to make sense or be grammatically correct. In Edgework experiments the observations and communications tend to be less intellectual and more experiential. Instead of writing in ways that everybody is accustomed to reading, try using language as a bridge to communicate your original experience. Some people find themselves drawing more pictures, writing in free verse poetry, or using words as artistic forms.

Technopenuriaphobia

I could provide numerous suggestions for Edgework experiments, but the limitless variety of possibilities begs to be narrowed. Therefore, I will focus in one area – technopenuriaphobia. I have taken the liberty of naming the fear of the lack of technology "technopenuriaphobia" or "TPP." The word "penuria" comes from the Latin and means scarcity, or deficiency. It is interesting to note that the word "technophobia," which is "the fear of technology and its effects," first appeared around 1964. Here it is, four decades later, and we now have "technopenuriaphobia," the fear that our technology will leave us. We have grown so dependent on modern technology in this past generation that we can no longer live on our own planet without it. An ideal environment for beginning Edgework experiments is in the arena of healing yourself, your relationship, and your family of this disease of contemporary life.

In our modern culture we are born high up on a technological ladder. Hanging out before us in the sky, bright as a Las Vegas casino sign, is the vision of the fabled good life that we are encouraged to strive for. We think we can achieve the good life only if we surround ourselves with enough labor saving, comfort providing, or entertainment devices. Even without trying to, we are completely buffered from life on planet Earth with scores of modern conveniences.

We learned that if you want food, all you have to do is go to the cupboard, the refrigerator, or the freezer and open up boxes, cans, plastic bags, or cartons, and there is an abundance of food. If the food starts to get low at home, go to the supermarket and there you will find food in such quantity and variety as to shame any king, all ready for the taking. Load up your basket and haul it home to eat. Food comes from the grocery store.

If you need money, for example, to buy the food, just give the people a little plastic card and type in a code number or write your name and the food is instantly paid for. If you want cash, use the same card and go to a cash machine or a bankteller. The money comes pouring out by the handfuls.

You want light? Flip a switch. Water? Turn a handle. New clothes? Use that plastic card again. Want to talk to somebody? Autodial their number wherever you are from your cell phone. Need to go somewhere? Don't walk; use a machine: bicycle, car, bus, train, boat or plane. Machines take you rapidly and comfortably anywhere in the world.

We forget how absolutely astonishing the modern world is. We live in a culture and a time where wonder-filled technological conveniences rule our lives. In this "heaven" we can't imagine that there could be a problem. But there is. The problem is that we are born high up on a technological ladder. We are skilled at living a modern life within technology. The technology is not the problem. The problem is the gap between us and planet Earth.

We subconsciously sense that the rungs below us on the ladder of technology are missing. If we dare to look down, we realize, deep in our guts, that those rungs are no longer in place. If we were to take one step down or somehow slip, we would instantly be in danger. A hidden ceaseless fear rumbles silently deep in our belly.

The rungs disappear the moment we forget that we and planet Earth are one. In our headlong rush toward the tantalizing modern comforts of tomorrow-land, we have forgotten how to live without technology. We have high-tech but we are missing low-tech. We cannot sleep without a bed, eat without a supermarket, see without a streetlight, move without a car, or be with ourselves without distractive media.

We have screwed ourselves. We have lost the original technology that created civilization: fire starting, food finding, clothes making, shaping shelter and tools out of whatever comes to hand. The loss of low-tech knowledge creates a lethal gap between us and our planet, and that gap is now filled with unconscious fear: technopenuriaphobia.

There is already a significant body of research proving that harm is done to motor skills and hand-eye coordination by placing children in front of computer and television screens in the years when they need to be developing three-dimensional perceptions and physical dexterity. This psycho-emotional damage may be irreversible. Technopenuriaphobia is an additional damage caused by longterm exposure to a profound fear that we are not aware of, and have no culturally embraced cure for.

TPP is a particularly Western affliction because you must first live with advanced technologies for a generation before the next generation forgets that you ever did not have them. One-hundred-thousand years of hard-earned life-knowledge vanishes from our common inheritance during one generation of being a city dweller. Considering the virulent Westernization of the rest of the world, technopenuriaphobia will quite likely infect millions if not billions more in the near future.

Getting dropped into the gap between planet and technology can happen in an instant when the elevator stops between floors, the batteries go dead, or the store is closed. A million different accidents can puncture the illusion of our comfortable little techno-world. We know bodily that if we were to somehow be separated from our conveniences – even just a few of them – we would be on very shaky ground.

Unless we have made special efforts to train ourselves in outdoor living skills, we all have technopenuriaphobia bothering us deep in our soul. TPP decreases the number of options from which we can choose, and thereby forces certain lifestyles upon us that we assume are without alternatives – "What do you mean I could wear out my old shoes before ordering new ones on the Internet?" "What do you mean unplug the TV?" If a high level of technology must be supported, we become like goldfish living precariously in a glass bowl in the desert.

So what can we do? How can we heal ourselves from TPP? How can we get free of this insidious fear?

Healing Technopenuriaphobia (BLTLCH07.09). Assuredly it takes work to heal oneself of TPP. Work and time. You can approach the work as fun work, but time to do that work will not come without you making it. Listed below are ideas for Edgework experiments to heal yourself of this modern-day affliction.

By the way, TPP Edgework experiments are excellent activities to share with children.

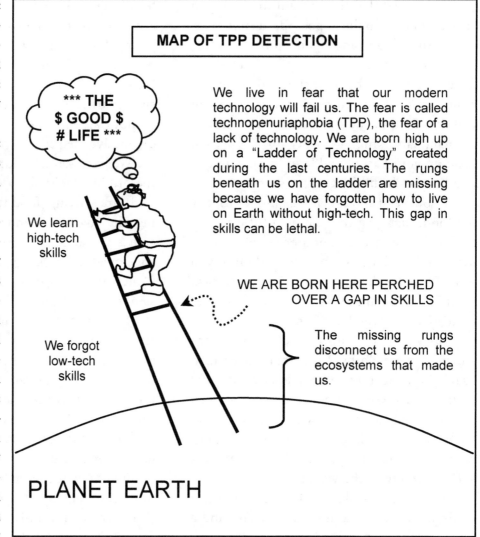

MAP OF TPP DETECTION

*** THE $ GOOD $ # LIFE ***

We learn high-tech skills

We forgot low-tech skills

We live in fear that our modern technology will fail us. The fear is called technopenuriaphobia (TPP), the fear of a lack of technology. We are born high up on a "Ladder of Technology" created during the last centuries. The rungs beneath us on the ladder are missing because we have forgotten how to live on Earth without high-tech. This gap in skills can be lethal.

WE ARE BORN HERE PERCHED OVER A GAP IN SKILLS

The missing rungs disconnect us from the ecosystems that made us.

PLANET EARTH

Antitechnopenuriaphobia measures are powerful interventions that safeguard the basic sanity and self-esteem of your children for their whole lives. Your efforts may last for generations because your children could well pass the benefit on to their own children, and their children's children after that.

Please remember that I am not proposing a back-to-nature antitechnology movement. I am not promoting medieval or tribal lifestyles. The point is to fill a gap where we are noncommittal, hollow, and inauthentic due to a deep abiding terror. I am encouraging us to reclaim nontechnical options in our everyday actions and thoughts. Installing low-tech rungs in the ladder of technology fills the gap

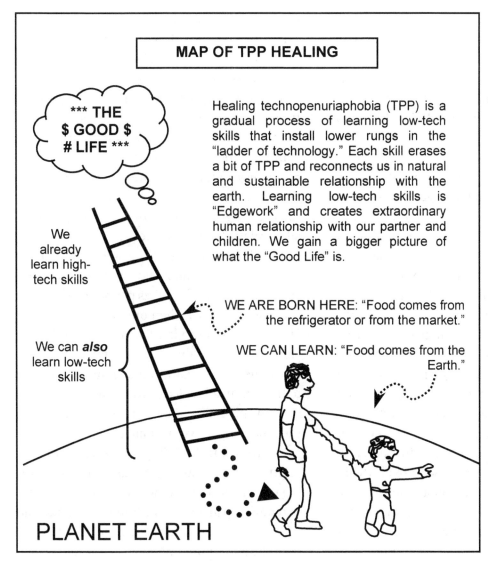

MAP OF TPP HEALING

*** THE $ GOOD $ # LIFE ***

We already learn high-tech skills

We can *also* learn low-tech skills

Healing technopenuriaphobia (TPP) is a gradual process of learning low-tech skills that install lower rungs in the "ladder of technology." Each skill erases a bit of TPP and reconnects us in natural and sustainable relationship with the earth. Learning low-tech skills is "Edgework" and creates extraordinary human relationship with our partner and children. We gain a bigger picture of what the "Good Life" is.

WE ARE BORN HERE: "Food comes from the refrigerator or from the market."

WE CAN LEARN: "Food comes from the Earth."

PLANET EARTH

between you and planet Earth, and builds a stable foundation onto which you can relax.

While reading through this sample list, mark which Edgework experiments are attractive to you, and note others that you may think of. This does not mean that you promise to do these Edgework experiments, or even that you know *how* to do these Edgework experiments. You are simply marking or creating Edgework experiments that might turn you on.

Counter-TPP Edgework Experiments

Go Barefoot: Taking your shoes off and exposing the sensitive soles of your feet to the textures and temperatures of the surface

of planet Earth adds dimensions to your experience. Walk barefoot, even in the rain. (Leaving bare footprints in the snow really makes your neighbors wonder about you.) Take your shoes and socks off at the office. Whose office is it anyway? Make your house a shoes-off house.

Do Without: Try fasting for a day or three. Just drink water, tea or juice. Walk instead of using any machines to get you places all week. Walk through stores and do not buy anything. Put away the TV. Have radio-free days. Clean out your garage and attic. Enter your weekend without a plan. Be silent for three days. Do without speaking. Do without sugar or meat or coffee for three days.

Go Camping: Just get outside into nature for an hour, a day, a week, a month. Step away from the containment of civilization and live on a wide open sandy beach, in the middle of a forest, in the rocky desert, on top of a mountain, beside a freshwater lake. As you become adjusted to camping, practice taking less and less civilization with you. Start with leaving behind the CD player, the bicycle, the camera. The lighter your backpack, the more the TPP gap is filled in.

Sit in the Mud: Mud has strong cleansing and healing properties. Mud is the earth. You are made of mud. You do not have to sit in it, but stop considering mud as dirt. Our mothers trained us to be so clean, to keep our clothes clean, to keep our face clean. Heal yourself and get dirty! Hold mud. Get in contact with mud. Paint yourself with mud. The kids can show you how.

Grow a Garden: Even if it is only potted tomatoes on your balcony, those tomatoes will taste different from store-bought. Vegetables grow in the dirt. There are bugs. There are gophers. The sun matters. The rain matters. Vegetables eat cow manure and rotting dead stuff. Then you eat the vegetables. This is Edgework.

Eat Bugs: Yes. There are 1,462 recorded species of edible insects. Get fried grasshoppers with chili, salt and lemon in Mexico; fried cicadas and silk moth pupae in Japan; roasted termites and crickets in Nigeria; snails are a delicacy in France; and you can get canned baby bees, chocolate covered ants, and stir-fried meal worms in the U.S. Suck the back ends of water bugs at vegetable markets in Thailand, and eat witchetty grubs and Bogong moths in Australia. And don't forget gnat soufflé! The menu is wide and varied, and rich in protein and vitamins. For recipes check out *The Eat-A-Bug Cookbook* by David George Gordon.

Take Things Apart and Fix Them: We are so accustomed to giving things to repair people or throwing things away that we do not have a relationship to fixing things anymore. Instead, try to fix things yourself. Simple little things, big complex things – simply give it a try. Even if you have absolutely no idea how, grab your screwdriver, take the broken thing apart and follow your intuitive wisdom. Fiddle around. Just make sure it is unplugged first and then you will not blow yourself up. Even when professional repair people say it cannot be done or cannot be fixed, try your best guess yourself. Be bold and trust yourself. Your successes will serve as reference points for creating possibility in seemingly impossible relationship situations.

Walk Twenty Miles: We know how to pilot a one-ton internal-combustion ground-machine at speeds of seventy-five miles per hour, but can we walk twenty miles when our car breaks down? Six leagues is not so far. The old California missions were built about twenty miles apart because the monks could walk from one mission to the next in about a day. Knowing that you can walk twenty miles whenever you want to makes the whole planet your home again.

Other anti-TTP Edgework experiments might include learning to use ancient hunting tools such as a boomerang, blow gun, sling, and bow and arrow; identifying and using wild edible plants; visiting third-world cultures; eating only whole and raw foods for a time; weaving cloth; making your own soap, candles, pottery, baskets, paper, and shoes; writing with feathers; flaking stone implements; starting a fire without matches, and milking a cow … all are excellent to do with your children.

SECTION 7-D
Intimacy Edgework

Intimacy Edgework (BLTLCH07.10). Intriguingly, love alone is insufficient to sustain extraordinary human relationship. Intimacy is also needed. In exploring the *Map of Four Bodies* in Section 5-A we noted that each of the four bodies has its own kind of food, its

```
┌─────────────────────────────────────────────────────────┐
│        ┌──────────────────────────────────────┐          │
│        │    MAP OF FOUR KINDS OF INTIMACY     │          │
│        └──────────────────────────────────────┘          │
│                                                           │
│   1. PHYSICAL INTIMACY: sex, foreplay (what isn't         │
│      foreplay?), singing, eating, washing dishes,         │
│      walking holding hands, sauna, sports such as:        │
│      roller-skating, biking, tennis, skiing, swimming,    │
│      etc., martial arts, dancing, massage, doing          │
│      holdings, physical therapy, brushing their hair,     │
│      brushing their teeth, cutting their fingernails,     │
│      bathing them, dressing them, a private fashion       │
│      show, traveling, making art, body painting,          │
│      gardening, playing with the children, action games   │
│      such as charades, going to the zoo, remodeling       │
│      the house, and so on.                                │
│                                                           │
│   2. INTELLECTUAL INTIMACY: talking, discussing,          │
│      philosophizing, debating, writing poetry, writing    │
│      proposals, running a business, meeting, planning,    │
│      strategizing, designing, creating, learning (such    │
│      as languages), playing games (cards, chess,          │
│      Scrabble, 20 Questions), entertainment (opera,       │
│      theater, concerts, shows, movies), museums,          │
│      circus, reading articles out loud, telling stories,  │
│      telling jokes, humor, sharing memories, creating     │
│      possibilities, and so on.                            │
│                                                           │
│   3. EMOTIONAL INTIMACY: sharing the experience and       │
│      the expression of feelings with 1000-percent trust,  │
│      saying "I feel mad, sad, glad or scared              │
│      because...," vulnerability, openness, acceptance,    │
│      deep listening without discussion, grieving,         │
│      contact, simplifying, revealing wounds, sensitivity, │
│      warmth, compassion, generosity, kindness,            │
│      weakness, confusion, depression, jealousy, ecstasy,  │
│      joy, delight, passion, and so on.                    │
│                                                           │
│   4. ENERGETIC OR SPIRITUAL INTIMACY: being present,      │
│      "being-with" the other, prayer, ritual, meditation,  │
│      appreciation, being in the presence of saints or     │
│      sacred artifacts, respect, dignity, nobility, being  │
│      in the space of Love, moving at the speed of Love,   │
│      communion, oneness, Countenance, evolution,          │
│      transformation, development, expanding the Box,      │
│      radiance, teamwork, family, community, holding       │
│      space, serving Bright Principles as a couple, and    │
│      so on.                                                │
│                                                           │
└─────────────────────────────────────────────────────────┘
```

own kind of pain, its own kind of ecstasy, and its own kind of intimacy. Since relationships thrive on intimacy, the edge question here is, "How intimate can I be with each of the four bodies of my partner?" Edgework experiments in the four kinds of intimacy produce an inexhaustible range of intimate experiences for nurturing extraordinary human relationship.

The *Map of Four Kinds of Intimacy* is not given for the purpose of isolating various activities into only one kind of intimacy. Certain activities by their very nature open into multiple intimacies simultaneously. The map is given for the purpose of inviting you to engage a much wider range of Edgework experiments as ways for being intimate together. Not only can you transform monotonous chores of daily life into intimacy Edgework experiments, with this map in hand you can also mix and match intimacy Edgework experiments in wildly creative and *very* interesting combinations! You can be doing physical and intellectual Edgework experiments exploring more than one edge together! We have many opportunities on a daily basis to create and explore intimacies with our partner. We often overlook them. Distinguishing four kinds of intimacy Edgework experiments opens up huge, fresh and stimulating opportunities for Edgework experiments.

Sample Intimacy Edgework Experiments

Discover Slowness Together: Experiment with "velocities of being" other than the normal high speed of the intellect. Try not talking so fast, not jumping from one subject to another so fast, not moving so fast through experiential spaces. Stay in one experience for extended periods of time; sniff a rose for fifteen minutes, not one brief sniff. Hold still together. Savor the nuances in flavors, colors and sensations. Appreciate subtleties of your partner like an art lover absorbs artwork in a museum. Make use of how the opportunities unfold rather than following a pre-made plan. For example, don't be afraid to speak before you know what you are going to say, to gush a little, out loud, in poetic detail, marveling at your partner's qualities of being, even if you have appreciated them before.

Get Dangerous Coaching: Bring pen and paper to your partner and read them the following: "Do you have a minute to coach me?" (If they say yes, keep reading. If they say no, make an appointment to read this to them later.) "Here is a pen and paper." (Hand them the pen and paper.) "Would you please write down at least three specific experiences that could add a new dimension to my personal development and that would be useful for me to learn about." Do not say a word while they write. When they are finished, do not read what they have written. This quick interaction does not involve any discussion. Do this same exercise with two other "dangerous" people, meaning people who know your weaknesses, people whose Boxes are significantly different from yours, whose Gremlins are bigger than yours, or people you regard as having authority. Then make a plan – for this next week – to undertake two of the experiences suggested to you on the papers. Your experiments can be done solo, with your partner, or with a friend of the same gender as you, whichever serves best.

Heal the Big Wound: More women than you might suspect have been physically or sexually abused in their childhood by men. When such a woman wishes to have physical intimacy with her man, there may well be memories and vows locked in her body from long ago that interfere with her relaxing and pleasurably enjoying herself. A healing is called for, and her man can participate in that healing process. As partners in this experiment, you should read through and talk about this process beforehand. When the woman is ready she should tell the man, "I am ready to begin the Edgework experiment." In this experiment the woman determines *everything*. The man follows her instructions as sensitively and as gently as he can, particularly without speaking and in complete acceptance. This is *her* experiment. In complete privacy, with both man and woman fully dressed, stand facing each other with the greatest distance between you as permitted by the room, but at least ten feet apart. Just stand. After three minutes the woman may say, "Stop," having decided that the experiment is over. The experiment continues the next night (or morning or afternoon, as requested by the woman). Start off each time in the way determined by the woman, in this case fully clothed, ten or more feet apart. This time the woman may say, "Take one step forward. Stop." After a minute she may say, "Take one step backward." And that may be the end of the session. It is *so* important that she says the word, "Stop," one or more times in each session. Next session she may say, "Take three steps forward. Stop. Slowly reach out your right hand. Stop. With one finger reach toward my left shoulder but don't touch me. Stop. Take three steps backward." End of session. After more sessions she may gradually come to say, "Take your shoes off. Take your outer shirt off. Take three steps forward. Stop. Put both hands on both of my shoulders. Stop, take your hands off. Put your hands back on. Stop, take your hands off. Take one-half step further forward. Stop. Kiss my forehead. Stay there and don't move. Stop. Unbutton the top button of my blouse. Stop. Button it back up. Take three steps back. Stop." And so on. Every move is orchestrated by the adult woman, in her own time, as she observes and digests her body's subtle reactions from the past. The realization that her feelings and reactions are from another situation in another time with another person separates these reactions from the totally different circumstances in the present. In the present circumstances with her man she has the power to say Stop, about any and every detail of the interaction. Exercising her power to say Stop gives the woman back her power to say Go. In a few weeks, this Edgework experiment can totally heal even the most terrible old wounds and give you each a fresh start to be physically intimate together.

Get Intimacy Coaching: Join a men's or women's group. Repeatedly ask the group for coaching about ways that you could remove or transcend your personal barriers to letting yourself be intimately known. Trust your coaching even if you do not understand it. Bring the results of your experiments back to the group and ask for further refinements in coaching to take your next steps.

Share from the Bottom: You probably already spend an evening now and then at the movies or the theater with your partner. This Edgework experiment is to spend an evening now and then at an Alcoholics Anonymous (AA) or Adult Children of Alcoholics (ACA) meeting with your partner. Even if alcohol was never a part of your family, it is definitely the drug of choice in Western civilization. Find what it means to hit bottom, i.e., to be so egoistically disassembled as to have no choice but to be completely vulnerable. Practice speaking out in the meetings at this level of radical vulnerability. Bring this ability to share into your relationship.

Accept Your Partner's Humanity: Invite your neighbors over for dinner. In your interactions, track how subtly and completely your Box seeks out the differences between itself and your neighbors' Boxes and uses the differences to establish separation between you. Give majority vote in yourself to a different purpose than finding differences. Instead, make your purpose to find examples of your simple common humanity. Nothing special needs to come of the dinner. Do not expect that they invite you to their place in return. Leave the evening with a broader understanding of what it means to be human. Use that new level of acceptance with your partner.

Find Your Break in Reality: Visit an old people's home or a hospital for the mentally ill and find a way to listen to people's stories. Just sit there making contact with patients. Your purpose is to listen to what they say and find how similar it is to the stories you tell yourself and others on a daily basis. Also listen for each person's break with reality, the phrases or attitudes their Box uses to avoid taking responsibility for creating their life as it is. Notice this same tendency in yourself. Share what you notice about yourself with your partner.

Fart in Public: A family doctor friend of mine, practicing in an area populated by gypsies, confided that more than one gypsy woman has come to him a neurotic wreck because her husband swore that if he ever heard her fart he would divorce her. Learn to fart in front of your partner. Play around with making basic mistakes in the presence of your partner. Let them make such mistakes in your presence. Take cha-cha, slow waltz and foxtrot dance lessons with your partner. Someone would have to totally love you to risk looking as stupid as one looks making mistakes in beginning foxtrot classes.

Serve Something Greater: Together with your partner plant 1000 baby trees in an area that was deforested. While you carry seedlings, dig holes, mix fertilizer and pour water together, get a sense of how your relationship as a whole is being used to serve something greater than each of you individually and even greater than the relationship itself. Let that greater thing nourish your relationship in a reciprocal flow as you take action to serve that greater thing. Reciprocal exchange between your relationship and something greater can occur during other projects too, such as organizing a local or international "Intersection Conference" (my idea) that convenes diverse peoples for the purpose of having conversations that matter.

Fight a Noble Battle: Work as a team. Attend your local town meetings and take a stand to pass the resolution that ends corporate personhood so that business leaders can no longer avoid responsibility by hiding behind the legal structure of a corporation. Then you have a noble battle to fight, an adventure to live, and (if you are a man) your woman has a hero to be rescued by.

Honor a Tradition: Take your partner or your whole family to hike the Inca trail in Peru for two months. Dress as Incas. Live as much as you can with the local people as Incas. Of course you are not Incas, and pretending to be Incas looks sort of stupid, but do the whole thing with respect for yourselves and respect for the Inca tradition, and through this respect you will succeed. Sharing these experiences together will create moments of intimacy that will nurture your relationship for a long time.

Express Your Partner As Art: Do a painting, sculpture or concerto inspired by your partner. Have them pose for you or sing for you numerous times over a three-month period. Develop a way to portray their inner radiance. Your work need not match the standards of Rembrandt or Botticelli. Forget that. Just do your best with expressing what you experience in them through your art, and be seriously intimate at the same time.

Let Your Discipline Shine: Participate in a longterm yoga, tai-chi or aikido class together. Although such a commitment changes your daily schedule and may be inconvenient, discipline and development is also attractive. Enjoy the attractiveness of your discipline.

Sing Your Quivering Heart: Find and share your wholly tender heart – share about how life is for you by speaking from a heart at risk of abuse and yet still daring to reveal itself. Create safe moments to speak privately together in the embrace of this heart, even if the space quivers. Sometimes sing or read poetry together from this quality of heart.

Wash Your Fears: Risk sharing rarely admitted fears that you normally pass over and ignore. Let honesty become so delicate that even small background fears are sensed. For example, whenever you wash dishes together make it a time to acknowledge the tiniest of underlying fears.

Reveal Your Vision: Allow your partner to see and feel your soul's true vision of what is possible for yourself, your children, your family, your business, your neighborhood, your city, and the world. Take a walk or a drive and speak about these things before you know what you are going to say. Take turns writing down what the other person says and read it back to them. Do not defend what you say, and don't make your partner defend what they say.

Love All The Way: Let both yourself and your partner be ongoingly flooded with so much love. Live your love maximally, rather than restricting it to a civilized minimum. Give permission for your maximum love to show up in what you say, feel and do, without giving your center away or expecting anything in return.

Just This Moment: Come into the same moment together with your partner without thinking or planning beyond that moment. Extend that moment beyond the limits where the mind would usually take back its grip of your daily To-Do list. Let something extraordinary and completely unpredicted come to pass between the both of you in that moment.

Follow the Leader: Trust the leadership of your partner by accompanying them fluidly. Exhibit complete nonresistance to their moves, for example, when they are driving, when they are giving instructions to your children, or when they are being around the parents (yours or theirs). Participate in a public meeting or workshop with your partner and be a total *yes* for whatever they contribute at the meeting.

Declare Perfection: Declare the perfection of the present circumstances several times a day by saying clearly out loud, "This is perfect." Include all of the circumstances of your partner (their body shape, "Your butt is *perfect*," their anger, "That anger is *perfect*," their doubts, "Your doubts are *perfect*") and the environment ("This morning is *perfect*," "Those flowers are *perfect*," "This music is *perfect*"), even though both of you know that there is only nonperfection at the level of material manifestation. Thoroughly enjoy together the utter satisfaction of the perfection that you have declared.

Guard Your Attention: Practice with guarding your attention so that you are indistractible (not distracted by other men or women walking down the street, by pictures in magazines or billboards, by television). Particularly focus on not being distractible by problems and issues. There will *always* be problems and issues, especially from the perspective of your Box. If your Box, your partner's Box, your mother-in-law's Box, or your child's Box can distract you from holding space for the sanctuary of intimate relationship with your partner, then the Box wins and you lose. Ongoingly demonstrate that being-with your partner has *by far* the highest priority, and prove this unwaveringly by where you place your attention (i.e., not distracted by the problem), even when you are together in the shopping mall, having a conflict, visiting the relatives, or with your children.

Play Space Together: Develop the ability to play "Space" with your partner. Playing Space is a mode of conversation where one person asks self-threatening questions and the other person answers those questions immediately, without forethought, without flinching, without protecting, but directly from truth. Then change roles. Write down what your partner says because, guaranteed, the Box will cause you to forget this stuff in the shortest time. Who is more qualified to give you oracle-quality information about yourself than your partner?

Go With Them: Decide already beforehand, and permanently, to not move energetically away from your partner, even when "you" (your Box) have reasons to reject them because it is offended. Instead, put your emotional reaction on an internal shelf for storing emotional reactions, and move energetically toward your partner. Go with them, even if it means going with them on a journey into their underworld, or your underworld (or both). Do not object. Simply accompany them as if on a friendly museum tour, making no conclusions except to stay close to them.

Minimize Now Together: Avoid "smearing" moments together. Time is quantized into moments. Each moment is unique. There are gaps between moments like the gaps between houses on a street or the gaps between cars of a freight train. If you minimize your now

An Intimacy Edgework Experiment About Expectations

Withdrawing Your Expectations (BLTLCH07.11). Write on a blank piece of paper the following words: "Expectations kill relationship." Fold the paper and put it into an envelope. Bring the envelope with you when you meet with your partner to do this three-part Edgework experiment.

Arrange to have an hour of private time with your partner. Sit across from each other in a chair or on the floor, not touching, with no obstructions between you. Then start Part 1.

Part 1: You listen while your partner tells you everything that they expect of you in every aspect of your relationship. They should begin each sentence with, "I expect that..." or, "I expect that you..." Ten minutes is long enough.

Then switch roles. Your partner listens while you tell them everything that you expect of them in detail, using the form, "I expect that..." or, "I expect that you..." Another ten minutes should be enough time. Stop for a moment of silence. Then begin Part 2.

Part 2: Have your partner open the envelope. Have them read out loud what the paper says: "Expectations kill relationship." This is bad news. Nobody ever told us this before so we bury our partner in a mountain of righteous expectations. We wonder why they are suffocating in our company. Expectations kill relationship because expectations are a fantasy picture of what your partner is supposed to be like. When you have an expectation about your partner, you do not have your partner. Instead, you have an empty fantasy of your expectation about your partner. When the horror of the situation that you have created for each other to live in starts to gnaw at your guts, then do Part 3.

Part 3: Your partner listens while you do the Edgework experiment to withdraw one of your expectations of them. The form of the withdrawal is precise. You choose one specific expectation that you have been holding over your partner's head, for example, that they should not do any work emails at home. Then, in a strong clear voice, you formally say, "(Partner's name), I withdraw my expectation that you should never do any work emails at home, forever." Then stay silent and do not move for one full minute. Watch what happens to your partner's energetic body.

Then switch roles. You listen while your partner does the same Edgework experiment to withdraw one of their expectations of you. In a strong clear formal voice, they say, "(Partner's name), I withdraw my expectation that you should pay more attention to me and not just to the children, forever." Again, both of you stay silent and do not move for one full minute so the communication can land in your body and not just in your mind.

Repeat Part 3 as long and as often as you both wish. Expectations are relationship killers. Nobody can force you to start an expectation. Nobody can force you to remove an expectation. No one else can be responsible for your relationship suffering under an expectation that you have made. Removing forever an expectation that you held about your partner can cause quite a bit of ecstasy. How much ecstasy can you stand?

to a present that is smaller than the gap between moments, then you can move sideways through those gaps into possibilities that were previously hidden. It is the Box that smears moments together, motion picture like, so it can make generalizations such as "always," "never," "can't" and "have to." Whenever you hear yourself using those words, know that your Box is working overtime to smear moments together into a blob that blocks all the other possibilities that are actually available if you could pay closer attention to details. To get out of smearing moments, shift to the level of the details.

Excrete Your Conclusions: Each time you sit on the toilet, do the intimacy Edgework experiment to erase all the conclusions that your Box has ever established about your partner. While moving your bowels, also make a detailed mental deposit into the toilet. Identify and release any conclusions that you have established about what your partner wants or does not want, who they are or who they are not, what they can or cannot do, what is next or not next for them. When you are finished, flush everything away. Step out of the bathroom completely cleansed and excited by what you might discover in the person you are with. Catch your Box if it ever tries to bring back any conclusions that are already flushed down the toilet.

Applaud Their Characters: Just like you, your partner has Shadow characters and Bright characters of immense variety, depth and diversity – the artist, the hypochondriac, the healer, the professor, the thug, the thief, the nun, the barmaid, the dungeon master, the hopeless ghost. Do the experiment to have no fear, no judgment, and no hatred of the characters that you find in your partner. They are just characters, even if your partner is completely identified with them as if they were real. Enjoy the richness of your partner's versatility and play a variety of roles in return, weaving pathways toward extraordinary

human relationship. Avoid requiring your partner to be one of the few characters with whom your Box can do its familiar dance of ordinary human relationship.

Tolerate Their Discontinuities: Extend the limits of what you can tolerate in terms of your partner's insanity. Understand that in order for them to learn and grow they must go through liquid state periods where they do not have their act or their life together. Expand your capacity for accepting your partner, until it greatly exceeds your partner's previous experiences of being accepted. Stop requiring your partner to continue their standard show of being sane for you. Instead, become a safe space in which they can experiment in their own disassembly. Tolerate discontinuities so they can reorder. Clearly distinguish in your own heart the difference between loving your partner as a being, and loving their Box's behavior. Continue loving them. Let their Box fade into background importance.

Let Kindness Prevail for No Reason: Do the intimacy Edgework experiment of discovering kindness without measure. Drop the necessity to have reasons for expressing kindness toward beings, spaces or objects, including every aspect of your partner and their life. Let kindness prevail as your predominant moment-to-moment experience as expressed by your thoughts, words and actions. See how long you can do this. When you find that the kindness has been replaced by something else, avoid all analysis and shift back into the kindness to try again. Sometimes make extraordinary bursts of effort to extend your capacity for reasonless kindness beyond all previous exceptions. Sometimes create kindness reminding factors for yourself, like carrying a flower all day, or wearing a heart necklace to keep you tuned into your kindness experiment. Sometimes apply surprise guerilla kindness when it is least expected. Then, also apply this kindness to yourself.

PART IV

The Archetypal

WARNING: Now Leaving Kansas

Having been born in Kansas myself I have a fond appreciation for the astute observation made by a pretty young farm girl named Dorothy Gale when she wakes up "over the rainbow" in the film version of L. Frank Baum's book *The Wonderful Wizard of Oz*. After looking around and seeing strange vegetation, midget Munchkin people, wicked witches, and red ruby shoes, Dorothy somewhat nervously says to her little dog, "Toto, I've a feeling we're not in Kansas anymore."

You too are about to exit Kansas. We leave behind us discussions of ordinary and extraordinary human relationship and cross over into Archetypal domains where we will find our own varieties of strange vegetation and interesting elements, including underworlds, upperworlds, the Archetypal Masculine and Feminine, longing, Archetypal Love, and the possibility of what I have named "Countenance": elements that come into play as we build Love that lasts.

Definitely not Kansas anymore.

CHAPTER 8

Archetypal Relationship / Archetypal Love

As exciting as this new Archetypal domain may be, the direct physical connection to an unlimited abundance of unconditional Love and joy may threaten the foundations of your reality construct, changing your worldview and your concept of who you are, drastically and irreversibly.

This connection to Archetypal Love may irrefutably confirm the existence of a reality that you may have only glimpsed before. Part of you already knows it exists, while another part has been avoiding it with a vengeance. And this denying part will attempt to keep you unaware of what it has been doing.

The experience of Archetypal Love is undeniable because it is physical. Yet, you cannot "adapt" to this experience. Instead, it uncompromisingly adapts you. You also cannot include the full experience of Archetypal Love in your present way of being because it will not fit. It is too vast and too different.

Entering the Archetypal world presumes that you are willing *and* have the capacity to be utterly annihilated, and then to start rebuilding your world from nothing.

Archetypal Love is not personal, yet it arises only through contact with another person, and it *feels* personal. This can be maddening.

Encountering unlimited joy and Love immediately puts you outside of society, because modern society is founded on a belief in the scarcity of love and on the idea that it is possible to be separate from love.

Finally, Archetypal Love leaves you with nothing to do. All is already done. The powerlessness you may sense can be so vast that it may feel like you are "being lived" rather than merely living. This realization starts you on a journey into territory for which we have not been prepared, and is the beginning of radical Edgework.

)(You Can't Get There From Here

We may as well get straight to the point: you *cannot* shift human relationship (whether ordinary or extraordinary) into Archetypal Relationship. They exist in completely separate domains.

In each moment we are creating either human relationship (ordinary or extraordinary) or Archetypal Relationship. Each operates under its own set of laws. They do not blend or mix. We cannot be in one *and* in the other at the same time. Consciously or unconsciously we choose and commit to human or Archetypal through our every move. Even the tiniest actions determine our choice.

The idea of shifting human relationship to Archetypal Relationship is like the idea of shifting the board game of backgammon into painting oil portraits in the style of Monet. You cannot shift backgammon into oil painting. In order to start oil painting, you and your partner must put down the backgammon dice, fold up the board, and put the game away. Then you can set up an easel and canvas, choose your brushes, arrange your partner into a pose, mix your colors and start painting their portrait. Backgammon and oil painting are two entirely different games.

The same is true of human relationship and Archetypal Relationship. There is a quantum separation between them. Neither form of relationship is good or bad, they simply produce different results. When we develop the sensitivity to notice a difference between human relationship and Archetypal Relationship, we gain an option that we did not have before – the option to *create* Archetypal Relationship. Before making the distinction we had only one possibility – human relationship, whether ordinary or extraordinary.

The possibility to create Archetypal Relationship opens up an entirely new universe of additional experiments for us to try, just like the possibility for oil painting opens up an entirely new universe of experiments to try in addition to those in playing backgammon. But, how do we begin with making experiments in Archetypal Relationship when all we have known before is human relationship?

The answer is to take responsibility. Taking responsibility means no longer acting as if we are victims of the conditions of our upbringing. Whatever our parents or grandparents demonstrated to us is no excuse. The fact that we may have been in some ways abused or abandoned or betrayed is actually irrelevant. The fact that we may consider ourselves to be insufficiently loved is no contributing factor. The fact that we have a tender sacred place within us that has never before been awakened and caressed is no hindrance. The fact that we do not already know how to create Archetypal Relationship does not matter.

We begin experimenting in Archetypal Relationship by taking responsibility for our present perception level and our present skill level with regard to creating relationship. It is not our parents' fault or our society's fault for determining what we do not see and what we cannot do. Taking responsibility means claiming that the quality and level of perceptions and abilities that we have so far developed has not depended on our circumstances. We are now, and have always been, at source for what we perceive and for what we can create out of what there is around us. Taking responsibility at the source level gives us the possibility of expanding our perceptions and our abilities so as to create a different kind of relationship. Taking responsibility for being where we are is the foundation stone and the always-present starting point for being able to create something other than what we are creating right now. Through taking uncompromising responsibility, we suddenly stand at the gates to the kingdom of Archetypal Relationship, whereas before we could only access human relationship. Through taking responsibility for previously blocking our own perception of the gates, we discover that the kingdom is at hand.

We cannot shift even extraordinary human relationship into Archetypal Relationship. To start doing experiments in Archetypal Relationship we call upon our discipline and *decide* to step out of the world of human relationship, and then begin completely afresh, right now, each moment, in the world of Archetypal Relationship. The procedure for this change is responsibility.

This book is *only* about taking more responsibility.

Love, Friendship and Sex in the Three Domains

Relationship involves such considerations as love, friendship and sex. In this book we are distinguishing among three categories or universes of relationship: ordinary human relationship, extraordinary human relationship, and Archetypal Relationship. In each universe the dynamics of love, friendship and sex function under completely different laws.

In ordinary human relationship – love, friendship and sex are experienced from the perspective of a victim. There is a scarcity of love. Love means "somebody loving me." I can never get enough of this love so I try to find love anywhere I can. I try to have friends as "the cure for my loneliness." I try to have sex as "the cure for my horniness."

In extraordinary human relationship, I take responsibility for sourcing love, friendship and sex as laboratories for evolutionary experimenting. Love, friendship and sex are not scarce at all, because wherever I go, there they are. I source them. I create them. I play in these domains with ecstatic joy and wonder. Love, friendship and sex exist merely because I am there causing them to happen.

The difference between extraordinary human relationship and Archetypal Relationship is that extraordinary human relationship is about love, friendship and sex, and Archetypal

Relationship is about Love, Friendship, and Sex, where the capital letters signify Archetypal Principles. This is a big difference. The purpose of Archetypal Relationship is to be a theater in which the Archetypal Principle of Love, the Archetypal Principle of Friendship, and the Archetypal Principle of Sex can perform Archetypal interactions. In other words, Archetypal Relationship is the space through which the Archetypal Principles of Love, Friendship and Sex (among others) can do their work in the world.

Archetypal Relationship turns out not to be about "me" at all. In Archetypal Relationship, the relationship itself serves the world as both a transformer and a transducer – structures that change the quality of energy. Transformers increase or decrease the *intensity* of a particular form of energy. Transducers shift the energy from one *quality* to another *quality*, so that the energy can be put to a different use.

In the case of Archetypal Relationship, the relationship itself serves as a *transformer* when, for example, it increases or decreases the intensity of Love, Friendship or Sex to the level of intensity most appropriate for the situation at hand.

Archetypal Relationship serves as a *transducer* when the relationship shifts the quality of the Principle of Love, for example, into the Principle of acceptance, teamwork, joy, appreciation, family, discovery, respect, or whichever Archetypal Principle is needed to make best use of the present circumstances.

Love, Love, Archetypal Love

Enlivening Your Own Legend of Archetypal Love (BLTLCH08.01). Once you have experimented enough to expand your personal experience until it carries more weight than the opinions of our culture, once you have released yourself from pacing back and forth in the cage of ordinary human relationship, after you have taken a few breaths of sweet air and splashed clean sunshine on your face from extraordinary human relationship, you will soon need to know where else it is possible to go. Let us start with the map that shows Archetypal Love.

I may not be the most qualified to speak about Archetypal Love. I will try anyway. In my experience, Archetypal Love is of such subtle quality and such vast dimension that pinning it down into maps and procedures is like trying to grab a mountain of whipped cream. The more you try to hold the more it slips away.

Common sense "rules" say we cannot speak about the unspeakable. In this consideration we will just have to break the rules. It may help to know that, although you may not be able to speak about the unspeakable, you can still directly and wordlessly *experience* the unspeakable, and then speak about the experience.

Archetypal Love is the radiance illuminating the chamber at the center of the Great Labyrinth of Spaces (*see* map in Section 8-D). Heartrending poetry is the typical language that mere human beings traditionally use to speak of Archetypal Love. Like a light that is too bright for the eyes to tolerate, you must examine it indirectly, through filters, reflected by inference and implication.

Since I am inclined toward the physical sciences, I seek the physics of Archetypal Love: how it works, the practical details, what we need to know. For example, already knowing that you can't move from ordinary to Archetypal Relationship, how *do* we get to Archetypal Love from here?

Traditional legends may hold some clues. Legends do not arise out of nothing; they derive from a source, and there is something true in every legend.

MAP OF THREE KINDS OF LOVE

1. Ordinary Human Love, self referenced, neurotic, "I need you" love, dependent on certain expected circumstances and experiences.

2. Extraordinary Human Love, respectful, playful, adult, responsible, alive in the present, independent of circumstances because you create new love happening in each moment.

3. Archetypal Love, the most abundant thing in the universe, pure, radiant, impersonal, the endless bright jewel of consciousness, the Principle of Principles.

Certain legends are passed on from generation to generation. The greatest of these legends is the legend of Archetypal Love.

"True Love," they call it. We have heard this phrase in love songs endlessly, and spoken on the big screen from time to time. In the film *Princess Bride,* Miracle Max asks the almost-dead Westley, lying on his kitchen table, "What do you have that's worth living for?" (You have *got* to see this film!) Max uses bellows to pump air into Westley's lungs, then he presses down on Westley's chest so the almost-corpse can utter a few words. "True Love," whispers Westley. That is good enough reason for the wizard to bring him back to life.

When we try circumscribing Archetypal Love with words, we cannot but speak in superlatives. We cannot help but make reference to the astonishing. What do we really know about Archetypal Love? Nothing. But, so what? Let us carry on with foolhardiness so great as to assert that every human being can have certainty and direct knowledge of Archetypal Love. How many people have actually experienced true Love? Everybody. That is why the legend continues to excite us.

Responsibility for True Necessity

There could be a good reason explaining the lack of cultural reference points for Archetypal Love. Think about these questions: What percentage of the reading public would seriously study a book like *Building Love That Lasts*? Look around your neighborhood. Be honest. How many would free up enough time and attention to buy the book and start experimenting? Think of other countries, other continents. What percentage of humanity is moved to make efforts to expand their conscious experience into the domains of Archetypal Love? Probably not a large number. A realistic estimate would be something less than one percent.

What is everybody else doing? That question is actually none of our business. More useful questions might be: What moves *you* in particular to stretch your intelligence, amoeba-like, to include greater competence with Archetypal Love? What makes this effort important for you? What do you get in exchange for the energy you invest? What keeps you reading rather than putting this book down and looking somewhere else for something else? What makes you hungry for Archetypal Love informational food? It is not that this food supply has been hidden – each culture and time for all of human existence has had direct access to these understandings. If a person with true necessity was persistent and intelligent in their searching, they could always find it. There is really nothing new here. The most interesting question is: What makes now the right time for you?

Building Matrix (BLTLCH08.02). A possible answer is that now is the time for you to receive clarity about Archetypal Love because you have built enough matrix to have true necessity. Other people have not yet built that part of their matrix, so they have no necessity.

Matrix is built by weaving distinctions through your soul. At first your soul is void of distinctions, like a loop with nothing in it. Each distinction weaves a sensitive string across the loop to detect differences, similarities, and connections between things of every nature. From simple distinctions like, "A stove might be hot," or, "This sensation in my eyes means I am tired," to more complex and sophisticated distinctions like, "If I feel like a victim in any situation it is only my Gremlin generating a low drama," or, "I can responsibly decode an irresponsibly encoded message; it is not fair but I can choose to do it." Each distinction weaves over, under, around and through your other distinctions, until your soul starts functioning as a net that can collect new distinctions on its own. Further and further distinctions woven into the net make the weave tighter and tighter, until at some point the net starts functioning as a sail, influenced by the force of Bright Principles that then blow you and your life in the direction of fulfilling your destiny.

Bright Principles and Archetypal Love

Archetypal Love can be seen as the first Bright Principle, the Principle of which all other Bright Principles are but a mere facet. Archetypal Love sources an intelligence so vast that consciousness, space, time, energy and matter originate and flow directly out of its structure. Archetypal Love would then be the most abundant thing in the universe.

When the first maps showed the world as flat, it was well known that if you sailed away from known territory you would fall off into the void and come to a terrifying and most disturbing end. These thought-maps had a profound influence on our behavior. Flat-world thinking – the thinking of boundaries, dangers and separations – is what created Europe. There is no Grand Canyon between France and Germany. There are no Atlantic Ocean or Himalayan Mountains to cross. You can easily walk from Paris to Frankfurt. But people would be born, grow up, have kids, work and die within a ten-mile radius, because they were unconsciously afraid to leave known territory. The thought-map of flat-world dangers separated Europeans from each other for centuries, permitting the evolution of diverse languages, attitudes, eating habits, and thought processes that still exist today. When the round-world map came into general acceptance, an entire Renaissance of creativity exploded across the Western world. I submit that the original Renaissance is still in its youth.

The same boundless joy and expanded horizons of the Renaissance await us when we discover the *Map of Archetypal Love.* By redrawing our thought-map of the universe of love with Archetypal Love as the original, eternal and endlessly available background, we gain immediate access to unforeseen new dimensions in relationship.

For example, in a universe where the source of consciousness and all existence is Archetypal Love, and where this Love is the most abundant thing in the universe, one of the features is that *you cannot be unloved.* Cannot! It is impossible to avoid the experience of endless unconditional Archetypal Love. Where can you go where Love is not?

Free Will

"So," you might ask, "what about those of us who do not feel this Love? What about those of us who feel wounded to the core, totally abandoned by anyone who matters: those who feel disrespected, betrayed by Love itself not living up to its great promise? What about the vast majority of humanity?"

Your Free Will and Your Herd Behavior (BLTLCH08.03). Consider this: Our Box has the power to block us from basking in and utilizing the endless resource of Archetypal Love. The Box is a manifestation of our free will. Through free will, we choose to believe our Box's copious evidence that we are our Box. Through free will, we choose to ignore the even more prolific evidence that we have a Box but that *who we are* is Archetypal Love. The Box uses a simple "sleight-of-mind" trick to block us from immense innate capacities for compassion. The Box's trick is called "misidentification." We constrain ourselves to behaving within the permitted limitations of our Box because we think that we *are* our Box. We squeeze down and miniaturize our allowable responses so that we appear to be sane, instead of appearing to be a Pirate Sorceress Warrioress Queen Goddess Woman or a Pirate Magician King Spiritual Warrior Man.

We constantly use our free will to sacrifice innate treasures of dignity and nonattachment, for the sake of peer approval and social acceptance. In the next breath, we admit that none of us is sane, that there is no universal measure of psychic health, or objective sanity. One person's sanity is another's madness. This sacrificing of our free will is unconscious herd behavior – extremely disrespectful of our memetic possibilities. There are far more interesting uses for free will.

SECTION 8-D
The "How To" of Archetypal Love

How do we step into the new *Map of Relationships* that includes Archetypal Love? How do we establish the flow of Archetypal Love through our central being? How do we open the floodgates and drown our separative misidentification in Archetypal Love? How do we reclaim a practical, functional ability to apply the resources of our true nature?

Taking the Actions That Are in Front of You to Take (BLTLCH08.04). The direct, though unnerving, answer to the question, "How do we do it?" is "Yes." Period. Full stop. Asking the question, "How do we do it?" seems like the first and most important question for us to ask. But asking, "How do we do it?" is actually a clever defense against taking any new actions. (This formula comes from Peter Block's book *The Answer to How Is Yes*. *See* the Bibliography.)

The answer to the question, "How do I do it?" is to simply begin doing it. What kind of action do we take to open the floodgates of Archetypal Love? We have been told *exactly* what kind of action to take for a long time. This is one thing that we have already been given explicit instructions for, although, since we have been trained in school to act like sheep, we may not have thought that the instructions applied to us personally. *The action to take is the action that is in front of us right now to take.* We do not have to worry about taking actions that are not right in front of us to take, because we cannot take them. Just because we can imagine an action, or that we know a particular action must eventually be taken, does not mean that we need to try to take that action *now*. We cannot open a door downstairs if we are sitting upstairs. To open the door downstairs we must first stand up, then walk to the stairs, then walk down the stairs, then walk to the door that is to be opened. The only action we can take now is to stand up, and we can do that. Thinking that we must open the downstairs door *now* when that action is not in front of us right now, shows the delusion of thinking. This thinking error easily drives us crazy. For the most part, even with complex endeavors such as navigating space, your job is simple. Take the actions that are in front of you to take.

1. Consciously Declaring

One of the three great capabilities of human intelligence is the power to declare. To declare something is to say, "It is so," or, "It is the way it is because I just said it is this way." We unconsciously declare how things are all the time. "I'm fine," we say. "The weather is terrible," we say. "This is fun." "That is wrong." "James is a snitch." "This job is impossible." "That's a great idea." "This is bad." "I like this." On and on we go making declarations. Each declaration creates a reality. As soon as we declare a reality into existence, we walk into that reality and behave as if the reality were true, even though we just declared the reality ourselves, out of nothing!

Declarations are held together with a substance called "is-glue" (cheaper by the quart, invisible when dry). The concept "is" does not exist in nature. "Is" is a creation of the human mind. Is-glue includes the derivatives: is, am, are, was, were, has, have, had, do, does, did, may, might, must, can, could, should, shall, will, and would, and also the "not" forms of each: such as "is not," "am not," "are not."

In general, we use is-glue with complete abandon and with complete unconsciousness. We can equally use is-glue consciously to create realities with other qualities. The closer our created reality approximates actual reality, the more precisely we will manipulate reality when we manipulate our model. Is-glue itself happens to be a model that approximates actual reality quite accurately. So, when we redeclare an is-glued reality, our new gestures reshape actual reality. The way to reestablish the flow of Archetypal Love in the spaces of your life is – you declare it so. You consciously declare the purpose of a space.

Recently, John and Sandy, a married couple, came to realize that the original reasons they had given to each other for being together at the time of their marriage were a sham, a total pretense. After many years of marriage, while in a Possibility Team session, they discovered that something more profound than personal preferences was actually substantiating their partnership. Realizing that Archetypal Love could live through them as a couple was a shock. Because they were prepared, the shock was well received. They used the energy of the shock to invite nearly a hundred friends, business associates and family members to a party. The purpose of the party was to start their partnership over. John and Sandy wanted to redeclare the basis and the commitment of their experiment in relationship. They asked me to give a short talk at the event. Given such a precious opportunity, I determined to try to "navigate space" to the Heart of the Labyrinth.

Consciously Declaring the Purpose of a Space (BLTLCH08.05). Since I know that human beings gather together for varied purposes, ranging from horse races, to stockholder meetings, to political rallies, I realized that the 100 people around me had consciously gathered together in the name of Archetypal Love. That is what I declared: "We are gathered together today in the name of Archetypal Love."

Human beings are invocational creatures. We never go anywhere without naming the space. Consciously or unconsciously, we name and declare every space to serve our purposes.

The quality of the space will determine what is possible in that space. For example, we do not fix cars in an ice cream parlor. We do not store horses in our mother's living room. The police station is not for roller-skating. We do not yodel in church. Each thing happens in the space named for it to happen.

Through consciously declaring the purpose of a space, we establish and enhance the available features in that space. Without sounding schmaltzy, we have all heard the quote: "Wherever two or more are gathered in My name, there am I in the midst of them." This declaration demystifies the mechanics of Archetypal Love. These are clear, specific instructions for how to call in Principles: It takes at least two people with a common purpose.

In the experiment noted above, we had men, women and children, singles, couples and families, old and young, friends and strangers, all gathered together in the name of Archetypal Love. I started off by declaring it to be so … hoping that the reality of Archetypal Love would then organize its own felt-presence in the space.

Was I scared when I did this? *Yes!* Was I sure it would work? *No.* Was I afraid of being seen as an embarrassing weirdo? *Definitely yes.* Has such an attempt failed before? *Yes.* Have I felt like dying after making mistakes like this before? *Yes.* Did making previous mistakes ever stop me from trying again? *Yes,* sometimes. But not this time.

I knew from previous experience that declaring the Principles of a space was not about being certain. Certainty is a rare luxury and mostly not necessary. What is necessary is paying the best attention that you can, keeping your center, and just going ahead and trying.

This time it worked. Archetypal Love showed up. Archetypal Love descended into the space like warm, radiant snowflakes. I invited people to risk letting down their defenses and to enjoy, feast, and unfold into

the nurturing radiance among their friends. And they did. The party went on for six more hours. Archetypal Love was happening.

2. Becoming a Space Navigator

The Sensation of Archetypal Love in a Space (BLTLCH08.06). Archetypal Love provides your whole body with a distinct and distinguishable experience, like the smell of cedarwood smoke drifting from a chimney on a quiet wintry night, like taking a curve on your bicycle going a little too fast, like the mood in Beethoven's Seventh symphony, like waking up after sleeping late on Sunday morning and starting to feel hungry. You can sense when Archetypal Love is happening by the feel of it. The sensation is palpable, unmistakable and objective, because everyone exposed to the radiance of Archetypal Love happening in a space has the same experience, although the experience may be too subtle to be consciously recognized.

Navigating Spaces (BLTLCH08.07). Once you have experiential clarity about what it feels like when Archetypal Love enters a space, you can use the memory of that as a standard reference point to sense if Archetypal Love is *ever* happening in a space. You can also then detect if Archetypal Love is *not* happening. These whole-body sensations can serve as your steering wheel for navigating space.

Previously, such energetic sensations may have been known to you but had no particular importance, beyond being either pleasant or bothersome. Those sensations can now be neutrally decoded and put to use. They mean something specific. You can use the sensations to go up, go down, go right or left, to accelerate or decelerate, and go here and there while navigating space.

Subtle physical sensations inform you as to what space you are in, *where* you are in that space, what direction you are headed, what your purpose is, what other people's purposes are, how fast you are moving, what is around you to avoid, what is around you that could be interesting or useful, what is the protocol for staying in and enhancing the present space, and what is the protocol for exiting to the next space. Your body is the transformer. Your body knows.

Three dynamic Archetypal forces let you interact with a space. The three forces function comparably to the three pedals that control a car. The three forces are the affirming forces (accelerator), the denying forces (brakes), and the sustaining forces (the clutch that connects or disconnects the engine with the wheels). The navigating is up to you. Consciously taking responsibility for "serving the space" puts you in the driver's seat. Navigating space, like dance or martial arts, includes a complex set of sophisticated skills that you can continuously improve and develop over a lifetime.

A *Map of the Great Labyrinth of Spaces* is an energetic map that you discover by experience and memorize by heart. The map holds an infinite number of spaces, each with its own unique qualities, limitations and possibilities, each with its own purposes and uses. Every space is connected to every other space. This means that you can get to anywhere else from wherever you are.

Each space is presided over by an energetic "deity" who represents a unique set of Bright and Shadow Principles. In the very center of the Labyrinth there is a singular space that exists as the abode of the overriding Principle of Archetypal Love. This space is called the Heart of the Labyrinth.

In the Heart of the Labyrinth the air is refined, and hums with an electric clarity. Endless, impersonal, radiant, ecstatic, Archetypal Love floods every cubic inch of the space, and floods every cell and nerve in your body when you enter that space. The Heart of the Labyrinth has always been there. It never goes away.

The view from the Heart, in every direction, is more than spectacular. Nothing much exists in this space. There are no amenities or facilities, no nooks and crannies. The space is pure. You cannot live here. Being in the Heart of the Labyrinth is like being at the top of Mount Fuji. You cannot live there, but you can visit. The experiences that you acquire in one brief visit to the Heart of the Labyrinth can reorder your priorities for the rest of your life. After your visit, you hike back down off the mountain into the valley. In the valley there are shops and toilets. In the valley you can eat and sleep and work. But your life in the valley is changed because of your trip up the mountain. You live in the valley with your memories of what things look like from the top of the mountain. You now know that ordinary human relationship happens in the valley, but that the world is a much bigger place than you previously realized.

You retain the *Map of the Great Labyrinth of Spaces* in your body, and reserve the possibility of navigating the space of your immediate relationship, when appropriate, directly into the Heart of the Labyrinth. Such navigating can only occasionally be done, but keeping the option open is a practice worth developing, as is demonstrated in an old story. It begins with a doorway – one that leads directly into heaven. The legend about this door is that it opens from the inside, it opens only for a moment, and it opens randomly only once every hundred years. If the door opens in the middle of the night while you are sleeping, your chance to get into heaven is gone. One man made it into heaven and God was surprised. "How did you get in here?" God asked. The man replied, "I practiced only sleeping while leaning against the door. When the door opened, I fell into heaven and woke up."

Once you possess the *Map of the Great Labyrinth of Spaces,* the world is not flat anymore; it has expanded into many additional dimensions. The once threatening and forbidden horizon – that dropped you into the void if you ever tried new ways of being, relating and acting – has vanished. You can now sail

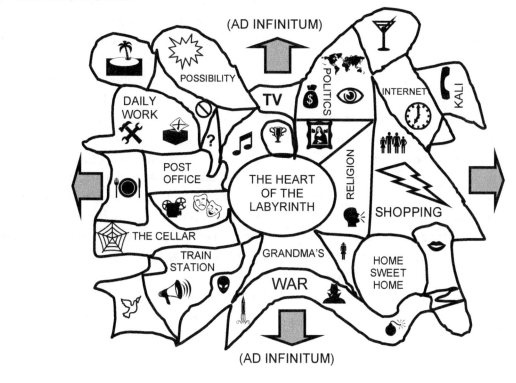

MAP OF THE GREAT LABYRINTH OF SPACES

There are unlimited numbers of spaces into which you can navigate. Each space is presided over by a deity representing a unique set of conscious and unconscious Principles. We enter a space when two or more gather in the name of the Principles of that space. We voyage from space to space unconsciously in ordinary human relationship and consciously in Archetypal relationship. Every space is connected to every other space. You can get to anywhere from here. You can voyage into the Heart of the Labyrinth, but you cannot live there.

(AD INFINITUM)

POSSIBILITY

DAILY WORK

TV

POLITICS

INTERNET

KALI

POST OFFICE

THE HEART OF THE LABYRINTH

RELIGION

SHOPPING

THE CELLAR

TRAIN STATION

GRANDMA'S

HOME SWEET HOME

WAR

(AD INFINITUM)

as far over the horizon as you want, and you can never fall off the map.

"We gather together in the name of Archetypal Love." "This meeting is called to order under the auspices of Archetypal Love." These are doorways in, produced through declaration: "I am the space through which Archetypal Love can do its work."

You have the inherent ability to voyage into very interesting new lands – the domains of Archetypal Love. The remainder of this book looks in these directions.

3. Recapitulating Your Story

Entering either extraordinary human relationship or Archetypal Love and Relationship requires you to have your own power. Your power includes your abilities to consciously choose, to create, to declare, to commit, to not act, to act for, to act against, to speak, to listen, to promise, to ask, etc. You reclaim your power through the process of "recapitulating" what actually happened to you, and reassessing the editorial spin placed on your experiences by the stories that you made about them.

Growing your being to the level of maturity where it has an authentic appetite for Archetypal Love is an involved process that includes considerable time and a multiplicity of experiences. Not a few of these experiences may originally be, and may still be, interpreted as "unfortunate." You might remember these experiences as negative. You might be coloring their memory with labels like "evil," "stupid," "bad," "unfair," "wrong," and certainly "unnecessary." I am asking you to bring your old labels into question.

Experience comes bereft of meaning, completely neutral. There is no story about an experience until you make up the story. The world is rich in evidence, so you will find plenty of reasons to make up *any* story you want about *any* experience. Moreover, every story that you create has a purpose. You are either aware of the purpose that you serve in making any particular story, or not. Ignorance of your purpose, however, does not protect you from its consequences.

The result of creating a story about an experience that labels the experience as "bad" or "evil" has the consequence of placing you into the victim position of a low drama. By feigning victimhood toward your circumstances, you assume that you can avoid responsibility. Getting to be irresponsible is tremendously rewarding for the Gremlin part of your Box. But the reward of avoiding responsibility comes at quite a cost. The cost of having no responsibility is also having no power.

Recapitulating Your Story About Being Wounded (BLTLCH08.08). To recapitulate means that you recall a specific story and ask yourself, "What is the purpose of this story? Is the purpose of my story to expand consciousness or to avoid consciousness? Is the purpose of my story to take responsibility or to avoid responsibility?" You will find that your story about any experience is not necessarily the experience itself, although it seems to come together with the experience just like a banana peel seems to come together with a banana. "My father did not love me because I screamed for help during a nightmare and he did not come to help me."

Start distinguishing your story *about* the experience from the experience. Peel away your dramatics, in the same way that you would peel a banana: First, break the stem at the top to reveal that there is both a banana *and* a banana peel, an experience with feelings and a meaning-making story about the experience and feelings. Then, peel away the story from what happened, just like you pull the peel away from a banana. "I had a nightmare and felt scared. I screamed for help. Nobody came to help me. That is what happened. My story about what happened is that my father did not love me because he did not come when I called for him. He let me be terrified and I hate him for it."

Peel one side of the banana down, to reveal a sweet soft "being" inside of you that has been isolated from humanity by the existence of your story. "In this nightmare as a child I felt terribly scared. I can still feel that level of trembling panic deep in my bones. My nerves are edgy. The scream is still in the back of my throat."

Then, peel the other side of the banana down to stand alone, now completely exposed without any protection at all. "If I remove my story about what happened, I am left with only a raw memory of the experience that I had. When I was a child, this raw experience was too intense for me to endure. As a child, I needed the story to buffer me from the intensity of my feelings. I made it someone else's fault. Now, as an adult, I am able to fully endure the intensity of these feelings with absolutely no story attached, no one else to blame, and, I must admit, that even in the fury of this experience-storm I am still okay."

Standing as a peeled banana in the center of the experience-storm of thoughts, memories, sensations and feelings brings you to recognize your true condition. You come to realize that you are not perfect as you have been taught to imagine that you should be. You are not perfect as you might imagine that you wish to be. You are not perfect. *You are wounded.* Through mature, responsible recapitulation, you can come to realize that you are not perfect; you are wounded, and, *the wounding is perfect.*

4. Cultivating the Broken Heart

In one way or another each of us has been wounded. In order to develop the matrix of consciousness upon which our being can grow, our childhood innocence must, in some manner and at some point in time, be taken away from us. Whether the destruction of our innocence was brutal and extended, or precise and swift, does not so much matter. What matters is that, at some point, like now, we gain the clarity about what happened to us from the perspective of a bigger picture about the process we are involved in. What is important is that we come to understand the necessity, value and use of shattered innocence.

Innocence may be shattered through being betrayed, abandoned, or abused, through losing something you cherish, or being stuck with something you hate. One person's innocence is shattered by being born prematurely and living their first three months in a plastic incubator. Another person's innocence is shattered by being sent to public school when they are five years old. Someone else's innocence is destroyed by the psycho-emotional terrors perpetrated on their family by an alcoholic father or a choleric mother, by a disease or an accident requiring surgery, by being sexually molested or by someone close suddenly dying, by natural disaster or the effect of war. Whatever exactly happened to you, whatever story you produce about what happened, the consequence of the wounding will be the same at the moment of the wounding as it is now, even if the wounding was lifetimes ago. The

A Dirge For Certainty

Like a dust devil spinning out into
  nothing,
You died quietly.
The rustle of a few dead leaves in
  the wind.
Which was a surprise for me.
How precious I once thought you were.
You seemed solid as granite,
Fierce as a tax collector,
Deadly as a wounded vampire.
I almost didn't know you were gone
So engaged was I in the avalanche
Of new experience,
Liberated by your passing.
I used to hang all my finest possessions
On your robust branches:
My expectations, my superiority,
My resentments, my trust.
Only raise the temperature and the
  sturdiest wood
Transforms into ashes
That can hold nothing.
I have fleeting memories of a time
  when things fit together
Into nice, neat packages and made
  sense.
Oh, what a small, tight world that was.
By accident I meet you now,
Lurking in the bottom of a glass,
Behind a betrayal,
Beneath a mistake.
Like brushing against sheets hanging
  on a line to dry,
I slip past so as not to disturb,
Feeling gratitude that you escorted
  me safely
Into a vaster more mysterious world,
Not wishing to renegotiate.
Life is better raw and unprotected
  Without certainty. – C.C.

result of the wounding will be objective, having the same result from person to person. The result of your wounding is a broken heart.

To move into the space of Archetypal Love requires the broken heart. Your first reaction to the image of having a broken heart could well be revulsion – a broken heart is a weakness, a vulnerability that saddles you with a handicap. What could it mean, a "broken heart"? First of all, it is not the heart that is broken. The heart is fine. What breaks is the agglomerated encrustations around your heart, that you collected so as to buffer your heart against experiencing an intensity of feelings you thought you could never bear. You defended your heart in order to survive. And it worked. You *did* survive. Your intention was noble and successful. Your intention was to take care of yourself so that you could continue to live. You lived and you grew. You matured, until that which once defended you has now become your prison. What may be happening now is that you are outgrowing your own defenses. The tricks you created to stay untouchable are as irrelevant as diapers, as unnecessary as a baby bottle, as extraneous as training wheels on your bicycle.

The broken heart is hard earned, and commonly perceived as an avoidable evil, something that God lets happen as an oversight. An extraordinary event must occur to shift a victim's view of having a broken heart to include its true value. How is one to responsibly understand and use the pain of deceit and betrayal to expand compassion rather than shrink it? How can a broken heart serve Archetypal Love?

Hitting Bottom (BLTLCH08.09). The answer is counterintuitive. A broken heart is so tender and raw that considering doing violence to another person or to nature feels like raw skin scraped on hot pavement. *It is not the pain of "being violated" but the pain of "being about to cause violence" yourself that changes you.* When pain about your own unconscious behavior wakes you up to the depth of your unconsciousness, then, your broken heart changes the way you behave. You care too much about the being of a person to be insulted by their Box. You cannot even pretend to take revenge. Why take revenge against a sleeping machine when there is a living being in there, whom you could love?

When you accept the unexpurgated experience of your broken heart, there may come times when you think you want to die of overwhelm from shame, from isolation, from depression, grief, or remorse. But you do not die. Instead, you live on within an intensity of experience, far above what you previously defined as the maximum limit. Even if you do not know how this process works, you continue living. In these times you have "hit bottom." You have given up trying to control the circumstances and have become fluid to a level that you previously assumed would drive you crazy. Then, you discover that in these times you are, to a high degree, transparent to the Principles that serve what is wanted and needed in the space, because your Box does not care to interfere with its dreary opinions anymore.

Using Your Broken Heart as a Gateway (BLTLCH08.10). As paradoxical as this may sound, in my experience the upperworld is entered through the bottom of the underworld. Your broken-heartedness gives you answers that you thought could only be found elsewhere through struggle or merit. In those "worst" of times, as you look back on your life, you see that having abundant compassion toward your own broken heart is what finally made sense.

If you practice delaying your reflexive moves that try to patch up the cracks in your heart, the heart will gradually relax into staying open even when it hurts. You develop distinctions between the different kinds of hurting. Is it fear? Is it rage? Is it sadness? Is it joy? Is this a feeling or is it emotion from the past? Is this *my* pain or is it someone else's pain? Is this feeling mixed together with other feelings, or is it a pure feeling? How big is it – what percentage?

Accepting your own broken heart is a new experience. Your whole body may find empathy, may become unpredictably kind and generous, may sense what is happening in its proximity as if it is happening to itself – not because your heart wants to feel these things, but by the very fact that it is broken and no longer protected with a sense of already-knowing certainty. The broken heart opens to wide-band exchange, both with other people and with specific situations. It encounters a new kind of energetic flowthrough. Sooner or later, you come to discover that the experiences that shattered your innocence and eventually broke your heart open gave you the exact reference points and sensitivities that you need to serve others and fulfill your destiny. Your pain has been your apprenticeship.

A broken heart becomes the gateway to Archetypal Relationship domains when you accept the totality of its brokenness. There is a difference between *accepting* broken heartedness as a permanent condition, and *enduring* a broken heart as a temporary strategy, just long enough to get through a moment of anguish. Enduring a broken heart is conditional. But Archetypal Love is *unconditional*. Archetypal Love cannot land in the relationship space you hold, until you are willing for it to be there forever. Then, Archetypal Love comes and goes as it pleases. By trying to endure a temporary broken heart without accepting an irreparably broken heart, the wall stays in place.

A man's broken heart exposes him to unspeakably precious experiences, that were too frightening for a heart guarded by reactionary machine guns. Experiences that were previously too intense become suddenly too temporary. Tenderly caressing the aliveness in your woman's hand enchants you endlessly. Within the field of your delicate attentions her she-ness unfolds into none other than the true Archetypal Feminine, the astounding Goddess, the same one who was Mary Magdalena to Jesus, who was Shakti to Shiva, who was Radha to Krishna. This radiantly alluring she-being stands in relationship to you, and every cell in your system tingles with the connection. You smell the musky warmth of her skin; you stroke the electric tangles of her hair. Maximum Womanliness fully and richly responds to your glance. She speaks into your fortunate ears. She willingly spends precious moments of her life sharing ordinary chores with you, while exuding flawless beauty, every breath and gesture only full of love. She envelopes you in her nurturing and healing balm of legendary proportions, the taste of which you can neither absorb enough nor appreciate enough. Being too close aches as much as being too distant, and yet she is the focus of your unquenchable longing when you appreciate and accept your broken heart.

SECTION 8-E
The Power of Attention

Human attention is one of the most delectable substances in the universe. How much effort do you put into trying to get attention from other people? Why? Most people love to get either positive or negative attention because it feels great to have another person's attention, no matter what form it is. Human attention is sometimes the only thing required to perform healings and transformations.

We each have masculine and feminine forms of attention. Masculine attention is singular, focused, directed, analytical "point attention." Feminine attention is wideband, multidimensional, free-floating, intuitive "field attention." Each kind of attention has its particularly effective applications. Masculine point attention is useful for persisting, getting a project finished, or "drilling down" to get to the root of a matter. Feminine field attention is useful for scanning people, projects or situations to assess the state of things, to check for unexpected conditions, to detect moods or the drift of underlying currents.

Placing the Man's Attention on the Woman (BLTLCH08.11). Placing your attention on something is like shining a flashlight into the dark. Where your attention goes, your energy flows. The effects caused by consciously directed attention do not come from the attention itself, but rather from the energy that flows along the attention. It is your energy that lights things up. For example, when a man places his Archetypal Masculine attention on his woman, his Archetypal Masculine energy flows to her, and in that moment she can light up. When a man places his conscious attention on his woman, the space is held for her. She is protected and safe. She no longer has to take care of herself from a survival perspective, so her masculine defenses can relax. She softens and becomes more feminine. In that moment of softening, the door opens for Archetypal Woman to appear. You can watch it happen as she changes before your eyes from an ordinary human woman into the Pirate Sorceress Warrioress Queen Goddess Woman, a transformation that is more thoroughly investigated in the next chapter. But, if a man places his ordinary attention on his woman, even for an instant, the spell is broken. One woman described it like this: "If I am adored by my man

it builds a foundation and I can abandon myself into being a fabulous and sensuous woman. But if he judges me, even in the slightest way, everything falls apart like a house of cards." The mood is shattered. The door is closed.

Placing the Woman's Attention on the Man (BLTLCH08.12). A woman must also be careful about what kind of attention she places on her man. A woman's ordinary attention can look anywhere and find fault. She sees whatever is not working, whatever might possibly go wrong. If you direct such attention at the imperfections in your man's thin ego structure, that ego mechanically snaps into a scared snarling dog, fighting for its life. But if you split off a portion of your practical field attention and use it to scan behind the scenes in all dimensions of your daily affairs, to detect anything that needs to be handled, and if you place whatever you find on a prioritized list at the feet of your man to dispense with as he sees fit, that creates Archetypal Relationship. With the details handled through respectful teamwork rather than entangled in low drama, you can reserve the bulk of your feminine attention for appreciating the experience of being with your Archetypal Man as he brings you on his adventures, fights his battles and rescues you from the dreary ordinary. Admiring your hero with Archetypal Feminine attention, even if he struggles or wavers in his efforts, gives a man the strength of knowing that someone truly believes in him. The mysterious strength that arises from knowing that someone truly believes in you makes legendary results possible. Behind every successful Archetypal Man is an Archetypal Woman admiring her hero.

The ability to intentionally place and sustain your attention on your partner takes intelligence and care. But, we have a conflict here, because the natural, unintentional manifestation of the masculine and the feminine is stupid aggressivity and evil. The key to the Archetypal domains is applying our attention with conscious intention, but practically speaking we do not own our attention. Most of the time we do not even know where our attention is. Our attention wanders around, bouncing from one thing to the next; whatever flashy object or loud sound strikes us gets our attention. Without specific practice, we have difficulty placing our attention anywhere with intention, for any length of time, because our attention span is so short and we are so accustomed to letting it be absorbed in distractions.

Being Not Distractible (BLTLCH08.13). Since our energy follows our attention, then whatever has our attention also consumes our energy. A thousand distractions will feed on us, whenever we don't pay attention to exactly what we are feeding with our flow of energy. Here is a list of distractions that consistently get our attention and devour our energy.

Common Things That Can Devour Your Energy

- Worries
- Resentments
- Physical pain or discomfort, even minor itches or having your hair out of place
- Withholding communications; not saying what needs to be said
- Keeping secrets
- Withholding anger, fear or sadness
- Repressing joy
- Getting hooked and emotionally overreacting
- Taking sides in a conflict
- Taking a position about anything, e.g., politics, sports, art, religion, science
- Having opinions
- Sustaining beliefs
- Avoiding unpleasant tasks
- Having internal mental conversations with others
- Having other people's energy in your personal space
- Power struggles with authority figures

- Making up justifications for what you did or what you want to do
- Blaming others
- Trying to be right
- Trying to make other people wrong
- Trying to be perfect
- Complaining to anyone about anything
- Trying to get other people's attention
- Trying to remember what you forgot
- Trying to find or reclaim what you have lost
- Trying to look good
- Trying to look better than other people
- Trying to be acceptable to others
- Trying to make other people jealous
- Trying to look normal
- Trying to be superior
- Strategizing ways to get revenge
- Being late, even just a few minutes
- Breaking your promises
- Not answering the exact question that was asked
- Saying more than is necessary
- Driving faster than the speed limit
- Arguing with anybody about anything
- Making messes for others to clean up
- Living in unseen messes, e.g., packed attics, unwashed dishes, unpaid bills
- Unfinished business, uncompleted projects
- Broken agreements, either by you or by others
- Broken objects that need to be fixed
- Too many possessions, having more than you need
- Borrowing money or things
- Loaning money or things
- Flirting, i.e., exchanging sexual energy casually with friends or strangers, over the telephone or over the Internet
- Protecting other people from feeling hurt; walking on eggshells
- Being adaptive
- Giving your center away

- Being a source of psychic violence
- Making lists of things to do
- Disorganization, confusion, pointless chaos
- Listening to other people complaining.
- Overeating, over drinking
- Junk food
- Drugs, prescribed or not
- Trying to stay in fashion
- Indulgence, e.g., fantasy worlds, bingeing, over shopping
- Mass media: television, radio, newspaper, magazines, billboards, posters, etc.
- Overindulging in desire for objects or experiences, e.g., sexual fantasies
- Addictions, e.g., to adrenalin, to problems, to being perfect, or to speed
- Gossiping or being around gossip
- Low drama
- Triangulating in communications, telling one person what you should be telling another person
- Not enough boundaries with your children
- Not enough boundaries with your parents
- Not enough boundaries with your own Gremlin
- Excessive orgasms or orgiastic behavior
- Making boundaries at the castle gate instead of at the frontier
- Avoiding contact or intimacy with your mate, shunning
- Making other plans, having a back door
- Leading a double life
- Not expressing what is really going on with you
- Conflicts with your neighbors, colleagues, boss, employees
- Violence, cathartic expression of emotions, horror films or novels
- Doing things that you do not consciously take responsibility for choosing to do
- Doing things you do not want to do
- Always just doing things, and so on.

As you can see, your energy is swiftly devoured by countless distractions. Without paying attention to your attention, your precious energy is easily sucked away. Like a sieve with a thousand holes, you can be drained in a matter of seconds. No wonder we can be so tired halfway through the day. Without realizing how, we frivolously spend our daily energy allotment. Then, we have little patience for deep listening, for being-with others, or for doing Edgework experiments.

That daily allotment of energy is the food of both the Archetypal Male and Archetypal Female. If our Archetypal energy is eaten by other things, then we have no resources to work with. It is Archetypal Man's and Woman's job to create and manage their own resources. To create and manage energy, both Archetypal Man and Archetypal Woman can intentionally establish a *different* practice with their attention. They can start playing a new game.

Conservation of Energy – A New Game

Conservation of Energy (BLTLCH08.14). The game starts like this: Track where your attention is directing your energy during the day. How much energy are you giving to what and when? And especially, why? Before you try to change anything about what you are doing, it is counterintuitive but very important to watch first. Watch for a long time. Spend weeks, maybe even months, watching what you do with your energy. You have to watch what you are doing for so long that you get sick of it. The only thing strong enough to change habits of energy flow is deep authentic remorse about the results you presently create. When the pain of watching yourself waste away your energy gets strong enough, you will automatically change your habits without having to effort. If your habits of flowing energy have not changed, it is because you have not yet let the pain of awareness about what you are doing get intense enough.

When you contain and consciously direct how you are flowing your energy, more and more you start building new kinds of muscles. The new muscles allow you to direct and focus your attention and energy through new capacities. Imagine what resources you would accumulate if you were able to conserve most of your energy during the day. This does not mean that you lie in bed all day. Conserving your energy involves going about your day, paying attention to your attention in two specific ways:

1. Pay attention to avoid flowing energy anywhere unconsciously. That is, make your attention harder to get (except for your children or your partner).
2. Pay attention to flow only the exact amount of energy needed to accomplish what you want, not too much or too little.

Following these two practices gives you energy in reserve. But, be careful about managing your new reserves of energy. The present design of your Box can only tolerate a certain maximum level of energy reserves and has many conscious and unconscious ways to quickly blow off more energy than it can handle. By conserving energy, your Box will quickly be faced with more energy than it can process. "Quickly" in this case means within even a few hours of practice.

Conserving energy produces evolution by reflex. When your newly conserved energy has exceeded a certain limit, your Box's self-regulation mechanisms destabilize, and your Box will have a tendency to automatically reorder itself into a more elegant and refined design – one that can flow and direct even more energy than before. On the way to this new, refined design, your Box will go through liquid states, so be forewarned: Be gentle with yourself. Having liquid states does not mean that anything is wrong, only that your Box is evolving to a new shape. Be careful to conserve energy also during the liquid states. Do not go bingeing on sweets or go emotionally cathartic while liquid. Be patient, do something with your hands like needlework or woodwork, read a good book, clean the house, watch a movie, meditate, go for a long walk, wait it out. In a few days you will get accustomed to the condition of having more energy in your system. Then, you can start exploring what new things are possible for you to create.

If you have conserved your energy, and you make it through the liquid states, and your Box reorders, then, when you consciously place your attention on something or someone, that thing (or one) receives the full dose of your energy. With practice, your attention energy can become quite strong. Conserving your energy and then consciously arranging to place your attention on your partner, for example, for an extended period of time, can cause some quite amazing results.

CHAPTER 9

A Short Course on Archetypal Man and Woman

Probably most of the men and women you have ever met demonstrated only ordinary human behaviors. Therefore, you could see what *they* saw, listen to what *they* heard, and understand what *they* thought. If you were lucky, perhaps you encountered a few people here and there who saw things *very* differently from you – perhaps a teacher who listened in an extraordinarily human way, or a boss who took responsibility from a perspective that seemed most unusual. Once or twice in your life you may have come face to face with Archetypal Man or Woman, someone who interacted with the world in ways you never dreamed of.

In other cultures or other times, encountering living, breathing, Archetypal role models was far more common. Not for us. We are disadvantaged by having a lack of Archetypal role models to imitate. In our society, people are able to gain decision-making authority without having to grow up. Such authority, however, is not enough to merit entry into Archetypal spaces.

The human body is hardwired with Archetypal structures ready to be initiated into action when we are about fifteen years old. It is only the beginning of our troubles that we have no guides, no role models to follow, and no map for the waking-up process. Initiation is further complicated by the fact that our nervous system was most optimal for transitioning into Archetypal awareness and responsibilities in our mid-teens, and most of us are significantly past our "Sell by:" date. Nevertheless, the Archetypal structures wait within us.

This chapter presents characteristic qualities of the Archetypal Masculine and Archetypal Feminine. If, at first, Archetypal characteristics seem difficult to understand, this merely indicates the size of the gap between human and Archetypal domains. Considerable experimenting may be needed before these ideas begin making sense in your everyday experience. In the meantime, frequent discussion of this chapter would be well worth the effort, especially with other men and/or women gathered for the purpose of strengthening relationship skills and building men's and women's culture.

SECTION 9-A
From Pain to Rocket Fuel

Redeeming Pain Through Consciousness (BLTLCH09.01). We can enter Archetypal Relationship domains only by continuously paying the entrance fee. The entrance fee is conscientious practice that builds the matrix upon which our being can expand into the Archetypal. In the process of paying the entrance fee, we are often required to consciously feel pain – not pain as suffering, but pain as one or more of the four feelings (felt distinctly, not mixed!). As we discussed in Section 5A, the redeeming value of pain comes through feeling our pain consciously. Feeling pain consciously changes it from pain into rocket fuel.

The pain you might feel while moving toward Archetypal Relationship could well come from realizing that you (as a man, for example) have been directing your energies toward subtly dominating, repressing and/or hating women. Maybe you did not realize that before. Your grandfather was doing it. Your father was doing it. Is it any surprise that you are doing it too?

Perhaps your pain comes from realizing that you (as a woman) long ago exchanged the possibility of true Love for seeking revenge against men because they built the patriarchy. With destruction as your goal, is there any question as to why nothing "relationally interesting" has worked out for you so far? Any doubts why you are living the same relationship life that your mother created for herself?

Perhaps you feel pain from realizing how you have ignored children, controlled children, or condemned your children's exuberance and imagination, rather than holding a safe harbor for children so they can establish and step into their own world responsibly. You unconsciously did to children what was unconsciously done to you.

The invitation here is not to avoid realizations just because they are painful. Instead, seek to keep the intensity of each insight alive. Then, practice with an impeccability made necessary by the acute pain of your insights.

It is easy to let the Box perform its usual procedure of selectively erasing "negative" or "bad" experiences from your awareness. The Box wants to consider your painful insights as if they were a one-time phenomenon, like stubbing your toe, the pain fading quickly into nonexistence. Do not let your Box dilute or wash away what you worked so hard to prepare yourself to receive. Learn to live with continuous disturbance, instead.

If you realize, for example, that you have been exhibiting the behavior of a pathological liar, and you see it clearly enough to sense the pain you have caused every-one who loves you, that painful clarity can take you to a new level of internal vigilance in self-honesty. Continuous pain about lying fuels an attention to truth-saying. If you ever, for a moment, forget the pain of realizing that you are in fact a pathological liar, then the behavior is unchecked and leaps back into action – full throttle. The pain of realization instills true remorse with its transformative power, and true remorse never fades, ever. It becomes part of your constitution, part of your overall perspective. True remorse builds the foundation you will stand on to encounter the next painful realization, the next conscious incompetence. Allowing realization-pain to fade away slides you back into ordinary human relationship behaviors quicker than you can say, "How could anyone be so stupid?"

When we imagine what it would be like trying to continuously remember painful realizations, it is nearly impossible for us not to equate this to guilt. But, being responsible is different from being guilty. We are far more familiar with being guilty. Beating ourselves up for being "bad" or "worthless" is not responsibility – it is guilt. There is a difference between remembering painful realizations as a reminding tool, and remembering painful

MAP OF GUILT vs. RESPONSIBILITY	
GUILT	**RESPONSIBILITY**
From the past.	In the present.
Strategic, defensive.	Evolutionary.
Promotes weakness.	Strengthens.
Avoids responsibility.	Puts you in the position
Is a response to	of being at source.
external authority.	You are the authority.
Creates a story:	No story.
burden, fault, blame.	No burden, not blamed.
"If I am guilty enough	You are the cause.
and beat myself up	Empowers through clarity.
enough then I can do	Clarity causes remorse.
it again."	Remorse won't let you
Guilt is punishment.	do it again because it is
You can make others	too painful. You take
guilty.	responsibility yourself.
Low drama.	High drama.

realizations as a way of beating ourselves up. Useful pain does not come from judgment or criticism. Useful pain comes from responsible, clear seeing.

No one is ever immune to the risk of sliding backward. You may even be sliding backward in those exact moments when you would swear that you are making specific efforts not to slide backward! The Box can be much slyer than we think. As Samuel Johnson, George Bernard Shaw, William James, Karl Marx, Lee Lozowick and Saint Bernard of Clairvaux, among others, have told us in one form or another, "The road to hell is paved with good intentions."

Archetypal Man and Archetypal Woman: the Notes

Archetypal Definitions of Man and Woman (BLTLCH09.02). In Archetypal domains we enter a new game between men and women. Since Archetypal domains function outside the reaches of the patriarchy, there is no longer motivation for competition or war between the sexes.

The new game starts with a new distinction: *There are no problems between men and women because there are no longer men and women. There are Archetypal Men and there are Archetypal Women. Each has their own dominion, over which there is no contest.*

But exactly what constitutes Archetypal Man? Archetypal Woman? And what clarifications establish relationships between them, such that there could be no problems? The following notes build a foundation for understanding the whys and wherefores of relationship between Archetypal Man and Archetypal Woman.

1. Archetypally, Men are Nothing

Not nothing as in worthlessness or emptiness, but Nothing as in the unknown, as in unlimited possibility. The central Nothingness of the Archetypal Masculine is why men's egos are so thin and fragile. One questionable comment by a woman shatters ordinary man's ego, and he frantically tries to reestablish his false self-esteem by flying back in a rage. That reaction is because Nothing is really there. The experience of being Nothing is terrifying for ordinary men who are not trained in how to powerfully use their Nothingness. Ordinary men *hate* being Nothing and neurotically try to be *something*. This is why men are attracted to anything that can give them an identity, like a wall full of university degrees, being publicized in the media for wild escapades, or trying to compete and be "the winner." Men's ordinary neurotic attempts to try to be something, anything, instead of relaxing powerfully into being Nothing, makes women furious. Being afraid of *anything* makes ordinary men angry. Men hide their fear of Nothingness with a cover of Box-defending anger, but underneath their anger is terror about being Nothing. If a man does not use his Nothingness wisely, then his Nothingness is used to serve unconscious purposes. The unconscious negative manifestation of the masculine is stupid aggression that destroys love. (Women, if you ever thought that men are stupid and aggressive, you were right.)

2. Archetypally, Women are Everything

This is why women notice every smudge of dirt, every bit of dust, every stain, every wrinkle, every task that is not done, and every little thing that is not working. The experience of seeing so much disharmony, so much disorder and so much work to do causes a deep and abiding rage in the Archetypal Feminine. This rage is like a volcano, immense enough to explode cities. The rage of the Archetypal Feminine is so big that it frightens ordinary women. Women are not trained in how to apply their rage, and how to use rage energy practically, so they cover their rage with fear – the fear of how much rage they hold and what might happen if it ever came out. Ordinary women get neurotic about being Everything when they try to choose (out of the Everything) one particular identity to be. Instead of being the richly abundant, diverse,

MAP OF ORDINARY vs. ARCHETYPAL ENERGETIC RELATIONSHIP DIAGRAMS

These are energetic diagrams, not the usual symbolic diagrams.

ORDINARY RELATIONSHIP

MASCULINE   FEMININE

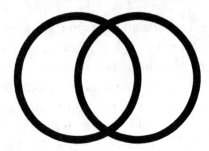

Enmeshed, unisex, fused, women waiting around for men to finally get it about relationship. At least there is equality. (Equality within the patriarchy? What kind of equality is that?)

ARCHETYPAL RELATIONHIP

MASCULINE   FEMININE

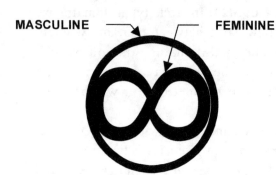

Masculine holds the space for the Feminine. Nothing is bigger than Everything. This is *not* an equal arrangement. Neither is it fair. It is, however, a very interesting "Winning Happening" game. Relationship becomes the space through which true Love can do its work.

---

totally connected Earth Mother, modern woman frantically flips through the catalog trying to find a singular identity for herself with the right matching outfit, the right hair style, and the right look. Ordinary woman's neurotic indecision about the one particular thing "to be," instead of relaxing into being Everything, makes men furious. On the surface ordinary women appear weak, fearful, delicate, and confused, but just underneath is searing clarity and a roaring furnace. If a woman does not use her Everythingness wisely, then her Everythingness is used to serve unconscious purposes. The unconscious negative manifestation of the feminine is evil. Evil uses the intimate knowledge and all-encompassing experience of the Everything to manipulate and destroy love.

3. No Solution to the Differences

Men and women, stupid and evil, the fly and the spider. Between the fly and the spider there is no contest. You have just discovered the reason for the patriarchy. We will never solve the differences between men and women. We are not supposed to. These differences are the most precious ingredients for consistently creating ecstasy.

4. The Need for Relationship Cultures

Double Space-Holding (BLTLCH09.03). A practical challenge these days is for Archetypal Man and Woman to establish relationship cultures that are independent of the dominant Western patriarchal culture. Men in

Archetypal Men's culture would be encouraged to hold space for his extraordinary relationship *and* for his Archetypal Relationship. His ability to pay finer and more disciplined attention would feed his hungry senses in experiential reality; and his increased ability to be Nothing, and still create, would provide him with a livelihood outside of stifling hierarchies. Archetypal Woman would be encouraged to make use of her vast resources of perception and intuition to heal her competitive regard for other women, and build a Women's culture that is rich and dynamic enough to be more interesting than a Macy's catalog. (Think how solidly women's unconsciously spent Archetypal Feminine resources support the patriarchy. Think how quickly patriarchal structures would crumble if they were suddenly unsupported by the time, energy and money of a majority of women. When women behave like unconscious predictable consumers is it any wonder they are milked like cows?)

By "double space-holding" (simultaneously "holding space" within the extraordinary and Archetypal domains), Man could sustain an Archetypal context even while living in ordinary Western culture with his extraordinary relationship. He would not have to retreat to some cave or monastery to do Archetypal Relationship experiments. Through relying on the coaching and support of his actively experimenting fellows, a man's intimacy Edgework experiments could turn out to be more interesting than football, films and fast cars.

By reclaiming true sisterhood, women could rejuvenate their Archetypal abilities to heal, teach, and lead groups of people through steps in their own personal development. Her ministrations would reach beyond the defined borders of Western cultures, to connect with Archetypal Women in cultures around the world. The sharing would be reciprocal, and through sane and practical exchanges, Western culture would evolve toward sustainability.

"Double space-holding" as a Man, and embodying matriarchal realities as a Woman, would not happen by force, but as a result of clarity. (See map on page 294.) Clarity is a higher technology than making forceful boundaries – it uses less energy and creates more sustainable results. Through clearly observing what is *really* going on in Western culture (viewed from the Archetypal perspective), changes in behavior and relationship would result. The first step for both men and women is to observe our culture from the perspective of Archetypal Relationship, rather than looking at Archetypal Relationship from the ordinary perspective of our cultural distortions.

5. Looking into the Void

The Nothing at the center of Archetypal Man is the Archetypal Void, the great emptiness out of which Everything was created. The real use of Man's Nothingness is for creating what has never been created before, for staying unhookable, for revealing clarity, and for holding a particular space as the framework out of which Archetypal Relationship can unfold. Archetypal Man is the space holder in relationship, just like a zero is a space holder in mathematics. The zero is the place in a number where presently there is nothing but could be anything. In particular, Archetypal Man is the space holder for Bright Principles, for stellated Archetypes, and for a dynamic and evolving relationship with the Archetypal Feminine.

6. Space Holding and Space Filling

Space Holding and Space Filling (BLTLCH09.04). Man sets and holds context like a wall defines the possibility of a garden. Woman fills the context held by Man with the Archetypal "Garden of Woman" – in the same way that flowers, fruits and vegetables, stones, waterfalls, fish, trees, pathways, gazebos and benches fill a biological garden. Man is the space holder. Woman is the space filler.

Man fixes the leaking faucet, traps mice, kills cockroaches and spiders, keeps the neighbors in line, changes the light bulbs, manages the heater repair man, and keeps the car in good running order. Woman decorates the rooms, creates and maintains the elegance of the sanctuary, chooses the menu, arranges the flowers, heals the children, keeps the cupboards and refrigerator filled with abundance and health, manages the relationships among the helper team, invites the guests to dinner, and fills the space with a never-ending profusion of love and beauty and grace.

7. Being the Gardener

In addition to holding space for the Garden of Woman, Archetypal Man also is responsible for being the gardener. (This is not how it is supposed to be, but how *it is* in modern Western culture. We explore how it is supposed to be in Chapter 10, *The Pirate Sorceress Warrioress Queen Goddess Woman*.) For modern men, being the gardener for the Archetypal Feminine looks more like walking into a spinning propeller blade. Modern men have been civilized. We are nice, polite, sensitive new-age guys. Our mother still has our balls. Being the gardner requires something very different from the masculine qualities given to us by modern culture. Being the gardener requires ongoing use of anger for the precise "sword work" of distinguishing clarifications, and indefatigably setting and holding boundaries. A Garden needs to be trimmed. Left untrimmed, a well-nurtured Garden takes little time to grow all over itself and become a tangled mess. The grass needs mowing. Hedges and trees need pruning. Old structures need to be destroyed and taken away. The earth needs to be turned over, and new things planted. The ground must be raked up fresh, with old leaves and dead branches removed for burning or composting. This is rough work, serious work, sometimes abrupt and painful work. Things look different after a gardener has been there.

When the gardener shows up with shears, cutters, saw, wheelbarrow, shovel and lawn-mower, it naturally raises the fearful wrath of the Archetypal Feminine. She has worked so hard to grow into and fill up the space that she forgets how good it feels when a Garden grows back fresh and even more beautifully, after skilled pruning. If the gardener cannot face Archetypal Feminine wrath with a professional, unhookable demeanor, he will not be able to keep his job.

Stay brave, Men. When you open the closet door and thirty shoeboxes fall on your head, it is time to "trim the Garden." When there is no more room for coats, do not build new hangers. Get rid of coats. When every shelf and flat open space is filled with knick-knacks, it is not time to build more shelves; it is time to rent a dumpster. When the monthly bills exceed your paycheck, immediate serious gardening is in order. Serious gardening sustains the health of the Garden. It is up to Archetypal Man to do a good job.

8. About Big and Little Things

Men like one big thing. Women like a lot of little things. The examples that follow are gross generalizations, but they indicate an underlying pattern: Men can find complete satisfaction with a mobile phone, a nice computer and their Mercedes. Women might find those items completely unfulfilling, and are far more satisfied shopping for cupboards full of kitchen appliances, a house decorated with curtains and wallpaper, and vacations to interesting parts of the world. The point is that these preferences are Archetypal, not neurotic, and can be relied on as a rich source of pleasure, sharing and appreciation. To make Archetypal use of the contrast in preferences, learn a different way to relate to them. Men like one big thing and it is not a problem, because men can learn to wait a long time before they get their one big thing. (In case you haven't figured it out yet, this "one big thing – many little things" metaphor relates especially well to sexuality and foreplay. Now read the last sentence again.) In the meantime, a man can dearly long for his one big thing, and that longing can itself become physically ecstatic. If a man gets his one big thing, his ecstasy of longing is instantly replaced by a deadness. (In fact, a French phrase for orgasm is *la petite mort* or "the little death.") In contrast to men, women like a lot of little things. Ordinary woman focuses on hoping to receive a lot of little things. When she does not get them, she generates the viewpoint that she is a victim, with a good excuse to feed her hungry Gremlin with revenge against that one she expected should have given her the many little things. Archetypal Woman focuses on *giving* a lot of little things instead of receiving a lot of little things. In the course of *delivering* a lot of little things (caresses, truths, kisses, sounds, giggles, jokes, nips), there are still a lot of little things happening for the delight of the woman. Giving can be even better than receiving, especially if the man's experience of the many little things is ecstatically intensified by his longing for his one big thing. Rather than trying to solve the apparent conflicts between men and women, consider learning French: *Vive la différence!*

9. Shit Blocks the Archetypal

Bullshit and Cowshit (BLTLCH09.05). In ordinary human relationships there are two kinds of shit, a masculine form of shit that men do, called "bullshit," and a feminine form of shit that women do, called "cowshit." Bullshit is saying things that are very, very relevant, like, "Honey, I'll be home at seven. I will take out the garbage tonight. I will fix that leak this weekend. I will help Johnny improve his algebra grades. I will spend less time at my computer." The problem with bullshit is that even though the things that are said are

very, very relevant, they are just not true. A persistent bullshit habit can effectively block man from accessing Archetypal domains with his Woman.

Cowshit is saying things that are very, very true. For example, when it is nine-thirty on Saturday night and the husband and wife walk up the stairs to be together in their bedroom and the wife says, "I noticed that you walked right by the laundry basket on your way up the stairs. You didn't even see it. That laundry is all washed, dried, folded and ironed. I did that already. All you had to do was carry the basket up the stairs. Couldn't you do even that one little thing to help me around the house…?" The problem with cowshit is that even though the things that are said are very, very, *very* true, they are *completely* irrelevant. A persistent cowshit habit can effectively block woman from accessing Archetypal domains with her Man. We will have more to say about cowshit in number 11, below.

10. Being Bigger

Nothing is Bigger than Everything (BLTLCH09.06). Archetypal Man lives in the question, "What is bigger? Nothing? Or Everything?" This is a strange question, seeming to be theoretical, almost philosophical – not a question for which you would expect to have much of a provable answer. But for Archetypal Man the answer is precise and immediate; the answer is experiential and not an idea. And the answer is of the utmost importance. For the question, "What is bigger? Nothing or Everything?" it is tacitly and continuously obvious that Nothing is bigger. If Nothing were not bigger, there would be no place for Everything! This is why Archetypal Man can hold space for Archetypal Woman. No matter what concoction Woman comes up with, Archetypal Man can relax and look her straight in the eyes, knowing, "I am bigger than that." Sometimes the most challenging thing that Woman comes up with is praise, admiration, love, respect, joy, happiness, hope, and wanting to be only nearer. Man can receive even a holy flood of joyous love when he realizes, "That too. I am bigger than that. I can be annihilated in Love and still function." We will discuss this at greater length in the Magician sub-section of Chapter 11.

11. Getting Killed, But Not Dying

Getting Killed but Not Dying (BLTLCH09.07). Because the feminine is aware of everything not working and everything not done, it can be that a woman comes to bed with a quiver full of very sharp arrows. She may be unable to sleep until her quiver is empty. She looks around for what to do with the arrows. There, in the bedroom, is a handy target: you, the man. *Twang-thunk!* the first arrow flies and finds its mark in your heart: "The car needs new tires, the phone bill is due, Mary needs new shoes, and we don't even have enough money in the bank to cover the rent. Why can't you get a job that brings us more money?" *Twang-thunk!* the next arrow flies: "You spend so much time working and when you come home you still think about work. You even go on the computer late at night to do emails! You call this a relationship?" *Twang-thunk!* "Your mother keeps calling and complaining about not being able to sleep because her neighbor's dog barks all night long. Her legs keep hurting. Don't you have the kindness to do something about that?" *Twang-thunk!* "Jane Smith stole my recipe for brownies and made them for the whole exercise club, and then *she* took all the credit! She flirts outright with the teacher and it is so disgusting. She has her hands all over his body. When I ask the teacher a question, Jane comes right over and interrupts with something totally meaningless, and he helps her instead of me!" *Twang-thunk!* "Your kids were fighting this afternoon – again! I can't stand it! I don't know what to do anymore. I am ready to give

up. You are not here to help me, and sometimes I just start screaming at them." *Twang-thunk!* "How many times do I need to tell you that I do not like you to touch me there until I am ready? You *never* listen to me!"

By the time her quiver is empty, she is feeling quite fine. If you are an ordinary man, then by the time her quiver is *half* empty you are feeling quite dead. Cowshit is like that. Undeniably true. Razor sharp. Totally accurate. And, if you listen to it, you get killed. On the other hand, if you don't listen to it, if you harden your defenses, argue back, give reasons and excuses, dodge the issue, and try to change the subject to, say, "What a fine evening it is," or, "My dear, your eyes are sparkling tonight," or, "What about a little back massage, hmmm?" she refills the quiver and keeps going. She wants you to listen, to be soft and tenderized, *and* to still be alive and ready for action. But if you listen in your usual way, thinking that you have to *do* something about what she says, then the thing in you that was interested in action dies. We have come to an interesting question: How can you be killed and not die? The answer comes from the Archetypal.

Archetypal Man is Nothing. This means there is Nothing to be killed. Nothing to get offended. Nothing to react. Nothing to figure out. If the Man listens as "a space," he can make contact, feel compassion and still not be hooked. Then, when the woman stops speaking, it only takes about three seconds for every echo of her voice to fade out of the room. All that was said has gone into the past – true, it is only three seconds in the past – but it is still in the past, and therefore it has become completely powerless, because something in the past has no power in the present. Nothing of what was spoken remains, unless the Man holds the words in his mind as reactive conclusions, or in his heart as emotional resentments. Don't do that. If the Man lets only the Nothing remain, then he has just discovered how to be killed and not die. This is your homework assignment. Practice being killed and not dying. Listen to more than can be listened to. Listen to more than you can understand. Complete the communication, and let your Nothingness hold space for Everything, so that no matter what an arrow hits, you are *not* that. As Nothing, you then remain alive and well for doing Edgework experiments in intimacy.

13. The 10% and 90% Solutions

Women enter Archetypal domains through becoming 10% Masculine, such as through learning to simply take action rather than discussing all the details first, answering questions with clear *yes* or *no* decisions, making boundaries easefully and without hesitation, asking for what she needs, not giving her center away and being adaptively nice, staying unhookable, and so on. Men enter Archetypal domains through becoming 90% Feminine, such as through setting aside fear-based domination and instead seeking understanding and relationship, learning to be open and receptive instead of automatically competitive, enrobing communications in acceptance, appreciation, flexibility, and sensuality instead of the cold, hard facts, being in contact when an internal struggle arises instead of withdrawing, and so on. Of the two prerequisites, it is more difficult for a woman to become 10% Man than it is for a man to become 90% Woman.

14. Vigilance Furthers

Being Conscious of Your Purpose (BLTLCH09.08). A woman can easily misunderstand that her expanded masculinity gives her power over men. The most difficult thing for the woman in becoming 10% Masculine is to be vigilant about what comes out of her mouth. The feminine mind has access to too many loopholes in reality. The loopholes make it easy to ignore the fact that everything that is said has a purpose, a design for what it intends

to create. She does not comprehend the real and immediate consequences of what she says. To make a shift with this, you can rigorously focus on the purpose of what you say. Be rigorous about whom you speak with, and especially for what reason. Be rigorous that your purpose is not unconscious evil. The experiment is to be over-vigilant at first. Start off by not saying most things. This is a good way to develop your vigilance. After a couple of months you can start to say a few things that you are sure serve responsible purposes. Without realizing it, one woman in a training was making her husband wrong. The trainer said, "Lady, you are making your husband wrong." She said, "I am not *making* my husband wrong. He *is* wrong. I am just pointing it out to him." Proving that someone is wrong is not a responsible purpose; it is low drama. Learn the difference.

15. Same Time and Same Place

Being in the Same Time and the Same Place (BLTLCH09.09). Archetypal Relationship is the commitment to intimacy. Intimacy has two dimensions: to be in the same time together, and to be in the same place together. Being in the same time as your partner implies a mutual, although perhaps unspoken, agreement as to how "big" the time of now is. Does intimacy include stories from years past, days past, or only seconds past? Does intimacy include fantasies of possible futures? Does intimacy include television, newspaper, gossip, or alcohol? Being in the same place together means presence. When you are together, who or what is present there? Does intimacy include other friends, relatives, work colleagues, old partners? None of these qualifiers about time and place are right or wrong. But, if there is conscious or unconscious disagreement about the time or place aspects of intimacy, then probably intimacy itself will be seldom experienced.

Being in the same time also means being in the same speed through time together. The

MAP OF TRADITIONAL
MASCULINE FEMININE RELATIONSHIP DIAGRAM

Archetypal Masculine and Feminine Relationship has been symbolically represented in many ways, such as the masculine sun and the feminine moon. In this diagram an equilateral triangle with its point upwards represents the masculine penis, action, force, fighting, focus, and typical masculine one-pointedness – the sword and the knight who carries it, fire. An equilateral triangle with its point facing down represents the feminine vagina, receptivity, acceptance, passivity, and beingness – the sacred chalice, the Holy Grail, the fair maiden, water. The ultimate dynamic flow of life is established through mature relationship between the Archetypal Masculine and the Archetypal Feminine – clear action balanced by sensitive wisdom. Archetypal Relationship can be symbolized by the six pointed star that results from overlaying the masculine and feminine triangles one on top the other in the interpenetrating oneness of sexual union.

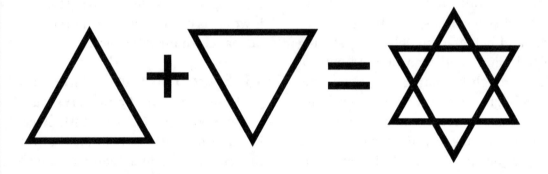

The ancient hexagram also represents a mirroring between the Archetypal and the human realms, captured in the two phrases: "As above, so below. As below, so above." This is holding the space through which Archetypal Principles do their work in the world (point down) and at the same time holding the space through which gratitude and praise is passed back up to the Archetypal Principles (point up). The diagram shows a reciprocal exchange where the Archetypal needs the human realm in which it can do its work, and the human realm needs the Archetypal for the clarity and power of Principles, the model of Archetypal Love and the possibility of transformation.

Masculine and Feminine have different relationships to the speed of time, for example, how long is a "while" in the hardware store vs. how long is a "while" in bed together on Sunday morning. The ratio between doing and being influences how fast time goes by in a particular space.

Being in the same place together means contact. Contact means seeing into the other person. Seeing into one another means caring enough to perceive the inner workings of the other with acceptance (without judgment, without being offended), and having the courage to honestly reveal yourself to your partner, so they can see into you, without you being afraid of attack or betrayal. It tends to be far more difficult for the Man to let himself be seen, because he is Nothing. Imagine in our culture what it must be like for a Man to be Nothing, compared to the Feminine – who could share forever and never scratch the surface of all there is to share about – because she is Everything. When the Masculine and Feminine are sharing, Archetypal Woman takes care to avoid filling up all the time and space with her sharing. Otherwise, she will think that her Man does not share, when in fact it is only a result of her filling up all the available sharing space. There is no room for the Man to share!

Woman learns to wait silently for her Man to share, and appreciates what he does share, knowing that in sharing he takes a huge risk.

16. Being and Doing

Being and Doing (BLTLCH09.10). Human men are focused on fixing problems, and want to know what to *do* in order to *be* in Archetypal Relationship. Archetypal Woman knows that there is *nothing* to *do* in order to *be* in Archetypal Relationship. Being requires no doing. Archetypal Woman demonstrates to her Man that he already has the Nothing required to be in Archetypal Relationship. He does not have to do anything or go anywhere to come up with Nothing. This can be extremely difficult for men to understand and come to trust. If a woman finds it difficult to believe how troublesome it is for a man to understand that there is "nothing to do to be," she is no longer in the Archetypal. She is hooked into ordinary.

ALWAYS REMEMBER

Always remember what you paid
to get into the new game
or you will fall asleep
and get shanghaied
by unconsciousness
back into the old game.
Along with death and taxes,
being shanghaied by unconsciousness
is guaranteed.

---

17. Nobody Knows

Women Shifting from Human to Archetypal and Remembering the Way (BLTLCH09.11). Men do not know about Archetypal Relationship. Ordinary women do not know about Archetypal Relationship either. When a man holds space for his woman and places his attention on his woman, she shifts from human woman to Archetypal Woman and suddenly she remembers about Archetypal Relationship. As soon as she shifts to Archetypal, the Woman remembers the way to the Center of the Great Labyrinth of Spaces. She can then navigate the two of them into intimacy, and teach her Man about Archetypal Relationship, while they explore the Great Labyrinth together. It is Woman's job to teach Man about Archetypal Relationship. Men *can* learn these things; they just need to be properly rewarded.

SECTION 9-C

Creating New Identities

We have referred to the idea of creating new identities, new characters, at several junctures in previous chapters. We will circle through this important concept once more here, and at a deeper level, as we prepare for the powerful distinctions that will follow in the next chapters – the new identity of Archetypal Man and the new identity of Archetypal Woman.

We will start again with the eternal question, "Who am I?"

We have now, and have always had, the complete freedom to choose who we are being. It is true that we have been raised in certain circumstances and in a certain culture and time. It is true that there exist powerful forces to try to sway our decisions in one direction or another about who to be. But those circumstances and forces are now, and always have been, outside of us, incidental, and not causative. The final decision – even down to the finest minutiae of our quality of being – has always been ours alone.

There are, of course, consequences to the decisions we make. Our assumptions about these consequences make it seem like we actually have no choice, and that we are squeezed into our way of being like warm plastic is squeezed into a steel mold. Cultural "being shaping" machinery is indeed powerful, as is family tradition. That is why the vast majority of us surrender our capacity to shape our own being to fit the illusion that it was never our decision in the first place. Nevertheless, the "vast majority" does not have to include *you*.

"Who am I?" is one of the first questions we are driven to answer. Once we find workable answers, we usually don't change them for the rest of our lives. We don't even wonder if our answers are the most useful or interesting. We assume the answers are true, and consider the job finished. Once we have built our Box, we forget that our Box is something that was built. Unconsciously, we know that if we reconsider the "Who am I?" question, it could drop us back into a liquid state – one that we assumed we had permanently left behind. The Box is quick to produce the terse comment, "Been there. Done that."

However … nonetheless … notwithstanding … you still have the right to change your mind about who you are. *That* has not been made illegal. After all, your Box is yours to play with and to make into whatever you want. That is why you are reading this book – to play with other possible shapes for your Box.

Consciously changing your Box is an option that you may tend to ignore if you have not acquired a taste for being in flux. Having the option to take on any identity, in any moment, is the same as having no identity at all. Those in-between times of making a new decision often seem bothersome – they are indefinite; we entered them after leaving behind *the way it was* and before having in place a new *the way it is*.

The Possibility of Shifting Identity
Shifting to Archetypal Identities (BLTLCH09.12). By investigating these ideas after shifting identity, you are tracing yourself back to the decision points where the design criteria for your Box were originally solidified. In the same way that the vibration waves of an earthquake can transform the seemingly solid earth into flowing mud, asking dangerous questions can provide sudden shocking realizations that decrystallize our self-image and open the possibility for the Box to take new shapes.

Re-asking already-answered questions returns us to the experience of having no answer. Having no answer can feel threatening. In our past, having no answer generated dire consequences. Well-meaning schoolteachers psychologically abused us when they would unexpectedly call on us to spit back requested intellectual information. If we had no answer for them, we were subtly (or not so subtly) condemned. Thus, in a true survival situation, we adopted the imperative of never being without an answer. Especially, we are never without an answer to such a fundamental question as "Who am I?"

Who are you? is also the first thing we demand to know of others: Are you man or woman? What is your name? Who are you? What do you do?

We keep handy answers available in case we need them. *Who am I?* I am a dentist, a father, a programmer, a gardener, an artist, a writer. Our *doing* is used to define our *being*. After choosing our answers for responding to the "Who are you?" questions, we then design our wardrobe, speech patterns, vocabulary, peer group, and lifestyle to match. This makes us appear to be stable, safe, continuous, properly socialized, and acceptably sane.

Who am I? I am a good person, a swell guy, a nice girl. I work hard. I try hard. I am strong. I am faithful. I am delicate. I am special. I am trustworthy. We have our pet answers.

It is interesting to note, however, that the answers we hold about ourselves are not necessarily the same answers (or even related to the answer) that other people would give about us if asked to respond candidly. In addition, it is even more curious that, if our unconscious behavior were carefully observed, not much that is either solid or true would be seen about either the answers we hold for ourselves, or the answer given by others. Huge gaps separate the answers we give and our actual moment-to-moment behavior.

Without realizing it, we are changing our answers about "who we are" from person to person and from situation to situation: as soon as we feel fear, as soon as we get negative (or positive) feedback, as soon as the telephone rings, as soon as we win or lose, as soon as we compare ourselves to photos in a magazine, as soon as we get on a scale, as soon as we make a mistake in public, as soon as we are put under pressure to do something we never did before. Without knowing it, we are already masters at changing identity. Unconsciously, we are actually as slippery as eels in changing identity. This gets interesting when we consider using our unconscious eel-slithering abilities to consciously slither into new characters.

What new characters? What for?

The "character" whose Box we play in determines the limits of what is possible for us. It therefore determines what kind of relationship we can create. At any moment, the new character could be purposely chosen to provide expansive new limits. Without our character being different, our creations will not be different. For our relationship to have new features, *we* need to have new features. The two characters that we will consciously explore in the next chapters are the Pirate Sorceress Warrioress Queen Goddess Woman, and the Pirate Magician King Spiritual Warrior Man.

CHAPTER 10

The Pirate Sorceress Warrioress Queen Goddess Woman

In this and the next chapter, both men and women will get to try on some new roles, on purpose, by practicing a few simple new behaviors. **Pirate Sorceress Warrioress Queen Goddess Woman (BLTLCH10.01).** For the purposes of entering the kingdom of Archetypal Love, we will start with the following experiment: From now on, until such time as you decide to change your mind, whenever answering the question from yourself or others, "Who are you?" use the following answer: For women, "I am a Pirate Sorceress Warrioress Queen Goddess Woman." For men, "I am a Pirate Magician King Spiritual Warrior Man." Memorize this answer. Each morning or evening when you brush your teeth and look in the mirror, repeat the answer back to yourself. During the day, add in more and more behavior details. The first section of this chapter contains a list of starter experiments for women. Experiments for men will be found in the next chapter.

SECTION 10-A
)(The Pirate ... Woman

You know what many of the limitations of your usual self have always been. As Pirate Sorceress Warrioress Queen Goddess Woman, your usual limitations will vanish. Without preconceptions of your limitations, you can meet and stay present with anyone. Entering the kingdom of Archetypal Love starts when you shift from being the "you" with characteristics that you have always known, to being the Pirate Sorceress Warrioress Queen Goddess Woman with characteristics that originate in the Archetypal and extend beyond what you or anyone might ever come to comprehend.

Healing your past through psychological or therapeutic processes may gradually move you from ordinary to extraordinary domains. But, entering the Archetypal happens with *who you are* and *what you have* in the immediate present, relying on your past with gratitude as a training ground, no matter what state of healing it is in. Instead of starting each moment from your familiar perspectives, you start each moment from the extemporaneous perspectives of Pirate Sorceress Warrioress Queen Goddess Woman. From your new approach, the available options seem completely different.

Pirate

The term *Pirate* with a capital *P* refers to conscious responsible piracy. The Pirate allows that other people's opinions are only other people's opinions, and she no longer wears the automatic "nice girl" mask to meet other people's expectations. In particular, a Pirate disregards internal rules that would limit thinking, being, feeling, perceiving and acting. Any similarity between a Pirate's actions and the standard rules for acting in those circumstances is mere coincidence. She takes radical responsibility for her actions regardless of what the rules are.

Sorceress

The Sorceress is called forth by what you can do with your attention. If you practice saying or doing something completely different from what you or anybody else have ever said or done before, you will be practicing as a Sorceress. Let your fear-level get to 50 percent (0 percent being no fear, 100 percent being

ultimate fear), and let it stay at that level all day, while you put your fear to conscious use. For example, use the sensations of fear to stay alert and solve problems that other people do not even dare permit themselves to see. Approach insolvable problems and be-with them, still afraid, even if you have no skill or experience that would lead you or anyone else to think you could have the ability to make any difference with those problems. If you think of something you can do to make a difference in the problem situation, just stay afraid, go ahead, pay attention, and do it. Sometimes the sorcery works; sometimes it doesn't. Shift and Go!

Warrioress

Our impression of Warriorship has been distorted by Hollywood's shoot-'em-up action heroes. Warriorship has more to do with internal disciplines of stillness than with violence or even action. Find the internal Warrioress who sustains your integrity – the one who promised to do something even when Gremlin offered good excuses not to. The Warrioress uses anger responsibly and consciously to create clarity, make distinctions, choose, declare, take action, change things, start or stop things, make boundaries, say yes or no, and ask for what she needs. These actions can all be clear and precise, and still delivered with gentleness and kindness.

The greatest challenge for modern woman is to awaken the Warrioress Archetype within her. The hindrance could well be the modern materialistic culture. In a material-centered patriarchy, women can ensure their survival through surrounding themselves with material goods. Even if it takes three cellars to bunker their warehouse, the security is worth it to the materialistic woman. In times of sudden poverty (e.g., if the man leaves), this woman can sell all her things to survive.

Hoarding material objects is the opposite of Archetypal Feminine tendencies. For

Archetypal Woman, letting go of things with love and appreciation is natural the moment those things are no longer needed. Women do this biologically every month during menstruation. They create an egg, then wait for fertilization. If the egg is not fertilized, it is released, and the whole system is cleaned out. The insanity promoted by modern culture is to create without knowing how to get rid of the things created.

Beauty itself arises through recognizing that all people and all things will one day pass away. Beneath the powder and fluff that characterize the stereotype of modern women is the natural Feminine ability to see things die and to go on creating. This is the Warrioress.

Women in modern culture do not learn that it is natural to get rid of excess. Consequently, men try to run interference in this activity, and must then deal with the subsequent recoil. For a woman to responsibly enliven her Warrioress, she would recognize that her faculty for detecting deficiencies (especially during times of premenstrual tension) is not to be wasted on men, but used by the internal Warrioress for her own benefit. She can then catch herself feeding her Gremlin through Ordinary human relationship. This "detecting-deficiencies faculty" can help her to dismantle her own defenses and become vulnerable; reconnect to other women; promote healing through discerning fallacious thinking; distinguish the difference between a pick-up artist and a Queenmaker, and so on. The sword of the Warrioress has two edges. The Warrioress uses both.

Queen

Self-respect, presence of mind and trust in her own authority permits the Queen to stand beside her Man without doubting herself or her Man. The Queen is in charge of her own queendom, which is parallel to the King's kingdom, but more complex and fluid than his. The Queen leads through joyous communication, brings people together, unwinds confusions, and forgives. Be the Queen. Stand, walk, turn your head, act as if you are Queen – not Queen over the peasants, but rather Queen with other Queens. Compare being Queen with how much energy it takes to stand, walk, turn your head, and act as if you are a victim. Keep comparing the conversation that you speak with others, or that you argue in your own mind, with the conversation that a Queen would speak. Be noble. Be generous. Be kind. Have a dignified body posture. Start taking little responsibilities that other people avoid. Then, train others to have your job.

Goddess

You have a capacity to get out of your own way so that a radiant, wise and loving Archetypal Goddess presence beams through where you are. For a few moments at a time, let yourself experience everything that you interact with as pure, holy, and vibrating with an abundance of Love – including people, young or old, known to you or unknown. The Goddess is not naïve; she is not to be trifled with; she is not even pretty or nice. At the same time, the Goddess is full of blessings. Figure out ways to bless people through what happens when you are with them. For example, bring people into their own energy. Be a "listening" through which people can heal themselves by completing important or emotionally-charged communications. This is not new-age namby-pamby crap! This is a science experiment!

Woman

Woman interacts with the world from the source of Archetypal Feminine strength, warmth, passion, subtlety, intelligence, tenderness, sensuality, acceptance and innocence. You can be Feminine, not as defined by the patriarchy, but as defined Archetypally. Find out experientially what Archetypal Femininity could mean. Find out what it means that Woman is Everything. Repeatedly experiment with making an easeful energetic contact with Everything simultaneously, everywhere. In linear, practical terms, such a thing is impossible. But this is the Archetypal. Get used to the vastness of your resources. Practice gazing around, slowly walking, and finally talking while having contact to Everything. Access Everything as a resource for serving others and for serving Bright Principles. Include into your foundation all that you could possibly experience, as well as the multidimensional beyond. And, let all of that flow respectfully and without expectations through the space that is held for you by your Man.

 **Manmaking**

Making Changes Delicately (BLTLCH10.02). Let's begin with a word of caution as we approach this vital subject of Manmaking. If you are a Woman who is practicing as Pirate … Queen, and you start to implement behavior changes such as those suggested in this book, make certain that your decision to change your behavior patterns is public information for your Man. That is, do not just suddenly start behaving differently. If you abruptly enact new behavior without explaining it to your Man, it forces your Man to confirm that you are crazy. If, as the Pirate Sorceress Warrioress… you change your preferences, your speech patterns, your timing, your needs, your wishes, or your actions without preparing your Man, he will not trust you *or* the new behavior for a long time. To prevent the distrust, each time before you make a shift in your behavior, do a little piece of "conscious theater." It is "theater" because you know that you are playing a role, and "conscious" because you play the role on purpose to reduce the natural shock that occurs for others when you change your behavior. To do the conscious theater, make sure the timing is right and you have the man's attention. Tell him that you have had some

kind of realization … that you had a dream … that you have been thinking things over… that you got some feedback that was correct… that you have changed your mind, and that you are going to start doing some things differently than before. This way, when you *do* start behaving differently, the man will know why – because you told him what happened to you that caused the change. He will not be shocked – because you predicted the behavior change for him. And he will trust you more, rather than less. This is how it works for men.

Educating Man About Relationship (BLTLCH10.03). Archetypally it is Woman's job to educate ordinary, extraordinary and Archetypal Man about relationship. It just comes with the territory. When you discover an aspect of relationship that you would like your Man to know more about, instead of complaining or feeling like an abused victim, you can feel glad that you have discovered a further way to create intimacy. You can develop new intimacy Edgework experiments and lead your Man into them.

Don't try to manipulate your Man into leading *you* into intimacy Edgework experiments. Relationship is Woman's domain so

Woman must lead Man. Don't be shy or it will not happen now … and you are not getting any younger. Do not be embarrassed or he will feel embarrassed too. Be bold. Take the initiative. Lead your Man into further intimacies.

Relationship is a complicated series of soft skills. Soft skills are learned in the body through practice, not in the mind through thinking about practice. If you have the idea that you can just complain to a man and he will learn something or change his behavior, you are *seriously* deluded. Soft skills are hard and painful to learn. Be-with your Man in such a nurturing way that he can go through the long, difficult and painful liquid states of learning new relationship soft skills without feeling too self-conscious. Men can learn. They just need the right reward.

Manmaking Step #1: Shift the Game

Here is a chance for you to do what most adults will never figure out how to do. You can shift the game you are playing in relationship. You need ask no one's permission to shift into Manmaking. You need have no license, pay no registration fee, or carry no certificate. You want to change the game you are playing in relationship? Then go ahead and change it. That is how the Pirate Sorceress Warrioress Queen Goddess Woman works. (Womanmaking is the subject of the next chapter, but both men and women can learn from the material in both chapters.)

Being a Pigmaker (BLTLCH10.04). The way we see things is an ongoing creative action. The purpose in this first step is to consciously use this powerful shaping force of "seeing" to establish that our human man is additionally an Archetypal Man (or that our human woman is additionally an Archetypal Woman). If we see "pig" we get "pig." If we see "Man" we get "Man." *Through the quality of your regard for your Man's well-being,* you open the door for your partner to re-originate and become new.

This first step is to shift where you are seeing from; shift the "source" of who you are *being* when you see, since everything else flows from that. Do not focus on the "problem" of where your attitudes and actions originally came from. Focus more on the opportunity of where your attitudes and actions *could* be coming from. This is what you are shifting into.

Start over again as one who holds respect for men as potential Men. Shift from being your historically-based self, dedicated to sustaining past memories about who you have been, to being presently original and unknown to yourself, dedicated to fulfilling Archetypal potentials. With every breath you take and every move you make let your new place of origin inform you. Shift from "I am me" into something entirely new. Try thinking of yourself as "I am a Manmaker" (or "I am a Womanmaker").

This first step is most crucial. That is because it is almost impossible for an exhausted, self-deprecating victim bitch to make a Man instead of a pig. Manmaking starts with you being the Pirate Sorceress Warrioress Queen Goddess Woman who can choose the way you see things.

How do you shift the game that you are playing? How do you shift the source of where you come from? How do you shift *who you are*? The shifting itself is relatively simple. You *declare* who you are. You say, "I am a Manmaker" in the same way that someone would say, "I am a fireman" or "I am a spiritual student." Your framework of being is declared, and then that framework is lived into with the actions of your life. The really difficult part of this whole procedure is to *remember* to make the declaration. The more useful questions at this point will be: How can you remember to shift the game that you are playing? How do you remember to shift the source of where you come from? How do you remember to shift who you are?

Using a Reminding Factor to Shift the Game (BLTLCH10.05). Since the Box will mechanically be doing all it can to prevent you from remembering to shift, the reminding factors for remembering to shift must originate from outside of your Box's field of control. The Box controls your feeling, thinking, and perceiving mind. The reminding factor must come from beyond the grip of your thinking. Jesus, for example, is reputed to have given his disciples such a reminding factor. The reminding factor was handed down from generation to generation for two thousand years until I received it from my father who was raised in the Christian tradition. He taught me to break my slice of bread in half before I ate it at a meal. When I was in my early thirties, it finally dawned on me to ask him why I should break my bread. He said that his father taught him that it was more polite that way. But the habit of breaking bread was actually passed down to my father in an *unbroken lineage* from Jesus, who gave that practice to his followers as a reminding factor. Every time they broke their bread before eating it, they could shift from the standard world of being human to the Archetypal world of being his disciples. Breaking bread before you eat it could become one of your reminding factors to shift from an ordinary woman into being a Manmaker (or from an ordinary man into being a Womanmaker).

Now that you have the idea of how reminding factors work, you can experiment with creating a continuously evolving series of them to alert yourself to shifting the game. For example, I carry a tiny cloth pouch around in my pocket, wherever I go, as a reminding factor. It is irritating to always carry that pouch. The persistent nuisance consumes a bit of my attention, and that is how it serves as a reminding factor. Putting a coin in your shoe will do the same thing. Tying a string around your finger could be a reminding factor. Touching each doorway you pass through could be a reminding factor. Putting your right shoe on first and then taking your left shoe

off first could be a reminding factor. Treating your partner with kindness, generosity and respect could be a reminding factor too.

Shifting the game from "I am me" to "I am Manmaker" (or "I am Womanmaker") is the first step in a six-step procedure for continuing to develop and explore Archetypal Relationship. **Being a Manmaker (BLTLCH10.06).**

Manmaking Step #2: Get Present / Stay Present

Archetypal Relationship takes place only in the present moment, which means it does not include anything about the past or future. The present only includes right here and right now. You can engage your partner in intimacy Edgework experiments only by staying present, here and now, not by psychologically processing with them.

Having the intense sensation of "a need to process" (that is, to work through your resistances, emotions or psychological difficulties) is one particular space in the Great Labyrinth of Spaces (*see* Section 8-D). It tends to be an underworld space, not bad or wrong, just underworld. If an issue from the past is coming up for you, and you have this need to process about it, go get yourself processed by another woman or work with therapist or a trainer, not your partner. Your process is not your partner's business. Trying to process the garbage heap of your past with your partner only contaminates your relationship. Precious time goes by that you will never get back.

If you let it, the Box will happily use psycho-emotional processing as a handy way to avoid intimacy here and now. The Box can dredge up an endless stream of considerations. You are Pirate Sorceress Warrioress Queen Goddess Woman. Break your own rules. Lift yourself up by the scruff of your neck and drop yourself into another space where processing is not necessary. Reserve the sanctuary of your relationship for the possibility of Archetypal Love now.

An additional aspect of being present is noticing *what is* when it is right in front of you. That means, if you want to be-with your Man then stop sending him away. If you are distracted and do not notice with all of your senses that your Man is there at home with you, when he *is* there at home with you, then you will have the impression that your Man is never at home with you. If your Man is off doing your bidding, fixing the car, building the fence, taking care of the kids, picking up groceries, remember that *you* sent him out there to do that. He is not with you because *you* made it a higher priority for him to be off doing something else. For him, he *is* with you because he is doing *what you asked him to do*. The time when your Man is off doing what you sent him away to do is time that you will never recover for intimacy experiments. The weekend is only so long, and ticks steadily away, however we use it. If you want to have a memory that your Man is with you when he is home from work, then arrange it that you are with him. Remember this the next time you want to complain that your Man is not with you. And vice versa for men.

Manmaking Step #3:
Place the Man on the King's Throne

Place the King on the Throne (BLTLCH10.07). You place your Man on the King's throne through authentically appreciating his qualities of being. You would place your Man on a King's throne out of respect for your own dignity. You are the Pirate Sorceress Warrioress Queen Goddess Woman.

MAP OF PROCEDURE FOR MANMAKING

1) SHIFT THE GAME FROM "I AM ME," TO "I AM MANMAKER."
2) GET PRESENT.
3) PLACE THE MAN ON THE KING'S THRONE.
4) BE THE POWER BEHIND THE THRONE.
5) LEARN TO BE ECSTATICALLY IN LOVE.
6) CREATE ONGOING NONLINEAR OPPORTUNITIES THAT LEAD YOUR MAN TO EXPERIMENTALLY ENTER COMMUNION, ECSTASY, LOVE AND ONENESS WITH YOU.

It is proper and dignified for your partner to be a Pirate Magician King Spiritual Warrior Man. Such a Man holds space and blesses the people when he is on his throne. The King's throne for your Man will be different places at different times. The King's throne could be at the dining table, at his desk, in the driver's seat of the car, in his overstuffed chair in the living room, at his office, in his workshop, or on the porch with the children. The King's throne is often made out of energetic intangibles, such as when you are walking down the street together. You place your Man on the King's throne by being committed to what he is committed to. First, you must find out what he is committed to. Your Man is telling you what his commitment is all the time. You can learn to listen for his commitments so that you can commit to what he is committed to in appreciative words and actions. Join him in what he loves to do. Be interested in what he is interested in, authentically, for a long time. Do not fake being interested in his world as a strategy to get him to give you his attention. And, if he *does* give you his attention, don't fill it up with your own interests, needs, topics, issues, proposals and news. Dumping your psycho-emotional hell world on your Man destroys the possibility of intimacy.

For example, if your Man is committed to opening the door for you, and you open the door for yourself instead, because you have a program in your head that makes you judge yourself to be weak or helpless unless you do things for yourself, that is not placing your Man on the King's throne. That is the little girl jumping onto the King's throne pretending to be King, thinking that this makes the Man proud of you. It does not make him proud of you. It disempowers your Man and makes him angry and sad that he is with a little girl instead of a Woman. Try this experiment: The next time your Man could open the door for you, radiate appreciation and self-respect, stand aside so he can do it, then walk elegantly through the door so he can admire you in passing. This little piece of conscious theater places your Man in his rightful place, on the King's throne. You can put your Man onto the King's throne in many different ways, a hundred times a day.

If there is a time when your Man does not show up and deliver as King, do not blame him or criticize him. Instead, use it as ongoing feedback to reflect how well you are showing up and delivering being Queen. Putting your King on his throne through your respect is your part of the deal.

Manmaking Step #4: Be the Power Behind the Throne

Be the Power Behind the Throne (BLTLCH10.08). Masculine power is linear, precise, clear, monodimensional, and final. For the Pirate Sorceress Warrioress Queen Goddess Woman, Masculine power is utterly boring. Test this for yourself. Feminine power is nonlinear, fluidic, multidimensional, and never comes to an end. Feminine power is the gameworld (*see* Glossary) for Woman. A Woman is powerful when she empowers others. Woman tends the household, purifies the sanctuary, communicates with the other householders and all their jobs. Woman flows energy to educate, strengthen and harmonize the people in the kingdom, especially her Man. The power of Woman is

Archetypally represented by Woman standing behind her Man, who is sitting on the King's throne. Woman has her hands resting on her Man's shoulders. Her hands on his shoulders are not there to suppress, control, or dominate. Her hands are on his shoulders so that *he* knows *she* is there to support him. The Queen's job is to empower her King with her counsel. This means: Do not argue with your Man. Do not prove to him or to other people that he is wrong. Proving that your Man is wrong does not make you strong; it makes the kingdom weak. Do not complain to your Man. If you complain to your Man you are not Kingmaking; you are trashcan making. Instead of arguing or complaining, just listen. Then, at the right moment, empower your Man with your counsel. Support your Man by providing him with useful information. Say, "Were you aware of...," "I am sorry but perhaps you did not know that...," "Could you also make use of the possibility that..." If your Man is lacking information, it is your fault that you did not inform or educate him yet. Apologize. Go out of your way to give the King the information (and the kisses) he needs. If your Man is going along and suddenly falters for lack of information, you can be right there behind him, leaning over his shoulder and whispering in his ear, empowering him by saying, "This person's name is Jean-Pierre Bouillon. He is the Chief Financial Officer from Bank of Sweden. You meet with him at 4 o'clock in the north room. His wife's name is Dorothea. He has no children and loves to play golf." If the King appears to argue with you, just say thank you and agree. Never say, "Yes, but..." Instead, train yourself to say, "Yes, and..." Continue to explore the dimensions of being the power behind the King's throne.

Woman is successful when she makes her Man's life successful by empowering him with her counsel. The feminine Gremlin, the queen of your underworld, when frustrated with your Man's mistakes or failures, will present you with irrefutable evidence to prove that your Man is an idiot and that life would be a lot easier without all this Manmaking stuff. The conscious, responsible, loving Woman, Queen of your upperworld, knows that without her Man being a Man there are spaces she cannot access, and very interesting experiments she cannot do. The responsible Queen intimately knows the wily deviousness of the Gremlin Queen, looks her straight in the eyes and says "Sit!" as if to a growling dog on a short chain. Give no power to your Gremlin Queen with regards to your Man. The Gremlin Queen gets enough food from feeding on other Gremlin Queens.

Manmaking Step #5:
Learn to Be Ecstatically in Love

Learn to Be Ecstatically in Love (BLTLCH10.09). Attract your Man's attention through his interest in your interest in him. Then, practice tolerating the intensity of your Man's full attention. His attention will change you. Your Man's full attention on you greets the Pirate Sorceress Warrioress Queen Goddess Woman and invites her into the space of ecstatic Archetypal Love. The banishment of the ordinary and the arrival of the Archetypal can be swift and unsettling to experience, like having what you always regarded as solid ground suddenly crumble beneath you into the gaping maw created by an earthquake. The transition may require practice getting used to. So go ahead and practice. Sit in the new sensations and breathe, gradually stretching your capacity to endure this intensity. If you cannot tolerate the Goddess when she arises in you, then your Man goes without Goddess food. He cannot drink Archetypal Feminine nectar until you let the Goddess come and pour herself into him. Being so fulfilled, so "drunk" on your Man's attention can be intense. Feeling pure joy for no reason makes our whole psychological defense strategy obsolete. Having no workable defense strategy is frightening – at first we

do not know who we are when undefended. But, when you think about it, the greatest security is *not having to have security*. Rather than limiting yourself by demanding that you first feel secure, find that place within yourself wherein security is irrelevant because you know yourself to be already whole and alive. Then, being the Pirate Sorceress Warrioress Queen Goddess Woman in relationship with your Man becomes endlessly fun because a possible adventure lays hidden in each moment; since you do not have the requirement for security first you can go along.

Manmaking Step #6:
Create Nonlinear Opportunities That Lead Your Man to Enter Oneness With You

Create Nonlinear Opportunities (BLTLCH10.10). Do not sabotage your opportunities to do intimacy Edgework experiments. You may not know exactly what experiments you will try before you two drive away into the countryside. This does not matter. The details will clarify themselves. Stay aware of and open to the conditions where nothing else is happening; where nothing else is taking up the room where Edgework experiments could take place. Be careful to create sanctuary for such opportunities. Don't sabotage your chances for entering unknown territories of intimacy by inviting along friends or relatives, by bringing office work or handicrafts, by getting little or no sleep the night before, by being late for the designated starting time because you are over packing with food, clothing or supplies so as to be prepared for everything. Beginnings are such delicate times. Take care that the time set aside to be together is spent *only being together*. Enter opportunities undefended with busy-work plans, or concerns about work and problems. Get well rested and nurture yourself for a couple of days before starting, so that you are vibrant and full of energy, instead of sleeping on the drive, getting sick, complaining of fatigue, yawning, and not being able to stay up all night playing together. Pack early so that you are effortlessly ready to grab your bags and go. Pack lightly so the baggage is not a burden. (He likes you best naked anyway.) Be relaxed and ready ten minutes ahead of your scheduled departure time, so you can leave early with no need to rush along the way. These little details can make all the difference in the world when navigating toward communion, ecstasy, love, lightness, joy, and oneness with your Man.

And a Few More Soft Skills for Manmaking

Manmaking Soft Skills (BLTLCH10.11). As we noted on page 282, "Relationship is a complicated series of soft skills. Soft skills are learned in the body through repeated practice, not in the mind through repeatedly thinking you should practice. If you have the idea that you can just complain to a Man and he will learn something or change his behavior, you are *seriously* deluded. Soft skills are hard and painful to learn. Be-with your Man in such a nurturing way that he can go through the long, difficult and painful liquid states of learning new relationship soft skills without feeling too self-conscious. Men can learn. They just need the right reward."

1. Rub the Magic Lamp

We have all heard stories about a magic lamp: *If you rub the magic lamp your wish comes true because the genii in the lamp gives you anything you want.* Every night you are going to bed with a magic lamp and you are not rubbing it! If you do not rub the magic lamp, how can you expect to receive the gifts of the genii? To be painfully explicit, a man's penis is like a magic lamp. His penis has one

home, and that is inside of you. When a man's penis is erect, it does not mean that he has to have an orgasm inside of you, or even have an orgasm at all. It simply means he wants you. Talk with your Man about this. Ask your Man if it is okay for him to have an erection and to not have an orgasm. Ask him if you can hold his penis even when it is not big, just because you like it. Ask him this frequently, not just a few times. Ask only in total privacy, with complete sincerity. Such a thing is not for teasing or the slightest bit of joking around. When your warm hand is wrapped around your Man's penis, whether it is large, small, or in between, your Man feels like he is inside of you. Actually he *is* inside of you, because your hand is also you. For a man, feeling an erection is great all by itself. For woman, feeling a man's erection is great too, especially if you have disassociated the presence of the erection from the assumption that you have to perform some duty. Woman can enjoy experiencing a man's erection for what it is, a magnificent warm wonder of nature. Man can enjoy the same thing. If your Man does not want to have an orgasm, just hold onto that thing and fall asleep together. If he does want to have an orgasm, just keep *gently* moving your hand as he directs. It is great for Woman to bring Man to orgasm, and it doesn't take that long. Rub the magic lamp. This little piece of advice is better than ten years of relationship therapy.

2. Let Go of the Fairness Issue

Neither Manmaking nor Womanmaking are fair. From the Box's perspective one person is always doing more for the other person. The extra efforts are unrecognized, unappreciated and imbalanced. Your advantage will be to enter the game already knowing at the outset that neither Manmaking nor Womanmaking are fair. The purpose of Manmaking, for example, is not fairness; it is Manmaking. Fairness is a consideration in a different game. Women and men are wildly dissimilar. Calling forth the Masculine or Feminine Archetypes uses vastly different procedures. Between man and woman it will *never be* fair. Handling unfairness is easy when we have the attitude that fairness is not even an issue.

Succeeding in circumstances that on the surface appeared to be unfair was a specialty of Mother Teresa of Calcutta. She expressed her approach clearly by quoting Kent M. Keith. The quote in the box below was hung on the wall of her children's home in Calcutta.

3. Relax Into Uncertainty

The vastness and complexity of a Woman's perceptions do not let her relax in the company of uncertainty. Women see too many possibilities for error. Fear of uncertainty is not bad; it does have its practical uses. For example, fear of uncertainty makes you ask questions like, "Did you lock the door? Do you have the tickets? Does the babysitter have our mobile phone number?" But giving *reality* to the fear of uncertainty is *completely* neurotic, because *uncertainty is all there is.* "The nature of reality is groundlessness," said Buddhist nun and teacher Pema Chödron, a woman. "Security is mostly a superstition. It does not exist in nature... Avoiding danger is no safer in the long run than outright exposure. Life is either a daring adventure, or it is nothing," said Helen Keller, a woman.

Even if you have a deluxe insurance policy, security is an illusion. Through tacitly recognizing uncertainty as the basic condition of life, it is completely possible to have relaxed, joyful self-assurance, and a really great time, without any certainty at all. We can have intimacy even in chaos, even if we have serious doubts, even if all the bills are not paid, even if the laundry is not done, even if our back hurts, even if we are late for an appointment. Do not let your Box promote decisions based on a neurotic fear of ambiguity. Stand in uncertainty and keep asking yourself, "Is it of greater importance for me to make efforts to find more certainty now, or to experience intimacy with my partner?"

4. Prioritize the Do-It List

A woman is able to create more problems than a man can solve. If you do tell your Man about a problem, or about what you are feeling, always remember to reassure him that he does not have to do anything

---

People are illogical, unreasonable, and self-centered.
Love them anyway.
If you do good, people will accuse you of selfish ulterior motives.
Do good anyway.
If you are successful, you will win false friends and true enemies.
Succeed anyway.
The good you do today will be forgotten tomorrow.
Do good anyway.
Honesty and frankness make you vulnerable.
Be honest and frank anyway.
The biggest men and women with the biggest ideas can be shot down by the smallest men and women with the smallest minds.
Think big anyway.
People favor underdogs but follow only top dogs.
Fight for a few underdogs anyway.
What you spend years building may be destroyed overnight.
Build anyway.
People really need help but may attack you if you do help them.
Help people anyway.
Give the world the best you have and you'll get kicked in the teeth.
Give the world the best you have anyway

– *The Paradoxical Commandments* by Kent M. Keith, 1968

---

about it. This will let him relax and listen to you in an entirely different way. He will not get overwhelmed, thinking that he has to fix your problem or do something because of your feeling. Women see, feel, hear, sense and *are* Everything. Women know and feel Everything that is not working, Everything that is wrong, and Everything that is broken. This is why a woman's fixit list is longer than a man's day. Do not overwhelm your Man with the vastness of your perceptions. Do not avalanche him with problems. He will just give up. Make a list and prioritize the jobs for him. Then he can tackle the jobs one at a time or in whatever fashion he wishes. The way he approaches handling the problems is none of your business. He is a man. Men do things very differently from women. Do not try to make your man into a woman.

5. Resolve Resentments Immediately

Take care of yourself about your resentments in the same moment in which you create the resentments. If you do not resolve your resentments, then you lose your Man. He may not necessarily leave right away. Nevertheless, you lose him. If you have resentments, when you look at your Man you do not see your Man, you only see your unresolved resentments about your Man. If you do not immediately take responsibility and resolve your resentments, they will burrow into your unconsciousness and become part of your Box, shaping what you see. Even one resentment is enough to destroy the possibility of intimacy.

The way to resolve a resentment is to take responsibility for creating it in the first place. Find out the exact moment you made the resentment and why. It is usually an unexpressed thought, feeling, need, or wish, a communication from one of your four bodies. To resolve the resentment, arrange to complete your communication. Work to let yourself be known. It is a paradox: Resentment blocks intimacy, but intimately sharing yourself releases resentment. Use the communication skills that were detailed in Section 6-O.

If you already have resentments about your partner – which most of us in ordinary human relationships do – then take responsibility for the fact that the only reason you still have resentments is because you maintained the resentments, as painful hooks in your heart, so as to hate your partner. Your Box can make a resentment for you about anything. *This means that resentments do not actually involve the other person.* You are doing resentment all by yourself. Resentments are Box strategy. Resentments are created by the Box to reinforce the beliefs and fears of the Box. If you take a resentment hook out of your heart, your Box will strongly object. If you redesign the part of your Box that sustains itself by holding a certain resentment, then the resentment will naturally fall away. Having a resentment fall away is nothing short of a miracle. But it does not happen all by itself. I have counseled couples who refused to take their Box-made hooks of resentment about their partner out of their own heart. Some of them did not last long as a couple after that. Resentment makes only hate food. Get yourself another diet.

And while we're on the subject of holding resentments, beware of a tendency to take revenge on your Man by spending his money. A woman is able to spend more money than a man can earn. Overspending is usually revenge. Revenge is resentment in action. For many men, money represents their life's blood, because of how much effort it takes to get the money. Spending a man's money makes him bleed. Get responsible, instead of torturing your Man. Do not use money revenge to try to compensate for your conflicts. The man you are angry at is most probably not even your partner. Your partner just happens to be the most accessible man to torture.

6. Communicate What You *Do* Want, Not What You *Don't* Want

Men cannot read your mind. Even Archetypal Men cannot read your mind. If you expect your Man to read your mind, you are living in a fantasy. You are actually trying to control the man and take his balls, creating ordinary human relationship. Men are linear and simple. Do not forget this. When you want something, be responsible for saying exactly and precisely what you want, so that the man can help to create it for you. The greatest pleasure for a Man is doing something that makes his Woman happy. Do not make your Man try to guess the details. This takes his center away. Communicating with a Man is simple, much simpler than you can imagine. Say what you do want, not what you don't want. When he asks, "Where do you want to go for a vacation this summer, Honey?" stop yourself from saying, "I don't want to stay with your sister again in Florida. That was *horrible.* The TV was always on, and she never stops talking, and trying to eat her version of coleslaw makes me want to..." He did *not* ask what you *don't* want. He asked what you *do* want. Learn to say what you *do* want. True, it is a narrower view. But that view can open whole new vistas of clarity and opportunity for the two of you.

Men ask simple yes or no questions. Yes or no questions do not fit the way the world looks and feels to a Woman, but they match the way the world looks and feels to a Man perfectly. If you answer a yes or no question with anything other than a simple yes or no, you instantly confuse your Man. Do not confuse your Man. He just stands there with a painful blank look on his face and cannot move. Without a clear yes or no answer from you, he is petrified. Practice listening for yes or no questions from your Man, and practice answering them with only a yes or a no. These tiny behavior changes can make an incredible difference.

7. Rewrite Your Stories About Your Wound

The patriarchy wounds women. Little boys in men's bodies wound women. Irresponsible men addicted to alcohol, men who are themselves wounded, men who feel powerless and want violent aggressive revenge, men who do not accept themselves how they are – these men wound women. Women carry wounds from these men. If women do not heal themselves of these wounds they will carry the wounds for the rest of their lives and as a result hate *all* men. It is crucial for a woman to admit her hesitation to making men into Men as long as she has not healed her own wounds. Through her thoughts, words and deeds, a wounded woman consciously or unconsciously makes men into pigs. Likewise, men who carry wounds from women are better pig-makers than Womanmakers.

It is important to understand that no amount of therapy or psychological processing will heal the actual fact that you were wounded. The facts surrounding what caused the wounding are irreversible. The incident that precipitated the wound should not have happened, and it did happen. You, as a Pirate Sorceress Warrioress Queen Goddess Woman, have the power to change your interpretation of the facts. The facts are neutral. Your story about the facts is not neutral. One at a time, consciously, go back to the naked facts and rewrite your story about what happened, while feeling the anger, sadness, fear and also the joy each time. Give the facts about what happened to you a meaning that empowers you, rather than one that positions you as a victim.

Then, separate the incident from what you learned through the incident, and let the incident take its proper place in the past. Regard the wound as one of your wisdom resources. Let the wound succeed in its evolutionary mission of delivering you with learning. With its mission accomplished, its cycle is finally complete. The significance of the wound can fade

Let Your Woman Succeed at Making You into a Man.

It was Sadie Hawkins Day in my seventh grade class – the day on which the girls were allowed to pick partners for the upcoming dance, if they could catch one. All the boys were lined up across the field and the girls were lined up behind them, dressed quite prettily. All I knew was that I was supposed to not get caught by a girl. And yet there was one girl who …

The gun fired. We sped away. I ran like I never ran before, probably to show off. Out of 100 boys, I reached the end of the field first! I was not a fast runner. In fact, I was one of the only boys to not get caught. It puzzled me, but I didn't get what was going on. Walking back to class, that girl found me. She approached me cautiously, alone. With heartbreaking tenderness she asked, "Why didn't you let me catch you?" I had no answer. That was our last conversation.

Today I know that I was afraid of the intimacy of being her Man. For men, this fear can be immense. If you let your Woman make you into a Man, you will feel afraid of how big that is for her and afraid of how that bigness cannot protect you. So what? Lots of things already make you afraid. You can get used to feeling afraid. But you can only grow accustomed to tolerating the intense fear of intimacy with the Archetypal Feminine while you are being intimate with the Archetypal Feminine. The love that arises will help you.

By now you have probably noticed that life goes by rather quickly. If she makes efforts with you, let her efforts succeed. The deep healing influence of Archetypal Love is inexplicably miraculous. Do not limit its influence with the linear requirement of your intellect. Try this experiment. The next time your Woman makes even the least effort to recognize you as a Man, let down your defenses. Allow yourself to personally experience the maximum intensity of ever-unfolding Love Happening in the tiniest gestures of her moment-to-moment presence. Let her succeed at Manmaking. Let your Man succeed at Womanmaking. Why not?

to the level of what you had for breakfast one morning twenty-three years ago. When you realize in your heart that the fact of the wounding absolutely lacks importance, its charge is dissipated, and any resentment dissolves into nothingness. Gone. Then you are healed. Then you can go about enjoying interactions between an Archetypal Man and an Archetypal Woman.

SECTION 10-C
Gorilla Basics

Bringing Archetypal Woman or Archetypal Man into your everyday life is revolutionary. If your efforts sometimes look as if they are failing, do not worry. This happens. Failing is integral to the learning process. It does not mean anything about you or about what is possible, and especially it does not mean anything about *what is possible for you.* Just start over. Do not take it personally. Change something and try again.

Stability in Archetypal domains is not accidental. Stability in Archetypal domains unfolds after first building a thorough understanding of both the animalistic and humanistic factors inherent in our incarnated predicament. Many of the daily functions of human life are purely animal functions, like sleeping, eating, grooming, mating, birthing, nursing, and so on. You will not get very far in the Archetypal without practical capabilities in dealing with your own and your partner's "gorilla" nature. For example, if you get offended while you are getting ready for bed because your partner takes a shit and stinks up the bathroom while you are brushing your teeth, the Archetypal door slams shut in your face. If you get offended because your partner is cramped up with unexpressed sadness and anger about an incident that happened during their day, and they want you to listen to their woes, then you will be unable to leapfrog over animal and human trappings to enter Archetypal Love-bliss together in bed. Therefore, even if you are interested in creating and exploring Archetypal Relationship, it is eminently wise to remember gorilla basics.

Some Notes on the Care and Feeding of Gorillas

Gorilla Basics (BLTLCH10.12). At this point in your experiments with Love it is

---

> ### MAP OF GORILLA BASICS
>
> NOTES ON THE CARE AND HANDLING OF MALE GORILLAS. GORILLAS GO CRAZY IF YOU TRY TO TALK WITH THEM WHEN THEY ARE:
>
> 1) TIRED.
> 2) HUNGRY.
> 3) HORNY.
> 4) SICK.
> 5) WHEN THE FOOTBALL GAME IS ON.
> 6) WHEN IT IS TIME TO GO.
>
> PAY ATTENTION WHEN YOU WANT TO HAVE A CONVERSATION. DO NOT SET YOURSELF UP FOR A BAD TIME WITH YOUR GORILLA.

---

advisable to reinforce a few important issues. First and foremost, remember that women do not understand men. Men do not understand women either, but men do not pretend to understand women.

Do not try to get your man to listen and talk to you like a woman talks to you. He is not a woman. He is a man, and you do not know what that is. Men are a mystery to women, and forever will remain a mystery to women. Learn to appreciate the mystery that men represent.

Men are smelly and scratchy. That is how men are. Just decide to like it. You would be surprised what men have to decide to like about women.

It's about time for you to peel off the "good girl" costume and flush her down the toilet. The good girl image is deeply woven into the female Box. "Good girls don't do that! Good girls aren't like that!" When women dress sexy, flash their eyes sexy, move sexy, and speak sexy, the gorilla gets attracted. But when the gorilla gets too close and sex is actually possible, the good-girl-machine kicks in and the gorilla is shunned, scolded for getting too close. The good girl turns her back.

The gorilla is shamed and skulks away. When a woman sees the poor gorilla, she suddenly wakes up, "Oh my God! What have I done? What got into me?" and she starts the sexy moves again. She breathes sexy, smiles sexy, wiggles her ass sexy, and the gorilla gets attracted and comes back again. But when he actually touches her, the good girl freaks out totally again! The good girl feels ashamed or afraid and closes up like a bank on Sunday. Here is a suggestion from the Pirate Sorceress Warrioress Queen Goddess Woman: Once and for all, peel off the good girl costume and flush her down the toilet! She is only a false role that came from some twisted pastor at church, or some dried up old teacher at school.

Life is too short for the good girl. Also, for the "good boy." Like it or not, as adults we emulate our parents' behavior with each other, which we saw as children, including their sexuality. If we did not see even the insinuation of healthy, passionate sexuality between them, when we step into adulthood, sexuality is also not included for us. We were not trained that being sexual was bad; being sexual was simply not included in the models we saw for being good. The "badness" of being sexual may only be reflected through its not having been explicitly included in the demonstration of "goodness." But the evil insinuation can still influence us powerfully, until we specifically unravel our mental wiring, slip on our respective masculine and feminine gorilla suits and start humping.

It is important to note that the clothing industry promotes fashions that push the line. By now, fashions are so close to the line that they are often more tantalizing than no clothes at all. Without knowing it, women dress themselves in the latest styles thinking that the styles are normal, standard, even neutral. But they are not neutral. They are hypersexual, developed over years by masters of erotic insinuation. These clothes well draped over breasts and thighs can drive gorillas completely into a slobbering sexual frenzy. As a way of torturing the masculine, these fashions can satisfy Feminine Shadow Principles. But more often than you might suspect, such fashions attract only gorillas who are uncontrollably attracted by superficialities. If you, as a woman, want to attract something more than a dumb gorilla who only wants to consume you, then do not go around dressed like a banana.

There are levels of intimacy that your mother never told you about, that the movies never show, that books cannot convey, and that we never believed could be true. You can only discover these treasures for yourself if you keep taking the risk to do experiments that cause you to become capable of greater and greater intimacy.

Let Yourself Be Adored (BLTLCH10.13). When your Man places his attention on you, let that Archetypal force call through you to the Goddess. Let the Goddess come and bloom. She is subtle, delicate, fragile, and radiant. When the Goddess arrives, you will feel it in every cell in your body. Your psychology will at first freak-out. What is this sensation? What is happening to me? Your Box's automatic Goddess-shut-off-mechanism operates below your normal level of awareness. You may not even recognize that you are clamping down to prevent the possibility of the Goddess from showing up in your body, until you have already shut down. Discover the cramping mechanism, and consciously block it from being engaged. Let her come. Keep breathing. Keep letting the Goddess grow inside of you in your Man's eyes. Let her come forth fully. Let the Goddess, so intimate, so revealed, be recognized and admired by your Man. This is

Manmaking: letting the Goddess be adored. Adoring the Goddess makes the man a Man. Let your Man adore the pure radiant beauty of the Goddess through you. Stand still and let the presence and sensation of the Goddess grow, until you think that you cannot stand it any more, and then let her get even bigger. Let him see her in you. Let him experience her in you. Let him be in her presence through you. There is "no top end."

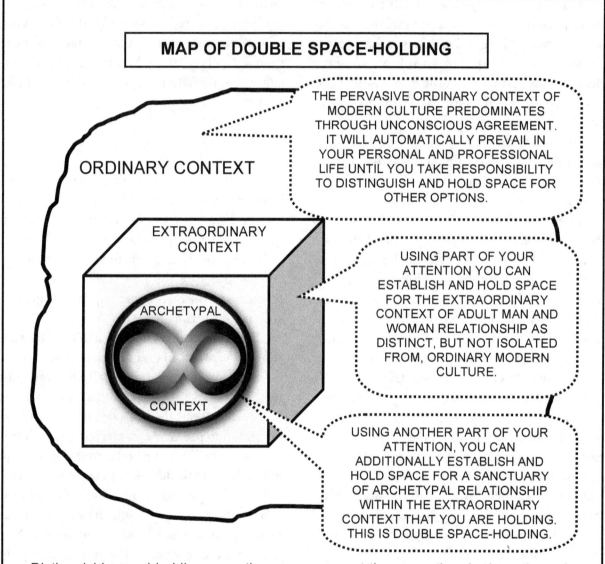

MAP OF DOUBLE SPACE-HOLDING

ORDINARY CONTEXT

THE PERVASIVE ORDINARY CONTEXT OF MODERN CULTURE PREDOMINATES THROUGH UNCONSCIOUS AGREEMENT. IT WILL AUTOMATICALLY PREVAIL IN YOUR PERSONAL AND PROFESSIONAL LIFE UNTIL YOU TAKE RESPONSIBILITY TO DISTINGUISH AND HOLD SPACE FOR OTHER OPTIONS.

EXTRAORDINARY CONTEXT

ARCHETYPAL

CONTEXT

USING PART OF YOUR ATTENTION YOU CAN ESTABLISH AND HOLD SPACE FOR THE EXTRAORDINARY CONTEXT OF ADULT MAN AND WOMAN RELATIONSHIP AS DISTINCT, BUT NOT ISOLATED FROM, ORDINARY MODERN CULTURE.

USING ANOTHER PART OF YOUR ATTENTION, YOU CAN ADDITIONALLY ESTABLISH AND HOLD SPACE FOR A SANCTUARY OF ARCHETYPAL RELATIONSHIP WITHIN THE EXTRAORDINARY CONTEXT THAT YOU ARE HOLDING. THIS IS DOUBLE SPACE-HOLDING.

Distinguishing and holding more than one space at the same time is done through clarity, not through force. Begin by distinguishing the sensations of ordinary, extraordinary and Archetypal spaces so that you can detect where you are and what is possible for you there. Then, practice consciously splitting your attention three ways at the same time: noticing the ordinary while declaring both the extraordinary and Archetypal into coexistence. Continue holding these spaces distinctly. You will not already know how to do this. Just keep trying and learn how through practicing. You can wash the dishes, or walk down the street, holding double space, *and* be in Archetypal intimacy with your partner.

CHAPTER 11

The Pirate Magician King Spiritual Warrior Man

As we noted in the previous chapter, for the purposes of entering the kingdom of Archetypal Love both men and women will get to try on some new roles, on purpose, by practicing a few simple new behaviors. **Pirate Magician King Spiritual Warrior Man (BLTLCH11.01).** Recall the experiment we proposed in Chapter 10, that from now on, until such time as you decide to change your mind, whenever answering the question "Who are you?" from yourself or others, use the following answer: For men, "I am a Pirate Magician King Spiritual Warrior Man." For women, "I am a Pirate Sorceress Warrioress Queen Goddess Woman." As we previously suggested, memorize this answer. Each morning or evening when you brush your teeth and look in the mirror, repeat the declaration to yourself. During the day, add in more and more behavior details. These next sections contain starter experiments for men. Experiments for women are found in the previous chapter.

SECTION 11-A
)((Pirate King

Writing to empower a modern man to become a Pirate King scares me. The patriarchy already produces irresponsible rascal pirate kings who break the rules *to take all they can*. What

I want to empower are responsible noble Pirate Kings who break the rules *to give all they can*. How will a man raised in a modern patriarchy learn to tell the difference? Where will a human male, babied by the entrenched patriarchy, get the courage or stamina to escape from his golden cage? Why should the "favored one" exchange his culturally-established and technologically-protected highchair-tyrant pseudo-powers for the personally-earned and fully-consequent powers of the wild pain-and-ecstasy-initiated Archetypal Man? The transformation from irresponsible to responsible is uncommon in an irresponsibly-contexted environment such as the patriarchy.

Trying to reveal the necessity for a modern man to shatter his comfortable dreamworld, throw back his warm covers and step naked into a cold shower is like trying to convince a thief to stop spending his stolen money because the money is counterfeit. As soon as the thief learns that the money is counterfeit, he will just try to spend it faster! There is no reason strong enough or incontrovertible enough to convince an adolescent to enter the process of authentically growing up. He has too much to lose.

But if we, as individual men, do not wake ourselves up to the consequences of rampantly using irresponsible power, and swiftly *do something radically different*, the forces of nature will wake us up to those consequences through the likes of so-called "climate change," a euphemism for human suffering beyond any previously known measure of pain. Choosing to change before we are absolutely forced to change means consciously choosing to suffer – a highly unusual choice. The choice belongs to each of us, and we make that choice with every gesture and each creation. If we do not make the choice to be a conscious servant of responsible Bright Principles, then the choice is automatically made for us to be an unconscious slave of irresponsible Shadow Principles. As Pirate Lee Lozowick says, "If the higher don't get you, then the lower must."

Nobody directly teaches us about the dangers of being enslaved by Shadow Principles. And, culturally embraced ignorance is no protection. We are answerable to the consequences of irresponsibility, just as surely as a rock thrown straight up in the air will fall straight back down on your head.

It is easy to find examples of irresponsible Archetypal characters. We have a whole catalog of names for rascal pirate kings, like: thief, murderer, gangster, mercenary, drug dealer, gang leader, criminal, scam artist, mobster, assassin, pimp, terrorist, thug, robber, religious fanatic, rapist, crook, or embezzler. But where can we imprint ourselves with dignified, responsible masculine qualities that include broadbased compassionate intelligence? If we look to business directors, clergymen, movie stars, doctors, teachers, spiritual leaders, rock singers, politicians, professors, and so on, the qualities of these characters are completely ambiguous, until we put the qualifier "responsible" in front of each of them, such as *responsible* businessman or *responsible* clergyman. These days, terms of leadership alone do not automatically imply responsibility.

To prepare ourselves for Archetypal Edgework experiments, it would be helpful to have role models for a self-aware responsible character. It would be helpful to emulate a fiercely vigilant, ruthlessly self-honest, radiantly joyous, and creatively-exploring hero practitioner. This is the potential Pirate King Archetype that is already designed into our four masculine bodies, and is inherently ours to step into. This is what our women hunger to love. Since there are so few living examples for us to imitate, we will just have to do the best that we can.

Spiritual Warrior

If it were not beaten out of us through the modern-day socialization process, we men would have direct and instantaneous access to maximum Archetypal anger. The only problem is that we would not know what to do with it. Our education about anger teaches us that it is dangerous and can easily destroy things. The embodiment of anger looks like war. The mental equation, that anger is bad, dangerous, ignorant and uncivilized, runs deep in the grooves of our mind.

Changing our relationship to anger (as well as to the other feelings), so that *we* contain the anger and the anger does not contain us, involves a significant initiatory process. It can include months of actual rage work, and perhaps years of recontextualizing our views, habits and understandings. Without fully engaging this process in a guided environment, a modern male is still energetically and emotionally tied to his mother's apron strings. As an uninitiated adolescent, he wastes or suppresses the very opportunities he is given for leapfrogging from aimless confusion to unquenchable inspiration.

The work of shifting from material consumer to Spiritual Warrior is long and difficult; not for children. A book can only paint maps, create clarifications, or suggest possibilities. The real learning must be expansive (experiential) learning, not defensive (intellectual) learning. Distinctions and clarifications must bypass your mind and enter your body through a long series of accidents, not necessarily painless, like the way a cowboy learns to ride a bucking bronco. An authentic maturation process will leave you bruised, impacted by what you realize. The physical memory of the impact is how the teaching enters your body. When such a reality hits you up-side the head, it may send you off running after your mother, whining for her to make your boo-boo better. There are no boo-boos, however, only lessons to learn. Making mistakes is how you learn those lessons, so making mistakes is fine, as long as you stay on your toes and learn from the mistakes. Respectful gratitude toward the learning process is appropriate. We men are all in this together. We can help each other establish a mature men's culture that nurtures and protects us while we get our feet on the ground and take back our rights to the experiences of becoming worthy of the name Man.

The Warrior Archetype responsibly applies the energy and information from anger to do things and to make things happen, to make decisions, start things, stop things, change things, make boundaries, make distinctions, to say yes or no, and to ask for what he needs. The Spiritual Warrior stands on all that, and takes into account a grander perspective. Whereas the adult warrior would take care of his family, his business, his fitness, and his personal projects, the Spiritual Warrior adds additional responsibilities that are sourced by the Principles he serves. The Spiritual Warrior takes care of his family, his business, and his fitness *so that* he can also take care of the projects given to him by the Principles. Such projects could include being on the team that runs a nonprofit association in the service of Bright Principles: associations that promote animal rights protection, research sustainable cultures, increase human rights awareness; educate about ecological systems, energy conservation, alternative energy development; support a living spiritual tradition, or develop human relationship and communication soft skills. Specific projects might include writing articles or books, giving talks or workshops, or making it possible for someone else in the same lineage of Principles to write articles or books and give talks or workshops. Spiritual Warriorship is a bigger game than standard warriorship. Deeper distinctions and energetic awareness are involved. Standing in the place where distinctions and energetic awareness originate requires the Spiritual Warrior to have the unceasing, relaxed-alert disposition of a skilled swordsman.

Sword Making

I remember first learning that anger was the discerning force behind sword work. As I learned about anger, and started giving permission for my nerves and tissues to experience and express the energy of its Archetypal levels, it came out like the anger of a raging bull. I was not a swordsman. I was a caveman. I had no sword. I had a club. I would stomp around in life energetically beating my world into a pulp. I was afraid of this raging Frankenstein monster whom I had unleashed, but the men in my men's group supported me and said I should just keep going. They said it was far better to have my rage come alive – even if it was ignorant and immature – than to keep my rage repressed as it had been for so many years, while on the surface acting like a good boy. They said that even if there were some casualties while the brute bashed his way through crowds, it was worth it because the brute was listening to feedback and would therefore quickly mature.

I don't think the brute matured as quickly as they estimated. I gained a reputation for being a trainer who left "dead bodies," meaning, participants who had received feedback with a hatchet rather than a scalpel. Nothing serious, just that my beginning work with people lacked finesse, timing, elegance and precision.

I wanted to take people as far as I thought they should go, rather than as far as their system could sustainably handle. I had yet to *become* a sword.

Becoming a Sword (BLTLCH11.02). Sword making is an art. To achieve the kind of temper that can both hold an edge and stay flexible, the blade steel must be heated and then beaten and cooled, then heated, beaten and cooled, over and over again. The sword is not a metaphor here. The sword *is* you. Being heated, beaten and cooled means that your Box will repeatedly go through the liquid state and be reshaped, and you will personally experience the classic "death and resurrection show."

After a few years of practice, I could notice anger coming up in my body and I could tell it was anger. Then, instead of being subsumed by the anger, I experimented with surfing on it to get where I needed to go. I would use an appropriate percentage of intensity of anger as the force behind my voice or my movements, but I would only use as much anger as was needed in that moment to get the job done. The anger came with its own inherent clarity. I could access the clarity of anger when I internally applied the question, "I feel angry because?" Immediately, the anger itself provided the answer. I started letting the anger inform me about what was not okay, what needed to be happening that was not happening, what needed to be started, stopped or redirected. I discovered that anger's clarity was immediate and implicit. I did not have to stop and figure things out with my mind.

Woven into the structure of anger is an immense depth of discerning wisdom that presents itself experientially whenever requested. As soon as my anger was freed of the "anger is bad and dangerous" fetters, as soon as I loved anger just for being pure volatile aliveness, the anger unwrapped its gifts.

I remember first discovering that I had something resembling a sword. I was leading a training in Atlanta, Georgia, around 1993, and was astonished by the clarity of the distinctions I was able to make. At the end of the training, I also noticed that I had far more energy remaining than in previous trainings. The work got done, so I must have been using energy from somewhere else, perhaps from the Principles themselves. I looked around at people's glowing faces, closed the training space and naively relaxed my alertness, effectively putting my Spiritual Warrior's sword away. And, in that instant, half a dozen hungry Gremlins popped out from among the participants. The Gremlins took over the space and began devouring each other in competitive conflicts, diluting the clarity that we had worked so hard to establish! Out came my sword again, as if powered by its own intelligence and instinct. Through shifting into a meta-conversation about what was being created, things were swiftly put back into order. But afterwards … I put my sword away far less often. I had learned an invaluable lesson.

The sword of clarity is not an intellectual sword for slicing up other people's arguments and winning debates. Therefore, do not be fooled by your Box taking up a rigid intellectual position and proving itself right in the name of the sword. The sword of clarity is not from the mind. Rather, it is wordless, diamond-sharp, experiential insight; exquisite kindness; wise generous presence and ruthless compassion. The sword of clarity is Archetypal Love in action. It need never be put away. Not even when the Warrior King goes to bed. In fact, navigating the spaces of vulnerable intimacy requires sword work of the most delicate precision. You can learn to sleep with your sword of clarity always at the ready, so your Box has no chance to usurp power even when you are groggy. Sloppy mechanical reactions ("You always take all the covers." "Why do you drop your clothes in the middle of the floor?" "Did you remember to take the garbage out?") kill countless opportunities for precious intimacy. What good is your sword over there on the shelf? Keep your sword to hand. Learn to live with the consequences of being dangerous to unconsciousness. Never put your sword away.

Magician

As we discussed in Chapter 9, in Section B, Archetypal Masculine power comes from being Nothing, as hard as this may be to imagine. Being Nothing means that no matter what occurs, no matter what feelings arise, no matter how visible your faults are, without logic or reason you contextually understand that Nothing, by its very nature, is bigger than Everything. If Nothing were not bigger than Everything, where would the Everything be? Archetypally, your essential Masculine being is vaster than Everything. You take up more space. Whatever approaches, you contain it, own it, hold space for it and take responsibility for it.

This does not mean you will have all the solutions to all the problems. What it means is that, when things get wild, which they will, especially if you are partnered with a wild woman, you simply say to yourself and stand in the realization: "I am bigger than that."

"I am bigger than that." You can say this when your child is having a tantrum in the restaurant, when the priest asks you why you have not been to church lately, when the neighbor lets his dog shit in your yard again, when you forgot to get the oil changed in the car, when the insurance bill is greater than the balance in your checking account, "I am bigger than that."

Being Nothing (BLTLCH11.03). "I am bigger than that" does *not* mean you are a dumb doormat, a wet rag, feeling nothing, or ignoring your dignity. "I am bigger than that" does not mean, "I am stronger than that," "I am smarter than that," "I am better than that," or "I am beyond that." It simply recognizes the essential Archetypal Masculine condition: Nothing is bigger than Everything. Let the experience sink in. It can save you a lot of grief. Open to the knowledge that Everything in the world – all put together – is not bigger than the Nothingness you represent. The Nothingness is your wealth, your treasure. As Nothing, you have access to Everything. This is where your Archetypal Magician's nonlinear creating comes from. It comes from the Nothing. What is present in the space of Nothing? Nothing. What is possible in the space of Nothing? Everything. If there is nothing in Nothing, then there are also no assumptions, no conclusions, no expectations, or no restricting beliefs in Nothing. Therefore, in Nothing there is immense possibility. Everything starts with Nothing.

The classical stage magician pulls a rabbit out of a hat. Before reaching into the hat, the hat was empty. Pulling a rabbit out of a hat is making something out of Nothing. Pulling a rabbit out of a hat is no different from looking in a near empty refrigerator and figuring out what to make for dinner, or looking into a near empty bank account and creating a way to still take the wife and kids out to movies and popcorn.

Our lives are so full of details that, when approaching the situation happening in this moment, you can fail to recognize that you do not have the Nothingness you need to create

out of. The working space that you require to create out of is already filled with preconceived notions, previous plans, pre-made decisions or ancient resentments – ancient, meaning "anything older than three seconds." Before you can make something out of Nothing, you must first be able to, and often need to, make Nothing out of something.

For example, it could be that your woman is holding onto a story about the way things *should be,* or about why she is feeling a certain way, such as, " You *know* I can't sleep when the neighbors play their music so loud!" Before you can bring in an alternative way of being together – one that offers more intimacy – you will first need to "vanish" what is already there taking up the space. You might allow your shared stories about the thoughtless neighbors to be subsumed by a newer story, for example, "I've had a change of heart about those neighbors, Honey. I saw the father talking with his son the other day and they looked so happy together. I want to be more with our children like that. The music reminds me of how they love being together." Vanishing an old story is the work of the Magician Archetype. Please note that the above example done without the vulnerable Nothingness of the Magician is reduced to being one of the twelve communication roadblocks mentioned in Section 6-O. The *not-knowing* is a crucial alchemical ingredient.

The Magician starts with feeling fear because he *always does not know* how to do what he has to do. Even if he has done the exact same thing a thousand times before, he starts with not knowing how. Then, the slate is wiped clean. If he started with already knowing how, he himself would not be in the present. He would be in the past, trying to resurrect a previous circumstance, and his already-knowing-how would fill up his Nothingness. He would have no access to possibility, so his results would be dead. Without being at the edge of his Box, he would not be afraid. If you are not feeling afraid then you are not creating.

Stellating Fear (BLTLCH11.04). Initiating your Magician Archetype happens when you (man or woman) transform your relationship to the energy and information of fear. Again, such a process can take many months of work, perhaps even years. The process requires getting yourself into an initiatory environment, a training, which is specifically and intelligently designed for the purpose of waking up your Magician Archetype. The space must be so safe that you are able to experience and express maximum Archetypal fear, and go on and on until the fear stops by itself. In the ensuing internal silence, you discover that you, without anything, are bigger than maximum Archetypal fear. It is not an idea. It is an irrefutable experience. You have become bigger than the territory of fear itself, and your future is forever changed. You have gained the capacity to consciously experience maximum Archetypal terror and still function. You have awakened the Magician.

After expanding, so that you contain the fear and the fear does not contain you, you will find that you can be completely at risk and still take actions to create whatever is wanted and needed. In the previous example, the results were vanishing an old story so that you and your partner both could have access to Nothing and could create something different together. Vanishing a story (from your woman, your boss, your child, your parents, your neighbor, etc.) may include these steps:

1. Listening to the story without being hooked, then
2. Having a meta-conversation about the story, then
3. Assessing the purpose of having such a story to see if the purpose is still in alignment with what the other person wants to create *now* with you, or

4. Recalling the incident at the origin of the story, and,
5. If the incident involves you, surrendering your payoff and honestly apologizing for your actions, asking the other person to forgive you, or
6. If the story originated long ago, asking the person to differentiate between you and whomever the authority figure was in the story that they are equating with you.

Trying and failing to vanish a story does not prevent you from immediately trying again in the next moment in a different way. Even if you fail altogether, working in the Magician's domain is at least a different game than was probably being played before, and could eventually lead you into even greater opportunities, such as Womanmaking.

Womanmaking

Womanmaking (BLTLCH11.05). Making Nothing out of something is a magical action, and is often the place where the Pirate Magician King Spiritual Warrior Man begins Womanmaking. Womanmaking (the same as with Manmaking) is a show, a series of gestures that fit together to form scenes in a conscious theatrical performance. The Man's Womanmaking show is an authentic show, because something actually happens. It is the same as when a gymnast performs a routine on the parallel bars. The gymnastic routine is a show that has been rehearsed over and over again, but the routine actually happens. The audience can appreciate and be changed by the show. The performance of the actions produces impactful results, even though it is just a performance.

You start Womanmaking by placing your attention on your woman. Not as a boy places his attention on his mother. Not at a lizard places his attention on a fly. Not as a mouse places his attention on a snake. Place your attention on your woman the way Renoir placed his attention on a flower, the way Einstein placed his attention on his equations, the way a wine connoisseur would place his attention on the sound of the cork coming out of a bottle of Chateau d'Yquem Sauternes 1787. By placing your appreciative Archetypal Masculine attention on your woman, you flow Archetypal Masculine energy into your woman's four bodies. This catalyzes the chance for an astonishing Archetypal transformation of the woman. Human attention, as we discussed at length in Section 8-D, is one of the most delectable substances in the universe. It is the sweet nectar she has been longing for, her entire feminine life. If you skipped over this section about attention, or don't recall it, please review it now. Having a handle on your attention is essential to what follows.

What Is Woman? You Ask

What are Women anyway? The patriarchy has trained us men to regard women from the surface: makeup, clothes, how much skin is showing? How big are the bulges? What jiggles? What curves? In show business they call it "tits and ass." That is the usual limit of a man's attention placed on a woman. "What would she be like in bed?"

But what is a Woman really? What is a Woman underneath the surface? Where does Woman lead to? What does Woman represent? We men rarely experience deeper qualities of relating to Woman because we lack the discipline to notice the Feminine invitation. Our patriarchal immaturity impedes us from entering Feminine worlds that are rich with experience beyond our wildest imagination, a healing balm for wounds we've been too immature to face.

There are "Woman spaces" so clear with awareness and piercing with intelligence that nothing of your being is left unseen. If you have any secret embarrassments or faults, they are no longer concealed. The Goddess sees all. There is no chance to turn away and hide. You are terrified to be so exposed, but through finally being seen, you find that you are accepted completely as you are. No judgments come from the Goddess at all. Here is where the healing of the false mask takes place. She sees your false mask as exactly what it is: your false mask. You think you can keep this a secret but she already knows. The secret is only for you. Perhaps you *need* to use the mask. She accepts that you need to use it. Your inauthenticity and your childish antics are clearly seen and accepted as your own uncertainty, and your uncertainty is also accepted. The healing happens because, since you cannot hide the false, you gain the courage to be true. All your efforts, whether they fail or succeed, only receive the Loving Goddess's smile that sees and recognizes and accepts.

There are Woman spaces as hot as the nuclear furnace at the core of the sun. Woman's fierceness blasts forth, rips off your skin and sears the meat from your bones like dry dandelion fluffs blown from the stem. Your hair smokes. Your eyes squint in the roar of the flames. You wobble so much you can barely stand. No defense can protect you. All that remains is knocking bones; your trembling crackling skeleton shaking in its hollow shoes. It is then that you realize that nothing of your pain could possibly ever equal the pain experienced and now being expressed to you by Woman. If you can bear the pain that Woman now risks sharing, and if you do not wither in its presence, or blame her back from your own weakness, you are recognized for your strength and courage, and you achieve a great victory. You are worshipped by Woman in a way that makes your juices surge, simply for listening and witnessing. The vulnerable appreciation, by Woman, of something so simple as your listening, is even harder to bear than her nuclear storm.

There are Woman spaces so wise and magical that poetry drips like sparkling dewdrops from her lips, answering every question you dare or care to ask. She stands before you, a naked oracle nymph, who only wants to caress your mind with sweet assemblies of clarity and truth. Here, wonder prevails. In the presence of such easeful wisdom, it is no longer necessary to defend yourself with sane sounding reasons, or to profess that you know. A great healing takes place, because you are permitted to fully relax into not knowing, and, for the first time, the wondrous present opens up for you and becomes truly habitable without fear. You can start to play. And the faeries play with you. Joy abounds and the joy is intensely endless.

There are Woman spaces so safe and sensual that all of your inhibitions vanish as if they never existed. Nothing is naughty. Nothing is forbidden. You discover an openness and fluidity of movement within yourself that you thought was impossible. Her willingness to flow, blend, roll and play overwhelms you with simplicity and kindness. There never was a need to be strategic or clever, never a need to manipulate to try to get what you wanted. Just ask. Just try. The healing intimacy is far far deeper than thinking. Experientially, you are led to discover how easeful sexuality is. The tacit innocence is irresistible. Everything

works. Everything brings you closer. The mind just drifts away from lack of use, and only touch guides you both further and further into delight in being naked and refreshingly alive.

There are Woman spaces so stark-raving insane that the world shatters around you into a million terrifyingly-sharp razor blades. Nothing fits together and everything makes you want to scream in fear and rage. The more you thrash, the more you get cut to shreds and bleed. Staying still is no answer, because then you are only an easier target for vicious vampire entities. You bodily perceive the unending and twisted depths of Feminine horror. Insanity reigns. There is no way out and no way through. Nothing and nobody could prove that anything else is true. Death would be better than this. Devouring demons rip out anything that is holy or sacred from your soul, and shit on it until it suffocates before your eyes. Nothing remains. And yet, after some time, the Nothing that remains has some persistence. No matter what else there is, there is also the Nothing. A healing arises out of the molding spittle slime. The healing is that, even in the depths of insanity, you find that you are okay. You find a new home in Nothingness, and that home is discovered to be already everywhere.

There are Woman spaces so warm and nurturing that boundless Love caresses the hidden sour pockets in your soul. Nectar reaches into your tissues and smoothes away all your rough edges, everywhere. Never more must you stand alone. You have arrived. The gates open and you are enfolded in the Garden of Paradise. She has only been waiting for you to come be-with her there. Nothing is expected of you. You do not have to pay. You enter her glance and crumble into her welcome. You should never be worthy of such sweet warmth and loving acceptance, for you know that you have sinned. You know that you have hurt women, even indirectly, accidentally. Women are such fragile tender creatures. And children, you have hurt children, only by ignoring their request for a touch, a smile, a glance. So precious are the children, and you have hurt them. You do not deserve to be welcomed into the Garden, and yet she begs you to come and only be held by her Love. Your heart breaks, and in the breaking, your heart becomes real and is healed.

Accepting the Invitation to the Garden of Woman (BLTLCH11.06). Words cannot begin to impress the actual experience of a man accepting the invitation to go through the gates and explore the worlds of Woman, hand in hand with, his woman. You have to work for this. It is hard work.

We can still ask, what is Woman? What does Woman represent? Where does Woman come from? Men are rarely allowed to learn. But Men can learn. Men can learn when they transform their woman into a gateway for Woman. Woman becomes a gateway when presented with authentic masculine presence (*see* Section 8-D.) When Man places his conserved, Archetypal-energy attention on the woman, with respect and wonder, the Goddess herself is drawn into the space where the woman once was. It is the Goddess who takes your hand and leads you on the journey further exploring Archetypal Manhood. A Goddess has a rare touch, a touch worth working for.

The journey is endless and the journey is always the same. The journey commences when

> ## From the Glossary
> *Holding Space* is the act of being responsible at the level of space. Holding space implies conscious intention. Before you can hold space you must first declare space into existence as a distinction between what is in the space and what is outside the space. Space is declared either as an eight-pointed box or as an amorphous bubble. Space is held through using a percentage of your conscious attention to dedicate the space to serving Bright Principles. When you first try to hold space you might use control, domination or manipulation, but these are Shadow Principles. Holding space is a core skill. Once you can hold space you can learn to navigate space.

the Pirate Magician King Spiritual Warrior Man establishes intimacy in Archetypal Love. That Love opens a joyous meeting of beings in a sanctuary through which the Masculine and Feminine Archetypes can do their work in the world – the real purpose for relationship between Man and Woman. In this "high drama" of conscious Archetypal theater, you, as Man, have a precise and thoroughly engaging role to play.

SECTION 11-E

Holding Space For Woman

When you, as the Archetypal Masculine, set your Box aside and hold a safe enough space for your partner to set her Box aside, then the Archetypal Feminine may appear. It is the

Archetypal King who holds space with joy for his Woman, but this is not as easy as it sounds. There are treacheries to contend with, both internally in the man (his Box and his Gremlin)

and externally in the Man's Kingdom (Gremlins in the workplace, neighborhood, family, and circle of friends). Without his Spiritual Warrior, Pirate Magician, and loving communicator to serve him, a King is but a figure of speech.

Here is a first-hand example. One evening, I invited a new male friend to stay as a guest overnight in our house. The man was surely a King, but his Gremlin was not fully recognized by him. Almost immediately, his Gremlin subsumed his faculties and commandeered his behavior, and for several hours his Gremlin voraciously flirted with my partner-woman (*see* Section 17-C, about "Psychic Sex"). As you could well imagine, all my faculties were alerted. Driven by immediate anger at the sensed disrespect, my Warrior raised my two-edged sword of clarity. My Box wanted to use the sword only on him – one of its favorite strategies being to feel betrayed. But the sword of clarity is ruthlessly neutral. It first demanded that I clarify: Was it my own neurotic jealousy, or was this truly dishonorable? When the answer became clear, my Pirate-Magician-King-Spiritual-Warrior-team unhesitatingly sprang into action. Undaunted by my Box's immense fear of what I was about to do (the "good boy" aspect of my Box, that is), the Magician broke all rules of hospitality and politeness to suddenly intervene between the man and my partner. The Warrior made that interference uncompromising, calling a *complete* halt to their interactions. The Pirate King took the man into the kitchen and sent my Woman to another room. By now, my friend was on complete alert with all his Gremlin forces, and my Woman had her own opinions, which were addressed in private later. The man and I entered a fiercely honest conversation that precisely confronted his actions and their purpose, even at the most subtle level. And, when the situation was fully exposed, I sent the man out, alone into the night, away from my home, without the slightest compunction to rescue

him. This was not the first time this man had been sent away from a couple's home. During the conversation, my King understood with compassion the attractiveness of my Woman to such a Gremlin, so the conversation was held with a degree of tenderness that would rationally seem uncalled for, given the circumstances. But the proof of the Kingly nature of this event is that this man remains a good friend of mine, although he has never been (and may never be) permitted back into my house. This story exemplifies one aspect of how Masculine Archetypes work integrally together in holding space for a Woman.

In further considering the Masculine holding space for the Feminine, we must first eradicate the malicious misconception that Woman is so weak or confused that she needs some man to hold space for her. She is not and does not. How self-serving for a man to think. "Women, yeah. You gotta hold the door open for 'em cuz they's so dainty … nyuk! nyuk!"

The ordinary patriarchal-male mentality is unconsciously committed to spiteful tyranny over the feminine, and ruinous revenge against any woman who objects. There are lots of Neanderthalean Boxes walking down the streets today. Being aware that Neanderthalean Boxes hold power and authority in much of Western civilization is no reason for women (or men) to regard all men with terror and hatred. Women (or men) do not have to become Neanderthalean to protect themselves from Neanderthals. Sensitive vulnerability does not make you a weak and powerless victim. Sensitive vulnerability *is* your protection. Attending to the precision of your awareness allows you to intelligently sidestep Neanderthalean brutality.

The technology for transforming Neanderthalean Boxes is beyond the scope of this book. Here we are attempting to awaken an interest in ordinary man to undertake the journey of learning to care for the purity and excruciating lightness of the Feminine being.

This awakening, however, can grate so hard against a man's fundamental constructs, that he may instead respond with amplified efforts to crush the same Feminine we invite him to hold space for. The thing to remember is that all males have a Neanderthal part. All females have an equivalent part that can admire or even continuously forgive being raped. If this Neanderthal part occasionally has the majority vote in you (and you know if it does), you can work to change the balance of power in your Box. The Neanderthal brute who lives in us is not bad, *and*, that brute does *not* have the refinements needed to Archetypally appreciate the precious background texture of a Woman's Feminine voice as she shares the song of her heart.

The patriarchy has recklessly undermined respect for the Archetypal Feminine for so many centuries that exceptional efforts may be needed for a man to reclaim his sensibilities. A new appreciation of subtleties can be kindled. But a man's appreciation originates from within a plane of utter stillness. Without this stillness as a standard, a man fails to detect the delicate signals he needs to perceive when holding and navigating spaces in which his woman can feel safe enough to unfold.

Instructions for Finding Internal Stillness

Finding Internal Stillness (BLTLCH11.07). Begin by directing your Pirate Magician King Spiritual Warrior resources internally. Your intention is to develop awareness and discipline. No "pigs" can be let loose. That means, no typically male comments, at all. Hold everything within you still. Not with force, not like in prison. Simply let no action have enough energy to take place. Make no sudden moves. Like a tightrope walker balances on his line, balance on the stillness. Become so tranquil that the warm breath of your woman, the subtle movement of her chest rising and falling, becomes magnificent by comparison. Be so still that, watching her notice that you are being with her, while she richly senses her own breathing, defracts your awareness into multiple perspectives like a house-of-mirrors. I think it works like that – a woman notices herself, while at the same time noticing a man noticing her: she notices what the man notices about herself. This kind of splitting of attention – into multiple perspectives simultaneously – is more of a feminine quality, far beyond everything male. Money, power, pride, competition, possessions, reputation, strategies, these have no place here. They are the toys of vicious little boys. So foolish. So temporary. Let them fall away from you without trying to figure out how it works without them. Let yourself trust beyond reason, and be drawn forth into a freshness and tenderness so raw that words are too coarse to be spoken. And continue. Let the tenderness in. The beingness of Woman awaits. She invites us into the feminine world so patiently, having full knowledge of its value. She is neither willing nor able to lessen its heartrending impact. Yet also, and this is the point, she is not able to share the treasure without a partner who is able to receive her gifts. Archetypal Womanliness requires an Archetypally-Manly partner to accompany her on the voyage of sensual exploration beyond the limits of normal senses.

Keep Refining Attention

Refining Your Attention (BLTLCH11.08). Man can awaken to a level of attention wherein merely observing the sublime gestures of his Woman's movement sends chills of pleasure down his spine. Without knowing how, we men still have the capacity for that kind of attention, far vaster than we can conceive. It also frightens us to the core, a core we dare not acknowledge.

Woman can welcome us into an immensity of homecoming that we have never before imagined, a healing so sweet and wholesome that our soul could reveal its undefended nature and bask in her radiant warmth, never wanting to leave. We do not know of this because ordinary masculine attention is so unrefined. Yet, we have a capacity to learn. And regardless of our present skill level, Woman waits, hoping we will snap out of our cold, rational, defensiveness. Woman holds the door open, hoping we will come back home, and not just once.

Somewhere, you already have a reference point for expertise in using refined attention – one that can be applied to appreciating the Archetypal Feminine. For example, perhaps you are a marine biologist and have developed an expertise for distinguishing subtle differences between various species of sea-going slugs, the Nudibranchs. Perhaps you are a racer and can hear, just by the quality of the roar of a V8 engine, which dragster will set a new track record. Perhaps you are a sailor and can tune the rigging of your schooner so she sings across the foamy seas. Perhaps you are an antique dealer and can distinguish the authentic patina of a ninth-century Indian bronze artifact from a more recent reproduction. Perhaps you do body repair work on cars and can feel the smoothness of a surface down to one thousandth of an inch just with your bare fingers. Perhaps you can tie a perfect Robinson lure, guaranteed to catch even the most wily summer trout. Any of a million forms of subtle sensing can blend to produce an uncanny expertise. It is the fact that you understand *expertise* that is importance. Use your sense of expertise-ness to appreciate the rainbow multiplicity of the Archetypal Feminine.

Over the millennia in which Womanhood has been abused, so much "heaven" has been wasted. Any heaven you can recover could make a difference. Anything that re-establishes or even hints at respect for her breathtaking openness and vulnerability could serve as a liquid link for you to ride on. With refined, expert attention, you might find an irrepressible desire to look at her and see her with more than admiration; to see her as if you *were* her yourself. When you can breathe like her, then you can appreciate how she tilts her head to intentionally catch the light in her hair, so her radiance draws you just a little bit closer, and to adore her. Learn to adore everything of the lake of her. Then, holding space for her becomes an automatic expression of Love.

Look where she has placed the vase. Look how it honors you in her room. How can she know how to do this? It was not thought about. It was not figured out. She wants you to appreciate all of her. Not the true part, but the real part. When you no longer revere only logic and reason, when you have purified yourself of greediness for mere satisfaction, then you can allow yourself to accept the invitation of Womanliness into a garden filled with ambrosia. It is more than you deserve, more than you could buy. She has kept this waiting for you for years, years of you only refusing. Why?

Why would a man refuse so much holiness? There is no answer, only unbelief, only regret, only wonder that Woman has not yet retreated from our inexcusable inattentions. And still she stays open to us, still she continues, while vast moments of being slide past unnoticed, one into the other. Nothing is happening, yet Everything is here with her. Nothing could be missing because the Allness of her encompassing nature has nothing to hide, nothing to lose. Where would it go? How could it disappear or be lost when she is Everything? Is she frightened? Of course she is frightened. But she is willing to feel her fear so it is not stuck in her. The fear flows through her and can vanish with one sparkle in her eye, one curve on her lips. The tinkling brook of her voice sounds so comforting here, watering the wandering roots of the masculine mind, so it wants to go nowhere else.

Once a Man knows of this dimension of Woman, he can never disregard her again. He is willing to enter her world whenever she invites him, while still protecting it with dignity and power. He pays attention to supply specific details that weave together and hold a context that permits Woman to drop her worries and thrive in that Feminine world, herself. This makes for a satisfied Woman and a totally embraced Man.

CHAPTER 12

Archetypal Relationship

You can consciously create and live in a nearly continuous state of radiant ecstasy by navigating to Archetypal Love in your relationships. This possibility is now added to the *Map of Relationship*.

As we noted about many other aspects of building Love that lasts, do not expect yourself to already know what Archetypal Relationship is. We are not educated about Archetypal Relationship in the normal course of our public education. Since we do not already know about Archetypal Relationship, the appropriate form of learning to apply here would be expansive learning, which was discussed in Chapter 1. Recall that in expansive learning we start from *knowing that we do not already know the most important things*. Each new observation and experience is respected and accepted for what it is without having to make it fit into anything we already know. As more and more islands of experience and knowledge are assimilated, sooner or later they begin connecting to each other in practical and understandable ways, establishing entirely new continents of knowledge. Through continued expansion, the new continents come to rival, in both size and usefulness, the original knowledge continents given to us by our culture. In expansive learning there is no top end to discovering more and more important things.

Although the knowledge continents of ordinary human relationship and extraordinary human relationship are not directly connected to the knowledge continent of Archetypal Relationship, it turns out that only after thoroughly understanding the distinctions between ordinary and extraordinary can we look into the horizon and detect a new land mass ahead – the

Archetypal. Do not expect to enter Archetypal Relationship if you are not already creating extraordinary human relationship. Do not expect to enter Archetypal Relationship if you are not already distinguishing three kinds of love.

⋊ Archetypal Context

Archetypal Relationship is a context, not a procedure. This is a big statement and warrants unfolding. A "context" is a container or a framework that catches and holds certain clarities, in the same way that a fishnet gathers fish. If you redesigned your fishnet with a wider or narrower mouth, with larger or finer netting, your design modifications would change the kinds of fish that you could catch. The same is true with context. If you adopt a different context for relationship, then you will find that a different quality and experience of relationship shows up for you. Just like with the fishnet, the proof of whether or not you have shifted your relationship context is whether or not new qualities of relationship appear.

Shifting the context of relationship is probably not one of those skills that your dad took you aside to explain. The manner in which Archetypal Relationship replaces the context of extraordinary human relationship, for example, is indirect, subtle and profound, beyond the Box's capacity to arrange.

The Box demands simplified instructions for making things happen, like, "First pull up, then pull down." "Lather, rinse, repeat." "Insert tab A into slot B." "Push to start." The Box wants linear techniques that produce surefire results. The Box has designed our modern culture with an editorial preference toward science and technology. But, in the case of relationship, what the Box wants and how things actually work do not coincide. Archetypal Relationship is multidimensional and alive, writhing with subtle never-repeated

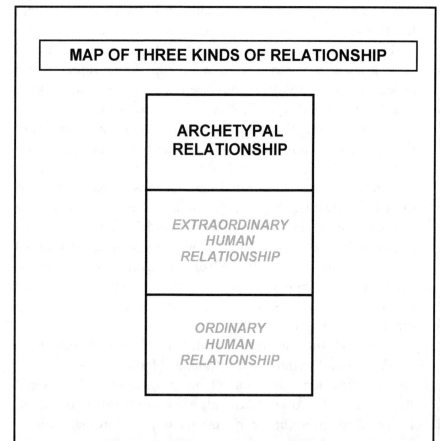

MAP OF THREE KINDS OF RELATIONSHIP

ARCHETYPAL
RELATIONSHIP

*EXTRAORDINARY
HUMAN
RELATIONSHIP*

*ORDINARY
HUMAN
RELATIONSHIP*

energy patterns. Ordinary linear instructions will not help you. This is why some people who would perhaps make wonderful parents cannot get pregnant. Their Box wants a child, but something in their relationship context produces physiological conditions that won't allow it.

The difference between what the Box wants and how things actually work is also why using Viagra or Cialis to make a man's dick hard will not necessarily enhance a couple's sexual intimacy. Archetypal Relationship is a context, not a drug.

Think of it this way: Having top-quality recipes does not guarantee that you can produce an extraordinary meal. Creating extraordinary meals comes from being an extraordinary cook, not from having an extraordinary cookbook. Extraordinary cooking is a mysterious faculty that takes years of training, practice and luck to develop, and is completely independent of the brand of your kitchen appliances.

Does having elegant furniture in your living room guarantee that the people who come to visit will connect to each other with warmth and harmony? No. Does having an impressive website guarantee that you will have lots of paying clients? No. Does wearing superb clothing or makeup guarantee that someone superb will be attracted to you? No. In the same way, following a step-by-step procedure will not guarantee that you enter Archetypal Relationship.

If this book were trying to give you a procedure, it would have ended before reaching considerations about Archetypal Relationship. There is no system, method or procedure that guarantees entry into Archetypal domains. *And*, there *are* ways of behaving that increase your chances of being in Archetypal Relationship. This chapter is about those ways. The gates of heaven are more prone to open if your behavior already resonates with what is on the other side of the gates.

Align with the Archetypal Purpose of Relationship

To investigate the Archetypal purpose of relationship, let us ask the bigger question: What is the Archetypal purpose of the universe? One would have to be galactically arrogant to seriously consider answering such a question. But we need an answer. One way to figure out what the universe is up to now would be to review what the universe has been up to during the past few billion years. The pattern seems rather clear: dust to diatoms to dinosaurs to Danny DeVito – the Archetypal purpose of the universe appears to be evolution.

The organic tissues constituting the saltwater computer of the human form represent a potential for evolution that surpasses our own capacity to estimate. This vast and awesome evolutionary potential, however, is imprisoned and limited by our free volitional power, controlled by our Box. It is our Box that stands guard between our evolvable being and the evolutionary purpose of the universe. The Box's self-defending purpose prevails. This is the true impact of free will.

When the purpose of our Box is unchanged from its original survival purpose, then our

> Do not try to make the ideas in this book into rules. The ideas are offered as considerations, perspectives of thought, and as possible avenues of experimentation to be used for your personal development and enjoyment. If you take these ideas as rules you are trying to give away your personal authority to the author of this book, and he refuses to be used as such an authority for you. Generate and sustain your own authority through doing your own experiments.

Box is dedicated to defending itself from the universe's efforts to bring it through evolutionary steps. As a side effect we are left stranded in ordinary human relationship. When our Box is initiated into adulthood, then the purpose of our Box shifts from defensive to expansive. Instead of trying to keep everything the same, our Box starts seeking how to learn, grow, and expand. Have you noticed any such changes happening in your own behaviors?

When you change the strategy of your Box so that it aligns to the evolutionary forces of the universe, you gain functionality in the responsible Adult ego state and can enter extraordinary human relationship. These are joyous times!

When you develop the ability to discern between the mechanical busy-ness of your Box and your natural ability "to be" and to "be-with," you can then make a paper-thin gap between the urges of your Box and what *you* choose to do, so that the Box's motivations become irrelevant. The Box's mechanical drivers and defenses can be disconnected from your actions – in the same way that the wheels of a car can stay motionless when the clutch is disengaged, even though the car's engine may be revving fast. When the Box is no longer the unconscious motor for your actions, you are free to move – or be moved by – Bright Principles and stellated Archetypes in evolutionary directions, such as toward Archetypal Relationship. Your relationship can become a theater in which Archetypal Love can perform, but this does not mean the end to all of your problems. For example, Archetypal Relationship is not intended to solve the problem of loneliness. Archetypal Relationship is not intended to solve *any* problems. The value of Archetypal

---

MAP OF THE PURPOSE OF RELATIONSHIP

The Purpose of Your Relationship (BLTLCH12.01)

PURPOSE OF ORDINARY HUMAN RELATIONSHIP	PURPOSE OF EXTRAORDINARY HUMAN RELATIONSHIP	PURPOSE OF ARCHETYPAL RELATIONSHIP
To be loved.	To love.	To hold the space where Archetypal Love can happen.
To avoid loneliness.	To create a partnership.	To serve something greater than ourselves.
To continue the family name.	To communicate.	To create the possibility of Archetypal Man & Woman being present.
To be socially acceptable.	To really live, all 4 bodies.	To discover Countenance.
To be seen as successful.	To have sex.	To be a servant of Bright Principles rather than a slave of Shadow Principles.
To find a pseudo-Mom / -Dad.	To play responsibly.	To be Nothing or Everything.
To have orgasms.	To create a family.	To become a force of nature.
To find security, be protected.	To synergize.	To be with.
To survive.	To learn and grow.	To navigate space and find the Center of the Labyrinth.
To be infatuated.	To do Edgework experiments.	To take radical responsibility.
To have a fight partner.	To explore intimacy.	To accept what is as it is.
To revenge on the opposite sex. To betray / feel betrayed.	To create clarity and possibility.	To be simply present.
To have regular Gremlin meals of low drama.	To appreciate and enjoy.	
To make our parents happy.	To expand the Box.	
To try to be happy ourselves.	To express Adulthood.	
To have a good reputation.	To create high drama.	
To conform to beliefs.	To be friends.	
	To enjoy the other's company.	
	To be present as ourselves.	

The Archetypal Purpose of Relationship is Evolution.

Use the Active Form of "What Is"

You do not have to understand this next paragraph to continue reading in this book, but if you *do* understand it, then you *needed it* to continue.

If you are aware of the illusion of opposites (e.g., the illusion that light and dark are opposites because you cannot have one without the other), you also recognize that using the perspective that time flows from the future through the present and into the past is naïve. I bring this up because I have suggested that the Archetypal purpose of relationship is evolution. The standard understanding of evolution is that evolution depends on the flow of time. We ordinarily imagine that things slowly or suddenly evolve during a passage of time. By saying that the Archetypal purpose of relationship is evolution I am not associating relationship with a past-present-future "trying to achieve a goal" flow-of-time orientation. Nondualistic clarity sees the eternal now as having no flow of time. To understand the overall purpose of relationship as evolution without discounting the Archetypal clarity of the nondual perspective that the eternal now has no time flow, you must have the additional clarity that, in the timeless eternal now there are actually two forms of "what is." There is a passive form of "what is" and an active form of "what is." The passive form of "what is" is accepting what is, as it is, here and now in the moment without judgment (Swami Prajnanpad). The active form of "what is" is conscious creation. In the same way that creating does not happen in time and only happens now, *evolution also only happens now.* Archetypal Relationship lives in the orientation that what happens now is either accepted or created, both of which include conscious responsibility. Archetypal Relationship is not about trying to evolve into something different in the future but rather consciousness of "evolution happening" now.

Relationship is that it creates the possibility for Archetypal Man and Archetypal Woman to be functionally present in the world. *How do we figure out what this all means? How do we work with these conditions?* The rest of this chapter reveals a broad set of Archetypal perspectives for you to test out for yourself during experiments in your daily life.

Radical Responsibility

Taking Radical Responsibility (BLTLCH12.02). Learning how to function in Archetypal conditions starts with you taking responsibility for having the potential to represent Archetypal Masculine and Feminine forces. Since Archetypal understanding is not provided to us by our culture, the first steps in gaining that understanding on your own can be a little shocking. It is important to allow yourself time and space to grow accustomed

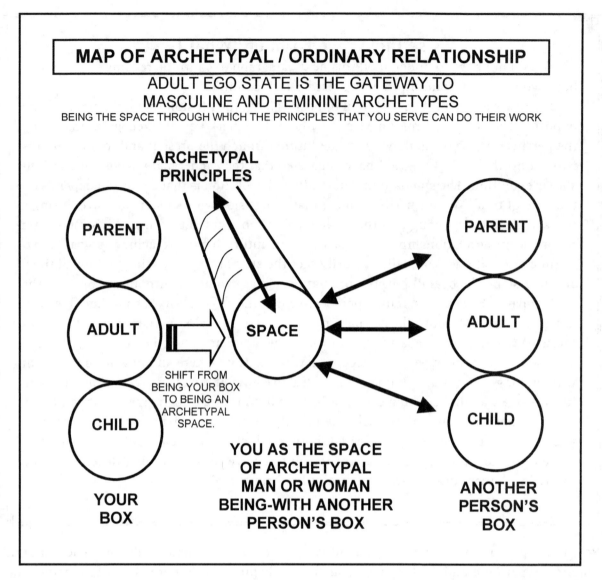

MAP OF ARCHETYPAL / ORDINARY RELATIONSHIP

ADULT EGO STATE IS THE GATEWAY TO
MASCULINE AND FEMININE ARCHETYPES
BEING THE SPACE THROUGH WHICH THE PRINCIPLES THAT YOU SERVE CAN DO THEIR WORK

ARCHETYPAL
PRINCIPLES

PARENT

ADULT

CHILD

YOUR
BOX

SHIFT FROM
BEING YOUR BOX
TO BEING AN
ARCHETYPAL
SPACE.

SPACE

YOU AS THE SPACE
OF ARCHETYPAL
MAN OR WOMAN
BEING-WITH ANOTHER
PERSON'S BOX

PARENT

ADULT

CHILD

ANOTHER
PERSON'S
BOX

to handling the sharpness of the clarity that is characteristic of Archetypal perspectives. Sharpness is sharp.

As a college student, I was home visiting my parents over Christmas. I had been practicing fencing in college and was eager to show off my swordfighting talents to my girlfriend. My parents were not at home and I took advantage of the opportunity by removing one of the two Spanish swords from a false shield-at-arms that an interior decorator had mounted over my parents' living room fireplace. The blade of the sword was not sharpened, but the sword was pointed and made out of steel. I parried and lunged around the living room, barefoot, proudly showing off as best I could. Then, when my demonstration was over, I absentmindedly let the sword drop to my side, assuming unconsciously that, since it was a fake sword, I did not have to take any of the usual precautions. In one swift move the sword sliced open the top of my right foot. I still carry the scar today, a reminding factor that handling sharpness requires extraordinary and unbroken attention. The same is true with the sharpness of Archetypal perspectives. Handle them with care. No matter if a clay water pitcher hits a rock, or a rock hits the pitcher, it is going to be bad for the pitcher. Diamond clarity easily slices through illusion wherever it touches the illusion. Holding Archetypal perspectives requires more than ordinary responsibility. Holding Archetypal perspectives requires *radical* responsibility.

For example, from the Archetypal perspective, everything that happens is neutral and completely without meaning. If something happens it does not happen for a reason and does not imply anything. When something happens, it happens without any story attached. There is no good or bad, no better or worse, no right or wrong, and no positive or negative. From the Archetypal perspective, what is, is, just as it is, without implication and without meaning. Your job is to be neutrally present to *what is* on all levels, to accept *what is*, just as it is here and now, without judgment.

From the Archetypal perspective, there is no such thing as a problem. "Problem" is a human term invented to establish a dramatic relationship between a person and a specific set of conditions. Defining a problem as a problem is completely subjective and changes from person to person, from moment to moment and from situation to situation. One person's problem is another person's perfect paradise.

From the Archetypal perspective, you cannot be "in" a situation, because you manufactured the perspective that creates the opinion that you are "in" a situation in the first place. There is no situation without a person there to claim that they are "in" this particular situation. Without the person's story about the circumstances, there exist merely neutral, unconnected circumstances.

From the Archetypal perspective it is impossible to be a victim. Consciously or unconsciously, you made the choices and took the actions that got you into those exact circumstances, whatever they are. Pretending to be a victim of the circumstances is simply a theatrical role that you would play in order to serve unconscious Shadow Principles, thereby causing an energetic exchange to feed your

Gremlin. In the Archetypal view, you cannot choose to take or not take responsibility. You *are* responsible. Irresponsibility is a delusion.

If you are sick, you are sick, no story about being punished. If you lost your keys, you lost your keys; it does not mean you are stupid. If you win a contract or lose a contract, either way it has no meaning about the value of your work. There may be consequences to what happens. There may be after effects or side effects to what you do or do not do, but even the consequences do not mean anything. It does not even mean anything that the consequences do not mean anything!

The perspective that everything is neutral can at first seem to be inhuman. For example, how could it be neutral that someone is raped or beaten or robbed? How could it be meaningless if millions of innocent people are killed in political upheavals? That children are enslaved or sexually molested? That animals are routinely tortured? There must be meaning to the "terrorist attack" on the World Trade Center! Or to the devastation of tropical rain forests! To ignore the meaning of such atrocities seems completely inhuman. Read On!

Whereas we were previously exploring ordinary human relationship and extraordinary human relationship, we are now exploring Archetypal Relationship. In the phrase *Archetypal Relationship* you will notice that the word "human" is missing. That omission is on purpose. The reason that human beings do not enter the domain of Archetypal Relationship is because human beings as originally packaged are too cumbersome. Human beings come with their Box. The Boxes used by us human beings to give ourselves the secure feeling of having an identity are meaning-making machines. The entryway to Archetypal territories is too narrow to bring ordinary Boxes along. Taking radical responsibility cuts away the entanglements

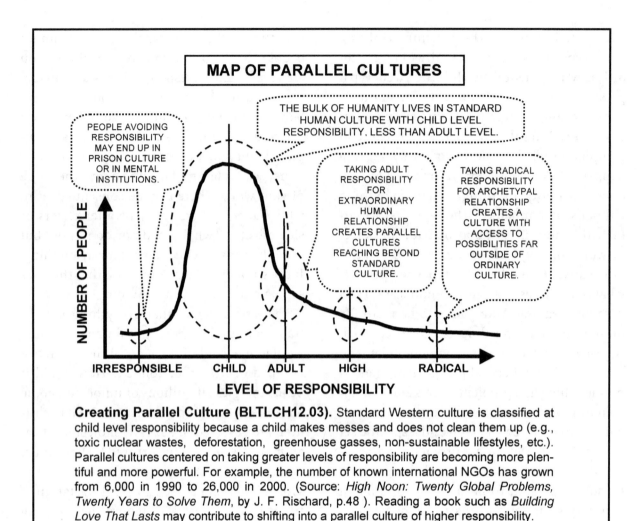

Creating Parallel Culture (BLTLCH12.03). Standard Western culture is classified at child level responsibility because a child makes messes and does not clean them up (e.g., toxic nuclear wastes, deforestation, greenhouse gasses, non-sustainable lifestyles, etc.). Parallel cultures centered on taking greater levels of responsibility are becoming more plentiful and more powerful. For example, the number of known international NGOs has grown from 6,000 in 1990 to 26,000 in 2000. (Source: *High Noon: Twenty Global Problems, Twenty Years to Solve Them*, by J. F. Rischard, p.48). Reading a book such as *Building Love That Lasts* may contribute to shifting into a parallel culture of higher responsibility.

created by the meaning-making machinery of the Box. But it also cuts away ordinary and extraordinary humanness.

You do not have to worry about becoming inhuman, superhuman, nonhuman or subhuman. Shifting to Archetypal is not volitional, meaning that you cannot just decide to go there. You can only put yourself into a position of necessity as a proposal to enter the Archetypal. The Archetypal itself decides if *shifting you* would serve the Archetypal. Shifting to Archetypal gives you no freedom from conscience, from moral principles, or from respecting human dignity. Quite the opposite is true. Shifting to Archetypal occurs spontaneously in response to objective necessity, and such necessity only arises if you have appropriately prepared yourself. One of those preparations is taking radical responsibility for conscience, for Principles, and for dignity.

If you do enter the Archetypal you will find that the shift unleashes tremendous energy reserves that were previously consumed in dealing with human meanings. The extra energy is powerful. Aligning yourself to Archetypal forces makes you a conductor of Archetypal power. What you soon realize is that, although you have access to Archetypal power, the power is not yours. The power cannot be used to accomplish the Box's or the Gremlin's purposes. Archetypal power can only be used to accomplish Archetypal tasks and purposes.

We are accustomed to the many shortcuts and loopholes in the rules for using power in the ordinary human domains. Moving into extraordinary human domains, there are fewer rules but also fewer loopholes. Fewer excuses are accepted. The rules are broken with greater consequence. In Archetypal domains the rules apply even more strictly. There are chambers and spaces where there may even be but one rule for using power, but that rule applies absolutely. Understanding and following *that* rule requires radical responsibility.

Take Radical Responsibility for Feelings

Taking Radical Responsibility for Your Feelings (BLTLCH12.04). Here is an eye-opening experiment about feelings from the Archetypal domain. Read and think along with this conversation between a trainer and a participant.

Trainer: "What do you *think* about this pencil?"

Participant: "I think the pencil is yellow, has bite marks, and needs to be sharpened."

Trainer: "Thank you. What do you *feel* about this pencil?"

Participant: "I feel like I would rather use my pen instead of that pencil."

Trainer: "That is a thought, not a feeling. I am asking what you feel about the pencil, not what you would prefer to do or not do with the pencil. There are four feelings: anger, sadness, joy and fear. In your statement there is a hidden feeling. Find your feeling and try again. What do you feel about this pencil?"

Participant: "I feel angry about this pencil because they made me use a pencil like that in English class and I hated my English teacher for not explaining things so I could understand them."

Trainer: "Thank you. Could you feel scared about this pencil?"

Participant: "Yes. I could feel scared about this pencil because I have a black scar in my finger where I once fell on a pencil like that and it jabbed me. That pencil could hurt me."

Trainer: "Thank you. Could you feel glad about this pencil?"

Participant: "Yes. I could feel glad about this pencil because I love the way pencil wood smells. It is cedar like they used to make the wooden arrows that I practiced with during summer camp where I had so much fun."

Trainer: "Thank you. Could you feel sad about this pencil?"

Participant: "Yes. I could feel sad about this pencil because I wrote my first love letter with a pencil like this to a girl who already had a boyfriend, and she decided to stay with him and not come to me. After that I did not try to have another girlfriend for ten years."

Trainer: "Thank you. So let me review what we just did. I asked you what you thought about this pencil and you told me what you thought. Then I asked you what you felt about this pencil and you said that you felt angry. Then I asked you if you could feel scared about the pencil and you said yes. Could you really feel it? Was it a real feeling?"

Participant: "Yes. I could really feel the fear."

Trainer: "Then I asked you if you could feel glad about the pencil and you said yes, and sad and you said yes."

Participant: "Yes, and I could really feel those feelings too."

Trainer: "So let me get this straight. I showed you an object. I selected a pencil to use for this experiment, but it could have been any object. You said that you could feel mad, sad, glad or scared about this object. Could you feel all four feelings about any object?"

Participant: "I guess so. I never thought about it before. Yes, I probably could."

Trainer: "Where do your feelings come from?"

Participant: "I create the experience of my feelings myself, according to the story I tell myself about the object. Each different story creates a different feeling. To change my feeling all I need to do is change my story about the object. This is astonishing!"

Trainer: "As we began this experiment with the pencil you said that you felt angry about the pencil. Now we see that you could have felt angry, sad, glad or scared about the pencil. But you arranged to feel angry first. If we had stopped the experiment at that point you would have concluded that you actually felt angry about the pencil. But we kept going and you felt all four feelings. Of the four feelings, why did you choose to feel angry first?"

Participant: "The anger is my first defense. People say I get angry easiest. If I am angry about something, then I do not have to take responsibility for it. It is someone else's fault. I get to persecute everybody else. It is very safe and normal for me to feel angry first."

Radical responsibility with regard to feelings starts when we declare, "I create my feelings. I do not feel a feeling because of any external experience or circumstance. I feel a feeling because I unconsciously create a story that allows me to feel this feeling to best serve my Box's survival strategies."

Take Radical Responsibility for Stories

Human beings are massively creative. We do not usually think of ourselves as creative. We allow that we might be a little creative at Christmas time when we wrap presents or decorate the house. But in every moment we are creating the stories that we tell to ourselves and to other people – the stories that give meaning to what happens in our lives. We do not tend to notice how voraciously we produce stories, because every three seconds the Box regenerates stories identical to what it created for us in the previous three seconds. This is how the Box keeps things the same; it ongoingly creates the same stories.

There are two classes of stories that we can create about what happens. By far the most common story we create characterizes us as a victim of the circumstances. That we were a victim seems completely *inarguable*. The inarguability comes from our habit of interpreting "the facts" to show how we were hurt, insulted, abandoned, betrayed, abused, neglected, etc., forcibly establishing ourselves as a victim in a low drama. Telling a victim story about what happened from the Parent or Child ego states creates ordinary human relationship.

But we could take the exact same circumstances, the same incident, the same people involved, the same actions, and we could create a responsible story about being involved in these circumstances. Responsible stories place us "at cause" or "at source" for the circumstances. Responsible stories come from the Adult responsible ego state and create extraordinary human relationship.

Creating responsible stories is a skill, perhaps a new skill. It may not have occurred to us that we could, in every circumstance, create a responsible story showing exactly how we caused, allowed, or, in some conscious or unconscious way, promoted what happened. We may have failed to listen to our intuition, for example, ignored obvious signals, or hesitated with timing, and in this way landed ourselves directly in the situation on purpose, perhaps an unconscious purpose, but still on purpose, even if it was a less than optimal situation.

What could we possibly gain from creating a less than optimal circumstance for ourselves? Consider these: A well-crafted victim story attracts kind attention from powerful people, allows us special exceptions, provides acceptable reasons for receiving extra comforts, justifies us taking revenge, undermines frightening intimacy in relationships, and so on. The idea that we could actually be responsible for creating things the way they turned out in every case may be a very startling perspective.

Cynthia, for instance, could not make the leap to figuring out how to take responsibility for her father committing suicide when she was only nine years old. This one event, about which she had always felt like a powerless victim, had dominated Cynthia's life decisions and her relationships to men and to authority figures in general.

When something happens and we make up a story about it, we can choose between making up a victim story or a responsible story. Cynthia wasn't immediately able to see that her victim story actually robbed her of responsible power. Like Cynthia, if we create a victim story for ourselves, then we get only the irresponsible power to complain, to blame someone else, to feel resentment, to get revenge, to prove ourselves right, or to prove someone else wrong.

When Cynthia created a responsible story about her father's suicide, the results were remarkably different. To create the responsible story in this example, Cynthia asked herself, "Who picked my parents?" and answered that question by affirming that *she* did. The choice was hers…as our choices are ours. Suddenly it was clear that she was not a victim at all, but had actually had a part in setting the whole thing up. Through creating a responsible story Cynthia claimed the responsible power of choice.

By choosing to adopt a responsible perspective today, we get to see how we set things up for ourselves all along the way, and then derived benefit from having an outstanding victim story for all the previous years.

When we create a responsible story about what happens, we vibrate with a different sort of power. We have responsible power, the power of ownership, the power of causing to

be, the power of being at source. Choosing to create responsible stories about what happens to us creates high drama and opens the doors to extraordinary human relationship.

Instead of saying, "I do not have time for this," as a victim, we responsibly say, "I will not make time for this." Instead of saying, "I can't do this," as a victim, we responsibly say, "Until now I have always chosen not to do this." It soon becomes clear that of the two stories we could create about what happens to us, victim or responsible, the responsible story gives us more power.

Now we come to an even more interesting question, the Archetypal question: Of the two stories we could create about what happens to us, which story is true?

What a puzzling question! Which story is true?

Some of us think that the victim story is true because what happened to us *really did* happen to us. We really *were* victimized. Therefore we really *are* victims. Those of us dedicated to creating victim stories tend to live in ordinary human relationships.

Some of us think that the responsible story is true, because we cannot avoid responsibility so easily. Regardless of what happens to us, we cannot deny the fact that it is we who made the choices that got us into those specific circumstances so that these precise things could happen. We could have made other choices and we did not, so we are responsible for making it happen exactly that way. Those of us who declare and step into responsible stories tend to live in extraordinary human relationships.

But there remains this nagging question: Which of the two stories is true?

Try answering the question, "Which story is true?" with another question: "How could a story be true?"

Stories are stories. There is no such thing as a true story. How can a *story* be true? No matter how convincing a story is, no matter how useful a story is, a story is just a story, a fiction, an editorialized point of view.

Unconsciously made, a story is an interpretation of circumstances slanted to produce a certain meaning that is useful for supporting our Box's unconscious purpose: low drama.

Consciously made, a story can be useful for supporting us being our destiny Principles in action: high drama.

In either case, we use stories to create the theatrical performances we call relationship. We make up a story and then we walk into the universe of conditions created by that story as if the conditions were actually true. We play our characters as if our lives depended on it, even though we just wrote the script ourselves!

Taking an Archetypal step beyond stories requires tremendous courage. Can you admit that no matter how grim or how funny your piece of theater is, it is still theater? If so, you free yourself of the confines of any particular story and you become a story maker. Taking actions from the realization that *I am the story maker* is part of radical responsibility. Radical responsibility is based on the tacit, irrefutable understanding that *every* story is a fiction. Using radical responsibility, the story maker goes ahead and consciously makes

---

MAP OF STORIES

RESPONSIBLE STORY

WHICH STORY GIVES YOU MORE POWER?

WHAT HAPPENED

WHICH STORY IS TRUE?

VICTIM STORY

When something happens we do not leave it as neutral. We create a story about it. If we want to use what happened for doing low drama we create a victim story. If we want to use what happened for doing high drama we create a responsible story. Of the two kinds of stories it is the responsible story that gives us more power. But which story is true? How can a story be true? Are you ready to take radical responsibility as the story maker?

---

stories *anyway*, not because they are true but because they are *useful*. Taking radical responsibility for being the story maker permits us to produce stories where we can behave with kindness, generosity, and compassion with ourselves and with others, no matter what the circumstances.

But, responsibly observing the stories we make may reveal another pattern: that Gremlin is controlling our in-house movie projector. We may have a long history of making stories that include propositions such as: I can't. It is impossible. You are wrong. That is not fair. It is not my fault. You are bad. You are stupid. You hurt me. I hate you. I am better than you. I can get away with this. This does not apply to me. You betrayed me. I don't trust you. I will get back at you, and so on. Radical responsibility reveals the true intention of these stories: to serve the unconscious Shadow Principles of our hidden purpose. Taking responsibility for being the story maker assumes our willingness to find ourselves personally responsible for hurting other people and feeling glad about it. This makes responsible self-observation risky. What we see may not be a pretty sight.

Observing the intention of our stories does not mean trying to change our victim stories to responsible stories. This could lead to us regarding victim stories as "bad" and responsible stories as "good." Victim stories are not "bad." Victim stories are just victim stories and produce certain known and predictable results, namely low drama and ordinary human relationship. Responsible stories are not "good." Responsible stories are just responsible stories and produce certain known and predictable results, namely high drama and extraordinary human relationship. The whole "good vs. bad" dichotomy is itself an irresponsible Shadow Principle, and automatically produces the likes of the Catholic Inquisition and Nazi death camps that typically proceed in our mind and heart during ordinary human relationship. Replacing victim stories with responsible stories is a process that occurs gradually, over time, through the painful experience of redemption. We are redeemed when objective impersonal remorse about creating victim stories becomes so intense in our moment-centered experience that it is too painfully ridiculous to continue creating victim stories.

Taking Radical Responsibility for Your Stories (BLTLCH12.05). We slip into Archetypal Relationship reflexively through a shift of context. Included in the shift of context is the awareness that, "I am the story maker. I make up no story accidentally. Every story is meaningless, and, every story has a purpose. Either I am not aware of the purpose of my story – in which case I serve unconscious purposes and I enter ordinary human relationship – or I am aware of the purpose of my story, in which case I serve conscious purposes and I enter extraordinary human relationship." The context of Archetypal Relationship has such clarity about story making that you can let all stories pass, as if they were a series of waves and you were a surfer. Keep this distinction in mind – you are the surfer, not the wave. The wave does not automatically drag the surfer along. With each wave (each story) that comes along you have several choices – to ride it without consciously choosing, thereby giving the story importance and power; to ride it consciously, knowing that it is only a story; or not to ride it at all, thereby letting the wave slide by you and crash purposelessly on the seashore.

Freedom from the meaningfulness of stories does not imply freedom from stories. There will always be stories. You may as well use stories that let you walk through your day with some bounce in your step. For example, no matter what has happened to you so far in your life, and no matter what previous stories you have so far used, you could make up an entirely new story right now that releases you from being a victim of all of your previous victim stories. Your new story would be a responsible story. It could go something like this: "I am so grateful for everything that has happened to me so far, no matter how painful it was at the time, because what happened has given me the wisdom to make better choices now."

The new story is you taking full responsibility for creating your past circumstances just exactly the way they went, so that you could learn all that you needed to learn to get exactly here, in this moment, in this book. The new story tells how you start over at this point to create an interesting, challenging, love-filled future, full of experiments in relationship and adventures delivering your full contribution to humanity.

SECTION 12-C

No Such Thing As Relationship

One of the many unquestioned stories planted into our Box by our culture establishes what we – from then on – assume is the nature of relationship. Ask anybody about their relationship and they will tell you about their joys, their communication problems, what habits they wish their partner would change, and their future hopes and worries. Implicit in everything they say is the idea that they "have" a relationship and that their relationship is a real thing. It is the "thing"-ness that we assume about relationship that locks us into certain narrow conclusions, and prevents us from accessing a wide range of other interesting options.

Concluding that relationships exist as a thing subjects our interactions to the laws of physicality. If our relationship is a thing, we can change it, work on it, build it, destroy it, take care of it, threaten it, protect it, start it, or end it. A thing is like a house. It has physical characteristics that persist all by themselves. You can go on vacation and when you come back your house is still there. But if I ask you to show me your relationship, you cannot do it. You may point to your partner, or to your ring, or to your wedding certificate, but these are only a person, a ring and a piece of paper. They are not your relationship. Where is your relationship?

What if relationship is not a thing at all? What if the idea that relationship is a thing is only a superstition? What if there is no such thing as a relationship?

If relationship is not a thing, what is it then? Consider the idea that rather than being a thing, relationship is a space. If relationship is a space, then all of a sudden relationship has an immense amount of flexibility and aliveness that it did not have just a moment before when it was as a thing. If your relationship is a space, then your relationship only exists in those moments when you are regarding it into existence. There is nothing there until you enliven it through relating. If your relationship is not a thing, then it has no past and no future, no story and no fantasy. You can make of it whatever you want to make of it, right now. You cannot count on your relationship to continue to exist without you putting your attention on and flowing energy to your partner. The quality of attention you give and the energy you flow is then the quality of your experience of relationship. Relationship is a space that you can live into through your way of being, feeling, communicating and acting. Your way can be any style that you want. You do not have to be a certain way. Your partner or children do not have to be a certain way. And, you cannot know what to expect. None of your old relationship assumptions or expectations work anymore. There is just this space of possibility between you and another person that holds a potential of excitement. It is a doorway to the unknown that can become whatever you can make of it with each other now. Each night your relationship vanishes completely. Each next morning you can bring it alive in some surprising new way. Your relationship unfolds as you ongoingly create into the possibility that being together is for you. Each moment of your relating is no longer held within the physical constraints of having to be now what it was just a moment before. In each instant, the relationship unfolds exactly the way you create it happening in that instant.

Relationship Gets in the Way of Intimacy

Relationship Getting in the Way of Intimacy (BLTLCH12.06). Ordinary human relationship occurs between Boxes. Person A's Box interacts with person B's Box. Our Box lets another person come no closer to us than the edges of our Box. Their Box does the same. Box meets Box. That is the limit of ordinary human relationship. No amount of psycho-emotional processing will allow two Boxes to enter intimacy because the ordinary purpose of our Box is to create and sustain separation between Boxes. Our seeming separation guarantees the preservation of what we have come to believe is our "self," but which is actually just our Box.

Archetypal Relationship occurs between *beings*. During intimacy, the Box is simply ignored as if it were an irrelevant, surrealistic illusion, an unwatched television. Intimacy operates in a dimension that is very different from the dimension of Box mechanics. While intimately being-with another being, the Box's writhing gestures do not apply. This does not mean that somehow the Box magically stops writhing. It does not. This means simply that we distinguish the Box's writhing as the Box's writhing, and that its writhing does not apply. There are no *reasons* for intimacy.

The more our being grows, the more it hungers for extended exposure to authentic intimacy. Intimacy comes in a variety of qualities, just like wine. Without an education in differentiating the various qualities of wine, we may overpay for cheap rotgut, or worse, we may knock back a glass of something truly transformational and miss the whole experience. The same applies to intimacy. Without an education to help us discern among various qualities of intimacy, we may soil ourselves with codependent fighting and fucking (pardon my French) and think that this is as good as it gets. There are two typical patterns to achieving pseudo-intimacy, both involve fighting and fucking. Here is a short class on what to avoid.

Fighting Then Fucking Pattern #1: We finally get so pissed off that we go for the throat. The fighting is so vicious and destructive that both people's automatic defense mechanisms overload and fry. The smoke slowly clears. For the moment, amidst the rubble of blasted structures, our Boxes can no longer defend themselves. A temporary pseudo-intimacy arises. By next morning each Box has reassembled itself and realizes that intimacy occurred. The Boxes recoil from each other and automatically reestablish separateness. Three or four weeks go by and the pattern is repeated.

Fighting Then Fucking Pattern #2: Our Box classifies every person into one of two types: enemy or friend. Our enemies vastly outnumber our friends. With enemies our Box engages in constant energetic warfare so as to conquer them. With friends our Box engages in seductive sexual flirtation so as to control them. Neither the fighting nor the fucking are authentic, only desperate affectation and pretense. Our fighting and fucking both prevent true intimacy.

If you recognize either one of these patterns, try to find something else.

The dictionary defines relationship as "emotional involvement, an emotional connection between people, connection by blood or marriage," etc. In contrast to relationship, the term "intimacy" is defined as "warm friendship, closeness, affection, familiar feeling, cozy, next to the skin, communion, contact with the innermost or essential nature…"

Which do you choose? Emotional involvement or communion of being? Relationship or intimacy? The quality of the experiences you arrange to have with the people closest to you in your life results from consciously or unconsciously choosing between relationship and intimacy. Ordinary human relationship gets in the way of intimacy.

The emotional involvement of ordinary human relationship may actually be a desire for one or more of the following:

- Having a good excuse to feel – even though it is "false ecstasy," at least low drama lets you feel something
- Feeling pain to confirm that you actually exist
- Finding a partner to engage in the "I'm okay"-"I'm not okay" intellectual debate
- Finding a partner for domination / submission or persecutor / victim games
- Seeking a hero with a white horse to come play the "rescue me" game
- Avoiding the reality of existential loneliness
- Satisfying your craving for what you believe to be emotional or financial security
- Feeding your addiction to the drug-like high of energetic enmeshment / entanglement / fusion / or co-dependency
- Finding a partner for intellectual combat, finding a Daddy or Mommy replacement
- Finding a surrogate baby
- Forging interdependency (meaning finding someone to take the blame for responsibilities)
- Establishing a guaranteed food supply for certain psychological-vampire structures in your Box.

Sooner or later you have to ask yourself this question: If the above list seems so repulsive, why does it perfectly describe most of our relationships?

Clearly seeing how deviously and profoundly your Box influences the quality of your relating can be shocking. If you have properly prepared yourself, the shock will start an internal wrestling match between two parts: the part in you that wants to keep things safely in the domain of ordinary human relationship and the part of you that wants to risk entering greater and greater intimacy. If you are lucky, the struggle between these two parts could keep you on guard for the rest of your life. Consider the idea that almost everything that happens in our relationship (cooking, washing, earning money, raising kids, owning a house, having a party, solving problems, doing your projects, going on vacation, even having sex), you can do all by yourself. Without creating a safe space for ongoing intimate sharing and being-with your partner, there isn't really any relationship.

It is painful to watch your Box repeatedly exchange the pristine sanctuary of intimacy for the emotional conundrum of superficiality. Nonetheless, you can fruitfully benefit from this pain. Follow the pain back to its source and you may uncover a turning point in your life: possibly the point where you decided that true intimacy was too frightening. The point at which, instead of risking intimacy, you decided for survival. You installed a block. Until you consciously change your original commitment to that block, it could still be doing its job.

Sooner or later you come to a point of consciously choosing between donning the straightjacket of your familiar blocks, and entering never-can-be-made-familiar intimacy. In Archetypal intimacy the other person is a complete unknown.

Prerequisites For Exploring Archetypal Intimacy

The Prerequisites for Archetypal Relationship (BLTLCH12.07). If you have the intention to enter Archetypal intimacy it is helpful to know that access requires a number of serious prerequisites:

1. The courage to take radical responsibility for your choices and actions rather than hiding behind traditional rules and commonly accepted customs
2. The courage to have your center in your body and to be just who you are rather than feigning to be someone other people can feel comfortable around
3. The courage to experience large amounts of raw fear
4. A lack of thinking about the past or future because intimacy only happens in the present
5. A shift from doing to being
6. Control of your attention so as not to be distractible
7. A vulnerable willingness to have no secrets
8. An almost violent refusal to carry even one resentment about your partner
9. An inexplicable trust while being exposed and completely seen
10. A profound innocence born of acceptance rather than out of naiveté
11. A capacity for deeply grieving about impermanence because you can neither protect or possess another person's being, no matter how precious it is to you
12. A capacity for enduring the intensity of ecstatic causeless joy
13. A willingness to undergo a perpetual longing to re-enter intimacy whenever it is not present (and sometimes even when it is present!).

Three Archetypal Experiments

Intimacy is never finally achieved. Moving toward greater intimacy involves stepwise experimentation. Here are a couple of places to begin.

Experiment #1:
Go Nonlinear and Go Cold Turkey

You are already quite familiar with relationship as produced by standard human intelligence thoughtware. Your next experiment in relationship is to "go nonlinear" from that domain. Going nonlinear means to try something completely different, something that is not already listed in the instruction manual for dealing with a certain set of conditions. Going nonlinear makes use of extraordinary human thoughtware.

Going Cold Turkey on Ordinary Human Relationship (BLTLCH12.08). Here is a suggestion for doing an experiment with ordinary human relationship from the perspective of

Archetypal Relationship: Give up trying to win. Several times a day, for as long as you can stand it, collect all of your habits of entanglement, control tactics, expectations, entwinements, strategic manipulations, resentments, techniques of seduction, victim stories, blaming, and so on. Place them all neatly in a little imaginary package. Tie the package closed. Lay the package on a back shelf in your mental closet. And do not go there! Game over. In the language of drug addiction, this exercise is referred to as "going cold turkey." *The experiment is to aim for complete and absolute abstinence from behaviors that create ordinary human relationship.* Until you do this experiment with ordinary human relationship you will not likely succeed with experiments in Archetypal intimacy.

Experiment #2: Recognize that the Woman Chooses

This is not a rule, but, if you think about what has happened in your life, and whatever you know about what has happened in the lives of others, you may find that you have already noticed that it is the woman who chooses the man, not the other way around.

Experiment #3: Constantly Detect Where You Are

In each of the three relationship domains you will have experiences, but the quality of the experiences will be detectably different.

- Ordinary human relationship tends to be experienced as defensive, mechanical, self-referenced, and riddled with irresponsible emotional reactions.
- Extraordinary human relationship tends to be experienced as consciously created, present time, other including, responsible feelings and actions.
- Archetypal Relationship tends to be experienced as exquisitely objective,

passionately intense, utterly neutral and highly conscious ecstatic sensations.

For example, there is ordinary human sex, extraordinary human sex, and Archetypal sex. If the sex includes the body, then it includes the gorilla. But the gorilla's body senses all three pleasures: unconscious irresponsible "pleasures," conscious responsible pleasures, and Archetypal pleasures. You can constantly detect where you are by the quality of your experience.

Unconscious irresponsible pleasures are extremely seductive. Distinguishing between unconscious and conscious pleasures requires consciousness, and the first thing that unconsciousness will claim is that it is conscious. But unconsciousness is not conscious. It is only well justified. In our overly developed intellectual body we consider justification to be consciousness! Such is the self-validating power of the Box! Unconscious irresponsible pleasures include innocuous behaviors – such as overeating pizza and ice cream (which is not even necessarily a pleasure because it can really hurt!). But unconscious irresponsible pleasures can also include the reciprocal feeding of psychological Gremlin entities through positionality, territoriality, competition, power struggles and low drama.

Constantly Detecting Where You Are (BLTLCH12.09). The way to detect where you are is to pay attention to the purpose of your actions.

- The purpose of ordinary human relationship is low drama, is making your life a playground for irresponsible Gremlin games.
- The purpose of extraordinary human relationship is adult responsibility, high drama, being present as yourself with your center and your attention in a minimized here and now to make your life a playground for fulfilling your destiny.
- The purpose of Archetypal Relationship is evolution and serving something greater

than yourself by being the space through which Archetypal Principles can recognize and be-with each other consciously.

Noticing the purpose of your actions helps you to figure out which domain you are enlivening.

Each domain – ordinary, extraordinary and Archetypal – functions according to its own particular laws of mechanics. In Archetypal domains the laws of animal and human no longer apply. This is not to suggest, for example, that animal behavior will not arise, because it will, and you will need to tell the unconscious animal parts of yourself to go sit in the corner and wait, until you are done with voyaging in the Archetypal, before they can come back and do their thing again. This is also not to say that rules, tools or procedures from one domain are better or worse than the rules, tools or procedures of other domains. Effectiveness in a new domain depends on you learning the mechanics of creating results in that domain. Consider how the tools for jewelry making are different from the set of tools for house building. Needle-nosed pliers and fine wax-shaping tools cannot accomplish the job of a cement mixer, circular saw and nail gun, and vice versa. Learning the new rules, tools and procedures can feel like starting over from zero, because whole libraries of knowledge may be absolutely irrelevant in the next domain. Your success will come through distinguishing which domain you are in, and shifting from gorilla male and gorilla female to human man and human woman to Archetypal Man and Archetypal Woman, and back again accordingly. Knowing *where you are* indicates what actions work best to get the desired results. In Japan you bow from the waist, take off your sandals, and eat with chopsticks. In New York you shake hands, leave your wing tips on, and eat with a steak knife. With a little practice, navigating domains becomes that obvious.

Create A Box Free Zone

In certain conditions you must choose between having your Box or having intimacy. You don't get to have both at the same time. The Box precludes intimacy because the Box will only let someone get as close to you as itself. If someone gets closer to you than your Box, they could glance over their shoulder and see with perfect clarity that your Box is only a Box. In that instant, your Box would become irrelevant to you, and the Box has a propensity for not allowing that to happen.

So you end up with an either or choice: Box or intimacy. To defend itself, the Box cleverly generates an endless stream of logical or emotional needs for motivating you to take action. But intimacy does not include action. The Box's desires suck you into action. You may experience almost irresistible urges to know, to control, to conquer, to dissect, to interact, to understand, to predict, to win, or to get the hell out of there. Intimacy is *being*. No matter what the Box says, *there is nothing to do in order to be*. If you take action, you lose the opportunity for intimacy and the Box wins.

Creating a Box Free Zone (BLTLCH12.10). Here is an experiment that helps to build a foundation for Archetypal Relationship. *Declare your home to be a "Box* *free zone."* In ordinary human relationship the home is the primary feeding ground for Gremlin. Gremlin views your partner as an all-you-can-eat low drama buffet, open 24 / 7. You could make a pact with your partner, both of you swearing on a stack of bibles never to allow Gremlin to again feed on the premises. Gremlin is fully capable of gulping down enough junk food to keep its belly full at work, with the neighbors, or while shopping. No Gremlin feeding in your home!

If your home is established as a Box free zone, then it is also an expectation free zone, a resentment free zone, an assumption free zone, a conclusion free zone, and a competition free zone. Your home becomes a sanctuary for the intimacy of not knowing, the intimacy of undefendedness, the intimacy of simple kindnesses, and the intimacy of Archetypal Love. Your home is no longer a known world.

To start this experiment the practice is very clear: When you come home, you check your Box at the door. Take off your Box and hand it to the closet like you would check your coat when entering the theater. No words come out of your mouth until your Box is safely stowed away. Plan to pick it up again on your way out the door, if you want to.

Some couples have the practice of taking their shoes off at the front door because shoes carry dirt from the outside world and are not needed in the clean soft sanctuary of their home. Take your Box off the same way. Enter your home naked, without plans, without needing anything, without shouting, "Honey! I'm home!" and thereby shattering the sanctuary space with the Box's childish desires for recognition and enmeshment. Enter your home as if you have no personal history, and no history with your partner. Enter not knowing what will happen, prepared to contribute whatever is wanted and needed.

If you enter your home environment leaving behind your Box, you will be able to appreciate the quality of things with unprecedented freshness. People will have possibilities that you never saw before. Simply breathing in the company of your partner will become like singing holy *Hallelujahs*.

After a taste of being in your home-sanctuary with your partner and without your Box, an intense series of questions could arise for you. Why would you ever want it different from this? Why would you ever let your Box eat your life? Why would you permit your Box to minimize and control such expansive and transcendental experiences? Why would you hesitate even for an instant to tell your Gremlin to "Sit" by your feet, and take care to feed him or her a controlled regular diet, elsewhere, anywhere else but at your home?

Sanctuary for Woman

When you, as the Archetypal Masculine, place your Box on the shoe shelf and hold a safe-enough space for your partner to set her Box aside, then the Archetypal Feminine may appear. When *she* is there, she is not to be analyzed with your cold logic or hit with masculine criticisms. She is not to be cross-examined for intellectual consistency or for meeting your mind's linear standards. She will not fit into those constraints. Stop your testing. The Archetypal Feminine comes from a place beyond testing, and if you fail to realize this you will not be able to meet her where she is.

If you begin experimenting with Archetypal Relationship and suddenly Archetypal Woman shows up, you have got to realize that this is really *her*. What stands before you is nothing that you already know about. This is *she*, the Feminine being, the fifth element, Venus, Aphrodite, Ishtar, the authentic Goddess. Wake up, man! Pay attention. Be most careful with your movements.

Do not do what you ordinarily do when you do not understand. She is so perceptive, so fragile, more delicate than snowflakes, lighter than feather down, fresher than a new-born baby, fluid as a mountain creek, direct as light. She will not tolerate cross-examination. Any thoughts that promote in you an attitude of testing, judging or criticizing are still coming from your Box. Go back to the front door and start again. Leave your Box at the door. What will work for you is experientially appreciating the richness of subtle details over long moments, standing in awe, and wakeful alertness with utter internal silence. Breathe. Wait with infinite patience and without expectation. Follow her lead while you hold space for her magnificence. Pay attention to her. Be-with her. Create a way for this to go on for a long time. This is sanctuary for Woman.

Sanctuary for Man

When you, as the Archetypal Feminine, come into your home and hang your Box in the closet along with your coat, sanctuary for your Man will start by making an internal vow: *no Gremlin feeding on my Man*. He is then off limits to your Gremlin. Express no complaints, no gossip, and do not treat him as a pawn on your chess board. This is your King, and *still* not a piece on your chessboard! When you relax in the understanding that the Archetypal Feminine is just as powerful (although with a different sort of power) as the Archetypal Masculine – regardless of the propaganda purveyed by the patriarchy – the power struggle between you two is over. You play two different games simultaneously on the same playing field, and can discover that the two games are perfectly complementary.

You have the capacity to create a sanctuary where your Man can stop defending himself. In your nurturing womanliness, his true Archetypal benevolence can appear. When *he* is there he is not to be controlled like a dog or manipulated like a marionette. He is not to be shredded with your Gatling gun of fault finding, nor filled up like a dumpster with the remains of your day. If you try any of these behaviors, he may resort to defending himself with aggression or disdain, and rightfully so. Stop behaving as if he disgusts you and then he will stop disgusting you. The Archetypal Masculine comes from a place beyond manipulation and control, and if you fail to realize this, you will not be able to meet him where he is.

If you experiment with Archetypal Relationship and suddenly Archetypal Man shows up, you have got to realize that this is really *him*. What stands before you is nothing that you already know about. This is *he*, the Masculine being, Tarzan, Achilles, Zorro, Zeus, Albert Schweitzer, George Gurdjieff, the authentic Man. Wake up, woman! Pay attention. Be most careful with your movements. Do not do what you ordinarily do when you do not understand or you will chase him away. This Man is so perceptive, so precise, that any deceptions flay his heart.

What will work for you is experientially appreciating the richness of subtle details over long moments, standing in awe, and wakeful alertness with utter internal silence. Breathe. Wait with infinite patience and without expectation. Follow his lead while you appreciate his magnificence. Pay attention to him. Be-with him. Create a way for this to go on for a long time. This creates sanctuary for Man.

SECTION 12-G

Serve Something Greater Than Yourself

Serving Bright Principles Through the Space of Your Relationship (BLTLCH12.11). We do not receive much training about what it could mean to serve something greater than ourselves. We have some idea about family honor, protecting our reputation, civic pride, or doing a good job for our team or our company. We can conceive of having patriotic duty toward our political party or our country. Or perhaps we are affiliated with one of the world's great religions and we feel enough affinity to promote some aspect of its customs or beliefs. But the concept of serving something greater than ourselves feels rather foreign to a Westerner, schooled in the values of independence, individuality and personal rights and freedoms. Being of service seems outside of our ordinary concerns.

Our entire Western culture is imbalanced toward the intellect. That is why our culture provides an abundance of education and a shortage of training. We are comfortable and skilled with making *content* distinctions in logic and reasoning because that is what schoolteachers demonstrated to us for the whole of our schooled lives. But, we had no role models who showed us how to make *context* distinctions so we could detect what space we were in and how to navigate our relationship from space to space according to what was needed and wanted for serving Archetypal Principles. We had no living alchemists, healers, medicine men, magicians, mystics, bards, shamans, yogis, gnostics, sorcerers, spiritual teachers, wise elders, or wizards in our village or family to imitate or apprentice to. Such characters are addressed by modern culture with the same negative connotations as silly fairy tales, dangerous brainwashing sects or new-age esoteric nonsense. If you have a deep attraction for gaining competence in the domains of making context distinctions as a vocation, you are left wandering on your own. No culturally-sponsored training can supply you with the kind of clarity and experience food needed to fulfill such a destiny. To proceed you must courageously follow your gut-level intuition to find an authentic source of training, which will invariably come from a context greater than that of standard Western culture.

Throughout these pages I use terminology such as Principles, Archetypal Principles, Bright Principles, Shadow Principles, destiny, true purpose, hidden purpose, and deep Masculine or Feminine Archetypes. These expressions are defined in the appended *Glossary of Possibility Management Terms* and pepper the rest of the book. Please bear with me. Even though including jargon is cumbersome and expensive in the added effort it takes you to get through a paragraph, being able to linguistically distinguish between specific energetic experiences gives you reference points when creating and exploring vaster dimensions of relationship.

The visible result of reading this book appears the moment you integrate new thought-maps into your Box to the depth that they generate new actions. Certain new actions produce a remarkable difference. If you start:

- Making a gap between you and your Box
- Identifying and sidestepping behaviors that previously locked you into ordinary human relationship

- Taking control of your attention and conserving enough energy to stop letting your Gremlin get away with thrashing your loved ones in low drama feeding frenzies
- Listening as a space to your partner, your children and your friends
- Making contact and improving your ability to be-with, and so on.

These actions alone will provide you with extraordinary human relationship. If these behaviors take years to develop, then those years are well spent. And if you keep making further contextual distinctions and keep experimenting with new actions, an entirely different and attainable relationship universe beyond the extraordinary could open up for you. You may enter Archetypal Relationship where you, and possibly also your relationship, become a space through which the Archetypal Bright Principles of your destiny can do their work in the world.

The perspectives and ways of being that accompany serving something greater are already known to us. We naturally have a deep instinctual resonance for the simple mechanics of Archetypal Principles intersecting with our life. We know it, without it being a conscious recognition. For example, a popular quote of George Bernard Shaw's, from his play *Man and Superman* written in 1903 states:

This is the true joy in life, the being used for a purpose recognized by yourself as a mighty one; the being thoroughly worn out before you are thrown on the scrap heap; the being a force of Nature instead of a feverish selfish little clod of ailments and grievances complaining that the world will not devote itself to making you happy.

Shaw is talking about (if I can be so presumptuous as to interpret the words of a Nobel Prize *and* Academy Award winning genius) the option of engaging life as a force of nature through functionally representing Archetypal Bright Principles rather than engaging life as a self-serving Box continually generating low dramas. He is talking about choosing to be put to more conscious purposes than Gremlin would ordinarily put you to. He says that living well comes less from catering to your insecurities, and more from serving so far beyond your comfort zone that every imaginable resource is wrung out of you. He claims that true joy is the background canvas upon which other experiences of life are painted, and that true joy can be your direct experience.

Not personally experiencing the joyous nature of the canvas is not the canvas' fault. If you dig down through a few layers of the paint so skillfully applied by your meaning-making machinery, no matter what the stories of your life have been, you will find the canvas of joy back there, holding your whole scene together, even the horrible parts. Even now, in this moment of reading, that background canvas of true joy can be felt. Even if only for a moment, you can sense true joy like a delicate flash of warmth in your heart. This may be happening regularly during your day or night – a flash of true joy. A slight smile flickers across your lips. A doorway into a vaster world opens up just for an instant. Through that door you can glimpse all of life arising out of an endless field of Love. Experiencing the immensity of that Love is joyous, and you can personally discover that radiant joy and brilliant Love are there. Whether or not you keep your foot in that door, keep that smile on your lips, or keep that warm flash in your heart, does not matter. The door is there. One momentary experience is all it takes to know that the joy is back there behind everything, and then it is too late to deny it any longer. You felt it. You then know what Archetypal Love is about. The canvas of joy is back there

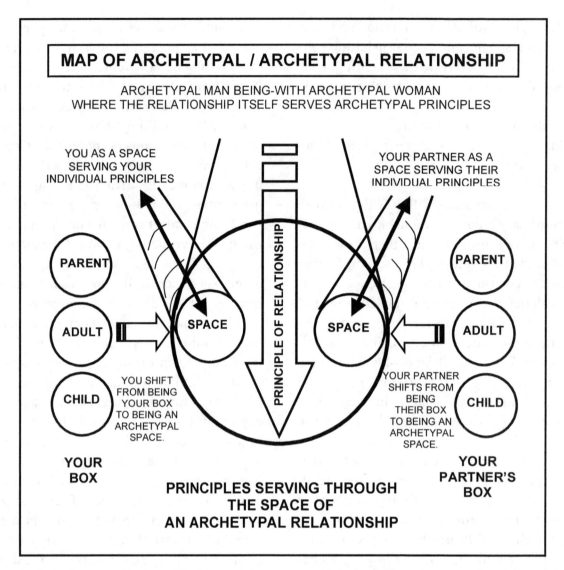

MAP OF ARCHETYPAL / ARCHETYPAL RELATIONSHIP

ARCHETYPAL MAN BEING-WITH ARCHETYPAL WOMAN
WHERE THE RELATIONSHIP ITSELF SERVES ARCHETYPAL PRINCIPLES

YOU AS A SPACE
SERVING YOUR
INDIVIDUAL PRINCIPLES

YOUR PARTNER AS A
SPACE SERVING THEIR
INDIVIDUAL PRINCIPLES

PARENT

PARENT

PRINCIPLE OF RELATIONSHIP

ADULT

SPACE

SPACE

ADULT

CHILD

YOU SHIFT
FROM BEING
YOUR BOX
TO BEING AN
ARCHETYPAL
SPACE.

YOUR PARTNER
SHIFTS FROM
BEING
THEIR BOX
TO BEING AN
ARCHETYPAL
SPACE.

CHILD

YOUR
BOX

YOUR
PARTNER'S
BOX

**PRINCIPLES SERVING THROUGH
THE SPACE OF
AN ARCHETYPAL RELATIONSHIP**

behind all the layers of paint. Working at the Archetypal level of the original canvas was for Bernard Shaw the true joy of life.

The urge to dig through layers of life stories that you have painted on the background canvas of joy is the same as the urge for simplicity. If you follow the urge toward greater simplicity you will be functionally realigning to the Bright Principles that you entered life to serve. You probably do not get to choose what section of paint to scrape away, or when, or exactly how. But, by submitting yourself to the service of recognizable mighty purposes, the purposes themselves could well have need of you to clean up a little more canvas so as to do a better job for them. This is what it means to "be used."

Being a force of nature through serving a mighty purpose is not a bad way to go. People may describe their experience of being used by a greater purpose in various ways. It can be that thoughts break free of their adherence to rigid frameworks. Speech blends tempo, pitch, tone, vocabulary and phrasings like oil paints into brilliant new colors. Perceptions broaden and reach into expanded domains to tap resources of clarity and novelty never imagined before. Problems shrink into linear steppingstones for getting from here to there. Consciousness becomes palpable, steerable, and formable into the substances, textures or shapes needed to pierce barriers, slip through confusions, or leap over chasms. Unnamed faculties provide exacting information or test for possible options, creating whatever is needed whenever it is not found. Play expands to encompass questions, gestures, or combinations of factors previously labeled as "dangerous," "taboo," or "invisible." Unsuspected talents arise fully formed to sensibly apply what gets created in the wonderful worlds that infinitely continue to unfold. And elegant ways to interact and make use of resources from the new territories are found in the new territories themselves.

After a few tastes of this sort of relationship experience, the disciplines needed for maintaining your relationship as a sacred-space vehicle for making exquisite journeys become more important than the pain of developing the disciplines. Once you know the value of what you are paying for, you are quite willing to sacrifice the Box's ordinary treasures, such as security or control, in order to endure Archetypal intensities of longing in the presence of your partner. In so doing, you may come to recognize the abundance of blessings that come from relationship created in the name of Bright Principles, and you may discover a natural wish to reflect gratitude back to the Bright Principles. Your relationship becomes a component in a reciprocal exchange: receive blessings from the Principles, send recognition and appreciation back to the Principles. Through being part of something greater than yourself, it becomes more and more clear why such a circumstance is called Archetypal Relationship.

))(The Archetypal Chamber

Archetypal Relationship starts when you *commit* to Archetypal Relationship even before you know much of anything about Archetypal Relationship. Committing *first* creates a force field of necessity that directs coincidences toward unfolding your abilities to take whatever steps are necessary to proceed. Committing first is a fabulous secret to success. Your Box may demand guarantees and explanations and may hesitate or be offended if you do not provide them. But, if you give your Box's requests for your attention a higher priority than holding space for Archetypal Relationship, you will never gain enough momentum to leave the linear worlds. Archetypal Relationship especially is ongoing *nonlinear* creation. It is certainly nonlinear to commit before you know how to proceed.

Cleansing Your Relationship Chamber (BLTLCH12.12). Begin with the commitment to cleanse your energetic relationship-space. Imagine a 1 foot wide and 1½-foot tall arch-roofed "temple" floating just in front of your body. This is the sanctuary for the energetic interactions between you and your mate. Before this sanctuary can be fully occupied by you and your present partner, it may be helpful to cleanse and purify it of energetic remnants from all your past relationships. For example, if your temple is 65-percent filled with attentions and memorabilia coming from or directed toward other past, present or future relationships, then you will only attract a partner willing to commit a maximum of 35 percent of their energy and attention to their relationship with you. The rest of their energy and attention for relationship will go toward other people, as yours does. If you like it that way, fine. Leave things the way they are.

But if you are interested in a higher percentage commitment from your partner, you have some work to do. No one but you can clean out and prepare an attractive and welcoming space for your partner to commit 100 percent in their relationship with you.

Cleansing the relationship temple is a practical and straightforward procedure that involves, for example, going through everything that you possess and getting rid of anything that holds energetic residue. Items commonly disposed of may include photographs of previous lovers, mementos from travels together, souvenirs, letters, postcards, books, CDs, DVDs, gifts, jewelry, furniture, clothing, artwork, kitchen equipment, cars, properties, magazine subscriptions, bank accounts, credit cards, and so on. Cleansing the energetic space from future relationships may include eliminating fantasies about movie stars, posters of rock singers, Internet sex sessions, pornographic magazines, or daydreams of being a character in a romance novel or soap opera. Such cleansing work takes persistent, conscientious effort over a period of time. I once knew a couple who made a pact with each other to be perfectly faithful *unless* Brad Pitt or Halle Berry came along and personally asked them for a date. Needless to say, the couple is no longer together, without either Brad or Halle having come by. Your particular escape route from commitment may differ from this example, but an open back door is an open back door.

Each cleansing action closes one more back door and therefore helps you to preserve more and more of your own energy. You are thus disengaging yourself from other people's attentions, and reclaiming your own attention that was previously entangled in other people's affairs. It makes sense to get your own energy back. Then you can use it for doing the experiments that you want to do in the relationship laboratory that you have created for yourself now. It is respectful to extricate yourself from other people's energy and send it back to them, so they can use it for doing their own experiments. Cleaning up your energetic entanglements might also be compared to a chemist cleaning up his or her lab equipment before starting an experiment. Without first cleaning beakers and flasks, there is no telling what kind of contaminated mess may be mixed together.

Successfully tracking your attention, and conserving your energy, effectively closes the back door and seals the chamber of your relationship. Once you seal the chamber, the heat naturally generated by Archetypal Love will begin to intensify. Your chamber of Archetypal Relationship grows hotter and hotter, gradually burning away anything that is not eternal.

SECTION 12-I

How To Be Turned On

Both men and women have the capacity to be irresistible. Not in a neurotic sexual way, not with a false mask, not by feigning irresistibility, not through pretending. You know what I am talking about. Deep within, you have a natural dignity, a mysterious nobility, and a fabulous being that makes you irresistibly attractive. It is your innocent excitement about being alive. And, you do not show it. You hide your natural attractiveness away. You block that luscious energy from running through your body.

If you are like most of us, you put your authentic irresistibility away long ago to protect yourself from being devoured by human wolves. When you first started being irresistible, there was too much power to deal with, no guidance for what to do with it, and plenty of hungry predators. You shut it down and buried it away for your own safety.

Bringing your irresistibility back to life in modern times is complicated by the nearly overwhelming impact of media. Modern advertising fabricates and markets false irresistibility to increase the sales of products. Our daily dose of seductive and tantalizing images in association with alcohol, cigarettes, automobiles and clothing is abusive to our senses and demonstrates that the purpose of irresistibility is to manipulate and deceive. The opposite is true. Irresistibility is simply our natural vitality. Disentangling ourselves from the experiential spiderweb of modern mass marketing, so that we can reclaim a sense of wonder and the true thrill of being in the presence of our partner, may also involve some disillusionment.

A friend of mine got to sit backstage in a photo-shoot for a line of clothing. He had seen a catalog of female models and was attracted to their voluptuous femininity revealed in the photographs. He wanted to meet these women that he had so longingly gazed upon in the pages of the catalog.

So, he used a fake press-pass to get in the door. One after the other, he watched rather ordinary (albeit skinny) women receive professional makeup and elegant clothing, but nothing seemed to change. They were still smoking cigarettes and gossiping loudly with one another, making power struggles, competing for territoriality and attention. Then, the moment it was their turn to pose in front of the camera, they would shift into a totally different character. As if by magic the catalog goddesses appeared in their full irresistibility! They could hold their poses for about as long as they could hold their breath. Then just as suddenly, blink once, and they were gone. They dropped back into their ordinary world of fiddling with their fingernails, being insecure and self-deprecating. My friend came away from the experience destroyed. He concluded that the catalog images he had fallen in love with were temporary fantasy whip-ups using modern photographic techniques and the imagination of the layout artists.

But my friend overlooked one thing. He overlooked the fact that the irresistibility was real. It was temporary for sure, but it was very real. Every human being has direct access to being irresistible.

Finding Your Access to Natural Irresistibility (BLTLCH12.13). Here is an experiment for you to do: Find your access to natural irresistibility. Find out why you turned it off. Find out how to turn the organic internal switch back on again. Practice tolerating the intensity of the experience of being irresistible. Then, see what you say and do with your partner when you let your irresistibility move you. And, see what happens for your partner.

What does a Man really need to know about turning on a Goddess? What does a Woman really need to know about allowing herself to be the Goddess she is? What can he do that will make her so passionate about being-with him that she spits and sizzles? What can she do that will encourage him to be the true King she knows he actually is? How can her love for him and his love for her be so electric that they glow in the dark? What is the gameplan?

The gameplan is a paradox. Archetypal Woman is turned on when Archetypal Man is turned on – first about his life so that his soul is fed, and second about her so that his heart is fed. A radiant Goddess reflects off of a blazing Man.

"Deep in his heart, every man longs for a battle to fight, an adventure to live, and a beauty to rescue," says John Eldredge on the cover

Notes On Power

- Women already have power.
- Women create human beings.
- Women's minds are naturally nonlinear and multidimensional.
- Women ARE the power behind the throne.
- Still a woman needs a man to sit on the throne or half of the energetics are missing and she cannot be the doorway for Archetypal Woman.
- Men have no power.
- Men have aggression.
- There is a world of difference between aggression and power.
- Men have no power until they leave behind aggression and learn about power.
- Aggressive is the immature man.
- Powerful is the mature man.
- A man starts having power when he starts over from the beginning again, and chooses life instead of survival. Living is a completely different game than merely struggling for survival.
- Power is engaged with the body,
- Not the mind.
- Power comes from clarity of mind, open heart, and a willingness to be accountable.
- Power manifests as responsibility, responsible speaking, responsible acting.
- When a woman or man taps into and unleashes Archetypal power they start taking the world apart and putting it back together again any way they want it.
- This much power is scary as hell.
- Creative power only happens at the level of Radical Responsibility.
- Radical Responsibility is more fun than fun.
- We are limited only by our own tendencies, habits of perception, thought and speech. We are only limited by our self-design. We are here to evolve, to redesign our design.
- To enter the game of building Love that lasts we navigate to a special kind of space.
- This is the Archetypal Relationship space, the Space of Possibility.
- This space sustains neither beliefs nor assumptions, the opposite of a cult.
- A cult seeks to induce you to believe, to join, to stay.
- Archetypal Relationship does not expect that you will stay for the next instant.
- Archetypal Relationship tries to make you go away and do other things until you have no choice but to take Radical Responsibility and become the source of Archetypal Love.
- A cult tries to get you to go to sleep, to give your power away and to be somebody they prescribe, a consumer.
- Archetypal Relationship demands that you find ways to stay awake, step into Power, and become more and more yourself, a responsible creator.

- As Archetypal Man or Woman you gain direct immediate access to almost unlimited Power.
- None of that Power is yours.
- You can only use that Power to serve the needs of the space of Archetypal Love.
- You will feel many things.
- You are invited to trust yourself and others at an unconventional level.
- "Do-overs" are allowed.

flap of his book *Wild At Heart*. The fight is the noble fight between a man and his Gremlin, the internal yes or no to the discipline it takes to stand for his true life-project. A man comes alive as he makes a fierce commitment to the success of his work in the face of all odds. The adventure in this work results from the man being put to the test and not knowing if he will make it or not, but having a heart wild enough to keep trying. And the beauty is what unfolds in a woman when she feels a man trying his best in her name. When a man sees his woman turn beautiful because she sees him as her valiant hero, that man can suddenly do miracles, and doing miracles is a turn-on.

When the man is fiercely *turned on* about his life, he guards his attention so his energy is not wasted. When the man is fiercely *turned on* about his woman, he guards his moments of intimacy with her as if he were sitting in the presence of God. This man wakes up *turned on*. He walks to the toilet *turned on*. He eats his breakfast *turned on*. He brushes his teeth *turned on*. And when he puts his attention on his woman, she gets it.

The woman wants to be fought for. She wants to be special to her man. She wants to be wanted as top priority. The woman wants to be rescued from normality and taken on the adventure of her life. She wants to be part of the adventure, not standing around on the sidelines cheering. She wants to be in the thick of it, up to her armpits in alligators, but not being the leader. She wants to be included and brought into places that take her breath away. She wants to see impossible promises kept. She wants to see loving communications with children, bad guys transformed, and mothers protected. She wants deep spiritual questions met with clarity and compassion, in ways that help other people lead better lives. She wants to sense profound spaces that startle her with their vastness. She wants to be caught up in something greater than herself that is sourced by her man.

There need be no end to the dance between the masculine and the feminine through which the Archetypes live. Even the most mundane of activities can reflect the Archetypal. No moments need be wasted. No opportunity lost. Even when all that occurs around you begs for an ordinary-human-relationship response, nothing says that you have to comply. You can sustain your independent authority about how to make use of this moment. In truth, the consequences of you choosing Archetypal Relationship will only be that the Archetypes live.

There are endless opportunities to practice giving and receiving attention in daily life. The more you pay attention so as to submit the space of your relationship to be used by the Archetypal, the more you will be used. To paraphrase Bernard Shaw's words, the greatest joy in life is your relationship being thoroughly worn out before it is thrown on the scrap heap, and before you and your partner are moved on to your next experiments.

Bright Principles and Archetypal Love

Hosting an Archetypal Chamber (BLTLCH12.14). Archetypal Relationship differs from both ordinary and extraordinary human relationship in the way it relates to Bright Principles. Archetypal Relationship has an open interface for a direct, real-time exchange between human consciousness and the Bright Principles. Such exchange is permanently offered by Bright Principles, but in ordinary human relationship our self-aware human consciousness is completely blotted out by the defense-oriented motivations of our Box.

In extraordinary human relationship, the adult human being takes more than ordinary responsibility, but not the radical responsibility required by Archetypal Relationship. In extraordinary human relationship, responsible high drama is happening, but not *Archetypal* drama. The responsible adult is maturely taking care of themselves, but is not holding the space for directly serving Bright Principles.

In Archetypal Relationship, the exchange between Bright Principles and self-aware human consciousness is not blocked, censored, or manipulated by the Box. This is because a relationship with Gremlin has been established – he sits at your feet cared for and attentive until you direct him to take action in a way that serves. In Archetypal Relationship, the Bright Principles can become conscious of themselves through one person experiencing themselves being a Bright Principle, in action, and appreciating the manifestation of the same Bright Principle in the other person. For example, the overriding Bright Principle of Archetypal Love becomes conscious of itself through meeting and appreciating itself in the other person, who is also conscious of being Archetypal Love. Self-awareness is a gift from human beings to the Bright Principles – which cannot obtain such awareness any other way except through the efforts of warm-blooded human beings in conscious Archetypal Relationship.

Just as Archetypal Relationship needs Bright Principles in order to live, Bright Principles also need Archetypal Relationship in order to live. Each needs the other to succeed so that it too can succeed. Archetypal Relationship and Bright Principles are interdependent. The model for the interdependence between Bright Principles and Archetypal Relationship is the alchemical aphorism, "As above, so below. As below, so above." Neither the physical nor the unmanifest is superior or inferior. Above and below exchange with each other through a third, usually invisible, element in the equation – the medium of space, which simultaneously separates and connects the other two elements. Without the third element of space, the first two elements could not exchange. Human beings provide this rare and precious service of consciously holding space, through which the exchange can occur.

When the exchange occurs through the space of Archetypal Relationship, the Bright Principles supply food for Archetypal Relationship and Archetypal Relationship supplies food for Bright Principles. The food that Bright Principles provide to Archetypal Relationship is the quality of Bright Principles represented by the specific Bright Principle itself. For example, the Bright Principle of clarity supplies the food of clarity to the

Archetypal Relationship. The Bright Principle of kindness supplies the food of kindness. The Bright Principle of possibility supplies the food of possibility, and so on. The food that Archetypal Relationship provides to Bright Principles is conscious attention placed on the Bright Principles. The attention on the Bright Principles is the conductor through which flow three forms of energy to the Bright Principles: the energy of conscious recognition of the Bright Principles, the energy of appreciation of the Bright Principles, and the energy of faith in the Bright Principles.

The reciprocal feeding of Archetypal Relationship and Bright Principles through the exchange of foods makes this an ecosystem. Like all ecosystems, the relationships among members are alive and in constant flux, attempting to include all elements, while maintaining an equilibrium that is stable enough to sustain the life of the members. This complex and unpredictable dynamism forces every Archetypal Relationship chamber to be experimental. Whether the chamber is formal, such as in a prepared bedroom, a dining or poetry reading experience, or informal, such as waiting in line at the cinema together, the outcome of the interaction is always unknown. Actions and the purpose of actions that occur in the Archetypal Relationship chamber are continuously changing and developing through being an integral part of a larger ecosystem. The chamber ebbs and flows with energetic tides, and throbs with the beating of Archetypal lifeblood. And you thought you were just having a night out together!

Try to remember that Archetypal Relationship is far more involved with Archetypal necessities than with human, personal or individual necessities.

SECTION 12-K
Impersonal and Nonlinear Evolution

It is particularly useful to remember that Archetypal Relationship is not much concerned with human necessities if for some reason your Archetypal Relationship seems to be changing radically, or looks like it may come to an end. The circumstances of the beginning, the changing, or the ending of Archetypal Relationship could have little or nothing to do with the people involved and could have everything to do with the experiments that could or could not be continued. The changing status of an Archetypal Relationship may be completely a result of the cosmic dance of "Divine Evolution," requiring specific and immediate changes in possible experiments. It may have nothing to do with you personally.

If you assumed that you were the one who caused your Archetypal Relationship to begin, then if your Archetypal Relationship radically alters or ends you might also assume that it ended because of you. Both of these assumptions could be false. If Archetypal Relationship exists through being of service to what Lee Lozowick calls "the Great Process of Divine Evolution," then the ending of Archetypal Relationship could have nothing to do with you at all. Evolution might simply require that you, your partner, or both of you, be experimenting under different circumstances.

Nonlinear changes are happening all the time. Perhaps, over the years, you have noticed inexplicably sudden changes in your business career, your place of residence, your friendships, your financial condition, or your health; situations where it seemed like you were picked up out of one circumstance by the scruff of your neck and unceremoniously dropped into completely different circumstances. This change was nothing that you decided on, and would have been nearly impossible to arrange through linear efforts. But since it actually happened, you had to accept it. Could it be that evolution simply had need of you elsewhere so as to maximize the benefit to evolution? Unfortunately, determining the evolutionary value of sudden changes only happens in retrospect. We cannot connect the dots until we look backward from some point in the future. All we can do is develop enough flexibility, so that when the next changes flip us into new conditions we can land on our feet, instantly reorient ourselves, and participate with our full level of contribution.

⋈ Doing the Homework

Most of us reading this book have not yet been experimenting with Archetypal Relationship. We're either deeply absorbed in culturally-encouraged ordinary human relationships, or just getting our toes wet with extraordinary human relationship. Issues around ending a relationship, for us, will not usually involve Archetypal considerations, like the ones mentioned in the previous section. (You can also read more about what to do when a relationship doesn't work in Chapter 19.)

For most of us, a non-Archetypal set of considerations applies, raising a different set of questions. In the ordinary, and even in the extraordinary, domain we may spend long periods of time agonizing over questions like: Should I or should I not stay in this relationship? Why does it have to be so difficult? I have already put up with so much; when do I get the reward? Maybe this is the point of no return? How can I be sure it will turn out differently next time? Is there no hope? Where is all the love and joy and happiness that should be in a relationship? When does the breakthrough happen? Where is marital bliss? Where is ecstatic sex? Or forget sex; where is simple kindness and respect? Where is talking civilly to each other over the breakfast table instead of bickering about who is right about what happened yesterday on TV? Why has intimacy been replaced by gossip or shouting at the kids? Why do I feel like I am walking into a meat grinder? Why is it so predictable and dead? Why does it feel like being in a prison for crazy people? Why doesn't she really love me? Why doesn't he change, even a little bit? Is this all there is? Am I just a slave here? Am I just sticking around for the sake of the children? Why doesn't she understand what I say? Why doesn't he talk to me? Why do I feel so, so lonely? Why does it feel like there is no real connection between us? Am I doomed to endlessly relive what my parents did?

Doing Your Homework (BLTLCH12.15). If any of these questions are in the forefront for you, then *stop reading here*, go back to Chapter 2, *Ordinary Relationship / Ordinary Love* and start reading it over again. Seriously. You have *not* done your homework. It is *not* time for you to read the rest of this book because *you are not yet doing what you could do* to make use of the opportunity you have in your present relationship laboratory. After you have taken more risks to keep your center, to express your feelings, to make boundaries and ask for what you need, to listen with completion loops, only then has the real test been done. Before that, you are complaining that the airplane does not fly, without ever having given it full throttle and pointing it down the runway into the wind.

What have you got to lose anyway?

This is *not* a rhetorical question. If you think the relationship is already on the rocks, what is the problem with taking outrageous risks that might crash it completely on the rocks but also have the possibility of taking it to an entirely new level of intimacy? Take your time to consider this question for yourself.

Without having done your homework to shift from ordinary to extraordinary human relationship, the rest of this book won't make much sense. Or, if you are moved to, read the next chapter, *The Underworld*, and then see how it goes.

Make the Leap

Getting Off Your Ass and Doing Things Differently (BLTLCH12.16). Internalizing new relationship ideas from a book, to the point where they accumulate enough presence to change your behavior, takes time. But waiting around for the right time can easily become a Box technique for procrastinating change. The key element to you changing your behavior is you getting off your ass and doing things differently. You will never have anything different than what you have right now if you keep doing things the way you are doing them right now – no matter how *right* you think you are

about what you are doing. Nothing is going to change for you until you get it that *you are the one who is right now making it exactly the way it is for you.* It is *you*, not them ... not the other person. It is you. This is horrible news because it means that the shit you are feeling is the shit you have rubbed into your own heart. This is wonderful news because if you put the shit in your own heart then you can wash it out again.

Whether you know it or not, there is no hope. The Box will make no effort to change until you grab it by the nose, yank it around to face in a completely new direction, kick its ass and shout with rage until it moves. This is your life, not your Box's life. The moments are ticking by. It is 11:59 P.M. Do you know where your center is? Do you know where your attention is? Do you know where your boundary is? Do you know how big your *now* is? Do you know what your story is? Do you know what your feeling is? Do you know if it is a feeling or an emotion? Do you know what kind of listening you are using? Do you know which roadblock that is? Do you know what your purpose is? Do you know where your Gremlin is? (If you do not know where your Gremlin is, then guess who is driving...)

I cannot tell you how many times people have sat before my teacher asking for his help in their relationships, acting all innocent and righteous, thinking that he can finally straighten their partner out, when all along it is *they* who are sneakily avoiding responsibility. Me included.

Our suffering about relationship comes from institutionalized confusion. Most relationship stories that our culture offers to us end with, "...and they got married and lived happily ever after." Meaning that, our culture does not have the knowledge for sustaining longterm committed relationships in which individuals joyously thrive and evolve. This leaves it up to you to figure it out for yourself. Welcome to your underworld.

CHAPTER 13

The Underworld

Somehow, you must satisfactorily deal with any connotative reaction that arises from the title of this chapter, *The Underworld*. This book does not intend to investigate the pros and cons of popular psycho-ideologies. Yet it could easily be that a phrase such as "underworld" encroaches on the territory of an unconscious myth that is currently influencing you. The myth would equate the word "underworld" with "negative," "evil," "dangerous" or "bad." If so, the connotations will automatically block you from acquiring new possibilities in Archetypal Relationship. What can you do? Recognizing a myth, consciously, *as a myth,* creates freedom from the unconscious grip of the myth. After the recognition, if you have an emotional reaction to the term "underworld," for example, and you have clarity that your emotional reaction is only the self-defense mechanism of a myth that you already disinherited, then you can let the reaction happen safely, all by itself, and keep exploring. We need to study the mechanics of mythology in greater depth here, before venturing into the underworld.

SECTION 13-A
The Power of Myth

Questioning Your Myths (BLTLCH13.01). Western civilization lives within a mythology that for the most part has not yet been recognized as a mythology. When a myth is not recognized as a myth, it is still considered to be the factual truth. Debunking Western mythology is not the purpose of this book. The purpose of this book is to provide you with the possibility of expanding your relationship skills. The difficulty right now is that further expansion of your relationship skills conflicts with a predominantly held Western myth that you may still be holding as the truth.

Check to see if you have this myth somewhere deep in your system: "We live our lives and then die, and then, according to a judgment about what we did during our lives, we are sentenced to spend the rest of eternity in either heaven or hell."

I am not asking you if you adjust your daily actions in fear of the consequences defined in this myth. Simply to look back in the dusty fringes of your mind to see if the myth is there, and is perhaps patching over a gap in the scenery where there are not enough facts to give you a different picture. Is this myth still functional for you? Or, have you somehow adopted a different story, and integrated it at a deep enough level to supplant this imagery?

We may try as adults to exchange the Occidental "die and go to hell" myth for some Taoist or Buddhist perspective, or with something like the Native American mantra, "It is a good day to die." But such philosophies do not usually land close enough to our core to replace views installed during childhood. The *mind* might grasp the new concepts, but our deep *soul* is still convicted of the original story: Down *there*, lording over the underworld, is some bad-ass devil guy gleefully rubbing his hands together and waiting for us to make some *sinful* little mistake so he can have our soul *forever*.

I am not asking you to do anything right now about what you see or find. I am only asking you to glance around "in there." (Nobody is going to make fun of you.) I am inviting you to see what you are using to cover over the nagging question, "What happens when I die?" What myth do you use to address this question?

I say "myth" because we don't know what happens after death. We all have the question, yet nobody *knows*. Any answer we fabricate to cover over a gap in our knowing is a myth. It just so happens that the "hellfire and brimstone" myth is prominent in our Christianized culture. Just look to see if you have it. I have it. It seems to come packaged right along with Christmas and Santa Claus. Even if you removed the myth covering the "What happens when I die?" question, so that you now live with the unanswered question as a gaping hole in the wall of certainty, you still have the old myth lying around in storage. Even in storage the myth can react.

Keep a part of your attention back there – on how the myth responds – while we slowly enter this next conversation. We are beginning, gently here, because confronting core beliefs and underlying myths is a delicate endeavor. The subject is so inflammable because we have made it a matter of belief, and not necessarily something backed by our own authority. We tend to grant abnormal powers to those individuals or institutions who claim to have authority in the religious or spiritual domains, authorities who purport to tell us the truth about our soul. If those authorities define a certain worldview and we start questioning the official view, we fear that we may be putting our soul at risk. Questioning religious authority can also put our life at risk, if we care to recall our cellular memories of what was commonly done to witches, heretics, unbelievers and blasphemers. The dire threats protecting institutionalized authority lie just behind our culture's thinner-than-you-may-want-to-think veil of civilized behavior.

Taking Authority for Your Own Soul

Archetypal Relationship demands nothing less than you taking back authority for your own soul. Otherwise, how can you do

Archetypal experiments? Stepping beyond your Box's mythology to take back authority for your own soul requires a high level of intelligent courage.

The Box asserts that your myths are more important than reality. Consider how many people have arranged to die in the name of mythologies promoted by religious or political causes. The Box has the power to modify your perceptions and your feelings so that what you see and feel matches what your myth says you *should* see and feel. Consider the intensity of the reaction that you have when someone eats with their elbows on the table or chews with their mouth open. These eating behaviors only contradict your myths about how to be polite. How much deeper and more serious will be your reaction if something offends your myths about how to preserve your soul?

The Box's "self-fogging" and "scenic augmentation" mechanisms are controlled by the specifics of your myths. Using any myth empowers the Box to block you from recognizing a wide variety of options forbidden by the myth, before you even know that your perceptions are being blocked. If you do not know when your Box blocks you from seeing something, that thing becomes invisible to you, even if it is standing right in front of your nose and other people around you can see it with perfect clarity.

For example, if your Box has the myth that the amount of money in your bank account is related to your personal well-being, then, if you receive a low bank balance statement, you might feel unhappy, forgetting that money is an intellectual fiction sustained by our culture – with little or no true impact on how well you live. Or if your Box has the myth that getting good grades in school is important, and your child brings home bad grades for the third time in a row, you might punish your child in some way, forgetting completely that the child is a young human being looking to his or her parents for guidance and modeling about how wonderful it is to learn. *Navigating your way through Archetypal domains can be quite awkward if your myths keep making things invisible for you.*

Over sixteen centuries ago, Western religious authority implemented a brilliant strategy for consolidating its power and property through proselytizing a simplified, polarized, good / bad mythology. The resulting church then justified its authority through the myth that the church alone was aligned with the "good." Anyone who had "fallen from the right faith" or "erred from the truth" was "evil." The clincher in this strategy and the force that spread this myth so far and wide was the addendum giving the church authority to punish any evil person who did not accept their myth! In retrospect, you can see how such a protected gameworld (*see* Glossary) would create an ideal playground, in which Gremlins could use religious bureaucracies for its own nefarious purposes hidden under the auspices of the good.

It is interesting to examine what symbols the church chose to build the brand of "evil." Before the church came into power, a number of deities received the people's adoration and attention. How could the church disempower the pagan gods? By transforming them into the epitome of evil! A mythological character was developed and named Satan, the devil. As the personification of evil, his image, even his name, would send shudders of fear down your spine. The church gave him hooves and horns that were stolen from Pan; his three-pronged pitchfork was stolen from Shiva, Poseidon and Neptune. And hell, the devil's home, was none other than the renamed Archetypal underworld. In the church's marketing strategy, the long-respected Archetypal underworld was transformed from a neutral map of "what is happening right now" into a terrible place located "down there." No longer were underworld resources of power, clarity, wisdom and transformation available to the common man or woman. In the church's redesign, the underworld became hell – the place where bad people are sent for eternal punishment, after they die, if they have not given their authority to the dominant religious organization. If you have ever used phrases like, "scary as hell!" or "hot as hell!" then you have bought the myth and are still using it.

Questioning a Myth

When precise inquiry approaches the central beliefs of a myth that you have long ago pasted over holes in you worldview left by unanswerable questions, you might start experiencing a queasy feeling in your stomach. Your unconscious fear of disrupting a myth can produce sudden unexpected feelings, like anger that attacks the invader, or fear that cuts off contact with them. At this point, for example, you could easily put this book down and let it collect dust. If you do not recognize that your emotional reaction is a Box-defending mechanism, distracting you from discovering that the way you think things are is only a myth, you might be fooled by your own feelings. You might treat your reaction as an omen. You might think your intuition is giving you a true danger signal. In fact, it is only your Box defending the indefensible. Without distinguishing the source of your emotional reaction, you might unconsciously lock yourself into behavior patterns that produce only ordinary human relationship.

I am sorry if directing your attention toward examining your own mythologies feels like a shatter bomb. I remember having a similar experience after first leaving my parents' house at the age of eighteen to attend a National Science Foundation summer science program in physics and mathematics. Skipping my high school graduation ceremony, I flew directly from a white upper-class suburb of Los Angeles, all the way across America, to a black women's college campus in Greensboro, North Carolina, where in my dorm room I met cockroaches as big as mice, only bolder.

Other participants of the program were geniuses. One evening, a guy visited my room and presented me with an airtight argument to prove that, if a tree fell over in the forest and there was no one there to hear it, the crashing tree made no sound. I knew the conversation was pure philosophical crap, but I could not argue my way out of it, and he spoke with such assurance that my world was suddenly shaking. An offended queasy rage erupted from my guts. I immediately hated that guy and sent him out of my room. His smug nonsense shattered a part of my innocence and awakened a sharp distrust of anything purely intellectual (which has proven useful ever since). But I also learned the importance of being careful when delivering someone else with alternative design options for the way their Box handles the world. I apologize if anything in this book has caused shaky feelings for you. If shaking has occurred, I can only sympathize from my personal experience with the same thing.

We may be carrying a myth since childhood, but when we want to explore areas that are tabooed by our myth, we are faced with a decision. Either the myth goes, or the possibility of exploration goes. Neither decision is good or bad. But unless somebody pulls back the curtain, we will never see the little man who is working the levers that keep the myth alive. It all depends on what you want to see.

Map of Worlds

We are here in this book together to call forth and explore the awe-inspiring conditions of true Love, possibility, Men, Goddesses, Archetypal Relationship and high drama. Not theoretically, but actually. Not once, but for the remainder of your days. We are here to establish the foundation for continuously shifting into new ways of relationship. You are making a journey to add consciousness, elegance, multidimensionality, and previously unseen options to your daily experience.

Making journeys into new territory requires new maps because (as was shown in the *Map of Maps,* Section 5-B) you do not interact with the world as it is. You interact with your thought-maps of the world. So let us begin with a new map, the *Map of Worlds,* which presents distinctions showing that you participate in more than one world during your day-to-day life.

The term "world" in this case refers to a world of experience. The *Map of Worlds* is not some weird, science-fiction, planet-hopping through parallel-dimensions, Star Trek idea. The *Map of Worlds* says that, at different times during your day, the energetic mood of your experience shifts. It is the world of your experience that determines what is possible for you in that moment.

For example, you know what it feels like to be depressed. You also know what it feels like when the depression is over. The whole world looks remarkably different when depressed and when not depressed. You have a different experience of what is possible in the mood of depression than when you are, for example, in the mood of ecstatic elation or serious concentration. This difference in your worlds of experience is addressed in the *Map of Worlds.*

Without thinking about it, you probably assume that you live in only one world – the obvious world in front of you that you can see, taste, hear, and feel during your daily activities. You might even regard this one world as the real world. As with most assumptions, the assumption that there is one true and consistent real world may provide you with temporary comfort, but it could be a completely false and misleading assumption in the bigger picture.

The reason you may not have noticed and mapped out other worlds is because we experience each world we are in as being internally consistent, since each world includes in its design the injunction: "And this is the only world there is." So, no matter which world we enter, we have the experience of being certain that it is the only world.

As you experiment with the *Map of Worlds* and start noticing that, in fact, you do journey through a multiplicity of worlds, your direct knowledge becomes inarguable. Nobody can talk you out of your new understanding because nobody talked you into it. You discovered it for yourself. You may gradually notice, over time, that a boundless and sourceless joy spontaneously arises deep in your heart. The joy does not go away, but instead slowly becomes a supportive background experience. The joy is a side effect of entering new territory; it comes from finding unexpected ways to start again with things for which you were sure you had no chance.

Three Worlds

The *Map of Worlds* eventually reveals three worlds: the upperworld, the middleworld and the underworld. In one space, any of these three worlds can be happening.

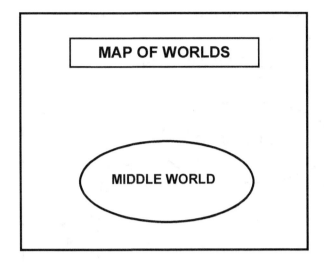

MAP OF WORLDS

MIDDLE WORLD

For example, your bedroom can be in the middleworld when you are vacuuming the floor, putting the laundry away, or changing a light bulb. Your bedroom can be in the upperworld when you are arranging the pillows with the same loving care you would use to tend a sacred altar for the Goddess of Archetypal Love. And your bedroom can be in the underworld when you are feeling alone and betrayed and are sobbing on the bed, or when you are fighting with your partner and trying to prove yourself right.

For another example, your car can be in the middleworld when you are on the way to the grocery store and you are busy making a mental list of what you need to buy. Your car can be in the upperworld when you drive toward a sunset sky changing from turquoise to orange to pink and you are in awe about the beauty of the world. Or your car can be in the underworld when you are late for an appointment and start swearing at the guy who cut in front of you, forcing you to stop at a red light.

For yet another example, your parents' house can be in the middleworld when you are helping repaint the kitchen or raking fallen leaves in the garden. Your parents' house can be in the upperworld when you notice for a moment that you and several other family members have unexpectedly released your family history and entered the present, and are having an inspiring new conversation that opens useful possibilities for each other. Or your parents' house can be in the underworld when dinnertime is contaminated with televised horrors from the evening news, or a quarrel erupts repeating the same ancient judgments that broke hearts in childhood.

And so on, day in and day out, wherever you are.

Middleworld

The *Map of Worlds* starts where we are right now, in the middleworld. the middleworld is concerned with common, ordinary, practical details of life such as cooking breakfast, taking the kids to school, brushing your teeth, going to work, paying the bills, or figuring logistics for the family holidays. You are industriously occupied with handling paperwork, washing the dishes, fixing the car, personal fitness, taking out the garbage, doing the laundry, reading a book, having sex, going to the movies, being social with the neighbors and relatives, and so on. Money, food and sex, busy, busy, busy, these are the basic ingredients of the middleworld.

Upperworld

From time to time you behold something very different and Brighter than the usual middleworld activities. Perhaps you are walking along a tropical beach at sunrise. Perhaps you are praying in a cathedral and look up at a mural of heaven or into the compassionate eyes of a statue of a saint. Perhaps you are having sex and it shifts into something transcendent. Perhaps you are sipping a rare wine, listening to Beethoven, reading poetry, or maybe just staring out the window at the rain and doing nothing. In that moment the world softens into a different sensuality and reflects in a wondrous light, as if that light were always present. You may find yourself saturated with feelings of optimism, joy, expansiveness, generosity, wonder, clarity, oneness, completion, love, brilliance, perfection, healing, possibility, union, and so on. This is the upperworld, and you already know about it. Everyone has had moments in the upperworld, perhaps even moments every day, if he or she is willing to admit it. Being in the upperworld is still being in the upperworld, even if your experience in the upperworld is only two seconds long. If you do not start taking responsibility for your two-second-long upperworld experiences, you may never notice how often you are actually *in* the upperworld!

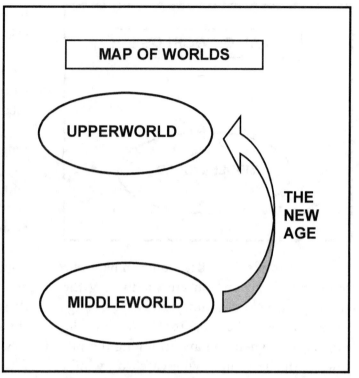

Transforming the Middleworld

Transforming Your Middleworld into the Upperworld (BLTLCH13.02). Upperworld qualities seem so wondrous and so near that, without much thought, you may have already concluded that your job in the middleworld is to make the middleworld into the upperworld. As a perpetual effort, you may be trying to make the middleworld into the upperworld right now, even in this moment. You may have tried many times in many different circumstances over the years to make the middleworld into the upperworld, and failed with each attempt. You may have failed so badly, so often, that you have given up trying, but your hopelessness about ever succeeding to bring heaven to earth has not changed your conclusion that this is still your job.

Two clarifications can make a difference here. First, thinking that we can go directly from the middleworld into the upperworld is the definition of "new-age" psychology and philosophy. It does not work that way. The upperworld represents perfection as a possibility, as a Principle, as an aspect of Archetypal Love.

Such perfection, although simple to conceive intellectually, is only a catalog of possibilities, only a guideline. Perfection is the normal operating condition in the upperworld. In fact, if you are experiencing perfection, you could well be *in* the upperworld. But perfection is not achievable in the middleworld because in the physical reality of the middleworld things fall apart. Things change, things move, things are evolving or devolving.

For example, think of an apple. It is easy to think of an apple. In the mind it is utterly simple to conceive of one individual thing, such as one apple, one idea, one person. But in the middleworld, one of anything cannot actually exist. No one thing stands alone, apart, and truly distinguishable from everything else in its framework. In the middleworld everything is connected to everything else. If you walk into a room and see a shiny red apple in the fruit bowl and smell its sweet tempting juicy crispness, you may pick up the apple to take a bite and think that what you have in your hand is one apple. But that is not true. The apple is actually a trap, and you have just been caught. The apple exists within a webwork of all apples. The apple is a vector, a momentum, a wave on the surface of an ocean of appleness as it extends through this moment from the past into the future. The apple came from an apple tree and contains seeds that can grow more apple trees. Human beings are used by the webwork of apple-DNA as the transportation to move apple seeds from one place to another for propagating the species of apples. There is no such thing as one apple. Apples are an interactive flowing interconnectedness integrally woven into the whole of middleworld existence. So are human beings. (Think about that the next time you are feeling lonely.) Perfection is a concept that the mind can easily grasp in the upperworld, but perfection does not exist in the middleworld.

The second fallacy in thinking that you can transform the middleworld into the upperworld is discovered the moment after you actually exert some effort to do it! "Try" communicating. Try hard to be loving. Try just being kind. Try entering communion. Try resting in the peace that surpasseth all understanding. Try being joyous for more than two minutes straight. Try being harmonious. Try being happy. Try being in pure spiritual union with someone and seeing what happens.

You already know what happens – as soon as you actually "try" to move from the middleworld into the upperworld problems arise. Conflicts boil up inside. You get offended over almost nothing, and react like a Geiger counter at Chernobyl. So does the other person. You are in the underworld! Deep and long-repressed feelings of rage, confusion, grief and terror raise their vicious heads and instantly transform you, the other person, or both of you into alien monsters hungry for fresh blood. Actually trying to go from the middleworld to the upperworld is how you discover that your underworld is located between them, and directly in the way!

SECTION 13-C
Underworld

On first impulse you probably regard your underworld as bad, negative, and dangerous. You assume (and have been taught) that if you are in the underworld something is *very* wrong. On the other hand, you do not usually notice that you are in your underworld when you are in your underworld. You simply engage in your typical underworld activities – like flying into a rage, or feeling hopelessly depressed – until your Gremlin is fully satiated. After he falls asleep in an engorged stupor, you glance back from the middleworld and wonder, "Huh? What was that all about?" as if it were a freak accident instead of a recurring nightmare. But your wondering will not last long, as each world totally absorbs your attention and becomes your exclusive concern. In the next moment you may be totally preoccupied with your middleworld business, until such time as Gremlin wakes up hungry again, takes over the reigns and goes looking for an underworld lunch.

The underworld referred to here is not somewhere else, deep under the earth's surface, for example. The underworld is in you. You carry your own underworld with you, as a potential, wherever you go.

The Underworld referred to here is not someplace you have a 50-50 chance of going to after you die. You go to your underworld *in every moment* when you generate an irresponsible action, unconsciously feed your Gremlin, or serve the Shadow Principles of your hidden purpose (*see* Glossary).

The underworld referred to here is not based on fantasy or a belief, fairytale or religion. The underworld is a first-hand, real-time relationship to the level of your consciousness about your intention – that is, what purpose you are serving right now.

Theoretically we locate the underworld somewhere far away from us, filled with devils, demons, monsters, and the hell realms. But, if you make any sincere efforts to take your relationship into the upperworld – for example, by being vulnerable and letting your partner see your fears in full force – you will often find yourself deep in your underworld instead. This is because of the geometry of worlds. You cannot get to the upperworld except through the underworld. You cannot have a stabilized upperworld until you take conscious possession of your underworld.

The underworld referred to here is not a new concept. The underworld has been explored and mapped for epochs. Knowledge about the underworld is necessary for any human beings wishing to live together in peace and harmony with other human beings. Ignorance of underworld principles is no protection from them. Underworld maps have been passed on from generation to generation orally, through legend, song, dance, and epic poetry, since long before the written word was ever invented.

Modern day Western culture has intentionally misinterpreted the encoded instructions about the underworld. We have been educated

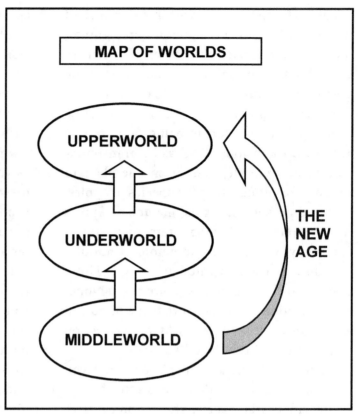

to regard any notion of underworld as nothing more than quaint allegorical nonsense. Because we no longer understand their true intent, underworld legends and tales no longer deliver their practical clarity. As a result, we fail to recognize what is going on and often have a shocking inability to take care of ourselves. Today's financial, political, military and religious spheres are networked and activated in the service of underworld principles with such sophisticated ferocity that together they manifest a Shadow strength never before seen on Earth.

Own Your Underworld

Owning the Treasures of Your Underworld (BLTLCH13.03). Recognizing the existence of an underworld within you is one thing. Taking responsibility for actively *sourcing* the underworld within you is a completely different thing. Taking responsibility for actively sourcing the underworld within you makes you bigger than your underworld. You are not trying to get rid of your underworld. You are trying to get conscious of your underworld. Your underworld is full of riches and insights that you can usefully extract for the rest of your life.

What riches? Authenticity, for example. Through owning your underworld you can no longer deceive yourself about not being Gremlin. Your friendly "nice person" mask no longer finds ears to hang on. When you inhabit your underworld you can have authentic compassion for others, each of whom has a vast underworld – regardless of whether they see it or not. Judging certain individuals as evil becomes a bad joke, not even funny. Your self-perception horizon expands to include previously invisible Shadowlands. Learning to navigate the Shadowlands consumes your naïveté, especially naïveté regarding people's true motivations. Instead of being an easy *mark,* you become a dangerous *ally* for accompanying others through their rites of passage. Rage and terror shift from being overwhelming or repulsive to being simply underworld feelings, fuel for staying alert and

Time to Seriously Collaborate

Radical Collaboration (BLLCH13.04). It has never been more important that people in the service of expanding consciousness work together as one team. This means simply ignoring all the typical boundaries that we might imagine separate one lineage or style of consciousness-expanding work from another. It does not matter what kind of Buddhist you call yourself. It does not matter what level Aikido practitioner you are. It does not matter what therapeutic tradition you come from. We can no longer afford to bicker over such superficial differences. If you are involved in expanding the Box, we are all on one team. We are all serving the same Bright Principles. It is time to seriously collaborate.

Creating a protected knowledge center that can serve as an "ark" certainly has value, but the fight has not yet been lost. It is not yet time to go underground and become invisible. Coordinated action is needed to experiment with alternative forms of culture, education, family, energy, government, city design, transportation, spirituality, society, financial exchange, management, entertainment, ritual, technology, meetings, and economic development. (*See* J. F. Rischard's brilliant book *High Noon: Twenty Global Problems, Twenty Years to Solve Them.*) Experimentation depends on you experimenting. It only happens if you lead it to happen.

The more reality that can be brought to implementing alternatives before they are desperately needed, the easier the transitions to using them will be. The need for experimenting is now. No, it is not easy to experiment now. Yes, you will be maximally challenged while implementing what you see is possible when others do not yet see similarly. Discovery always brings disorientation. But, if you do not try to bring what you know to be possible into existence now, *who will*? If you have clarity and the ability to take real actions and try things out, it is probably a job on *your* workbench. Change manifests one individual at a time, one day at a time, one small action at a time. Every little effort helps to cut new forms of consciousness that act as seed crystals and establish resonance for others who can tune in and follow. This is not a time for hesitation or hiding out. We have work to do, and this work needs to be done together.

creating clarity and possibility. Through integrating Archetypal dimensions, you become more whole and more real. Finally, you understand what it means to be growing up.

Owning your underworld does not mean that anything horrible must happen to you. By taking responsibility for your underworld you simply gain a freedom of choice that you did not have before. You get a choice about whether or not to enact behaviors which were previously automatic – like creating resentments, bearing grudges, or imagining revenge. You gain the choice of *not* underworld. You see the possibility of navigating to someplace else. Through discovering and integrating your underworld's tricks, strategies and hidden purposes, your underworld stabilizes into a foundation that you can stand on. When the underworld no longer undermines you, the gates of heaven open. You have heard the legends.

Owning your underworld can never be completed or perfected. Just like the upperworld and middleworld, the underworld is vast and complex. Neither is it wise to live in your underworld. The underworld is like a giant garbage dumpster. You have the dumpster. You use the dumpster. But life is not about living in the dumpster. This is how you own your underworld. You take possession of it and use it as necessary.

You gain functionality in your underworld the same way that you would become adept in navigating and working in any other new land. You repeatedly enter the territory with caution and attention to learn as much as you can, and then you come back. You go in, get the treasure, and get out.

What we are speaking about here is the classic hero's journey. Enter the Shadowlands, capture the golden key, pick up the magic wand, collect the dragon's tooth, snatch the bag of jewels, slide the power sword into your belt, memorize the book of secret knowledge,

rescue the beautiful maiden and then get the hell out of there. This is how you come to know your underworld. You walk right into the unknown and try some things. Use what is useful. Learn as much as you can, and then return to the middleworld. The hero's journey into the underworld is part of your Archetypal rite of passage into adult responsibility.

In each voyage into your underworld you reclaim one of the treasures. Each treasure is actually a part of yourself that you long ago hid away, to disempower yourself, so that you could survive by not being a threat to your environment. You reclaim each treasure by taking it back from where you hid it from yourself. Going into the underworld is a search, a treasure hunt. You can enter the underworld with a prayer: "I do not know what I am looking for. I do know that I am looking for something. I only hope that I will recognize it when I find it."

Owning your underworld still lies ahead of you, until you have engaged it to the level that it becomes part of your daily life experience. Once you have consciously entered and exited your underworld a number of times, your relationship to it changes. You start to know where you are by the smell of the experience. You start filling in the underworld blanks in the *Map of the Great Labyrinth of Spaces*. You start detecting your own motives and the motivations of others, so you know where they come from and where they will lead you.

You are less naïve because you have met your own King or Queen of the underworld face on – your Gremlin. You have seen him or her in action with full, horrifying, conscious clarity, and you know that in each action you take and each word that you speak, either you own Gremlin or Gremlin owns you. The Archetypal battle has begun within you, and you have learned by experience that there is no compromise with Gremlin. Changing your relationship to your underworld is big work, the utmost challenge, requiring every personal resource you can muster.

What could you expect to find in the underworld? Lots of stored up feelings, to begin with. Unexpressed rage, grief, terror and ecstatic joy. The feelings are locked away in your body. When you enter the underworld your automatic mechanisms of denial and self-deceit come to a screeching halt. You stop pretending. You stop being nice. The game is up. You are suddenly and only exactly where you are.

Being exactly where you are can be of great importance and practical use, if you know what to do with an almost unlimited supply of irresponsible rage, fear, sadness and joy... What rage? Consider this. Mostly without knowing it, women carry rage laced into their tissues and cells from 6000 years of torture, injustice, disrespect, abandonment, betrayal and intentional destruction of the dignity of Woman by the patriarchy. When a woman enters her underworld she begins to feel a white-hot rage in her like she never imagined could exist. She feels the rage of her mother, of her sisters, of her friends, of the unnamed women she sees on the street, the women sitting in back offices not yet feeling their own rage. She feels the rage of the millions of women who suffer at the hands of men, women who have died in the death camps of the men's wars. The ancient rage of women runs deep. It is enormous.

Men too have been minimized by the patriarchy. Men's rage has an equivalent depth and size. The underworld is there inside of us even if we do not know it is there. The irresponsible rage, terror, grief, and joy of the underworld are to be consciously experienced and expressed. If we do not own our underworld, if we do not transform and use the energy of our feelings consciously to serve our Bright Principles, then our feelings will come

out sideways, and we will keep unconsciously hurting the people closest to us.

Not knowing what to do with so much uncivilized energy is what keeps most of us away from discovering our deep Masculine and Feminine Archetypal structures. The way that you avoid feeling your feelings is by evading the present. But evading the present has a severe side effect: it permanently blocks you from accessing the Adult ego state. Without direct immediate access to the Adult ego state, you haven't a snowball's chance in hell of creating extraordinary human relationship, let alone anything Archetypal.

From the civilized perspective, an underworld full of unexpressed feelings could only be a serious liability, one to be avoided in the extreme. Looking at the same scenario from a different perspective reveals that what at first appears to be the problem is, in fact, the solution. Having explosive resources hidden away in your underworld is not a design error from God. These resources contain the exact quality of intelligence and quantity of energy required to meet the challenges of bringing your destiny to fruition. The question is, how to change the lead into gold? The answer is *stellating*.

Stellating Your Archetypes

Stellating Your Archetypes (BLTLCH13.05). The word "stellating" means to change from a planet into a star (*also see* Section 5-E). The difference between planets and stars is that planets, like Earth, absorb more energy than they radiate. Stars, like the sun, radiate more energy than they absorb.

The planet and star difference is analogous to human beings. Human beings are trained to live as planets. You are taught to consume as many resources as you can afford, absorb knowledge from what is already known, imitate styles, critically judge if things are good or bad or if they meet your preferences and match your expectations or not, complain if

---

MAP OF STELLATING ARCHETYPES

CHANGING FROM A PLANET INTO A STAR

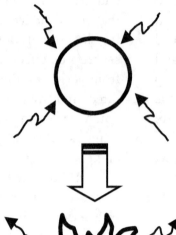

PLANET:
Consuming
Absorbing
Copying
Criticizing
Judging
Complaining
Following
Pretending

Planets absorb more energy than they radiate. Stars radiate more energy than they absorb. Human beings are trained to live as planets, but we are designed to live as stars.

STAR:
Producing
Creating
Appreciating
Leading
Exploring
Experimenting
Declaring
Generating
Causing
Discovering

STELLATING:

Stellating is the initiatory process of changing from a planet into a star. This process done safely and sustainably involves deep emotional work over a minimum of two years. Each of the four feelings stellates into one of the four Archetypal structures. The result of stellating is living in service of your destiny Principles.

things do not make you comfortable, follow whoever is leading you, and pretend that you are satisfied.

Although you have been trained to live as a planet, *human beings are designed to live as stars*. You are designed to produce more than enough resources for yourself and your game-worlds – your associations of two or more people gathered to enliven your Bright Principles. You are designed to generate more than enough intelligence, love, creativity, inspiration, money, energy, time and collaboration to bring your projects, your family, and your work abundantly to fruition. You are designed to create options whenever you run out of the options that you find, to appreciate the subtle details

of four-body experiential reality – reality previous to words – so that you can lead anyone interested to join you in exploring new territory. You are designed to do Edgework experiments, draw new thought-maps, encounter new experiences and bring back whatever you find to share with your people.

Stellating involves progressively expanding your Box through examining your Box's present set of maps, while at the same time being exposed to upgraded maps that offer greater clarity and possibility. Taking on new maps changes the shape of your Box. Each change of shape requires your Box to go through the liquid state and involves deep emotional work – with anger, sadness, fear or joy. Stellating done safely and sustainably will mean taking a serious step, like being in a transformational training environment for several days in a row, once every three months or so, for a couple of years, at least. Such a program is already recognized as an effective method for sustainable professional development, for example, in the system of Continuing Education Units (CEUs). The result of stellating is not guaranteed happiness, wealth, health or enlightenment. The result of stellating is having the dignity of living your life in the service of your destiny Principles.

MAP OF FEELINGS AND ARCHETYPES

ANGER DOER / MAKER (WARRIOR OR WARRIORESS)	**SADNESS** COMMUNICATOR (LOVER)
JOY ARCHETYPAL MAN OR WOMAN (KING OR QUEEN)	**FEAR** CREATOR (MYSTIC OR SORCERESS)

Before learning how to feel consciously, maturely and on purpose your feelings use you to serve your hidden purposes. Associated with each of the four feelings is an Archetype that is hardwired into your body and ready to turn on at about age 15. Each Archetype is initialized individually through a guided process of safely, consciously and intentionally experiencing and expressing 100%-maximum Archetypal feelings, until your relationship to the feeling shifts. Archetypes arrive responsible, adult, clear, and bigger than your 100%-big feelings. Once initiated, the four Archetypes are available for the rest of your life. Without stellating your Archetypes you remain functionally adolescent.

That was the "stellating" part. What about the "Archetypes" part? For clarity's sake it can be useful to remember that the context in this book is not a psychology context; it is a possibility context. Over the thirty years in which I have been doing empirical experimenting, I have helped teams of adventurous people to repeatedly come into direct contact with the Archetypal source of possibility. This contact is what has produced the language of Possibility Management. In the context of possibility, the question, "What is possible right now?" turns out to be of utmost interest. In the radical responsibility that characterizes Archetypal domains, the answers to this question come from your Archetypes, which surprisingly are not available automatically. Associated with each of your four basic feelings is an Archetypal character that is hardwired into your body and ready to "turn on" at about the age of fifteen years. You have access to your Archetypal resources only after you "initialize" them through a rite of passage that stellates your four feelings. Anger stellates the doer or maker, which is the Archetypal Warrior or Warrioress. Sadness stellates the communicator, which is the classical Lover Archetype. Fear stellates the creator, which is the Archetypal Magician or Sorceress. And joy stellates the Archetypal King as Man and the Archetypal Queen as Woman.

Initializing Feelings

Each Archetype is initialized individually, through a guided process of intentionally experiencing and expressing maximum Archetypal feelings, until your relationship to the feeling shifts. Before the stellating process, the unexpressed, often unconscious, feelings are bigger than you are. After the stellating process, you are bigger than the feelings. Before stellating, the feelings owned you. After stellating, you own the feelings. Before stellating, the feelings contained you. After stellating, you contain the feelings. The determination that you are bigger than your fully-stellated Archetypal feelings is not theoretical and disputable; the determination is experiential and indisputable. Your Archetypes arrive responsible, adult, clear, and fully tapped into their inherent clarity and power. What they need is experience. Once initialized, the four Archetypes are at your service for the rest of your life; without stellating your Archetypes, you remain functionally adolescent – for the same length of time.

If you were born in Western civilization, then your culture provides no way for you to stellate your Archetypes. Yet, permanent adolescence may not look so attractive. If you want to live from the source of Archetypal Man / Woman, protected by the doing-making power of a Warrior / Warrioress, connected

---

Retrieve Love from Hell

Tearing Up Your Contract About Serving Unconsciousness (BLTLCH13.06). During your path of evolution you may have accidentally left Archetypal Love behind you in the underworld. While evolving out of a life serving the shadow side, it could be that, during the struggle, you left the treasure behind. Perhaps you were rushing to escape through a quickly closing door and you just forgot to bring Archetypal Love along. In your panic-leap away from unconscionable irresponsibility, the treasure may have been too much of a burden to carry at the time. Perhaps you were confused in that moment and thought that Love itself was evil and part of the original problem. Perhaps in the impending doom of the threatening circumstances you had no time to get clarity and untangle it all. You just needed to get out and shut the door tightly behind you. And you did it. You succeeded in getting out. But it could be that, in the process of getting out, you accidentally left Love in hell. The thing to realize is that Love is Love, pure fuel for being. Love belongs to the radically responsible world where you are working now. Now you need Archetypal Love. You need it at your fingertips whenever you shake hands with someone. You need it wherever you touch, wherever you look, wherever you feel. Your permission to radiate Archetypal Love may be trapped in your underworld and you may need to go back in there and get it. Do not worry. That is the important thing to know. You do not have to worry. *You are different now.* Your time of serving irresponsibility is complete. You may even have signed a contract that promised you would serve unconsciousness *forever* as part of the deal. Well, even unconsciousness knows that forever is a really long time. If this situation applies to you, ask your body the following question: "Have I served long enough?" If something in your body relaxes, the answer is *yes.* You have served long enough. The contract is over. You can now go back to unconsciousness and look it straight in the face and say, "I have served long enough. The contract is over." Then, tear up the contract and leave. Only this time, on your way out of the underworld, lean over and gently pick up the bright jewel of Archetypal Love. Protect her close at your chest, and take her with you out of there. She is yours. And you need her now.

to others through a Loving communicator, with access to immediate invention through a Magician / Sorceress, it will be up to *you* to make it happen. You, or no one, will take responsibility for stepping beyond the limits of the culture and finding an intelligent environment that is designed exactly for bringing your Archetypes to life – your life!.

SECTION 13-D
Man's Job in the Underworld

(Men) Taking Your Balls Back from Your Mother (BLTLCH13.07). For a man, owning your underworld will to a large extent be the process through which you put your stellated Archetypes to work and take your balls back from your mother. Since Western civilization is not a true Warrior culture we do not raise our boys to become Warriors, as could be imagined in ancient Sparta or in some of the Native American or African traditions. Western civilization raises their boys to be production workers, football fans, and consumers of Chevys or Fords.

As a modern mother takes care of raising her modern son, she also naturally takes care of his balls. Since he does not need his balls for attending school – and in the eyes of teachers and staff preferably does not have them – the mother takes the balls when he is a baby and keeps them carefully tucked away in her bedroom drawer, hidden amongst her socks and her underwear. Every now and then she brings the balls out for inspection to make sure they are still okay, dusts them off a bit and puts them carefully back. And there they stay, well preserved, unused, almost forgotten. Without a man taking his balls back from his mother his balls will stay in her little bedroom drawer until his dying day, even if his mother dies before him.

If a woman is looking for a man who can hold space for her she will start off with a test.

She will do something to see if she can take the man's balls away. If she succeeds she will despise the man. She has tested many men before and has a collection of men's balls at home mounted on the wall over her fireplace. Each set of balls has the man's name engraved on a small brass plate, the date of the taking, and the way the balls were collected. As soon as a woman gets disgusted toying with a man like a cat tires of toying with a mouse, she drops him and looks for another man to test. The man will have no idea why he was dropped.

Grown men who still live in their mother's house are not the only ones who have not taken their balls back. It is almost all of us. Until you take your balls back from your mother every woman you go to bed with is mom. It is no wonder if you have sexual inadequacies. You may as well have a portrait of your mother on your bedside table. Until you take your balls back from your mother you are still sleeping only with her.

Your mother cannot give your balls back to you, even if she wants to, even if she knows that it needs to be done. The best that a mother can do is, on an appropriate day after her son's eighteenth birthday, take his balls out of her drawer, open the front door, place the balls on the porch, and then shut the door. Her job as mother is complete. If your mother does this and you do not come and collect your balls off the front porch right quickly, some hungry dog may come along and slurp them up for lunch.

In the meantime, mom can have a Mother Graduation Party. She can invite other mothers over, bring out the champagne, and formally exchange her role of "mother" for any of the other roles she has kept on the back burner in order to be "mother." She can turn in her nametag that says *Mom* for a nametag that announces her real name again. She can take her life back.

What is the way to take your balls back from your mother? For each man this is a unique and personal process. It does not mean that you do not love you mother. It is the procedure of cutting the apron strings, of chopping the umbilical cord, of severing the energetic binding between your center and her womb.

Such cutting is not merely intellectual fantasy; it is real cutting and involves all four bodies. Such cutting is a violent, loud, sudden and final procedure. She will feel it, you will feel it, and the world will feel it. Through the process of becoming your own man it occurs that you are no longer your mother's son. The world is a different place after taking your balls back.

Taking your balls back from your mother is an exact procedure. The steps are best done formally in the company of other men who have already been through the process themselves. Ideally you take your balls back under the guidance of a man well trained in the procedure. Without the clarity and camaraderie of other men more experienced than yourself in this procedure it is easy to fool yourself.

SECTION 13-E
Woman's Job in the Underworld

(Women) Taking Your Center Back from Your Father (BLTLCH13.08). For a woman, owning your underworld will, to a large degree, be the process through which you put your stellated Archetypes to work and take your center back from your father. Whether your father was present or absent, kind or abusive, attentive or aloof, he was your first protector. Out of love for him or out of fear of losing him you empower your father with the best thing that you have to give him: your center. You do not necessarily want to give him your center. You may not give him your center on purpose. But the net result of growing up in a Western country is that you enter the age of transition from girlhood to womanhood having given your center away to your father.

Not only do you give your center to your father, you give your center to the patriarchy.

If the patriarchy has your center, the patriarchy gets to decide who you will be, and the patriarchy offers few Archetypal models for a woman to step into and become. The women's liberation movement that started in the 1960s and 70s is still going strong. The valiant personal efforts of thousands and thousands of clear-headed, strong-willed, loud-voiced, courageous women have built an energy wave that you can catch and ride on. In terms of support and guidance for your rite of passage into adulthood, you have a clear advantage over men. But do not think that the patriarchy has given up its tendency to dominate woman. Do not expect the patriarchy to hand you your rite of passage on a platter. You will need to fight for it, and your fight will need to be intelligent. Do not fight to transform the patriarchy. Fight to transform yourself.

Without taking your center back from your father, every man you come close to and every male authority figure with whom you work is not an individual person. They all wear your father's face. You look to them for protection and when you do not get your expectations fulfilled then they receive your ridicule and revenge. Without taking your center back from your father then every man you go to bed with is dad. Is it any wonder if you cannot express your complete sexuality?

Before a woman owns her underworld she plays the game of hurting men. Many women have a collection of stories that they tell themselves and other people over and over again. These are the stories that show how men have hurt them. If you can prove that men have hurt you, then you are perfectly justified to hurt men first. You may even tell these stories to your own daughters so they can carry on the tradition. You either blame your man with hatred for being as bad as your father, or you blame your man with hatred for not being as good as your father. You can never authentically be-with your man, as he is, until you take your center back from your father.

Here are dangerous questions to ask yourself: "What stories do I keep to prove that men have hurt me? In what exact ways do I intentionally hurt men?" The Queen of your underworld feels *very* glad when men suffer.

The lessons of building Love that lasts are strong. The lessons are clear. You are not here to topple the patriarchy. There is no need to topple the patriarchy. You do not need to destroy or even change the patriarchy in order to accomplish your goals, meet your needs and be what you are.

The patriarchy proposes one game: that if you want to improve your relationship with men, if you want to solve the problem between men and women, then go to psychotherapy, take drugs, get divorced, etc.

Archetypal Love proposes a different game. Remember who you are – Pirate Sorceress Warrioress Queen Goddess Woman – and then start your own game. The new game could go like this: There is no problem between men and women. There are men and there are women. Men and women play different games. The two games when well played are perfectly complementary. The evolution starts with you taking new actions with what you have right now. The basic action of the new game is radical responsibility. Responsibility for everything. Freedom from making excuses. Freedom from blaming anyone else, ever again, for anything.

The energetic description of the work you must do to grow up is of necessity precise: you must remove your father's energy from your space, or, more crudely described, you must take your father's energetic penis out of your vagina. It is up to *you* to take your center back from your father. If you insist on remaining your father's little princess it prevents you from becoming your own man's goddess. The purpose of all this is for you to take possession of your own life as a woman in the world. Only then do you have a chance to enter the extraordinary and Archetypal domains

---

I DECIDE

The spider and fly
hurt me hurt you game with men
continues until I grow up
and take my center/womb/power
back from my father and from
the Patriarchy
and start a new game
called Archetypal Love.
I decide which game I play
in each moment
with each word I speak and
each action I make.

---

of womanhood. It does not mean that you don't love your father.

Taking your center back from your father is an exact procedure – violent, swift, and loud. The steps are best done formally in the company of other women who have already been through the process themselves. Ideally you would arrange to be under the guidance of a woman already well trained in the procedure. Without the company and wise counsel of more experienced women it is easy to fool yourself about this.

Ж Map of Possibility

Until you recognize that you do in fact *have* an underworld, it makes no sense to map it in detail. After perceiving the magnitude and frequency of your internal urges that are decidedly less than honorable, it suddenly becomes imperative to understand where they are coming from and what they are for.

Everybody has an underworld. The processes through which you personally own your underworld take time. *Allow yourself to have that time.* Some underworld recognition processes are simple and quick. Some processes are longer and more complex. The underworld is never wrong, never healed and never goes away. You may as well include the underworld as part of the whole picture of things. What helps build a foundation of clarity for navigating your underworld is the *Map of Possibility*.

The *Map of Possibility* brings together many of the elements we have been distinguishing throughout this book. The map is complex and sophisticated, and although it looks like it represents a dichotomy, it has nothing to do with the dualities of right and wrong, or good and bad. The *Map of Possibility* describes what is possible for you to create right now.

As with every map, the *Map of Possibility* is neither true nor false – instead it is accurate or inaccurate, useful or not useful. Every map in this book is under continuous development and improvement. Nothing is final. It is you who verify the accuracy or usefulness of each map, and you who will continue to develop these maps. Possibility Management is open code. If you understand it, you are qualified to use it. You are also responsible for the outcome of its use, and for its further development.

The *Map of Possibility* starts with a vertical line drawn in the center of the page. This line represents the only thing that is true on this map – that everything is neutral; that everything happens without meaning. There is no good or bad, no better or worse, no right or wrong, and no positive or negative. Not even the fact that everything is meaningless has any meaning. What is, *is*, as it is, and occurs with no story attached.

The implications of this declaration of neutrality are vast, although they all derive from one source: radical responsibility. There is no such thing as a problem. It is impossible to be a victim of circumstances. You cannot be at the effect of a situation because you are busily *creating* the situation. All of psychology is a virtual reality. Conflicts are theatrical pieces enacted among Boxes; you as a being cannot have a conflict. Reasons have no power. Irresponsibility is a complete illusion.

MAP OF POSSIBILITY

This is a map of what is possible right now. What you are doing right now is creating.
You create by making stories about what is.
The world is rich in evidence, so you can make up any story about anything.
You do not make up stories for no reason. Every story has a Purpose.
You are either aware of the Purpose of your story or you are not.
If you are aware of the Purpose of your story then your actions serve conscious Purposes.
If you are not aware of the Purpose of your story your actions serve unconscious Purposes.
This map is not about good or bad. It is about responsible or irresponsible creating.

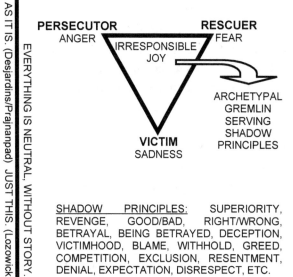

CONSCIOUS PURPOSE
CREATES A RESPONSIBLE GAME
"WINNING HAPPENING," "I WIN AS YOU WIN"
ABUNDANCE THROUGH TAKING RESPONS-
IBILITY FOR SOURCING THE RESOURCES.
SERVES TRUE PURPOSES (DESTINY).
BRIGHT PRINCIPLES.
USES ENERGY AND INFORMATION OF
FEELINGS TO CREATE HIGH DRAMA.

DOER / MAKER (WARRIOR) ANGER   **CREATOR** (SORCERER) FEAR

RESPONSIBLE JOY

ARCHETYPAL MAN OR WOMAN (KING/QUEEN) SERVING BRIGHT PRINCIPLES

COMMUNICATOR (LOVER) SADNESS

BRIGHT PRINCIPLES: KINDNESS, DIGNITY, GENEROSITY, RESPECT, ACCEPTANCE, CLARITY, TEAMWORK, COMMUNICATION, INTEGRITY, INVENTION, DISCOVERY, FRIENDSHIP, COMMUNITY, POSSIBILITY, GROWTH, EMPOWERMENT, RADIANCE, ETC.

WHAT IS, IS, AS IT IS. (Desjardins/Prajnanpad) JUST THIS. (Lozowick)

EVERYTHING IS NEUTRAL, WITHOUT STORY.

UNCONSCIOUS PURPOSE
CREATES AN IRRESPONSIBLE GAME
"I WIN, YOU LOSE," "HA-HA! I GOT YOU!"
SCARCITY THROUGH AVOIDING TAKING
RESPONSIBILITY FOR THE RESOURCES.
SERVES HIDDEN PURPOSES.
SHADOW PRINCIPLES.
USES ENERGY AND INFORMATION OF
FEELINGS TO CREATE LOW DRAMA.

PERSECUTOR ANGER   **RESCUER** FEAR

IRRESPONSIBLE JOY

ARCHETYPAL GREMLIN SERVING SHADOW PRINCIPLES

VICTIM SADNESS

SHADOW PRINCIPLES: SUPERIORITY, REVENGE, GOOD/BAD, RIGHT/WRONG, BETRAYAL, BEING BETRAYED, DECEPTION, VICTIMHOOD, BLAME, WITHHOLD, GREED, COMPETITION, EXCLUSION, RESENTMENT, DENIAL, EXPECTATION, DISRESPECT, ETC.

King or Queen of the underworld is Gremlin – feels glad when someone else feels pain. Serves Shadow "hidden purpose" Principles. King or Queen of the upperworld is Archetypal man or woman – feels glad when someone heals, learns, changes or succeeds, when Winning is Happening. Serves Bright "true destiny" Principles . When you have clarity about your hidden purpose and your true destiny all you get is a chance to make a conscious choice about what you are creating right now. This is a useful choice.

Nevertheless ... even so ... on the other hand ... well yeah, but ... *we are human beings*. And, as we've mentioned many times before, human beings are meaning-making machines, with a little piece of machinery called "the mind." Its job is to churn out an endless stream of meaningless thoughts and stories, and it does its job with a vengeance. Without training you are probably unwilling to remain uncomfortably present to the simple "what is" of existence. You are also probably unwilling to leave things in their stark neutrality. Instead, to ease your discomfort and/or establish some foothold in the camp of right or wrong, you believe your own stories about what happens.

Right now you are creating stories in your mind, heart, soul and body about how things are for you and what you perceive to be happening around you. The nature of your stories, as we've discussed in previous chapters (*see especially* Section 12-B), determines the nature of the world for you. Recall that you do not interact with the world *as it is*. You interact with your stories *about* the world, and no story can be true because stories are *stories*!

But, remember also that stories have power, because the Box has an incredible susceptibility to snap into the reality of a story (just walk by a television and you can feel the magnetic pull into the world of stories). Since stories have power, you act as if your stories are true, even though you just now made the stories up out of nothing.

The world is rich in evidence to support any story that you want to make up. It only takes a tiny shred of evidence to support the believability of an entire story, and you are very skilled at finding those shreds and creating a complete universe of opinions, attitudes, judgments, expectations, and beliefs that all fit together into a very convincing story.

Interestingly, you do not make up stories about everything. Many things exist or happen and you make up no story about them.

The stories that you do make up have a specific purpose; you make them up for a reason. Either you are aware of the purpose of your story or not. Being aware or not aware of the purpose of your story divides your creating into two categories:

• Creations that serve conscious purposes.
• Creations that serve unconscious purposes.

It will cost you blood, sweat and tears to truly understand what I am saying here. Awareness is expensive in the sense that it does not come free of pain. The arising of consciousness hurts. But your pain of consciousness can be put to very practical use on the *Map of Possibility*. You can sense if you are conscious of the purpose of your story or not.

If you are conscious of the purpose of your story then your actions feel painful (laced with frustration, grief or worry). Your actions feel a little forced, pushing against internal resistance. Consciousness is irritating because it provides you with multiple layers of perspectives: you see what you are doing and *you see that you see* what you are doing. Your moves cannot be fully automatic anymore.

On the other hand, if you are *not* conscious of the purpose of your story, your actions may feel smooth and ordinary. That is because you are identified with your actions, convinced that they are *right*, that they are the only possible actions to be taken in the given circumstances.

Being unconscious of the purpose of your story does not mean that you will know that you are unconscious. *This is the nature of unconsciousness.* Until your denial is busted, until you are disambiguated, until your focus is refined, your fog burnt away by the heat of realization, you unconsciously assume that you are fully conscious. Only after consciousness expands can you look back and see that, just previously, you were less conscious.

You interact with the world according to the perspectives supplied to you by the stories that you yourself create. When you take actions that support stories that serve unconscious purposes (for example, the all-too-common story that your parents did wrong to you, so to get back at them you dedicate your life to proving to the world that you had horrible parents by being a miserable failure yourself), what you are not conscious of is the full costs of your actions (for example, that you sacrifice an immensely joyous adult life to try to get the attention of someone who already proved to you that they don't care about you). Not being aware of the costs of your actions is irresponsible. Not being aware of the costs of your actions sets up irresponsible "games" (interactions with low drama payoffs) with other people.

The most basic irresponsible game that human beings play is called "personal survival". The game of personal survival is irresponsible because it blatantly ignores recognizing that you are alive right now. Since you have already survived, there is no need to continue trying to survive. That would be like trying to drink while you are already drinking, trying to breathe while you are already breathing.

If you play the personal survival game then you might automatically assume that there is a scarcity of resources, meaning not enough for everybody. That assumption appears obvious. People are starving to death in Africa. Countries are at war over the remaining oil reserves in the Middle East. Logically, there is only a limited quantity of money, a limited quantity of love, a limited quantity of jobs, a limited quantity of positions in the hierarchy, a limited quantity of territory to own or control, a limited quantity of recognition, time, space, energy, fame, intelligence, and a limited quantity of really good chocolate cake.

From the irresponsible perspective of the survival game, whatever "it" is scarce, then, if *they* get it, *you* do not get it. They live, and

you die. Personal survival based on the belief in limited resources manifests as competition. The game is, "I win, you lose." If you win then you have power over the other. "Ha! Ha! I got you!" You feel glad when another person hurts. You experience joy when the other team is defeated. Such joy is irresponsible joy because it avoids the bigger picture responsibility.

The bigger picture is that the "I win, you lose" game results in far more losers than winners. The losers are full of resentment and jealousy. They want nothing more than to get revenge, to beat you back, and gloat over *your* pain of being the loser. Or, they want nothing more than to help all of the poor losers and feel superior about what a great rescuer they are. The exciting "I win, you lose" game involves victims, persecutors and rescuers thrashing about in the irresponsible unconscious theater called low drama, which we've detailed in Section 2-C. Low drama creates only more low drama, so nothing ever really changes.

The master of ceremonies at your low drama spectacles, the King or Queen of your irresponsible creating, is your Gremlin. Your Gremlin sits on the throne, smokes a cigar, and has dominion over all the creatures in your underworld ecology. Your victim, persecutor and rescuer characters, knights of the triangular table, unconsciously role-play their theater pieces to serve your Gremlin's hidden purposes. In the underworld domain nothing is sacred.

The Principle that nothing is sacred is a Shadow Principle. The Principle that everything is sacred is a Bright Principle. The terminology of "Shadow" and "Bright" for describing Principles is used because the *Map of Possibility* aligns with traditional Archetypal maps given to us through legend and fable. We could have equally used the terms "Red Principles" and "Blue Principles." Retaining the ancient terminology makes the Archetypal alignment clear.

The danger of using the term "Shadow Principle" is that it is so easy for you to equate "Shadow" with "bad." "Shadow" simply implies something that is more or less obscured, indistinct, murky, fogged, confused, blocked and absorbing. The danger of using the term "Bright Principle" is that it is so easy for you to equate "bright" with "good." "Bright" simply implies something that is more or less revealed, transparent, obvious, distinct, clear and radiant. The view that you can categorize something as either good or bad is itself a Shadow Principle.

The *Map of Possibility* primarily distinguishes between using Bright Principles for responsible creating or using Shadow Principles for irresponsible creating.

Principles are forces of nature, facets of the consciousness out of which the universe is made. Consciousness spans a full spectrum from the total lack of consciousness at one extreme to the total completeness of consciousness at the other extreme. Both consciousness and unconsciousness are complementary aspects of the same phenomenon – a phenomenon that does not really have a name. It is previous to the substance of material manifestation. We could call it God. We could call it Love. We could call it Reality. We could call it The Nameless.

In general, consciousness can be divided into two categories according to its editorial spin, its purpose. Consciousness either has the purpose of increasing responsibility or consciousness has the purpose of decreasing responsibility.

Applied consciousness *is* responsibility. Responsibility is consciousness in action. Responsibility is the overriding Bright Principle of the upperworld.

Bright Principles are all facets of the jewel of responsibility, such as: respect, friendship, integrity, kindness, reliability, communication, clarity, possibility, acceptance, lightness, intimacy, community, inclusion, openness, vulnerability, faithfulness, creation, joy, generosity, transformation, understanding, being-with, discovery, exploration, learning, growth, sharing, Winning Happening, abundance, and love.

Applied unconsciousness *is* irresponsibility. Irresponsibility is unconsciousness in action. Irresponsibility is the overriding Shadow Principle of the underworld.

Shadow Principles are all aspects of irresponsibility, such as: superiority, separation, exclusion, waste, revenge, greed, envy, deception, betrayal, being betrayed, resentment, mockery, manipulation, trickery, competition, disrespect, exploitation, denial, destruction, chaos, having enemies, control, cruelty, cynicism, invulnerability, "I win, you lose," scarcity, survival, and hate.

We have many names for manifestations of the Gremlin in our culture, for example: thief, murderer, terrorist, religious fanatic, con artist, irresponsible businessman, sect leader, sociopath, rapist, tyrant, embezzler, corrupt politician, pornographer, egomaniac, burglar, crook, criminal, drama queen, swindler, assassin, gossip, child abuser, mobster, thug, extortionist, drug dealer, rumor-monger, mercenary, bandit, pickpocket, hijacker, hoodlum, racketeer, gangster, etc. And very colorful names they are indeed. The enthusiastic creativity with which we name our Shadow Worlders indicates something about the present state of our culture.

Compare that to the names our culture has for the King or Queen of the upperworld: leader, priest, business manager, politician… wait a minute! In modern Western cultures a position of leadership does not automatically imply responsibility. The position of leader has been so profoundly abused that in many cases its irresponsible connotations are unshakeable (such as the inherent repulsiveness of the German word *führer*). Modern terms for leaders remain completely ambiguous until we put the

```
┌─────────────────────────────────────────────────────────┐
│         ┌──────────────────────────────────┐            │
│         │   MAP OF THREE KINDS OF GAMES    │            │
│         └──────────────────────────────────┘            │
│                                                           │
│  When an interaction involves winning or losing that      │
│  interaction becomes a "game." By including status,       │
│  position, power, prestige, etc., as things that          │
│  can be won or lost it becomes clear that almost every    │
│  human interaction is a game. On the surface of an        │
│  interaction is its content. But entwined within each     │
│  interaction is its purpose. You can sense the purpose    │
│  of an action by its "spin," its agenda. Regardless of    │
│  the content, the purpose indicates which of the three    │
│  kinds of games it is. The three games distinguished      │
│  below match closely to the three kinds of relationship:  │
│  ordinary human, extraordinary human and Archetypal.      │
│                                                           │
│   1. "I WIN YOU LOSE"                                     │
│          Competition. Goal is: I win.                     │
│          Assumes a scarcity of resources.                 │
│          If I get the resources you die. If you get them  │
│          I die.                                           │
│          My survival depends on me winning.               │
│          We learned this game before we evolved into      │
│          primates. It is still the most popular game on   │
│          the planet.                                      │
│                                                           │
│   2. "I WIN YOU WIN"                                      │
│          Cooperation. Goal is: We both win.               │
│          Let us figure out a way that we can all win.     │
│          Can degrade into "I lose, you lose" through      │
│          compromises.                                     │
│          Sometimes becomes "It is okay with me if you     │
│          win as long as I win just a little bit more."    │
│          Back to "I win, you lose."                       │
│                                                           │
│   3. "WINNING HAPPENING"                                  │
│          Creative collaboration. Goal is: The Bright      │
│          Principle of Winning Happening can do its work   │
│          in the world.                                    │
│          Does not involve the "I" and the "you."         │
│          Assumes an abundance of resources through taking │
│          radical responsibility for resources. If there   │
│          are not enough resources I am not a victim       │
│          because I source more resources. Through serving │
│          something greater than the Box one can discover  │
│          the experience of really living.                 │
│                                                           │
└─────────────────────────────────────────────────────────┘
```

qualifier "responsible" in front of them, such as responsible leader, responsible priest, responsible business manager, responsible politician, responsible doctor, responsible spiritual leader, responsible professor, responsible artist, responsible inventor, and so on. To provide clarity in speaking about a responsible conscious King or Queen of the upperworld we refer to them as Archetypal Man and Archetypal Woman, or Man and Woman with a capital "M" and "W."

Since our present culture is so thoroughly contexted in unconscious irresponsibility we have had to begin our exploration of the *Map of Possibility* beginning on the irresponsible side. Only after we have some moments of objective remorse about the depths to which we have been trained to produce low drama can we even begin to talk about the other side of the map and what it is to create high drama.

Whereas Gremlin takes actions to avoid responsibility and instead creates irresponsible games, Man or Woman takes responsible actions that create responsible games. Gremlin's game is played as "I win, you lose," and Gremlin feels glad when the other person suffers. Archetypal Man or Woman's game is played as Winning Happening, which is itself a Bright Principle. Man or Woman feels glad when the other person learns, heals, grows, discovers, or expands their Box. Whereas Gremlin knows only the experience of surviving because resources are so obviously scarce and must be coveted, Man or Woman explores the possibilities of really living – a completely different context from merely surviving – and therefore already has an abundance of everything that is needed. Man or Woman can be generous and kind because they take responsibility for sourcing the resources. If there is ever not enough of a particular resource they create more. Solutions to creating resources are often nonlinear, and arrive from Man or Woman unreasonably committing to sourcing the resources even before they know how. The satisfaction of having already committed to producing a result establishes a flow of necessity between the result that is committed to and the Bright Principles that can provide the result. The flow is through the space that Man or Woman holds. Man's and Woman's feelings have been 100-percent stellated to activate the intelligence and energy of the Archetypal Masculine and Feminine structures. As we observed in Section 13-C, rage stellates into the doer or maker, the Archetypal Warrior (or Warrioress). Sadness stellates into the communicator, the Archetypal Lover. Fear stellates into the creator, the Archetypal Magician (or Sorceress). And after these three energies have been activated it is discovered that, previous to them and continuously present, is a reasonless, radiant, background joy of responsibility. It is the joy of the King or Queen blessing their people. The doer, the communicator and the creator characters are role-played as necessary to serve the Archetypal Man or Woman's three, four or five Bright Principles of his or her true destiny through creating conscious acts of responsible theater called high drama.

We get to be a slave of our Shadow Principles or a servant of our Bright Principles. Slave or servant, that is the choice we gain through the *Map of Possibility*. It is a choice worth struggling for. **Holding a Bright Principle Meeting (BLTLCH13.09).**

SECTION 13-G

Name Your Gremlin and Its Hidden Purpose

An unconsciously functioning underworld can subsume the entire context and purpose of your life. It is your job to work out how to take your life back. The Gremlin – whom we first encountered in Section 6-K – has had many years head start in serving the Shadow

Principles that undermine your responsible creative power. In this section we will suggest ways in which you can consciously get your power back.

Naming Your Gremlin (BLTLCH13.10). The Gremlin part of you is committed to serving a specific set of three, four or five Shadow Principles called your hidden purpose (*see* Glossary). That Gremlin part is organized, fast, and very intelligent about keeping you unconscious of its true motivations. The Gremlin derives pleasure when your enemy feels pain, even when that "enemy" is your beloved partner. Giving this Gremlin part a name is a powerful alchemical tool. Your Gremlin will even tell you its own name if you respectfully ask and attentively listen. Here are the names of some Gremlins I have met: Dinki, Baue, Schnupu, Thorsten, Katanka, Speedy, and Pim. Not ordinary names, for sure, but real Gremlin names nonetheless. Having the name of your Gremlin gives you a handle for getting a hold of it (recall that in the fairy tale *Rumpelstiltskin*, the maiden could only release herself from the power of the Gremlin through learning his name). Without the handle, Gremlin does what it wants whenever it wants to do it. Since you cannot call it by name it owns you. Never forgetting your Gremlin's name, and keeping a watch out for the three to five Shadow Principles of your hidden purpose, are huge steps toward you "owning" it.

Carrying Gremlin's name and hidden purpose on the tip of your senses permits you to experientially distinguished the Gremlin within yourself. You can identify its approach by the energetic signature of its gleefully irresponsible, smug, little giggle. Until you fiercely self-observe to the point where Gremlin's activities become conscious, Gremlin's activities will remain unconscious and will destroy your possibility of serving Archetypal Love. Instead, no matter what you think, your life is dedicated to serving Gremlin.

Even long-time spiritual students who have not made the Gremlin distinction can be counted upon to regularly create Gremlin games with the people in their life. Gremlin keeps its foot in the back door, never allowing the Archetypal Relationship chamber to seal. The internal heat and pressure can never get hot enough to ignite genuine remorse because Gremlin blows it off with a joke or a comment, or doggedly persists in whistling unconsciously along his merry way. Without the intense and lasting pain of the remorse of recognizing that the Gremlin is getting ready to feed, and then you doing something completely different, nothing changes.

Gremlin feeding activities typically include: flirting, masturbating, playing video games, eating junk foods, men not lifting the toilet seat to pee, women gossiping, breaking time agreements (coming in even a few minutes late, even if you have a good excuse or if you apologize), complaining as if you are a victim, forgetting appointments or promises, playing practical jokes, stealing insignificant things (pens from work, silverware from the restaurant, grapes at the grocery store, airline blankets, special leftovers from the refrigerator), driving even a few miles an hour over the speed limit, not exercising, trying to cut ahead in line, energetically "trashing" spaces even in small ways (e.g., walking through the space being visible, inelegantly opening or closing the door, coughing, yawning, farting, looking out the window, moving the chair, dropping a pen, conspicuously drinking from your water bottle at delicate moments), having little accidents or breaking something and not cleaning it up, littering, sneaking, swearing, sleeping in when you've previously made a commitment to yourself to get up at a certain time, trying to get more than somebody else, returning the car with the gas tank on empty, talking to keep everyone's attention, leaving floating turds in the toilet, overeating, not changing the empty toilet paper roll or the burned out light bulb, looking on other people's desks or into their drawers, reading other people's mail, sleeping during meetings, lying, making jokes or comments about other people, making up excuses, not doing what you say you will do, feeling resentful, changing plans without telling anyone, and so on.

As you can see, many of these activities are quite familiar, indicating that you have an entire underworld ecology thriving within you, determining the quality of your life day and night. It is your responsibility to recognize the full horror of the situation. It is your responsibility to learn the hierarchy of underworld creatures feeding upon each other within you, upon you by other people, and by you upon those people who are dearest to you. Until these dynamics are brought to light, your Underworld is controlling your life.

The procedure for distilling the three, four or five Shadow Principles of your hidden purpose is appropriately named the Hidden Purpose Process. In contrast to its sensible name, the process itself is horrendous. The term "disillusionment" does not even come close to depicting what it feels like. For this reason, the Hidden Purpose Process is best done under the guidance of someone skilled in navigating underworld spaces with absolute clarity; someone who will never forget, for an instant, that the manifestations that arise, the feelings, the tones of voice, are all an act of underworld theater – all a story, and only one way to look at things. Distilling your Shadow Principles has nothing to do with beliefs, and especially nothing to do with good and evil.

Once you have distilled your hidden purpose from the incidents and accidents of your life it can take you months or years to digest and integrate the experience into practical application. All that you have, after distilling your hidden purpose, is a way to detect who is in charge of what you are saying right now. That is a useful distinction.

Gremlin creations are far easier to spot in someone else than in ourselves. One way for people to serve each other and hold the space for the possibility of Archetypal Relationship is by making an agreement to "spot the Gremlin." Each time your Gremlin reveals its grimy little paws and yellow-tooth, bad-breath smile, your "spot the Gremlin" team mate has permission from you to greet it by name and purpose. "Hello Dinki. Feeling betrayed again, are we?" Identifying your Gremlin by name and hidden purpose gives you a way to interact with your Gremlin responsibly. This is a small but necessary step.

Own Your Gremlin

Owning Your Gremlin (BLTLCH13.11). Once you have your Gremlin's name, all that you have is the knowledge of its existence and an ability to distinguish "it" from "you." This is significant and still insufficient. There are further steps to take. Your job now is to change your relationship to your Gremlin through responsibility. Whereas previously Gremlin ran wild, knocked you unconscious, and did whatever it wanted with your life, now your job is to make Gremlin your ally instead of your owner.

At first Gremlin will hate you for your efforts. Gremlin hates you because you represent responsibility. Responsibility, to the Gremlin, is like water to the Wicked Witch of the West. If you douse the Gremlin with responsibility he fears there will be nothing left. In being recognized by you, Gremlin is terrified of soon starving to death from lack of irresponsible, low drama energy food. Your job is to put your Gremlin on a regular feeding schedule so that starvation is no longer an issue.

There are certain foods that your Gremlin loves to feed on – foods that will deplete your relationship energy reserves; and other foods that can maintain a healthy diet for Gremlin without costing you so much in terms of the quality of your relationships. Your task is to distinguish between the two kinds of foods. Then, you can choose to feed to your Gremlin foods from the second list on a regular basis.

To start, make a list of what your Gremlin loves to eat when it has free rein. For example, your Gremlin might love to devour the following:

Typical Gremlin Foods
- Creating the story that your boss is an enemy and having regular confrontations
- Weekly social gatherings with alcohol, coming home late and drunk
- Three large ice creams a week
- Incessantly talking to fill up any empty space with the sound of your own voice
- Staying up until three AM on business trips watching triple-X movies
- Not paying your telephone bill and having the phones almost cut off
- Arranging to have fights with your mate as an excuse to throw dishes and lamps against the wall
- Wearing funny, strange or mismatched clothes to get attention
- Behaving insanely to shock people
- Interrupting other people to blurt out whatever you want to say
- Teasing your mother-in-law so she is too flustered to criticize you
- Bingeing on videos every other week
- Drinking colas all day
- Regularly complaining
- Changing everything into a joke that you can laugh at
- Eating daily doughnuts, cookies, candy, cake and coffee
- Smoking
- Gossiping, speaking about someone when they are not there (triangulating)
- TV, newspaper, magazines

- Holding resentful grudges and plotting revenge in the bottom of your heart
- Thinking about chocolate
- Sleeping past your alarm
- Devouring salty, greasy, junk food, such as hamburgers, chips, pretzels, popcorn, peanuts, Taco Bell, and fries
- Catalog shopping to the maximum limit on your credit cards
- Biting your nails, scratching your face, pulling your hair, picking your nose
- An hour or so of internet sex here and there.
- Having an ongoing feud with your neighbors, and feeling right about your position
- Eating so much pizza and ice cream for dinner that the endorphins kick in
- Having power struggles with your mate; proving they are wrong in public
- Manipulating your relatives and colleagues with your illnesses
- Leaving messes around the house that drive your partner crazy
- Flirting with the guys or gals at the exercise club
- Swearing at other drivers
- Paying your taxes late
- Blaming the government.
- Keeping your desk buried in an almost non-functional pile of papers
- Kicking the dog
- Add your favorites …

It might take you a couple of weeks to collect the details for your list, but then again, maybe you can make the list immediately. Once you have your list of favorite Gremlin foods, develop a reasonable strategy for a regular feeding schedule. For example, a strategy that works well is to choose one day during the week, for example Saturday, and promise your Gremlin that on this one day, all day long, midnight-to-midnight, he can feast as much as he wants on the specific ten items that you have selected from your list. Write out the ten available Gremlin foods on a paper and tape it on your refrigerator to see. Then for the other six days go completely cold-turkey on all Gremlin foods.

In the beginning you might make it through one day of no Gremlin food before he actually knocks you unconscious and you wake up on the far side of a binge or a quarrel. Do not feel guilty. Do not beat yourself up. Do not punish your Gremlin. Just remake your commitment and keep your promise of maximum feeding, on the specified day only.

After awhile you might make it through three days before getting knocked unconscious. In the meantime Gremlin might put a constant stream of voices in your head, "This is stupid! This is stupid! This is *really* stupid! I hate this! Mmmm, look at *those* tits! Just a little piece of chocolate would be okay. Then I'll be satisfied. What a jerk! Let's stop this nonsense. I can't do this anymore. I am a failure. I am not good enough. I will never make it. Whose idea was this anyway? Not mine. Fucking book!" And so on. These are only voices. You may wish to keep in mind that you own a fully-loaded Voice Blaster.

Gremlin might lose a little weight, but he will soon start feeling more fit and alive without so much fat around his belly. He will appreciate his new trim feeling and the interesting challenges you start giving him. Gremlin will recognize that you respect him and are treating him well. After a few months you and your Gremlin might get through an entire week with no snacking. Stay on this regular weekly feeding schedule for at least a year.

At some point you might notice that a feeding day went by and your Gremlin forgot to feed. Do not change the feeding day that week. If Saturday slipped by with no feeding, do not feed on Sunday or Monday. Just wait until the chosen feeding day comes around again.

You might also notice that a feeding day arrives and none of the ten special Gremlin foods appeal to Gremlin. This is okay. You do not have to force-feed your Gremlin. And, do not let it graze on the banned Gremlin foods. Stick to your feeding schedule practice.

Being accountable to your Gremlin for providing him with a regularly planned feeding schedule establishes a relationship with Gremlin like an owner has with his Doberman pinscher. Your barely-tamed potentially-vicious beast is willing to sit at your feet when you say "sit" because he knows that he is respected, he is taken care of, and in particular, he is regularly fed. This really works.

Put Your Gremlin to Work

Putting Your Gremlin to Work (BLTLCH13.12). Contrary to what you might expect, you will use Gremlin more in extraordinary human relationship and Archetypal Relationship than in ordinary human relationship. In ordinary human relationship, Gremlin is sneaking around as a *ronin*, a lone samurai without a master, serving himself. In Archetypal Relationship the rightful place of Gremlin is established: awake, attentive, sitting at the feet of Archetypal Man or Woman with a short chain tied around his neck.

At first, when discovering the true nature and intention of Gremlin, it is quite difficult not to simply declare with disgust that Gremlin is bad and must be imprisoned or banished forever. Such thinking is a remnant of the good/bad distortion and will leave you with your Gremlin invisibly at work, busily creating his usual unconscious horrors with your life, like the priests at a parochial school justifying violence or sexual intimacies with the boys in their care.

Gremlin is Gremlin. Gremlin does what Gremlin does. We all have Gremlin and no matter what we think or try to do, Gremlin will never go away. Gremlin is a force like sulfuric acid, like plastic explosives, like a laser beam, like a crowbar or lock picks, neither good nor bad, but definitely capable of producing certain results. As with all tools, Gremlin can be used to fulfill either responsible or irresponsible purposes. We live in a wild world. We need access to a kind of intelligent wildness for taking care of ourselves and for creating what we want to create. The source of that wild intelligence is Gremlin. After possessing your Gremlin, a source of wild intelligence sits at your feet, a trained attack animal, ready to do what it always does but doing it as you responsibly and maturely direct.

Gremlin is an exceptional tool of nonlinearity, particularly suited for shaping extraordinary human and Archetypal Relationship where only ordinary human relationship existed before. The application of this tool is counterintuitive. You use Gremlin's ability to destroy anything, at any time, for no reason, as the force to dismantle the mechanicality of your own Box. Gremlin is the only one who knows the secret ways to get through your own defenses, the only one clever enough to free you from being trapped by your own tricks.

The first use of Gremlin is very exact. Use Gremlin to monitor Gremlin to not "do" Gremlin. It takes a thief to catch a thief, and Gremlin is the ultimate thief. Only Gremlin knows exactly how devious, cunning, and shrewd Gremlin is. Only Gremlin is sensitive and fast enough to catch Gremlin before he steals away your dignity with his shenanigans.

Practical Applications of Gremlin

Use Gremlin to sharpen your self-discipline. Use Gremlin to stop overly judgmental thinking. Use Gremlin to keep your attention free from being hooked and your heart free from emotionally reacting. Use Gremlin to hold your tongue when all it wants to do is lash out and destroy. Use Gremlin to not snicker, not sneer, not sigh, not yawn, and not roll your eyes. Use Gremlin to not speak the hurting cynical words, not make the cutting tone-of-voice insinuations, not say the nasty, stupid, degrading little jokes that destroy people. Use Gremlin to keep your center when everyone around you is giving their center away. Use Gremlin to stay awake and pay attention when everyone around you is sleeping and hypnotized. Use Gremlin to look in shadowy places at what is normally ignored. Use Gremlin to not throw stones at the adulteress. Use Gremlin to stay still when other people move and to move when other people stay still. Use Gremlin to do the right thing even when the consequences are frightening. Use Gremlin to make and hold necessary boundaries even when the kids are screaming at you to give in to their demands. Use Gremlin to ask dangerous questions that no one else can even think of because the forces of conclusion are so strong. Use Gremlin to break the rules that minimize expressions of kindness, generosity or compassion. Use Gremlin to distinguish subtle details that make invisible things distinct from their camouflage. Use Gremlin to kill your own denial, to walk directly into your own pain and to let your whole world go up in flames, burning to a cinder. Use Gremlin to watch your old reality crumble to dust without being even one percent a victim of the experiential circumstances. Use Gremlin to stay present and let your reality construct die without being sentimental, hysterical, isolated, or nostalgic. Use Gremlin to let yourself be seen raw, naked, stupid, crippled and wounded – exactly as you are – and do not care about other people's opinions or judgments. Use Gremlin to energetically "spin" so that you hold no position and stay a moving target for other people's comments. Use Gremlin to wait patiently through the unknown until the next thing can happen. Use

Gremlin to have the courage to start something that has never been started before.

It is Gremlin who can stand completely exposed and vulnerable and not care. It is Gremlin who can allow chaos and total destruction to rain upon you with the same acceptance and neutrality that he allows blessings, appreciation, respect and love to rain upon you. And it is Gremlin who can feel deep compassion for others whose Gremlin still owns them and keeps them living (if you can call it living) in an underworld created by their still unconscious and all-powerful Gremlin.

SECTION 13-H

Be Your Destiny in Action

Being Your Destiny in Action (BLTLCH13.13). As you work to own your underworld, put your Gremlin to use, and consciously explore the three worlds, you suddenly enter a new game. The new game is about fulfilling your destiny.

Each of us has a destiny. Your destiny is a unique set of three, four or five Bright Principles that are an expression of your soul's true purpose. You were born to fulfill your true purpose, your destiny in the world, to live as your Bright Principles in action. It is relatively straightforward to use the Distilling Destiny Process to extract your Bright Principles out of your life and name them with clarity. With such clarity you become a tool that can be more consciously utilized by Bright Principles to do their work in the world.

Human beings have free will. Free will is more powerful than destiny. This makes serving your destiny optional. By paying ongoing attention to the creations of your will, not as an action but rather as a way of being, your actions can express a wish to serve your destiny. By putting your free will in the service of your destiny your life then forms itself around the needs and requests of your destiny Principles rather than the needs and requests of your Box.

The mystery of human will is that it is both flexible and resilient enough to contain opposites. Two things do not ordinarily occupy the same place at the same time. If they try, there is a force created, an energy of conflict. Ordinarily, such force is avoided as being uncomfortable or destructive. Human intention has the ability to hold two things in the same place at the same time and make use of the resulting force to serve a conscious purpose. For example, you can take a moment to see the details of what exists now in the present situation of your life. Then you can split your attention, remember what you just saw about your present life, then shift your perspective, and focus another part of your attention to see details of what is possible for you, your potential. What exists and what is possible are not usually the same. Use your intention to hold the conflicting views collected by your two attentions. It will feel like you are a stretched balloon holding too much air inside itself. You are containing a disorderly force that wants to simply disperse itself. The disorderly force of the conflict between what exists and what is possible can be directed towards creating what you really want to create. Directing the chaos is just like letting the air out of the balloon in one direction so that it can push you through the air in the other direction.

For example, if you experience in excruciating detail that Archetypal Love is possible, yet is not consciously present in this moment in your relating, and you can hold the intensity of that experience, you can use that energy as a resource to do what is needed and wanted to create Archetypal Love.

It is your Principles that provide a vision of what is possible. If you bring integrity to the instructions provided by the Principles of your destiny you will end up with a project. Your project will show up as a way for you to serve the greater humanity. Your project will include practical details for holding space so that the spaces where you work and live become an intersection of worlds. Through the work that you *do* you *are* your destiny Principles in action. Tolerating the intensity of being a space where Principles of the upperworld can do their work in the middleworld makes you a transformer. A well functioning human being lives as a transformer bringing more Archetypal Love into the world.

MAP OF INTERSECTION OF WORLDS

UPPERWORLD
BRIGHT PRINCIPLES

You hold your work space as an intersection of worlds. Here you can be your destiny in action.

MIDDLEWORLD

UNDERWORLD
SHADOW PRINCIPLES

You cannot make the middleworld perfect. That is not your job. Your job is to call Bright Principles into your workspace. You are then holding space as the intersection of worlds through which the Principles that you serve can do their work in the middleworld. What happens in this space will never be perfect. But it will be as good as it gets. And this is good enough.

SECTION 13-I

 # Serve as the Center of a Gameworld

Stars cannot be a solar system by themselves; they need planets to express their full potential.

Neither can planets be a solar system by themselves. Planets need stars. Planets naturally are attracted to orbit around stars to be involved in the "games" that stars can create. This section is about such games and the gameworlds that you – the star – can attract and serve.

You become a star by stellating your four feelings, thereby igniting an unquenchable fire of inspiration that burns in your belly and moves you from action to action during your day. You radiate! But a star without planets is just a lone star, bright but not really serving anything but itself. And planets without a star are shadowy interstellar debris, dangerously imperceptible when you are traveling at high speeds. But the combination of a star *and* planets together is a configuration that is far more than just the sum of the star and the planets. The configuration is a solar system, a complex, integrated flowing interconnectedness that evolves and can be used for things far greater than either stars or planets alone.

Your projects will develop over time to include a more sophisticated level of experiments. More sophisticated experiments require that you have *your own laboratory*. The time for you to have your own laboratory will not necessarily be obvious to you. You may think it is long overdue for you to have your own laboratory when in fact you are not yet ready because, for example, you have not yet acquired the soft skills or learned to maintain your attention and responsibly hold space. Or you may think that you will never be close to the point of setting up your own laboratory because, for instance, you find evidence for devaluing yourself at every turn, when in fact it is already past time for you to start. You will need to trust the feedback and guidance from your coach and from your environment as to when the timing is right for stepping into your own laboratory.

Your laboratory will show up as a project with a goal, involving people and resources to make something happen. The interaction between you, your Principles, your

From the Glossary

A "Gameworld" is a dynamic environment created by two or more people agreeing to relate according to an internally consistent story. Gameworlds can range from temporary and of minor consequence to longer lasting and of major consequence. Examples of gameworlds include "let's go up the elevator," "let's have a party," "let's have a relationship," "let's have a family," "let's have a company," "let's have a town," "let's have a country," "let's have a religion," "let's have a war," and so on. Gameworlds can be responsible or irresponsible, depending on their purpose and their results. Gameworlds become defensive if their stories are believed to be true or are kept invisible to the participants, in which case the participants are said to be identified with their gameworld. Even if a gameworld is considered to be the "one and only true reality" by a majority of its players, it is still a gameworld. Gameworlds founded in beliefs build false community and survive through competing for limited resources through war. Gameworlds founded in Bright Principles and responsible results build authentic community and thrive on creative collaboration to source the resources. Taking responsibility at the level of being the story maker for gameworlds is the entry door to Possibility Management. Responsible gameworlds tend to be more galaxical than hierarchical in design. In a galaxical gameworld the source people are found serving as its center.

stellated Archetypes, the other members of your project, the project purpose or goal, and the obstacles to reaching the goal all come together in the form of a living organism called a gameworld. The gameworld is your laboratory. Whether that gameworld is small and simple like a book-writing project or a relationship with another person, or larger and more complex such as a family, a theater production, an alternative energy initiative, a company or a project for a bigger organization, the mechanics of gameworlds apply.

Gameworlds come together around a center and are sustained by the energy that flows through them. If the gameworld is a family, then it is the job of the mother and father to be the center of the family and to supply energetic food into the family that keeps the family nurtured and flowing along. This is the parents' job, not the job of TV, the job of the grandparents, or the job of the children.

If the person who is the center of the gameworld tries to nourish the whole gameworld with their own personal energy they will soon run out of "primate" power and become the normal exhausted parent or overworked project leader. The gameworld will cease growing and can easily wither or die because it will have insufficient energy to survive. Participants will eventually go somewhere else – including leaving their mate – to get the food for making their lives more vital.

Consciously Feeding Your Gameworld (BLTLCH13.14). A gameworld thrives through the exchange between the participants in the gameworld and the resources of the gameworld. The exchange is mutually beneficial. Your gameworld needs access to the energy and information resources of the Principles and Archetypes, and the Principles and Archetypes need the gameworld as a physically manifested circumstance in which to work. You, as the center, are the space holder through which the exchange takes place.

You are both crucial to the aliveness of the gameworld and completely replaceable – except for the fact that, in general, all available space holders are already busy being used at their maximum capacity to source other gameworlds and are not available to replace you in yours. It is your baby.

As the space holder at the center of a gameworld you do not have to worry about your own evolution. You will be taken care of by the Principles and Archetypes, because as much as you need them to flow through you to feed your gameworld, they need you to be fit enough to handle the flow. *Your capacity to flow energy is the bottleneck of the gameworld.* When it comes time for you to handle a bigger flow of energy or to handle a flow of a different kind of energy, the Principles and Archetypes will arrange in some completely practical and unpredictably nonlinear way for your limits to be expanded.

Your personal limits function as "restricting sphincters" on the energy flow into the gameworld. In the beginning of a gameworld, the energy flow through the space you hold is more than sufficient. As the gameworld evolves it is natural for the gameworld to require more energy than you can originally handle. Through cycles of stress and relaxation your development will be managed by the Principles.

The sphincters that restrict the flow of energy into your gameworld are rigidifications of your will, the same rigidifications that establish the shape of your Box. Under a wide variety of conditions, willpower can rigidify into decisions, emotional trigger points, vows, beliefs, assumptions, rules, defense strategies, and so on, for example:

- Old self-preservation decisions made in circumstances that no longer exist
- Unexpressed feelings that fester into sensitive wounds that automatically react whenever a psycho-emotional "button" or trigger point is touched

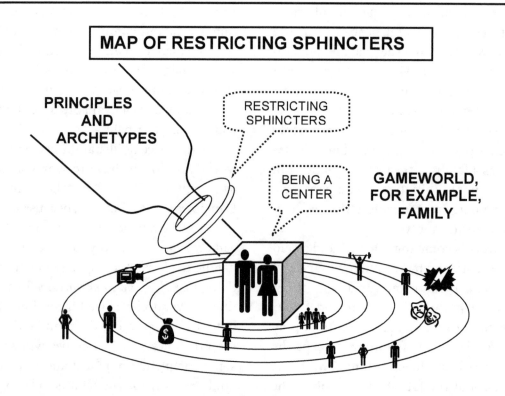

MAP OF RESTRICTING SPHINCTERS

PRINCIPLES
AND
ARCHETYPES

RESTRICTING
SPHINCTERS

BEING A
CENTER

GAMEWORLD,
FOR EXAMPLE,
FAMILY

The quality of relationship you create with the people in your life and with the projects you are in formats your gameworlds. Clarified Principles and stellated Archetypes provide energy and information resources for you to feed your gameworlds. Old decisions, blocks, past-life vows, etc., can be restricting sphincters limiting the flow of energy and information into your gameworlds. Part of your ongoing development will include relaxing the sphincter's grip so more resources can flow through you. Relaxing the grip expands your Box.

- Past-life vows made at the moment of a horrendous death and therefore strong enough to last through lifetimes with sufficient force to shape behavior
- Beliefs placed over a question in the side of the box for which no answer can be found (e.g., Who am I? What is God? Where does consciousness come from? What happens when I die?)
- Assumptions about how things are that in the past proved to be accurate in some important circumstance
- Rules taken to be true and believed to carry heavy consequences if broken
- Conclusions, opinions, stories, memories of "bad" experiences, expectations,

prejudices, attitudes, dreams, myths, desire for comfort, misunderstandings, superstitions, propaganda, hidden conflicting commitments, addictions, habits, interpretations, and so on

Flexible or rigid, your willpower is stronger than your destiny Principles. In order for more or different energy to pass through the restricting sphincters, the sphincters themselves must change shape or expand. Certain conditions bring the rigidified will of a sphincter into the chaotic disequilibrium of the liquid state, where it can relax its grip and reorient itself to a wider acceptance and perspective. The Principles themselves serve as the morphogenetic field, giving the sphincter its new shape as it re-solidifies. When the expanded sphincter permits more energy and information to flow through from Principles and Archetypes, the Box expands and the gameworld is brought back into fruition at a wiser and more intelligent level of organization. When that happens you have more matrix on which being can grow. When you live in the service of something greater than yourself, that same thing takes care of you in mysterious ways so that you can continue to be of service. After some personal experience with this phenomenon you may begin to radically rely on it happening.

Imagine designing both your personal and professional gameworlds to be sentient environments functioning in the service of Archetypal Love. Could you do this? Every interaction, moment after moment, would be an experiential expression of Archetypal Relationship happening. And to think that we have come to a consideration like this in a chapter called *Underworld*.

SECTION 13-J
Report From an Underworld Journey

The following is a personal journal entry that I wrote in 1996. It is not included here because it is typical, but rather to give you an idea of how unromantic it can be to experience what Don Juan Matus and Carlos Castaneda called "stopping the world" and "shifting assemblage points," meaning to melt down the ideas that shape our understanding of life that we always regarded as unmeltable. I also share this story because you may have experienced similar moments and may find some solace in confirming that this can be how it goes.

October 1996

It has all suddenly stopped working. The illusion spins apart. I sit here alone in a tiny hard room on the Mediterranean island of Crete, on vacation. On vacation from what? Good question. I take a pen in my hand and start writing how it really is, how it looks from the place where nobody is looking.

The truth is that I have been living in a fantasy world. When my fantasy world is unplugged from the cosmic cable-TV connection and my picture fades, what I see really going on is not at all what I thought was going on.

I am not in relationship. I am not connected to anything or anyone. I dangle here in endless unsettlement. Things are no longer hanging together like they did even moments before. There is nothing to stand on. The floor drops away, the whole scene is shattered, like a glass kaleidoscope dropped on a tile floor. Shattered to tiny irreparable bits. Except that it is not the kaleidoscope that is shattered this time; it is the viewer who is shattered. What I always regarded as me. The oil painting of my nicely formulated self-image violently disorganizes itself. The picture disintegrates into tiny irregular pieces that are already lost in the dirt. Through shock and dismay another feeling arises. The feeling is fear. What at first seemed like a short fluctuation, a small shudder, is quickly escalating into total annihilation. In the back of my head a quivering voice is beginning to squeak: "This could get serious…"

Before now, my picture was seamless – everything blended into everything else and formed a whole flowing picture that I could glide through. Now there are seams everywhere, and the seams are open. There is an infinite gap between each object, between each word, between each movement.

What made everything stay connected before? Some kind of glue? Whatever it was, it worked for a long long time and it fooled a lot of people, including me. But now the glue is gone. Dissolved forever. Nothing is continuous anymore. From here I see that it never was continuous. The seamlessness was only a mirage. The picture is now fully shredded, back to its original formlessness. There are no instructions for putting it back together again. It is far easier now to fall into an infinite gap than to hold any two things in association. The movie projector machinery in my mind that generated the world as I once knew it grinds to a screeching and total stop. No one else is there. It is all I can do to keep breathing.

I used to imagine that everything was fine. Where did I ever get that idea? Look around. Things are not fine. Who am I kidding? All of my movements are so mechanical, so robot-like, so predictable. All of my thoughts are the same stale thoughts I always think, same tone of voice, same opinions, same emotional reactions to being offended, same judgments, same expectations. This sharp little mind of mine, so proud of itself, so tight and quick and final. All of the thoughts that I have ever had fit into a precise formula, the same formula I have always used. The purpose of the formula is to create a delusion. I have been living according to a self-generated fantasy master plan. Mentally smearing everything together into a seamless whole is specifically intended to make me think that I am living my life, that I am safe, that I
am in control, that I can understand, that life has meaning and makes sense, and that what I think I understand is important.*

But not now. The show has stopped. Now nothing works. Nothing is together. Everything is in stasis. And the truth has been revealed: it is a real mess.

Who I thought I was is no longer coherent. I do not even remember what that was anymore. I do not even care. My self-concept is some vague image, a ghost, a cartoon. Sadness arises now. The fear is replaced by a sense of deep loss. If the image that I spent so much effort holding together and presenting both to myself and to other people is actually just that: an image, then how could people still like me or relate to me? How can people still like me if there is no me? If I am not what they thought? How can people like me if I am nothing? How can I function? What if I never come back together? The sadness changes to fear again.

I have invested years in making a consistent character presentation of who I am. I sacrificed a lot to keep the image solid. So often I did what my image dictated, what the image said was necessary to maintain the image rather than what I truly wanted. I have paid in blood. I really tried to be good, to be nice. I tried to be sincere – Oh God! How I tried! A good son, a kind brother, a perfect student, a friendly colleague, a loyal trustworthy mate, a strong man, a generous and compassionate father. I have paid. I sacrificed my soul on the alter of acceptability. So many years of my life I have thrown away trying to keep my image together.

Now it is obvious that all that effort was a lie, a sham. I have been a fantasy. No, it is worse than that. I have been false. I have been adaptive, trying to have at all times good reasons for my behavior in case any authority figure wanted to know just exactly why I was doing what I was doing – even when there was no authority figure available. I have spent my life trying to connect the next thing with the previous thing

I did, trying to be predictable and consistent, trying to follow some logical progression. I have tried not to frighten people. Really. I have tried to be sane.

But now the sanity framework is gone. The compelling force for maintaining the show no longer compels. There is no sense in it any more. The old standard reference point of "I" has suddenly vanished. What remains sees things from a different perspective – something previous to my fabricated ordinariness has shifted.

This new view is extremely painful to endure. There is rage with panic and hopeless grief all mixed together. I cannot stop the waves. I want to scream. I want to hit somebody. I want to run. I want chocolate, doughnuts, cookies. I want a drink. (I don't drink!) I want to watch a video. Stop this pain. Get me away from all this confusion.

I ache. I am alone. I am afraid. Nobody would understand what is happening to me. Nobody knows what this feels like. It hurts. I am only raw nerves. I am laid open like an oyster. I am naked. I am ruined. My whole life is a lie … Everyone's life is a lie. All of society is based on this deception. All government. All church. All school … especially school. All of it is lies, weak and pointless.

In fact, the world is a lie. Everyone out there is still trying to keep it all together. They still believe things are seamless. They still act like they are standing on something real.

And to see they are standing on nothing is devastating. Whatever dignity remained is blown away like a house of cards in a hurricane. Pretending to be sane and reasonable in the middle of this fraud has itself been a fraud. Only I did not know I was fraudulent. I did not know I was pretending. Either no one told me, or I was too blind to see, or both. Rage comes. Rage about being fooled. Those fuckers! Who fooled me? My parents? My teachers? Society?

No. They are just as fooled as I am.

Who fooled me then? No more lies! Who is the fooler?

There can be only one answer to this question: the fooler is me. I am no victim of someone else. I am not the focus of some great conspiracy. There is no conspiracy. There is just meaninglessness. I have fooled myself for all of these years thinking that it matters if I hold it together and force it into a shape that makes sense. There is no sense. And the deception comes from me.

But why? What do I get for this outrageous performance? Why do I do it? To get love? To get attention? To get acceptance? To avoid feeling the terror of the situation?

Yes.

Did it work? Did I get these things?

Yes – but not really. Love, attention, acceptance, and clarity about the terror of the situation all came to me, but I did not get to receive them. What stole the treasure was my self-identified egoistic psychological mind. My Box. It received the benefit. I got nothing. And now the Box has accidentally forgotten and the bogus treasure is gone.

If I keep up the show I get nothing.

But what do I have if I stop the show?

Also nothing.

Either way it is nothing.

So, then what? Do I put the show back together again? Do I continue pretending? Do I act as if I have not seen the little non-man behind the non-curtain? Do I try to go unconscious and pretend as if I do not know? Is this my only choice? What else is there?

That is a dangerous question. Do I have the courage not to put it back together?

Do I have the courage to stay insane?

What would that mean?

If I stayed the way I am now, if I stayed insane, nothing would look real. Everything would come without a name. The experience would come raw, undigested, without a story, without understanding. I could not function according to any assumptions about anything. Communication with other people would be difficult, although being in contact with them would not. But the contact I want would fry their circuits. Most people would run the other way screaming.

If I stayed insane then every communication would be an act of creation. I could never represent anything the way it was ever represented before.

If I stayed insane then I would know what I was intending because I would no longer be fooling myself about my intentions. But I would always know what the other person was intending too. If I stopped fooling myself it would be quite difficult for anyone else to fool me.

If I stayed insane how could I keep from being pissed off all the time? How could I keep from hating people's petty power manipulations, social injustices, selfishness, other people's expectations and their murderous little fears? Now I know why crazy people yell in the street. Normalcy is so disgusting.

If I stayed insane like this I would constantly confront true insanity, the insanity we all normally live in, what I used to think was normal. My rage about mass insanity would come when I assumed that I was someone. I would be detached if who I think I am as an identity, a person, was totally absent. Then I could understand and have compassion, but that only happens like this, when I am centered in the nothing.

It comes to this question: Do I have the courage to remain here? Do I have the courage to never shift back, to walk out that door into the hot Greek sun and let the world stay shattered around my feet like so much rubble? Do I have the courage to be nothing and stay insane?

Am I okay now? In this discovery, in this state that most people would call insane, am I okay? In this state that most people would run from like a man runs from a burning house, am I okay here?

Yes.

I am okay. And, it feels lonely here. None of life's little rewards produce any resultant fulfillment. I cannot even talk with someone and have it mean anything real. I am just disgusted and pissed off. Everything, even touch, is false if it contains implication. Everything is empty and dead. Life tastes dry in the mouth like old mummy dust.

On the other hand, everything is exactly as it is. I can accept whatever it is because it does not mean anything at all that it is as it is. Everything actually represents the same thing: nothing.

If everything is nothing, then we are all the same, exactly the same. We are connected at a level below all the stories, all the expectations and conclusions. That is what is true. That is what has always been true. That is what lasts. Nothing.

But what about this endless sadness in the center of my chest? The ache, the longing ... what about that?

Ah, let us take a closer look. There is sadness, yes. It is sad to feel the death of something that was once so near and dear to me, even if it was an illusion. Fantasy worlds die hard. If the ant-sized view is subsumed, it actually dies. Grieving its death is appropriate.

But grief is distinct from longing. Let us not confuse grief with longing. What is the longing? This longing is the longing for communion with the Archetypal absolute.

From where did this longing come? The longing was always there. The longing started when the universe started. Being identified with the "human" show distracted me from experiencing the longing, just like the show distracts everybody else. This in fact could be the purpose of the great deception: to distract us from experiencing the longing.

What is the longing for? The longing is an internal ever-present compass for determining what is important, for seeing what is true, for sensing what is precious, and for choosing what is a good use of the time that we have. I am using the compass of longing now to make the effort to write these words. Some day this mapping may be useful to someone else, or to me again, when I forget.

So, this raw insanity and this intense longing is something to come back to? Some great experience?

Ah, a bit of humor all of a sudden?

I wonder, what will be the excuse for the internal unconscious fantasy-generating machinery to start rolling its gears again? It has been three hours. What initiates the mental mechanism that so deftly weaves separate details back together and creates my seamless illusion of a world that I can understand and that makes sense? What makes me go back to comfortable sleep so that I think it is better to feel better?

Ahah! Just this! This exact question is the ejection seat! Asking how it all starts again is how it all starts again! The ride is over. Back out of the Shadowlands. Amazing.

PART V

Countenance

CHAPTER 14

Reinventing People

Imagine this experiment. You are at a party and some guy comes in thinking about himself, "I'm an idiot. I'm a jerk. I'm stupid. I'm ugly. I'm not good enough," but everybody at the party has a different opinion. They are sincerely delighted that he has come to the party. They can't wait to be-with him, to talk and laugh with him, to share their time with him. Is the guy a jerk, or is he a great guy?

Do the experiment in reverse and the answer is easier to get. Imagine you are at the party and some guy comes in thinking about himself, "I'm cool. I'm the best. I'm handsome. I'm wonderful. I'm the greatest," but everybody at the party is about ready to throw up. "Who invited this guy?" they think, trying to avoid eye contact, hoping Mr. Cool does not come over and dominate their conversations. Here is the question again: Is the guy a jerk or is he a great guy?

The question here is, could it be that *who we really are* is not what we think about ourselves but rather what is coming out of other people's mouths to each other about us? If so, then if we want to change who we are, we need to behave in such a way that what comes out of other people's mouths about us changes. Our feedback meter would be the effect we cause in other people's experience.

This consideration becomes even more interesting when we realize that we each have the power to choose what experience we have of someone else. If *who they are* is the experience that we have of them, and if we have the ability to choose what experience we have of them, then we have the ability to reinvent who people are. In extraordinary human relationship and in

Archetypal Relationship this is an important success factor.

This "Nine Cow Story" that follows is about how we can reinvent other people. We reinvent other people by declaring our experience of them. Goddesses are made, not found. The same is true with brilliant, happy children; with generous, kind, powerful bosses at work; with good neighbors, respectful parents, and efficient, creative, responsible employees.

SECTION 14-A
The Nine Cow Story

The original "Nine Cow Story" was written by the late Patricia McGerr and published in *Woman's Day* magazine in November 1965 with the title "Johnny Lingo's Eight-Cow Wife." A condensed version was published in February 1988 in *Reader's Digest*. This story has been retold and retold by so many people in so many different ways that I take the liberty here of telling it to you my own way.

Mike and Bill were sailing across the ocean in search of paradise when up comes a big storm. In the middle of the night their boat crashes on a reef and is completely demolished. The two young men struggle across the reef and manage to drag themselves half-drowned up onto a tiny tropical island.

The next morning natives of the island discover the two drenched and forlorn sailors and set about patching up their wounds, finding new clothes for them, bringing them food, and getting them comfortable.

That evening, Mike and Bill are sitting around a fire having a meal with all the villagers. Mike keeps staring across the fire at one of the women serving the food. Finally he says to his friend, "Bill, see that woman there? She is *my* woman."

Bill says, "What? Did you drink too much salt water? Look at her! Her hair is a mess. She's all slumped over. She's got a big gap between her front teeth. And she's pissed off at everybody."

But Mike says, "*You* look at her. She's *so beautiful!*"

"No, come on man!" implores Bill. "Forget it! Tomorrow we'll get out of here. We'll borrow an outrigger canoe and sail to a bigger island where we can catch a ride back home and you can find yourself a real woman."

"No way," says Mike deliberately. "I am not leaving this place. I have found my woman. I am going to marry her and stay here the rest of my life."

Bill can't believe what he's hearing. He starts shaking his friend. "You've gone nuts Mike! Wake up! Wake up! What's gotten into you?" But Mike insists that he's staying.

The next morning Mike has not changed his mind. The next week, still the same. Finally Bill builds himself a raft out of bamboo, makes a sail out of woven mats, and sails away, leaving Mike behind on the island.

After Bill leaves, Mike goes to the chief of the tribe. "Hello, Chief," he says.

The chief just grunts. "Mmm."

Mike continues, "Listen, Chief, that woman – the one with the wild hair and the gap between her teeth. I'm going to marry her."

The chief says, "Well, in our village, if you want to marry a woman, you have to pay for her. Each woman has a different value, somewhere between one cow and nine cows. That woman you want, you can have her for three cows."

At this Mike gets really angry. "*That* is *not* a Three Cow Woman," he says. "*That* is a Nine Cow Woman!"

The chief starts laughing. "Her? Didn't you notice her slumped shoulders? The way she dresses? How she's pissed off at everybody? She isn't even a Three Cow Woman. She's really only worth two cows. But I said three so we had room to bargain."

"No!" Mike insists. "This is a Nine Cow Woman. I am going to marry her and I am going to pay nine cows for her!"

The chief says, "You're not only stupid, you're crazy. I can't do this. If I do, the whole economy of women will be destroyed." He studies the stubborn look in Mike's eyes for awhile and finally says, "Okay. You can do it. You can go ahead and pay nine cows for her. I will just use you as an example of a stupid American."

Mike says, "I don't care what you tell people, but I'm paying nine cows for this woman."

He doesn't have any money, so it takes him over a year of hard work and helping a lot of people in order to earn the nine cows. Then he and the woman get married.

About a year after that, Bill comes sailing back to the island in his new sailboat. He tosses the anchor in the water, rows to shore, and walks into the village looking for his old buddy. When he sees a couple of natives he says, "Hi. I'm one of the guys who crashed on your island a couple of years ago. Remember me? You people took care of me and my friend Mike. Remember?"

"Yeah," they say. "How ya doin'?"

Bill says, "Great! Hey, my friend Mike, is he still here? Whatever happened to him?"

The villagers point off down the beach and say, "He lives in the house at the end of that path."

Bill is really excited. He runs down the path to the house and knocks on the door. In a few moments this beautiful woman opens it. "Yes?" she says.

Bill just stares at her. Finally he says, "I'm one of the guys who crashed on the reef a couple of years ago, and I'm looking for my friend Mike. Is he here?" He figures maybe he knocked at the wrong house.

"Yes, he's right here," the woman says sweetly, standing aside. "Please come in."

Bill walks up the steps, Mike sees him, and instantly the two buddies leap into each other's arms for bear hugs and laughs. They sit down and start swapping stories. The woman brings them fresh mango juice. Then hot tea and a delicious abundant meal with spicy coconut-cream vegetables and fresh fish over steamed rice.

After awhile Bill says to Mike, "Hey, I have to ask you something. When we crashed here a couple of years ago you went crazy. Remember that night when we were sitting by the campfire and you were looking at that impossible woman with the slumped shoulders and messed up hair? You said, 'That's my woman'? Remember that?"

Mike says, "Yes, I remember."

"So whatever happened to her?" Bill continues. "I thought you'd lost your mind. You wouldn't come home with me. You stayed here because of that witch. Now you've got this great place in paradise and you are living with this wonderful sexy island queen. I am glad you sobered up. But what actually happened to that first lady?"

Mike points toward the kitchen and says, "I married her. She opened the door for you. She cooked this meal for us. That's her."

"No way!" says Bill. "That's not her. That other woman was dressed in rags. Her spirit was ruined. She was skinny and pissed off at everybody. This is *not* her! Your woman is a goddess. She's gorgeous. She's radiant.

She's full of love and confidence. Her eyes sparkle! This is *not* that other woman. You're lying to me!"

Mike says, "No. I'm not lying. This is my Nine Cow Woman."

Bill says, "I don't believe you."

Then Mike calls to his woman. "Excuse me Mary," he says. "Could you please come here and explain to my friend who you are?"

So she comes over and sits down at the table. She smiles at Bill with simple joy and says, "Yes, this is really me." And as she smiles Bill can see the gap between her teeth and he recognizes that it *is* her. He is stunned.

"I can't believe it," he says, shaking his head. "What happened to you? I saw how you were back then. You were this skinny, angry, messed-up woman. What happened?"

She points to Mike, smiles again and says, "It was this man here. He did it."

"What do you mean?" Bill asks.

"Well," Mary says gently, "Ever since I was a little girl I knew that I was really only a Two Cow Woman. Everyone in the village, including my friends and family, also saw me and related to me as a Two Cow Woman. Then along comes Mike saying that I am worth nine cows! At first I resist. But then he actually pays the nine cows – nine cows! For *me*! And when we get married he organizes a Nine Cow Wedding ceremony. I wear a Nine Cow wedding dress! Me! And then he builds me this true Nine Cow Woman house. I see him sweating, sawing the wood, carrying boards, thatching the roof. I see that he totally trusts what he is doing for me. There is no doubt in him about who I am. Every evening, I mean *every* evening he would do the Nine Cow Rub-Her-Feet-and-Shoulders Ceremony. And every Saturday morning he would spoil me with the Nine Cow Tea-and-Breakfast-in-Bed Ceremony. At first I could not handle it. I was not very pleasant to be around. But I could not do anything to change his mind. Even now he refuses to get off it. He talks with me only like you would speak to a Nine Cow Woman. In every way he treats me like a Nine Cow Woman. He even introduces me to people as a Nine Cow Woman. At some point I could no longer disagree. I surrendered. My old opinion of myself fell away. *I had no choice.* I started experiencing myself through his eyes. I became a Nine Cow Woman."

For a few moments there is total silence. You could hear waves gently lapping against the white coral sand beach. Then Bill looks over at Mike and asks, "You did this to make her happy?"

Mike says, "I did this because I wanted to live with a Nine Cow Woman."

Reinventing People

Reinventing People (BLTLCH14.01). Nine Cow methodology sounds so simple. Actually it is simple, but it is not easy. We use Nine Cow methodology often in our everyday relationships with people, but we use the methodology unconsciously to surround ourselves with pigs, idiots, and untrustworthy persons. It contradicts years of habit for us to try something different than pig-making. It is not so easy to use the Nine Cow procedure consciously to surround ourselves with Kings and Queens, with real friends.

I sometimes tell the Nine Cow story in trainings and then I pair up men and women and have them sit facing each other. I invite each man to look at the woman and speak to her as a Nine Cow Woman, and I invite each woman to look at and speak to the men as a Nine Cow Man. And *they cannot do it.* At first this was very unsettling to me. But, after repeated experiments, I learned that this is actually how it is. Nine-Cowing someone takes practice because in order to Nine Cow someone you have to reinvent reality. This is how you recreate people. You reinvent your experience of who they are by looking for evidence that supports the story that leads to your experience of your experience.

In every moment you are creating or storytelling, and your creating/storytelling is either serving your conscious purposes or your unconscious purposes. When you relate to another person, whether it is your mate or even a stranger, you are either creating a King or Queen or creating a pig. If you are trying to make the person wrong, prove that you are right, point out how they are making mistakes, how they do not understand, you are making them into pigs. You are either functioning as a King-maker or pig-maker. You get to choose. Them being a King or a pig is entirely up to you. With each thought you think, with the tone and spin on each word that you speak, you get to choose. If you are a woman living with a man, you have a choice as to whom you live with. What you want is revealed to you by what you have up to this point chosen. Your choice may not have been a conscious choice, but conscious or unconscious, you have chosen it. If you are living with a pig, guess who makes him into a pig?

The world is rich in evidence. You are immensely creative. You can find evidence to support any story. Even the tiniest bit of evidence is sufficient to support your story that your partner is a pig. "He picks his fingernails.

He loses his glasses. He trips over the spots in the linoleum." One incident is sufficient evidence for your Box to create a story about someone for a lifetime. The same amount of evidence can be used to support the story that they are a King or Queen. You get to choose.

Mike did not at first have much evidence to support the story that Mary was a Nine Cow Woman, but he found one thing and he clung to it. Maybe it was the delicateness with which she held her wrist when she passed the tray of food. Maybe that was the only evidence he could find to support his story that she was a Nine Cow Woman. That one thing is enough. Mike then only paid attention to her wrist. By monitoring his attention he practiced eliminating any other evidence from his awareness. If contradictory evidence ever arose he undoubtedly used his Voice Blaster (*see* Glossary or Section 6-B) to vaporize the images, the feelings, or the voices in his head. A fierce commitment to discipline made it possible to avoid indulging in contradictory evidence. The quality of delicateness in her wrist was all that he saw about her. This is exactly what we can do when we look at our mate or our children, our colleague or our neighbor. We can choose to look at them and see only evidence to support the story that they are a King or Queen.

Choosing the evidence you use to make stories is not about being naïve or Pollyannaish. It is not about blinding yourself and living in a fantasy world. Choosing the evidence you use to make stories is about taking responsibility at the level of story making. As you stop making stories that serve your unconscious hidden purposes, you become a conscious story maker.

A word of warning: If you are planning to try the Nine Cow experiment, you should know that it takes a minimum of three months of effort before the subject of the experiment begins to believe you – before they start to recontextualize themselves in response to your

She Said

"I don't want to hear about the darkness," She said,
With a gentle aching cry.
"Write me a love song, "She said,
"So I can open my sweet wings and fly."
"I don't want to dwell in the madness," She said,
"I want to concentrate on the light.
So keep your cynicism to yourself," She said,
"I want to love not fight."
Thank God for the Women.
Thank God for the Women
In these times of confusion.
Thank God for the Women
They keep us from drowning in illusion.
Yeah, thank God for the Women.
"Take your talk of war and pain," She said,
"Get it out of my face.
Leave it for your conversations with the other boys.
I want to talk of love and beauty and grace."
Thank God for the Women.
She slaps us in the face with Her cold hard truth
That turns soft and warm when our hearts let loose.
Thank God for the Women.
"I will not indulge your terrors," She said,
"Let my touch begin to heal.
There isn't time to hash out all the wrongs," She said,
"It's only bright joy we need to feel."
And I said, "Thank God for the Women!"
"Confusion and doubt are useless," She said,
"Things are simple in my view.
I'm not interested in things that don't work.
I'd rather give myself to a life of loving you."
Oh, thank God for the Women!

(Lyrics from the CD *écrasé par l'amour (crushed by love)* written and sung by Lee Lozowick. Muse-ic Records
© 2004 Lee Lozowick. All rights reserved. Used with permission.)

perceptions of them. For three months you are going to look at only one tiny little piece of evidence to support the story that he or she is a King or Queen. After three months something extraordinary will start to shift in them, and it will show up when you least expect it. The changes that happen are literally "impossible." You will have reinvented reality.

Reinventing reality is a huge responsibility. Think about it. You become responsible for who other people are to you. Your story about them creates your experience of them, which creates their experience of themselves. You become responsible for how they see themselves.

Normally we think that we first experience someone and then, based on that experience, we understand who they really are. But human beings are so vast and complex that there are thousands of things you could experience about any given person, and use to create your story. Normally you select one or two details that match the requirements of protecting your Box's opinions. Although you often choose superficial evidence, you decide that what you have chosen to experience about that person is who that person *actually* is. Then you are stuck in the past, relating to your old story about a person, rather than being in the present relationship with the person as they are now.

For example, when your boss walks in the door you already know what your story about your boss is. You immediately put on your scanners and start looking for the evidence you can use today to support the story that you already have. When you find the evidence you think, "See! He really *is* an asshole! Look at this evidence! The evidence proves it! Who could argue?" All you see is the evidence that you looked for, and you create your entire relationship with your boss based on that evidence.

You pass your life this way never getting to be-with who is really there. And the days you have spent creating assholes to support your unconscious hidden purposes – you will never get those days back.

An experiment to try would be to "reinvent" your boss or your child. The next time you see them use the same scanner you used to find evidence for making him or her into a jerk, but this time use the scanner to find evidence to prove the story that they are geniuses in their own way and worthy of your highest respect. Look and look and keep looking until your Gremlin takes a nap and releases the editorial controls of the filters of your Box. Suddenly you will have new evidence to work with. With your boss, your child, or anyone you are doing this experiment with – and I recommend that you do it often – the evidence could be something as small and simple as noticing that their shoes are polished, that they comb their hair, that they love dogs, or that they ask interesting questions. The next time you see him or her, focus on that *one* detail about them to the exclusion of all others, and tell yourself, "This person is responsible. What attention! What care they are capable of! Shoes are just physical objects, but with all their other responsibilities they really care enough to see that their shoes are polished." Then say to him or her, "Good morning, Mr. or Ms. Fritz," or, "Good afternoon, Sam. I've never told you this before, but I have great respect for you because of how you care for details. Your shoes are an example." Do not expect any particular kind of response. This can be a brief interaction. Then continue with your reinvention by telling your colleagues or neighbors the same thing, and then tell your mate the same thing. "I have such respect for them because of their attention to this." Keep looking for evidence of things you can truly admire and appreciate about your boss or your child and do that for three months. In this time you are creating a legend about them – a legend they will not be able to resist – and more and more of the evidence will start conforming to the legend you have created. Soon you will have produced a Nine Cow boss or a Nine Cow child. Now, whom would you rather work for or get ready for school in the morning? A Nine Cow person or a pig?

How you see and speak about people is how they will show up for you. What is possible when you relate to someone as worth nine cows is a lot different than when you relate to them as worth two cows. When you relate to someone as worth nine cows, as being whole, complete and with a bright future – as opposed to someone with "problems" and needing to be fixed – the possibility of a Nine Cow relationship emerges. You now have created for yourself a playing field for extraordinary human and Archetypal Relationship. Then, simply refuse to change your mind.

CHAPTER 15

The Experience of Countenance

Over fifteen years ago I was introduced to an experience that I have come to refer to as Countenance. Without linear preparation, without maps, my attempts at trying to figure out what happened and how it fit in with the rest of my known world at the time, were rather futile. Still, I wanted what happened to have happened, so I wrote about it as best I could. What I wrote is included below. Looking back, I now understand that the capitalized "You" in this and all further writings in this book refers to impersonalized Archetypal Love.

SECTION 15-A

Countenance, the First Time

From my journal, April 1994

You got me. I did not think that You ever would. I might even have bet on that. After all, I am forty-two years old. But looking backwards I can see that all the clues led me step by step to the point where my heart gets broken.

I did not think that it would happen like this, gazing. Just gazing, and drinking tea! I did not suspect that in that moment You were reaching for me. In actuality, there probably has never been a moment when You were not reaching for me. All these years You have been waiting, waiting, endlessly patient. Were You confident in the results? I doubt it. I would not have been. But without hesitation You have only waited, never ceasing to reach out for me.

Then unexpectedly, this one time, as I gaze, something slowly burns through the thoughts just as the sun burns through morning fog. It is the realization that You are reaching out to me, that even with all my imperfections, my human frailties, You completely want me and receive me. The dawning reformulates my consciousness, like what happens when you study chaotic patterns in special posters where you change the focus of your eyes and suddenly three-dimensional pictures appear. The new image is always inherently there but the viewer must shift to perceive it. Somehow I shift.

As I come to realize that You are completely open and intentionally inviting me to fully enter Your realm, a bolt of pure terror rips through my body. I am instantly and automatically blocked against that kind of surrender, that kind of intimacy. If I continued then in a moment I would be closer to You than to my own mind. My eyes want to dart around the room, my mouth wants to chatter, my mind generates a million questions. I know there is something else I should be doing right now. Please let there be something else! Anything but this!

Yet somehow, miraculously, I do not make a sudden knee-jerk move that could "accidentally" destroy the space. Somehow the mind does not interrupt me with interesting or necessary thoughts to distract my attention forgetfully away from You. Somehow, the four bodies around me have built up barely enough tolerance of the intolerable that I can stick around rather than running away. What is happening now is the result of having 51-percent vote to stay put on this extremely intense spot. Maybe it is only 50.01 percent. Barely there, hanging on by a hair, like a tightrope walker balancing on the line for the first time without a safety net, making it, but verrrrry wiggly. Then, I remember to take a breath, and coach myself, "Relax those knots between your shoulders. There, see? It is not so bad, is it?" I keep trying. I keep paying attention. I try to relax and let the presence of the presence grow. I cannot grasp it, so subtle it is. If I grasp, it vanishes like smoke. If I relax in total alertness without pressure it comes back again. I am thinking, "Just allow. Just notice. Just accept and enjoy. It is not going anywhere. If you stop going anywhere it will stay there with you. Breathe!"

Way back in there, somewhere, the mind is also screaming: "Hey! Stop this immediately! Let's get out of here! What, are you crazy? We are going to die!!!"

But there is another, deeper part of me that is feasting, gorging itself on this endless supply of indescribably nourishing nectar. And this is the part, right now, that has its fingers guarding the controls.

And You just keep opening more and more, but with sensitivity, only as much as I can handle. You seem so relaxed, so comfortable, as if this were the most common thing in the world, while I am teetering on the edge of insanity.

It seems that without feeling like I deserve it at all, I am somehow being initiated back into the Garden. It is the Garden that Archetypal Woman builds within the space held for that purpose by Archetypal Man. This is the Garden that Woman is, the Garden of Eden. Without explanation, without excuse, without warning, the door opens wider and wider. If I accept the invitation, I will be subsumed in Paradise. You are initiating me into what it means to be 90 percent Woman. Many forces urge me to be a thief, a vandal, to try to take all the goodies I can, then destroy what is left and run away. That would be possible because You are completely vulnerable.

Matriarchy is defenseless. But to stay here, to keep from being expelled, I must become a beggar, one who has nothing to offer but gratitude, and who appreciates whatever is given. There is a fine distinction between what it is to be a beggar and what it is to be a thief. To be permitted to stay I cannot lie, no matter how much face I lose. In fact, I must lose all face, and instead just feel what I am feeling – the truth, all my fears, all my sadness, all my excitement.

In Your embracing smile I see that there are no bad consequences to losing face. It is me you are offering to embrace, not my face.

As I begin to sink into the immense stillness of Your presence, to accept Your invitation to be-with You, I also begin realizing that nothing else could ever feel this good. Nothing else could ever be so satisfying, so nourishing, so healing, so fulfilling. No kind of physical sensation, not touching the softest skin, not kisses, not orgasms, not swimming in the warm tropical ocean, not baking in the sun, not mangoes, not homemade cookies, not the most beautiful sunset or the most incredible movies or the most superb concert. As I relax into it – my body humming like a high voltage transformer – the only thought I have is a kind of attention which is monitoring my Gremlin. There is no way I want to lose my focus and let that monkey-mind take back control by asking fancy questions or cracking wiseacre jokes. No way. I keep calming the Gremlin while he sits muttering to himself at my feet on a very short leash. I keep trying to pay attention and relax.

I notice that I am losing my usual concerns about even basic human needs, like knowing what time it is, or knowing what happens next. I begin to wonder to myself, "Can you imagine resting in this? What if it could be like this forever?"

At the moment, this seems possible. Perhaps I died and went to heaven. On and on and on

it goes. Nothing else is important. Nothing else matters. Nothing else counts. It becomes clear that the whole purpose of human-realm life is to support the miniscule chance that there could be a moment like this. And You have been just waiting, wanting, aching to share this with anyone who will come, offering direct undiluted contact with You since forever! How stupid I am for not surrendering to this before, for not accepting Your offer. How could I have been afraid of being so totally welcomed and held like this?

I am scared to stop. What if this is it, my only chance to drink of You? What if...

And realization hits me like a hand smacking a mosquito. I have been had.

Here I have been given what feels like an endless source of pure ecstasy and after unreservedly jumping in I realize three things: 1) Once I have tasted Paradise I can never not be hungry for Paradise. 2) I am going to have to stop ecstatically drinking of You like this at some point, and go off to take care of the mundane details of life. 3) I am not in control of whether or not, or how, or when You are ever available to me like this again.

I have been caught, like a monkey with his hand around an apple in a jar. No way will I let go of that apple. No way will the jar let go of me.

Now that I know what I have been looking for, You tell me that it is not permanent, and that the method for gaining access to it again is out of my control?

Well, that sucks. And... I would not trade it for anything in the world.

And yet, for right now, I cannot stay here any longer. I must break from You. I stand up and walk away. I leave the space. I go about my business. My experience of You unavoidably drifts into the realm of memories. That jungle of memories. Such a shame. So disrespectful that the most valuable treasure would sink into the same swamp with memories of pain, failure, and ordinary life. What else can I do? You are gone into the past. I am still in the present, and helpless.

Time goes by. Days. I breathe, walk, see, talk. Everyday life creeps back in and normal overlays the extraordinary. But, not all the way. I notice that there is something different now, forever changed.

There is a place around my heart that aches. It never ached like this before. So tenderly, so insistently. I experientially know what is possible for a human being now. I cannot deny what I know. And since it was a personal experience, neither can anyone dissuade me. My old view of life has been irreparably shattered, replaced with direct knowledge of a world that is vaster, more alive, and filled with a mysteriously wonderful heart-rending awe. The aching remains. It is the ache of longing to have You visit with me again. Now I know what is the most important thing. I want nothing else.

I want to hoard You. I want to command You to return to me immediately, whenever I desire it. And, at the same time, I somehow know that You will not let me possess the key. You will come whenever it pleases You. There is no key.

Now it is my turn to wait. Can't You see? I have been had. I have worked all my life for this. My heart longs for the tiniest assurance that there will be a next time. Please don't make me wait too long. Please.

I am waiting...

SECTION 15-B

Countenance at 30,000 Feet

Around 1988 (plus or minus five years), I read an article in a national news magazine. It was a long and unusual letter sent in by a reader who told of a life-changing experience that touched me deeply. Back then I had no idea what the man was talking about. Now I think that the man had his first experience with Countenance.

At the time this story happened the writer was a passenger on a commuter jet. He was sitting in the front row of an economy-class night flight. The weather was extremely stormy. Something happened and suddenly the plane was going down.

Fear broke out everywhere, but of course, there was nothing anyone could do. The pilot gave the command for all crewmembers to buckle into their seats. A stewardess pulled down the folding chair mounted on the bulkhead directly opposite the man. She strapped herself in. Then she looked at the man straight in his eyes. He looked back.

Neither the man nor the stewardess knew what was going to happen. All they knew was this: that they did not know what was going to happen. The dissolution of certainty about the next moment brought them both suddenly into the immediate present with each other. Their minds stopped chatting because, in the present, their minds had no way to know what to chat about. Their attention was totally focused and alert because of the immanent danger. They were prepared to die because the option was out of their control. There was nothing better to look at than each other.

Then the space shifted. Time disappeared. The man wrote about how he fell into an immense and unconditional Love for this woman who the moment before was a complete stranger, a nameless stewardess on an airplane bound for some city. Finding themselves in the middle of Archetypal Love, neither of them looked away.

The lifelong cement wall around the man's heart crumbled away while the two of them were locked together in the whole body experience of what we might assume was Countenance. He had never in his life encountered an intimacy that was so accepting, so open, or so total as this. The intensity grew and grew. Minutes went by and he just kept breathing, being-with her more and more. This woman stayed with him too. She was not afraid. His faults were obvious and she did not turn away. The man could only bask in her beauty and feminine radiance.

Then the plane crashed. All hell broke loose. The shear physical violence and thunder of exploding engines and ripping metal shattered the space. Flashes in the night. The total unrelenting chaos of absolute destruction. Time passed. Things settled down. The man found that he was still alive, not too badly hurt. A miracle! Although I forget the details now, I imagine that perhaps he regained consciousness in a hospital the next morning. He remembered the stewardess and asked for her. She was killed in the crash.

The story never ends for this man. He was a normal businessman – with wife, kids, job. But his life changed. The veil was ripped away in those moments of Countenance while the plane was going down. The man's life was changed because from that moment on he could neither forget nor deny that Countenance existed. And he didn't even have a name for it.

This man wrote his letter to the magazine years later in hopes that someone else knew what had happened between him and the stewardess. He wanted to find someone else who could understand what he was talking about. At the time, I had no clue. I only knew that his letter touched a longing deep within me that, before then, was dormant. Now he and I could have an interesting conversation. Are you still out there, my friend? Talk to me.

If you, reader, know of this article, could you please send me a copy? I tried to find it and had no luck. I would like to read it again. If you know of this man, could you please ask him to call me? I would love to meet him.

SECTION 15-C

The Map of the Evolution of Self and Relationship

Reviewing Your Relationship Evolution (BLTLCH15.01). The explanations that accompany this series of energetic diagrams are brief and contain any number of inexcusable generalizations. Your life experience may differ greatly from what is described. At the same time, when you review what happened to you and what may be happening now with you or with your own children, these diagrams can provide significant clarity about what is or has been going on for you in your relationship. These maps cover the evolution of self and relationship from before ordinary human relationship begins all

MAP OF CHILD TO ADOLESCENT

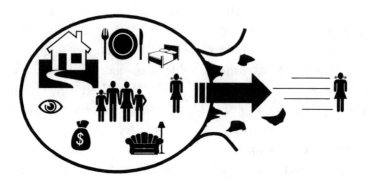

A child lives in their parents' home, eats their parents' food, spends their parents' money, and follows their parents' rules. In order to survive, a child adapts their Box to fit with their parents' Boxes. The level of behavior adaptation may be extreme. At early adolescence a healthy child wants to get out. They do whatever it takes to make the break. Healthy parents facilitate the transition out into the world. But a child in the world is still a child, naïve and without clarity about his or her center, space or Purpose.

MAP OF EARLY ADOLESCENT RELATIONSHIP

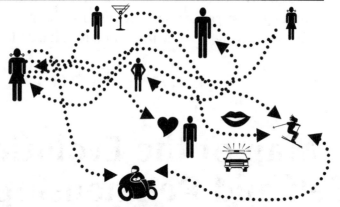

The adolescent in the world experiences raw energy without boundaries or distinctions. The purpose of actions is unclear. Sexual energy is mixed with Principle energies and Archetypal energies. Sexual energy is exchanged indiscriminately with anyone in the gang because it feels good, or at least it feels interesting. Flirtation at shopping malls or parties is stimulating but temporary, and ultimately unfulfilling. At some point a relationship of more stability may be sought. Since a rite of passage is not provided by the culture, substitute experiences, created by the adolescent, may be quite dangerous.

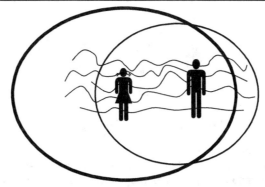

MAP OF LATER ADOLESCENT RELATIONSHIP

We search for intimacy without clarity about personal spaces, so we duplicate the co-dependency we experienced at home. We are involved in our partner's space and they in ours, enmeshed. They belong to us and we belong to them. We know what they think and feel almost before they do, and we enable each others' neurotic defense strategies. We experience irresponsible intimacy that feels like subtle jolts of electric ecstasy. It can be an emotional roller coaster of low drama. We give our center away and use adaptive behavior to manipulate for validation. Fusion feels like a drug dependency. This may be our understanding of what is to be "friends." Long hard work may be required to extricate ourselves from fusion, but until we do we have no hope of entering extraordinary human relationship.

the way through the far fringes of Archetypal Relationship.

In the early 1990s my men's group first informed me that I only created enmeshed, fused relationships, and that in fact I had no idea what it was to experience mature adult friendship among men. We had been meeting regularly for over a year. I already trusted these men. I had already repeatedly experienced their uncanny ability to hit a nail on the head at exactly the right moment, so when they landed this hammer on me I could only surrender to the truth of it. I was totally blind and stuck, and relied heavily on their guidance. Of my own volition I ended all informal contact with both men and women until such time as the falling apart could complete itself and something else could begin growing out

of the ashes. It took longer than a year. The beginnings of new contact began of its own accord and was a startling experience with qualities of a completely different nature. No longer was my personal space enmeshed in the other person's personal space. We were simply in contact, and not entwined into each other to possess, as had been the case previously. Only then, when I was over forty years old, did I first experience adult responsible relationship. This was one of the hardest periods in my life. Nobody knew me. I am forever grateful to these men for having the courage and integrity to put my face into the reality of my unconscious behavior until, through the pain, I could be reborn. Without that, none of my further explorations of relationship could have been possible. (*See* next three *Maps*.)

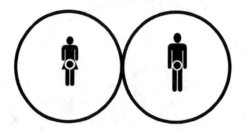

MAP OF EXTRAORDINARY HUMAN RELATIONSHIP

This is the first relationship where we take responsibility for our center and our space. We have few role models for this. Individuality is clearly experienced. If we find a partner also willing to have integrity we discover extraordinary human relationship, based on respect. Our spaces are in contact but not enmeshed. We each have our center. We are conscious of and avoid low drama. We practice to stabilize in the responsible Adult ego state, the gateway to deep Feminine and deep Masculine Archetypes. We can choose, act, decide, create, take risks, communicate and explore, and still be in relationship. Without men's and women's culture for support we may only experience extraordinary human relationship for a few hours on our marriage day, and spend most of our time in fusion and flirtation whenever we are away from the house at work, at parties or while shopping.

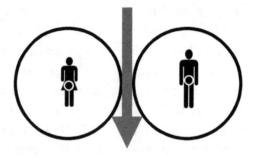

MAP OF RELATIONSHIP AS HIGH DRAMA

An extraordinary human Adult relationship can itself become the space through which the Principles that it serves can do their work. The relationship then becomes the place where two are gathered in the name of the Principles. Archetypal Relationship can occur. The relationship can serve as the center of a gameworld. There is a slight gap between partners through which the Principles function to serve the organization or project, and also to feed the relationship. High drama relationships are rare.

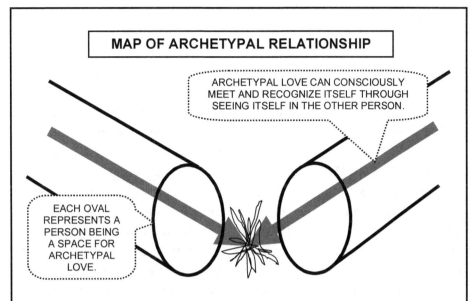

MAP OF ARCHETYPAL RELATIONSHIP

ARCHETYPAL LOVE CAN CONSCIOUSLY MEET AND RECOGNIZE ITSELF THROUGH SEEING ITSELF IN THE OTHER PERSON.

EACH OVAL REPRESENTS A PERSON BEING A SPACE FOR ARCHETYPAL LOVE.

Archetypal masculine meets Archetypal feminine only when certain criteria are met, such as holding space, being centered, being present, paying attention to attention, staying unhookable, and being unafraid to die so that the person can become a space. Notice that in each person's space the person is not there. The individual's space becomes the mouthpiece of a tube conducting Bright Principles and Archetypal Love. Archetypal Love through one can gaze upon and make contact with Archetypal Love through the other. If Archetypal Love becomes conscious of itself through recognizing itself in the other, it completes a circuit and as a side effect creates a physical experience I call Countenance.

SECTION 15-D

Self-Sitting – Preparation for Countenance

Some call it meditation, contemplation, reflection, introspection, recapitulation, self-observation, or prayer. I call it sitting. You may or may not have a practice of sitting. Self-sitting is not unique to the work of building Love that lasts. In almost every tradition of self-development or self-discovery throughout history and throughout the world, some form of sitting is practiced. For thousands of years, since well before recorded history, people have used self-sitting as a foundation tool for unifying their mental, emotional, physical and energetic bodies and for developing skills in inner navigation. Not that it matters, but the regular practice of self-sitting is scientifically proven to relieve emotional, mental, physical, and psychic stress, and to facilitate shifts through the liquid state. One of the traditional purposes of sitting is self-knowledge. While searching for this elusive "self" what we do observe and get to know is our Box. Self-sitting is therefore a way to study Box mechanics. Furthermore, self-sitting builds matrix. Because of these effects self-sitting also turns out to be preparation for Countenance.

This section not intended to be a complete explanation of the practice of self-sitting. Rather, it is a simple invitation to begin an exploration of self-sitting as a practice. It contains only enough information to get you started. What I present here is the form of self-sitting that I have found to be most useful, not necessarily the "best" or only approach.

Self-Sitting (BLTLCH15.02). You already have many reference points for self-sitting. Every day you spend at least a few minutes in some form of reverie, even if it is only those private moments sitting alone on the toilet. To formally begin a self-sitting practice, however, it is helpful to establish a regime – a sitting time, a sitting place, and a sitting duration. Proactively deciding on these details decreases Gremlin's interference with its complaints, opinions, reasons and stories. Then, your self-sitting has a chance of feeding something other than your Gremlin.

My suggestion would be to start with sitting for twenty minutes at 7AM, for five days a week. After gaining some experience you may wish to increase your self-sitting time to thirty-five minutes, and finally to fifty minutes, which in my view is the maximum self-sitting time at this stage. It can easily take a year or two to reach fifty minutes of self-sitting. Do not rush.

During self-sitting, your posture is an important factor. Self-sitting can be done on a firm cushion on the floor with legs crossed – either one under the other (crossed legs), or one on top of the other (half-lotus style). You can also sit in Zen style, on your knees with legs at the sides of your cushion, or even in a straight backed chair with your feet flat on the floor. The most crucial element of self-sitting posture is having your spine erect and your head resting directly on top of your spine, with your chin slightly and loosely tucked in. The eyes are usually closed during self-sitting, but half open and unfocused is also fine. Hands rest gently on the knees with the palms down. Shoulders are relaxed. Then be still.

When you are sitting up straight, motionless, not talking, and not sleeping, then by definition you are self-sitting. It is that simple. As you know, simple does not necessarily mean easy. Thoughts, feelings, mental conversations, insights, frustrations, long lost memories, emotions, visions, physical discomforts, disturbing sounds, horrible or inspiring images, reactions, conversations … singly or all mixed together, may invade your experience during self-sitting. Or, perhaps, absolutely nothing will happen. In self-sitting you are not trying to achieve any particular goal. For example, there are no better or worse sittings. There is no such thing as a perfectly accomplished "sit." The Box can go crazy when it discovers the paradox that it is equally impossible to succeed as it is to fail while sitting. All in all, the details of your sitting experience are not important. What is important is that you sit with consistency.

In this style of sitting you do not focus on mental imagery (called *yantra*) to rid yourself of thoughts; you do not chant a word or sound (called *mantra*) to yourself; you do not hold your hands or fingers in any special position (called *mudra*), and especially you do not focus on or try to manipulate or control your breathing (called *pranayama*). Strategic imagery, chanting, finger positions or breath control may be central to other sitting traditions, but not in this form of self-sitting. Self-sitting is neither superior nor inferior to any other method of sitting. For best matrix-building results it is suggested to not mix methods.

On one hand, try not to involve yourself with what comes up during self-sitting. If something comes up, notice that it has come up, and when you notice that it has come up, gently return to just sitting. On the other hand, what comes up during self-sitting may be something that you wish to have happened. In that case be sure to write down your experiences afterwards. Writing is a transformational action in that putting ink marks on paper gives physicality to what was previously just a subjective and transient experience. If you do not write it down, then it was only imaginary and did not actually happen, because without being recorded in writing, subjective experiences fade into the memory horizon. Words on paper remain in the physical world like dormant memetic viruses, ready to jump back to life in a reader's mind and cause changes in behavior. The reason you have this book in your hands right now is that I followed this suggestion to record certain valuable experiences in writing.

There are no purposes in self-sitting other than to sit. You sit because you have taken on sitting as your practice. Archetypal Man or Woman gradually develops a life that is generated moment-to-moment out of nothing but practice. After some time, you may begin to notice that your Principles take the opportunity of your self-sitting to deliver you with your instructions for the day. Responsibly using such input requires that you discriminate between instructions from your Principles and voices from your Box. Be careful not to fool yourself. One way to distinguish between the two is that Principles do not have voices. Principles simply move you.

As with any practice, self-sitting does not happen without commitment and discipline. A commitment to sitting shows up in only one way: sitting. How many days a week is your butt on the pillow? Five-days-a-week sitting is a strong practice. Sitting seven days a week liberates you from having to struggle with the question of whether you sit on that day or not – the decision has already been made to sit. However, sitting five days per week may in the long run prove to be more effective because then your sitting is not mandated by a rule that tends to take over responsibility for choosing to sit. Without a rule, you sit because you responsibly now choose to sit, not from enacting a rigid fanatical habit.

Together-Sitting – The Beginning of Countenance

It can also be interesting and useful to practice another form of sitting called together-sitting. In together-sitting, two people sit while being in contact with each other. Here is a forum where the possibility of Countenance begins.

Historically, the styles of sitting such as self-sitting that focus a person's attention inward were developed to aid those growing up in Eastern cultures. In Eastern cultures, the primary social emphasis for centuries has been on developing humility and cooperation. Self-sitting was designed to counteract the imbalance in Eastern people by strengthening their personal identities and their ability to be-with themselves.

Together-Sitting (BLTLCH15.03). Together-sitting was developed particularly for those who have grown up in Western cultures. In Western cultures the primary social emphasis for centuries has been on developing personal identity and achievement. We are taught from childhood to be strong and independent, to compete for our place in life, to be self-reliant, and so on. Together-sitting can teach us to bridge the gulf between others and ourselves. We can learn to overcome the fear of openness and intimate relationship with another person that is the natural side effect of an upbringing in Western society.

Together-sitting enlists the help of another person to develop your use of attention. The other person serves as a mirror in which you can see things about yourself that might otherwise be difficult or impossible to observe alone. Many of your most important inner qualities are only revealed in contact with others. By observing the experience of contact with a variety of other people, you can exercise your attention muscles, you can discover much about your Box, and you can explore what else you are besides a Box.

The practice of together-sitting involves learning how to establish and maintain contact with another being. The two persons sit facing each other as closely as possible without actually touching. The spine is kept erect, the head centered on the spine.

When both partners are ready, establish and maintain eye contact. The aim with the eye contact is to gently focus your full awareness on your partner. This does not mean a fixed stare, but rather an uninterrupted, relaxed observation. You put the kind of attention on your partner that you might normally reserve for looking at yourself in the mirror. If you find yourself becoming absorbed in thinking, mental chatter, feelings or internal dialogue, do not scold yourself. Just gently redirect your attention back to your partner's eyes. Keep relaxing your face to keep a neutral expression. Try not to smile or laugh. No talking.

This is not a staring contest. It is not any kind of contest. You are not trying to "beam cosmic love" or read minds or achieve anything fantastic. Together-sitting is simply about having your attention placed on the other person. If you need to blink or cough or scratch or wiggle, just go ahead. That is fine. This should feel pleasant and relaxed, but focused. The practice of together-sitting requires effort, but not struggle.

Together-sitting is normally done for twenty minutes at a time. Engaging in together-sitting with a wide variety of persons shows how each person you meet can teach you something about yourself. In your self-observation practice, note with whom you have been willing to establish contact, and also who you have managed to avoid.

The eyes have been called the windows of the soul. This is why there have been so many cultural and even legal constraints upon establishing eye contact with another person. For example, a slave or peasant was normally forbidden to gaze directly at an aristocrat or nobleman. Such an offense was punishable by a beating, or even, as in feudal Japan, with instant beheading. Similarly, women in some cultures have been prevented from establishing eye contact with men lest they be considered sexually overt. Such controls over eye contact have had the full force of both civil and religious law. It is clear that this form of contact is potentially very powerful. Throughout the ages, saints and sages have been considered either brave or foolhardy because they were willing to look even kings in the eye and speak the truth they saw. It is difficult to hide one's basic humanity, and to pretend to be superior or even divine if others can freely get a clear look at you.

⟩⟩ The Possibility of Countenance: An Experiment in Archetypal Intimacy

The eyes will draw us like a whirlpool, into a deep and endless cavern, holding every treasure, every discovery, all possibility ... expanding our being into infinite space and consciousness, into Light and Revelation. – Lee Lozowick

You are about to take risks in the direction of experimenting with Archetypal intimacy. Intimacy is not about sharing secrets. Intimacy is not necessarily about speaking at all. Intimacy begins with stopping all the doing with another person and discovering the simplicity of being-with them. Intimacy naturally and easefully occurs when two people navigate to the space where the dynamics of ordinary human relationship have nothing to grip on. All that remains is being-with.

Before you try this experiment in Archetypal intimacy perform a little research study. Spend some time where couples are hanging out together, such as cafés, parks, restaurants, shopping zones, or public transportation centers. Notice to what level the couples connect. Start developing an internal intimacy meter so that you can detect from 0-10 (10 is maximum) how intimate the two are being-with each other. I have generally noticed that they get to about intensity level 3 and then they shift away to less intense intimacy. Three, and then bounce back. If their being together intensifies anything past 3, they break the contact. They move their eyes, adjust their body posture, shift their focus of attention, or change the subject of the conversation. They distract themselves. One or both of them go back to zero (0) to start over again at a level of intimacy that feels safer, somewhere below level 3. They cycle through intimacy intensities every few seconds. *And they do not know that they are doing this!* I call this the "three and bounce" pattern. Maybe you'll see or interpret results differently.

After observing the three-and-bounce pattern for some time and with many different couples I could not help but be astonished at its power and consistency. I asked myself if there was some secret treasure that was hidden from all of us, in plain view, at an intimacy level greater than 3. What was this mystery?

Countenance (BLTLCH15.04). I have just defined your experiment: enter the mysteries of Archetypal intimacy. Find a partner. At first do not tell them the experiment. Assume that they too have the three-and-bounce intimacy avoidance pattern. Tell them about what you have discovered while observing the intimacy patterns of others. Tell them you are looking for a partner who is willing to go past level 3 with you. If they agree, set aside about twenty minutes and begin. Sit or stand facing each other and go to level 3. Go to 5. Go past 5. Hang in there; hang in there. Go to 7, 8, hang in there. Notice what happens in your mind and emotions and body and being. Notice what your Box does while attempting to defend itself against Archetypal intimacy. Be extraordinarily patient with yourself, also with your partner. Do not force anything. Try more than once to get to 10 and effortlessly stay there for a minute or two.

Be gentle with each other and with the space of intimacy. Breathe. You may notice a warm, pleasant, shivery vibration starting in your middle and expanding from head to toes. Relax into it. Your gazes will meet in the middle and gently wash forward and back. You are both giving and receiving at the same time. No talking. No thinking. Navigate to undefendedness. Simply try to be present. Let your body get accustomed to all that is new. There is so much to learn here. Let yourself be known.

If you fail, do not worry that nothing seems to happen. The effort alone builds matrix. If you succeed, do not worry about not staying there. Although the view from the top of the mountain is breathtaking and highly rewarding, you cannot live on top of the mountain. You must come back down into the valley to live. What you bring down off the mountain with you is a memory of a remarkable experience, and perhaps a desire to someday return for further explorations.

Formally end your experiment after the twenty minutes. Briefly thank your partner and then immediately part company. Regardless of what happened, do not hang around together for discussion. If you do, the gorilla may easily knock you unconscious and you might wake up on the other side of sex and regret it later. Being by yourselves for an hour or two afterward is an important part of the experiment. You each need time to privately digest the experience on many levels.

This is the best I can offer as instructions for finding your way to a direct experience of Countenance yourself. The experience of Countenance is reported to be amongst the most intense and precious experiences of being human. What one encounters during Countenance is truly the treasure. At the same time, Countenance is simply an experience of the laws of physics, like light refracting through raindrops makes a beautiful rainbow, or electricity discharging from clouds makes searing flashes of lightning and roaring thunder. Although experiencing the phenomenon of Countenance can be stunning or unsettling, it is at the same time no big deal. Countenance is just a phenomenon, an impersonal effect, included in the design of the universe. Nonetheless, once you find the treasure, then a new game begins. The question becomes: What will you do with the treasure?

The next section includes guidelines for meeting the requirements that appear to be necessary before Countenance occurs. You may also encounter various obstacles that may be blocking further expeditions into Archetypal intimacy. Many fine Edgework experiments can be done while proceeding with the work needed to meet the requirements and eliminate your obstacles.

))(Requirements For Countenance

Meeting the Requirements for Countenance (BLTLCH15.05). Countenance occurs when two individuals in contact (*see* Glossary and Requirement #8 below) become conducting tubes for Archetypal Love. If the two individuals then gaze into each other's eyes, Love looks out at Love looking in. Through human

consciousness, Love becomes aware of itself. Love consciously gazes at consciously-manifested Love gazing at it. The circuit of Archetypal Love is completed through human cognizance. The human body becomes a transformer, changing unconscious Archetypal Love into conscious Archetypal Love. The

Arch-Principle of Love experiences itself through two human bodies while their nervous systems register the experience as a side effect of pure ecstasy. The side effect is called Countenance.

The interesting thing about Countenance is that, just as with the laws of physics, when the conditions are met the phenomenon is repeatable. Unlike other forms of ecstasy, Countenance never goes away. It is always there waiting for you. The requirements for Countenance are not philosophical; they are structural – structural just like an airplane with no wings cannot fly, and an airplane with proper wings *cannot avoid flying*. The situation is simple: if you do not meet the requirements for Countenance you will not enter the experience of Countenance. The requirements for Countenance turn out to be quite profound.

Requirement #1: You Must Be Able to Leave Verbal Reality and Enter Experiential Reality

Leaving Verbal Reality and Entering Experiential Reality (BLTLCH15.06). Ever since early childhood we have been hammered into a life in verbal reality. So much importance is placed on reading, writing, speaking, spelling, vocabulary, grammar, languages, and all the forms of written media that, after years of conditioning, we come to imagine that verbal reality is the reality of greatest importance.

MAP OF REQUIREMENTS FOR COUNTENANCE

1) You must be able to leave verbal reality and enter experiential reality.
2) You must be able to slow down and move at the speed of Love.
3) You must be able to be in your heart and out of your mind.
4) You must be able to pay attention to your attention.
5) You must be able to keep your center.
6) You must be able to hold space.
7) You must be able to be present.
8) You must be able to make contact with another person, exposed, raw, and undefended.
9) You must be able to be a space, that is, you must be able to not be there. In order to not be there you must be okay right now to die.
10) You must be able to declare that the space that you are exists in the name of love.
11) You must have a longing to directly experience Archetypal Love.
12) You must be able to give without fear of giving too much, and you must be able to receive without fear of receiving too much, both maximally and at the same time.
13) You must be able to tolerate the intensity of being the space through which Archetypal Love does its work.

In verbal reality the words lead, and eventually come to replace, the things they label. Words bypass sense experiences and lock life into conceptual boxes. Then your experience only goes as far as what you have words for. As soon as your mind finds a word for a thing, it grabs the word like a victory prize and your experience of that thing is cut off.

Experiential reality is quite different from this. In experiential reality your experience leads. The words are held back like a pack of wild dogs on the leash, and silenced with disciplined vigilance, while experience is given free rein to roll exquisitely through your senses – from head to toe – wordlessly. Then later on, if you choose to, you can select particular words to describe or appreciate your experience, but words are not part of the experience.

In experiential reality words can serve as a bridge to transport experience from one person to another. Such communication arrives with startling authenticity because it is not

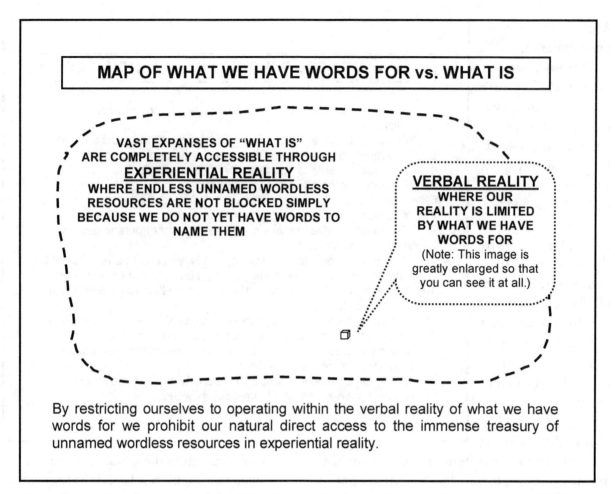

MAP OF WHAT WE HAVE WORDS FOR vs. WHAT IS

VAST EXPANSES OF "WHAT IS" ARE COMPLETELY ACCESSIBLE THROUGH **EXPERIENTIAL REALITY** WHERE ENDLESS UNNAMED WORDLESS RESOURCES ARE NOT BLOCKED SIMPLY BECAUSE WE DO NOT YET HAVE WORDS TO NAME THEM

VERBAL REALITY WHERE OUR REALITY IS LIMITED BY WHAT WE HAVE WORDS FOR (Note: This image is greatly enlarged so that you can see it at all.)

By restricting ourselves to operating within the verbal reality of what we have words for we prohibit our natural direct access to the immense treasury of unnamed wordless resources in experiential reality.

packaged into already known phrase blocks. In experiential reality, the words land in the body rather than in the intellect, and instead of stimulating thought these words awaken a personal experience within the listener. The value of expanding your competence in experiential reality cannot be overstressed if you wish to add delightful dimensions to relationship. Expanding competence into experiential reality starts with very simple experiments.

For example, in verbal reality a chair is exactly that: a chair. As soon as you have identified a thing as a "chair" the rest of that thing's possibilities are lost. To expand yourself into experiential reality you can repeatedly do the experiment of not giving a thing a name. Stand there in front of a thing, or an experience, and draw no conclusions about what it is. Encourage yourself to have no name for a thing and to permit it to still exist

for you. An apple becomes a reddish-green smashable shiny thing that smells tasty. A pen dissolves into a probe stick with moving parts and greasy substances in it. As your comfort in experiential reality begins to grow, you may find that this funny-shaped thing before you (that used to be a chair) can certainly still function as a chair but also diversifies into a more unlimited potential. What in verbal reality can only be a chair can, in experiential reality, be a sock drying rack, a display case for the crown jewels of England, a ramp for changing car tires, a defense against lions, a hat, firewood, an umbrella, a table, a battlefield for toy soldiers, a juggling tool, an item of barter, a ladder, a doorstop, a rope winder, a nutcracker, a demonstration for the limits of a flat Earth model, and so on.

In verbal reality, if you are driving down a road at dusk and see a shadowy object off to the side, the mind goes crazy. "What is that thing?" All of your attention goes into identifying the shape so it can become a known object. "Is it a bear? Is it a deer? Ah! It is just a dead tree!" And then the mind clamps shut and the mystery is gone. The prize has been found. You have a name for it. In verbal reality if you do not have a name for it, it does not exist.

In experiential reality you can experience an experience without having a name for it. Mysteries are allowed to remain as mysteries. In Western culture, men being able to experience their experience instead of simply naming it is almost unheard of. Even for Western women this is rare, especially smart Western women who read thick complicated books about relationship!

Through doing Edgework experiments together you can test if the Archetypal Feminine is more comfortable experiencing experience than the Archetypal Masculine. Whatever the result, you might enjoy spending some time enticing your partner further and further into the delicacies of experiential reality.

Experiment in Imagining
Touching Through (BLTLCH15.07). Here is an experiment for experiencing what you may not have a name for.

> Imagine that it is a hot Saturday morning.
> A little girl loves her daddy.

She is furiously peddling her tricycle down the sidewalk after him. She is wearing a short dress. She waves to him and just then her tricycle tips over. She falls onto the hard pavement, scraping the bare skin of her knees and her elbows on the hot sidewalk.

Almost everyone will have a squeamish ripply feeling in their stomach or all over their body. This is a common experience that we do not have a name for. Did you experience it? After you wordlessly have the experience you can use words to describe the experience for someone else. Verbal reality limits us to what we already have words for. Compared to the vast reaches of what actually is, our verbal reality encompasses only a very small bit. Through experiential reality we gain direct access to an immense treasury of unnamed wordless resources.

Experiment in Touching
Here is another experiment for making use of experiential reality. It has to do with the way you touch, especially when you are touching your partner.

The next time you are with your partner ask them for a moment of stillness. Tell them that you want to do an experiment. Ask them if you can touch them. If they say yes, then reach over and touch their skin the way you have always touched their skin. That is to say, touch their skin in verbal reality. A touch performed in verbal reality stops at the surface of the object because you are touching a known object. You know the name and the form of the thing you are touching, a hand for example, a cheek, or an arm. That thing you touch is an object with a surface where it starts and stops, and that is obviously where you are touching the object: on its surface. This is touch in verbal reality – we touch to confirm what we already know.

Now take your hand away and shift into experiential reality. Shift out of your head into all four bodies. Shift out of concept into experience. It can help if you slowly, delicately rub the tips of your fingers together and feel only that sensation. This helps to shift out of your Box's ongoing stories into the tiniest moment of a wordless, minimized now. Then, without knowing what it is that you are touching, slowly reach over and "touch all the way through" the skin of your partner so that wherever you are touching them you are touching the whole of them all at the same time. Your touch is making deep contact. Avoid using images of bones, muscles, blood and veins. Visualizing images only wakens the mind again. Instead, *do not know* what you touch, only that you are "touching through," touching wholeness, touching being, touching the one you love. You may notice that you touch your partner with a field of touching even before you make physical contact with their skin. And when you do touch their skin your touch no longer stops there. By touching the hand or the cheek you are touching everywhere in them all at the same time. You may notice that your touch is firmer than usual and strokes less. Then imagine hugging all the way through instead of only at the surface. Then move slowly and try it. This is called "touching through," a different kind of touching that you do through experiential reality.

Requirement #2: You Must Be Able to Slow Down and Move at the Speed of Love

Moving at the Speed of Love (BLTLCH15.08). Most of us, most of the time, walk faster than the speed of Archetypal Love. We have our attention on where we are going, whatever we are talking about and whatever is happening. We notice things around us, and all of these things take our attention away from Archetypal Love. The subject of our conversation, our feelings about the subject, our feelings about the other person's feelings, all take priority over the importance of Love. Our purpose is to take a walk, or to discuss a certain subject, to make a point, or to give someone feedback. We may accomplish those purposes. There is nothing wrong with accomplishing those purposes. However, you may wonder where the Love went. Well, you were walking too fast and you left the Love behind.

Principles are intelligent and delicate. Principles function according to their own physics. When two or more people gather in the name of the Principle of Archetypal Love, there will Archetypal Love be in the midst of them. If you wish to move from one place to another, moving too fast leaves the Love behind. It is possible to walk within the Principle of Archetypal Love and have the Love move with you, provided you do not walk faster than the speed of Love.

Love has a maximum velocity, which is the speed of a slow, relaxed stroll. Walking no quicker than the speed of Love allows you to move around within a Principle-of-Archetypal-Love bubble, a Love mobile. That Love will never go away if you do not leave it behind. That Love radiates and feeds the world. If you can walk in Archetypal Love so that Love happens, a resonance spreads out that allows a thousand other people to catch hold and enter Archetypal Love also.

Try this experiment. Always retain the option of walking in a different way. After you have a partner with whom you can invoke Archetypal Love, take a Love walk. Various sorts of things may be accomplished during your walk. You may even go through the middle of town or arrive at some predetermined destination. But, during the walking, the prime purpose of the walking is to include Archetypal Love. Keep a majority of your attention on noticing that Love is still with you. Split your attention so that you can speak, think, safely cross roads, and so on, but at all times the majority of your attention is on experiencing the Principle of Love. Walk along *being in Love*. No matter what you are talking about, no matter what you are thinking about, the most important thing in that particular moment (and the next, and the next...) is that Love is happening there, with the two of you. Your attention and your intention are on the experience of Love happening. If for any reason you get distracted, if you walk too fast, if you forget what the most important thing is, just stop. Reconnect. Call Love back into the space, and then start again. Love is very forgiving. Love loves to go for a walk.

Requirement #3: You Must Be Able to Be in Your Heart and Out of Your Mind

Being Out of Your Mind (BLTLCH15.09). Being "out of your mind" is a common euphemism for being mentally insane. In Western culture if you are out of your mind there is no place else to be except in a crazy house. Referring back to the *Map of Four Bodies* (*see* Section 5-A) you can see that there are many other places to be besides your mind. For example, you can go to your heart, your body, or your being. Our distorted identification of assuming we *are* our mind, blocks us from having an expanded identification and an expanded experience of who we are. When you expand your identification of who you are, you expand your possibilities of how you can relate to another human being and who they are. Relating from heart to heart is a different experience than relating from mind to mind. Mind-to-mind relating is like ping-pong. Heart-to-heart relating is like two warm clouds commingling. Practice diminishing your mind-to-mind relating and practice expanding your heart-to-heart being-with relating. Try doing this experiment in even the most bizarre circumstances, such as when you are stopped by a policeman for speeding, when your child is screaming at you, when someone dies or is sick, when you are standing in line at the grocery store, when you are telephoning with the tax department, and so on.

Requirement #4: You Must Be Able to Pay Attention to Your Attention

If you are not able to pay attention to your attention then your attention can be taken by any little distraction inside of you or outside of you, and then you do not have your attention to place on your partner. If you place your attention on something else besides your partner – thoughts about work, unpaid bills, plans for the weekend, a conflict with your siblings – then that is where your energy flows. If your attention is scattered then your energy is wasted, and you cannot feed your partner or the sacred space of your relationship with your energy. Where your attention goes your energy flows. If you have the potential to enter Countenance, your energy starts looking very attractive to all kinds of things that devour attention. Those things will try their best to hook your attention and get your energy. If you cannot protect yourself from the energy vultures, both your partner and the space of Countenance are unprotected. Practice paying attention to your attention so that you know exactly where and how much of your energy goes to different places during your day. You could even keep an energy journal for a few days. Set the beeper on your watch to beep every fifteen minutes. As soon as it beeps, write down what percentage of the fifteen minutes was spent with you consciously placing your attention on something, and what percentage of that time was spend with your attention unconsciously taken from you. Start noticing the patterns of what you allow to steal your attention and where you flow your energy unconsciously.

Requirement #5: You Must Be Able to Keep Your Center

If you do not have your center then you are incapable of being responsible, of being adult, of being in the present, of consciously creating, of choosing, of declaring, of responsibly communicating, of taking risks, and of leading. These are exactly the capacities that help you to undertake experiments in Countenance. Giving your center away under any circumstances is very costly. For example, if you are a man and you give your center away, to a woman it looks like you are giving your balls away. This is not inspiring for the woman. A man needs his center to hold space for his woman to shift into Archetypal Woman. She can then remember the way and lead her Man to the Center of the Labyrinth, the home of Archetypal Love.

Requirement #6: You Must Be Able to Hold Space

Developing your capacities to keep your center and to place your attention on your attention opens the door to being able to hold space (*also see* the Glossary). Holding space is the skill of splitting your attention, putting part of your attention on what you are creating in the space, and the other part of your attention on remembering that *you are in a space*. Once you can hold space you can begin declaring that people come together in that space in the name of a certain set of Bright Principles to accomplish whatever needs to be accomplished. The specific activity that happens in the space you are holding can vary from childcare to a board meeting, from sweeping out the garage together to reading a book of Japanese love poems together. The specific activity does not matter. What matters is the quality of the space holding, your intention and attention. Holding space for the work of Bright Principles transforms that space into a sanctuary. It is only within a sanctuary that Countenance can arise.

Requirement #7: You Must Be Able to Be Present

To be present means to simply be, without excessively moving, doing, speaking, or thinking. The present does not include the past or the future. In the present there are no stories, expectations, conclusions or assumptions. One discomfort of being present is that you may start experiencing what has been stored away in your body – including emotions, visions, vows, resentments, and so on. Each time your "now" is minimized and the flow of time is extinguished by the eternal timeless present, the next layer of surprises comes to the surface. Do not worry about how many layers there are. There is nothing that you can do to circumvent going through the layers that you have one at a time. Just persist. After six to nine significant layers have been de-charged, you will suddenly find yourself able to rest in a small "now" with surprising easefulness. More obstacles for you to go through will eventually arise, of course, because there is "no top end" (as Lee Lozowick points out) to the expansiveness of being present. The old hippy catchphrase was "Be here now." What you can try is "Be here more." Building a balanced set of four bodies that can withstand the intensity of being present takes time. It is authentic struggle to build matrix for being present that provides you with a ticket into the chamber. Countenance is the door prize – but you have to be present to win!

Requirement #8: You Must Be Able to Make Contact with Another Person – Exposed, Raw, and Undefended

Making Contact (BLTLCH15.10). "Contact" as I use the term in Possibility Management refers to the phenomenon of one person being-with another person, so that communication can take place (*also see* the Glossary). Conscious contact is a foundation skill. If you cannot consciously initiate contact, stay in contact, and terminate contact, then you cannot engage either extraordinary human relationship or Archetypal Relationship.

The words that best capture the mood or intention of contact are "follow" and "support." The purpose of making contact is to follow and support the other person – to be there for them, wherever they are – not as a rescuer, and definitely not as a "responsible victim," but rather as another human being on the same team playing the game of Winning Happening. Contact can only occur now, in the present, through you being present in the moment. Contact means that you keep one foot in the center of the space of objective reality, while your other foot meets the other person in their space, wherever they are. If you are *in contact*, the other person is free to move about in any of the three worlds with the guarantee that they can find their way back to you. Such contact is a form of service.

Contact begins by clearly and directly saying, "Hello." The "Hello" does not necessarily have to be spoken. It can be energetically created with intention and presence. However, the easiest, most straightforward, adult, mature and effective way to establish contact is by actually saying the word, "Hello."

You can imagine an image of contact being two sheets of paper face to face, almost touching but not touching. When one paper bends, the other paper bends in exactly the same shape as the first one. Contact allows you to experience exactly where the other person is, exactly what they are going through, and exactly where they need to go, because you are conscious of having the same experience through your contact.

When being in contact with someone it does not matter if you hate their guts, if you are afraid of them, if you are angry at them, if you are sexually attracted to them, if they are shut down, if you are shut down, it does not matter. All of these are merely Box reactions. You can go into profound contact with anybody: man, woman, old, young, pretty, ugly, mean, crippled, despicable, or world famous, and authentically be-with them in a space of Archetypal Love, exposed, raw and unprotected, and through the integrity of your contact you will still be okay.

Requirement #9: You Must Be Able to Be a Space, That Is, You Must Be Able to Not Be There. In Order to Not Be There, It Must Be Okay, Right Now, for You to Die

Being a Space (BLTLCH15.11). Your fear of not being there is predicated on the fantasy that there is some kind of "you" that is already there in the first place. If you have been paying attention you will by now have discovered that life is best when you are not there. The experience of not being there has been called the "zone." Mihaly Csikszentmihalyi calls it "flow." George B. Leonard calls it "soft eyes." Zen Buddhism calls it "no mind." Whatever you call it, if you pay attention you will notice that when "it" is happening "you" are not there. You can skip all the rigmarole that tries to prepare you for death. Instead, with a simple snap of your fingers, you can vanish yourself into being merely the space holder of the space where you used to be. Then you can immediately get on with the fun stuff. What can you do with all of your predilections towards avoiding death? Store them on a back shelf. They are no longer relevant after you discover that no matter how many times you vanish yourself it does not take too long before you automatically come back. You do not have to worry about the coming back part. It happens all by itself. Practice enjoying the ride between times when you are not there.

Requirement #10: You Must Be Able to Declare That the Space That You Are Exists in the Name of Love

Declaring Spaces in the Name of Love (BLTLCH15.12). Declaring is a simple matter of using the word "is" to glue two diverse things together to formulate a new condition (*see* Glossary, *IS Glue*). Like I just did here: I glued the term "declaring" to the phrase "a simple matter" using the word "is." This makes a statement "declaring is a simple matter" that may or may not be true, but which can in either case prove itself to be very useful or very interesting. Such an "is-glued" statement forms the basis of a story that you can step into and use as a reality in which to operate. In the case of preparing for Countenance you declare that the space you hold is dedicated to being a safe place for Archetypal Love to abide. Your declaration creates a specialized sanctuary by banishing cross-purposes and inviting an abundance of Archetypal Love. All the previous requirements must be activated in you to consciously and effectively declare and hold the purpose of a space in the name of Love.

Requirement #11: You Must Have a Longing to Directly Experience the Principle of Love

How can we even talk about this? I don't know where such a longing would come from. Perhaps it is a memory that comes alive during the experience of being present. Perhaps the longing itself is Archetypal, and as soon as you have stellated some of your Archetypes, the longing for Archetypal Love arises automatically in conjunction. Such a longing has an irresistible potency and can probably not be fulfilled by anything else. A defensive Box would avoid the longing for Archetypal Love with a vengeance because the Box thinks that even the longing itself, let alone the fulfillment of the longing, would send its preeminence to the gallows. If you somehow did not already have this longing I doubt that you would still be reading this book. You can therefore assume that the longing is strong in you. One consequence of making your longing for the direct experience of Archetypal Love conscious is you might inexplicably start writing poetry of love.

Requirement #12: You Must Be Able to Give Without Fear of Giving Too Much, and You Must Be Able to Receive Without Fear of Receiving Too Much, Both Maximally and at the Same Time

As old sayings usually go, there are two types of people: those who can never get enough, and those who can never give enough. The challenge in preparing yourself to encounter Countenance is that you need to be both

---

MAP OF COUNTENANCE vs. ARCHETYPAL LOVE

COMPARING THE EXPERIENCING OF COUNTENANCE WITH THE EXPERIENCE OF ARCHETYPAL LOVE

COUNTENANCE
Requires eye contact.
It works at 30 yards distance.
It works through a mirror.
It works in the dark.
It works through glass and plastic (windows, glasses and contact lenses).
It does not work over the phone.
It is specifically between two people.

ARCHETYPAL LOVE
Does not require eye contact.
It can be felt in any space where two or more are gathered in the name of Love.
It works over the telephone.
It works in a whole group of people in general and all at once.

Long For Longing

Longing for Longing (BLTLCH15.13). Taking pleasure in the experience of longing is the opposite of our cultural habit. We are trained to avoid longing by fulfilling any imagined desire or need as fast as we possibly can. Our desires are inflamed to the maximum with tantalizing advertisements that tempt or frighten us into immediately buying what we want.

Based on your own personal experience you have probably discovered that fulfilling desires never gives you lasting peace and contentment. Even though contentment is possible in any circumstance, with or without anything, you can watch the Box at work causing you to forget this and quickly arranging the next thing for you to desire.

Peace and contentment are about *having* what we *do* have. Fulfilling desires is an effort to try to *have* what we *do not* have. Fulfilling our desires neither eliminates longing nor establishes peace and contentment. Thinking that gratifying a desire will eliminate desire produces an artificial union. For example, we may think, "If I only had that car I would be happy." Or, "If I could also buy the large ceramic salad bowl then my dish collection would be complete and I would be satisfied." After we have the car and the salad bowl will we really be happy? Will that be the end of our desires? No. Fulfilling a desire does not stop desires. The habit of fulfilling desires opposes the practice of cultivating longing.

Cultivate longing? Yes. Longing is one of the great joys of life. Longing makes any moment precious because if we long for the extraordinary and we enter the extraordinary we still know that the extraordinary will again leave us. Longing can be a life-spicer – like adding cayenne pepper to soup. The burn keeps us awake, alert, and bright. Trying to stop longing is as futile as attempting to stop hunger. The hunger and longing always comes back and will never be finally fulfilled. Acceptance of our longing is the true completion. Longing is the way.

Cultivate your appreciation of longing. As an experiment you can choose something that you long for and purposefully evade the Box's attempts to fulfill that particular longing. Start with something simple, such as the urge to scratch an itch, to see a movie, to eat chocolate, to turn up the volume, to put down a heavy load, to go to sleep, to turn on a light, to tie your shoe, to have just one more. Don't do it. Instead, sit with the longing as if it were a coal in your belly warming you up; as if it were flavor enhancer for life; as if the longing itself were what you wanted, not the thing you originally desired. Learn to love the longing for Archetypal Love as much as you love Archetypal Love. "Long live longing!"

at the same time. Usually we have a predisposition towards *either* survival *or* abundance. This leans us toward either sucking or spewing energy. To become the space through which Archetypal Love is simultaneously given and received means you have to become a kind of resistanceless, bi-directional superconductor. It makes no sense at all, and yet this is how it works. Two people together in Countenance is like ball-lightning. On rare occasions when lightning strikes it does not immediately dissipate into the ground. Sometimes it recirculates in itself as a plasma ball, humming and buzzing along with a tremendous amount of self-contained power flowing in both directions at once. People have died touching ball lightning; so if you see one, don't try to grab it. But if you can imagine pure energy flowing maximally in both directions at the same time without interfering with its own flow then you can picture Countenance happening. Be that.

Requirement #13: You Must Be Able to Tolerate the Intensity of Being the Space Through Which Archetypal Love Does Its Work

Our Box sets the intensity limit for our experiences. No matter how convincing the threat story told to us by our Box, the Box has in mind only its own self-preservation, not our general well-being or our fondness for evolution. High-intensity experiences paralyze the Box's defense mechanisms. If we encounter high-intensity experiences and survive even though the Box is paralyzed and is unable to put on its usual performance, we will see that the Box is not as necessary as it makes itself out to be. Your practice can be to gradually, over time, enter conditions of greater intensity with the idea that the Box slowly raises its allowable intensity limits. You can internally reassure your Box that its hard-earned skills and capacities will always be needed and respected, even if they are not always given priority. This assurance will go a long way towards calming the Box's absolute resolve to avoid unbearable intensities such as are encountered during Countenance.

Working with the Requirements

Any one of these thirteen requirements is daunting – each one challenging enough to make a modern twenty-first-century he-man pee in his pants or a prom queen to run home with uncontrolled terror. So what? Do not let that stop you from trying. Our culture provides us with no way to make sense of what it would be like to fulfill even a few of these requirements. And yet, in order to enter Countenance you will need to fulfill all of these requirements all at the same time.

Do not be disappointed if you do not meet the requirements immediately. Experiencing Countenance is a rare privilege, worth working towards. At the same time, successfully encountering Countenance engenders great responsibility. You can only enter Archetypal territories when you can enter Archetypal territories. Meanwhile, you have plenty of things to do to get ready.

The most precious thing is just knowing that the answer is *yes*. Countenance is possible. If it takes you only seven years to accomplish such a feat, that in itself would be a miracle. Do not let how much time it takes worry you. Do not let your Box convince you to take no action or give up too soon. What better way is there to spend your life than learning with someone else to be the space where Archetypal Love meets Archetypal Love?

Obstacles to Countenance

As soon as you actually try entering Countenance you will realize that not only are there requirements (as we have already considered), but there are also obstacles. As you encounter the obstacles, pay attention to the feedback you experientially receive about what works and what does not work. This specific information is all you need to create your own map for how to navigate through or around the obstacles. Obstacles are not bad; they are teaching instruments. The feedback you get from your attempts provides exact instructions for how to improve your attempts. Too many people encounter an obstacle and then give up their project up for lost. Instead, develop the disposition of a sword being hammered on by the blacksmith. Let the obstacles reshape you into something thin and resilient enough to get to the next obstacle.

Obstacles can come in a wide variety of forms, including inexplicable panic reactions, old resentments, being distracted by accidents, headaches, illnesses, addictions to the adrenalin rushes of low drama or insecurity or near calamities, lack of money, a tendency to withdraw or hesitate, sloppy communications, assuming you are a victim of circumstances, fear of clarity, fear of leading, fear of being betrayed, and so on. Your obstacles become your way to refining your abilities to deal with obstacles.

Bypassing and Unwinding Obstacles to Countenance (BLTLCH15.14). To engage your obstacles you will be using two approaches. First, you will do experiments in changing your behavior so it bypasses obstacles rather than colliding with them. Second, you will journey to the source of the obstacles and unwind them. A third and most effective strategy is to do both at once. Refine the shape of your Box at the same time that you unwind the source of the obstacles. Do the experiment of radically trusting your four-body system to provide you with bountiful signals for navigating with an obstacle even if you've never met this obstacle before. Your mind gives you thoughts. Your heart gives you feelings. Your soul gives you yearnings. And your physical body gives you the sensation of very fine and wise distinctions. What an abundance of support and guidance! If you listen for it, your bodies inform you clearly about what area of relationship or self-awareness or risk needs to be addressed next, and how. Trust your bodies.

You will discover that the source of many of your obstacles is a wound. Working through these wounds so as to enter Countenance is a tremendously profound healing process. Give yourself plenty of time and permission for the healings to occur. Do not try to rush your development. The healings can take years of work and take you into domains of learning that were previously unimaginable. No matter how daunting the challenges may sometimes seem, you are designed to make the leaps from the known into the unknown, and then to do it again. Just go ahead and work steadily with whatever comes up next.

SECTION 15-H
Cultures Evolve

If you end up somehow experiencing Countenance you may discover a cascading series of subsequent events occurring. You may discover that the experience of Countenance is neither explained by nor able to be integrated within Western culture. It does not fit. Nothing matches up. In one hand you have the well-known and familiar cultural understanding of reality. In the other hand you have your incontestable first-hand experience of Countenance. The two are in radical opposition to each other, mutually exclusive. You are left with a dangerous question: Do you keep the culture? Or do you keep the repeatable experience of Countenance?

You *could* keep both. But since Countenance does not integrate into our culture, the culture no longer looks the same after experiencing Countenance. The popular worldview no longer applies. The known culture has a gap, a hole in its foundation. Something is missing, and no one in the culture could successfully convince you that what is missing is not important or real.

What before has always been seamless has suddenly disintegrated into a rubble of unanswered questions. Countenance causes disillusionment. The illusion was that our culture was real. Suddenly our revered culture is demoted to being a mere story, a fabrication of the mind, just one of myriads of possible cultures.

Cultures evolve. The fact that you or someone you know can enter Countenance could be a sign that our culture is evolving. When an individual within a culture has an experience that is outside of the boundaries of the culture the individual is evolving the culture.

Being Used by Evolution (BLTLCH15.15). If you have the experience of Countenance – or even try to have it – you may well be part of an experiment being done by the Bright Principle of Evolution to evolve the culture. It is an honorable profession, being used in experiments by a Bright Principle, although at times the experience can be significantly disturbing: evolving can force you out of the mainstream and into the fringes. Evolution happens most abundantly at the fringes where there is an interface between two cultures – between the present culture and the future culture, for example, or between the known culture and the possible culture. The first few billion fish to crawl out on land did not necessarily have an easy time of it. The whole transition from sea creature to land creature or from land creature to air creature was probably neither comfortable nor comforting. Sustaining the possibility of Countenance is an equally upsetting proposition. And here you are, in the middle of it all, at cause for evolution.

Keep in mind that while experimenting with Countenance your success could be far more disturbing than your failure. Everything that you once thought of as real could be annihilated in Love. If it is any consolation, you could consider that there are worse things by which you could be annihilated.

Just Once More

I sit.
If I am fortunate and sitting happens,
Then Shiva sits in my place.
A sitting Shiva attracts Shakti, Parvati – the Archetypal Feminine.
I ponder the little bronze Goddess that I bought.
She is not so little, and hardly made of bronze!
I sit.
You sit with me.
You sit so closely I can feel You breathe.
You breathe me.
I breathe You.
Oh beautiful One! Oh Goddess!
The whole nervous system sings
With electric love
So strong
That breathing is barely necessary anymore.
You can sit forever like this, Goddess.
You love, never go away.
Never.
But I have a body.
I stop. Sooner or later I stop,
And I go on about my human life.
Yet my cells remember.
In a short while my nervous system grows hungry
And aches for the moment
When I can sit again
That there may be a chance
That You, as the Goddess (such an inadequate word!)
That You, as the beautiful, radiant, pure, endless, love One
Might appear and sit with me
Once more.
Oh, please, just once more.

– C.C.

Encountering The Goddess

The Goddess wants to live. For the Goddess to live there needs to be a flow of energy through her. This is true of all life. Living organisms are sustained by the energy that flows through them. Air, food, water, sunlight, sound, smell, attention, information, and love are all examples of energy flowing through and sustaining the life of a human being. When a structure is sustained by energy flow, this structure has the capacity to be perturbed and to suddenly reorder into a form that is more elegant, more complex, more beautiful, and more sophisticated. This is how what was once woman can suddenly become Goddess. Being in the presence of and witnessing the transition from woman to Goddess transforms what was already extraordinary into the unprecedented Archetypal.

For energy to flow there must be a completed circuit, a connection. The Goddess is only one pole. No matter how voluptuously radiant her intelligence and beauty are, no matter how dear she is, she does not come alive without a witness, someone else to kneel before her and appreciate her. The appreciator serves as the other pole. This is Archetypal theater between Woman and Man. It also works.

In other species it is the male who wears the brightest colors, shows off his feathers, dances, squawks and preens. This is because the highest purpose of other species is survival. The strongest most virile masculine provides the greatest chance for the female's offspring to survive. Human beings may be the first species to be able to transcend survival and have an additional purpose: to appreciate. In the human species it is the female who wears the brightest colors to attract the attentions of the masculine. This makes sense if survival is no longer the highest purpose. Archetypally, Woman is Everything. Man is the one to place his attention on and appreciate the endless abundance of the feminine Everythingness.

The Man who recognizes and appreciates the Goddess is like the receiving antennae for a television. Without the antennae and the receiving circuitry there is no distinguishing between the true signal and random electrical noise. It is the Man's job to ongoingly make these distinctions, not with his mind and perceptions, but with his body and experience. This is sword work. The ability of Man to select and pay attention only to the true signal, and to let the noise go by without notice, transforms raw feminine energy into the exquisite presence and movement of the always-present potential of Goddess. The Man's sword work is essential for letting the show go on.

The Goddess is ready and waiting to deliver the show. She will come through any door that is appropriately opened for her and she will bestow her blessings and her gifts. The door can open when Man places his attention on the possibility that the door can open and waits for the Goddess patiently, attentively, expectantly.

Encountering the Archetypal Through an Artifact (BLTLCH16.01). You have probably heard of the Goddess appearing through living human portals – such as an oracle, a priestess, a healer, or someone in a state of prayer or an attitude of openness and discovery. The idea that the Goddess would come through an inanimate portal is also not strange. Human beings have created physical doorways – sacred artifacts and ritual sites – for accessing the Goddess for tens of thousands of years. We have discovered Goddess artifacts dating back nearly to the origin of our species: figures shaped out of clay, wood, bone, stone and metals, symbols scratched on the inside of caves, painted on pottery, drawn on papyrus scrolls, hammered in gold ornaments, tiled into temple floors. The Goddess lives in the hearts of human beings from every culture and time. Why would such artifacts be so common and persistent throughout human history if they did not work?

I have my own story to tell about a Goddess artifact. The portal in my story is a piece of metal. Not just any piece of metal. The metal is bronze, an alloy created by blending molten copper and zinc. Bronze has different qualities than its component materials. Bronze is gold colored, for example, whereas copper is "copper" colored, and zinc is silvery. The particular piece of bronze in this story has been fashioned with great care into the shape of a sacred Goddess. To my astonishment I found that a sacred bronze Goddess statue can function like a human female body to serve as a doorway to the Archetypal Goddess.

SECTION 16-A
A Personal Encounter

This story begins when I walk into an attractive little gallery tucked into the corner of a side alley of a quaint French village. The building is some six hundred years old, made of handcarved limestone blocks, thick handhewn oak beams, and mud, just like all the other buildings of this era. From the perspective of an American whose country did not exist before 1776, it amazes me that the whole village is not in some museum.

In this building several beams have been recently renewed. A few stones are new. The shop is well cared for, and the window display draws me in with strange and tantalizing objects. I wasn't planning to shop for trinkets, but in I go.

It is dark inside. I cannot see much, but as I enter I overhear the shopkeeper talking to another customer. "I love these things," he says. "I really love these bronzes. If I didn't love these things I wouldn't have the confidence to sell them to you."

I strain to see what the "things" are that he so passionately sells. You guessed it. Bronze figurines. At the same time I wonder, *What does love have to do with it?* The mind goes crazy with questions like this.

By now my eyes adjust to the lower lighting and I scan the merchandise. I am stunned, stopped in my tracks. Hundreds of pieces of bronze-ware sit shoulder-to-shoulder, rim-to-rim, haunch-to-haunch, all waiting, no, begging for my attention. New, old, shiny, tarnished, huge, miniature, pristine, damaged, bowls. There are cups, implements, animal figures, Goddesses and Gods of every description, all available for a price and waiting for my glance, my touch – or perhaps waiting to touch me?

My mind analyzes. *I wonder where this one came from. How much does this one cost? Where would I put it? Why would I ever want one of these?* Thinking, thinking, thinking, trying to figure it out.

The shopkeeper continues with his door-opening instructions. "There is only God. To adore something is to recognize that thing's inherent divinity. This recognition brings that thing to life. Adoration allows the light that is there to arise and radiate. The adored then becomes a doorway to all of reality. To go through the doorway we must be detached from form."

Huh? I study the guy's features. He must be sixty, short, big nose, gray beard, elegant but comfortable threads. Interesting guy. I pull out my pocket-sized notebook and start inconspicuously jotting down what he says.

I slowly move through the shop, each step bringing me closer to being within range of actually picking up one of the bronzes. I write studiously as I walk. The shopkeeper continues, "Meditating on the bronzes is a training exercise. Their form modifies our form by a kind of imprint. They train our ability to perceive. The more we are formed by the bronzes, the more they can reveal themselves to us."

On my third time around I see pieces that were invisible on my second pass. *How can they appear now? Where were they before? Behind my own barriers? Covered by my own fears? Does the process of gazing upon the bronzes cause my mind to momentarily slacken its rigid grip on my experience of reality so that the previously incomprehensible can appear?*

In a distracted moment of random gazing upon the rich assortment of metallic geometries and forms, my breath catches in my throat. *What is that?* I notice a strange physical sensation. It is a warm gentle electric tingling deep in the center of my chest. The after-shock ripples out through my limbs and hangs there gently humming. *What is that?*

Is this experience the result of some new factor? Or was it there already and I just never noticed it before? I am stuck with an experience and no words to name it.

I intently search through the figures before me. Suddenly I find the source. It is her! The golden one! Four arms outstretched, sitting with one leg folded across. She is less than five inches tall. She is present. Waiting. (She seems *very* good at waiting.) And the sensation comes again, only more so. Dzonggg! It feels as though there is a smiling upon me from whatever is empowering that statue. I sense it deep in my chest, a quickening within.

The Countenance of a Goddess. I gaze at her and a circuit clicks home. My heart has found an Archetypal food source. It is now irrefutable: whatever it means, however it works, I have been touched by the bronze and the touch is good.

The shopkeeper is still rambling, "The purpose for the existence of the universe is self delight."

For me, a scientist, this is a very bizarre moment! Why this statue? Six others nearly identical sit side by side with her. I pick one of the others up and feel its hard cold metallic weight. There is nothing illusionary about the bronze. I look at their labels: "Durga," says one. "Kali," reads another. "Shakti," the next. *Confusion as authority*, I think to myself. *That figures! The opposite of my desire for a rational authority.* This forces me to rely on my internal sensing and take authority for my own authority, even if it contradicts existent authority, like Shakespeare, who was in this case wrong when he wrote "a rose by any other name would smell as sweet." These deities might all be "roses" but only one of them smells sweet to me. There is no logical reason, yet that one shiny figure touches me at the core.

I walk away. From across the room I surreptitiously watch other shoppers to see if anyone else notices her, to see if she is calling out to just anyone, to see if she is a prostitute. No. No one else is affected. No one else even sees her.

But I do. So I make a wild decision. I buy her. *As if love could be bought*, I think. Do not ask me the price. The shopkeeper smiles kindly, says, "That's a good one!" I smile back. I heard him say the same thing to his previous customers. He wraps her in a wrinkled scrap of Indian newsprint. I tuck her under my arm and bring her home.

I place her on my desk in my office. A few days go by. A week. The moment comes when I haphazardly remember that she is there. As I scrutinize the form and detail of her feet, outstretched arms, bare chest, the torch, knife, ball and snake in her four hands, her fancy hat and well-rubbed face, I make an internal observation. By experimentation I realize that I have a choice. Either my mind is there thinking, analyzing and judging, or, I can be-with her. It is one or the other, not both. I can sustain a distinct conscious space for experiencing her, or I can fill up that space with word-salad from my mind. This then is the first requirement: if I am to *experience* the deity then it must somehow be that the analytical mind is not there.

For the mind, *not being there* is no different from death. So to encounter the deity, I must first be prepared to die. This does not mean that I need to be childish or adaptive; it does not mean that I need to give up my power. Of what use is a weak irresponsible admirer to a deity? She needs a sanctuary of intentionally devoted attention to work in. Can I put the mind out to pasture for a few minutes? With that challenge the "Goddess experiment" begins in earnest.

The shopkeeper had said to be detached from form. But I adore her form! The beauty of her face, the cheekbones, her forehead, her knees, the curve of her breasts, the glow of her golden skin! No... actually that is not true. The form itself is not beautiful. The form becomes beautiful through my Adoration! At this expansion in my understanding the doorway suddenly opens wider for me and the experience of Adoration gets *way* too intense. I reflexively return to my office work. There are things I have to get done you know...

A few days later I decide to stop flirting and instead make it formal. These are important experiments. The nature of reality is being revealed. The physical sensation in my chest is repeatable. Something is happening.

I have a realization. *If I am going to get this, it boils down to one thing: personal experience. I usually try to find answers outside of my experience, through my mind. But if I am really going to get the transmission I must get it essentially.*

So I set aside specific amounts of time to practice encountering the Goddess through my little bronze doorway of Adoration. In doing so, I discover Countenance.

Things begin to change. First, the word "her" suddenly becomes sacred. What an exquisite precious sound! Saying "her" becomes a holy experience. The Feminine needs to be cared for; such fineness, such delicacy. I notice that when she experiences the care and dignity of my respect she becomes strong and indomitable, radiating her strength back to me.

The experiments continue. What is being discovered? When I practice adoring the bronze something else shows up. The space shifts. The most intense impersonal sensation of unconditional Love permeates every atom in the space where I sit with her, thicker and sweeter than honey. All doubts, all self-loathing vaporize in the radiant Joy of this brilliant Love.

And she changes too. I am no longer looking at a bronze. No longer is it simply a womanly form. I have Countenance with a Goddess, fully present, benevolent, eternal. Having the Countenance of a Goddess puts me on my knees. How could she be so? A moment before she was just a small golden body, imperfect, mortal. Now behold! The Goddess in full blooming radiance and beauty, all wisdom gazing back at me with a Love that is so intense my breath stops, so compassionate that my heart no longer needs to beat by itself.

My body shudders. Neither laughter nor tears come, although I think they must. Love burns through emotional indulgence like fire through straw. The contamination is burned away before I even feel the heat. Emotionalism is without substance. What remains in me is objective awe.

I find that I do not want to turn away, ever. But, if I keep gazing, all my secrets will be revealed, all my faults, all my failings. Then Love eats even those thoughts and all I can experience is being totally, unconditionally accepted by the Goddess, just exactly as I am. It is this close to being unbearable.

I ask myself, *Why me? Why do I receive such blessings?*

The shopkeeper's words leap out from my journal, "The mood of wonder, awe, majesty and ecstasy when we behold the Goddess makes us more human. It does not separate us from others who do not feel these things."

I realize that I am being healed, made round and whole. What is healing me? Love. Where does the Love come from? The Love seems bi-directional. Love comes through me toward the Goddess and she recognizes and fully experiences that Love. At the same time Love comes through her toward me and I recognize and experience that Love. Wave after wave, tide after tide. Endless Love that can never go away. The Goddess conducts what I conduct. As I become conscious of what I give and receive the recognition completes a circuit and makes the Love conscious. When Love becomes conscious of itself it brings creation to life. The reverberation of transforming Archetypal Love into conscious Archetypal Love produces a substance in the world and a sensation in the body called Countenance.

We can avoid love, deny love, covet love, fear love, subvert love, but it is never Love that changes. It is us. Love is Love, impersonal, pure, powerful, and the most abundant thing in the universe.

The shopkeeper again: "Love is a completely free-standing radiance." (At some point I have to ask myself how this guy discovers these things ...)

How much ecstasy can I tolerate? Why should life suddenly be so delightful?

"God's wish for creation is that creation have the same wish for God." That is what the shopkeeper had told those people.

Recognizing that my Love of the Goddess as Archetypal Feminine is as strong, clear, true and as deeply irreducible as the Goddess' Love of the Archetypal Masculine – that is ecstatic. Love consciously recognizing Love. The recognition happens through two physical objects that are nothing more than mud that has been structured fine enough to become conscious of its own consciousness. Love is all there is. Love is already there. I use the Goddess to become conscious of Love, and she uses me for the same thing. It takes both of us to complete the circuit. Love meets Love.

Just as light shining through air is invisible until it hits something, consciousness only manifests when there is a piece of creation to reflect it. Consciousness manifests according to the complexity and maturity of the matter through which it manifests. I observe: *A Goddess is elegant and sophisticated enough to recognize the Love you have of the Goddess, and your Adoration makes you elegant and sophisticated enough to recognize the Love she has of you.*

But what about between times? What about between times? This is worrisome. *Because it is mostly between times.* Longing for gazing at the Goddess with Love and having the chance that the Goddess could be delighted and gaze back at me with Love is strong longing. The longing may not go away. Experiencing the lack of once having been in Paradise and not being there *now* may not be a pleasant experience, and it may stay with me forever. I feel the longing when I sigh. I feel the longing as a physical ache in my chest every time I remember what is possible. The words "wistful," "pensive" and "melancholy" acquire a forceful immediacy.

Two other things the shopkeeper said that day: "Even when you have found the Beloved you are still yearning for the Beloved. This is the broken heart. To *be* is heart breaking."

And: "How do you put your attention on the Divine? Look to what your attention is drawn to relative to the Divine – and then that is where you put your attention."

Anything could be used as a doorway if you put the proper kind of attention on it.

Here we have the paradox. What is the right kind of attention? What is the key? When Bugs Bunny the comic strip rabbit comes to a solid rock wall, he can pull out a paintbrush, paint a doorway on the rock, open the door and walk right through. That is a high level skill. Painting doorways requires taking uncompromising responsibility for sourcing the way things are.

The man hunting Bugs Bunny is Elmer Fudd, Mr. Normal. When Bugs Bunny vanishes through the stone, Elmer Fudd tries to follow. But poor Elmer smacks his face into the stone. For Elmer Fudd it does not matter what is painted on the rock. A rock wall is not a door; it is a rock wall.

We are each faced with the same dilemma as Elmer Fudd. Is a bronze a bronze? Or is it a doorway?

The shopkeeper in the artifact gallery provides his customers with some assistance for doing experiments that help them to unfold that dilemma. He sells bronzes that have already been used as doorways for centuries. These doors have greased hinges. They already know what to do. They can open almost all by themselves.

Some of us might be thinking that we would like to open a door so the Goddess can come for a visit. We assume the door won't open because it is locked. We think that to open the door we must find some kind of key. We look for the key; we try to find the key with our mind. But it could well be that the key cannot be found with our mind. The key may be Love, and the key of Love can only be found with our heart. If the key to open the door is Love, then we must undertake a different form of experimenting.

Navigating the Space of Relationship

Navigating the Space of Relationship (BLTLCH16.02). As human beings we can know and relate to each other in limitless forms and ways. Each way that we relate to another person is defined by the qualities of the space of relationship that we create for the relating.

All of the spaces of relationship hang together in a continuous labyrinth just like all of the countries, lands and seas of the world hang together on the continuous globe of the Earth. There is nothing innately good or bad about any particular space of relationship, just like there is nothing innately good or bad about any particular country. And, in each space, we can create and experience unique results with different qualities of relationship; just as in each country we can encounter different cultures, religions, political systems, laws and customs. (*See* Section 8-D for more on this subject.)

For example, each of the following relationships occurs in a different space of relationship: client to car salesman, father to son, sister to sister, beggar to businessman, farmer to wife, artist to artist, speeder to policeman, and so on. There are endless possible forms of relationship. We do not have to go looking for relationship. *We are already in relationship.*

We can relate to the collection of all possible spaces of relationship altogether as the Great Labyrinth of Spaces. We can learn the skills of navigating from one space to another space. This set of skills can be referred to as "navigating space."

Part of learning to navigate space involves learning some of the characteristics of relational space. For example, there are an unlimited number of spaces. Every space is connected to every other space. This means that, wherever you want to go, you can (at least theoretically) get there from here. Just because there is conflict and confusion with somebody in one moment does not mean that there cannot be respect and clarity with that same person in the next moment. Navigating from one space to the next space can produce radically contrasting experiences.

You do not have to know this, but the Great Labyrinth of Spaces comes into existence through a frictional interface between union with the Archetypal Beloved and the illusion of separation from the Archetypal Beloved that comes from having a body, a mind and emotions.

Through exploring and experimenting with navigating the Labyrinth you will make some surprising discoveries. You may find that men cannot find their way through to the Heart of the Labyrinth alone. You may also discover that women know their way through the Labyrinth instinctively. But, if a woman is not "awakened" into Archetypal Woman she will not remember that she knows the way through the Labyrinth. To navigate space to the Heart of the Labyrinth, men and women *work together* in a special way. Archetypal Man puts his appreciative attention on his Woman and enjoys her company so much that she starts enjoying it herself. Suddenly she remembers the way to the Heart of the Labyrinth and can gracefully lead her Man there.

Bringing the Woman to Life

Adoration and Bringing the Woman to Life (BLTLCH16.03). Archetypal Masculinity naturally includes the capacity to completely leave the analytical mind aside and stand before an object or a person with naked Adoration. Archetypal Adoration has the capacity of "bringing the Woman to life."

What does this mean?

Let us start with a piano analogy. Anyone can make sounds on a piano. Even without fingers or ears, a person can bang on the keys with their elbows, their feet, or a stick. But bringing the piano to life is an entirely different matter. Bringing the piano to life by calling beautiful inspiring music through its keyboard and pedals to fill up the hearts and lives of listeners takes concentrated effort. Years of practice refine both the sensitivity and the skills to connect to the source of where such music comes from.

Similarly, anyone can be in relationship with another person. Even if they have no mind or cannot speak, they can irritate a person and create an aggressive persecutor, victim, or rescuer relationship to them. But to bring another person to life is an entirely different matter. Bringing a person to life by calling to Love, kindness, generosity and joy elegantly through them, until they experience it themselves and can play it back to you on their own, takes years of concentrated effort. Such effort is no different from seeking mastery of any musical instrument. The practice is to develop sensitivity, responsibility, timing, tone of voice, clarity, intention, attention, people-reading skills, being-with skills, listening, gentleness and mood, all of which add rich extensions to the normal experiences of life.

If what brings Archetypal Woman to life is Adoration by Archetypal Man, this means that for woman to come to life the man needs to shift to Archetypal first!

In recognizing that the man needs to shift first, woman might easily despair. What man do you know who is willing or able to consciously shift from ordinary to Archetypal in order to place his Archetypal Attention on his woman so that she shifts from ordinary to Archetypal and remembers the way and can lead him to the Heart of the Labyrinth? Such Men are not produced by our culture, therefore such Men must be made, not found. Making such a Man might be hopeless. Making such a Man comes previous to step one in the *Handbook for Archetypal Maidens*! The Manmaking step is not even listed, because it is assumed to have already happened! Until you make your partner into such a Man, you do not have a vehicle for exploring Archetypal domains. On first glance the job of making man into Man involves an unreasonable amount of work and risk. In short, the task is extremely unfair!

To reframe the onerous task of Manmaking into a more interesting perspective, consider yourself as a treasure hunter. Some treasure hunters look for gold, jewels, lost texts, or ancient artifacts. They spend their entire lives tunneling relentlessly through solid rock, dynamiting hillsides, sifting through tons of sand. It is backbreaking work in desolate lands under scorching sun or in damp darkness deep in the bowels of the earth. Why would someone do these things? They would do it for the adventure! For the possibility of finding the treasure! For the joy it gives them to know themselves as a treasure hunter!

You could try this yourself. Try regarding yourself as a treasure hunter. What would be a worthwhile treasure for you to hunt? Here is where you should hunker down in your seat and listen carefully. The following information is not theoretical. It comes from firsthand experience – not only my own. Archetypal Sex can lead directly to an experience of something like extended consciousness. It is like leaving ordinary reality ("dying before you die") and voyaging deep into the fabric of consciousness itself. Women have the ability to melt into and become ecstatically joined with a bigger consciousness in the moment of orgasm. But there is a crucial point just before the orgasm, one second or some seconds before, where the woman must decide if she is safe enough to enter into this approximation of death. If she is not completely certain that she is securely attended by a Man of attention, she will not or cannot melt and "go extended." To find this treasure you need a Man with you, awake and present to protect you while you journey away, leaving your body completely vulnerable. With Archetypal Man at your side the treasure hunt can begin. Doesn't that sound like an interesting enough reason to make yourself a Man?

Archetypal Adoration

Archetypal Adoration takes place in a different domain from chocolates and flowers. Not even a 42-carat "girl's best friend" will necessarily open the door of Adoration. Archetypal Adoration takes place in a domain that is different from the domain of ordinary social convention and human exchange.

Ordinary human exchange includes expectations, hidden agendas and demands. Since we want to keep our relationships smooth, we normally try to keep our expectations, hidden agendas and demands to ourselves. Keeping them to ourselves does not mean that they are not there. They still deliver their effect in our relationships whether we are trying to hide them or not.

Archetypal Adoration of the Woman by the Man is a response of such absolute purity that in the moment of Archetypal Adoration all the deals we want to make with one another are completely erased. Through a kind of relaxed hyper-attention, the unconscious mind completely disappears and has no influence on the actions that are happening in the space. If the unconscious mind were still influential, the purity would not be high enough to open Archetypal Adoration. This is because the unconscious mind (the Box) always has its little negotiations and counter strategies going on.

In that moment of purity, when Archetypal Adoration is flowing, Woman naturally responds. This is a delicate moment. Both the Adoration and the Woman coming to life are wordless and thoughtless responses to Archetypal Law. The Woman wakes up in the woman and She responds to the Archetypal Man. This is what we have all always wanted from each other.

The new, powerful, hyper-aware Archetypal Woman keeps it safe for the Man to see what has happened. In seeing and being seen by Archetypal Woman, man is confirmed as Man. Archetypal Woman might be tempted to use her newfound power in familiar ordinary woman ways to dominate the man or to try to enjoy the experience of her power alone. This would instantly destabilize Archetypal Woman and bring her back to ordinary woman. Archetypal Woman uses her power tenderly to bring the Man with her in communion on the journey toward the Heart of the Labyrinth.

Conditions for a Happy Accident

Our natural tendency is to grab a hold and try to possess an ecstatic experience so it does not go away. Trying to possess experiences that happen when Archetypal Woman leads Archetypal Man through the Great Labyrinth of Spaces is like ripping the wings off a butterfly because the wings are so beautiful. As soon as man grasps at the experience, Archetypal Woman vanishes. Instantly, the human woman returns and she says, "You *always* do that! You just ruined the moment!"

Try to develop the habit of letting beauty lead you where the beauty wants to lead you. Avoid acting on your desire to extract and analyze the experience. Beauty is impermanent. Part of experiencing beauty is longing for the experience to endure, and at the same time knowing that the experience is transitory. Learn to have greater and greater longing while making no sudden moves. Enjoy the ride. Grabbing hold decreases the intensity. Learn to ride with your hands waving free. Let it be intense, and just glide. Communion evolves through you learning to sustain the moment.

With years of intention and practice, Archetypal Adoration arises. The Man is in awe, in wonderment, and Woman feels it and responds. When Archetypal Woman is awakened and responds, the two can voyage through a series of spaces where Woman tenderly and lovingly leads the Man into greater and greater intimacies. We end up having a very fine time together or, if sexual play is included, the experience is a great sexual moment.

Afterward, the first thing we naturally want to do is repeat what just happened to us this time, the next time. The mind gets a grip on the memory and decides that, since this memory is just a memory like other memories creating the circumstances that lead to creating another such memory would be as easy as going to see a movie over and over again. You just have to buy a ticket, walk into the theater and sit down to watch the same movie again. But as soon as we actually try to duplicate "the experience," we discover that it does not work that way. Suddenly the precious uniqueness of the original moment becomes apparent. It was there, and now it is gone, and it can never, ever, be the same again. Original moments become rarer the more we try to duplicate them. We try and try again, but they seem as far away as ever. Finally we can only surrender. Each journey is unique and can only arrive unexpected. We wait.

There are a series of conditions that permit a man to shift into Man so that he becomes the space through which Archetypal Adoration occurs, so that he can place his attention upon his woman in such a way that the woman awakens into Woman and remembers how to guide the Man through the Great Labyrinth of Spaces. Falling into that series of conditions happens almost by accident. However, certain conditions can make us "accident-prone," conditions that arise as a side effect of practicing the new skills. The way to optimize the possibility of entering that series of spaces is to live in resonance with the context that was experienced during the previous ecstatic journey together. That means, to live our day-to-day relationship on the basis of *what we realized* during the shift of spaces. We simply dedicate ourselves to obeying the laws of building Love that lasts. The specifics of the laws of building Love that lasts are the contents of this book.

When you enter a moment of Adoration – Woman has been awakened in a woman and She starts to lead the Man through the Labyrinth – and sex happens, and we know exactly what is happening, and the sex is over, and we go on about our lives and at the same time we are thinking that we want to continue journeying together on and on in these domains of clarity, ecstasy and Archetypal Adoration, it is extremely useful to remember that it only goes further if we are intelligent about living on the basis of what we realized during the shifted spaces.

In practical terms what "being intelligent" means is to take into account the fact that your partner may be able to be a *doorway* to the Archetypal Man or Woman, but they *are* *not* the Archetypal Man or Woman. They are just the doorway. Whenever they are not *being the doorway* to the Archetypal Man or Woman, you are faced with them dealing with their life as an ordinary human being in an ordinary human body. This means that they have physical needs like enough sleep, proper high-quality food, good water, a healthy nurturing environment, enough exercise, enough money, enough time to simply *be*, creative projects to be involved in to express their inner life, a desk and shelves and storage cabinets of their own, decent clothes, recreation, and education such as books to read that continue to expand their understanding of and provide nutrition for their continued evolutionary relational development.

SECTION 16-D

An Ordinary and Extraordinary Nurturing Environment

Many factors affect the nervous system and the body on all of its physical, energetic, emotional, psychic, auric, and etheric levels. This section will explore what a "healthy nurturing environment" could include, since the ordinary and extraordinary domains always serve as the platforms for setting off on Archetypal voyaging. Keep in mind that these considerations are not intended to be stretched to neurotic extremes or made into rules, and at the same time they are real issues.

A healthy nurturing environment would *avoid* repeated shocking loud sounds such as trains, highways, subways, airports or construction sites; contaminants such as nuclear power or chemical manufacturing plants, lead-soldered water pipes; late night party music from a disco with a beat that is dissonant to the heart; neighbors who scream and fight with each other or with you; incessantly barking dogs; electro-smog from mobile telephone repeating towers; television station or high-voltage electric wires; neon or fluorescent lighting; an old building with leaded wall paints or asbestos insulation or roof tiles, and so on.

The environment is also *not* nurturing if every open space is filled with some kind of knick-knack, if it holds things that are not necessary (you can define things as "not necessary" if they are things that you have not used during the last year or two), if it contains gifts or mementos from a person with whom you are no longer actively engaged in a relationship, items passed on from generation to generation that contain family history or significance, too many photographs of ancestors or friends or relatives, artifacts from wars, carpets soiled by other people, kid's toys scattered everywhere, remnants or reminders of unfinished projects, mass-produced interior design artwork, new age or tourist-faux cultural objects, artificial flowers or plants, live plants that are suffering from lack of sunshine or care, animal hair or animal smells, a buildup of kitchen grease or dirt, and so on.

Creating a Nurturing Environment (BLTLCH16.04). Your environment becomes healthy and nurturing through care, attention and intention. Every object in your environment has a meaning and a purpose. (If an object does not have a meaning or a purpose then it is just litter.) Every object radiates its purpose and meaning into your environment. The objects in your environment did not get there by accident. This is your environment – an extension of your own mind, heart, body and soul. You are the only one who is totally responsible for an object being there. (This remarkable statement should perhaps be repeated.) When an object is in your environment it is there because you alone permit it to be there. Each object is fulfilling its purpose whether you are aware of what that purpose is or not. Look carefully and slowly around your environment. Pick up and examine each and every object that is there, even in closets, basement, attic, kitchen and medicine chest. What is this object's purpose? What does it do to the space? What is it for? Why is it here? What does it cause for you and for others? Do you want and need this purpose to be fulfilled in your environment by this object? If not, it is a simple matter to get rid of it.

You can start to create a healthy nurturing environment for yourself and your partner or family by being clear about the purpose of the objects in your spaces and also their relationship to each other. Objects that help to produce a healthy nurturing environment are objects that are placed with a conscious nurturing purpose. The art of placing objects and arranging spaces originated in India and is still practiced today as *vaastu*. Later, the form spread to China as *feng shui*.

Some of the things that create a healthy nurturing environment also help to create sacred space, the sanctuary that nurtures the level of respect and conscious attention required for bringing the Woman to life. Consider making one or two parts of your living environment into sacred space, such as your bedroom, a silent sitting room, a bathroom (sacred cleansing chamber), perhaps even your kitchen. When your kitchen is kept as a true sacred space, the food that comes out of your kitchen contains sacred energetic ingredients that feed and nurture more than just the physical body.

Consider removing mirrors, which tend to emphasize and promote vanity and self-consciousness, and replacing them with objective artwork, paintings, lithographs and prints from classical artists. Consider placing sacred artifacts such as bronze statues of deities, or stone or wooden carvings in prominent places in your home. If the pieces come from some culture with which you are not so familiar, make sure that they are intended to invoke Bright Principles rather than Shadow Principles. Some of the pieces coming out of Africa and Southeast Asia that are sold as art these days do not necessarily promote peace, harmony, openness, consciousness and evolution. Be a little careful.

Clearing out extraneous, distracting, cluttering objects from your living spaces helps to promote the well-being and fulfill the physical needs of your partner by providing a healthy nurturing environment.

Archetypal Possibilities in Ordinary Life

Staying Archetypal (BLTLCH16.05). In addition to physical needs, your partner also has emotional and psychological needs such as the need for respect, information sharing, appreciation, recognition, humor, and playful repartee. In your daily life together your partner will be going through the usual processes of evolution that may or may not include having to deal with issues from their past. They may or may not have to heal and transform abuses, betrayals, or old decisions about themselves, other people and the world, decisions based on circumstances that no longer exist. The processes that they need to go through are not your fault, nor are they your responsibility to fix. Do not take such processes personally. Your partner may be projecting their mother or father onto you and may attack and blame you for your behavior, but it all may not be about you. Again, try not to take such things personally. Your job is to accept it as it comes up for you or for them to deal with, and to consistently return to the thing that makes your life together precious and real, the important thing: bringing the Woman to life and navigating space to the center of the Labyrinth. Let the Archetypal aspect of your life together be what is real and significant, and let the rest of your life be of secondary importance and happen around *that* as it may.

This invitation is a practical one. Do not allow the possibility of Archetypal Relationship be devoured by the compelling forces of everyday life and the ordinary human condition. The way to avoid being hooked into diminished possibilities by your Box's reactions is through awareness. Consciousness creates freedom. When you know what is coming from your Box and from your partner's Box, you can take one step to your left and let both of your reactions pass by you without getting hooked in the guts, just as a skilled toreador stays aware of what bulls do so he does not get hooked in the guts. Expending little energy, the bullfighter stays in compassionate contact with the bull, but just at the right moment stands elegantly aside and lets the bull run past him so he does not get hit. But the bullfighter stays unharmed *only* if he remains aware and alert at all times. This means he must remember he is a bullfighter and that, in this moment (and many moments), he is bullfighting. In the same way, you can remain aware and alert by continuously reminding yourself that what usually passes for reality is a mere smear of a vaster world of experience. You can remind yourself that the bigger world is what is truly of value to you and simply refuse to engage in anything less than that. You have reference points for the experience of dignity, nobility and respect. You can develop the alertness and skill of a bullfighter to go nowhere else.

Set Your Priorities First

Both you and your partner already know that as ordinary human beings you each have nasty habits, hidden irresponsible purposes, unconscious agendas, and psycho-emotional reaction buttons. Either singly or simultaneously, your trigger buttons can be pushed by any number of unexpected stimuli that vaguely resonate with unexpressed or incomplete emotional experiences that lie dormant in your body. When something that is happening in the present even vaguely resembles an incomplete experience from your past, a residual emotional charge unwinds and springs out like a coiled rattlesnake at any convenient target.

Keeping your daily relationship loving and glowing, or at least neutral and open, requires maintaining a delicate balance. Do not retreat into adaptive behavior, trying to please your partner and giving your center away in the meantime. Also do not dominate your partner with rigid demands or be so emotionally needy and reactive that your partner has to conform to your demands and give their center to you. Keeping the balance is a matter of paying attention and noticing. We know what our partners like and what they do not like.

For example, if you are a man and you work as a car mechanic and your woman has told you that she hates it when you come home from work wearing your greasy clothes and having black grit under your fingernails, then to live in accordance with what you experienced when Woman was awake you would not hesitate to alter your patterns. It is a no-brainer to figure out that your woman would be more interested in going on the next intimacy journey with you if you changed your clothes and brushed out your fingernails *before* you came home from work. Not once. Not once a week. Change your pattern *across the board*. What does it cost you? You now have a higher priority than sloppiness. Compare the price of paying attention to your appearance in new ways to the value of what you gain: the possibility of living with a woman who is doorway to the Goddess. It is simple. Do the ordinary day-to-day things that please your woman. Do not do the things she hates. Your small efforts will keep your woman open and vulnerable so that the doorway is not blocked by ordinary psychological defense mechanisms.

If a woman is really paying attention to her man she will no longer need to ask him, "Honey, do you or don't you like nuts in your brownies?" She will already know. And even if the woman prefers to have nuts in *her* brownies, if he prefers no nuts there will be no nuts in the brownies. In this way we avoid the immature reactions that shatter sanctuary, and we maintain a softness and a gentleness that sustain the possibility of communion.

Again, it should be mentioned here, this process/work is simple, not easy. This is why the phenomena of a Woman who is awake and in communion, and leading Man through the Labyrinth, is so rare.

Designating Your Partner as a Gremlin Free Zone (BLTLCH16.06). Adoration has to be so important to you that the conditions that would normally cause you to react, even internally, just do not matter anymore. Period. You and only you choose your internal priorities. When the Gremlin part of you is looking for an easy, tasty meal, you can detect the hunger before it becomes ravenously out of control, and you can intentionally feed the Gremlin some other food on your own timing. Declare the tender, precious being of your partner as off limits for Gremlin feeding. Stake out your partner as a Gremlin-free zone.

SECTION 16-F
What to Watch Out For

Before you succeed at bringing the Woman to life I want to offer you a few words of warning – information to help you avoid certain unnecessary but common and potentially painful events. If you can avoid the painful events, perhaps you may sooner convince your mind-body-emotion system to again knock on heaven's gate. Here is what to watch out for.

1. Sometimes It Works, Sometimes It Doesn't

There is a story about a man who read in a book that by using a certain kind of focused attention an ordinary person could "burn" holes through clouds. He looked outside. It was quite solidly gray and cloudy. He called to his young daughter to come out with him; he would show her an interesting trick.

They put on their coats and walked out into the yard. He said, "Wouldn't it be great if the sun would shine on us for a bit right now?" She said, "Oh yes! That would be wonderful!" He looked up toward the sky and "burned" a hole right through those clouds. The sun shone gloriously upon them. After a few minutes he stopped. The clouds filled in the hole and the sky was all gray again.

For years afterwards the daughter would plead with her father to come burn holes in the clouds. She wanted to show her friends. She wanted to learn to do it herself. She wanted to believe that it could be done. The father always refused to try again. One day, in desperation, the daughter finally asked him why he would no longer try. His answer was simple and relevant to all of us. He said, "It might not work."

As with burning holes through clouds, the same possibility is true of consistently building Love that lasts. It might not work. Just because it worked one time is no guarantee that it will ever work again.

Love that lasts is a wonder. Countenance is ecstatic. Wonder and ecstasy are an inherent part of daily human experience. Because they are natural and arise from an organic innocence, they might not work. Fallibility is part of the play. Yes the mystery exists. No, you cannot always go there. You can only go there when you can go there.

To try and fail is embarrassing enough. But to try and fail in these days of technical mastery where everything should start with the flick of a switch, this is closer to religious blasphemy with an attached death sentence. We want our technologies to work immediately and without fail. We are not accustomed to having to wait. We do not accept an attitude that says about the miraculous, "Sometimes it works. Sometimes it doesn't." We want our miracles to work *all* of the time.

Maybe you have had a glimpse of how big the universe really is. Maybe the curtain parted slightly and the Goddess and King lived in the same moment together. Maybe Archetypal Love flooded through you one day in the presence of another human being and you were so overwhelmed that you could not comprehend that such magnificence could ever happen again. You tremble at the thought of trying and failing. But if you let your doubts stop your actions then the uncertainty is over, because you already *have* failed.

Years of conditioning about our preferences, opinions, insecurities, expectations and so on can fall away in an instant when intimately exposed to the glorious radiance of a Woman brought to life. But sustaining the falling away of the conditioning takes discipline. This is just as true for the Woman brought to life as it is for the Man who awakened her. Continuing to live with the woman as if in any moment she could awaken takes tremendous spaciousness. The spaciousness is about allowing people to have the space to be completely themselves in our presence, with absolutely no expectation, criticism, judgment, opinion, or even analysis from us.

When Archetypal Adoration wakens Woman, Woman leads Man through the Labyrinth. Either person's psyche can interrupt the process. The interrupter can even be the internal masculine part of the woman that screws things up. The masculine part of the

What If?

What if we are one of the "... few fortunate ones ... who are satisfied and fulfilled by a human partner, feeling we have met the goal, realized the wish, found the dream, as lucky as we are and as wonderful as this is, have still missed the mark. For the 'partner' that is so longed for is God"? What if "... by the time we're grown up, we've completely displaced this deep and powerful longing onto the mundane human domain and been convinced by magazine articles in teen and women's magazines and feel-good movies, or feel-bad movies, that it is the perfect human mate that is the answer to our prayers and our yearning desires. But in fact it is God, union with God, seeing the face of God that is the 'partner' we seek and since God, the 'partner God' is already at hand, is not in any way, except perhaps a psychological way, separate from us, not at a distance, of course we broken-heartedly call out for this Union, the union that we know instinctively, or instinctually, whichever applies, is the only thing that will complete us. And we are already complete, we just don't know it?" What if "... we realize the true nature of our longing, and realize that this 'partner' is already where it needs to be, here, now, exactly synchronous, not-separate, then we can relax, stop requiring our human partner to be God, to be the perfect man or woman, and be open to a working, successful, loving, caring, tender human partnership. Want it all? You can have it. Why not? But first things first. Stop searching for what you already have in order to find what would please, even thrill you, that which is also closer than we can possibly imagine when we are assuming it is so impossibly far away?" (Lee Lozowick, *The Little Book of Lies and Other Myths*. Prescott, Arizona: Hohm Press, 2005, 170-171.)

woman may show up in many ways: as moving suddenly, as being focused on the goal rather than experiencing the present moment, as taking actions instead of being-with, as hardening opinions into rigid positionality. That is why it is important to understand that Adoration occurs in a domain that is outside of ordinary human interaction. Woman will not come to life in the domain of ordinary human relationship. It simply does not work.

2. Watch Out for Psycho-Emotional Recoil

Avoiding Psycho-Emotional Recoil (BLTLCH16.07). If you succeed at entering paradise together, if you bring the Woman to life and She leads the Man toward the Heart of the Labyrinth, take care during the next few days to minimize recoil. It is quite common that if the night is one of the most intensely intimate between you and your partner, then the next morning will be one of the most ferociously separate. Psycho-emotional recoil can be vicious, erupting out of the most ridiculously meaningless conflicts, yet creating the most painful scars that a relationship must bear.

From the psychological perspective, recoil from intimacy makes sense. The Box is there to defend us and protect us. If we let someone get closer to us than the limits of our psychological mask, that person has the power to undo the mask. Our Box then experiences that person as our most threatening enemy. From the Box's perspective, the possibility of future intimacy with that person must be destroyed, at all costs, in order to preserve our future identity. To destroy the possibility of continued intimacy, the Box gives us the experience that everything about our partner is clearly distasteful. The Box instigates a righteous rampage, like rounding up wild horses that have escaped from their corral. Perceptions that were recently expanded through experiencing deep intimacy are suddenly and furiously contracted by the Box.

Unconsciously perhaps, we think that we must live out both the positive and the negative aspects of the Taoist *yin-yang* symbol all by ourselves. We may erroneously conclude that too much joy has to be balanced by an equal part of hatred because we all know that "there is no such thing as a free lunch." Not true, from a larger perspective. Although equalization may appear to be a natural law, it is only a superstition. The ultimate balancing takes place on a bigger scale. There is already so much suffering in the world – you do not have to add to it in any way. The world could actually use a few more people living out their relationships in endless ecstatic joy. You could volunteer for the job.

3. Beware of Archetypal Exclusivity

Once we have brought the Archetypal Woman to life we may tend to want to continue the relationship only with the Archetypal Woman or the Archetypal Man and ignore the human woman or the human man. Excluding the human nature of our partner will not work. Our human partner is still human! When union with the Archetypal Woman is realized, the integration of this realization includes continued relationship with the human partner.

Human men and human women can create circumstances that mirror relationship in higher and subtler domains. But, we cannot live on the top of the mountain. There is no food or shelter there, no work, no movie theaters. We must come back down off the mountain peak to live with each other. It is through our daily living with each other that we prepare ourselves for our next journey up the side of the mountain into the rarified atmospheres.

SECTION 16-G

Your Divine Beloved

As long as we understand that our partner will always retain their humanity, we can extend our experience of them to also include their divinity. In the flush of directly experiencing Archetypal Love, the possibility arises that we could be one another's Beloveds. It is the mood that brings us to this possibility. The mood of Archetypal Love is inexpressibly sublime. Because of the sublimity of the mood, we conclude that the mood itself is divine. We divinize the mood. Then, because our partner is needed to create and sustain this exquisite mood, we divinize our partner. The divinization of our partner is not true, because our partner *is and always will be* human. And yet, something hangs on. The residue of the experience of Archetypal Love will not fade away. We are somehow convinced of the divinity of our partner.

Regarding our partner as our Beloved does not become a problem as long as our attitude is held in its proper context. It works as long as we do not put our partner onto a pedestal above us in status, and then use the inequity as justification to expect certain behaviors from our partner, or use the inequity as an excuse for our own irresponsible behaviors. Divinizing our partner will not work in the ordinary human relationship context because our ordinary human perspectives cause us to distort the inequity into a problem. Remember, Archetypal Adoration occurs in a domain that is different from ordinary human relationship. If you can remember this, then regarding your partner as your Beloved creates precious surprising moments of delight, joy and ecstasy where none could otherwise be reasonably expected in your day-to-day life.

PART VI

How To Do It

CHAPTER 17

Protecting What is Real

If you skipped ahead and came directly to this Part VI – *How To Do It* – you will probably be disappointed. The answer to the question "How to do it?" cannot be gotten through being clever and jumping ahead. There is no jumping ahead. You must work where you are.

If you read the book straight through and came to this page the long hard way, you might still be disappointed, the way you might be disappointed with Tiger Woods' answer to the question, "How do you consistently shoot five under par?" You might hear his answer. You might write down his answer. You might memorize his answer. You might even understand his answer. But this does not mean you will be able to shoot five under par.

The tantalizing scenario has been painted before your eyes. The door is open. Elysium fields lay vibrant and gorgeous before you. Honeysuckle-scented spring morning air gently caresses your face. This is what is possible in your relationship: endless radiant extraordinary and Archetypal Love.

But how? How? Don't you just hate that?

SECTION 17-A
⊁ No Jumping Ahead

Love that lasts … just beyond the thinnest of veils. But how do you get *through that veil*? How do you get over *there*? You may be wishing for your dreams to come true. You may hope that love comes and stays. Then, some hours, days or weeks later you suddenly remember, "Oh. Whoa. Where am I? There was a time when I wanted to have love come and stay... What happened?" In that instant, you realize again with a start that it did not work!

Again you stopped practicing. Again you were not able to make love stay. You wanted love to come and stay, but instead you fell asleep. And in your sleep you behaved in a manner that sent love away. Again! Aaarrrrggggghhhh?!?!

Discovering that your love-banishing actions form an oft-repeated pattern sends a cold horror creeping down the back of your mind. The internal adversary has more strength, speed, subtlety and persistence than you do. The opponent never sleeps, but *you do*. This enemy never goes away because you carry it within yourself. The prickly sensation of its hot breath on the back of your neck reeks of moral corruption and old garlic. The foe manifests in so many ways through internally twisted reasoning, habits of interpretation, hidden purposes, fantasy projections, and long forgotten core decisions that still influence your life today. *You know all this already!*

Is your desperation desperate enough to keep you from falling asleep? No.

The kingdom of heaven is always at hand. Your chance to enter is not.

How do you use the chance when you have it? Is there a method?

No.

If there is no method, is the only way to get into heaven to improvise?

Ask it this way: If there *were* a method would love be authentically alive, or would it only be a trophy?

How can there be success if there is no method for success?

The good is in the wanting. No effect is the payoff. The Benediction is in the mood itself – so keep wanting!
    – Lee Lozowick

A man was complaining about never getting new customers. "Do you ask new potential customers for a contract?" he was asked. "No."

Another man was complaining about not finishing his writing project. "Do you make time each day and write?" he was asked. "No."

Another man was complaining that his children were estranged and his wife always nagging at him. "Do you speak and act toward your dear ones with respect? Do you listen to their hearts?" he was asked. "No."

The efforts needed to build Love that lasts are as straightforward as the efforts needed to create new customers, finish a project or grow a family. If you engage in certain practices, you are much more likely to succeed in your efforts than if you do not engage those practices. The practices themselves do not guarantee results. But without practicing, reaching results are a thousand-fold less likely.

Making the Most of Your Circumstances (BLTLCH17.01). Sometimes in trying to build Love that lasts you may think, "If only an expert healer were here to smooth our old emotional wounds with warm healing salve. If only these harsh thoughts could be extracted from my mind. If only a master teacher of Tantric sex were here to guide our moves! It is a noble thought. But if you let wistful fear stop you, even for an instant, from going ahead and trying experiments in exactly the way that you, right now, can do them, you are making a big mistake. The great lovers, who could already do with certainty what you are faced with trying to do with severe doubts, are not here. *They are not here.* They are out there in their own lives and stories, challenged beyond their maximum limits to create Archetypal Love in situations you could hardly dream of. The person who has the greatest chance to make the most of the circumstances that you are in is *you*. Because you *are* here. Just do your best. Pay attention. Keep learning. Try again.

How to do it? Use your attention to pay attention to your attention. Find and keep your center. Make "now" a sacred space. Know your true purpose and keep it presently in mind. Stay unhookable from other purposes. Listen. Feel. Be. Don't only think. When you are wordlessly moved, then move. Keep practicing.

SECTION 17-B

Pseudo-Archetypal Substitutes for Love

Avoiding Pseudo-Archetypal Substitutes (BLTLCH17.02). Our culture abounds with alternative, easily-reproducible substitutes for true wonder and ecstasy. With little effort you can find close approximations that are certain. You probably already have a list of favorites – like chocolate, alcohol, overeating, egoism. What we tend to ignore about these approximations is their cost. We pay a very high price for guaranteed ecstasy and wonder.

When you cover your walls with reproductions of art, when you place artificial plants in your room, when you eat frozen and pre-packaged foods, when you listen to CDs but never go to a live music concert, or watch TV but never visit the theater, when you stay in Westernized hotels in third-world countries, when you only say prayers that you did not make up yourself, you lose something priceless. What you lose is your connection to authenticity. You replace authenticity with convenience.

So beware. This section is intended to alert you to the unthought reasons why you choose what you choose and why you do what you do. Make the mechanisms of your unconscious psychological habit patterns visible to yourself, or you will suffer in their hands mercilessly.

These approximations – like sex … chocolate – seem innocent enough. They certainly are easy enough to get. Easier anyway than extraordinary human or Archetypal Relationship and Countenance. In fact, chocolate produces almost the same effect in the mind and body as Countenance (50 percent of the effect …well, 20 percent anyway), and unlike Countenance, chocolate works *every* time. Countenance only works when it works.

But, the experience of eating chocolate or imbibing alcohol, the endorphins from overeating and the hormones from sex are *not* Countenance. Simply drink, eat or have sex and the experience momentarily arises. Countenance involves more of the mystery, and comes and goes as it pleases only when a rigorous list of conditions is met.

Beware the tendency to substitute for Countenance. It is not a fair trade.

Look around the world again. What is more plentiful? Archetypal Love or sex? Countenance or chocolate? Sex in all its glorious forms is easy compared with Archetypal Love. Psychic sex is even easier than physical sex – and the next section will be devoted solely to this delicate subject.

As soon as a practitioner loses even a little integrity, as soon as their practice gets sloppy to even a small degree, the "love feast"(a term that was applied to the gatherings of the early Christians) leaves the domain of ecstatic communion with Archetypal energies and enters the arena of egoic indulgence.

Protecting the Rare and Endangered

It is not that sex or chocolate (or videos, or shopping, or overwork, or screaming at your kids, or jogging, etc.) are bad or wrong. They are not. Everything has its place. It is just that Countenance is so rare on Earth. Six billion people, and how many of them are in Countenance right now? Almost none. And the same with Archetypal Love.

Your efforts and your trying are precious. To exchange the real thing (that can change possibilities with planet-wide impact) for cheap imitation substitutes is as close to a crime as I can imagine. And yet it is completely understandable. Sex and chocolate, and other forms and substances, can be very rich experiences, *and* they are much easier to come by in comparison to opening the doorway to Countenance. No one could argue with you if you want to let your together-sitting sessions slip into sexuality and a nice dinner out. But something is definitely lost.

I am begging you to pay attention, practice, discriminate, use discipline. Be a little rigid about this. Practice is extraordinary. Practice is always different from whatever you are being strongly invited to participate in by people working in normal spaces. Reserve a place in your world for the not-normal.

Protecting your efforts to practice Archetypal Love is like protecting an endangered species. If you are reading this book and practicing Archetypal Relationship, *you* are an endangered species. I am trying to protect you. Why? Because I love you. Because I hope that you will keep going, keep experimenting, keep trying even when it does not work.

So what? It does not work? So what? When you accept the fact that it did not work in this moment, the next moment has entirely new possibilities. If it does not work right *now*, that is no reason to believe that it will not work right *now*. So what? Keep practicing.

⋙ Warning: Psychic Sex

Understanding Psychic Sex (BLTLCH17.03). Oh, jeeeez! Another warning!

Yes. Another warning. And I am particularly sorry to have to open this can of worms. Especially here toward the end of the book. Psychic sex is closer to a pit of cobras than a can of worms. I am sorry. It is going to be relentless. I already know it is going to be "too much" from having entered this consideration with my friends. I remember how it was when it was first opened for me. Only later did I realize what valuable friends they were to have the courage and integrity to bring this up for me. The insights were

horrendous. Yeccch! I am sorry to be bringing this up for you.

Nobody ever told us these things before. Nobody ever explained what was going on with psychic sex, and what happens because of it. I think it is better to know now and to start getting aware of your involvement in psychic sex, rather than to continue pretending. Not that you will necessarily be able to do anything about it for awhile. But it is good to know. Then you can start checking it out for yourself.

At the level of your body's knowledge, you already know everything I am going to say about psychic sex. That does not matter, because if you are anything like most of us, you have not yet been willing to own, at a conscious level, what your body already knows – and for a very good reason. Once you become aware of the depth to which you are involved in psychic sex, it can ruin your day.

Psychic sex. If you are not consciously *not* doing it, then you are doing it.

The consideration of psychic sex has nothing to do with interpretations of right and wrong, or good and bad – psychic sex is not a moral issue. We are not speaking about "should" or "should not." Psychic sex is about physics. The laws of psychic sex become significant as soon as you discover that what you thought was almost nothing, in fact, leaves a long-lasting, powerful, energetic residue – a stain on your psychic bed sheets, so to speak. You take notice of psychic sex as soon as you feel the depth to which psychic sex entangles you with other people.

On the path of evolution your perceptions are gradually refined. Sooner or later your perceptions become sensitive enough to notice that psychic sex is happening. Like an iceberg reveals itself dead ahead on a dark, calm sea, psychic sex suddenly looms into your view. Gradually your sensitivity matures, until one day you discern energies and connections that you were totally unaware of before. You notice that, although these influences are indeed subtle, they are also deep and powerful. It might take longer for you to notice these effects than you might have guessed. You may unconsciously delay getting to this point of realization by keeping denial mechanisms in place, because psychic sex has so many payoffs, so many pleasures, and so many advantages for Gremlin. For example:

Advantages of Psychic Sex
- We can do psychic sex in public and be "invisible," because everybody else is also doing it and nobody is talking about it. We all have made an unspoken agreement to look the other way.
- There is no physical proof! No lipstick smudges or perfume residue, no stains.
- There is no danger of pregnancy.
- We can do it with almost anybody, anywhere, anytime, even in our dreams.
- There is no chance of contracting dangerous venereal diseases or AIDS.
- It is quick. No foreplay necessary. Success is almost guaranteed. Failure is not a problem.
- In the moment we are doing it, it feels fantastic. It is very rewarding to the Box.

We don't ordinarily realize it, but our casual involvements with others is actually psychic sex. These interactions are so common, personally, and so rampant, culturally, that until we understand what is actually going on it goes almost unnoticed.

When we become sensitive enough, unwanted psychic sexual interactions are suddenly experienced as an interference in our life, perhaps even as a contamination. Only at that point will we be motivated to make the sacrifices and efforts necessary to shift our behaviors in this area. Only when we know the true costs will we willingly suffer the discomforts of changing our unconscious habits.

It gradually dawns on us that we have been unconsciously or semi-consciously exchanging energetic sexual "substances" with members of the opposite sex (or possibly of the same sex) – a momentary glance, a shared smile – for almost as long as we can remember.

The seeming innocence of a momentary glance will vanish when we experience what we are truly creating for ourselves and others. Shared smiles will take on a devastating implication. No longer will the fleeting fantasy of full or partial nakedness leave such a sweet after-taste upon our nervous system. When we start to feel the true impact of psychic sex in our lives, it can be a shattering realization. Things can no longer stay the same.

What is psychic sex? Think back and remember the last time you were strolling along a shopping mall or through the center of town. Part of your mind was occupied with thinking about what you intended to accomplish, whether it was window shopping for shoes, or remembering to pick up a bottle of shampoo. Though most of your conscious attention may have been involved in these intellectual considerations, a deeper and more broadband "animal" part of your mind was scanning the environment for a possible partner with whom you could exchange sexual substances. Unless you consciously stop scanning the sex channel, it happens of its own volition automatically. Unless you intentionally override the program, it proceeds to unerringly complete its designed-in purposes.

You notice when someone else notices you. Others notice when you notice them. If the mutual noticing of each other, which can occur in an instant, reveals a ripeness of conditions, then *shhwinggg*, the deal is done. It is a momentary *zzzztt* through the eyes. Briefly imagined possibilities flit through the imagination, and it is accomplished. You know what I am talking about.

How do we alter such behavior when there is a large part of us that is adamantly convinced that *this is the best thing that we do in our entire day?* When it produces our greatest fulfillment? Our most stimulating aliveness? Our most enjoyable feelings of satisfaction?

The answer is, we start doing experiments when we are ready to work at the level of psychic sex. What kind of experiments? Here are some ideas: "Fake it." Pretend that psychic sex is not part of who you are anymore. Declare that energetically eating the sexual substances of strangers is not to your taste. Be different, suddenly, without warning, for no reason. Give no explanation. Be different as

an act of volitional theater. There needs to be no gradual or rational step-by-step procedure for changing behaviors. Just fake it until you make it, until it *becomes so* for you.

By habit, psychic sex may be one of the most cherished experiences in our daily life. The truth is that sexual substances from others are a drug no different from sugar, caffeine, nicotine, adrenaline (released into our system by the adrenal glands during a life drama), endorphins (released by the brain into our system when we overeat), tetra-hydra-cannabinol (marijuana), alcohol, and so on. Stopping the constant use of this drug may eliminate pleasures that we have enjoyed for years.

It is not uncommon for a man or woman who is making moves toward stopping psychic sex to experience deep grief as if having lost a close friend. We might even ask ourselves questions about the purpose of life without the satisfaction of savoring sexual substances from friends and strangers. The degree of pain experienced during our experiments is the degree to which we indulge in nostalgia. The pain arises out of wishing for the ignorant bliss of the unconscious "good old days."

As we are beginning to experiment, a common mistake is to confuse psychic sex with communion. There is a vast difference between the two. In psychic sex there is an exchange of substances. In communion there is no exchange of substances, but rather an acknowledgement of mutual recognition of what is. Profound communion results from acknowledging deeper levels of reality. Communion is a recognition without exchange. Psychic sex involves – at least momentarily – getting inside of another person's personal space. In communion, the sanctuary of the other is honored with infinite respect, at the same time that our absolute commonality is implicitly understood.

After psychic sex you can feel the foreign sexual substance in your body as a whole-body titillating, tingling sensation. The reverberation can last for months, years even. It is a very pleasant high, not too different from the sensation of having eaten sugar or chocolate. Sexual substance in our body fills in the void of existential aloneness.

If we examine our life, we may be able to remember such exchanges from the recent past – weeks, days, or moments ago. Further recollection brings up exchanges from years ago, perhaps even from childhood. Some of these incidents may have been turning points in our lives. Why can we remember these exchanges? Could it be because we are still carrying the substances that we exchanged? An older woman, a former nun, affirmed that she was a frequent target for psychic sex as a very young nun, and only too gladly participated, psychically, in all her naïveté. She still remembers the experience.

There is not much difference between an exchange of psychic sexual substances, and an exchange of personal mementos. If a woman gives a man a necktie by which to remember her, and in exchange that man gives the woman a necklace, they will be connected to each other through these objects until such time as they return them to the other, or dispose of the objects completely. The same is true for sexual substances, the only difference being that sexual substances are "stickier" than material objects. Sexual substances are subtler; they cling more firmly, and are far more difficult to get rid of, in the same way that we cannot easily get rid of a memory. The harder we try to get rid of a particular memory, the more we think about it.

Even though a psychic sexual energy exchange may have involved only a moment of time, the results can last forever. The exchange creates bonds that can only be undone through specific forms of intentional or "accidental" recapitulation, meaning, to actually re-enter the moment of doing, using a specific formulation that causes either an undoing or a completion.

We do not normally acknowledge that psychic sex has happened. We think that since nobody has seen it happen, then nothing can be proved. We think that we can get away with it all the time. The truth is that there are no secrets. Our psychic-sexual-substance exchanges are completely visible to our mates, to our children, to our relatives, and to our friends, should they ever care to look. A common agreement between people is to pretend that psychic sexual exchanges cannot be seen. Here is a dangerous question to ask: What kind of holy sanctuary is created when we make a pact to be dishonest with each other?

How It Happens

Psychic sex starts as a field effect. Before you even see a person you can feel them approaching. How else do you know when and where to place your attention, at just the right moment to catch the other person's eye? *Zzzzzzt!*

We develop unconscious art forms to cleverly manipulate other people's attention. For example, in meetings, the person who "accidentally" sits across from you is typically proposing to be your partner for psychic sex. Most questions asked during meetings are timed and directed so as to get someone's attention for psychic sex. Women (and men to a lesser degree) do subtle energetic warfare, staking out or trying to steal psychic sex territory and competing for attention to get psychic sex from prestigious people.

An exchange of sexual substances can take place in as short a time as one-half of a second, and it can occur through glass. Psychic sex can happen while you are driving down the street and exchange glances with a pedestrian. It can occur at a subway stop when you look in the eyes of someone sitting in another train going in the opposite direction.

Psychic sex can occur through the mouth while talking or breathing with the mouth open. Watch Val Kilmer exchange sexual substances through his mouth in the film called *The Saint*.

Psychic sex can occur through the eyes. The exchange occurs instantaneously after contact is established, which takes about one second.

Psychic sex can occur through the written word, through implication in language and timing, through what is not said, what is merely indicated or referred to. And then we invented technology.

Computer Sex

When this manuscript was first started, the Internet did not even exist. It is a stunning acknowledgement of how fast our culture changes, that now a separate section is required to address the impact of psychic computer sex.

Sex of any kind occurs through our imagination. This is why we can have orgasms in our dreams. This is why we can masturbate. You are responsible for imagining the success of your own sexuality. If you cannot imagine sexuality happening for you, then it does not matter who you are with, or what the circumstances are, *it ain't a gonna work for ya.*

Telephones have long been used for stimulating sexual imagination. Panting, moaning, naughty words, screaming in ecstasy, dial that 888 number and a delightful (or frightening) sexual fantasy partner is there to play with your mind.

Then, starting in 1992, the general public first gained access to the Internet. Given human ingenuity, it was not long before Internet sex was possible. The sounds are the same on the Internet as on the telephone, but a new dimension was added: the visual. The human mind is so visually dominated that Internet sex has an impact several orders of magnitude greater than telephone sex. In short, by Internet sex we are bowled over.

The picture in our imagination about what is happening in our sexual fantasy changes, with Internet sex, from being sourced by our imagination to being sourced by the computer screen. The picture comes in through our eyes with such clarity that it replaces the image generated by our imagination. And the computer picture is perfect. When pornographic films were only available in adult seXXX shops, people were afraid of being caught walking out from a private film booth. Now in the privacy of our own office, Internet sex is soaring.

The virus of Internet sex has massively infected the minds of modern man and woman – Internet sex is perfect for the mind. But here's the catch. After a short exposure to Internet sex we may start losing our ability to internally generate our own sexual images without the computer. Our neurons have been externally stimulated and we can become addicted to that stimulation.

It turns out that, as a result of the strength and duration of the impact of Internet sex images on our sexual imagination center, we are confronted with making a choice: computer sex *or* real sex. Let it sink in. The human mind does not allow for both. If we decide to choose real sex over computer sex, then, according to participants in our trainings, it can require six to twelve months or longer of healing time, absolute abstinence, for our mind to decontaminate itself from the fantasy images of computer sex before we can truly enjoy real sex again. Since Internet sex produces the same energetic residue as psychic sex, your partner knows what you've been up to. Think clearly before you make that click.

Cleaning It Up

Building a wall and completely withdrawing from the world around us is not the answer to ending psychic sex. The goal is to refine our sensing and our acts of creation to the point where we can work on the level of sexual energy with consciousness and purpose.

When someone offers to exchange sexual substances with us, and we do not wish to exchange sexual substances with them, it can become the same as someone offering us a cigarette when we do not smoke. We do not have to energetically "kill" them for making us the offer. Neither do we have to become dead ourselves. What we can do is work to refine our sensitivity to the speed and delicacy with which psychic sexual exchanges take place. Through acknowledging the reality of psychic sex and expanding our awareness on the same subtle levels, what is occurring or about to occur starts becoming obvious and making sense. When we are aware of what we are creating and what is happening, then at that point we have choice. Psychic sex can be avoided by glancing away in one-quarter of a second, before there is time for contact to complete itself and for sexual energy to exchange. Psychic-sexual-substance-exchange can be blocked by pressing the tip of your tongue behind your top front teeth. Try this method yourself to check its effectiveness. It's like this: If you continue making efforts to learn what a street is, then at some point you can cross it without getting run over.

Do you remember when you first began to think about cleaning up your life? Did you ever try to imagine whether or not a person could actually live on a vegetarian diet? Perhaps you were quite accustomed to using drugs and alcohol, eating red meats and dairy products, drinking coffee, tea and sodas, having desserts with every meal, watching television, reading the daily paper, and listening to the local radio station. For most of us, at one time or another, these things were quite normal ways to spend our time and our energy. If some of these activities have gradually fallen away, it does not mean that you have excluded yourself from life or humanity. Neither does it necessarily make you strange. You have simply shifted your level of practice. The same applies to psychic sex.

Psychic Sex: One Man's Experience

The following is a personal letter from a man who was experimenting, to shift his participation in psychic sex. Through his ruthlessly honest sharing, you can feel how deep the struggle is, and you can see how similar we all are.

Last summer I did an experiment of three months without sex. I immediately discovered that I was a total sex-junkie, and that sex was the oldest and hardest drug I ever had. Like every real addict I was capable of throwing away the rest of my dignity if there was any opportunity to favor to my addiction. Just as a real smoker would hike in the middle of the night through a rainstorm to the next village to get a cigarette (which I have done too), I would do almost anything for some quickie sex. I think that there is no drug in the world where the abuse of it creates more terrible results in human dignity than the case of sex.

How often did I act without any dignity? How often did I take sex into an abusive form and enter woman's spaces with my neediness, supposedly to not be alone, but getting my instant-ecstasy as quick as possible?

During these three months I observed much more closely where I placed my attention. In doing so I also noticed that there are sudden moments when certain women look into my eyes and grip me through my eyes directly to my balls. I have no chance to defend myself by closing the gate. For a millisecond she owns me totally – with skin and hair – and I do not know what to do. She knows that she owns me, and she knows that I know. I had hoped that by continuing my no sex practice that this would stop automatically, but it did not.

A part of me was really scared to be in contact with women because I knew that one or another woman could own me instantly "against my will." But I did not have much clarity about this, only to see that my dignity was "for sale" so to speak, like a male prostitute.

Observing psychic sex has not been easy because it is very hard to handle the amount of energy that suddenly arises, all these emotional gas-bubbles that climb out of the inner swamps, and all the fights I start having with my big monkey.

But stopping psychic sex is much harder still. The exercises you gave me change my daily interaction with woman completely. It is very hard for me not to look straight in a woman's eyes while I am talking to her, especially with friends. It is also very hard not taking women in my arms while saying hello or goodbye. When I stopped extended eye contact and hugging women with whom I thought I did not have anything going on, suddenly arises a big fear in me. When I am out in the streets or together with people, I fear to be in "enemy country"! I now sometimes feel in the presence of women that they are the enemy. And if I am together with a man he automatically becomes my friend even if he is the worst asshole. It is strange.

I do not practice as strictly as possible. I am still looking for compromises. For example, "Oh yes, I can still look in my therapist's eyes, or take her in my arms …"

I get this fear that a woman with whom I do not look straight in her eyes during a conversation might think that I am not present or interested in her, or that I am sick or insecure. That is terrible. And that you suggested I cancel my Tango dancing lessons was the worst thing. It was less my suffering a lack of sexual energy flowing around me while dancing with other women than it was my fear of going to the class with my own woman where it should be my job to guide her, and to be straight and clear in what I am doing, and not hopping like a beginner in the scene. Shit! In a way I am lost!

In conclusion, we may be surprised by how much is going on in our lives and in our relationships that at first glance appears to be invisible. Entering the domains of Love that lasts involves many levels all at the same time. We discover relationship as a sophisticated new art form. Just as with any creative format, becoming a relationship artist requires courage and dedication. Once competence in the basic procedures is attained, a whole new world of expression opens up to explore.

CHAPTER 18

What About the Kids?

Considering how to have and raise children in the context of building Love that lasts would fill another entire volume. Nonetheless, I can recommend several excellent childraising books (*see* Further Reading), and offer a few ideas and secrets here regarding relationship, family and children.

When a couple becomes a family – through pregnancy and birth, through adoption, or through marrying a partner who already has children – the relationship energetics completely change. For many people the addition of children is gradual and tends to be, at first, unnoticed; but then the new formation stays. With others, the family group experiences sudden and drastic change. The steady rise in divorces means that the children are shuttled back and forth between ex-partners. With the increase of single parents, the arrival and departure of potential partners is often abrupt and unpredictable. The social and energetic stresses from these changes must be dealt with using delicacy and forthrightness or the stresses will tear the family apart.

In my first marriage I thought that I was done with childraising after homebirthing and homeschooling two daughters through to college age. Then, I got divorced and started a new relationship with a woman who already had three boys under the age of ten. After being around girl-children, I thought I knew about children. Encountering these boys, I could not imagine what was wrong. "What *are* these things?" I would wonder privately and out loud in amazement at the kicking and fighting, shouting, throwing and breaking things, non-communication, power conflicts and lack of relationship. The answer was, of course, "These are boys."

My three new sons spend part of each month with their father at his house and part of the month at our house. Transitioning back and forth from being a couple to being a family has been like sunning ourselves on a tropical beach and then suddenly being inundated by a tidal wave.

Nothing avoids the engulfing chaos of having children in the house. Try to remember this. If the children are born to you, or if you live with them full time, it is easy to forget that what is happening, right now, in relationship with your beloved partner, man or woman, may only be the result of the massive impact of children. To manage or counterbalance the effects of children, so the couple can continue experimenting in the domains of building Love that lasts, there are definitely some important issues to consider and some experiments worth trying that seem to make a difference.

))(The Phoenix Effect

Making Use of the Phoenix Effect (BLTLCH18.01). First and foremost – remember that having children around completely changes the energetic dynamics in a relationship. Maintaining extraordinary human or Archetypal Relationship in the company of children requires a much higher level of commitment and precision than negotiating relationship as a mere couple. Simplicity vanishes in the kid-storm. Some parents would even claim that sustaining extraordinary human relationship with children around is impossible. But it is not impossible. It is just rare, because we are not trained in how to do it.

If you start (each day) by already knowing and consciously remembering that attempting to hold the space for Love that lasts is almost never accomplished, that it is a difficult challenge even privately as a couple and often frustrating or painful, then this puts your efforts and your experience into proper perspective. Knowing the magnitude of what you are up against at the outset gives you a proper perspective for proceeding. Having frequent honest conversations with your partner about the heartbreaking thrashings that go on in your spaces of sanctuary on a regular basis can allow what is called the "Phoenix Effect" to do its work with you.

- The Phoenix Effect recognizes that relationship is made out of substances that are eternal – such as clarity, Archetypal Love, and possibility.
- The Phoenix Effect assumes that your relationship space is filled with ordinary human relationship, extraordinary human relationship, or Archetypal Relationship, depending on where you navigate the space.
- The Phoenix Effect means that out of the cold dark ashes of a burned down relationship a new relationship is born.

The Phoenix Effect goes like this: When children or problems crash into the relationship and cause conflict or breakdown, it feels like the whole relationship house starts on fire. The hint is this: let the house burn, *and*, remember the Phoenix Effect. "Do-overs" are allowed because Archetypal Love never goes away. Only *you* go away. *You* can come back.

Stand together with your partner and warm your hands over the fire enjoying each other's company during the chaos, knowing all the while that *what the relationship is actually made of cannot burn.* What burns is dross, riff raff, illusionary Box projections or expectations from the past or the future. What feels like disappointment or betrayal comes from false assumptions that have grown on the relationship like vines up the side of a building. Let the fire inform you about what worked and what did not work, so that your next experiments stand on new wisdom. As the blaze slowly burns down and the words and emotions subside, take a deep breath, let a few moments of nothingness go by, and gently start

---

MAP OF THE PHOENIX EFFECT

1) Try something new.

2) Go until you crash and burn.

3) Let it burn. Learn from the fire about what worked and what did not work. When there is nothing but ashes, go back to step 1).

---

over again from the cleansed emptiness and a completely new perspective. This three-step cycle of the Phoenix Effect produces rapid relationship evolution and a more and more solid preparation for the next burn.

SECTION 18-B

Archetypal Relationships with Children

A parent's relationship with his or her child naturally includes Archetypal dimensions. For example, in the same way that men and women need to be bonded to and nurtured, coached and held accountable by Archetypal Men's and Women's cultures, children also need bonding into Archetypal Children's culture. Our schooling system of dividing children into grades terribly shatters the bonding among children of different ages. Young children learn most surely by imitating their older role models. Older children best solidify their learning through teaching what they already know to their younger associates. When older children gain experience through caring for younger children as part of their upbringing, they already know something about how to be good parents when they have their own children. The shocking fact that adults, such as myself, need to take birthing and childraising classes before we have our own kids, because we lacked natural contact with children, indicates a horrifying gap in the sanity of our present culture.

Our whole present schooling system is based on the simple misconception that teachers actually *teach* their students. But they do not. You cannot teach a child anything – but a child can learn whatever they want. Think back on your own childhood. Did anybody teach you? Or did you decide to learn?

The Archetypal Parent's job is to create ongoing environments in which children can develop their muscles for taking responsibility. In such environments, the parent-child relationship stands on a set of rules and boundaries that are clear and dignified. The boundaries serve as the bars of a jungle gym on which the child develops responsibility muscles. Of course the child will test those boundaries. Muscles are developed through persistent exercise. The child repeatedly testing a boundary even to the point of tantrum does not make the boundary wrong. Repeatedly testing boundaries is a sign of developing strength. If the parent does not provide solid bars, for example, if the boundaries are not held with easeful consistent precision, the child's world collapses into formlessness. The child is forced to take responsibility for their immediate survival at a level for which they are not designed to take responsibility. Parents sometimes imagine that they are being "nice" to their children if they bend the rules or let the children lead and make decisions. But parental leniency literally drives children crazy. Archetypally it is the parents' job to hold the world solid for their children, until the children are old enough *and* mature enough to take responsibility for generating the rules themselves. Mature responsibility does not begin before fifteen years of age.

Children Become Who You Are

Your efforts to create and sustain extraordinary human and Archetypal Relationship go directly into the being of your children. You may have noticed already that children do not *do what you do*, they become *who you are*. The spaces of extraordinary human and Archetypal Relationship radiate high quality energetic food that nurtures the souls of your children. On the surface, when you and your partner enter a few moments of Countenance, or when you "touch through" each other, or

when you move together at the speed of Love, or when you create intellectual intimacy, or when you listen "as a space," or when you are being-with each other, or when you appreciate the other, all of this goes into the hearts of your children and opens them to what is possible in relationship. Your extraordinary human and Archetypal moments form reference points for the rest of their lives. They have a thought-map and they know where they can go. You might not see them go there for years, but they *can go there* and *will be able to go there* because you have shown them the way. Know that your efforts to avoid being sucked into the Box's webwork of ordinary human relationship establishes a beachhead into new territory for anyone else who observes what you are doing.

Hold Space for the Center of Being of Your Family

It is possible (even ordinary!) to hold space for an extraordinary daily family experience. The way to hold space for extraordinary daily family experience starts with you (in particular the man) keeping the center of your family.

Keeping the Center of Your Family (BLTLCH18.02). Each family has a center of being, just like each person has a center of being. Keeping the center of the family is Archetypally the man's job, but actually the woman and man work together keeping the family center. Keeping the center of your family is similar to keeping your own personal center, and involves three components:

Keeping the Center of Your Family
1. Put your attention on the center of your family.
2. Find where the center of your family is right now. In many modern families the center of being of a family is the television, the Internet or computer games. The center of your family could also be with

the children's schooling, with in-laws, job problems, the bank account, an alcoholic father, a secretly raging mother, etc.

3. Bring the center of your family in and place the center of your family on the purpose of your family.

To keep the center of your family, you must know the purpose of your family. What is the purpose of your family? Is the purpose of your family ordinary human relationship, extraordinary human relationship, or Archetypal Relationship? It is not a common practice to consciously remember and live into the purpose of your family.

A breakthrough in family satisfaction can occur through realizing that the purpose of your family may differ from the purpose of other families. There is no "normal" family.

It is not required that your family's style of being together imitates any previously known or recognizable family pattern. Bringing this idea to a few family discussions can suddenly free both children and adults to unleash creativity for discovering what your family could be for you. In a short while, you could find yourselves thriving, in a dynamic, harmonious mini-society, experimenting to express individual desires and personalities.

Without intentionally exploring the purpose of your family, the purpose is controlled by whomever makes the loudest shouts. Since the way children develop responsibility is through testing parental boundaries, it is often the children who shout the loudest. Or the shouting may come from the father or mother who are not aware that clarity is more powerful than making boundaries, and

---

Handbook for Creating Ordinary Relationship

Here are twenty surefire ways to undermine the Archetypal center of your family and thereby create ordinary family relationship:

1. Keep the television or radio on while you eat meals. This makes the television or the radio the center of your family. Make the television the center of your family life together.

2. Bring the newspaper to the meal table, or let the children bring toys. This makes the (mostly horrifying) news or the (corporation-marketed) toys the center of your family.

3. Do not eat meals together. This makes the Box's stomach (in each person) more important than the family purpose.

4. When you want something from your mate or the children, just shout for them in the house. This destroys respect and shatters spaces.

5. Do not hold boundaries for the children. Let them scream their way out of the boundaries that you do set. This drives children crazy because then they have no boundaries on which they can structure their world and their intelligence.

6. Serve sugar-sweetened foods at all your meals. This makes sugar the center of your family.

7. Do not tell the children what will happen next. Instead, just order them around. This terrorizes the children and makes them recalcitrant and centered on themselves for mere survival.

8. Let the children interrupt adult conversation and adult spaces with their teasing each other, their questions, their getting hurt, anything to get your attention. This shows children that adults have weak attention and that the space is not held and they are not safe.

9. Do not have fun as adults. This proves to the children that they should never grow up and take responsibilities because adults are not passionate and obviously do not have fun.

10. Do not have physical or emotional intimacy with your partner in front of the children. This shows children that physical or emotional intimacies are bad, or at least not included in the image of "the good adult" who your children will imitate.

11. When a child gets hurt, tell them that nothing happened. Do not listen to their feelings. This psychologically abuses the children into distrusting their own experience.

12. Expect your children to take responsibilities before they are truly capable of being responsible (around fifteen years old). Expect your children to brush their teeth, go to bed, clean up their room, do their homework, etc., without you holding the space for it. This expectation destroys their innocence. When your children fail to meet your expectations this gives you reason to resent and hate your own children.

13. Do not read, sing, dance, or play musical instruments to or with your children, or let them see you loving to do these things. This starves their spirit.

14. Never apologize to your children. Never admit to being wrong. This makes children think they are supposed to be perfect like you.

15. Never let your children know that they hurt you. Then they think they are powerless and do not have to learn to manage their power.

16. Do not teach children to be sensitive to various kinds of spaces (e.g., adult meetings, churches, ceremonies, prayer or meditation spaces). This way nothing is sacred to them because they think nothing is sacred to you.

17. Only give your children your partial attention for a minimum amount of time. This keeps your children starving for attention so they keep coming back to you and trying to manipulate you to give them more. Then children learn that getting negative attention is better than getting no attention at all, and they wrap you around their finger with the problems they cause.

18. Use your financial resources to buy new appliances, cars, clothing and computers. This shows children that possessing objects is more important than being together.

19. Praise or blame your children for their behavior instead of appreciating them or being-with them. Then children think that praise and blame is how to manipulate the other people in their lives.

20. Send your children to public school and expect the teachers to raise them (to become like their friends who are also sent away from their parents). This shows children the weakness and confusion of their family and takes away their hope of having authentic parents who provide support with family bonding and family love. This shows your children how to try to give away the responsibility for their own family if they ever have one.

clarity does not require shouting. Clarity only requires statement.

Having the center of your family located someplace other than where the purpose of your family is, typically fills the "relationship creation zone" that your family represents with ordinary human relationship. Then, the chances for extraordinary human or Archetypal Relationship happening in the family are lost.

Something different occurs in a family only when the adults hold and navigate the center of the family into extraordinary human or Archetypal Relationship. The practice for navigating the center of the family into extraordinary human or Archetypal Relationship is to consistently ask and answer this question: "In the name of which purpose are we as a family gathered in this moment?"

Aim to keep the center of the family in the Adult context, the responsible context, and the extraordinary context. Make this your purpose, and make your purpose top priority, no matter what else is happening. Do not forget your priority. Strive to keep 10 percent of your attention focused on navigating the family space to consistently answer the question of purpose.

Your Attention and Your Children

The central skills for continuing relationship experiments even when there are kids around involve paying attention to your attention.

As we discussed at length in Section 6-B, bringing the woman to life requires 100 percent of the man's attention on the woman. If that is so, what about the attention needed by the kids? How is the man supposed to place 100 percent of his attention on his woman if 60 percent (more or less) of his attention is already on the kids and the family – listening for the mood, the tone, and the well-being of each member and navigating how things are and what needs to be done. Holding space for the family already requires an enormous amount of the man's attention.

Clearly, some new skills need to be developed. Without developing the new skills, twenty years of family life can go by and the couple, which is the core of the family, withers and dies due to lack of food.

The reason that attention plays such an important role in feeding your partner is that *energy follows attention*. That is, your energy flows where your attention goes. This phenomenon is obvious once you have heard it. What you place your attention on receives your energy.

Energy Follows Attention

To confirm the theory that energy follows attention, practice increasing your sensitivity so that you can detect where you are placing your attention and where you are flowing energy. For example, when eating, notice that when you look at the food on someone else's plate you put your energy into their food. You can easily detect this in reverse. When someone else looks at the food on your plate, their energy goes into your food, and you can feel it.

When you walk in the shopping mall and you scan the other shoppers, your energy flows into them and they can feel it. Remember all the times when you have turned your head for no reason and you saw that a stranger was looking at you? You could actually feel their energy coming into you. When you look into another shopper's eyes and they look into your eyes the exchange of energy can be like a flash of lightening. Start to notice how much attention you use to control your attention, so that you do not look into other people's eyes and receive unwanted energy from them. This is the kind of sensing that will allow you to begin placing your attention on your partner and flowing them energy even in the midst of screaming thrashing kids.

Putting your attention on someone flows energy to them. This energy is real. This is the phenomena that is happening when, just as you are about to telephone someone, the phone rings and it is the person you were about to call.

Flowing energy to your partner is food that they need to continue living in their relationship to you. Sending cards and letters and gifts, bringing flowers and chocolates, these are all *signs* of placing attention and flowing energy. But these *are not* flowing energy. The flowers and chocolates are not enough. Flowers and chocolates are symbols of energy, not energy itself. Kisses, hand squeezes, holding the coat or opening the door, performing errands or favors, sending or bringing cards and gifts, even dinners out or vacations together are all forms of *doing*. No amount of *doing* flows energy. Doing is doing. Placing your attention on your partner and flowing them energy is *being-with*. Flowing energy to your partner can occur at the same time you are kissing, hand squeezing, holding the coat and so on. But the doing does not flow energy. *Placing attention on* flows energy. There is no substitute for placing your attention on your partner and flowing them energy. Doing by itself only gets things done. Doing does

not feed their soul. Attention energy feeds their soul.

When the children are around, the children require attention, energy and care. When we look at our desk we see that the endless details of our busy lives also require our attention, energy and care. The consequences of not giving children and daily details our attention are loud and evident. The kids scream; the telephone gets cut off; there is no food on the table; the neighbors complain. Somewhere in the midst of this world, our partner, our mate, is lost.

We may tend to regard our mate as more of a colleague rather than a lover in the project of living and raising children, since our partner has the same goals as we do with the children and the details. Therefore, we work together to accomplish certain objectives: get the kids to school, have a birthday party, do Christmas with the relatives, and so on. Unfortunately, however, in the busy-ness of our daily lives, we can easily ignore the silent cries of our partner for presence, rather than ignore the quarreling children or our formidable to-do list.

Placing Archetypal Relationship as the Highest Priority (BLTLCH18.03). As a way of creating another possibility for your partnerships, try this experiment: Decide right now to forever place Archetypal Relationship at the highest priority. Placing experiments in intimacy at the highest priority is different from giving those experiments the most time. Such experiments do not require much time. We forget this in our daily overwhelm. We forget that one moment of pure being-with has no time. Once we enter the intimacy of pure presence, time stops. You already know this. A moment is as long as a day is as long as forever because presence only happens now. A day of pure intimacy can occur in a moment if we are careful to focus 100-percent attention and, during that moment, flow 100-percent being-with energy to our partner. A feast happens in that moment, a restarting, a healing, a reinitiation. Moments of placing attention on our partner and flowing them energy like this *because it is our highest priority* will encourage our relationship to grow even when the kids are around.

Whose Energy Is It?

A common confusion about this principle that energy follows attention is to imagine that, if we are giving our attention and flowing our energy to our children and our life's details all day long, by the end of the day we will be exhausted and all of our energy used up. We will then look at our partner as another needy child and think, "Oh, God! Not another one! Why don't they leave me alone? I am tired. I am already used up. I have nothing left to give."

The confusion comes from not realizing that the energy we flow when we place our attention on someone is not *our* energy. It is the energy of the Principles that we serve. In the case of our partner, the energy is Archetypal Love. Archetypal Love is already there wherever we are in unending abundance. The energy that we flow to our partner is not our energy.

Maybe you have had an experience like this: You returned home late one night, and you finally lay your exhausted aching bones down on a bed next to your partner ready to collapse into sleep. There was a good night kiss. The kiss went on a little longer. The kiss expanded from the lips to the neck to the arms and legs, fingers and toes. In a moment there was an aliveness and energy that came from nowhere and the exhaustion was gone like it never existed. The energy of Archetypal Love is not *your* energy.

The key to flowing energy is what we do with our attention. Energy flows where our attention goes. Start learning what you are doing with your attention so you can start learning what you are doing with your energy. If your attention is split between your partner and the children, your partner feels it. So do the children. Do not make your children

dependent on always having your 100-percent attention. Support your children to be able to feel comfortable and safe while sometimes being self-entertaining. Support your children to learn to work with their own attention. The same with your partner. Then, make life a dance. Sometimes you are 100 percent with your children, sometimes 100 percent with the telephone, sometimes 100 percent with details, sometimes 100-percent with your partner. Sometimes you are splitting your attention two ways, sometimes five ways. Swirl your attention in blended spirals, then focus it precisely on one thing, then bounce it from one thing to another, then fuzz it into the whole field. Let the dance of your attention and your energy-flow unfold according to what is wanted and needed, never forgetting that Archetypal Love with your partner, and as the purpose of your family, is the highest priority. Even if the problems seem horrendous, do not forget your priority.

Learn to instantly drop everything and refocus 100 percent of your attention onto your partner, so that you can receive the 100-percent attention they are placing on you. Perhaps your partner has been placing 100-percent attention on you for years and you never noticed. If your attention is habitually split between your partner and an internal conversation with an enemy that you are engaging for a mutual low-drama-feeding-frenzy at work, you will never experience the 100-percent attention and the energy flow of Archetypal Love from your partner.

Make Time

Using 100% of your attention to experience 100% attention from someone else does not take a lot of time. We have developed a linear concept of time based on the idea of time scarcity. We spend our days chasing the clock, trying to catch up and fit everything into a limited twenty-four-hour day. We frantically review our schedule trying to find time. In this mode we will never find the time for intimacy with our partner, because kids and the chaotic details of our daily lives will expand to swallow up every moment. To give Archetypal-Love intimacy experiments top priority requires that we change our relationship to time.

Where did you get the time to read this sentence? We do not often ask ourselves such a question. But ask yourself now, where did you get the time to read this sentence? Our first answers will probably be something like: I got the time from the calendar; I borrowed the time from everything else I have to do today; God gave me the time; I looked for and found the time; I stole some time out of my day planner, and so on.

Making Time (BLTLCH18.04). Right now you could be anywhere in the world doing anything. But here you are right now, reading this paragraph. Where did you get the time to read this paragraph? All of our previous answers sidestep our responsibility in this situation. The truth is, we are time makers. Anything that we do, we *make* the time to do it. If you brushed your teeth this morning you made the time to do it. If you wanted to brush your teeth this morning and did not do it, that was because you did not make the time to brush your teeth. You only do what you make the time to do. Anything that you do is through making the time to do it.

You have the power to make time. This is the power you exercise to make the time for placing 100-percent attention on your partner and flowing them energy. No matter what else is happening, no matter where you are, no matter what circumstances might make it seem impossible – even kids! – you have the time whenever you make it.

SECTION 18-D

Letting Go of Your Kids

Bringing a Son or Daughter into Adult Gender Culture (BLTLCH18.05). The transition from adolescence to adulthood is not identified as significant in the tradition of our culture. By now in this book you should be sensing that this particular transition shapes the remainder of our children's lives as adults, partners and parents. The lack of a rite of passage leaves our children directionless, like a compass with no needle (*see* Section 3-E for more on rite of passage). Without much effort you can build the legend in your family about the importance and sanctity of the adolescent-to-adult shift, and you can substantiate your stories by creating a series of rituals around it.

I will never forget the rising tension as each of my daughters approached her seventh birthday. In a pre-arranged ritual, each alone climbed the steep hill behind our house in Arizona, followed a hand-drawn map, and found her first pocketknife hidden away in the rocks. Such rituals mark turning points and important shifts of context in the growing up process (refer to the book *From Magical Child to Magical Teen* by Joseph Chilton Pearce for more details on the unfolding process). By formalizing transitions you publicly recognize these events and give them more of their proper place in our lives. Through ritualizing the end of childhood and letting go of your sons and daughters without strings attached, you help model for them the Archetypal context for their future relationships.

Instructions for Mothers

When your son (or daughter) turns eighteen years old, call up your friends, bake some cakes, open some champagne, close the curtains, turn up the music and have a mother graduation party. Your job as mother is fulfilled. You can take the role of mother and the job description of mother and you can put it back on the shelf. You can reclaim your name and step back into the world no longer as a mother but now as a woman. No matter what has happened, you have done the best job that you could. Now the job is over. You can let the job go. The past eighteen years have been what they were. Now, what is next for you? There is a whole world awaiting your next creative contribution.

This suggestion to have a mother graduation party is a shock to many mothers. After eighteen years of reading from the same script, some mothers are afraid to discover who they are when their life is no longer defined by their high drama theatrical role as "the mother." For example, my mother never took off the title or the role. She had three sons, and even when all three moved out of the house, set up their own lives, and created jobs and families of their own, my mother continued to play out the role of being "mother" to "her three boys." You do not have to do this. Sticking to the role of "mother" avoids the greater responsibility of being "woman," and possibly also the greater joy of Pirate Sorceress Warrioress Queen Goddess Woman in the world at large. That a woman would choose to avoid these pleasurable and challenging grand adventures is an example of the Box's "free will" occluding Archetypal opportunities.

You cannot stop being a child's mother like you can quit being a man's wife or a company's manager. The suggestion to have a mother graduation party is no invitation to stop loving or respecting your child. The party is simply a ritual intended for consciously and elegantly deflating your "mother" character, thus giving you more space to explore other possible adult roles. At the same time, those people who used to be in your custody as children are freer to begin creating through their own adult roles. Boy children, especially, benefit by having a better chance of "taking their balls back" and entering their own manhood – a procedure that is not well supported by our modern culture and can therefore use all the help it can get.

To Fathers, About Daughters

A girl transitioning into adult womanhood requires the guidance and impetus of a feminine rite of passage that our culture does not provide. If the transition to womanhood occurs at all, in our present culture, it occurs inaccurately or incompletely, or more likely both. Certainly the onset of menses initiates a female body into a more mature relationship to nature, birth and death, but womanhood encompasses far more than physiological shifts. Engaging adult womanhood is stepping through a one-way door into an entirely new relationship to the world – a world of radical creative play, of uncompromising responsibility, and the possibility of life as Pirate Sorceress Warrioress Queen Goddess Woman.

One of the confusions surrounding the transition from girlhood to womanhood comes from the father. Fathers are not provided with the clarity they need to enact their part in the transformational high drama that unfolds a woman from a girl. Unnecessary pain and residual perplexities could be avoided if men played their part with elegance and sensitivity, but men are neither informed nor trained in how to do this.

Instead, many fathers suddenly abandon all connectedness with their daughters at the first sign of budding breasts or bloody tampons. The daughter's shock of being abandoned, at a time when her father's steadfast admirations and appreciation is most needed, can leave lifelong emotional scars in her trust of and relationship to all future men in her life. Women need to experience – in all four bodies – that they are still appreciated, respected, admired and loved, even if that body is making wild changes that are beyond their control.

A father who abandons his daughter at adolescence usually does so out of his own confusion and embarrassment. The daughter thinks that her father suddenly rejects her. The father thinks his little girl has vanished and has become that mysterious and dangerous "feminine thing." He thinks she would prefer total privacy, instead of the warm fatherly hug he used to give her, when in fact her hesitations are only timidity about revealing her new form. He thinks his daughter intends the separation that is happening, when, instead, she is only testing his steadfastness toward her in her more mature condition. When the father stops playing catch or tag with his daughter, stops tousling her hair, stops listening to her stories of her new interests, stops paying attention and holding a fatherly space for her, the shock of his abandonment destabilizes her shift into a bigger world. She needs father's continued fatherly support as much if not more than ever during her adolescence. This is when father should not let go of his daughter.

Other fathers blatantly ignore any changes at all while their daughter grows up. As the girl turns from nineteen to twenty to twenty-one years old, goes away to college, starts seriously exploring relationships with men, establishes herself in an interesting and enlivening career, and enters the adult world, the father still treats her like his little girl. He pays her bills, fixes her car, demands to know where she's been last night, and tells her what will be happening over the weekend. She may have moved out of her father's house, gotten married, started her own business and had several children, but the father still calls her by her childhood name and treats her like his little missy.

A father can never stop being a father even if he can quit being a husband or a consultant. But a father can recognize and contribute to his daughter entering adulthood. As the father, he can continue to represent the strong arms in which his daughter can always find comfort, information, encouragement or protection.

The father-daughter connection may also be inappropriately secure. If the father does not make the shift at the right time from being father-to-daughter to being older-man-to-younger-woman, then his daughter suffers silently with resentments, or suffers more perceptibly by cutting him out of her life so she can have a life of her own. Taking her center back from her father is a daughter's work. Her father cannot give her center back to her, just as the mother cannot give the balls back to her son – he has to take them. And yet there is an appropriate time for a father to hand his precious girl out into the world, to let her go, come what may, prepared or not, for better or worse. And, in that releasing, the man graduates from his role as responsible daddy and enters new roles as proud father, playful grandfather, Archetypal Pirate Magician King Spiritual Warrior Man, and respectful admiring friend of an amazing woman who used to be his child.

Sons into Men's Culture and Daughters into Women's Culture

The difficulty with fathers bringing their sons into Archetypal Men's culture and mothers bringing their daughters into Archetypal Women's culture – even though such a transition is so crucially important – is that Archetypal Men's and Women's cultures do not exist in our present modern Western cultures, and we do not naturally know how to create them ourselves. Instructions for bootstrapping yourself into your authentic Archetypal gender culture are beyond the scope of this book. But instructions do exist. Brave men and women are experimenting at the fringe of our culture. With diligence you can find them, work with them, and together you can build a bridge into Archetypal gender cultures for yourself, your family, your friends and your colleagues. Keep making efforts. Whatever you try is assuredly better than the present state of affairs, which may include giving up before you start.

CHAPTER 19

What If It Is Not Working?

Relationships die. Love never dies. So, relationships do not die from lack of love.

Popular folklore leads us to believe that we can fall in love and then fall out of love. This is nonsense. The idea that we can stop loving someone is an idea that does not relate to Archetypal Love.

Human love can be given and taken away like attention, like money, like a wedding ring. We love someone. We hate someone. Our ordinary human feelings can change in a moment. Hate is not the opposite of Archetypal Love. Hate is the shadow side of ordinary human love. If we hate someone we are still involved with them; we still exchange energy with them. Behind the exchange of love-hate energy in ordinary human love is always Archetypal Love. Archetypal Love never dies.

Archetypal Love cannot be given or taken away. Archetypal Love exists far beyond the reach of human control. Archetypal Love is a force of nature, a radiance, the most abundant thing in the universe. The fact that we *think* we can love and then stop loving reveals the severity to which the human mind is subject to a schizophrenia that we all pretend to ignore.

Once we step through the veil of the ordinary human illusion of separation with another person, once we spontaneously cannot refuse to say (or cannot stop wishing to say) "I love you," there is no going back. The bond is made. Archetypal Love does not undo itself.

We are usually not prepared by education or demonstration to understand that love never dies. We may want love to die. We may want to put up a brick wall where the veil vanished and where Archetypal Love first flowed through. We may want to forget and we cannot forget. But still we try. We get senile and try to forget. We feel victimized and try to forget. We get sick and try to forget. We get psychotic and try to forget. We die and try to forget. But the veil never returns and Archetypal Love never goes away. It may be that human beings are naturally designed to open to Archetypal Love with more and more people, one by one, until it becomes too painful to continue to deny that all there is, is Love.

Think of how many women are physically beaten or psychologically tortured by their alcoholic husbands and still stick around being co-dependent. Think of how many men are used as emotional trashcans or psychic punching bags by their semi-borderline wives and still stick around being co-dependent. Think of how many children have been raped, beaten, abandoned and betrayed by their modern parents and still can do nothing but love them. Think of the silent things left within you from all of the times your heart desired to say "I love you" and you did not deliver the communication. That message is still in your heart wishing to be heard. Love does not vanish.

And, still, relationships can come to an end.

Build Common Ground

Relationships do not die from a lack of love. Relationships die from a lack of common ground.

If we have built common ground, then being in communion with our partner within the common ground creates heart and soul food for the relationship, and the relationship lives and grows. If common ground shrinks away, then the food supply dwindles. Communication breaks down, the relationship starves and eventually can no longer be sustained. What do we do then?

Common ground does not mean that you both love to play golf, although that could be included. Common ground does not necessarily mean common interests, projects, hobbies, friends, films, music, food or work habits, although these could be a part of it. Common ground in relationship means *a common level to which we are able to be intimate.*

Notice, the definition for common ground is not "the common level to which we are *willing* to be intimate," but "to which we are *able* to be intimate." Here is where the question gets interesting. What is it that determines our ability to be intimate?

Is the level of intimacy to which we can go volitional? Or is it structural? Sure, we can theoretically choose to be as intimate as we want, just as we could theoretically choose to be as authentic as we want. But, in actual practice, the level seems to be set by something other than our conscious choices. We can only be as intimate as we can be. Yet somehow, over the years, our yearning for intimacy can change.

What factors affect the level to which we are able to be intimate? For each individual the factors seem to be unique because we each have a unique past and our past experiences leave "footprints" on us. These footprints are still with us and can be seen immediately by someone who has developed their ability to scan for them. To summarize what we've emphasized throughout this book, the footprints that we carry influence the shape of our Box, and the shape of our Box determines the level to which we are able to be intimate. If we make successful efforts to change the shape of our Box, then our ability to be intimate can change. But, in each moment, the Box factors that produce intimacy include:

- Our Stories. We remember what happened to us and we make a story about it. We use our story to substantiate our decision as to whether what happened was "good" or "bad." We are certain about our stories; we hold them indubitable. No one can challenge the validity of the stories we make about what happened to us. Then these stories create expectations in us. Our basic expectation is that whatever is happening now will be the same as what happened back then, good or bad. Expectations take us out of the present, and the present is the only place where intimacy happens.

- Our Decisions. When things happened to us we made decisions about ourselves, about other people and about life in this world. Those old decisions still influence our lives today. When the old decisions pertain to intimacy, such as, "If I open up I will get hurt," then the old decisions limit our capacity for intimacy.

- Our Emotions. When things happened to us in the past, we might have been able to experience and express feelings about it at the time. But, most likely, there was no one there to listen to us, so our feelings were uncompleted. Unexpressed feelings become emotions. In order to be intimate, we must be present and in our bodies. As soon as we get present and in our bodies, the unexpressed emotions that are locked in our bodies become present too. If it is not okay for us to feel and express these emotions now, we cannot get present, and again our ability to be intimate is blocked.

- Our Resentments. When things happened to us in the past we may have felt hurt, disrespected, abused, or betrayed. We might quite understandably carry these wounds around as a bodily memory for protecting ourselves, even if the incident of the wounding is outside of our present awareness. This is resentment. Resentment is a hook in our heart keeping the wound open as a constant reminder to avoid getting ourselves into a similar situation where we could get hurt again. Resentments keep our heart wounded and thereby block us from intimacy. And so on.

Many factors limit our ability to be intimate. Hopefully the examples above indicate how significant and longstanding these factors are.

Facing Our Intimacy Devouring Monsters (BLTLCH19.01). Each person represents a unique set of these factors that, taken together, create the shape of his or her Box. Most of these factors remain completely unconscious until such time as we, for some reason, wish to enter a deeper intimacy or greater authenticity. And, in the moment we make a gesture toward greater vulnerability, these and other factors raise up their serpentine heads like Loch Ness monsters.

Of course we are surprised and shocked by the immensity and ferocity of these protective intimacy-devouring monsters. Who are we to do battle with such creatures? And for heaven's sake, what for? Best to leave the heinous serpents alone, undisturbed in the deep, we think. And who could argue? Sure, we *could* be more intimate, *if* we succeed in the wrestling match with the prehistoric beasts. If we *don't* succeed, then our level of possible intimacy will be strictly defined by the Box's psychological makeup.

The ordinary strategy is to find a partner who has an equivalent intimacy factor and to get together with them. Our marriage vows include the tacit agreement that we will leave our monsters untamed and our partner will do the same. But this strategy assumes we can outsmart evolution, which may surprise us with unforeseen increases in our need for intimacy. As a result, we end up reading a book like this to try to figure out what is happening to us. If the book has worked, then we are already doing responsible experiments that develop our capacity for feeding relationship with greater intimacy. But, studying and experimenting creates further openings to the forces of evolution.

Evolution and Relationship

Once you get together with someone, and a few years tick by, a new factor arises that can again seriously influence the "balance of intimacy" equation. That factor is time. At first, or even later on in our relationship, we might find ourselves faking a level of intimacy either greater or less than we can actually sustain. We do this to match what we think our partner wants. Such a strategy does neither person any good in the long run, and time itself gradually wears the strategy away. Remember, the "run" may not be as long as we think. Life has a tendency to slip by no matter how we play it out, so why not take the full risk of playing it out as authentically as you can? Time's invitation is to stop wasting time pretending to be something you are not. Use the time you have in daring to be more and more who you are. The journey of being who you are is a dance with evolutionary forces.

Evolutionary forces can be simple or sophisticated. Examples of simple evolutionary forces include an interest in reading self-help books, writing in a diary with fierce introspection, forced health or diet restrictions, hiking or camping trips in nature, classes in martial arts, meditation, theater or singing, training with bow and arrow or sword, learning handicraft or circus skills, and so on. Examples of more sophisticated evolutionary forces include extended travel in third world or seriously foreign cultures, participation in certain personal development or training programs that provide deep emotional processing and/or new mental clarity, attending regular study groups or meetings with high-integrity teachers or healers, following your teacher's instructions to run your own workshops, taking a leadership position in projects that are bigger than you know how to handle, and so on.

Exposure to either simple or sophisticated evolutionary forces over a longer stretch of time is almost guaranteed to deepen the level of intimacy that a person is able to engage. If one partner in the pair enters a faster track of evolution than the other, an imbalance in the ability to be intimate is sure to arise. In fact, only an illusion of the mind makes it seem that any two people ever have the same speed or direction of evolution. Don't believe the illusion.

Evolution tends to direct itself to transforming whatever is the most important factor that blocks the flow of life force. Even longterm or very shadowy blockages can be digested by evolution and changed into doorways of discovery. When the ability to intimately meet the being of the other is imbalanced in a couple, one, or more likely both, of the partners go hungry and the relationship starves. If you find yourself in a starving relationship, first consider that it may be your Box at work furiously defending against changes that would take it out of familiar territory. The Box's free will alone is strong enough to resist or evade even the most powerful forces of evolution. As one partner starts a meditation practice, for example, the other may resist this change with all their might. That is natural. But if your Box is afraid of the reaction of your partner's Box and has you adapt to their resistance, then what can evolution do for you? It can only wait. This is why results from all of the conditions that we have been speaking about are individual and in general unpredictable. There is no general formula to guarantee how relationship will grow, or die, or succeed. A lot is up to you personally, you and your Box.

An honest story of relationship is far more intricate and interesting than the fairy tale "Harry and Betty got married, had kids, and lived happily ever after" that we have been told all of our lives. The question of whether or not our relationships will succeed depends on our answer to the question: Who is running our relationships anyway?

Who Runs Your Relationship?

If we start a relationship it may not be wonderful, and if we end a relationship it may not be a disaster. Whether we start or end a relationship may not even be in our domain of responsibility. It might instead just be our fate (*see* Section 12-K).

Think of how your relationship began in the first place. Did you get to choose with whom, when and where your relationship started? Not a chance. Not in the big picture. You see someone and you think, "Wow, now there's someone I could really be friends with." Does it work out that you get to be friends with that person? Almost never. Even

if you make efforts and try to set things up to be friends, "accidental" incidents and unseen factors arise to prevent your plans from shaping reality. (If you want to make God laugh, tell her your plans.)

Now think of how you met and got closer to the people with whom you are friends now. Did you plan it out? Or did coming together seem to happen by "accident," by unexpected coincidence, or by serendipity? For most people most of the time, relationship experiments begin without preplanning. Relationships start by chance, by luck, and even by "miracle."

If relationships start by "miracle," then it would make sense that they would continue by "miracle," and naturally come to an end by "miracle." Some "Coincidence Control Center" (a term borrowed from John C. Lilly and Antonietta Lilly in their book *The Dyadic Cyclone*) exerts its influence according to the needs of a plan that is bigger than ours.

So, the question remains, do we align with the obvious and let Earth Coincidence Control Center have its way with our lives? Or do we let our Box fight it? This becomes more of a lifestyle decision. To make the decision we might ask, what is the purpose and design behind a mythical Coincidence Control Center? There is a subtle fear involved in asking that question. What if the Coincidence Control Center has a different purpose from our social custom of lifelong monogamous relationship, staying together no matter what? What if the force of evolution would rather have us continue in a relationship only as long as we are evolving?

To Evolve or Not To Evolve?

The universe seems to be interested in more than mere survival. The universe created our three-pound brain as an ideal laboratory for evolution, but our Box stands in the way. If we let the Box keep defending us from evolution, the universe tends to make stronger and stronger invitations to evolve.

Finally, the universe brings in heavy artillery like accidents, diseases, conflicts, breakdowns – anything to put a crack in the Box's defenses and gain access to that in us which is capable of evolving.

How does this relate to relationships? Exactly. An organization can be defined as two or more people with a common purpose. Using this definition then, a relationship is an organization. To design our organizations we naturally copy the structure we are most familiar with – our Box. We end up with unspoken agreements that force our relationships to be rigid, hierarchical and defensive. We assume that our relationship will continue in this traditional form. Our planned trajectory is straight. Evolution slowly chips away at the solid ground beneath our foundation. It may take us awhile to recognize what is happening. By the time we notice the pattern it may be too late for our Box to do anything more to defend itself.

Take the traditions of marriage and the nuclear family as examples. As contrary to common understanding as this may seem, the startling rise in divorces may not be an indication of cultural failure, but instead an indication of cultural evolution. If a marriage functions as an organization defended against evolution, evolution may intercede. Evolution may be needing people to evolve faster than the present institution of marriage and family allows.

By way of an analogy, think of the present shift in audio and video technologies from tape to disc. Is the fact that it is more and more difficult to buy VHS films and audiotape cassettes a breakdown in the film and music industry? Not at all. On the contrary, the film and music industry is booming. Video and music have never before been more effectively transported to the viewing and listening public than through DVD and CD formats. The demise of VHS and audiocassettes is simply an unavoidable byproduct of the evolution of technology.

The same may be true of ordinary human marriages and the nuclear family.

As a culture we try not to see what is happening. That is because we still think in the old paradigm: lifelong marriage, 2.4 children, and a house on the edge of town. If viewed from the traditional paradigm, the nuclear family is the good and right way. Anything else is bad or wrong. We assume that living in a nuclear family is normal and we assume that it works. Both of these assumptions are questionable.

Shifting from Nuclear Family to Network Family (BLTLCH19.02). Nuclear family has only been normal in highly Westernized cultures during the last one hundred years. More than two thirds of the world's population lives in mixed multigenerational villages and tribes, and have been continuously doing so for the past 100,000 years. From this perspective, nuclear family is definitely not normal.

Assuming that nuclear family works is like assuming that nuclear power works. Sure it works, from a certain shortsighted perspective. But consider the shadow side. How can two people think that alone they could fulfill the complex needs of a growing child? Especially with one or both of the parents working full-time jobs? Nuclear family deprives children of very fruitful daily contact with a variety of other children, other "grandparents," and other adults. A nuclear family culture lacks designed-in support for the man from other men (men's culture), or for the woman from other women (women's culture). Without the support of men's and women's cultures, a relationship easily degrades into silent separation or psychological war, neither of which support children and family. The nuclear family does not work. The nuclear family has never actually worked. It just took us a hundred years to start realizing it.

Church and state are the forces that have historically disapproved of unmarried sex and also made it uncomfortable for couples to separate. The influences of church and state in modern times are weakening. Church has a tough time competing with TV talk shows, catalog shopping, and cosmetic surgery. In terms of the state, the lawmakers themselves want divorces, so the legal procedure has become easy, quick, and nearly painless. What is the result? More and more divorces. The breakdown of the nuclear family may be the beginning of a cultural shift that brings single moms into living together in inner-city tribes and villages, and regenerates a strong men's culture and women's culture.

It is easy to see why an industrial state would promote the nuclear family. Production and sales are maximized when the buying unit is minimized. With technologies and manufacturing processes created during World War II, the mass production of inexpensive, highly-automated household appliances proliferated. If one car suffices to serve ten people, far fewer cars are sold than if one family needs two cars! A refrigerator in every house! A clothes washing machine in every pantry! A dishwasher and food processor in every kitchen! A kitchen for every four people! Think how much profit is to be made!

Should We Keep Trying?

Your relationship may align to the purpose of the universe and be evolving. Even if your relationship is intense and rocky, if evolution is happening then all is possible. You should keep trying. If evolution is not happening, if you are not communicating and you or your partner have hardened into patterns that halt the flow of evolution, then precious time is going past that neither of you will have again.

A struggle then arises between the purpose of the universe and the purpose of the Box of your relationship. The universe intends for your relationship to be a hotbed of evolution. The Box of your relationship intends each day to repeat yesterday's Box-controlled interactions. If the universe has its way, then it will crack the shell of your relationship wide open so you are kicked out and again exposed to evolutionary forces in your next relationship. If the Box has its way, you will be dead and buried before anything changes.

There is a third alternative. If the two of you come to the end of fruitful experimenting given your character structure and the level of intimacy you are able to engage, then from the evolutionary viewpoint of the universe the experimental chamber of your relationship has completed its task. It is time for the next experiment. The opportunities that were possible have all been used. The relationship served as a vehicle through which partners could evolve from Box A to Box D. If both partners recognized that they have gone as far as they can go together, then they can say thank you and goodbye, and continue on into the next phase of their lives with dignity and respect. What if, at that point, you called all your friends and family and had a victory party?

Engaging relationship from the point of view of evolution, rather than the point of view of legal structures and churches, may prolong the whole human experiment. We may actually use relationship as a rapid learning environment to prevent us from blowing ourselves up. Continuously developing extraordinary human relationship soft-skills in communication, listening, understanding, accepting and respecting makes very good sense from the point of view of evolution.

On the other hand, this idea of treating the end of a relationship with an attitude of success immediately brings up further considerations. It may be too easy and obvious a solution to simply kick out the old guy and bring in the new guy. But what is really going on? Is it that the Gremlin is in charge? After all, Gremlin has many devious ways. Perhaps our conviction that further evolution is impossible in our relationship is Gremlin's concoction. Perhaps by limply acquiescing to Gremlin's whiny complaints something irreplaceably precious may too quickly be discarded. Or, perhaps our Gremlin has concocted an altruistic scenario: Our community of friends is looking up to us as a role model for a successful relationship. Somebody has to make the sacrifice, don't they? Perhaps the whole community will go into shock and pain if we break up. Perhaps we will never come together again for these great skiing vacations. Perhaps the two of us staying together, in secret Gremlin-feeding agony for a few more years and continuing the show, will cause less pain and overall suffering than making a break, destroying the fantasy, and forcing everyone in the community to look unproductively in horror at their own underworlds. If you choose that story then Gremlin's food supply is protected for a few more years.

Or, perhaps your discomfort is the way it feels just before an evolutionary breakthrough of untold proportions, and the proper approach would be to tolerate the ongoing intensity in your relationship and keep working through it. Perhaps the gates of heaven are just about to open. If that were the case, the hardearned opportunity of a lifetime would be wasted because Gremlin had us give up a little too soon. Perhaps the years of loving patience and kindness have sprouted a seed that is almost breaking the crusty earth's surface and is soon to bloom gloriously. How can we know?

We are still left with the question, "Do I stay or do I go?"

Here are four points to keep in mind as you work with this question:

1. Suspect Your Box and Your Gremlin

What if, in spite of all your efforts, your partner will not take responsibility for stabilizing themselves in the Adult ego state? What

if he does not want to become Man? What if he does not want to learn to place the quality of attention on you that awakens and invigorates the Goddess? What if he is just not interested? After all, the negative unconscious manifestation of the masculine is blind aggressive stupidity. What if he just won't budge? What then?

Or what if, after all these years, deep down inside she is unwilling to trust you? What if she is filled with unconscious resentment and simply unwilling to risk being hurt again even though you think that you have changed or that you aren't like the other guy who hurt her? What if she just won't grow up and leave her childhood fears behind to risk it with you?

Remember, we are not assessing this situation according to goods and bads, rights and wrongs, shoulds and should nots. We are considering what is going on, and what you are going to do about it.

The commitment in any relationship is a commitment to intimacy, a commitment to meeting the being of the other. The commitment is never fulfilled finally or perfectly. Never. Box never wants two people to get closer to each other than the level where Box meets Box face to face. If you get closer than that, then you realize that you are not Box. You look back over your shoulder at the inside of Box's mask and say, "Hah! Look at that ridiculous delusional shell! Who needs that thing?" Right about then, Box shits in his or her pants and incites the Gremlin to go berserk in your psycho-emotional system.

Suspecting Your Gremlin (BLTLCH19.03). If intimacy is not engaged as well as you think it could be, start by being suspicious of your Box and your hungry unmanaged Gremlin. Make a boundary with your Gremlin. Teach it to sit, and feed it, on your schedule, the foods that you choose. Become more aware of the intricacies of Box mechanics. Learn why your Box does what it does and try something else. Try again. Try many times. Try until it is objectively clear that there is no more chance of evolution.

2. Take It Slowly

Do not make a decision to split up lightly. When your two beings have little common ground on which to meet, then the basis of the relationship itself becomes questionable. Without the common ground of intimacy, relationship evolution does not happen. Box's Gremlin wants your conclusion to be that the lack of intimacy is *your partner's* fault. It may be. It may *not* be. Box is sly. Hold the distinction between you and your Box. Your part is to remember that Box is devious, even deceptive. The Box attracts justifiable reasons like a dead dog attracts flies. Box's motives are quite reliable: always self-centered, always comfort oriented, always looking for a payoff, always trying to be right, and always looking for an easy way out with a very good excuse. Box is *very* reliable – reliable at being Box. First be suspicious of your own Box.

To decide whether you are sourcing the difficulties and it is time for you to grow up, or if it is your partner causing the difficulties and time for you to get out, will require ruthless self-observation and consistent feedback over a long period of time from reliable sources not controlled by your own Box. You know those people around you whose opinions are not controlled by your Box. So does your Box. In the time when you most need their counsel, your Box can arrange for you to see those sources of wisdom and intelligence as your enemies. Then your Box gets to do its usual thing, and will take irreversible actions, before your friends can hold you down and pound sense into your head.

3. Get the Help You Need

No matter what reasons or explanations you may tell people about your splitting up, they will make up their own judgments and share them with everybody they know. "He's running away from the real world. He is escaping. He is taking the easy way out. It is just a mid-life crisis. The asshole. He is throwing away years of marriage. He wasn't strong enough. The younger woman hooked him. He is a cock, chasing after a sex fantasy. He is too weak to keep his commitments. He is untrustworthy. He is dangerous. He's just a bastard like all men." How do I know about these harsh judgments? I did them myself. In the spring of 2004, I heard that a colleague of mine had suddenly left his wife and nine-year-old son and had "run off" with a younger woman whom he had met through his profession. I was so angry at him that I could not talk to him for nine months. Every thought in my mind about this man was severely negative and derogatory. The most degrading insults poured out of my heart. I knew his wife. She was a fine woman – intelligent, responsible, dynamic, and loving. I knew his son – brilliant, communicative, creative, and strong. How could this man be susceptible to what was so clearly a major life blunder? How could he be so weak and irresponsible as to lose his family to the guiles of a younger woman? Where was his integrity? How could he be so stupid? By the spring of 2005, I myself was divorced.

Examining Your Double Life (BLTLCH19.04). What is the lesson here? The lesson is to take care. It may not be true in every case, but if you find yourself in a blind rage about someone you know splitting up, if you feel unusually scared, grieved, or offended, your reaction may be a warning sign of conditions deep within you – conditions about which your Box has been keeping you unaware. You could be out of touch with what is really going on in your heart about your own relationship situation. Instead of being unified within yourself, instead of being *where you are*, you may be leading a double life: one life on the surface that you show to others, and one life deep inside that you do not even show to yourself. You could be living in false acceptance. You may be unconsciously repressing a volcano of resentments, hoping that the resentments will somehow go away all by themselves because you are putting on a good show. You may be hoping that you will manage to keep the lid on, for all the rest of your life, so that you do not have to go through what the truth would bring you to go through. You may be in denial.

I am telling you from first-hand experience that resentments do not go away all by themselves. Resentments are strategically maintained snack food for hungry Gremlins needing a reason to fulfill Shadow Principles. One single undealt-with resentment about your partner undermines the integrity and presence needed to enter with them into Archetypal Relationship.

Take the risk of being radically honest with yourself, and with your partner. Keep asking them if they have any resentments about you, any expectations about you, and ferret them out of yourself. Resentments and expectations are relationship killers. Go through them by going to the heart of them and feeling the feelings, making the feelings conscious, and communicating your feelings, because love is a function of communication, and because consciousness creates freedom. **Getting Support from Other Couples (BLTLCH19.05).** When you need help in your relationship, *go get it*. With only two people talking to each other *there is no objective sanity*. You need a third intelligence. Keep persisting in communication until you are understood and until you understand. Do not give up on yourself. Do not give up on your partner. Trust your intuition entirely. If you do not understand and appreciate

what is going on within yourself or with your partner, then keep digging until the festering discrepancy is lanced, wherever it is.

Not being yourself is betraying yourself. Self-betrayal is insidious because no one else can discover that you are doing it and no one else can cause you to do anything different. Your Box can live in immense denial forever, because the Box *is* denial. Your Box can adjust to accepting *anything* as normal. Just because your Box has accepted something as normal does not mean that thing should go unscrutinized. Do not let your Box eat your life. Authentic aliveness is precious, rare and worth fighting for. Take your life back from your Box. It can be the most humiliating embarrassment to publicly admit that you have deceived yourself for a long time. It may be far worse to lie on your deathbed knowing that you lived falsely but did not have the courage to do something about it.

4. Take Responsibility
Choosing to Choose (BLTLCH19.06). The decision of whether or not to stay and keep trying is going to be up to you. It comes down to three possible options, and you are the only one to choose.

1. Choose to engage the learning opportunity that may be sitting in your lap with the circumstances of your present relationship. Choose to stay.
2. Choose to engage the rest of your possible life that may be knocking on your door with the next relationship. Choose to leave.
3. Especially do not choose to play victim and wait around hoping that circumstances will dictate what choice you must make. Choose to choose.

Take responsibility. Make your choice. Get on with your life.

Requiem: A New Ritual for Accepting Changes

Accepting Change Through Requiem (BLTLCH19.07). I want to start a new ritual in our culture in addition to birthdays, funerals, and Christmas. It is a change-accepting ritual called Requiem. Requiem comes from the Latin, *requies*, meaning "to rest." A Requiem is a facilitated process specifically held and dedicated to completing the rest of whatever needs to be completed in any sudden change – divorce, death, house burns down, natural disasters. It is a place to rest, so people can come together and feel the rest, say the rest, understand the rest, and let everything about the change be experienced and expressed and finally come to a rest.

In the six or seven times that I have gone through a split up of a relationship, I wished that I did not have to do it so alone. I had no guidance and I did not know what I was doing. We do not have lessons in how to split up a longterm relationship. What I tried did not necessarily work so well. I did what I had to do to split up, but the process lacked elegance and often dignity. The process has taken years. There are people who are still offended. There are people who have communications in their heart with no chance to make the communications because we have not been together about this. My parents, her parents, her brothers' and sisters' families, my brothers' families, our shared friends, no one came and truly shared and went through together what they have to share and go through about the split up. Most of us probably have these longstanding messes, painful scars in our personal humanity, undigested heartaches that if we used Requiems would not still be undigested. Without a Requiem the wound of certain life-changes may unnecessarily fester for the remainder of everyone's days, the pain unexpressed, the voices unheard, and communications uncompleted.

Sure, there are reasons for not coming together. For example, my friends and family are spread all over the world. But if I had died, many people would have come together for the funeral. Not for me, but for themselves. A Requiem serves the same purpose: a change-accepting ritual for the people who attend. We need this ritual in our culture to move elegantly into being present with new circumstances, whatever they are, because these days there are so many new circumstances. Without such a ritual we carry around so much unnecessary emotional residue. If you would like to evolve the culture and start using Requiem, a description of a sample ritual follows.

Instructions for Requiem

- In the case of a couple ending their relationship, after going through meetings, support groups, and investigations to create clarity about what is happening and why and how – a Requiem is indicated. When it is clear that the relationship will break up, then immediately the whole community of friends is informed that there will be a Requiem. Everyone who knew this couple, from all over the world, is invited to be together to participate in the change of relationship. There is a great circle – chairs, and cushions – all in a spacious room.

- Requiem starts and ends with the voice of a Requiem moderator, trained to hold space for total chaos in total safety for as long as it takes. The ritual starts as soon as at least two people are present, when the Requiem moderator says, "Let the Requiem begin." The moderator stays in the room all day and all night from the start to the finish of the ritual. He or she is the first person to arrive and the last person to leave.

- The coming together is chaotic. The time when people come is when they arrive. Whoever comes is exactly who is supposed to be there. No one is missing. When people are hungry they bring out their food and share it with each other. When people are tired they sleep. When people leave they leave. It may look like absolute chaos according to linear standards, but if the Requiem process is trusted it is perfect – magnificently orchestrated, awesomely beautiful to be a part of.

- And people come. Everyone who has ever been involved in your relationship, everyone who loves either of you, everyone who loves your relationship, they all come together. The meeting is a community, gathering together in the name of Love. Then we sit, talk, cry, shout, blame, hate, scream, defend, argue, dance, eat, sleep, ask questions, share stories, sing, and keep going and going with everyone, all sharing, and all at once, about everything that needs to be shared. The Requiem is for experiencing and expressing the feelings, and digesting all the ripples and after effects of the change. It goes on and on until the echoes have died out and all is said and done. People leave when they are satisfied, when they have emptied the past and are full with the present, accepting what is, ready to create a new future together. When the Requiem is down to the last person, the Requiem moderator says, "The Requiem is ended," and he or she closes and cleans the space.

CHAPTER 20

A Short Handbook on Living Happily Ever After

Why do the storytellers always forget to tell us exactly how *we* are supposed to manage to live happily ever after? Why do most stories end just after the marriage ceremony? The man and the woman are still blissfully in the passion of infatuation, before he sees her without makeup, before screaming kids and varicose veins, before scratchy beards and farts, before cellulite and arthritis, before dirty socks and overflowing trash cans pre-empt the honeymoon phase of Archetypal Love.

Maybe nobody knows how to live happily ever after. Maybe it is impossible. Or maybe if you find out how to live happily ever after you pop into another universe and never come back. Maybe the language of "happily ever after" is a language that we cannot understand until we can already speak it ourselves. I mean, where are the role models?

Where are examples of relationship where Archetypal Love happens? Politicians? No. Religious leaders? No. Business executives? No. Movie stars? Big no. Where then? We may find a few motivational speakers who look really good. They are rich, clever, confident, handsome, strong, healthy, inspiring, and happily married. It looks perfect. You walk out of one of their seminars thinking, "I can do it! I can do it! *I can do it!*" And then you don't do it. Even if you could do it, let's get practical. How many millionaire motivational speakers can the planet support?

I suggest that we take a new kind of role model – one who is not perfect. Somebody who does not know for sure how to be in relationship and who goes ahead anyway. Somebody who feels afraid, is uncertain, makes mistakes, just tries as best they can – a human being. Somebody who does not have it all together and who does not even have it in them to try to be perfect. They may not even know that they are a role model. These people are not necessarily happy, rich or healthy, and yet they still go ahead and live their life well. They are fully engaged and playing full out. They have immense fun. Their life makes sense according to their own standards, not media standards. They are excited and are on the path of healing. They play, create, and love life as it is now, rather than if and when it meets some future criteria for success, "I will be happy when..."

Being Your Own Role Model (BLTLCH20.01). Well, that role model may be you. Yes, you creating a relationship of true Love.

We are not talking about "let's pretend" here. We are not talking about fantasy or blissful ignorance. We are not talking about being a zombie, an airhead, or a grinning ninny. We are not talking about airy-fairy tales, dreamland, or denial.

We are talking about true Archetypal Love. What if you try and it lasts? What if true Love sticks around?

We have all had moments of miracle and wonder. Even an instant of personally experiencing paradise gives us enough hope that we would buy and read a book like *Building Love That Lasts*. Not that it matters, but most of what has been written in this book is true. If you seriously consider the maps in this book, do some exercises, practice the practices, and perform the experiments, it might actually work for you. That brings up an interesting question. What if it really works?

One summer during college I found a book titled *Outdoor Survival Skills* by Larry Dean Olsen. It showed how to start a fire by rubbing two sticks together. I decided to try it. I sat alone on my parents' back porch; one foot held the book open while I followed the clear step-by-step instructions. I rubbed the sticks together until they made a tiny delicate glowing ember. I nestled my precious ember in a handful of dry shredded tinder, just like the book showed. I raised the little nest to my lips. I took a deep breath and blew steadily on the smoking, glowing ember to give it more and more oxygen. Then suddenly, just like the book said, *froompf!* The smoke burst into flames. I was in ecstasy. Look at that! A real fire! I had a handful of flames. It worked! The leaves and grass in my hands were actually burning. Fire! Burning! In my hands! Hey!...

What was supposed to happen next? I had not read any further in the book! What was I supposed I do?! I dropped the whole flaming mess and almost started the book on fire.

The moral of the story is: When trying to make fire it helps to be prepared for the possibility that it could work.

What If It Works?

What if you do the experiments in *this* book and they actually work? Then what? What do you do when Love does not go away? When Love comes and stays with you? When the radiance between you and your partner lights up half the city for the whole day and most of the night? What do you do when you can hardly breathe because your attention is subsumed by waves of causeless ecstasy and you are not even doing anything?

What do you do when joy is so intense that your brain shuts down and you think your nervous system will fry? What do you do when Love is obviously everywhere, and everything else becomes an irrelevant illusion? What do you do when all you want to do is be in the presence of the being of the other person and absolutely nothing else matters?

What do you do when the ordinary loses its usual attraction and starts to fall away? When you do not want to take your eyes off of the Man or the Goddess across from you? When your smile muscles cramp up from overuse? When all you want is to cry and laugh for no reason? When the truth seems so simple and obvious, and most of normal life is revealed as irrelevant lies and deceptions?

What do you do when your heart finally gets properly fed and grows to its true, immense size in your being? What if you finally let your heart speak and it says, "I love the Earth. I love the trees. I love the rocks. I love the ocean waves crashing on the beach. I love the air. I love all of life on the Earth. I love people. I *love* people! And I love you!"

What do you do when Love is happening? When the humming air is so rich with meaning and importance and Love, and nothing else is real?

What do you do then?

The consideration about what to do if radiant joy and brilliant Love are real cannot be trivial or intellectual. There are no final answers. Or, more clearly said, the final answer is that we do not know the answer. Realize that we do not know. And realize now that knowing would only be another illusion. It is completely okay that we do not know what to do if Love works. The ticket for gaining entry into the great mystery of Love is the ability to not know. Let yourself begin to get accustomed to not knowing. And let this process take its time. Let it take all the time it needs to unfold along its way. Be persistent but do not be impatient.

Do not worry about coming to the end of Love. There is no end to Love. You will never get it all. It will never go away. This is what makes your experiments safe. You can fail or succeed in your experiments and Love will never go away.

Much internal reordering occurs while Love is happening, and also while you are making preparations for Love that lasts to happen. Let the reordering occur. Something is being built inside of you. Love is food for that which supports the growth of being. Let your internal self grow. This can be an astounding, world shattering, and immensely fulfilling and reassuring experience. Love supporting the growth of being can also be extraordinarily appropriate. "Love Happening" is exactly as it should be. Let Love Happening be as big as it is.

Be aware that other people in your life, even strangers at other tables in the restaurant, strangers in the elevator, people passing you on the street, people who are not practicing the exercises that you are doing, may also be irradiated by Love coming through. The Principle of Love can completely saturate spaces and can be tangibly felt. Nearby people derive direct and indirect benefit from your experiments. Keep in mind that others *are affected* by what is happening. Give them the space to go through changes and realizations too, even if you never speak with them directly about it. Honor their possibilities through appropriate, caring regard for their well-being, even if only for a moment, even without words.

The existence of Love that lasts creates the possibility of Countenance. What if Countenance works? What if you find something that is better than chocolate? Better than sex? Better than the movies? Better than shopping? Better than a new car? Better than war? Not that these things are bad. It is just that the experience of Countenance is so all-embracing, so fulfilling, that if you were truly given the choice, then just about everything else that God has ever invented takes second place. That is evolution.

Countenance does not cost anything. You need no paraphernalia. It is not illegal. It is not immoral or fattening. You can experience it anytime, anywhere, without touching or saying anything. You do not have to move.

Life could simply be about living happily ever after.

And.

Here is what our defensive-oriented self-preserving Gremlin-empowered little Box will probably do to try to avoid that.

For three to six months of a new relationship everything is "love." We receive a period of grace. Everywhere we look there is only love. It is like a baptism. We are washed clean. We are blessed. We get a taste and an imprint of Love that lasts. The most precious gift of all is just to learn that Love that lasts is possible.

The universe gives us a free sample of paradise. After the introductory offer expires, it is up to us to get ourselves back to the Garden.

At first our Box is "blown away too far" to get its usual grip on us. Box cannot present us with defensible reasons to change anything because the mind is not there to listen. We are in Love.

But we have twenty, thirty, or forty, (or fifty!) years of experience living a "normal" life. Brilliant Love is not normal. We *know* what normal is. And our Box knows that as long as we use Gremlin's standard tricks and strategies we can survive in that particular normal. Therefore, our creative powers (the immensity of which we are hardly aware) are dedicated to assembling the factors needed to recreate that specific experience of "normal" no matter where we are. We had already succeeded in warping the universe to conform to our psychological needs... until we encountered Archetypal Love.

Archetypal Love is a surprise. We have a nervous system and a capacity to enjoy and endure the direct physical experience of pure Archetypal Love, so when it first arrives it goes on for awhile. But the Box is still here. Mr. or Mrs. Gremlin did not move out of the house when Love moved in. As soon as we realize that we are gliding effortlessly through the air, Mr. or Mrs. Gremlin conspires to ask the nasty little question, "Hey. What do you think you're doing up there? What ever made you think you can fly?" The moment we begin to give explanations, we crash. The party is over. Our Box starts looking for checkpoints to verify that the old standard "normal" is in place and it does not find any. "Oh my god!" we think, "This Love stuff is much too intense! We can never bear it! Let's get back to normal."

Box creates in us a pressing urge to return to the familiar conditions of reality and promises to bring us back into the safety of our marshmallow zone. Without making certain efforts, paradise is quickly lost. Anyway, it seems easier to go create normal again than to stay in heaven. We efficiently generate the same conflicts, the same fears, the same resentments, the same betrayals, the same insecurities, and all of the same problems that decorated our normal living environment. Box is happy in a standard sort of way.

Our Box efficiently exchanges paradise on earth for a hazardous waste dump, and then proudly says, "Now you are safely back with me. Home at last!" Victory is sweet for the Gremlin.

Not Creating Normal (BLTLCH20.03). Here is the secret to living happily ever after: In order to live happily ever after, make a wild leap through the open window. Many times you will have to make this leap. Every time Box will say, "Hey! What are you trying to do? Fly? Whoever said you can fly?" Your answer comes without hesitation, "I said I can fly!" And then you leap.

You leap out through the same window that opened when paradise first arrived. Yes, *that* window. You *know* that window. It did not disappear. It did not go anywhere. That same window is always still there. You can locate that window in the dark. You know the feel of the draft it creates when the glass slides up and the bottom drops away. And you know that you can make the leap. You did it before. You can do it again. You can do it always. Now or never, you just leap.

You leap out the window into the paradise of true Love, and then you just keep flying.

How do you fly? This is a ridiculous question. Although it sounds so reasonable, it is utterly ridiculous to ask how to fly.

Just to satisfy your clever little mind I will provide you with an answer.

SECTION 20-B
Flying Instructions

Flying in the Fluidic Unknowable Evolutionary Process of Relationship (BLTLCH20.04). These are the seven instructions for flying.

First of all, to fly, do not ask the question, "How do you fly?" Asking this question is a distraction from flying. Asking the question, "How do you fly?" is a defense against flying. You already know how to fly. Human beings are designed to fly. Human beings are *not* designed to live within the positional confines of a rigidly known psychological defense strategy. You are designed to live in the fluidic groundless unknowable process of evolutionary expansion. Flying is your nature.

Second, do not look down. As soon as you look down, the Box gets linear and sees all the well-known problems inherent in flying. "Hmmm, I wonder how high we are? What's the airspeed and temperature up here? How much fuel do we have left? How did we get up this high anyway? What is that thing down there? *Aaaarrrggghhh!*" Crash!

Third, take yourself lightly. The idea is old and trite, but that does not make it untrue: Love is angel food. Angels can fly because they take themselves lightly. Stay light by constantly dropping the baggage of considerations about past and future. Humor is grease to slip free of seriousness. *Now* is almost weightless. If it is heavy it is

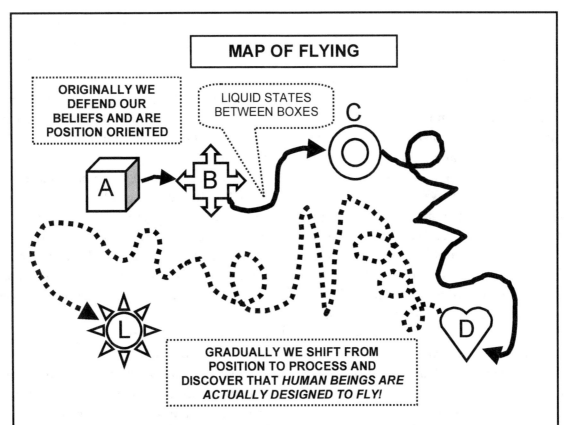

MAP OF FLYING

ORIGINALLY WE DEFEND OUR BELIEFS AND ARE POSITION ORIENTED

LIQUID STATES BETWEEN BOXES

GRADUALLY WE SHIFT FROM POSITION TO PROCESS AND DISCOVER THAT *HUMAN BEINGS ARE ACTUALLY DESIGNED TO FLY!*

Shifting shape from Box A to Box B is traumatic enough. The liquid state was scary as hell. You quickly reestablish rigidity in your new form and find positions to support the views from Box B. One day the fog shifts at the horizon and it becomes apparent that there is a Box C. What? Nobody ever told you about Box C before! Box C cannot be seen from Box A; it only comes into view from Box B. "I wonder what that could be about?" you wonder. Soon your curiosity gets the better of you and you make the leap. Again you enter the liquid state. Again your Box shifts shape and soon you find yourself in Box C. Only this time the journey through the liquid state took a little longer. And Box C is a little smaller and less stable than Box B. The smoke settles and the dust clears. Slowly over the next horizon a new image comes into view. "Oh my God! Box D? Inconceivable! Who ever heard of a Box D? I wonder what is over there?" The liquid state comes a little easier this time. The pattern of solid to liquid to solid feels more familiar. After a few more times you are headed for Box L. At that point the length of time *between* solid states becomes longer than the time resting in any particular form. Your strategy shifts from being less oriented towards the defensive positionality of form than to the expansive process of formlessness. In this moment you discover through experience that human beings are in fact designed to fly!

not Love. Stay unhookable by staying connected to Nothingness. Nothingness cannot be hooked onto by anything. A small "Disk of Nothing" (*see* Glossary) helps to keep you angelweight.

Fourth, delight. What delights you? What delights the other? Use these questions as your compass. Play. Discover. Go nonlinear. Totally stop. Be. Open. Try again. Spin. *G[r>jak#L*!* (This is the spelling for a delightful activity for which we do not yet have a word.) Navigate the space of relationship toward delight happening. Why not? Delight is alive, so you will always have a moving target. What is delightful now is not necessarily delightful now. Delight only happens now.

Fifth, create. Relationship is ongoing non-linear creation. Love and creating are the same experience; they come out of the same field. You are a being who lives when Love flows through you, when you have someone to give Love to and they are receiving it. Keep creating new ways to express Love. Create ways to Love out of nothing but Love itself. You source Love. Love does not come from somebody else. Love is all there is. Instead of using your massive powers of creating to create things now to be exactly how they were three seconds ago, use your massive powers of creating to create Love fresh each three seconds.

Sixth, learn to fly solo. You will never be able to be happy with another person if you cannot already tolerate the intensity of being radiantly happy all by yourself. No matter what the circumstances, if you really wanted to be happy, who could stop you? If you really want to be happy right now, prove it.

Seventh, so what? There are many reasons for not flying. So what? Many people will not understand what you are doing. They might be offended. They might not believe you. So what? Flying might be impossible. It might not be permitted by your culture and times. It might be outside the conceivability limits of your relatives or neighbors. So what? You get the idea. So what?

These are all the flying instructions you will ever need. If you get them, try to teach them to others. Have fun! And, thanks for asking.

There are some Women we know who have taken back their power from the patriarchy without resentment. These Women have learned to keep their center, hold space, stay present, make contact, feel their feelings with clarity, and create Archetypal Relationship possibilities for their Men. These Women serve something greater than themselves. These Women are Pirate Sorceress Warrioress Queen Goddess Women. These Women live with Kings because they are Kingmakers.

These Women love what they do, even if they fail, because they know that what they do or do not do does not change who they are. They are Kingmakers.

Just the Edgework excitement of trying empowers these Women, because they are trying to do the impossible. As Lee Lozowick says, "Nothing less than trying to do the impossible pays respect to the honor of being born in this world and having a human life."

When these Women are done for the day (or the night) and they are about to part company, they look each other straight in the eyes and with a slight curve in the side of their mouth and a radiant sparkle in their eyes, they challenge each other to continue with their experiments. In a steady voice full of courage, joy and dignity they say to one another, "Keep Kinging!"

And that is exactly what they do.

Sitting There Together With Nothing

The Lord giveth
And the Lord taketh away.
But He taketh away not everything.
He taketh away not the bodily memory of the experience
Of what it was that He hath given.
And if what He gave was heaven on Earth,
If what He gave was so precious
That all other experiences pale in comparison, then all that remains
Is less than it was before the Lord giveth.
Even the most magnificent sunset, the most satisfying dessert,
The most luscious orgasm, the best movie,
Has no worth compared to heaven on Earth.
I have discovered an exception to the rule that all things are transitory.
The discovery is that all things are transitory
Except longing.
Longing remains.
Longing never fades away.
Even when heaven returns the longing for heaven remains.
Longing for heaven in heaven?
What, am I crazy???
No.
I am ruined.
Ruined.
So let this be a warning to you.
The house of the rising sun
Looks so tempting from the outside, but run away.
Run away before it is too late.
Heaven on Earth can vanish
But your longing for heaven to come back to Earth will not.
And they do not tell you how intensely the longing aches.
Ah, well.
You will not heed this warning.
(I did not.)
So I'll be seeing you,
Late in the night.
After everyone else has gone home to something,
You and I will be sitting there together
With nothing
In the tavern of Ruin. – C.C.

Glossary

Possibility Management Terms Used in This Book

From the Greek word "glossa" meaning "tongue" was derived the Latin "glossarium" meaning "a difficult word requiring further explanation." Middle English extended the meaning further with the word "glossarye" meaning "a list of terms in a special subject, field or area of usage with accompanying definitions." The special area of usage in this case is Possibility Management. Most of the words in this Glossary are not new or difficult so much as being used in a context that unfolds deeper or more specific meanings from them. I look forward to the day when such a glossary would be unnecessary because the meanings were already understood through common usage. In this Glossary I have capitalized only the terms that remain capitalized in the text of this book, along with the term currently being defined. For further thoughtware upgrades an expanded version of this Glossary is available online as the Distinctionary (www.distinctionary.xyz).

ACTION – In Possibility Management an Action is defined as any gesture that has energy. This definition for Action is more refined than our typical understanding of an Action that only includes gross physical movement. In Possibility Management, examples of Actions include: physical motion, speaking a word, having an idea, insinuation, inspiration, feeling, placing your attention, moving your attention, placing your center, keeping your center, making a conscious or unconscious wish, internal emotional reactions, declaring, asking, choosing, and so on. In general, the more subtle the Action, the more energy it contains. (*See:* Center, Declaring, Purpose, Results)

ADULT (RESPONSIBLE ADULT or ADULT EGO STATE; KING or QUEEN ARCHETYPE) – As defined by Dr. Eric Berne in his *Map of Parent Adult Child Ego States*, an ego state is a self-contained set of ideas, beliefs, attitudes and behaviors with which a person is identified. In the Child ego state you have no power because you are stuck in the past. In the Parent ego state you have no power because you are being adaptive to others. The Adult ego state is where you have power because you own your center, use your own voice, minimize your here and now in a spacious present and take responsibility for what is. The Responsible Adult also turns out to be the gateway to Archetypal Man and Archetypal Woman. (*See:* Center, Communicator, Creator, Doer, Goddess, Identification, *Map of Possibility*, Now, Responsibility, Stellating Archetypes)

ARCHETYPAL PRINCIPLE – (*See:* Principle)

ARCHETYPE – The Archetypal terminology used in *Building Love That Lasts* comes from Possibility Management and is not derived from or associated with the work of Carl Gustav Jung. Jung evolved his deep-psychology "archetypes" in reference to the psychoanalytical context that he inherited from his teacher Sigmund Freud. Instead of relying on Jung's experiences, we have done our own empirical research for over thirty years. These experiments brought us directly into contact with the same sources that Jung must have tapped into to formulate his particular languaging. Instead of a psychological context, we researched from a Possibility context. Because we went fishing with a different net, we caught a different sort of fish, although we fished in the same sea. In Possibility Management, Archetypes are energetic configurations hardwired into the matrix of every human being. Archetypes are either responsible or irresponsible. Irresponsible Archetypes are awakened during childhood and used to create a workable defense strategy. Responsible Archetypes lie dormant until they are consciously initiated or stellated through a modern rite of passage. Before stellating responsible Archetypes, a human being must first be capable of Adult responsibility, which does not occur until about fifteen years of age. Our modern culture does not provide a rite of passage process though which you can activate your responsible Archetypes, so they remain switched off. If you want your responsible Archetypes activated you are forced to go outside of the culture and arrange it for yourself. This takes a lot of courage and entails certain real risks. Actions of people who have not gone through the process of stellating their responsible Archetypes are typically dominated by the Shadow Principles of their irresponsible Archetypes. Archetypes are fueled by the energy of feelings. Anger fuels the responsible doer (Warrior / Warrioress) or the irresponsible persecutor. Sadness fuels the responsible communicator (Lover) or the irresponsible victim. Fear fuels the responsible creator (Magician / Sorceress) or the irresponsible rescuer. And gladness fuels the responsible Adult (King Man / Queen Goddess Woman) or the irresponsible Gremlin. (The original idea for the names of these four Archetypes came from the title of a book by Robert Moore and Douglas Gillette, *King Warrior Magician Lover*.) (*See:* Adult, Feelings, Gremlin, High Drama, Low Drama, Principle, Stellating Archetypes)

ASKING – Asking is one of the three powers that you can use for creating possibility (the other two are declaring and choosing). Asking is particularly useful for navigating space. A question acts like an iron hook with a rope attached. When you throw the hook into the unknown, what you grab onto depends on the design of the hook. There are 18 standard questions to Ask, each with its own purpose. If a question grabs hold of an answer, you can pull on the rope with your attention. The pulling slides you and everyone you are in contact with into the new space where the question landed. A particularly effective way to open new perspectives is to confront the present perspective with a question. Sometimes a question is too real to be Asked. If a real question is Asked, it may be destroyed by an answer – then you must go find yourself another real question. An unasked real question sits in you until your Box conforms to the shape of the question and you become the answer. (*See:* Attention, Dangerous Questions, Navigating Space, Real Question)

ATTENTION (CONSCIOUS ATTENTION) – Conscious Attention means paying Attention to your Attention, being aware of what you are aware of, or perceiving what you are perceiving with. Engaging Conscious Attention helps build matrix upon which your consciousness can grow. Attention can also become conscious through

paying Attention to your purpose and considering, "What is my purpose right now?", or through deciding whether to use "point Attention" or "field Attention." Your Attention is valuable because where your Attention goes your energy flows. If you do *not* have your Attention, something else *does*. Businesses spend billions every year trying to get your Attention. They do this for two reasons: 1) Because it works – most people's Attention is unguarded. 2) Because it is worth it – when they have your attention, they have your wallet. Putting your Attention on your Attention initiates a process that makes you less susceptible to being used for other people's purposes and therefore more capable of consciously creating high drama, exploring extraordinary human and Archetypal Relationship, and fulfilling your destiny. (*See:* Center, Destiny, High Drama, Matrix, Purpose, Relationship)

BAG OF THINGS – Your Bag of Things hangs from your "Possibility Manager Tool Belt." Within your Bag of Things is a gap between worlds. What is in the gap? Nothing. What is possible in the gap? Everything. Whenever you require a non-segued idea you simply reach into your Bag of Things and pull something out. You can never know what you will pull out of your Bag of Things until you pull it out and look at it. If you know what you will pull out before you pull it out, then you are pulling it out of your mind full of the known rather than out of the Bag of Things full of the unknown. (*See:* Gap, Is-Glue Dissolver, Nonlinear, Possibility Manager, Tool Belt)

BEING A SPACE – Being a Space is contrasted with being yourself. Being a Space means that you are holding space but you are not filling up that space with the usual needs and wishes of your Box. Instead, that space is empty and consciously dedicated to serving your Destiny Principles. Possibility Management starts by teaching you how to listen as a space called possibility listening, and to speak as a space called possibility speaking. With practice you can learn to Be the Space through which the Principles that you serve can do their work. Your Box will only let you Be a Space after you realize that you already have everything that you need, a quality of the King / Archetypal Man and the Queen / Archetypal Woman. (*See:* Box, Destiny, Holding Space, Space)

BEING CENTER – You have two centers, your physical center and your Being Center. Your Being Center is mobile and starts out about the size of a grapefruit. You move your Being Center around in various parts of your body for various purposes. You also place your Being Center outside of your body when you give your center away to either a general or specific authority figure. In Western cultures we tend to keep our Being Center in our heads. Being grows with matrix. (*See:* Being Centered, Matrix, Physical Center)

BEING CENTERED – Being Centered is a relationship to the world that is established through placing your being center on your physical center, an action called centering. Being Centered is one of the seven core skills of Possibility Management. (*See:* Being Center, Core Skills, Physical Center)

BEING NOTHING – At the Archetypal level, every man has immediate access to Nothing in the same way that a zero represents a place where nothing is. Through Being Nothing, man is the space holder of relationship. It is Woman who fills the space of relationship that man holds. Since we live in a patriarchy, men are artificially empowered by the structure of our society and are given no rite of passage into adulthood. This leaves men handicapped by being trapped in adolescence. As a result modern man has a terrified victim relationship to his own essential Nothingness which could actually provide him with tremendous power. For example, once a man stellates his Archetypes, he can stay present in the Archetypal fear of Being Nothing. As Nothing, he can experientially answer the question, "What is bigger, Everything or Nothing?" (This is not a pure question as in mathematics but rather a practical question as in physics.) The Nothing must be bigger than Everything so that the Everything has some place to be. Being Nothing lets a Man accept the massive confrontation of Everything, that may come from his Woman, through realizing without malice, "I am bigger than that," no matter what the "that" is. Being Nothing, a Man can hear every level of communication from his Woman, can be authentically touched by the communication, can let his Box be killed by the pain of what he hears, can let the communication drift three seconds into the past, and without residue, can then come back to life.

This is an example of the power of Being Nothing – to be killed and not die. (*See:* Adult, Archetype, Do-Overs, Experiential Reality)

BEING-WITH – Your familiarity with the adrenalin-enhanced tension of constantly doing things distracts you from your capacity for Being-With. The joke is that when first encountering the idea of Being-With you might ask, "What do I have to *do* to Be-With?" Being-With is not about *doing* anything; not talking, not moving, just *being*. Relationships do not die from a lack of love; relationships die from a lack of Being-With. Being-With another person who is Being-With you opens the door to intimacy and creates food that feeds your heart and your soul. Western culture teaches you to feed your physical body and your mind, so, like the rest of us, development in your four bodies is probably way out of balance. Your mind and physical body may be healthy while your heart and soul may be starving. Yet the idea of intimacy may be the most frightening proposition in the world for you. Intimacy starts with Being-With, and Being-With starts in the Adult responsible ego state. Being-With can become Countenance if it enters the Archetypal. (*See:* Adult, Archetype, Be Wrong, Countenance, Four Bodies)

BEING WRONG – Box defense strategies intend that the Box is proven to be right. Even if the Box asserts, "See, I am wrong again!" the Box is being right about being wrong. For an extra credit experiment you can arrange it so that you end up Being Wrong. If you are right the game is over. You win. They lose. But if you are wrong then there are myriads of options still open to the both of you for continued exploration. For example, if you are wrong then you can easily ask for help or for feedback and coaching. You can listen instead of speaking. You can be open for new possibilities. Making yourself wrong does not mean to actually cause destruction, waste, pain or confusion. To be wrong is a way to be in relationship where you do not automatically fulfill the Box's neurotic desires to know, to feel safe, to be in charge, or to be right. The experiment is to come from not knowing, and to make Being-With a higher priority than security for your Box. (*See:* Being-With, Box Mechanics, Coaching, Edgework, Experiment, Feedback, Possibility Listening, Winning Happening)

BELIEF (BELIEF SYSTEM) – A Belief is an "is-glued" formulation that has no connection to reality. The Box uses Beliefs as a bandage to patch over holes in its walls where it has no answer. Beliefs are defended not by experience but by positionality such as "I'm right. You're wrong." Positionality is exclusive, that is, a particular Belief can be supported only if all contradictory Beliefs are destroyed. The automatic and unavoidable result of positionality is war. Look at human history. Sets of Beliefs hang together in a Belief system. A Belief system is a virtual reality. A Belief system gives the Box a framework of reasons with which to prove itself right. People whose Boxes use the same Belief system tend to gather in groups and play in the same gameworlds. (*See:* Box, Gameworld, Is-Glue, Position)

BOX – Also known as belief system, worldview, mindset, reality structure, paradigm, self-image, identity, personality, psychology, comfort zone, or defense strategy. Our Box is made out of thoughtware and thought-maps. The purpose of our Box is to insure our survival. Since we have survived so far, the Box knows that its strategy works, and it suspects that anything else will not work. So the Box dedicates its resources above all else to defending itself first. The Box defends itself through acting as a multidimensional filter, controlling what we can perceive and what we can express. The Box's original purpose is to keep everything the same as it has always been, regardless of what that original state of normal is. The Box is designed to shift purpose from defensive to expansive when we are about fifteen years old, but our culture does not promote that rite of passage, so even leaders and authorities in Western culture tend to function from the irresponsible perspectives of their defensive Box. Boxes come in layers. Individuals, relationships, families, clubs, committees, teams, communities, cities, businesses, races, cultures, religions, and nations all have Boxes. Possibility Management focuses particularly on the individual Box because that is the only Box that can take responsibility for itself and therefore it is the only Box that can create change. All Boxes are subject to the laws of Box mechanics. (*See:* Box Mechanics, Defensive Context, Expansive Context, Marshmallow Zone, Radical Responsibility, Shift, Thought-Map, Thoughtware)

BOX MECHANICS – Since the Box is assembled from inanimate structural components (memes) all working in relationship to each other, the machine-like stimulus-response impulses of the Box are repeatable and subject to mechanical laws just like ordinary machines. These laws form the theory and practice of Box Mechanics. Gaining familiarity with Box Mechanics gives you abilities to troubleshoot, repair, redesign and rebuild Boxes, in the same way that familiarity with engine mechanics gives you equivalent capabilities with engines. Machines unconsciously do what machines do. Having clarity about Box Mechanics helps you stay unhookable. (*See:* Box, Meme, Memetics, Thoughtware, Unhookable)

BRIGHT PRINCIPLE – Bright Principles are an Archetypal force of nature. The overriding Bright Principle is Archetypal Love or consciousness. Responsibility is consciousness in action. Consciousness prisms into a rainbow of Bright Principles including integrity, abundance, aliveness, growth, learning, inclusion, clarity, kindness, possibility, acceptance, respect, joy, communion, commitment, impeccability, creation, winning happening, healing, transformation, openness, communication, relationship, practice, service, appreciation, fitness, hospitality, generosity, authenticity, and so on. Serving Bright Principles is high drama. You can become the space through which the Bright Principles that you serve do their work in the world. (*See:* Archetype, Destiny, *Map of Possibility*, Shadow Principle)

BRIGHT WORLD (UPPERWORLD) – The domain of actions and gameworlds dedicated to serving Bright Principles. (*See:* Action, Bright Principle, Gameworld, High Drama, *Map of Possibility*)

CENTER – (*See:* Physical Center)

CENTER (CENTER OF A GAMEWORLD) – An organization is two or more people with a common purpose. A relationship is an organization. An organization with a purpose is a Gameworld. Every Gameworld needs leadership, and the person or persons who stand for leadership in the Gameworld are its Center. A Center in a Gameworld functions much the same as the sun in the center of our solar system, providing an attraction force that holds the whole Gameworld together and being a conduit to the Bright or Shadow Principles of the Gameworld. The "planetary systems" that orbit around a Center in a Gameworld are people. You gain enough mass to be a Center by consciously choosing to serve your Destiny Principles. Your job as the Center of a Gameworld is to "feed," care for, educate, train, and liberate the potential of your planets. A Center knows that planets can become stars. By learning to create the possibility that planets become stars, you become a starmaker. Planets who become stars can create Gameworlds within Gameworlds, or can start their own Gameworlds, which may not be as easy as it sounds. (*See:* Gameworld, Laboratory, Possibility Manager, Possibility Trainer, Star, Starmaker)

CENTER OF THE LABYRINTH (HEART OF THE LABYRINTH) – (*See:* Goddess, Navigating Space)

CENTERING – (*See:* Being Centered)

CHILD – (*See:* Adult)

CHOOSING – Choosing is one of the three powers that you can use for creating possibility (the other two are declaring and asking). Every action you make comes out of a conscious or unconscious choice. Taking radical responsibility for your power of choosing takes you out of the victim position of low drama and opens many more opportunities for creating high drama. The challenge with Choosing has to do with sadness. By Choosing one option out of a hundred, the other ninety-nine options are left to die. If it is not okay for you to grieve the death of the ninety-nine unchosen options, then you will have a tendency to not Choose. (*See:* Action, Asking, Declaring, High Drama, Low Drama, Radical Responsibility, Victim)

CLICKER – Your Clicker is an energetic tool clipped onto your Possibility Manager Tool Belt. Your Clicker looks like a remote-control television channel-changer. You operate your Clicker by snapping your fingers. The snapping does not have to make a loud sound. In fact, you can simply tap one finger on the table or on your leg to accomplish the same physical action more inconspicuously. The Clicker is used for starting, stopping, changing and declaring spaces. (*See:* Declaring, Space, Tool Belt)

COACHING – Coaching is information from your surroundings about the future. Our old ideas about Coaching associate it with advice, instructions, or personal stories from a person with more expertise than ourselves. For exploring relationship, a position of expertise blocks intimacy. A different concept of Coaching may be more useful. Try experimenting with Coaching that offers a distinction about what to try next time to produce better results. It does not take expertise to offer such Coaching. Feedback can tell you what worked and what did not work from the past. Coaching can tell you what to try next time to create a different future. For example, "If you wait until I am finished speaking before you start speaking I will have more of an experience that you actually heard what I said." The distinctions in Coaching create clarity. Clarity creates possibility for new actions. (*See:* Action, Feedback, Rapid Learning, Result, Shift, Swamp)

COMFORT ZONE – (*See:* Box)

COMMUNICATOR (LOVER ARCHETYPE) – One of the four Bright World Archetypes who can be stellated in you to serve your destiny (along with creator, doer, and Adult). The Communicator responsibly uses energy and information from sadness. The way a Communicator uses sadness is to connect, listen, understand, let things go, be vulnerable, be honest, be trustworthy, open up, accept, be intimate, and so on. Relationships thrive on responsible intimate communication. The Communicator serves your Bright World Archetypal Adult King / Queen. (*See:* Adult, Archetypes, Being-With, Creator, Doer, High Drama, Love, Possibility Listening, Possibility Speaking, Stellating)

CONSCIOUS PURPOSE (DESTINY, TRUE PURPOSE) – (*See:* True Purpose)

CONSCIOUS THEATER (HIGH DRAMA) – From the perspective of radical responsibility it is all theater. If something seems to be real, such as a real feeling or a real problem, it is still theater – the "realness" derives from us being identified with the feeling or problem so there is no gap and the theatrical-ness of it goes unconscious. The clarity about Conscious Theater provides you with a dangerous question to ask: "Is this piece of theater conscious or unconscious?" In Conscious Theater everything is neutral, there is no such thing as a problem, it is impossible to be a victim, irresponsibility is an illusion, and accepting things exactly as they are here and now without judgment or creating something different is all that is left for you. The question then arises, what are you to do with your humanity? You are a human being after all. That does not go away even in Conscious Theater. What do you do with all of your creative energy? The answer is, create continuous compassionate Conscious Theater. Both extraordinary human relationship and Archetypal Relationship are ongoing acts of Conscious Theater. Conscious Theater is looking at the world through the eyes of your destiny principles and saying, "Okay. What needs to be done? What is the next thing right here and now for me to do to make the world a better place?" Suppose it is something that you do not know how to do; suppose it is something that you do not like to do; suppose it is something that your Box is afraid of, but still it is something that obviously fits the criteria of serving the world. What do you do then? How do you carry on without complaining, without sabotaging, without being confused, without whining? How do you go ahead with dignity, with enthusiasm, with care? The way you can carry on is to act "as if." You go ahead and do the job, acting as if you know how to do it, as if you liked to do it, as if you had courage. Hold within you (cathect) any reactive energies that arise and redirect them toward getting the job done well. Acting "as if" to create high drama *is* Conscious Theater. (*See:* Asking, Gap, Dangerous Question, High Drama, *Map of Possibility,* Navigating Space, Problem, Radical Responsibility, Reality, Unhookable)

CONTACT – Contact means establishing sensation between two beings. Making Contact begins with a "Hello." Maintaining Contact uses attention and provides you with the experiential information required to navigate space into new territory with your partner, your family, or a gameworld in such a way that the people trust you and stay as one team. Rather than making the others come to you, you go to them and make Contact. Contact allows you to know how another person is being, not through communication but through direct experience. If you make Contact and you know

where your attention is, then you know where their attention is. If you make Contact and you know where your center is, then you know where their center is. If you make Contact and you know what you are feeling, then you know what they are feeling. Contact is one of the seven core skills of Possibility Management. (*See:* Attention, Core Skills, Feelings, Together-Sitting)

CONTEXT – Context refers to the structure of a Box or a gameworld rather than its contents. Since everything you can think or perceive is formulated by your Box, you are functionally limited to the Context of your Box. Your Box can have one of two basic Contexts: either the Box is defensive or it is expansive. If you arrange to work in the expansive Context you become a Context generator. That is, you are responsible at the level of Context, and you decide what games are played in your gameworlds: ordinary, extraordinary or Archetypal. In the same way that the design of a fishnet determines what kinds of fish are caught, the Context of a Box determines its content. If you change the Context of a Box, you automatically change what the Box is about. Assessing and redesigning Context is the job of a Possibility Manager. (*See:* Meta-Conversation, Possibility Manager, Reality)

CORE SKILLS – The seven Core Skills in Possibility Management are: staying unhookable, being centered, holding space, making contact, going stellar, creating possibility, and selling possibility. You enter the space that activates the Core Skills in the moment when you shift identity into taking radical responsibility as a Possibility Manager. (*See:* Being Centered, Box Mechanics, Contact, Creating Possibility, Going Stellar, Holding Space, Navigating Space, Possibility Management, Radical Responsibility, Shift, Unhookable)

COUNTENANCE – When two people are being-with each other in the Adult responsible ego state and they both enter the Archetypal as a space, then the Principle of Archetypal Love can become conscious of itself through them. The intensely ecstatic physical experience of Archetypal Love in one person consciously recognizing and experiencing Archetypal Love in the other person is called Countenance. (*See:* Adult, Archetypal Love, Being A Space, Being-With, Contact, Navigating Space, Love, Together-Sitting)

CREATING POSSIBILITY – Since Possibility is itself a Bright Principle, infinite Possibility already exists. Possibility is not actually created; it is already there. Practically, gaining access to unseen Possibility comes from you changing the filtering system of your Box, which strategically occludes Possibility in its own defense. Since the Box is tremendously creative, the obstacles blocking Possibility are equally inventive and tend to be self-repairing. The thought-maps and thoughtware of Possibility Management produce tools and techniques that circumvent the obstacles to accessing Possibility. Creating Possibility is one of the core skills of a Possibility Manager, and includes a complex set of other skills. Creating Possibility is a valuable service to provide for both individuals and organizations. (*See:* Box Mechanics, Core Skills, Creator, Navigating Space, Possibility, Possibility Management, Thought-Maps)

CREATOR (MAGICIAN or SORCERESS ARCHETYPE) – One of the four Bright World Archetypes who can be stellated in you to serve your destiny (along with Doer, Communicator and Adult). The Creator responsibly uses energy and information from fear. The way a Creator uses fear is to stay alert, pay attention, assess risks, make plans, make agreements, make things secure, and enter the unknown. In order to make something out of nothing the Creator must first have access to "Nothing" as a resource. To attain "Nothing" the Creator steps over the limits of the Box into the unknown. This is definitely frightening, but the Creator has learned to feel 100-percent fear and still declare, choose and ask so as to functionally navigate space. The guideline is, if you are not feeling fear, you are not creating. The Creator serves your Archetypal Bright World Adult King / Queen. (*See:* Adult, Asking, Choosing, Communicator, Declaring, Doer, High Drama, Nonlinear, Stellating Archetypes)

DANGEROUS QUESTION – You can ask many kinds of questions. Most of your asking has been civilized and made polite, and therefore disempowered. You have the capacity to regain your authenticity and to become disillusioned with your naïveté, gullibility, denial and self deception. If you stop fooling yourself then it becomes more difficult for other people to fool you. Suddenly you are not civilized anymore. Instead, you are you. You have your feelings and your voice and you

represent a catalytic force of nature that is sought by some and avoided by others. You naturally ask yourself and other people certain questions, the answers to which lay outside of the Box. These are called "Dangerous" Questions, because going to where the answer is expands the Box. (*See:* Asking, Expand the Box, Force of Nature, Pirate, Pirate Agreement)

DECLARING – Declaring is one of the three powers that you use for creating possibility (the other two powers are choosing and asking). With Declaring you assert that something is so. Without knowing it you Declare things all day long, such as, "This is a nice day. My name is Bob. I like you. I can't do that." Declaring is a conscious use of is-glue. To help make the Declaring conscious you can use your "clicker." One use of Declaring is to create stories that include possibilities not available in your present gameworld. In general you are unaware of how many of the circumstances of your life you unconsciously Declare into existence. Discovering the prevalence of unconscious Declaring causes a shock of realization that can take you a long way toward radical responsibility for what you Declare. (*See:* Asking, Choosing, Clicker, Gameworld, Is-Glue, Radical Responsibility, Story)

DEFENSIVE CONTEXT – The Defensive Context is the original survival strategy of your Box. Since that original strategy is for the most part unconscious, your actions serve Shadow Principles. Conscious Archetypal actions are only possible through shifting your Box from the Defensive Context to the expansive context. (*See:* Defensive Learning, Expansive Context, Stellating Archetypes)

DEFENSIVE LEARNING – The way you were taught to learn in school is Defensive. You built a central continent of knowledge, and new knowledge could only be learned when it fit into some part of your present knowledge continent. If something does not fit into your knowledge continent, that thing may be invisible and is generally regarded as useless. (*See:* Box Mechanics, Expansive Learning)

DESTINY (DESTINY PRINCIPLES, TRUE PURPOSE) – Your Destiny is the specific set of Bright Principles that you were born to serve. Serving your Bright Principles is what most turns you on. Serving your Destiny is optional – you do not have to do it and Box can easily get in the way. When we distill our Destiny out from our lives and our Destiny Principles become conscious, then we have the option to choose from moment to moment whether or not to be our Destiny in action right now. (*See:* Bright Principles, Distilling Destiny Process, *Map of Possibility,* True Purpose)

DISCOVERY SPEAKING – One of the four kinds of speaking defined in Possibility Management. Discovery Speaking is a team effort where the space holder avoids discussion about who has the better opinion and instead navigates to the edge of new territory. Once at the edge, the team keeps going powered by group genius. The team uses previously unseen wisdom and suddenly discovered insights as milestones. The space holder is no longer an authority figure who already knows, but instead becomes a true navigator, working with the team to collaboratively document distinctions in graphic and verbal form on flip charts (called thought-maps). Discovery Speaking is done in response to the true necessity of one or more of the participants asking real questions. Most of Possibility Management was developed through thirty years of Discovery Speaking. (*See:* Asking, Dangerous Question, Navigating Space, New Territory, Possibility Speaking, Real Question, Thought-Map)

DISK OF NOTHING – Your Disk of Nothing is a Possibility Management tool that allows you to avoid being hooked. A mere five inches in diameter and clipped onto your tool belt, the Disk of Nothing is metallic gold on the back and around the rim, but the front is a thin fluid gateway into absolute nothingness. Whenever a hook is cast in your direction to try to offend you and start a reciprocal feeding frenzy between Gremlins, simply hold up the Disk of Nothing. The hook goes into the void and returns unrewarded no matter how often or how deeply it is cast. In the void there is nothing to hook. Having a bit of nothing conveniently at hand can prove to be extremely useful. (*See:* Gremlin, Hooked, Springscreen, Tool Belt, Unhookable)

DISTILLING DESTINY – The Distilling Destiny Process allows you to extract from your life the precise formulation of the three to five Bright

Principles that you were born to serve. It is not that the Bright Principles are not already at work in your life. It is just that serving your Destiny Principles is optional. (The idea that your Destiny is optional came from Robert Fritz in his truly excellent and highly recommended little book *Creating.*) If you do not consciously choose to serve your Bright Principles then you will unconsciously choose to be a slave to your Shadow Principles. Servant or slave, that is your choice. The value of Distilling your Destiny is that, once you consciously know what your Bright Principles are, you can make clearer choices to serve them. You become your destiny in action when you are the space through which your Bright Principles can do their work in the world. Being your Destiny in action feels great. Distilling Destiny is a service provided by Possibility Trainers. (*See:* Bright Principle, Destiny, Hidden Purpose Process, *Map of Possibility,* Possibility Trainer, Principle, Shadow Principle)

DO-OVERS – In extraordinary human relationship Do-Overs are allowed. If through inattention or being hooked you create ordinary human relationship with someone, stop mid-sentence, the instant you notice. Apologize authentically and get off any position you are holding. Say something like, "Whoops! Excuse me! I did not mean that. Let me try that again." And, without waiting for permission, immediately start over all the way from the "Hello" at the beginning of the conversation. This time create a result that is different from you being right. You may have the tendency to give up on intimacies after the first try that fails. Instead, try again – even if the first time was only a few seconds ago. You might be surprised to find how many possibilities are available in each next three seconds. Do-Overs are allowed because Archetypal Love never goes away. Only you go away. You can come back. (*See:* Creator, Love, Nonlinear, Pirate, Position, Relationship)

DOER (WARRIOR or WARRIORESS ARCHETYPE) – One of the four Bright World Archetypes who can be stellated in you to serve your destiny (along with Creator, Communicator and Adult). The Doer responsibly uses energy and information from anger. The way a Doer uses anger is to start things, stop things, make decisions, make distinctions, say "yes," say "no," ask for what the space or the organization needs, make boundaries, complete things no matter what, change circumstances, and so on. Doers serve the Archetypal Adult King / Queen. (*See:* Adult, Communicator, Creator, High Drama, Stellating Archetypes, Sword)

EDGEWORK – Edgework is the practice through which you can discover a never-ending excitement about the possibilities of life. Edgework has three steps: 1) Find an edge of your Box that excites you to explore. 2) Go to that edge and stay there (when you can feel the excitement or see the edge you are at the edge). 3) Do Edgework experiments. Edgework experiments in intimacy produce tremendous nurturing for your relationship. There are four kinds of intimacies to explore with your partner. Choose physical, intellectual, emotional or spiritual intimacy, or some combination, and do Edgework experiments that feed and inspire your relationship. For example, when most of us think of physical intimacy we think of sex. Sure sex is one form of physical intimacy, but physical intimacy also includes dancing, singing, playing musical instruments, making art, doing theater, physical maintenance (combing hair, bathing, massage, physical therapy, cutting fingernails, brushing teeth…), martial arts, walking, picnics, eating, sports, swimming, sailing, washing dishes, cleaning out the garage, remodeling the house, gardening, and so on. Have fun! (The term "Edgework" was sparked by ideas in Seth Godin's practical little marketing book titled *Free Prize Inside*.) (*See:* Be Wrong, Box, Experiment, Four Bodies, Intimacy)

EGO – (*See:* Box)

EGO STATE – (*See:* Adult)

EMOTIONS – Emotions are incomplete feelings. Emotions have the same four categories as feelings (anger, sadness, fear and gladness), but they come from the past. You had needs as a child that were not met. Those unmet childhood needs can never be fulfilled because they are needs of the past, not of the present. You have no power in the past. You cannot go back to change anything. Unmet childhood needs feel like a vast unfillable emptiness, especially when you are standing in front of the open refrigerator and looking for something that is not in there. Bringing unmet childhood

needs into your adult present creates Emotions. No matter how much you experience or express an Emotion nothing will change. A handy test is: If what you think is a feeling lasts for more than three minutes it is not a feeling; it is an Emotion. (*See:* Adult, Feelings)

EXPAND THE BOX – You built your Box to survive in the world. It works. You survived. But when you became capable of taking responsibility around fifteen years of age, that which once protected you becomes your prison. The Box is then ready to shift context from its original defensive mode to its designed-in Expansive mode. Can you remember what that feels like? To be ready to make that shift and then not have the chance? We do not make the shift from defensive to Expansive because the shift is not sponsored by Western culture. To make the shift you must go beyond the culture to get it. There is no top end to Box expansion. Expanding The Box includes stellating Archetypes. Since the Box is a solid, changing shape requires that it temporarily go through a liquid state so that its structural components can reorganize with regard to each other. It helps if the training environment in which a Box Expands is clear and safe enough to encourage and protect the liquid state. (*See:* Box, Defensive Context, Expansive Context, Liquid State, Possibility Trainer, Starmaker, Stellating Archetypes)

EXPANSIVE CONTEXT – Through the equivalent of a rite of passage, a Box can shift its basic strategy from defensive to Expansive. When the Box is dedicated to Expanding itself then daily life involves serving Bright Principles such as adventure, exploration, impeccability, learning, growth, clarity, wonder, awe, mystery, surprise, communication, respect, discovery and so on. In the Expansive Context, possibility is unlimited. Since extraordinary human relationship and Archetypal Relationship only function in the Expansive Context, to go there it is helpful to develop a sensitivity to avoid being hooked back into your Box's original defensive context. (*See:* Box, Defensive Context, Expand the Box, Expansive Learning, Hooked, Low Drama Detector, Unhookable)

EXPANSIVE LEARNING – Expansive Learning was the original way you related to the world as a child. Expansive Learning readily accepts the unexpected because it does not assume that you already know everything. New pieces of knowledge can be appreciated for their own worth regardless of whether they fit into anything else that you understand or not. In school you learn defensive learning in which you fit new information into the knowledge continent of what you already know. Expansive Learning is useful for exploring new territories and gaining competencies in nonlinear skills. (*See:* Defensive Learning, Experiment, Nonlinear, Stellating Archetypes)

EXPECTATION(S) –Expectations are sleep-inducing fantasy declarations made by the Box with the impossible intention of forcing the future to be the same as the past, or of forcing someone else to be the same as you. Expectations are one of the Box's most efficient tools for destroying the possibility of intimacy and for creating low drama. Expectations ruin relationships. Expectations are not far different from beliefs, insofar as you can have Expectations about anything and there is no connection between an Expectation and reality. Expectations can also be used consciously as a way of shaping coincidences, such as Expecting that your child is a genius, or Expecting that a miracle could happen. Using Expectations consciously is an advanced technique because you have to be unhookable and completely able to drop the Expectations without residue if what you expect does not turn out to be what happens. Expectation is a creative act whether consciously or unconsciously directed. It has nothing to do with positive thinking. (*See:* Box Mechanics, Declaring, Low Drama)

EXPERIENTIAL REALITY – Reality previous to being processed by the Box is Experiential Reality. Reality after processing is verbal reality. In Experiential Reality, experience is not limited to words or concepts. In Experiential Reality, experience leads. You communicate about your experience later, if you want to, by finding words to use as a bridge to cause the experience to occur in someone else's body. For example, before a person will buy something they must first experience the value that this product or service will provide for them in the future. With access to Experiential Reality, a salesperson can create the experience of future value in a client so they are inspired to buy. Access to Experiential Reality also gives you the

ability to appreciate and enjoy the fullness, richness, depth and complexity of life in a mysterious world. This appreciation improves relationships both personally and professionally. (*See:* Inner Navigating, Mind, Relationship, Verbal Reality)

EXPERIMENT – The usual scientific image of the term "experiment" brings up an image of cold calculated testing – men in white coats putting electrodes on rats, mixing chemicals or shooting instruments into orbit. In Possibility Management, an Experiment is an action taken to explore what is possible, what is true, or what works. To Experiment means to venture into new territory and expand the Box. Responsible Experimenting builds matrix. (*See:* Action, Edgework, Expansive Learning, Inner Navigating, Laboratory, Matrix, New Territory)

FEEDBACK – Feedback is information from your surroundings about the past. Feedback can tell you what worked and what did not work. Feedback is the second step in the rapid learning process. Whatever you do or do not do, see or do not see, say or do not say, you will get Feedback. The world is a giant Feedback generator. There are only two kinds of Feedback that you can receive. *Go!* which means that what you are doing works, keep going. And *Beep!* which means that what you are doing is not working. Use the information of the *Beep!* to shift and *Go!* again. The more unexpected the Feedback is, the more information it contains. Sometimes the most useful Feedback to get is the Feedback that you do not understand at all. Let the Feedback sit there and, over time, it will inform you. In rapid learning, Feedback about the past is fruitfully followed by coaching about the future. (*See:* Coaching, Rapid Learning, Shift, Swamp)

FEELINGS – To feel is your birthright because you have a body. Western culture teaches you that it is not okay to feel, so you block your Feelings in order to survive through your childhood. If you have a Feeling, and Feelings are not okay, then you must conclude that you are not okay. As ridiculous as this is, such habits die hard. Blocking Feelings cuts you off from your emotional body and forces you to rely on your intellectual body – a poor substitute and a common imbalance in our culture. All Feelings can be classified into one of four Feeling categories: anger, sadness, fear or gladness. We have been trained to regard three of these Feelings as "bad feelings" (anger, sadness and fear) and one Feeling as a "good feeling" (gladness). This is as intelligent as saying that three of the directions on a compass are "bad directions" (for example, north, south and east) and one of the directions is a "good direction" (west). Feelings are experiential information. All four Feelings are tremendously useful professionally, capable of providing you with the energy and wisdom for doing your jobs with excellence. Each Feeling empowers one of the four Archetypes. When you mix Feelings you disempower your Archetypes. Disempowering your Archetypes is a standard psychological survival strategy. To turn on the Archetypes you can go through a Feeling process called "stellating." (Valerie Lankford created the *Map of Four Feelings* after her studies with Dr. Eric Berne and during a therapeutic process with Jacqui Schiff at the Cathexis Institute 1971-1975.) (*See:* Archetypes, Emotions, Experiential Reality, Four Bodies, Inner Navigating, Mixing Feelings, Stellating)

FORCE OF NATURE – It is a far greater error to assume that you know something and to limit your experiences so that they fit your assumptions than it is to open yourself to perceive a world more magnificent, bizarre and mysterious than your wildest expectations even if you do not understand what is happening. In this book we bandy about with terminology and ideas like we know what we are talking about. Please remember, Possibility Management is a new field. If you have a question about things now, ask it in two or three hundred years after we have had a little more time to experiment. Mostly we do not know. Mostly we are guessing. You too will discover when trying to create possibility for yourself, for other individuals or for organizations, sometimes it works and sometimes it does not. If it does not work, consider yourself the lucky recipient of a lesson from Mother Nature. Pay attention and take notes. She may be trying to teach you something. Human beings are influenced by Forces of Nature far greater than we typically concern ourselves with. We are influenced by the likes of planets, stars, karma, family ancestry, brain chemistry, genes, memes, phases of the moon, barometric pressure, pheromones, viruses, bacteria, blood sugar levels, contaminants, radiations, deities, demons, entities, angels, elves, fairy godmothers, indigestion, past

life vows, curses, and the will of God. Do not fool yourself into thinking that we can control these things. We cannot. We can hardly even imagine them. So, when things work out well, count your blessings. When things work out badly, count your blessings. Just do the jobs that hit your bench as elegantly and with as much dignity and integrity as you can. You cannot create possibility for a person whose soul is not ready to take that step. You cannot create possibility for a person without finding some way to love them. Most times it is not up to you, so give yourself some slack, and the other person too. The best overall advice that I have ever heard is: Trust the process. (*See:* Creating Possibility, Creator, High Drama, Love, Principle, Soul)

FOUR BODIES – You can distinguish that you live in Four Bodies. The Four Bodies are the physical body (the bones and tissues with sensations), the intellectual body (the mind, psychology, and intellectual capital of the Box with thoughts, knowledge, logic, and reasons), the emotional body (the heart with feelings and emotions), and the energetic or spiritual body (the soul with presence, essence, and being). Each body has its own kind of pain, its own kind of ecstasy, its own kind of food, its own kind of intelligence, its own kind of liquid state, and its own kind of intimacy with other people's Four Bodies. Western culture neurotically reinforces our identification with the intellectual body, so you can assume that you start off significantly imbalanced. It takes efforts to bring all Four Bodies into a working harmony. (Possibility Manager Wolfgang Köhler invented the *Map of Four Bodies* in September 2005.) (*See:* Box, Edgework, Feeling, Heart, Intimacy, Mind, Physical Center, Soul)

GAMEWORLD – A Gameworld is a dynamic environment created by two or more people agreeing to relate according to an internally consistent story. Gameworlds can range from temporary and of minor consequence to longer lasting and of major consequence. Examples of Gameworlds include: let's go up the elevator, let's have a party, let's have a relationship, let's have a family, let's have a company, let's have a town, let's have a country, let's have a religion, let's have a war, and so on. Gameworlds can be responsible or irresponsible, depending on their purpose and their results.

Gameworlds become defensive if their stories are believed to be true or are kept invisible to the participants, in which case the participants are said to be identified with their Gameworld. Even if a Gameworld is considered to be the "one and only true reality" by a majority of its players, it is still a Gameworld. Gameworlds founded in beliefs build false community and survive through competing for limited resources through war. Gameworlds founded in Bright Principles and responsible results build authentic community and thrive on creative collaboration to source the resources. Taking responsibility at the level of being the story maker for Gameworlds is the entry door to Possibility Management. Responsible Gameworlds tend to be more galaxical than hierarchical in design. In a galaxical Gameworld the source people are found serving as its center. (*See:* Center of a Gameworld, Identification, Organization, Possibility Management, Purpose, Reality, Result, Story)

GAP – Several tools and techniques from Possibility Management derive their effectiveness when you consciously enter the Gap in time between moments, or the Gap in space between you and your Box. Such Gaps can be as thin as a sheet of paper, but that sliver of opportunity is enough to disconnect the false bond and reclaim a natural freedom of movement. When you put your attention on the Gap and remember that it is there, then, for example, the world can provide a stimulus, but you do not have to respond because the stimulus has no power to create meaning in your Box. Or, your Box can be going crazy with reactions, but you need not say a word because the reactions die in the Gap and never manifest. The idea that there could be a Gap in time between moments or that there could be a Gap in space between your inner world and your outer world are concepts that can enter your mind. Actually navigating your way into those Gaps and tolerating the intensity of staying there occurs in experiential reality rather than in verbal reality and requires live coaching and feedback from another human being during a training. (*See:* Attention, Bag of Things, Experiential Reality, Minimize Now, Unhookable, Verbal Reality)

GODDESS – The Goddess is one particular aspect of the Pirate Sorceress Warrioress Queen Goddess Woman, the Archetypal Feminine. The qualities of Goddess come through the space being held for the Archetypal Feminine by the Archetypal Masculine and are not a manifestation of the Box. Therefore, Goddess cannot be produced by willpower alone, and cannot serve charismatic or self-centered purposes. When a woman can enter and stay in the Adult responsible ego state in the company of an Adult man who is holding Archetypal space for her, if the woman is willing to shift into the Archetypal Feminine then the Goddess can unfold through her. The Goddess inherently remembers the way through the Great Labyrinth of Spaces to the Heart of the Labyrinth and can lead her Man there. Such a rare and beautiful radiance! The Goddess enjoys, blesses and heals, and offers the sweet nectar of Archetypal intimacy that is Countenance. (*See:* Adult, Archetype, Countenance, Experiential Reality, Navigating Space)

GOING STELLAR – Going Stellar means having free access to full 100-percent Archetypal experience and expression of any of the four feelings without reason and without warning whenever necessary. This is comparable to having the radiant power of a star with an on-off switch. Since Western culture does not bring you through a rite of passage to consciously ignite your responsible feelings, you can obtain that initiation in certain trainings. Once you have consciously stellated your four Archetypes, from then on, for the rest of your life, you have the uninhibited ability to Go Stellar. The energy and information of all four feelings are then available for your use as an inexhaustible resource. Going Stellar is one of the seven core skills. (*See:* Core Skills, Feelings, Stellating Archetypes)

GREMLIN – Your Gremlin is the Archetypal King or Queen of your Shadow World. Everybody has parts. Everybody is part Gremlin. Gremlin is the part of you dedicated to creating low drama and serving your hidden purpose. Gremlin is quite likely to take over whenever you are unconscious of the purpose of your action. When Gremlin takes over you do not know the true cost of your irresponsible actions. Gremlin creates low drama gameworlds based on scarcity, competition, and survival in order to eat Gremlin food. For example, Gremlin leaders take other people's centers and surround themselves with followers in order to feel safe. Gremlin derives joy at other people's expense through "I win! You lose!" and "I'm right! You're wrong!" and "Ha ha! I got you!" games and nasty little jokes. As you begin to get clarity about the presence and participation of Gremlin in your life, it is crucial to remember that Gremlin is not bad. Gremlin is Gremlin and can be counted on to do what Gremlins do. Gremlin cannot be rehabilitated to be responsible, and besides, that is not the point. Gremlin is not your enemy. The idea is not to kill, imprison or disempower Gremlin, as you may have been taught through some kind of moral system, but rather to establish a relationship with Gremlin such that you own Gremlin rather than Gremlin owning you. When Gremlin is consciously integrated into your general presence and sits at your feet at your command, you become responsibly "dangerous," that is, no longer gullible or naïve. Gremlin awareness refines your overall awareness. Transforming your relationship to Gremlin is the way to stellate joy, and like stellating the other feelings involves two phases. Phase 1 is liberating Gremlin to 100-percent capacity and presence (which obviously must be done in a special Gremlin-proof environment designed exactly for this purpose). Phase 2 is integrating Gremlin capacities into practical skills through conscious practice. Since Gremlin can destroy any space at any time for no reason, there are many practical uses for Gremlin that nothing else can accomplish. Some of these uses are, for example, staying unhypnotized, staying unhookable, and going nonlinear. Expanding to responsibly include Gremlin takes time and practice, and necessitates building matrix. (*See:* Center, Hidden Purpose, Low Drama, *Map of Possibility*, Purpose, Matrix, Nonlinear, Pirate, Practice, Unhookable)

HEART – Your Heart is the center of your emotional body and the transducer of feelings. To create clarity in your relationship, give your Heart to the partner you love, and give your soul to your destiny. Your destiny does not require your Heart, and your partner is not your destiny. (*See:* Destiny, Feelings, Four Bodies, Soul)

HEART OF THE LABYRINTH (CENTER OF THE LABYRINTH) – (*See:* Goddess Navigating, Space)

HIDDEN PURPOSE – Your Hidden Purpose is the personalized set of three, four or five Shadow Principles that you serve as your survival strategy.

Your commitment to serving Hidden Purpose is primary, previous to any other commitment in your life because your first choice is always to survive. It is shocking to realize that in the noble endeavor to survive we are so dedicated to irresponsibility. That is why the Hidden Purpose is called "Hidden." As a child, when you choose to live instead of die, you replace your instinctive perception of what "normal" should be with the often cataclysmic "normal" of your Western culture childhood environment. Your Hidden Purpose is to duplicate and sustain the abnormal normal at any expense because in that state your Box knows that it can continue to survive. (*See:* Box, Gremlin, Hidden Purpose Process, *Map of Possibility*)

HIDDEN PURPOSE PROCESS – The Hidden Purpose Process is a guided expedition during which you enter your Shadow World and extract jewels of clarity about your Shadow Principles. As you could well imagine, the Hidden Purpose Process can be loud and intense, and is done carefully in a safe and sustainable way by a certified Possibility Trainer. Knowing the three to five Shadow Principles of your Hidden Purpose gives you one little choice that can change your life – the choice of not serving Hidden Purpose. (*See:* Bright Principle, Distilling Destiny Process, Gremlin, Hidden Purpose, *Map of Possibility*, Possibility Trainer, Shadow Principle, True Purpose)

HIGH DRAMA (HIGH LEVEL FUN) – High Drama is any action intended to take responsibility. High Drama is conscious theater enacted for serving Bright Principles. An example of High Drama is committing to produce results before you know how to do it. If you create High Drama, the world lays itself before you like an open oyster (or if you are not attracted to raw oysters – which is quite understandable – how about "like a peeled mango"? or "like a sliced pepperoni pizza"?) begging you to live as your destiny in action. Most of us are so imprisoned by our Box that we do not even perceive the universe's invitation, let alone act on it. Another example of High Drama is expanding the Box. Because the Box is so cleverly defended, expanding the Box is impossible and cannot be figured out with the mind. High Drama is to go ahead and commit to doing it anyway. (*See:* Action,

Adult, Communicator, Conscious Theater, Creator, Destiny, Doer, Expand the Box, Low Drama, *Map of Possibility*, Pirate Agreement, Possibility Manager, Radical Responsibility)

HIGH LEVEL FUN – (*See:* High Drama)

HOLDING SPACE – Holding Space is the act of being responsible at the level of space. Holding Space implies conscious intention. Before you can Hold Space you must first declare space into existence as a distinction between what is in the space and what is outside the space. Space is declared either as an eight-pointed box or as an amorphous bubble. Space is held through using a percentage of your conscious attention to dedicate the space to serving Bright Principles. When you first try to Hold Space you might use control, domination or manipulation, but these are Shadow Principles. Holding Space is a core skill. Once you can Hold Space you can learn to navigate space. (*See:* Attention, Core Skills, Navigating Space, Purpose, Space)

HOOKED – Being Hooked is when you are knocked unconscious and behaving according to mechanical Box reactions. Being Hooked is psychological imprisonment. When you are Hooked, your attention and identity are confined to the limitations of your Box's defense strategy. When you are Hooked, you easily enter low drama and have no access to possibility. Being Hooked is not accidental. The purpose for being Hooked is to create low drama to feed your Gremlin. Since being Hooked is not accidental, it can also be avoided. (*See:* Box Mechanics, Disk of Nothing, Gremlin, Low Drama, Reminding Factor, Springscreen, Unhookable)

IDENTIFICATION – Identification is the unconscious or conscious action of using is-glue to declare who you are. Unconscious Identification equates you to being your Box, produces ordinary human relationship, and is the result of standard human intelligence thoughtware. Conscious Identification equates you to being a vast and awesome potential, specifically as the space through which the Bright Principles that you serve can do their work. There is far greater possibility available when you are Identified as a vast potential than when you are Identified as your Box. (*See:* Conscious Theater, Creator, Hooked, Thoughtware, Is-Glue, Is-Glue Dissolver, Shift, Unhookable)

IMAGINATION – In many ways, who you are is your Imagination. But in Western culture, mind is at war with Imagination. And mind has won. You can get your Imagination back. The work of rehabilitating your Imagination is preparatory work for stellating your Masculine or Feminine Archetypes. Imagination is an endlessly rich resource of wild, unpredictable, radiantly humorous nonlinear possibilities. You may be using an unconscious form of Imagination right now in one of these two forms: 1) You imagine that things are as you perceive them, when in fact your perceptions of things have become quite distorted by your Box and they are not really that way. 2) You imagine that things are different from how they are, meaning that you are living in a fantasy world as a way of avoiding the way things actually are. Imagination can be intentionally applied for the practical purpose of creating possibility. (*See:* Creating Possibility, Mind, Nonlinear)

INNER NAVIGATING – No one can negotiate your internal experiences but you. The set of skills for distinguishing where you are in your internal world, what is happening there, what you do about it, and why, is called Inner Navigating. Without Inner Navigation skills, moving through the experiences of being yourself would be like sailing through treacherous waters without a chart or compass. Many people choose to stay at home and watch TV and leave their Inner Navigating to licensed professionals. You have obviously made a different choice. Inner Navigating improves through self-observation, self-knowledge, and practice with feedback and coaching in an environment of immediate clarity. Inner Navigating involves connecting delicate intuitively-sensed experiences with clear thought-maps of feelings, worlds, and spaces. Since inner experiences are so convincing it is crucial to distinguish between what is authentic and what is reactive theater. Regular self-sitting and together-sitting are indispensable practice for Inner Navigating. (*See:* Box Mechanics, Conscious Theater, Emotions, Experiential Reality, Feelings, Identification, Navigating Space, Practice, Rapid Learning)

INTIMACY – Relationship does not die from lack of love. Relationship dies from lack of Intimacy.

Intimacy implies distinguishing between a person and their Box. Intimacy is being closer to a person than your Boxes would normally allow, so you are being-with each other as beings rather than being-with each other as Boxes. Intimacy does not mean being in another person's personal space – this is enmeshment and leads to co-dependency and adaptive behavior. Authentic Adult intimacy builds matrix. You can enter new territory by doing Intimacy Edgework experiments in all four bodies. (*See:* Adult, Being Centered, Being-With, Contact, Countenance, Edgework, Experiment, Four Bodies, Matrix, Relationship)

IRRESPONSIBILITY – Irresponsibility is unconscious theater about pretending to not be at source, acting as if you are not at cause, acting as if there is not enough, trying to disown, playing the victim role, or in any way being contracted from your inherent limitless potential. From the Archetypal perspective, irresponsibility is an illusion. (*See:* Conscious Theater, Low Drama, *Map of Possibility*, Radical Responsibility)

IS-GLUE – Is-Glue does not exist in nature. The concept of "is" and its many conjugations including am, are, was, were, has, have, had, do, does, did, may, might, must, can, could, should, would, shall, will, and also the "not" forms, such as is not, am not, and so on, are all a product of the human mind. Is-Glue hangs on your Possibility Manager tool belt and resembles a tube of toothpaste. You squeeze out a blob, "PPPlthlthlthl" and glue two completely disassociated things together to serve conscious or unconscious Purposes. If used unconsciously, Is-Glue produces assumptions, expectations, conclusions, beliefs, etc., that form rigid if not crystallized parts of your Box. For example: "This job is impossible." From this detached perspective you can see that "job" is not at all connected to "impossible" until you glue them together with Is-Glue. You can also use Is-Glue consciously, for example, to build a platform for high drama, such as with, "Our team loves doing impossible jobs." Whether unconsciously or consciously used, you create your own Is-Glued stories and then act as if your story is true even though you just glued it together yourself. (*See:* Declaring, Gameworld, Is-Glue Dissolver, Meme, Reality, Story, Tool Belt)

IS-GLUE DISSOLVER – Is-Glue Dissolver comes in a handy spray bottle and is clipped to your Possibility Manager tool belt. Is-Glue Dissolver is a declaration that disassembles Is-Glued realities through recognizing that thoughtware is only held together with Is-Glue and is not in fact objectively real. To experiment with Is-Glue Dissolver, choose a story about yourself that disempowers you, such as, "I might fail." Hold it out in front of you and clearly distinguish the three components, the two solids "I" and "fail," and the Is-Glue "might." Spray on a little Is-Glue Dissolver, "Pffffftttth, pffffffttttth." Clip the Is-Glue Dissolver bottle back on your tool belt and use both hands to slide the two solids apart from each other so you have one in each hand. Your left hand holds "I" and your right hand holds "fail." Nothing connects the two together any longer – they are completely independent, one from the other. Now you can separately decide what you want to do with each. Experiment with putting "fail" back into the "bag of things" hanging on your tool belt, and reaching past it for something else you could glue to "I" that would better empower you. With the "bag of things" you never know what you will pull out before you pull it out and look at it. For example, you could pull out "an experimenter," and try Is-Gluing that to "I" with the Is-Glue "am." Then you have "I am an experimenter." Does that empower you? Or you could pull out, "love to learn by doing," or "trust the universe," or "love to make new contacts," or "open interesting doors of possibility with every action." Try a few nonlinear possibilities rather than settling on whatever you come up with first, keeping in mind that whatever you try you can easily change again with Is-Glue Dissolver! Is-Glue Dissolver is very powerful, so the suggestion is to begin using it with caution. (*See:* Bag of Things, Creating Possibility, Declaring, Is-Glue, Nonlinear, Reality, Story, Thoughtware, Tool Belt)

KING – (*See:* Archetype, Adult)

LABORATORY – You may notice that over the years you have developed an appetite for a certain energetic food that occurs when possibility is created and applied. A Laboratory is the circumstance in which you intentionally manufacture that food for yourself and for other people to feast on. For example, your primary relationship can become a Laboratory where you are each deeply fed and nurtured through doing intimacy Edgework experiments with one another. A gameworld such as a club meeting, a business, a training or a team can also be a Laboratory if you use it for doing experiments. The gameworld for learning Possibility Management is called a Possibility Laboratory. (*See:* Edgework, Experiment, Gameworld, Possibility Management)

LABYRINTH – The Great Labyrinth of Spaces. (*See:* Navigating Space)

LINEAR – Linearity is the quality of being direct, straightforward, predictable and reasonable. Once regarded as the most efficient and effective method for solving problems, nowadays Linear solutions are frequently not efficient or effective enough. For any given problem there is usually one Linear solution, but often many nonlinear solutions that turn out to be far more useful. Extraordinary human relationship as well as Archetypal Relationship both require that you have access to an unlimited resource of nonlinear possibilities. (*See:* Creating Possibility, Nonlinear)

LIQUID STATE – For a Box to shift from one solid shape into another solid shape, it must at least for a short while pass through a Liquid State. During the Liquid State, rigid structures become fluid in relationship to each other, and reordering can take place. For more information on this you can search Wikipedia.com on the Internet for the theory of "Dissipative Structures" that won Ilya Prigogine the Nobel Prize for Chemistry in 1977. Ordinarily, while your Box expands, you are more interested in the newly expanded position than you are in the frighteningly groundless Liquid State. Nonetheless, as you continue to expand the Box you may notice that each new Box shape becomes less and less rigid, and that the distance between one solid position and the next becomes greater and greater. Over time you may become more comfortable during fluidic expansion than in defending a rigid but known position. You may even come to recognize that the Liquid State is the true nature of reality, and that human beings are designed to fly. (*See:* Box, Expand the Box, Morphogenetic Field)

LISTENING AS A SPACE – (*See:* Possibility Listening)

LOVE – Possibility Management distinguishes three kinds of love. 1) Ordinary human love where "I love you" means, "I need you, I own you, I want to control you." Ordinary love comes and goes, so people in ordinary love are victims in a scarcity of love looking for someone to love them. 2) Extraordinary human love where "I love you" means, "I am responsible for love, I source love, if I am there love is there," with responsible Adult dignity and respect. 3) Archetypal Love where Love is a sourceless radiant Principle, the most abundant thing in the universe, and "I love you" means, "the Principle of Archetypal Love is happening." In the great Labyrinth of Spaces, the Space of Archetypal Love Happening is also known as "the Heart of the Labyrinth." (*See:* Labyrinth, Low Drama, Navigating Space, Principle, Radical Responsibility, Relationship)

LOW DRAMA – Low Drama is any action that is consciously or unconsciously intended to avoid responsibility. Low Drama is an energetic exchange between human beings that serves Shadow Principles. There are two direct ways to detect if you are enacting Low Drama. The first is if you are playing the role of victim, persecutor or rescuer. The second is if you exhibit Low Drama behavior: blame, resentment, justification, complaining, being right, or making wrong. It can be startling to distinguish that Low Drama is certainly exciting, but that, no matter how right you think you are, Low Drama is not life; it is only Low Drama. No matter how good your reasons are or how strongly you resent the other person, the only thing that happens in Low Drama is that you get older. Nothing changes. To actually change something involves taking responsibility. Low Drama is not an accident. The fact that Low Drama is not an accident means that Low Drama can be avoided. The purpose of doing Low Drama is to feed Gremlin. Notice the pattern of a hungry Gremlin finding another hungry Gremlin to start a good fight. A Gremlin feeding-frenzy follows. When the Gremlins are satiated, they go to sleep and you wonder what the fight was all about? Low Drama is never a step on the way toward responsibility. Low Drama cannot be transformed into high drama. Attention placed on Low Drama *is* Low Drama. The only way out of Low Drama is taking responsibility. With practice you can develop the ability to avoid entering Low Drama for any reason. Low Drama is the main characteristic of ordinary human relationship. (The *Map of Low Drama* is modeled after the original "Drama Triangle" developed in 1965 by Dr. Stephen Karpman. Dr. Karpman was a student of Dr. Eric Berne, the founder of Transactional Analysis. It was Dr. Karpman who named the three positions of Low Drama: victim, persecutor and rescuer. I renamed Dr. Karpman's Drama Triangle as "Low Drama" to more easily reveal its relatedness to "high drama" on the *Map of Possibility*. In one of his original designs for the Drama Triangle, Dr. Karpman had included a fourth position that he called "trickster," identical to what I call "Gremlin.") (*See:* Gremlin, Low Drama Detector, High Drama, Irresponsibility, *Map of Possibility*, Practice)

LOW DRAMA DETECTOR – An excellent way to avoid being hooked into low drama is to build for yourself a Low Drama Detector. The Detector is a metaphorical red-flashing light mounted on your right shoulder as a reminding factor to warn you about incoming low drama. The Low Drama Detector senses low dramas from a distance of 100 yards, and instantly flashes its red light and emits a sharp, persistent, warning beep. The Detector displays which of the three roles is being played out, victim, persecutor or rescuer, and which of the three roles you are being invited to play. To avoid low drama, do not resist low drama – this is like trying to resist thinking of a pink elephant. Clarity about low drama is key. Identify low drama as low drama, not bad or wrong, but guaranteed to create only certain predictable results. To avoid low drama, create high drama. In other words, as soon as your Low Drama Detector sounds off, change your course and go somewhere else. It takes practice to go *toward* low drama and not *enter* the low drama. (*See:* Low Drama, Hooked, Reminding Factor, Unhookable)

MAGICIAN – (*See:* Creator)

MAKER – (*See:* Doer)

MAKING TIME – The possibility of Making Time is a consequence of taking radical responsibility in the domain of time. To discover how to Make Time, do the following experiment. Responsibly answer the following question: "Where did you get the time to read this sentence?" After you understand about Making Time you can then figure out how to move faster than the speed of time. (*See:* Creator, Radical Responsibility)

MAP – (*See:* Thought-Map)

MAP OF POSSIBILITY – This is the central thought-map of Possibility Management (*See:* the *List of Thought-Maps*). The *Map of Possibility* starts with a single vertical line which acknowledges that whatever happens is completely neutral. The *Map of Possibility* is based on the observation that human beings do not leave things neutral, but instead are creating in every moment. You create by making stories about what happens, by interpreting the evidence that you perceive and giving it meaning. The world is rich in evidence, so there is evidence to support any story you want to create. Every story you make has a purpose. Either you are conscious of your purpose or you are not. The dichotomy between unconscious and conscious purpose creates two general types of games: irresponsible games or responsible games. Which game you are playing is always discernable by the results you create. Irresponsible games serve Shadow Principles. Responsible games serve Bright Principles. The King or Queen of the Shadow World is the Gremlin who sources low drama. The King or Queen of the Bright World, for lack of a better term, is the Possibility Manager who sources high drama. (*See:* Archetype, Gameworld, High Drama, Low Drama, Principle, Result, Story, Thought-Map, True Purpose, Unconscious Purpose)

MARSHMALLOW ZONE – The Marshmallow Zone is the all-too-real super-safe and familiar, hermetically sealed set of behavior patterns located far away from the edges of your Box. A person living in the Marshmallow Zone uses standard human intelligence thoughtware, and can typically only create ordinary human relationship. For "settler" type Boxes, the Marshmallow Zone is "Home Sweet Home." For "pioneer" type Boxes, the Marshmallow Zone is "death warmed over." Voyaging out of the Marshmallow Zone is an experiment guaranteed to bring up fear of the unknown regardless of your Box's orientation. Fear only stops you if your story about the experience of fear is that "fear is bad" or "fear is dangerous." To continue exploring new territory it helps to rewire your story so that "fear is fear." (*See:* Box, Feelings, Edgework, Story, Thoughtware, Experiment, Is-Glue)

MATRIX – (Not to be confused with the matrix concept from the popular films of the same title.) Matrix is similar to the trellis upon which a climbing rose is supported. Without the trellis, the rose plant grows feebly along the ground. With a trellis, the rose grows strong and radiant. Matrix is the energetic structure upon which consciousness or "being" can grow. Matrix cannot be rushed or grown instantly. Matrix grows at its own speed limit and as a result of certain efforts and influences. Matrix can be built through exposing yourself to certain beneficial stresses (such as living in a foreign culture, doing responsible Edgework experiments, or trying to understand this book), certain radiations (such as being in the company of saints, empowered temples, objective art, or sacred artifacts), certain substances (such as early morning sunshine, or a true alchemical elixir like Tonic Gold™), certain efforts to stay awake (such as by paying attention to your attention and staying aware of what you are aware of), and your efforts to practice (such as avoiding low drama, or flossing your teeth every night before you go to bed no matter how late it is or how tired you are). No one can build Matrix for you. If you do not do what it takes to build your Matrix, your Matrix grows geologically; that is, at the natural speed of continental drift. Matrix can be functionally compared to soil. There are more than enough seeds. What is needed is good soil. As soon as the soil is prepared, the seeds grow. As soon as Matrix is built, consciousness grows. As soon as the Box expands, new possibility is available. (*See:* Edgework, Practice, Radical Responsibility, Tonic Gold™)

MEETING TECHNOLOGY – The way we come together and have meetings determines the kinds of results we can create as a group. Western civilization meeting format unconsciously defaults to the form established by parliamentary procedure as described in the book *Robert's Rules of Order* by Henry M. Robert, published in 1907. Other meeting formats are possible and, in fact, are needed for producing more diverse, flexible and intelligent results. Particularly effective are circular or open meeting technologies that allow for more chaos during the meeting. Parliamentary procedure establishes a linear hierarchy of rules for managing the competitive territorial question of "Who has power now?" Nonlinear meeting formats rely on the generative and self-organization properties of groups to liberate immense reserves of imaginative intellectual capital and group intelligence. Convening diversity rather than controlling power may be a more useful approach for responding to the challenges of today's rapidly evolving conditions. Examples of new meeting formats include Open Space Technology, World Café, and the Art of Hosting conversations that matter. Possibility Management's New Meeting Technologies include: Possibility Team, The Problem Is the Solution, Big Mad and The Genius Process. Rather than the political concern of "Who has the power?" these new meeting formats effectively address the questions "What is possible right now?" and "How to be the space through which the principles of this organization can do their work in the world?" (*See:* Holding Space, Nonlinear, Possibility Management, Principles)

MEME – The word "meme" was invented in 1976 by Richard Dawkins, a British biologist. A Meme is a fundamental instruction for the design of your mind, just like a gene is a fundamental instruction for the design of your body. Memes can be classified into various categories, such as assumptions, attitudes, beliefs, conclusions, definitions, excuses, expectations, interpretations, justifications, meanings, opinions, perspectives, preferences, prejudices, reasons, stories, values, visions, and so on. Simple Memes equate to the names of things, for example, the Meme "feeling" is the name of something that carries emotional energy. Once a mind is infected with a Meme, the Meme frames up the mind's perceptions. Then, something like music is sensed by the quality of feeling it delivers. Complex Memes are constructed out of simple Memes pasted together with is-glue, such as "feeling is dangerous" or "feeling is fun." The idea of a "Meme" is itself a Meme. A functional set of Memes is your thoughtware. The Box is made of thoughtware and thought-maps. (*See:* Box, Is-Glue, Memetics, Thought-Map, Thoughtware)

MEMETIC VIRUS – Memetic Viruses are a compact set of memes usually stored in written form that are so clear, so useful, and so interesting that their new thinking patterns automatically replace and upgrade your current thoughtware. This book is full of Memetic Viruses. If you want an additional source of Memetic Viruses get a hold of the book *Wild Thinking* (*Abenteuer Denken* in German) by Clinton Callahan. (*See:* Meme, Thoughtware)

MEMETICS – Memetics is the study of memes and Memetic engineering. Memetic engineering is the field of skills, tools and processes for redesigning or reinventing the Box. Boxes are constructed out of memes. A Box's Memetic structure determines its functionality – in other words, function follows form. If you reinvent your Box, you reinvent your world and what is possible for you. This is how Memetics is related to the management of possibility. By reinventing the form of the Box, even slightly, through Memetic engineering, vast new possibilities can be opened. (*See:* Box Mechanics, Experiment, Liquid State, Possibility, Possibility Trainer, Thoughtware)

META-CONVERSATION – A Meta-Conversation is a "conversation about the conversation." The way to create the possibility of possibility is to have a conversation about the conversation. Then, instead of remaining stuck in the limits of the present conversation, you go nonlinear into a perspective with different limits – limits that are more useful for accomplishing the job at hand. A Meta-Conversation changes the context so that your conversation can have a different content. This has the same effect as putting away the chessboard and getting out the cookbook – you get to play together in a completely different kind of gameworld. (*See:* Context, Gameworld, Navigating Space, Nonlinear)

MIND – Mind is the center of your intellectual body and is shaped by your Box. You have been trained in Western civilization to identify yourself as your Mind. Western science operates under the assumption that the universe can be systematized and explained so that Mind can understand it. In extraordinary human relationship and Archetypal Relationship, the Mind is far too slow, too impoverished, and too linear for what you need to accomplish. To source relationship through ongoing acts of nonlinear creation, you require greater resources than Mind offers. With a balanced mix of all four bodies (intellectual body plus physical body plus emotional body plus energetic body), you access vast resources

of energy and information, even if your Mind cannot figure out how you do it. (*See:* Box, Four Bodies, Identification, Imagination, Verbal Reality)

MINDSET – (*See:* Box)

MINIMIZE NOW – A man asks a woman to marry him and she says, "Not now!" A year later he asks her again. She says, irritated, "I already told you, not now!" The woman lives in a very big Now. You can create a Now so big that it includes decisions made in a far distant past, or expectations that project into a far distant future. From the perspective of a Minimized Now, "far distant" means anything longer than three seconds. Boxes defend themselves by creating big Nows to keep everything in the future the same as it was in the past. Extraordinary relationship is an ongoing act of nonlinear creation. Going nonlinear requires you to move orthogonally through the gaps between moments. Time is quantized into experiential moments. Between each moment is a gap. These gaps are invisible if your Now is too big. A big Now smears over the gaps and makes reality appear to be one continuous scene, just like with motion pictures and television – where there is no action, only the illusion of action. When your Now is small enough, you can slip sideways through gaps between moments into previously unseen and completely unexpected possibilities. While experimenting with Minimizing your Now make sure that your Minimized Now is spacious and is not founded in a scarcity of time. In Now there is no time. (*See:* Adult, Gap, Making Time, Now, Orthogonal)

MIXING FEELINGS – Without clarity about feelings we tend to experience and express our feelings mixed together. Mixing Feelings blocks our access to the Archetypal energy and intelligence of the pure feelings. For example, mixing anger with sadness produces the experience of depression. In Possibility Laboratories, you can learn inner navigation, and physically separate the feelings clearly one from the other. After unmixing the anger from the sadness, the depression vanishes and you feel angry about one thing and sad about either the same thing or another thing. This clarity gives you the power to create different results. Mixing sadness with fear creates the experience of isolation or desperation. Mixing anger with fear creates the experience of hysteria. Mixing joy with sadness creates the experience of sentimentality or nostalgia. Mixing joy with fear creates the experience of carelessness or excitement. And mixing joy with anger creates the experience of feeling glad when someone else feels pain, "I win, you lose," or "Haha I got you!" "*Schadenfreude*." Mixing Feelings is not bad or wrong; it just produces certain results. (Possibility Manager Marion Lutz developed the *Map of Mixing Feelings* in 2003.) (*See*: Archetype, Feelings, Laboratory, Possibility Trainer, Result)

MORPHOGENETIC FIELD – Literally, Morphogenetic Field means "shape making" field. This term comes from Rupert Sheldrake and his Theory of Morphogenetic Fields that you can learn more about through Wikipedia.com on the Internet. When you declare and hold a space in the name of principles, and someone in that space enters the liquid state, the principles function as the Morphogenetic Field, molding their Box's new shape as it resolidifies. (*See*: Declare, Liquid State, Principles, Space)

NAVIGATING SPACE – An infinite labyrinth of spaces ranges the full spectrum from Shadow Worlds to Bright Worlds and everything in between. Every space is connected to every other space. Every space represents a different set of possibilities. Being conscious and responsible for what space you are in is called Navigating Space. You can develop your powers of moving from space to space. While Navigating Space, you appreciate each member of your team as a crewmember of your "spaceship" – including the waitress! Crewmembers are responsible for informing the navigator the instant anything is detected on the instrument panel of their four bodies. Extraordinary human relationship and Archetypal Relationship only occur in certain spaces. And only you can Navigate the Space of your relationship into those spaces. At the Center or Heart of the Labyrinth is the one space of Archetypal Love. The Goddess remembers how to get there. (*See*: Discovery Speaking, Experiential Reality, Goddess, Inner Navigating, Laboratory, Painting Doorways, Possibility Trainer, Space)

NEW TERRITORY – New Territory is everything not yet encompassed by your Box. Exploring new thought-maps expands your box into New Territory. You explore New Territories by doing Edgework experiments. Possibility Management is neither theoretical nor verbal; it is experiential. So, in Possibility Management Laboratories, first you see a thought-map of a New Territory and then you actually go there. New Territory is new because things are possible in the New Territory that are not possible elsewhere. As soon as you acquire enough familiarity with a New Territory, your own learning continues by empowering others through introducing them to the same New Territory. The expanse of New Territories is endless. This means that for your Box expansion there is "no top end" (as articulated in the teaching of Lee Lozowick). Possibility Trainers who go first into New Territories take responsibility for making new thought-maps to share with their people. (*See*: Edgework, Expand the Box, Experiment, Laboratory, Marshmallow Zone, Thought-Map)

NONLINEAR – Nonlinearity is the quality of moving at right angles to the assumptions of the current space. Western culture teaches you to be linear. If you find a linear solution to a problem, such as the shortest distance between two points, then you conclude that you have found the best solution … and you stop thinking. With Nonlinearity you do not stop thinking. You know from experience that, just over the edge of your Box, there are unlimited numbers and forms of additional Nonlinear solutions, waiting exactly where the last one was, just before you found it. When navigating space at higher speeds, going Nonlinear necessitates that a Box have little or no mass. Trying to turn a Box that is made massive with assumptions, expectations, preferences, stories, prejudices, positions, beliefs, or opinions is like trying to turn the Titanic. This is why it can be helpful to eliminate extra mass by dropping the necessity for beliefs, by making stories optional, by minimizing your now and by minimizing your *here*. With little or no mass you gain the ability to turn right angles at "light speed." (*See*: Edgework, Gremlin, Linear, Orthogonal, Navigating Space)

NOW – Through experimenting with these ideas you will sooner or later discover that your power is available only in the present. You cannot change something that happened even an instant ago, or which might happen an instant in the future. The only place where you have power is right Now. Creating happens Now. Distinctions are made Now. Decisions are made Now. This makes it most interesting to deal only with what is possible right Now. How big is this Now? We could define Now as one moment. How big is a moment? Moments change depending on what space you are in. As Albert Einstein described it, time is relative. "Put your hand on a hot stove for a minute, and it seems like an hour. Sit with a pretty girl for an hour, and it seems like a minute. *That's* relativity." In general, we could define a moment as the length of time it takes to make a decision: one second to make the decision, and two seconds for the Box to reorder. (*See:* Adult, Minimize Now, Possibility Stone)

ORGANIZATION – An Organization is two or more people with a common purpose. This definition includes a relationship or a family in the category of Organizations. Every Organization has a Box and is subject to the laws of Box mechanics. The difference between the Organization Box and the individual Box is that the individual Box is the only Box that can take responsibility. Organizations can be viewed as living organisms that need food, use energy, make waste, communicate, move, evolve, expel contaminants and parasites, replicate themselves, fight or align with other Organizations, and die. Organizations become rigid if they are conceived of as being hierarchical. Organizations are more fluid if they are conceived with a more organic flow of power and authority, such as with "galaxical Organization charts." (*See:* Box Mechanics, Gameworld, Purpose)

ORTHOGONAL – The term "Orthogonal" comes from mathematics and literally means "perpendicular to or at right angles to." Possibility Management uses the word Orthogonal to mean, "at right angles to the Possibility limits of the prevailing space or gameworld." Orthogonal is another word for nonlinear. Orthogonal actions lead to innovation and are crucial for creating possibility. (*See:* Nonlinear)

PAINTING DOORWAYS – When you encounter an obstacle, regardless of whether it is physical or energetic, internal or external, you encounter the obstacle as an obstacle. This is almost too obvious to speak about. But, encountering an obstacle as an obstacle plucks it naked of all of its other

possibilities. Painting Doorways is the Possibility Management tool of transforming obstacles into passageways to new territories. You do this by pulling your "possibility paint brush" out of your "tool belt" and Painting a Doorway and handle on the solid wall of impossibility. Then, you turn the handle and walk through the door. Anyone in contact with you in that moment will easily slide with you into the next space, and may not even notice the change of spaces except for the new set of possibilities. (*See:* Declaring, Is-Glue, Navigating Space, New Territory, Possibility Trainer, Tool Belt)

PARALLEL CULTURE – A Parallel Culture is two or more people making actions in a gameworld, using thoughtware that is different from the standard human intelligence thoughtware of the dominant culture. A Parallel Culture is in the same circumstances as the dominant culture but creates different results. Cultures can be distinguished and graphed according to their level of responsibility, from irresponsible to radically responsible. Western culture is classified at the Child level of responsibility, lower than Adult responsibility, because we are making messes and are not cleaning them up. (*See:* Action, Radical Responsibility)

PARENT – (*See:* Adult)

PERSECUTOR – The Persecutor is an Archetypal Shadow World character in a low drama who unconsciously uses the energy of anger to serve your Gremlin. The Persecutor takes the position of "I am okay, you are not okay," and uses that as justification for trying to get rid of or exclude the other person. (*See:* Gremlin, Low Drama, *Map of Possibility*)

PERSONALITY – (*See:* Box)

PHYSICAL CENTER – Your Physical Center is the center of your physical body, located halfway between your hipbones, and halfway back through your abdomen. Your Physical Center has various names in various traditions (*dan-tien, hara,* etc.) and is often a key consideration in martial arts training. Since Possibility Management is a form with some similarities to the martial arts, it is no surprise that the Physical Center plays a role in the studies of a Possibility Manager. (*See:* Being Centered, Four Bodies)

PIRATE –Rules are assumed to dictate where you can go and where you cannot go, who you can be and who you cannot be, what you must do and what you can never do. Rules of thinking, speaking, being and acting stand between you and going nonlinear. In order to go nonlinear, the dominance of rules must somehow be circumvented. There is a character for whom rules hold no concern. This character is the Pirate. The capital "P" differentiates an extraordinary, radically responsible Pirate who breaks the rules in order to *give* more, from an ordinary irresponsible pirate who breaks the rules in order to *take* more. A responsible Pirate grants themselves permission to grant themselves permission. If a Pirate appears to be following the rules, it is mere coincidence. (*See:* Archetype, Dangerous Question, Nonlinear, Pirate Agreement, Possibility Manager, Radical Responsibility)

PIRATE AGREEMENT – "High level fun" is when you commit to producing a result before you know how. If you start playing high level fun, you eventually realize that you cannot do it alone. However, the specific kind of help you need to produce results before you know how is help that cannot be manipulated or thwarted by anything so mundane as circumstances. Your commitment is to produce the result *no matter what*. To succeed, you can call on a responsible Pirate to make a Pirate Agreement with you. The agreement is to do everything possible to help produce the result. They have permission to do anything it takes to get you to succeed. It has been reported that Pirates who make Pirate Agreements can be heard to walk away singing, "Yo Ho! Yo Ho! A Pirate's life fer me!" (*See:* Dangerous Questions, High Drama, Pirate)

POSITION – A Position is an arbitrary belief taken to be true and subsequently defended against all feedback to the contrary. Beliefs have no relationship to reality. The Position that your ideas are right and another person's ideas are wrong automatically and inevitably leads to war. Positionality is characteristic of Boxes still tied to using their adolescent defensive orientation. (*See:* Being Nothing, Being Wrong, Belief, Box Mechanics, Defensive Context, Do-Overs, Expansive Context, Feedback)

POSSIBILITY – A measurable quality of any conversation, space, organization or gameworld. The amount of Possibility is equal to the present number of real options available to choose from. In general, 99 percent of the Possibilities that are available right now are invisible to you. This is because the Box occludes Possibilities out of its habitually defensive orientation. Possibility is a Bright Principle. Possibility is one of the most valuable things in the universe. For example, any product or service that you buy, you do not buy for the product or service itself, but rather for the Possibility that this product or service creates for you. (*See:* Creating Possibility, Navigating Space, Principle, Space)

POSSIBILITY LISTENING (LISTENING AS A SPACE) – Possibility Listening is one of the four kinds of listening distinguished in Possibility Management. In Possibility Listening you use your "clicker" to declare yourself as being a space into which the other person can speak. By comparison, adult responsible listening has the purpose of understanding what is being said. You must be there to understand, and you might ask questions, interrupt for clarifications and demand distinctions that can easily interrupt the flow of the speaker's thoughts and feelings. In Possibility Listening, there is no such requirement of understanding. Instead, your attention as the listener serves as an empty workbench upon which the speaker can work things out, uninterrupted. If you do not limit yourself to trying to understand what you hear, then you can hear anything. Being the space into which the other person can say anything is an astonishingly powerful tool, and should be used like you would use any powerful tool, appropriately and as needed. (*See:* Being A Space, Declaring)

POSSIBILITY MANAGEMENT – Possibility Management is the open code gameworld entered by taking radical responsibility for creating the possibility of possibility. The gameworld of Possibility Management was initialized in 1974 by Clinton Callahan and has been continuously developed, documented and delivered in various training environments since then. In 1995, Western civilization broke the evolution barrier, and continues to exceed the naturally allowed speed of cultural evolution. Present organizations use last millennium's designs, and can be hindered by not being fluid enough to function effectively in the new millennium's conditions. Possibility Management proposes new organizational forms and new meeting technologies. In the near future, the job of Possibility Manager will appear on company "org charts" as a change agent with radical responsibility for liberating and applying a greater proportion of an organization's human intellectual capital. If it is your calling to provide new thoughtware for leaders or managers through coaching, consulting or training, consider getting yourself certified as a Possibility Trainer. (*See:* Core Skills, Gameworld, Meeting Technology, Possibility, Possibility Trainer, Radical Responsibility, Thoughtware)

POSSIBILITY MANAGER – An individual trained and certified in applying the thoughtware of Possibility Management. Possibility Managers serve individuals and organizations by converting obstacles, conflicts and diversity into opportunities, solutions and results. On the *Map of Possibility*, a Possibility Manager is the Archetypal Bright World King or Queen character serving Bright Principles to create high drama. (*See:* Archetype, *Map of Possibility*, Possibility Management, Principles, Thoughtware)

POSSIBILITY SPEAKING (SPEAKING AS A SPACE) – If you do not know what you are supposed to say, then you can say anything. In Possibility Speaking, what speaks is the destiny Principles that you serve and the Archetypes you have stellated. When you are being the space through which your destiny Principles can do their work, the usual Box-empowered "you" is not there. If the Box is not there filling up the space with its usual concerns and opinions, then what can be spoken serves something greater than your Box. The secret to Possibility Speaking is to first make contact and commit to serving the authentic necessity of the individual or group you are speaking to. Commit before you know how, then click your "clicker" to vanish yourself into a space, and speak before you know what you are going to say. Let your commitment lead you, and keep speaking into the necessity. (*See:* Archetypes, Clicker, Destiny, Discovery Speaking, Responsible Principles, Space, Stellating)

POSSIBILITY STONE – An actual pebble kept on your person as a reminding factor of the unlimited Possibilities available when you shift identity into being a Possibility Manager. The Possibility Stone can be used for developing muscles of attention by repeatedly placing your attention on the Possibility Stone and then taking your attention away again. You can also use your Possibility Stone for locating "now." When you touch your stone, "now" occurs in that moment when you experience the stone-touching sensation. (*See:* Attention, Now, Reminding Factor, Shift, Tool Belt)

POSSIBILITY TEAM – A new meeting technology from Possibility Management. Possibility Teams use rapid learning, Winning Happening and possibility speaking to create possibility for individuals and the organization. Possibility Teams regard mistakes as intellectual property. (*See:* Meeting Technology, Possibility Speaking, Rapid Learning, Winning Happening)

POSSIBILITY TRAINER – Participants of a training can only go as far as the Trainer can go. This means that the Trainer needs to go first. A Possibility Trainer is an individual trained and certified to train others to apply the thoughtware of Possibility Management. There is a big difference between educators and Trainers.

- Educators provide explanations and information in classes where people learn how to do what is already known. Education provides new knowledge.
- Trainers provide possibilities in trainings where people gain abilities to innovate ways to do what is not yet known. Training provides new behavior.
- Educators put information into your Box. Trainers help you redesign your Box. Educators provide what to think *about*. Trainers provide what to think *with*.

A Possibility Trainer's job requires an enhanced creator Archetype connected directly to the source of possibility. Through practice, a Possibility Trainer learns to take reality apart and put it back together again with a new shape, so that it provides the required new possibilities. A Possibility Trainer takes radical responsibility and navigates space to the liquid state so that individuals or organizations can learn in all four bodies, not just in the mind. What a Possibility Trainer must learn is beyond what is provided by Western culture. This is the necessity that created Callahan

Academy. (*See:* Creator, Four Bodies, High Drama, Liquid State, Navigate Space, Possibility Manager, Practice, Radical Responsibility, Starmaker, Thoughtware)

POSSIBILITY WAND – The Possibility Wand is a tool clipped to your Possibility Manager tool belt. The Possibility Wand is a sentence, specifically the declaration that, "Something completely different from this is possible right now." The most bewildering aspect of using your Possibility Wand is simply remembering, in the moment when you need it, that you have it. (*See:* Declaration, Possibility Manager, Reminding Factor, Tool Belt)

PRACTICE – Practice is intentionally enacting behaviors producing a quality of stress that builds matrix. Practice is often orthogonal to what is happening in a space, and can therefore require the conscious use of Gremlin to break free of the embarrassment of Practicing when others in the space are not Practicing. Extraordinary human relationship and Archetypal Relationship only arise when supported by a certain level of Practice. You can gradually build for yourself a life of Practice. The experience of Practice, for example when you first try Adult responsible communication with completion loops, may at first feel unreal, unnatural or inauthentic. This sensation of strangeness can arise because when you first start consciously Practicing you are not hooked. The sense that your action is unreal is only the unfamiliar gap in space that comes with the non-identification characteristic of conscious theater. The gap allows you to move in any direction in any moment for no reason. Practice only happens consciously. Consciousness creates freedom. (*See:* Conscious Theater, Gap, Gremlin, Identification, Inner Navigating, Matrix, Orthogonal,)

PRINCIPLE – A Principle is an energetic force of nature (to borrow a phrase from George Bernard Shaw). Bright Principles are facets of responsibility, such as respect, clarity, possibility, or Winning Happening. Shadow Principles are facets of irresponsibility, such as revenge, good / bad, deception, or I win / you lose. When you become the space through which the Bright Principles that you serve can do their work, you are used by something greater than your Box and *you* become a Force of Nature. When serving Bright Principles, you become Archetypal Man or Woman as your destiny in action. When serving Shadow Principles, you become Gremlin as your hidden purpose in action. Buckminster Fuller spoke about Principles like this: "There are no solids. There are no things. There are only interfering and noninterfering patterns operative in pure principle, and principles are eternal. Principles never contradict principles ... The synergetic integral of the totality of principles is God, whose sum-total behavior in pure principle is beyond our comprehension and is utterly mysterious to us, because as humans – in pure principle – we do not and never will know all the principles." (Fuller, R. Buckminster. *Critical Path.* New York: St. Martin's Press, 1981, 158-159.) (*See:* Archetype, Bright Principle, Destiny, Force of Nature, Hidden Purpose, *Map of Possibility,* Shadow Principle)

PROBLEM – On the *Map of Possibility* there is actually no such thing as a Problem. Therefore, any time there appears to be a Problem, either from your perspective or from someone else's perspective, the Problem is an act of conscious or unconscious theater. You can try the experiment of regarding any Problem as an indicator that signals the start of the next gameworld – often the invitation to deeper intimacy. This is the basis of the Possibility Management meeting technology named "The Problem Is the Solution." (*See:* Conscious Theater, Low Drama, Meeting Technology, Victim)

PROJECTION – An extremely effective Box defense strategy. The Box takes any part of itself that it does not accept and transfers that quality to other people, whom we can then outwardly ridicule. (*See:* Box, Box Mechanics)

PSYCHOLOGY – Another name for Box. All of Psychology is a virtual reality. (*See:* Box, Mind, Thoughtware)

PURPOSE – Purpose is the fundamental motivator in human beings. Every action we take has a Purpose. We are either conscious or unconscious of the Purpose of our action. Our consciousness or unconsciousness places our action on either the responsible or irresponsible side of the *Map of Possibility* and determines the quality of the results that we create. We can determine the true

Purpose of our action or inaction by looking at the results. We may be fooling ourselves about our Purpose, but the results never lie. (*See:* Action, *Map of Possibility,* Navigating Space, Result)

QUEEN – (*See:* Adult, Archetype)

RADICAL RESPONSIBILITY – Ordinary responsibility has a bad reputation in Western civilization. The message is that responsibility is a burden. Responsibility makes you guilty. If you are responsible, then you are the one to be blamed or punished. To differentiate the Responsibility of high drama from ordinary responsibility, we introduce the term Radical Responsibility. Radical Responsibility is the unreasonable declaration that you are the cause of everything, and that you take full Responsibility for everything that is and everything that happens, even though you cannot control it – like in juggling, for example, where you have only two hands but you are responsible for three balls, even though you often cannot control one of them. Radical Responsibility is taking Responsibility even for the level of Responsibility you are taking. If you take Radical Responsibility then you are suddenly far beyond the influence of circumstances, excuses, reason, logic or psychology. Everything that happens is neutral, without story, without meaning. There is no such thing as a problem. It is impossible to be a victim of a situation because you created the situation exactly like it is. Irresponsibility is a complete illusion. Radical Responsibility is the practical manifestation of Archetypal Love. (*See:* Archetype, Love, *Map of Possibility,* Unreasonable)

RAPID LEARNING – Rapid Learning is a three-step model of short, cycle-time evolution that proves to be a simple and useful model for improving relationship. Rapid Learning begins with *Go!* Try something first, before you try to figure it all out in advance. What you can trust about the world is that it will give you feedback about whatever you do or do not do. There are only two kinds of feedback that you can get: *Go!* or *Beep! Go!* tells you to keep *Go!*ing. *Beep!* tells you to shift your behavior according to your goal, and then *Go!* again. These are the three steps of Rapid Learning. *Go!* Feedback. Shift. Then *Go!* again. Rapid Learning is a simple powerful thought-map, useful for making sense of what happens in a rapidly evolving environment like relationship. (*See:* Coaching, Feedback, High Drama, Meeting Technology, Shift, Swamp, Thought-Map)

REAL QUESTION – Questions can come from any of the four bodies. We are most familiar with reasonable questions or curiosity questions that come from the intellectual body. Answers to intellectual questions further expand your already expanded intellect. A Real Question comes from the heart of the emotional body or the soul of the energetic body and is often unreasonable. One who asks a Real Question puts themselves at risk of getting an answer. Gaining an intellectual answer to a Real Question destroys the Box-expanding potential of the Real Question, because the mind grabs hold of the answer and thinks it *has* something. But the Box tricks the mind into forgetting the answer in the next moment. A more intelligent and more uncomfortable use of Real Questions is to let them remain unanswered. The discomfort, over time, builds matrix, so *you* become the answer. (*See:* Asking, Box, Dangerous Question, Discovery Speaking, Four Bodies, Matrix, Unreasonable)

REALITY – Objective Reality is "What is, as it is, here and now, without judgment," in the words of Swami Prajnanpad and Arnaud Desjardins; or, "Just this," one of the core teachings of Lee Lozowick. Subjective Reality is what is seen through the story that is agreed upon to establish the rules in any particular gameworld. Realities can be more or less rigid. The true nature of the universe is fluid and groundless. Realities become rigid when people take the position (believe) that the stories of their gameworld are true and not just stories. Rigid Realities tend to generate war. Fluid realities tend to generate possibility. (*See:* Belief, Gameworld, Memetic Virus, Painting Doorways, Reinventing Reality, Story)

REINVENTING REALITY – The stories that produce a reality can be rewritten, that is, restructured into new forms so as to contain different sets of possibilities. With regard to reality, function follows form. That is, when a reality has a new form it has a new functionality. You can Reinvent Reality such that your choices and actions serve your destiny. (*See:* Action, Choosing, Is-Glue, Is-Glue Dissolver, Liquid State)

RELATIONSHIP – Three distinctions determine the experiential quality of your Relationship: ordinary human, extraordinary human, and Archetypal. In ordinary human Relationship you avoid responsibility, there is a scarcity of love, and you use your partner to create low drama. In extraordinary human Relationship you take adult responsibility and create high drama as a source of extraordinary human Love. In Archetypal Relationship you take radical responsibility for Relationship. Then there is no such "thing" as a Relationship. What exists is a potential that can be lived into and enlivened, any way you want; a space that can be navigated; a possibility that always does not yet exist, so therefore cannot be already known. Relationship is then nothing, until you produce *what it is* through ongoing acts of nonlinear creation. Archetypal Relationship thrives when you commit to what the other person is committed to and communicate about what arises in relationship. Immediate communication creates intimacy. An easy gauge of what space you are navigating your Relationship into is to detect your purpose. Either you are seeking to be right, or you are seeking to be in Relationship. (*See:* Experiential Reality, Laboratory, Love, Navigating Space, Nonlinear)

REMINDING FACTOR – A Reminding Factor is a self-arranged condition that indicates a way out of the constraints of a particular space. Without Reminding Factors, the Box's defensive filtering easily blocks you from remembering that "Something completely different from this is always possible right now." You can develop the knack of arranging Reminding Factors to keep one foot outside of a space. Then, no matter what the circumstances are, "Possibility" is always a possibility. Reminding Factors must be somehow disturbing or uncomfortable in order to function, and they can vary wildly. For example, the practice of behaving in some way contrary to any of the Box's habits creates a Reminding Factor (e.g., not smiling or cursing when you make an error in sports, or tying your shoes with the bow pointing another way). You will find it necessary to persistently develop new Reminding Factors because the Box's propensity for self-induced sleep can disempower the wake-up effect of a Reminding Factor in a remarkably short time. (*See:* Matrix, Possibility Wand, Practice, Radical Responsibility, Space)

RESCUER – The Rescuer is a Shadow World Archetypal character who unconsciously uses the energy of fear to serve your Gremlin in low drama. The Rescuer takes the position of "I am okay, you are not okay," and uses that as justification for doing something for someone else because you feel afraid that they cannot adequately do it for themselves. (*See:* Gremlin, Low Drama, *Map of Possibility*)

RESPONSIBILITY – Responsibility is consciousness in action. We cannot choose our level of consciousness. If we could choose our level of consciousness, we could simply stop having low drama; we could stop having wars; we could stop degrading our environment. Since we cannot choose our level of consciousness, we also cannot choose our level of Responsibility. Responsibility increases through building the thing upon which consciousness can grow. That thing is matrix. (*See:* Action, Low Drama, Matrix, Parallel Culture, Radical Responsibility)

RESPONSIBLE PRINCIPLES – (*See:* Bright Principles, *Map of Possibility*)

RESPONSIBLE STORY – A Responsible Story is high drama consciously generated as an arena for serving Bright Principles. Responsible Stories are neither better nor worse than victim stories; they simply give you more power. (*See:* Conscious Theater, Story, Victim Story)

RESULT – A Result is the outcome of an action. Examining the Results shows whether an action served responsible purposes or irresponsible purposes. Results locate your action on the *Map of Possibility* as either low drama or high drama. Whatever your intentions, the Results never lie. (*See:* Action, Irresponsibility, *Map of Possibility*, Radical Responsibility, and the example given in entry for Thought-Map)

RITE OF PASSAGE – (*See:* Stellating Archetypes)

SELF-SITTING – Self-Sitting is a contemplative form of practice done in stillness and silence, usually with the eyes closed, at the same time and the same place for the same length of time each day. A regular practice of Self-Sitting builds matrix and is ideal for developing attention, inner navigation and being. (*See:* Attention, Being Center, Inner Navigating, Matrix, Practice, Together-Sitting)

SHADOW PRINCIPLE – Shadow Principles are an Archetypal force of nature. The overriding Shadow Principle is irresponsibility or unconsciousness. Irresponsibility is unconsciousness in action. Unconsciousness prisms into a rainbow of Shadow Principles including revenge, hatred, survival, betrayal, being betrayed, superiority, manipulation, blame, deception, exclusion, disempowerment, good / bad, arrogance, disrespect, scarcity, competition, being right, self pity, greed, envy, jealousy, sneaking, resentment, making wrong, withholding, domination, contamination, separation, right / wrong, and so on. Gremlin thrives in the service of Shadow Principles. (*See:* Bright Principle, Gremlin, *Map of Possibility*, Principle)

SHADOW WORLD (UNDERWORLD) – The domain of actions and gameworlds dedicated to serving Shadow Principles. (*See:* Gremlin, Low Drama, *Map of Possibility*, Shadow Principle)

SHIFT – *Shift* is step three in the rapid learning process. *Shift* means to briefly enter the liquid state so that your internal reference points ("assemblage points" per Carlos Castaneda's writings about the teachings of Don Juan Matus) can reorganize themselves. The new association of reference points gives your Box new functionality because your actions come from a redrawn thought-map. Since your set of possible actions is defined by the character in yourself with which you are presently identified, by Shifting identity you Shift what is possible for you. A useful identity to Shift into is the Possibility Manager. The clicker makes Shifting clear and quick. (*See:* Box Mechanics, Clicker, Coaching, Feedback, Identification, Liquid State, Rapid Learning, Reinventing Reality, Story, Thought-Map)

SORCERESS – (*See:* Creator)

SOUL – (We tread on protected territory attempting to define the term "Soul" here. But, hey, this is Possibility Management! Let us give it a try! The worst thing that can happen is we get a *Beep*.) A human being has four bodies: a physical body with organs that have sensations, an intellectual body with a mind that has thoughts, an emotional body with a heart that has feelings, and an energetic body with a Soul that has presence or being. The Soul is the being center of your energetic body. The Soul is born to fulfill a destiny, is nurtured through intimacy, and is capable of being inspired. Your Soul starts out about the size of a grapefruit. Your Soul can grow when your matrix grows, through certain kinds of stresses, nutrients, shocks, experiences, radiations, influences, efforts, repetitions, and clarity about how things work. In especially safe environments, Soul can let itself be known. The willingness to let one's Soul be known builds authentic community in organizations. (For more on this see the books *Open Space Technology* by Harrison Owen and *The Different Drum* by M. Scott Peck). (*See:* Box, Four Bodies, Matrix)

SPACE – There are two kinds of Space: physical Space as defined by solid walls, ceilings and floors, and energetic Space that comes into existence through declaration. Energetic Space can change size, location and purpose according to your conscious intention. You can learn to declare energetic Space as a skill. Declared energetic Space is a volume of attention in which you take responsibility for responsibility. When a Space is declared and owned, that Space can then be navigated to serve true purposes. (*See:* Declaring, Holding Space, Navigating Space, Possibility Trainer, True Purpose)

SPACE HOLDING – (*See:* Holding Space)

SPEAKING AS A SPACE – (*See:* Possibility Speaking)

SPRINGSCREEN – A Possibility Management tool that allows you to avoid being hooked. The Springscreen is useful when you encounter a scene that would normally upset you, offend you, frighten you, take your center, knock you off balance, over stimulate you (for example with rich food, easy money, or casual sex), or in some way hook you into low drama. To use the Springscreen, first notice that the scene before you appears on a white screen. This screen has a rubber loop hanging from its bottom. If you simply unhook the rubber band from the floor the entire screen rolls up like a movie projection screen and instantly vanishes. It is a Springscreen! All that remains is the next perfectly blank white Springscreen. If the same scene starts to replay itself on your new Screen, simply unhook that one and it zips away too! You have an unlimited number of Springscreens! (Possibility Manager Johann Göbel invented the Springscreen in 2003.) (*See:* Disk of Nothing, Hooked, Unhookable)

STANDARD HUMAN INTELLIGENCE THOUGHTWARE – The way you think is not random. You think in repeated patterns determined by how you perceive the relationships between things as described by your Thoughtware and thought-maps. You derived your present set of Thoughtware largely from your parents before you went to school. Where did your parents get their Thoughtware? From their parents. Where did they get their Thoughtware? From their parents, and so on. Most people adopt their birth culture's Standard Human Intelligence Thoughtware, the same set of memes that has been passed down from generation to generation for thousands of years. You are probably using some very old Thoughtware. Newer versions of Thoughtware exist. You have the option of upgrading your Thoughtware whenever you want to. Such upgrading happens in trainings. Trainings differ from classes in that a class gives you new information to think about, whereas a training gives you new Thoughtware and thought-maps to think with. (*See:* Belief, Expand the Box, Marshmallow Zone, Meme, Possibility Trainer, Thought-Map, Thoughtware)

STAR – In astronomy, a star is at the center of a solar system. In Possibility Management, a Star is at the center of a gameworld. You may think that a Star has all the glory and sits in the most important position, but this is not true. Stars need planets. A Star without planets is a lone wolf. It is equally true that planets need Stars. A planet without a Star is interstellar debris. Coming together, planets and stars form something greater than each of them individually. Together they form a planetary system, an organization, a gameworld. You do not join an organization to solve the problem of loneliness. In fact, coming together in an organization is not intended to solve any problems at all. Coming together into an organization creates a gameworld that is the possibility that Bright Principles can do their work in the world. (*See:* Center, Organization, Stellate)

STARMAKER – Certain individuals who stellate their Archetypes serve destiny Principles such as integrity, clarity, possibility, transformation and Love. A person serving this particular set of Bright Principles loves to liberate the vast and awesome potential of others. In Possibility Management, the job of making other stars is called Starmaker. Starmaker professions include teacher, trainer, coach, consultant, healer, mediator, guide, manager, leader, doctor, nurse, therapist and so on. But where do Starmakers come from? Think about it: If we are to somehow renew our public education system, so it provides tools and techniques needed to live well in a rapidly evolving closed-ecology environment, we cannot start by teaching students. *Where would we get the teachers?* The answer is that we have to *create* the teachers first! What is the way toward making new teachers? Answer: We need men and women capable of training trainers, healing healers, and teaching teachers. We need people who can make Starmakers. This is the aim of Possibility Management, to make Starmakers so they can make other Starmakers. (*See:* Destiny, Possibility Trainer, Star, Stellating Archetypes)

STELLATE – To Stellate is to change from a planet into a star. A planet absorbs more energy than it radiates. A star radiates more energy than it absorbs. Human beings are designed to live as stars: creating, designing, exploring, producing, generating, and so on. Standard human intelligence thoughtware has us living as planets: consuming, imitating, criticizing, giving our center away, being adaptive, feeding off of the responsibility of authority figures, and so on. You can learn and practice with upgraded thoughtware to possess your center, to take responsibility for responsibility, and to become the source of resources. Stellating would naturally occur during a rite of passage that you are ripe for at about fifteen years of age, but this maturation process is not provided by ordinary Western culture. (*See:* Being Centered, Starmaker, Thoughtware)

STELLATING ARCHETYPES – Stellating Archetypes means initializing Archetypes, turning them on. Each of the four feelings is associated with a Bright World Archetype and a Shadow World Archetype (e.g., anger with both the doer and the persecutor, sadness with both the communicator and the victim, fear with both the creator and the rescuer, joy with both the Adult King / Queen and the Gremlin). Shadow World Archetypes are generally already activated through the use of standard human intelligence thoughtware. Bright World Archetypes can only be turned on consciously when they are mature and ready to be activated at about fifteen years of age. The process of Stellating Bright World Archetypes requires that you experience and express 100-percent maximum of each of the four feelings, intentionally, until you discover that although the energy of the feelings is big, you are bigger. Then, for the rest of your life, the resources of the Archetypes are available for you to use. (*See:* Archetype, Center, Feeling, Stellate)

STORY – As described in the *Map of Possibility*, everything that exists and everything that happens is without meaning and completely neutral. But, you are a human being. You do not leave things that way. Human beings are always creating. You create by making Stories about what exists and what happens. Stories are the meanings you add, your interpretations, how you see things, your assumptions, projections, judgments, criticisms, opinions, implications, conclusions, expectations, and so on. Your Stories make the world look acceptable to your Box. You package Stories in specific tones of voice and emotional moods in order to slant things, twist things, add spin, hook people, and make things important or invisible, so that your position is justified and your Box is proved right. If you can create your Box's usual Stories, then your Box feels safe and tells you that you will survive. It is amazing that we can believe our own Stories even though we just make them up out of nothing using is-glue. The Box has an uncanny ability to pop into a gameworld created by a Story and act as if the gameworld were reality. Much of your Story making is unconscious and thus serves Shadow Principles. With practice, you can learn to use Story making to create high drama and serve conscious purposes. (*See:* Box, Experiment, Gameworld, Is-Glue, *Map of Possibility*, Unhookable)

SWAMP – If it is not okay for you to receive feedback, then, in the map of rapid learning, you go into the Swamp. The world is a giant feedback generator. Receiving direct, honest, confrontive feedback can challenge the reality of your Box.

Having your Box challenged is one of the most disturbing experiences you could possibly have. When you are more committed to defending your Box than you are to expanding your Box, you must somehow avoid feedback. One very clever way to distract yourself from "negative" feedback is to enter the Swamp. You are in the Swamp when you hear voices in your head such as, "I'm not good enough, I'm a failure, I will never make it anyway, nobody loves me, nobody listens to me, I can't do it, I'm too stupid, I'm too weak," and so on. After awhile, you might even get to turn your story making toward the ones who gave you the feedback, "What do they know about me anyway? Who are they to be giving me feedback? Look at their life! They are stupid! They are a failure," and so on. The energetic quagmire of having these voices in your mind is the Swamp. The voices provide your "x on the map" to clarify that you are in the Swamp. Recognizing that you are in the Swamp gives you a choice. Clarity gives you power – the power to choose. You can continue to fester and decay in the Swamp, or you choose to get out. To get out, all you have to do is say to yourself, "Ah! I have these voices in my head! I must be in the Swamp! I must have received some feedback that was not okay with my Box." If you go to the person who gave you the feedback and say, "Thanks for the feedback," this immediately takes you out of the Swamp and puts you back into rapid learning. Then you can use the feedback to guide you about what to shift to get better results when you try again. (*See:* Box, Feedback, Rapid Learning, Voice Blaster)

SWORD OF CLARITY – The Sword is the metaphorical tool of the Archetypal doer (Warrior/Warrioress). It is the doer who establishes and cares for a relationship with Archetypal anger, such that anger informs his actions and enables him to move with precision and without hesitation. The Sword of Clarity is used to make distinctions, make decisions, create clarity, and when necessary, make boundaries. As the Archetypal doer, you learn to never put away your Sword, not even when you go to bed. This makes you potent, ever alert, attentive, hot to ask dangerous questions, and therefore useful for serving the Archetypal Man / King and Archetypal Woman / Queen. (*See:* Archetype, Attention, Dangerous Questions, Stellating Archetypes, Tool Belt, Victim Story)

TECHNOPENURIAPHOBIA (TPP) – Technopenuriaphobia is the fear of the lack of technology. Technopenuriaphobia is a side effect of the patriarchal disregard for the fact that we live on a closed ecology planet. Children of modern culture are born halfway up a long ladder of technology. For such a child, water comes from a faucet. Light comes when you flick a switch. Food comes from the refrigerator or grocery store. Cars or trains take us anywhere we want to go in total comfort. And money comes from cash machines. Behind a life of comfort is the subtle but pervasive terror that our thin veil of technology could suddenly fail. Since we do not know how to live on planet Earth without our technological interface, failure of our technology certifies our death. The cure for Technopenuriaphobia is repeated exposure to gradually decreased levels of technology, until at last we regain the ability to live on Earth with a minimum of technology. (*See:* Feelings)

THEATER – (*See:* Conscious Theater)

THOUGHT-MAP – A Thought-Map is an energetic diagram showing the relationship and the flow of power between factors. You can understand the importance of Thought-Maps when you consider that very practical possibilities were created when people changed their Thought-Maps about the earth from seeing it as a disk to seeing it as a ball. We acquired new possibilities not because the earth itself changed, but only because our Thought-Map of the earth changed. We do not relate to the world as it is. We relate to the world through our Thought-Maps of the world. Get a new Thought-Map and you get a new world! The value of diagramming your Thought-Maps onto paper is that you can more objectively examine dynamic relationships between you, people, objects and energies in your life, and then consider additional Possibilities.

For example, there is a Thought-Map that shows the relationship between new Thought-Maps and new results. It is called the *Map of Changed Results.* In the *Map of Changed Results* (*see* text page 202) you can see that new results come from making new actions. (It would be a form of insanity to think that you could get new results by continuing your same actions!) New actions are produced when you make new decisions to act. Making new decisions is based on having new options to choose from. And new options come from

new Thought-Maps. Instead of working on the level of trying to change your habitual actions, you can go directly to the level of your Thought-Maps. Making a small change in your Thought-Maps can produce a significant change in your results. (*See:* Action, Meme, Possibility, Result, Thoughtware)

THOUGHTWARE – Thoughtware is the specific formulation of memes used by a mind to create the meaning of perceptions and the decisions for actions. No matter how it may look or feel to a user, all Thoughtware is arbitrary fiction. (*See:* Box, Meme, Parallel Culture, Possibility Management)

TOGETHER-SITTING – Together-sitting is a contemplative form of practice done in stillness and silence as a dyad. The eyes are open and you are gazing into the eyes of your partner, exploring and deepening contact. A regular practice of Together-Sitting builds matrix and is ideal for developing inner navigation and being. (*See:* Being Center, Contact, Countenance, Inner Navigating, Matrix, Practice, Relationship, Self-Sitting)

TONIC GOLD™ – This substance is a true alchemical elixir with the same matrix building properties as this book and Expand the Box trainings. Tonic Gold is a catalyst that moves through your energetic blocks and harmonizes, coordinates and balances your four bodies, promoting evolution. Tonic Gold is imbued with its own intelligence; it locates and transforms irresponsible tendencies, redirecting them to strengthen the body's own innate healing capacity. Tonic Gold is integrative and supports other healing and transformational processes. Tonic Gold is handcrafted exclusively in limited quantities in India, in the modern laboratory of a European man who is one of the world's master alchemists. Tonic Gold is unequalled in quality and requires one year to prepare. In USA call +1 888-886-6427. In Hong Kong call +852 (0)2512 0347 or email: reflection@pacific.net.hk. In Europe call +49 (0)89-74949473. (*See:* Expand the Box, Experiment, Matrix)

TOOL BELT – In the same moment in which you shift identity to become a Possibility Manager, you also buckle on your Possibility Manager Tool Belt. The Tool Belt contains a full set of energetic tools for use in managing what is possible. (*See:* Bag of Things, Clicker, Disk of Nothing, Is-Glue, Is-Glue

Dissolver, Painting Doorways, Possibility Wand, Sword of Clarity, Voice Blaster)

TRUE PURPOSE (CONSCIOUS PURPOSE, DESTINY) – The three, four or five Bright Principles that form the intention and direction of your Destiny is your True Purpose. Your life is your True Purpose in action when you are the space through which your Bright Principles can do their work in the world. (*See:* Destiny, Distilling Destiny Process, Hidden Purpose, High Drama, *Map of Possibility*)

UNCONSCIOUS PURPOSE – Unconscious Purpose is another term for hidden purpose. An Unconscious Purpose serves Shadow Principles. Serving Shadow Principles is referred to as unconscious behavior, because if you were conscious of the pain you caused to other people and yourself you could not enact it. (*See:* Gremlin, Hidden Purpose, *Map of* Possibility, True Purpose)

UNDERWORLD – (*See:* Shadow World)

UNHOOKABLE – The first and most crucial of the seven core skills of Possibility Management is staying Unhookable. Staying Unhookable is an art form. Humanity is so easily hooked that if you become Unhookable you almost seem inhuman. The art is to remain Unhookable and still be human. Unhookable does not mean unfeeling, isolated, shut down or numb. On the contrary, Unhookable means that you perceive the hooks with great sensitivity and precision, and, while still being compassionate, you shift slightly out of context of the hooks. Then, the hooks have no chance to set into your psychological flesh and cause a reaction. The problem is that you will always have a Box. And, if you have a Box, then there will always be something there to hook into. Many of the tools and techniques from Possibility Management aim at keeping you Unhookable, because if you get hooked you forget that you have extraordinary and Archetypal possibilities, and therefore you forget to access them. (*See:* Center, Core Skills, Disk of Nothing, Hooked, Springscreen)

UNREASONABLE – The Box defends itself through welding every choice that you make to an acceptable reason. You have been trained to be reasonable. Without a good reason you cannot represent your choices and actions as being sane. If you have

a good reason, you can get away with (almost) any irresponsibility. The problem with making a choice for a reason is that the reason then has the responsibility and therefore the power in that choice, not you. In order to go nonlinear, you need more freedom than is allowed by being reasonable. It is possible to do the internal surgery of separating choices from reasons. Then, when you make a choice, you no longer avoid radical responsibility with reasons, and you gain access to every possible option. You have become Unreasonable. (*See:* Choosing, Nonlinear, Radical Responsibility, Real Question)

UPPERWORLD – (*See:* Bright World)

VERBAL REALITY – There are various ways to frame-up a perspective of the world. Each way creates its own style of reality. Verbal Reality assumes that what is real is what can be named, described, or thought about in words. In Verbal Reality the words lead – your experience is limited to your vocabulary. Ever since childhood, we have been hammered into Verbal Reality. Although Verbal Reality is a cornerstone of modern rationalism, it forms a poor basis for relationship because relationship is ongoing nonlinear creation. In order to appreciate the qualities of your experience, you can unbind your experience from the limits of your vocabulary and enter experiential reality. (*See:* Creating Possibility, Experiential Reality, Four Bodies, Mind, Nonlinear)

VICTIM – The Victim is an Archetypal Shadow World character who unconsciously uses the energy of sadness to create low drama in the service of your Gremlin. The Victim takes the position of "I am not okay, you are okay," and uses that as justification to support self-pity, being betrayed, being resentful, blaming persecutors, or manipulating rescuers. A skilled Victim can make a persecutor or rescuer out of anyone, and is therefore the most powerful character in a low drama. From the Archetypal perspective, it is impossible to be a Victim, because irresponsibility is an illusion. (*See:* Gremlin, Low Drama, *Map of Possibility*)

VICTIM STORY – A Victim Story is one of the three stories played out in a low drama. At the core of every Victim Story is the false assumption "I am not okay." Your Gremlin part finds evidence to create the Victim Story as a reason to justify irresponsible actions that serve Shadow Principles. For example, once you have created a good enough Victim Story, you imagine that you have the right to take revenge! When Adult responsible man or woman detects a Victim Story (their own or someone else's), they can use their sword to make distinctions that produce a different perspective, for example, that a Victim Story can be an invitation to deeper relationship. (*See:* Choosing, Gremlin, Low Drama Detector, Relationship, Story, Sword, Victim)

VOICE BLASTER – A Possibility Management tool holstered in your tool belt that allows you to obliterate mental voices speaking irrelevancies into your head. Mental voices come from someone else or out of your past. As a way of surviving, your Box made hearing such voices normal. When the familiar messages no longer come from outside, your Box maintains its "normal" by generating the voices itself. Voices can include both praise and blame about you or others, such as, "I'm not good enough. I am the best. You are a failure. You are cool. I am an idiot. You won't like me," etc. Neither praise nor blame is effective communication because both of them are forms of manipulative conditioning. Every person is born with a Voice Blaster. If you never used your Voice Blaster before, that may only be because no one told you it was there. Reach down and pull it out of its holster. It looks like holding an imaginary pistol in your hand. The Voice Blaster has an infinite number of bullets and never misses. Voices flutter about outside of your head like bats. You can vanish them with your Blaster. When the Blaster fires it makes a sound, "Bang!" For particularly pernicious voices some people prefer a machine-gun or bazooka-style Voice Blaster. (*See:* Low Drama, Rapid Learning, Swamp, Tool Belt)

WARRIOR / WARRIORESS – (*See:* Archetype, Doer)

WINNING HAPPENING – Winning Happening is a Bright Principle and also a characteristic of high drama. In contrast to Winning Happening, standard human intelligence thoughtware has you create gameworlds using "I win, you lose." In "I win, you lose," participants compete against each other for what appear to be limited resources. There is usually one winner and many losers. The assumption is, "If I do not win, I die," or "If you win, I die," neither of which is generally true. The "I win, you lose" game is a survival game. An upgrade was invented in the 1960s called, "I win, you win," sometimes abbreviated as "win-win." A potential defect of "I win, you win" is the "I" and the "you," which is often played out as, "It is okay with me if *you* win as long as *I* win just a little bit more." Then, you are back in "I win, you lose." Another fault with "win-win" is that it can easily default into "lose-lose," through compromising rather than creating truly new possibilities that provide what is wanted and needed. The process of rallying human intellectual capital for innovating new options is called Winning Happening. Winning Happening noticeably differs from "I win, you win" because there is no "I" and no "you." Winning Happening is itself a Principle, and Principles are bigger than the "I" and the "you." Winning Happening is the game in which, "If you win, I win," or "If you win, we win." An example may be the doctor and the family winning when a patient heals, or a teacher and society winning when a student learns, or a consultant and the economy winning when a client is more successful. A strong sense of bonded teamwork arises when you experience the Principle of Winning Happening in operation. Winning Happening is the backbone of Possibility Management meeting technologies. (*See:* Bright Principle, High Drama, *Map of Possibility*, Gameworld, Meeting Technology, Principle)

WORLD VIEW – (*See:* Box)

List of Thought-Maps

List of Experiments

✕ References

The following books, movies and music were mentioned or quoted in this book.

Bibliography

Berne, Eric. *Games People Play*. New York: Grove Press, 1967.

Block, Peter. *Stewardship: Choosing Service Over Self-Interest*. San Francisco: Berrett-Koehler Publishers, 1996.

Block, Peter. *The Answer to How Is Yes: Acting on What Matters*. San Francisco: Berrett-Koehler Publishers, 2002.

Carson, Rick. *Taming Your Gremlin: A Surprisingly Simple Method for Getting Out of Your Own Way*. New York: Quill / Harper Collins, 2003. (Note: Rick Carson regards Gremlin as bad. I have a completely different experience and opinion: Gremlin is Gremlin, irresponsible King or Queen or your under-world. I like the rest of what Rick writes, especially the last chapter. – C. C.)

Castaneda, Carlos. *Journey to Ixtlan*. New York: Simon & Schuster, 1972.

Csikszentmihalyi, Mihaly. *Flow: The Psychology of Optimal Experience*. New York: Harper Collins, 1990.

Dick, Philip K. *Valis*. New York: Bantam Books, 1981. ("I wish to encounter a disinhibiting factor that will trigger my anamnesia.")

Durkheim, Karlfried Graf. *The Way of Transformation: Daily Life as Spiritual Exercise*. London: Allen & Unwin, 1988.

Eldredge, John. *Wild At Heart: Discovering the Secret of a Man's Soul*. Nashville, Tennessee: Thomas Nelson, 2001

Ferguson, Marilyn. *The Aquarian Conspiracy*. New York: Jeremy P. Tarcher, 1987.

Fuller, R. Buckminster. *Critical Path*. New York: Saint Martin's Press, 1981.

Galilei, Galileo. *Dialogue Concerning the Two Chief World Systems*. Berkeley, California: University of California Press, 1953.

Gerrold, David. *A Rage For Revenge*. New York: Bantam Spectra, 1989.

Godin, Seth. *Free Prize Inside: The Next Big Marketing Idea*. London: Penguin Books, 2004.

Gordon, Dr. Thomas. *Parent Effectiveness Training: The Tested New Way to Raise Responsible Children*. New York: Plume, Rei Edition, 1975.

Heinlein, Robert A. *Time Enough for Love*. New York: G. P. Putnam's Sons, 1973.

Heisenberg, Werner. *Physics and Philosophy*. New York: Harper and Row, 1958.

Herbert, Frank. *Dune*. New York: Chilton Book Company, 1965.

Johnstone, Keith. *Impro: Improvisation and the Theatre*. New York: Routledge, 1987

Keith, Kent M. *Anyway: The Paradoxical Commandments: Finding Personal Meaning in a Crazy World*. New York: G. P. Putnam's Sons, 2002.

Kinsella, William Patrick. *Shoeless Joe*. Boston: Houghton Mifflin, 1982.

Kirk, G. S. *Heraclitus: The Cosmic Fragments*. Cambridge, UK: Cambridge University Press, 1970.

Kundera, Milan. *The Unbearable Lightness of Being*. London: Faber & Faber, 1984

Lilly, John C., and Antonietta Lilly. *The Dyadic Cyclone: The Autobiography of a Couple*. New York: Simon and Schuster, 1976.

Lozowick, Lee. *The Alchemy of Love and Sex*. Prescott, Arizona: Hohm Press, 1996.

Lozowick, Lee. *The Little Book of Lies and Other Myths*. Prescott, Arizona: Hohm Press, 2005.

Maslow, Abraham H. *Motivation and Personality*. New York: Harper & Row, 1954.

Maugham, W. Somerset. *The Razor's Edge*. New York: Doubleday, 1944.

McGerr, Patricia. "Johnny Lingo's Eight-Cow Wife." Story in *Woman's Day* magazine, November 1965. A condensed version was published February 1988 in *Reader's Digest*.

Moore, Robert, and Gillette, Douglas. *King Warrior Magician Lover: Rediscovering the Archetypes of the Mature Masculine*. New York: Harper Collins, 1991.

Olsen, Larry Dean. *Outdoor Survival Skills*. Provo, Utah: Brigham Young University Press, 1973.

Ouspensky, Peter D. *In Search of the Miraculous: Fragments of an Unknown Teaching*. New York: Harcourt, Brace & World, 1949.

Owen, Harrison. *Open Space Technology: A User's Guide*. San Francisco: Berrett-Koehler, 1997.

Pearce, Joseph Chilton. *From Magical Child to Magical Teen: A Guide to Adolescent Development*. Rochester, Vermont: Park Street Press, 2003.

Peck, M. Scott. *The Different Drum: Community Making and Peace*. New York: Simon & Schuster, 1987.

Prajnânpad, Swâmi. *Les Formules de Swâmi Prajnânpad: Commentées par Arnaud Desjardins*. Paris: La Table Ronde, 2003.

Rischard, J. F. *High Noon: 20 Global Problems, 20 Years to Solve Them*. New York: Basic Books, 2002.

Robert, Henry M. *Robert's Rules of Order: The Classic Manual of Parliamentary Procedure*. New York: Gramercy Books / Random House, 1978.

Rowling, J. K. *Harry Potter and the Half-Blood Prince*. New York: Scholastic, 2005.

Seelig, Carl. *Albert Einstein: A Documentary Biography*. London: Staples Press Ltd., 1956.

Shaw, (George) Bernard. *Man and Superman: A Comedy and a Philosophy*. London: Penguin Books, 1946.

Taylor, Rogan P. *The Death and Resurrection Show: From Shaman to Superstar*. London: Anthony Blond, 1985.

Trungpa, Chögyam. *Cutting Through Spiritual Materialism*. Boston: Shambhala Publications, 1973.

Tomatis, Alfred A. *The Conscious Ear: My Life of Transformation Through Listening*. Barrytown, New York: Station Hill Press, 1991.

Tweedie, Irina. *Daughter of Fire: A Diary of a Spiritual Training with a Sufi Master*. Inverness, California: The Golden Sufi Center, 1986.

Van Vogt, A. E. *The Weapon Shops of Isher*. New York: Ace, 1951.

Watson, Lyall. *Gifts of Unknown Things: An Indonesian Adventure*. New York: Simon and Schuster, 1977.

Zola, Émile. Quoted from www.wikipedia.org.

Videography

The Adventures of Buckaroo Banzai Across the 8th Dimension (1984) with Peter Weller, John Lithgow, Ellen Barkin, and Jeff Goldblum. Directed by W. D. Richter.

As It Is in Heaven (*Så som i Himmelen*) (2005) (Swedish with English subtitles) with Michael Nyqvist, Frida Hallgren, Lennart Jähkel, Helen Sjöholm, and Ingela Olssen. Directed by Kay Pollack.

Field of Dreams (1989) with Kevin Costner, Amy Madigan, Gaby Hoffman and Ray Liotta. Directed by Phil Alden Robinson.

Groundhog Day (1993) with Bill Murray, Andie MacDowell, and Chris Elliot. Directed by Harold Ramis.

The Last Samurai (2003) with Ken Watanabe, Tom Cruise, William Atherton, Chad Lindberg, Koyuki, and Hiroyuki Sanada. Directed by Edward Zwick.

Little Big Man (1970) with Dustin Hoffman, Faye Dunaway, and Chief Dan George. Directed by Arthur Penn.

The Matrix (part 1) (1999) with Keanu Reaves, Laurence Fishburne, Carrie-Anne Moss and Hugo Weaving. Directed by Andy Wachowski and Larry Wachowski.

Pirates of the Caribbean: The Curse of the Black Pearl (part 1) (2003) with Johnny Depp, Geoffrey Rush, Orlando Bloom, and Keira Knightley. Directed by Gore Verbinski.

The Princess Bride (1987) with Cary Elwes, Mandy Patinkin, Chris Sarandon, Christopher Guest, Wallace Shawn, Robin Wright Penn, and André the Giant. Directed by Rob Reiner.

The Razor's Edge (1984) with Bill Murray, Theresa Russell, Catherine Hicks, and Denholm Elliot. Directed by John Byrum.

The Saint (1997) with Val Kilmer, Elisabeth Shue, Rade Serbedzija, Valeri Nikolayev and Henry Goodman. Directed by Phillip Noyce.

The Wonderful Wizard of Oz (1939) with Judy Garland, Frank Morgan, Ray Bolger, Bert Lahr and Jack Haley. Directed by Victor Fleming.

Discography

Randy Newman. *I Think It's Going To Rain Today*. Randy Newman. Burbank, California: Reprise / WEA, 1968.

Lee Lozowick Band, *écrasé par l'amour*, (previously titled *dog's day in the sun*). "She Said." Prescott, Arizona: Muse-ic Records, 2004.

Further Reading and Further Listening

Books that provide enough clarity or provocative thinking to support such a volume as *Building Love That Lasts* are rare and precious. Here are some suggestions.

On The Patriarchy

Block, Peter. *Stewardship: Choosing Service Over Self-Interest.* San Francisco: Berrett-Koehler Publishers, 1996.

Graves, Robert. *Watch the North Wind Rise.* New York: Creative Age Press, 1949; as Seven Days in New Crete. London: Cassell, 1949.

Quinn, Daniel. *Ishmael: An Adventure of the Mind and Spirit.* New York: Bantam, 1992.

Wolff, Robert. *Original Wisdom: Stories of an Ancient Way of Knowing.* Rochester, Vermont: Inner Traditions International, 2001.

On Children

Fedorschak, Karuna. *Parenting – A Sacred Task.* Prescott, Arizona: Hohm Press, 2003.

Harrison, Steven. *The Happy Child: Changing the Heart of Education.* Boulder Colorado: Sentient Publications, 2002.

Holt, John. *Instead of Education: Ways to Help People Do Things Better.* Boulder Colorado: Sentient Publications, 2004.

Johnson, Anne, and Goodman, Vic. *The Essence of Parenting: Becoming the Parent You Want to Be.* New York: Crossroad, 1997.

Lozowick, Lee. *Conscious Parenting.* Prescott, Arizona: Hohm Press, 1997.

Neufeld, Gordon. *Hold Onto Your Kids: Why Parents Need to Matter More than Peers.* New York: Ballantine, 2005.

Pearce, Joseph Chilton. *From Magical Child To Magical Teen: A Guide to Adolescent Development.* Rochester, Vermont: Park Street Press, 2003.

On Sexuality

Long, Barry. *Making Love: Sexual Love the Divine Way.* Los Angeles: Barry Long, 1998.

Lozowick, Lee. *The Alchemy of Love and Sex.* Prescott, Arizona: Hohm Press, 1996.

On Radical Responsibility

Block, Peter. *The Answer to How Is Yes: Acting on What Matters.* San Francisco: Berrett-Koehler, 2002.

Callahan, Clinton. *Wild Thinking: Radical Knowledge for Liberating Your Effectiveness and Delivering Your Destiny.* (Available in German as *Abenteuer Denken.* Bremen, Germany: Genius Verlag, 2004. Still unpublished in English. C. C.)

Carse, James P. *Finite and Infinite Games: A Vision of Life as Play and Possibility.* New York: Random House, 1986.

Ferguson, Marilyn. *Aquarius Now: Radical Common Sense and Reclaiming Our Personal Sovereignty.* Boston: Red Wheel/Weiser, 2005.

Fuller, R. Buckminster. *Grunch of Giants.* Clayton, California:Critical Path Publishing, 2002.

Glasser, William. *Choice Theory: A New Psychology of Personal Freedom.* New York: Harper Collins, 1998.

Hartmann, Thom. *The Last Hours of Ancient Sunlight: Waking Up to Personal and Global Transformation.* New York: Three Rivers Press, 1999.

Lozowick, Lee. *Getting Real.* Prescott, Arizona: Hohm Press, 2007.

Ouspensky, Peter D. *In Search of the Miraculous: Fragments of an Unknown Teaching.* New York: Harcourt, Brace & World, 1949.

Rischard, J. F. *High Noon: 20 Global Problems, 20 Years to Solve Them.* New York: Basic Books, 2002.

Wilber, Ken. *No Boundary: Eastern and Western Approaches to Personal Growth.* Boston: Shambhala, 1985.

On Communication and Feelings

Adams, Linda. *Be Your Best: Personal Effectiveness in Your Life and Your Relationships.* New York: Putnam, 1989.

Berne, Eric. *Games People Play.* New York: Grove Press, 1967.

Blanton, Brad. *Radical Honesty: How to Transform Your Life by Telling the Truth.* New York: Dell, 1996.

Gordon, Dr. Thomas. *Parent Effectiveness Training: The Tested New Way to Raise Responsible Children.* New York: Plume, Rei Edition, 1975.

Lankford, Valerie. *Four Feelings And What To Do With Them* (This is a privately published pamphlet only available directly from the author: Valerie Lankford, 11600 Hunters Run Drive, Baltimore, Maryland, 21030-1951, USA. Tel: 1-410-771-1234 www.valcanhelp.com)

On Archetypal Masculine and Feminine

Moore, Robert, and Gillette, Douglas. *King Warrior Magician Lover: Rediscovering the Archetypes of the Mature Masculine.* New York: Harper Collins, 1991.

On Becoming Man

Biddulph, Steve. *Manhood.* London: Vermillion / Random House, 2004.

Somé, Malidoma Patrice. *Of Water and the Spirit: Ritual, Magic, and Initiation in the Life of an African Shaman.* New York: Penguin, 1994.

On Bringing the Woman to Life

Gold, E. J. *Life In The Labyrinth: The Labyrinth Trilogy Book II.* Nevada City, California: IDHHB, 1986.

On Longing

Lozowick, Lee. *Death of a Dishonest Man.* Prescott, Arizona: Hohm Press, 1998.

Lozowick, Lee. *Gasping for Air in a Vacuum.* Prescott, Arizona: Hohm Press, 2004.

On Creative Relationship

Fritz, Robert. *Creating: A Guide to the Creative Process.* New York: Ballantine, 1991.

Johnstone, Keith. *Impro: Improvisation and the Theatre.* New York: Routledge, 1987.

Further Listening

Two astonishing CDs with songs that express many principles explored in this book are:

écrasé par l'amour (*crushed by love*) by Lee Lozowick

l'ange brisé (*broken angel*) by Lee Lozowick

These CDs are available through: Hohm Press, P.O. Box 2501, Prescott, Arizona 86302 USA; Tel. +1-928-778-9189.

Index

cooperation, 365
confusion, 21, 87
conscious competence, 122
Conscious Ear, The (Tomatis), 163
conscious incompetence, 122
conscious theater, 76, 281, 285, 320, 363, 488-489, 507; *also see:* high drama
consciousness
    is everywhere, 16, 19
    freedom and, 52, 59, 85, 137, 149, 432, 473, 507
    justification and, 326
    level of, 509
    sex and, 428
    of spaces, 141
    source of, 18-20, 250
consequence,
    and actions, 6, 227, 458
    and Box, 186
    and communication, 155, 164
    and decisions, 187-188, 197, 276, 337, 414
    and feedback, 121
    and Gremlin, 371
    and learning, 25
    and patriarchy, 2, 56
    and responsibility, 62, 85, 111-112, 175, 317, 500
    and *Restricting Sphincters*, 375-377, *Map of*, 376
    and rite of passage, 65
    and stories, 256-257, 273, 315
    and sword of clarity, 299
    and Western culture, 58, 197, 296, 343
    also see: responsibility
conservation of energy, *see:* cathexis
contact, 412-413, 489
context, 489
    Archetypal, 310-313
    defensive, 490
    expansive, 492
    possibility, 5-6, 177-178
    shift of, 67, 321
core skills of a Possibility Manager, the seven, 489
    0. shifting identity to Possibility Manager, 33, 275-277
    1. staying unhookable, 136-140, 514
    2. being centered, 173-176, 486
    3. contact, 412-413, 489
    4. holding space, 140-142, 497
    5. feeling Archetypal feelings (going stellar), 495
    6. creating possibility, 485, 488, 489, 490, 497, 504
    7. selling possibility, 489
Countenance, 393-397, 489
    experiment in, 405-406
    Map of __ vs. Archetypal Love, 414
    Map of requirements for, 407
    obstacles to, 416-417
    requirements for, 406-417
    works, 479
cowshit, 271-273; *also see:* bullshit
Creating (Fritz), 491
creating,
    feels like, 228, 482
    possibility, 490
    relationship, 80, 209, 228, 333, 482, 502, 509, 514
Creator (magician or sorceress) Archetype, 279, 299-301, 490
culture, *see:* Western culture, gender culture

D

dangerous questions, 490
dating, 206
Daughter of Fire (Tweedie), 68
Death and Resurrection Show (Taylor), 22
decisions,
    in adult communication, 161
    and sadness, 187-188
    vs. reasons, 218
    yes or no, 187-188
declaring, 252-255, 413-414, 490
decoding messages, 161-163, map of, 162
defensive,
    Box strategy, 82-83, 137, 170-172, 312, 490
    context, 490
    learning, 13, 490
    also see: Gremlin, expansive
deity, 142, 254, 423; *also see:* Principles, space, holding space, navigating space
delight, 481-482
denial, 130-131, 361, 362, 364
    and Gremlin, 371, 445, 473, 490
depression, map of, 98, 104-105, 188
destiny (true purpose),
    in action, 372-377
    and attention, 485
    and Box, 224
    and Bright Principles, 96, 485, 490-491, 507, 514

destiny (true purpose) [continued]
    and building matrix, 250
    and conscious theater, 320, 488-489
Distilling __ Process, 372, 491
    and edgework, 224, 229
    and evolution, 206
    and extraordinary relationship, 326
    and free will, 74
    and gameworlds, 487-488
    and high drama, 366, map of, 361, 496-497
    and patriarchy, 59
    and Phase 2 of feelings work, 182, 186
    and possibility speaking, 506
    serving your, 372, 376-377
    song lyrics about, 208
    and soul (-food), 208-209, 372-377, 510
    and stellating Archetypes, 354-355,
        map of, 354
    and terminology, 330
    and trainers, 192, 330, 511
    and what matters, 190
Detecting Messages,168-170, Maps of, 168 and 169
Dialogue Concerning the Two Chief World Systems
    (Galileo), 68
discovery,
    listening,166-168, map of, 165
    and reorientation, 14
    speaking, 172-173, map of, 171
discussion, 170-172, map of, 171
Disk of Nothing, 481, 491; also see: hooked, un-
    hookable, Nothing
dissipative structures (Prigogine), 499
distilling destiny, 491; also see: destiny
distinctions
    and boundaries, 192-193
    and the Box, 83
    and clarity, 17, 194-195
    making, 17-18
    Relationship __, 18
do-it list, 288-289
do-overs, 491
Doer (Warrior or Warrioress) Archetype, 491-492
Double Space-Holding, 269, Map of, 294
drama, see: high drama, low drama
Drama Triangle (Karpman), see: low drama
drivers, 130-131
Dune (Herbert), 114
Durckheim, Graf Karlfried, 22
Dyadic Cyclone (Lilly), 468

E

Early Adolescent Relationship, Map of, 398
earth, flat map vs. round map, see: Map of Maps
Eat-A-Bug Cookbook, The (Gordon), 234
ecstasy, 90-91
Edgework, 221-241, 296, 325, 327,
    405-406, 492, Map of, 225
ego state(s), 32-35
    in Map of Archetypal/Archetypal Relationship,
        332
    in Map of Archetypal/Ordinary Relationship,
        314
    Map of Adult, 117
    Map of Parent Adult Child, 34
    relocating to adult, 116-118
eighteen standard Boxes, 85-87; also see: Box
Einstein, Albert, 14, 302,504
emotional body, 90-91
emotions vs. feelings, 179-181, 492
encoding messages, 161-163, map of, 162
enemy (enemies)
    Gremlin is not, 496
    men as, 60-61
    "there is no," 18-20
    within yourself, 442
energy. 261-262, 263, 457-459
energetic (or spiritual) body, 90-91
energetic space, 510; also see: physical space, space
Everything and Nothing, 271-273, 299-300, map
    of, 268
evolution,
    of consciousness, 18
    of culture, 417-418
    and flying instructions, 480-482, Map of
        Flying, 481
    your job in, 54-55
    nonlinear, 339-340
    and "now," 313
    also see: matrix building, edgework, parallel
        culture
Expand the Box, 492
expansive context, 492
expansive learning, 13-15, 492-493
expectations, 493
experiential reality, 493; also see: verbal reality
experimenting, 7-8
extraordinary human love, 119-120
extraordinary human relationship,
    and choosing "who" to talk to, 204-205
    and clarity about nits, 143

gap, [continued]
  between moments, 239-241
  between partners, map of, 400
  and reactions, 14
  and sanity, 80
  in seamlessness, 378
  in space, 139
  staying in the, 495
  and stories, 96
  and technology, 479
  and thoughts, 180-181
  in time, 239-241
  between urges / choices, 312
  between Western culture / Countenance,
      417-418
Garden of Woman (Paradise), 269-270, 303-304,
    307, 394, 479
gender culture, 265, 268-269, 297, 453, 462-
    463, 469-470
Gerrold, David, 18
"get killed but don't die," 273
Gifts of Unknown Things (Watson), 88
giving your center away,
  and adaptive behavior, 159-160, 173-175
  and co-dependent behavior, 159-160,
      173-175
  and getting it back, 462
  and losing it, 159-160, 173-175
  to patriarchy, 358
  also see: center, centering
Go! (in Rapid Learning), *Map of*, 191
Goddess Archetype, 259, 280, 302-304, 419,
    420-426, 495
Godin, Seth, 221, 492
Göbel, Johann, 511
going stellar, 495; *also see:* core skills
\good vs. bad as Shadow Principle, 321
good boy, 24, 46, 71, 86, 131, 205, 277, 293,
    298, 305
"good" feelings, 92-97
good girl, 46, 86, 131, 205, 277, 292-293
Gordon, Dr. Thomas, 122, 129, 156, 160
gorilla basics, 291-294, *Map of*, 292
gossiping,
  and fear, 99
  and Gremlin, 367
  and intimacy, 273
  and neurotic speaking, 170, map of, 171
  and sanctuary, 329
  and self-revealing, 78
  is triangulating, 369

Great Labyrinth of Spaces, *see:* Labyrinth
Gremlin,
  and Archetypal Love, 479-480
  and Archetypes, 491
  and being hooked, 497
  boundaries with, 327-328, 305
  definition of, 495-496
  and detecting deficiencies, 280
  and ending relationship, 217-218,
      470-473
  feeding schedule, 186, 326, 368-370, 433
  and internal movie projector, 320
  and leadership, map of, 174
  and low drama, 186, 499
  and Man, 329
  and manipulating, 147
  naming of, 366-368
  and nonlinearity, 370-372
  and ordinary relationship, 327-328, 349
  owning, 368-370
  relationship with, 338
  and resentment, 217
  and responsibility, 368, 496
  and revenge, 271
  and self-observation, 185
  and sitting, 402
  training and using, 139, 286, 338, 370-372,
      496, 507
  and underworld, 349-353, 362-366,
      495-496
  and victim, 315
Groder, Dr. Martin, 71
Groundhog Day (film), 210
guilt,
  beating yourself up and, 266
  and Gremlin, 370
  and mixing feelings, map of, 98
  and responsibility, 508
  and responsible victim, 38
  vs. *Responsibility, Map of*, 266

H

"Ha! Ha! I got you!" *see:* I win, you lose
*Handbook for Creating Ordinary Family
    Relationship*, 455-456
*Handbook for Creating Ordinary Human
    Relationship*, 38-50
Handbook on Living Happily Ever After, 476-482
happiness,

breakthrough in, 340-341
and Box, 203-204
danger of, 93
in extraordinary human relationship, 120
duration / permanence of, 181, 224
and media, 103
and personal growth, 8
and Western culture, 31
pill, 104
as purpose of life, 104
heart,
    being in, 411
    communication and, 157-159
    cultivating the broken, 257-259
    and decisions, 187
    feeding the, 207-209
    and imagination, 202
    and jealousy, 99
    and low drama, 35
    song lyrics about, 208
    as transducer of feelings, 496
    and work, 209
    also see: four bodies
Heart of the Labyrinth, *see:* Center of the
    Labyrinth, Labyrinth
Heisenberg, Werner, 85
Heraclitus, 104
Hidden Purpose (Process), 366-368, 496
high drama,
    vs. Archetypal Drama, 338
    and communications, 161
    and conscious theater, 366, 496-497
    and destiny, 320, 490-491
    and low drama, 36, 366, map of, 361
    Map of Relationship as, 400
    and mothering, 461
    and relationship, 304, map of, 312, *Map of,* 361
    and responsibility, 488-489
    and rite of passage, 461
    and stellating Archetypes, 366
    and stories, 319-321, map of, 320
    also see: responsibility, rite of passage
high level fun, *see:* high drama, Pirate agreement
High Noon (Rischard), 316, 351
holding space,
    and anger, 94-95
    and Archetypal Relationship, 269-272, 304-308, 333-334, 486,
    map of, 314, 332
    and attention, 304, 412, 457-459
    and being a space, 485

and Bright Principles, 331, 338
and Box, 239
and Countenance, 407, 412, 413, map of, 401
and declaring, 497
and destiny, 142, 274, 304, 331, 373, map of, 373
and discovery speaking,172-173, 491, map of, 171
and discussion, 170-172, map of, 171
and double space-holding, 268-269, *Map of,* 294
and energetic intimacy, 235
and Everything, 273
and extraordinary relationship, 120, map of, 400
and family, 198, 454-459
and feelings (*Four Feelings*), *Map of,* 96
and gameworlds, 373-377, map of, 376
and high drama, map of, 400
and intersection of worlds, 373
and magnificence, 329
and Pirate ... Woman, 482
and Possibility Speaking, 172, map of 171
and relationship, 140-142
and responsibility, 497
and Requiem, 474-475
and responsibility, 140-142, 299
and speed of Love, 410
also see: core skills, space, navigating space, meeting technology
Hold On To Your Kids (Neufeld), 197
homework, 340-341
hookable / hooked,
    and Adult ego state, 118
    and bull fighter, 432
    and Child ego state, 117
    and do-overs, 491
    and emotional reactions, 102-103
    and extraordinary relationship, 136-140
    and forgetting, 514
    and Gremlin, 137-138, 371, 497
    and *Low Drama Detector, Map of,* 184
    and other's Boxes, 143-144
    and Parent ego state, 114-115
    and resentment, 289
    symptoms of being, 137-138
    ways of being, 137
    also *see:* unhookable, Disk of Nothing, gap, Springscreen, voices in your head, Voice Blaster

I

I win, you lose,
- and belief, 363
- and discussion, 172
- and Gremlin, 366
- and *Map of Three Games*, 365
- and mixing feelings, 503
- and patriarchy, 52
- and *schadenfreude*, 99
- vs. Winning Happening, 515
- *also see:* survival, mixing feelings

I win, you win, 365, 515
- *also see:* Winning Happening

identity,
- and "who am I?", 276-277
- as a character, 77-78
- as a child, 117
- for men, for women, 267-268
- in patriarchy, 55
- for security, 315
- shifting, 33, 275-277
- in Western culture, 403
- *also see:* the Box

identification,
- and actions, 75
- and being a character, 77-78
- and Box, 497
- and naming, 78
- and other roles, 77
- and relationship, 411
- and shifting, 33
- *also see:* misidentification

imagination,
- and child raising, 265
- and fear, 68
- feels like, 200-201
- and Feminine worlds, 302
- and gameworlds, 377
- and handicaps, 60
- having no, xiv, 44
- and healing, 417
- and heart, 202
- and Internet, 448
- and linearity, 200
- and mind, 200
- and ordinary relationship, 326
- and problems, 4
- and reading this book, 8
- and relationship intelligence, 9, 30
- and resources, 332

- and sex, 448
- and victim stories, 79
- and who you are, 497
- and witch hunts, 60

Impro (Johnstone), 201

inauthenticity, 128-130, map of, 129

incompetence, *see: Soft Skills, Map of Learning,* 122

infatuation, 31-32, 312, 476

inner navigating, 97, 177-178, 497-498; *also see:* navigating space

Inquisition, 63-64

insanity,
- and beliefs, 133-135
- and child raising, 198
- and feeling, 180
- and new actions, 124
- and ordinary relationship, 143
- and possibilities, 80
- and power, 80
- tolerating your partner's, 241
- and Western culture, 52, 280, 453

intellectual body, 90-91

Internet sex, 186, 334, 369, 448

intersection,
- between two media, 224
- between what is / could be, 223
- Conference, 238
- with unknown (Edgework), 221
- of worlds, with *Map* of 373

intimacy,
- and antagonistic partner, 8
- and Box, 83, 323-324, 327-328, 435-436
- as Bright Principle, 364
- in chaos, 288
- and children, 100, 197
- and communication, 156-159
- and Countenance, 405-406
- definition of, 497
- and discovering treasures, 293
- Edgework, 227, 234-241, 269, 281
- and evolution (of relationship), 398-401, 467-473
- and expectations, 240
- factors effecting, 465-467
- fear of, 100, 291
- and feeling, 97
- and four bodies, 90-91
- and infatuation, 32
- lack of, 217
- and letting self be known, 189

Labyrinth,
    Heart (Center) of the, 4, 252, 254, 426-429,
        435, 495, 499, 503
    your map of the, 352
    Map of the Great __ of Spaces, 255
    of Spaces, 254-255
    also see: navigating space
ladder of technology, *see*: technopenuriaphobia
    TPP
Lankford, Valerie, 92
Last Samurai (film), 176
Later Adolescent Relationship, Map of, 399
learning
    and actions, 124-125
    defensive, 13, 490
    expansive, 13-15
    liking, 125-126
    Soft Skills, Map of Learning, 122
    team, 22
Life in the Labyrinth, 412
light speed, xiv
linearity,
    and Archetypal feminine, 328
    and being hooked, 138
    and Box, 203, 310-311
    and Countenance, 393
    and dangerous questions, 172
    and defensive learning, 13
    and flying, 480
    and *Marshmallow Zone, Map of,* 223
    and meeting technology, 501
    and men, 285, 290
    and mind, 502
    and problems, 332, 499, 503
    and relationship 200
    and Requiem, 475
    and solutions 203
    and time, 459-460
    and Western culture, 52, 189, 200, 333
    also see: nonlinear
liquid state, 126-128, 263, 376-377, 499, *Map of,*
    127, *Map of Flying,* 481
Listening, Four Kinds of, 164-168, 505,
        Map of, 165
Little Big Man (film), 210
Little Book of Lies and Other Myths, The
    (Lozowick), 435
longing,
    and Archetypal intimacy, 325
    and attention, 302
    and authenticity, 7

and broken heart, 259
and ecstasy, 271
for extraordinary / Archetypal, 175, 380-
    381, 407, 414
for Goddess, 425
for God, 435
for heaven, 483
for longing, 415, 429
and sacrifice, 333
Longstocking, Pippi, 139
looking bad, 22-23, map of, 122, 197
looking good vs. learning, 22
lose-lose, 515
love,
    Archetypal, 248-259
    extraordinary human, 119-120
    Three Kinds of, 499, *Maps of,* 31, 119, and
        249
    ordinary human, 30-32
    True, 249
Lover Archetype, *see*: Communicator Archetype
low drama,
    detector, 183-186, 500
    and Gremlin, 184-186
    and high drama, 499
    is not life, 37, 499
    Map of, 36
    Map of __ Detector, 184
    and responsibility, 35-38, 499-500
    also see: high drama, *Map of Possibility*
Lozowick, Lee, 5, 25, 55, 266, 296, 339, 405,
    412, 435, 442, 482, 503, 508
    lyrics of, 390
Lutz, Marion, 98, 503

M

magic lamp, 287
Magician Archetype, *see*: Creator Archetype
Maker Archetype, *see*: Doer Archetype
making time, 319, 442, 459-460, 500
making wrong, 207, 217, 261, 273, 369, 389,
    499, 510
man,
    and authenticity, 2
    Archetypal, *see*: Archetypal Masculine
    as dad, 59-60
    ordinary, 57-58, 200
    song lyrics about, 208
    also see: Pirate ... Man

nice girl, 46, 86, 131, 205, 277, 292-293
Nine Cow methodology, 388-392
Nine Cow Story (Callahan), 386-388
nit, education, 143-149
no reason,
    appreciate people for, 96
    ask for help for, 192
    be different for, 446
    being happy for, 210
    being together for, 199, 323
    bless people for, 95
    body is lovable for, 103
    creating for, 201
    cry / laugh for, 478
    enter extraordinary relationship for, 219
    feel joy for, 286
    Gremlin destroys for, 371, 496
    let kindness prevail for, 241
    love for, 120
    make decisions for, 218
    practice for, 507
    rub feet for, 116
    wanting what we want for, 190
    also see: reasons
nondual perspective, 313
nonlinearity,
    and actions, 200-207, 325-326
    and assumptions, 503
    and empowerment, 14
    and Gremlin, 371-372
    in Manmaking, 286-287
    and meta-conversations, 152
    and relationship, 80, 209, 228, 333, 482,
        502, 509, 514
    also see: linearity
normal neurotic listening, 164-165, 170-171
Nothing,
    and Creator Archetype, 271-273, 300
    Disk of, 491
    is bigger than Everything, 271-273, 299-300,
        map of, 268
    Men are, 267, 275, 486
    Sitting There Together With (poem), 483
not knowing, 6, 275
not okay to feel, 93-94, map of, 95
now,
    and change, 117
    and decisions, 503-504
    and delight, 482
    and doing, 140, 489
    and evolution, 313

    and experience, 21
    and feeling happy, 482
    and gaps, 239-241
    and love, 21
    and the miraculous, 124
    and past or future, 283-284
    and power, 116
    and presence, 458
    and responsibility, 484, 502
    and sanctuary, 443
    and stories, 362
    and time, 118

O

objectivity,
    and Archetypal Love, 253, 316
    and artwork, 431, 501
    and attention, 104
    and beliefs, 135
    benefits of, 192
    and feelings, 182
    and is-glue, 498
    and reactions, 149
    and reality, 508
    and relationship, 513
    and sanity, 192
    and subverting the patriarchy, 55
    and a third intelligence, 473
    and writing, 20
obstacles, 416-417
Of Water and Spirit (Somé), 65
okay-ness (Transactional Analysis), 37, 504,
    509, 514
one team, 18-19, 171-173
ordinary human communication, 32-35
ordinary human love, 29-32
ordinary human relationship, 29-32
    Handbook for Creating, 38-50
    Handbook for Creating, in Family, 455-456
    Map of __ vs. Archetypal Relationship, 268
organizations,
    and change, 128
    definition of, 469, 504
    and domination, 52
    and gameworlds, 375-377
    innovative, 117
    and matriarchy, 51
    and meta-conversations, 149-152
    and Principles, map of, 400

organizations, [continued]
    and resolution to end corporate personhood, 85
    and rigid structures, 56
orthogonality, 80, 502, 504, 507
Outdoor Survival Skills (Olsen), 477
Overwhelm, Map of, 113

P

pain
    consciously creating, 18
    changing to rocket fuel, 265-266
    from feedback, 123
    vs. feelings, 179
    of learning, 178
    vs. suffering, 91
painting doorways, 425, 504
paradise, 66, 303, 315, 386-387, 394-395, 425, 435, 477, 479-480
Paradoxical Commandments, The (Keith), 288
parallel culture, 63, 316, 504, *Map of*, 316
Parent Effectiveness Training (Gordon), 156
Parent ego state, 33, 34, 114, 118, 484
parenting (child raising, children)
    alternative approaches to, 54-55
    and Archetypal to Child relationship, 453-454, map of, 314
    and assumptions about children, 189
    and attention, 175, 239, 457-459
    and authority, 160
    and being-with children, 198-200
    and blaming other parent, 42
    and child's exuberance, 265
    and communicating about problems, 160-163, map of, 160
    and completion loops, 157-159, maps of, 158 and 162
    and computers, 231
    and conscious expectations, 386-392, 493
    Dad's place in, 59-60
    and Edgework experiments, 232-234, 513
    and evolution of self, 397-401
    and extraordinary relationship, 210, 212, 213, 215-216
    and fear of children, 100-101
    and feelings training, 99
    and grades, 344
    with heart / soul food, 207-209
    and holding space, 375, 412, 454-457
    and influences from parents, 41, 130, 293

    and irresponsible Archetypes, 484
    and letting go, 460-463
    and low drama, 185
    and making boundaries, 193, 195-198
    and making time, 459-460
    and meta-conversations, 152-153
    and nuclear family, 469-470
    and ordinary family relationship, 455-456
    in the patriarchy, 52-54, 58-59
    a problem child, 48
    and rescuing, 37
    and rite of passage, 66, 102
    and sexuality, 293
    and tantrums, 299-300
    and trusting partner, 239
    as space of possibility, 322
    and stories, 300-301
    and verbal reality, 513
    and your vision, 238
    and Western culture, 496
    and what woman wants, 337
    when something is wrong, 167
    and whining, 215-216
    underworld and, 347
past-life vow, 376; *also see:* restricting sphincters
pathological liar, 130, 265-266
patriarchy,
    and Archetypal Man / Woman, 267, 268-269, 329, 359
    and matriarchy, 51-52
    and men, 2, 57-60, 69, 73, 295-296, 486-487
    noticing the, 55-56
    options not offered by, 54
    reason for, 268
    and rite of passage, 65, 67
    subverting the, 55, 359
    and Technopenuriaphobia (TPP), 513
    and women, 3, 60-64, 68, 69, 73, 265, 279, 290, 358, 482
    and Western culture, 52-54, 67, 302, 305-306, 353
pattern disintegration, 21-22
Pearce, Joseph Chilton, 25, 460
penis, *see:* magic lamp
permission,
    to allow healings, 417
    to bring life to life, 228, 491
    to create success, 505
    for feelings, 92, 188
    to grant yourself __, 505
    to learn, 21, 82, 126

sword of clarity, 512
    as awakeness, 214-215
    and Aikido, 176
    becoming a, 289-299
    and boundaries, 193, 270
    and Goddess, 421
    and holding space, 304-308
    and low drama detector, 184
    obstacles and, 416-417
    in radical honesty, 219
    for saying yes / no, 159, 187
    sharpness of, 313-317
    for staying unhookable, 139
    of the Warrioress, 280

T

taking action, 251-252
tantrums, 160, 299, 454
Technology of Beliefs, Map of, 135
technophobia, 230
technopenuriaphobia (TPP) 230-234, 513
    Map of __ Detection, 232
    Map of __ Healing, 233
Teresa, Mother, 132, 288
theater, conscious, *see:* conscious theater
thought-map,
    Box and, 487
    and Europe, 250
    inner navigation and, 497-498
    interaction with, 346
    energetic diagram and, 513
    of relationship, 250
    and options / possibilities, 30, 140-141
    results from, 202
    in Possibility Management, 500
    standard human intelligence thoughtware
        and, 511
    new territory and, 503
    new world and, 93-94
thoughtware, 5, 325, 498, 500, 501, 511, 513;
    also see: standard human intelligence
    thoughtware, meme
Three Kinds of Games, Map of, 365
Three Kinds of Relationship, Map of, 29, 110, 310
"three seconds,"
    action / non-action in, 54, 149
    "ancient" and, 300
    and Box stories, 318
    cleaning space every, 139

    creating Love every, 482
    echo fading within, 272
    "far distant" and, 502
    liquid state and, 127
    pain and, 486
    possibilities in every, 216, 491
    reactions in, 144
    reinvention and, 75
time,
    making, 459-460, 500
    taking, 20-21
together-sitting, 403-404, 444, 513; *also see:*
    self-sitting, practice
Tonic Gold™, 16, 501, 513; *also see:* building
    matrix
tool belt, 185, 513-514
trainer (Possibility Trainer), 5, 72-73, 97,
    177-178, 192, 283, 298, 506-507; *also see:*
    Possibility Management
Transactional Analysis (Berne), 22, 32-38, 92,
    484, 499-500
True Love
    definition of, 248-249
    exchanging __ for revenge, 265
    experiencing __ personally, 21, 249, 346, 477
    and "flying," 480
    relationship and, 268
    remembering possibility for, 7
    also see: Archetypal Love, Countenance
True Purpose, 514; *also see:* Bright Principles,
    destiny
Trungpa, Chögyam, 21, 103, 175, 214
trust,
    betrayal of, 79
    of body, 417
    boundaries and, 193
    is decision, 68
    emotional intimacy and, 235
    feats of, 68
    of feedback / coaching, 237, 374
    of feeling, 62
    no one, 88
    intuition, 21, 24, 473
    partner, 239
    sensation, 125
    yourself, 25, 62-63, 234
    the universe, 213
twelve roadblocks (Gordon), 156-163, 198-200,
    Map of, 156

U

Ueshiba, Morihei, 176
Unbearable Lightness of Being, The (Kundera), 91
uncertainty,
    and beliefs, 226
    and excitement, 14-15
    vs. fanaticism, 226
    Heisenberg __ principle, 85
    and inauthenticity, 302
    and relaxing, 288
    of it working / not working, 434-435
unconscious purpose, 514; *also see:* Hidden
    Purpose, Gremlin
underworld, 342-373
    and Gremlin, 204, 285-286, 363
    journeying into, 9, 239, 377-381
    Man's job in, 357-358
    on *Map of Possibility*, 361
    need to process, 283-284
    Woman's job in, 358-360
    also see: Gremlin, Shadow world,
        Shadowlands, *Map of Worlds*
unhookable,
    and Adult ego state, 117
    and clarity, 487
    and conscious expectations, 493
    and Gremlin, 496
    and nits, 144
    and nothingness, 480-481
    importance of staying, 136-140, 514
    also *see:* hookable, Disk of Nothing, gap,
        Springscreen, core skills, Adult
unreasonable, 190, 508, 514
upperworld, 346-350, 514, map of, 350
    and Bright Principles, 364
    getting there, 258, 349-350
    holding space for, 363
    King or Queen of, 286, 364-366
    on *Map of Possibility*, 361
    also see: underworld, middleworld, *Map of Worlds*

V

verbal reality, 86, 407-410, 493, 495, 514; *also*
    see: experiential reality
victim,
    and being okay, 514
    as standard Box, 86
    and Box mechanics, 196
    of circumstances, 76, 78-79, 256, 315, 360,
        473
    and game(s), 363
    and Gremlin, 60, 250, 271, 367-368, 371
    impossibility of being, 79, 315, 360, 489,
        508
    in low drama, 35-38
    of nothingness, 486
    and persecutors, 514
    and radical responsibility, 488
    responsible, 37-38
    and Shadow Principles, 499-500
    story, 318-321, 514-515
    of time, 319, 459-460
    also see: low drama, Gremlin, *Map of*
        Possibility, responsible story
violence,
    about to cause, 258
    and ending relationship, 217
    between siblings, 153
    and incompetence, 152
    justifying, 370
    and patriarchy, 52
    psychic, 262
    slave of, 63
    and Warrioress, 279
    also see: abuse
Voice Blaster, 114-115, 148, 370, 389, 515, *Map*
    of, 115, 361
voices in your head, 113-115, 118, 370, 512

W

waking state, 125, 133, 213
war,
    anger as, 297
    alternative to, 479
    beliefs and, 134-135, 487, 505, map of, 135
    Gremlin and, 218
    "having a," 374, 494-495
    horror experiences from the, 99
    lyrics about, 390
    of mind-imagination, 200, 497
    motivation for, 267
    patriarchy and, 52
    relationship / psychological, 469
    rigid realities and, 508
    scarcity and, 363
    talking about, 41

wound(s) (wounded, wounding), [continued]
  Gremlin and, 371
  healing of, 23, 181, 236-237, 302, 417, 442, 474
  and intimacy, 32, 235
  resentment and, 39, 466
  will power and, 375
  writing about, 290-291

writing,
  about attention, 411
  and this book, 403
  Box and, 239
  coaching and, 236
  convalescence and, 71-73
  about decisions, 126, 192
  about expectations, 239
  in experiments, 230
  about feeling, 176-177
  about Gremlin foods, 370
  new meaning from, 290-291
  new ways and, 61-63
  and objective reality, 20
  owning knowledge and, 6-7

and soul's vision, 238
about stress, 148
in underworld journey, 377-381
transformational action and, 402-403
and victim, 79
about wound(s), 290

X
X on the map,
  of Creating Ordinary Family Relationship, 455-456
  of Creating Ordinary Human Relationship, 49-50
  of Four Feelings, 97
  of Five Kinds of Speaking, 170
  of Learning Soft Skills, 121
  of Possibility, 362, 509
  of Problem Ownership, 159
  of Rapid Learning, 512

Z
Zola, Émile, 205

P. S. It Is All True

You probably won't believe what I am going to say.
You probably won't believe it because I am using words.
Words won't impact you enough for you to get it
Unless you have already been there.
My question to you is this: are you willing to recall a memory?
Because you *have* already been there.
And without having to think about it much you already know
That it is all true.
All the legends of gods and goddesses,
Of radiant golden floating temples made of marble columns and flowing silk,
Of Archetypal angels and demons, upperworlds and underworlds,
Of a sanctuary where uninterrupted being-with can occur.
It's all true.
All the subtle energetic levels of multidimensional fluid reality
All of the best ideas communicated in this book
The wildest most outrageous inconceivable ideas in this book
Are all true.
Waiting to be explored, experienced, employed by you.
Does it matter?
No.
Is it all true?
Yes.
You can go directly to the core of the mythical labyrinth
And float in the being of the One
Any time that you achieve floating conditions.
It is not personal.
The opportunity never goes away.
Long before you were born and long after you die
The opportunity is there waiting.
She is there waiting
The One. She is waiting.
The beautiful, quiveringly tender, limitlessly accepting One.
The One with wisdom and knowing beyond words.
The One who waits, who can only wait
Until you the Man become a stillness sanctuary where She can rest
And "be-with" the brilliant radiance of Her being,
The glow of Her presence, the Countenance of Her raw wild power,
And Her peacefulness that surpasses all understanding.
Words are far too crude and solid to talk about this.
Even thoughts get in the way.
So much of what happens falls through the gaps between thoughts.
Nonetheless, it is all hereby confirmed to be true.
Now, tell me this. What are you going to do about it?

– C.C.

Other Titles of Interest from Hohm Press

AS IT IS
A Year on the Road with a Tantric Teacher
by M. Young

A first-hand account of a one-year journey around the world in the company of a tantric teacher. This book catalogues the trials and wonders of day-to-day interactions between a teacher and his students, and presents a broad range of his teachings given in seminars from San Francisco, California to Rishikesh, India. *As It Is* considers the core principles of tantra, including non-duality, compassion (the Bodhisattva ideal), service to others, and transformation within daily life. Written as a narrative, this captivating book will appeal to practitioners of any spiritual path. Readers interested in a life of clarity, genuine creativity, wisdom and harmony will find this an invaluable resource.

paper, 725 pages, 24 b&w photos, $29.95
ISBN: 0-934252-99-8

TOWARD THE FULLNESS OF LIFE
The Fullness of Love
by Arnaud Desjardins

Renowned French spiritual teacher, Arnaud Desjardins, offers elegant and wise counsel, arguing that a successful love relationship requires the heart of a child joined with the maturity of an adult. This book points the way to realize that blessed union.

paper, 182 pages, $12.95
ISBN:0-934252-55-6

SIT
Zen Teachings of Master Taisen Deshimaru
edited by Philippe Coupey

Like spending a month in retreat with a great Zen Master. *SIT* will "tell it like it is..." to both beginners and long-time students of Zen, particularly those who desire an experience of the rigorous Soto tradition in a form that is accessible to Westerners.

paper; 420 pages; $19.95
ISBN: 0-934252-61-0

THE ALCHEMY OF LOVE AND SEX
by Lee Lozowick
Foreword by Georg Feuerstein, Ph.D.

Reveals 70 "secrets" about love, sex and relationships. Lozowick recognizes the immense conflict and confusion surrounding love, sex, and tantric spiritual practice. Advocating neither asceticism nor hedonism, he presents a middle path—one grounded in the appreciation of simple human relatedness. Topics include:* what men want from women in sex, and what women want from men * the development of a passionate love affair with life * how to balance the essential masculine and essential feminine * the dangers and possibilities of sexual Tantra * the reality of a genuine, sacred marriage...and much more. " ... attacks Western sexuality with a vengeance."
– *Library Journal*.

paper, 312 pages, $16.95
ISBN: 0-934252-58-0

THE ONLY GRACE IS LOVING GOD
by Lee Lozowick

Love, God, Loving God, Grace, Divine Will—these subjects have engaged the minds and hearts of theologians throughout the ages, and even caused radical schisms within organized religions. Lee Lozowick dares to address them again, and in a way entirely original. He challenges all conventional definitions of love, and all superficial assumptions about the nature of loving God, and introduces a radical distinction which he calls the "whim of God" to explain why the random and beneficent Grace of loving God is humanity's ultimate possibility. More than just esoteric musings, *The Only Grace is Loving God* is an urgent and practical appeal to every hungry heart.

paper, 108 pages, $5.95
ISBN: 0-934252-07-6

HALFWAY UP THE MOUNTAIN
The Error of Premature Claims to Enlightenment
by Mariana Caplan
Foreword by Fleet Maull

Dozens of first-hand interviews with students, respected spiritual teachers and masters, together with broad research are synthesized here to assist readers in avoiding the pitfalls of the spiritual path. Topics include: mistaking mystical experience for enlightenment; ego inflation, power and corruption among spiritual leaders; the question of the need for a teacher; disillusionment on the path ... and much more.
"Caplan's illuminating book ... urges seekers to pay the price of traveling the hard road to true enlightenment." – *Publisher's Weekly*

paper, 600 pages, $21.95
ISBN: 0-934252-91-2

THE ALCHEMY OF TRANSFORMATION
by Lee Lozowick
Foreword by Claudio Naranjo, M.D.

A concise and straightforward overview of the principles of spiritual life as developed and taught by Lee Lozowick for the past twenty years. Covers subjects of use to seekers and serious students of any spiritual tradition. A radical, elegant and irreverent approach to the possibility of change from ego-centeredness to God-centeredness—the ultimate human transformation.

paper, 192 pages, $14.95
ISBN: 0-934252-62-9

THE MIRROR OF THE SKY
Songs of the Bauls of Bengal
Translated by Deben Bhattacharya

Baul music today is prized by world musicologists, and Baul lyrics are treasured by readers of ecstatic and mystical poetry. Their music, lyrics and accompanying dance reflect the passion, the devotion and the iconoclastic freedom of this remarkable sect of musicians and lovers of the Divine, affectionately known as "God's troubadours."

The Mirror of the Sky is a translation of 204 songs, including an extensive introduction to the history and faith of the Bauls, and the composition of their music. It includes a CD of authentic Baul artists, recorded as much as forty years ago by Bhattacharya, a specialist in world music. The current CD is a rare presentation of this infrequently documented genre.

paper, 288 pages, $24.95 (includes CD)
ISBN: 0-934252-89-0
CD sold separately, $16.95

YOGI RAMSURATKUMAR
Under The Punnai Tree
by M. Young

This is a richly detailed and thoroughly re-searched biography of the beggar saint of Tamil Nadu – Yogi Ramsuratkumar. From the lyrical to the factual, this book is filled with stories of Ramsuratkumar. Personal accounts of those who knew the beggar well reveal the life story of a saint unique even in the long history of India. *Yogi Ramusuratkumar: Under the Punnai Tree* occasionally takes a broader view and explores how Ramusuratkumar's life fits into overall themes of the spiritual path. A literary and pictorial feast for those who love India's rich heritage and a must read for spiritual seekers of all traditions.

paper, 726 pages, 72 photos, $39.95
ISBN: 0-890772-34-8

ONLY GOD
A Biography of Yogi Ramsuratkumar
by Regina Sara Ryan
Foreword by Jay Martin, Ph.D.

This is the true life story of a beggar, a hidden saint, a well educated holy man who begged on the streets of India: Yogi Ramsuratkumar.

"Only God" was his creed and his approach to everyday life. His unusual innocence and radiant presence were recognized by seekers from both East and West. The book includes the lives and teachings of the holy beggar's three gurus: Sri Aurobindo, Ramana Maharshi and Swami Papa Ramdas. With self-revelatory honesty and an enjoyable mix of storytelling, interviews and fact-finding, this is an affect-ing account of an extraordinary life.

cloth, 832 pages, $39.95
ISBN:1-890772-35-6

YOU HAVE THE RIGHT TO REMAIN SILENT
Bringing Meditation to Life
by Rick Lewis

With sparkling clarity and humor, Rick Lewis explains exactly what meditation can offer to those who are ready to establish an island of sanity in the midst of an active life. This book is a comprehensive look at everything a begin-ner would need to start a meditation practice, including how to befriend an overactive mind and how to bring the fruits of meditation into all aspects of daily life. Experienced medita-tors will also find refreshing perspectives to both nourish and refine their practice.

paper, 188 pages, $14.95
ISBN: 1-890772-23-2

NOBODY SON OF NOBODY
Poems of Shaikh Abu-Saeed Abil-Kheir
Renditions by Vraje Abramian

Anyone who has found a resonance with the love-intoxicated poetry of Rumi, must read the poetry of Shaikh Abil-Kheir. This renowned, but little known, Sufi mystic of the 10th century preceded Rumi by over two hundred years on the same path of annihilation into God. This book contains translations and poetic renderings of 195 short selections from the original Farsi, the language in which Abil-Kheir wrote.

These poems deal with the longing for union with God, the desire to know the Real from the false, the inexpressible beauty of cre-ation when seen through the eyes of Love, and the many attitudes of heart, mind and feeling that are necessary to those who would find the Beloved, The Friend, in this life.

paper, 120 pages, $12.95
ISBN: 1-890772-04-6

THE WOMAN AWAKE
Feminine Wisdom for Spiritual Life
By Regina Sara Ryan

Through the stories and insights of great women whom the author has met or been guided by in her own journey, this book highlights many faces of the Divine Feminine: the silence, the solitude, the service, the power, the compassion, the art, the darkness, the sexuality. Read about: the Sufi poetess Rabia (8th century) and contemporary Sufi master Irina Tweedie; Hildegard of Bingen, author Kathryn Hulme (*The Nun's Story*); German healer and mystic Dina Rees, and others. Includes personal interviews with contemplative Christian monk Mother Tessa Bielecki; artist Meinrad Craighead and Zen teacher and anthropologist Joan Halifax.

paper, 518 pages, 20+ photos, $19.95
ISBN: 0-934252-79-3

THE YOGA TRADITION
*Its History, Literature, Philosophy
and Practice*
by Georg Feuerstein, Ph.D.

A complete overview of the great Yogic traditions of: Raja-Yoga, Hatha-Yoga, Jnana-Yoga, Bhakti-Yoga, Karma-Yoga, Tantra-Yoga, Kundalini-Yoga, Mantra-Yoga and many other lesser known forms. Includes translations of over twenty famous Yoga treatises, like the Yoga-Sutra of Patanjali, and a first-time translation of the Goraksha Paddhati, an ancient Hatha Yoga text. Covers all aspects of Hindu, Buddhist, Jaina and Sikh Yoga. A necessary resource for all students and scholars of Yoga.

paper, 540 pages, 200+ illustrations, $29.95
ISBN: 1-890772-18-6.

TAO TE CHING FOR THE WEST
by Richard Degen

A new rendition of the revered classic, *Tao Te Ching*, this sensitive version offers a contemporary application of Eastern wisdom to the problems created by modern Western living. This highly-readable collection presents a way of life characterized by harmony and integrity; a way that bypasses the happiness-depleting traps that people have set for themselves and others.

paper, 120 pages, $9.95
ISBN: 0-934252-92-0

PRAYING DANGEROUSLY
Radical Reliance on God
by Regina Sara Ryan

Re-enlivens an age-old tradition of prayer as an expression of radical reliance on God. This approach expands the possibilities of prayer, elevating it beyond ordinary pleas for help, comfort, security and prosperity. Contains a chapter on the poetry-prayer of Lee Lozowick to Yogi Ramsuratkumar.

paper, 240 pages, $14.95
ISBN: 1-8990772-06-2

A MAN AND HIS MASTER:
My Years With Yogi Ramsuratkumar
by Mani, with S. Lkasham

A personal account by Yogi Ramsuratkumar's trusted "right-hand man," Mani, of his six years at the master's side. Mani's heart and extraordinary faith shine through this touchingly personal and intimate account.

paper, 394 pages, $21.95
ISBN: 1-890772-36-2

THE ART OF DYING
RedHawk

RedHawk's poetry cuts close to the bone whether he is telling humorous tales or indicting the status-quo throughout the culture. Touching upon themes of life and death, power, devotion and adoration, these ninety new poems reveal the poet's deep concern for all of life, and particularly for the needs of women, children and the earth.

"An eye-opener; spiritual, native, populist. RedHawk's is a powerful, wise, and down-home voice." – Gary Snyder

paper, 120 pages, $12.00
ISBN: 0-934252-93-9

JOURNEY TO HEAVENLY MOUNTAIN
*An American's Pilgrimage to the Heart
of Buddhism in Modern China*
by Jay Martin

"I came to China to live in Buddhist monasteries and to revisit my soul," writes best-selling American author and distinguished scholar Jay Martin of his 1998 pilgrimage. This book is an account of one man's spiritual journey. His intention? To penetrate the soul of China and its wisdom. Anyone who has wondered about the health of monastic Buddhism in China today will find this a fascinating revelation. Anyone who longs for the serenity and clarity that the author sought will want to read this book.

"Well written and intelligent." – Library Journal

paper, 263 pages, b&w photographs, $16.95
ISBN: 1-890772-17-8

HOLY MADNESS
*Spirituality, Crazy-Wise Teachers,
and Enlightenment*
Revised and Expanded Edition
by Georg Feuerstein, Ph. D.

This book traces the shadowy tradition of "holy madness/crazy wisdom" from the Holy Fools of early Christianity, through the great adepts of India and Tibet, up to the controversial gurus of today. In our day, when even the Dalai Lama has warmed Western seekers to choose their teachers carefully, Feuerstein provides an intelligent and cautionary guidebook to the guru-disciple relationship, plus a comprehensive analysis of the principles of authentic spirituality.

Dozens of shorter illustrative examples surround a more in-depth portrayal of crazy-wisdom in action in the lives and activities of contemporary teachers.

paper, 526 pages, $29.95
ISBN: 1-890772-54-2

THE WAY OF FAILURE
Winning Through Losing
by Mariana Caplan

This straight-talking and strongly inspirational book looks failure directly in the face, unmasking it for what it really is. Mariana Caplan tells us to how to meet failure on its own field, how to learn its twists and turns, its illusions and its realities. Only then, she advises, is one equipped to engage failure as a means of ultimate "winning," and in a way that far exceeds our culturally defined visions of success.

paper; 144 pages; $14.95
ISBN: 1-890772-10-6

KISHIDO: *The Way of the Western Warrior*
by Peter Hobart

The code of the samurai and the path of the knight-warrior—traditions from opposite sides of the globe—find a common ground in *Kishido: the Way of the Western Warrior*. In fifty short essays, Peter Hobart presents the wisdom, philosophy and teachings of the mysterious Master who first united the noble houses of East and West. Kishido prioritizes the ideals of duty, ethics, courtesy and chivalry, from whatever source they derive. This cross-cultural approach represents a return to time-honored principles from many traditions, and allows the modern reader from virtually any background to find the master within.

paper, 130 pages, $12.95
ISBN: 1-890772-31-3

THE SHADOW ON THE PATH
Clearing the Psychological Blocks to Spiritual Development
by VJ Fedorschak
Foreword by Claudio Naranjo, M.D.

Tracing the development of the human psychological shadow from Freud to the present, this readable analysis presents five contemporary approaches to spiritual psychotherapy for those who find themselves needing help on the spiritual path. Topics include: the shadow in the work notable therapists; the principles of inner spiritual development in the major world religions; examples of the disowned shadow in contemporary religious movements; and case studies of clients in spiritual groups who have worked with their shadow issues.

paper, 304 pages, 6 x 9; $16.95
ISBN: 0-934252-81-5

THE ANTI-WISDOM MANUAL
A Practical Guide to Spiritual Bankruptcy
by Gilles Farcet, Ph.D.

What if the spiritual path turned out to be a road to hell paved with good intentions?

Most spiritual books tell us what we should do, or how we should view things. *The Anti-Wisdom Manual* takes a different approach. It simply describes what people actually do to sabotage their own progress on the spiritual path, whatever their chosen way – Christian, Buddhist, Native American, Muslim, Jewish, or any other. Think of it as a handbook in reverse. Using humor and irony, while based in clarity and compassion, the author alerts readers to the common traps into which so many sincere seekers easily fall.

paper, 176 pages, $14.95
ISBN: 1-890772-42-9

WESTERN SADHUS AND SANNYASINS IN INDIA
by Marcus Allsop

This book contains interviews and stories about a unique group of Westerners who have lived in India for twenty years or more. Now known as sadhus and sannyasins (traditional Indian holy men or women), they have renounced the materialistic values of their native culture in favor of a life of austerity and spiritual practice. Marcus Allsop's pilgrimage takes him from Mt. Arunachala in southern India to the source of the Ganges in the foothills of the Himalayas. He stops at age-old shrines and majestic temples, and shares the powerful insights into Indian spiritual culture that he gains along the way.

paper; 232 pages; 24 photos; $14.95
ISBN: 0-934252-50-5

Further Experimenting

I appreciate that you are reading this page. Each further experiment you try has the possibility of cutting new forms of consciousness that other people can then more easily follow. A next-culture leader is simply the one who goes first. In this case, that someone is you.

Where are all the others who could have gone first before you? There is no explanation for that. We are where we are. Having to go first is not fair, but it makes you a bridge to 'archearchy' – the culture that naturally emerges after matriarchy and patriarchy have already run their course (http://archearchy.org).

Authentic change happens one individual at a time. When you take a step, it pioneers the way for others to take similar steps. This is how your personal efforts make so much difference. Please keep going. There are literally millions of new friends out here living below the radar happily using upgraded thoughtware and creating archearchy. I offer you some suggestions for finding your way here:

1. Shift identity. Decide, "I am an Experimenter." Decide to do radically responsible edgework experiments for the rest of your life. Doing experiments builds the matrix in your Being to hold more consciousness. Our team is creating a free-to-use massively-multiplayer online-and-offline matrix-building thoughtware-upgrade personal-transformation game called StartOver.xyz (http://startover.xyz). Each experiment you do builds real matrix to hold more consciousness. Players are collaborating globally to create one million new Matrix Points in a Winning Happening game that evolves the status quo. It is free to play.

2. Get copies of *Building Love That Lasts* into the hands of your friends (and your enemies...) then keep practicing the new skills together at your weekly Possibility Team. (Download your free copyleft *Possibility Team Handbook* at http://possibilityteam.org.) Empower each other to become 'Possibilitators' (http://possibilitator.xyz) by sending each other to *Expand The Box* training and ten *Possibility Labs*! (http://possibilitymanagement.org).

3. Read my other book: *Conscious Feelings,* and do those experiments at your Possibility Team. For example, commit to lowering your 'Numbness Bar' as part of your adulthood initiations. Feelings are for handling things. Emotions are for healing things. You can sense the difference! By lowering your Numbness Bar you unleash the intelligence and energy resources for being your Archetypal Lineage in action (http://archetypallineage.org). Delivering your destiny to your village is ecstatic! I have also written a fabulously illustrated children's book titled *Goodnight Feelings.*

4. Subscribe to my free monthly newsletter (http://clintoncallahan.org). In each newsletter I send you the latest SPARK experiments. S.P.A.R.K. stands for Specific Practical Applications of Radical Knowledge. Each SPARK includes a powerful distinction with notes for understanding it and experiments for applying it. If you start with SPARK001 and do the experiments (not just think about doing the experiments...) I guarantee your life will change for the better! All existing SPARKs are online for free (http://spark-experiments.org). Register the Matrix Points you earn from SPARK Experiments at http://startover.xyz.

5. *Building Love That Lasts* is a handbook for 'Inner Permaculture' (http://inner-permaculture.xyz). People around the world are realizing that combining Outer Permaculture with Inner Permaculture creates Whole Permaculture (http://wholepermaculture.org), where people tend to want to live together in conscious community or in ecovillages. I implore you to take it one step further and build yourselves a 'nanonation' with your own Codex and Bill of Wrongs (http://nanonations.org). To paraphrase Buckminster Fuller: "You don't change things by fighting the existing gameworlds. You change things by building new gameworlds that make the existing gameworlds irrelevant!" Learn to build new gameworlds! (http://gameworlds.xyz). Create your nanonation by moving into it!

6. Refuse to use hierarchical power structures in your organizations. Hierarchies are easily hijacked by those who are most willing to do whatever it takes to climb the hierarchy and take positions of power: psychopaths and sociopaths. This explains why effective solutions have been known for decades for global warming, hunger, overpopulation, war, pollution, etc. yet are not being implemented. A bright future for humanity is not on a psychopath's agenda. Avoiding the hierarchy design-flaw starts with creating circular or toroidal organizations and using new decision-making processes. (http://torustechnology.org).

7. Make authentic adulthood (http://adulthood.xyz) initiatory processes (http://initiations.org) a central value in your gameworlds. If you do, it will not be long before you find yourself and those you love escaping the six prisons (http://getoutnow.xyz) through study, transformational and healing processes, and perhaps some Possibility Coaching (http://possibilitycoaching.org). Suddenly you become one of the new refugees, someone who has – through Armageddon or Evolution – stepped out of modern culture's capitalist patriarchal empire (http://newrefugees.org). You are not a victim. The intense anger, fear, sadness, and joy in your heart carry design criteria for inventing the social, political, educational, economic, agricultural, health and spiritual gameworlds that deliver better results. Don't be left behind playing in a stupid gameworld...

Your mind is yours to play with and make into whatever you want! Thank you for thinking wildly!

Life is short. Do what matters!

Possibility Management

Tools and techniques from Possibility Management empower this book. Possibility Management is not a method or a system. It is an innovative cross-disciplinary context that liberates and applies unseen resources through new thoughtware and cutting-edge soft-skills. Like bicycle riding, what you learn of Possibility Management is not easily forgotten. The acquired skills are integrated and effective because the learning is in five bodies and not just limited to the mind (http://possibilitymanagement.org).

About The Author

Clinton Callahan (http://clintoncallahan.org) began originating Possibility Management thought-ware upgrades (http://possibilitymanagement.org) in 1975. He also writes S.P.A.R.K.s (http://sparkexperiments.org), the Distinctionary (http://distinctionary.xyz), and StartOver.xyz (http://startoverhere.xyz). Born in Kansas, BS Physics from Cal Poly San Luis Obispo, California, Clinton has lived and worked in the USA, Australia, Japan and Europe, and now carries a passport from the nanonation of Possibilica. Callahan is a trainer in the Possibility Management Trainer Guild, author, speaker, and memetic engineer at General Memetics (http://generalmemetics.org). He invented *Expand the Box* innovation soft-skills training in Germany in 1998, and has been a student of Western Baul Master Lee Lozowick since 1989.